Dear Students and Families,

Welcome to *Into Geometry*! In this program, you will develop skills and make sense of mathematics by solving real-world problems, using tools and strategies, and collaborating with your classmates.

Every lesson includes Spark Your Learning, Build Understanding, and Step It Out tasks. A Spark Your Learning task provides an opportunity to make sense of the mathematics using concepts and procedures you know to try and solve it. The Build Understanding tasks guided by your teacher focus on understanding new concepts, and Step It Out tasks guided by your teacher focus on building efficient procedures and applying those procedures.

With the support of your teacher and by engaging with meaningful practice, you will learn to persevere when solving problems. *Into Geometry* will not only help you deepen your understanding of mathematics, but also build your confidence as a learner of mathematics.

We want you to be successful in learning math because it opens up a world of possibilities to you. By engaging and persevering in the learning tasks in *Into Geometry*, you will be well on the path to becoming college, career, and civic ready in mathematics. Enjoy your time with *Into Geometry*!

Sincerely,
The Authors

Authors

Edward B. Burger, PhD
President, Southwestern University
Georgetown, Texas

Robert Kaplinsky, MEd
Mathematics Educator
Long Beach, California

Juli K. Dixon, PhD
Professor, Mathematics Education
University of Central Florida
Orlando, Florida

Matthew R. Larson, PhD
Past-President, National Council
of Teachers of Mathematics
Lincoln Public Schools
Lincoln, Nebraska

Timothy D. Kanold, PhD
Mathematics Educator
Chicago, Illinois

Steven J. Leinwand
Principal Research Analyst
American Institutes for Research
Washington, DC

Consultants

English Language Development Consultant

Harold Asturias
Director, Center for Mathematics
Excellence and Equity
Lawrence Hall of Science, University of California
Berkeley, California

Program Consultant

David Dockterman, EdD
Lecturer, Harvard Graduate School of Education
Cambridge, Massachusetts

Blended Learning Consultant

Weston Kiercshneck
Senior Fellow
International Center for Leadership in Education
Littleton, Colorado

Open Middle™ Consultant

Nanette Johnson, MEd
Secondary Mathematics Educator
Downey, California

STEM Consultants

Michael A. DiSpezio
Global Educator
North Falmouth, Massachusetts

Marjorie Frank
Science Writer and
Content-Area Reading Specialist
Brooklyn, New York

Bernadine Okoro
Access and Equity and
STEM Learning Advocate and Consultant
Washington, DC

Cary I. Sneider, PhD
Associate Research Professor
Portland State University
Portland, Oregon

Essentials of Geometry

MODULE 1 Geometry in the Plane

(l) ©HelloRF Zcool/Shutterstock; (r) ©Philip Mugridge/Alamy

Build Conceptual Understanding   Connect Concepts and Skills   Apply and Practice

MODULE 2 Tools for Reasoning and Proof

©Neirfy/Shutterstock

○ Build Conceptual Understanding   ○ Connect Concepts and Skills   ○ Apply and Practice

3 Transformations

MODULE 5 Transformations that Preserve Size and Shape

MODULE 6 Transformations that Change Size and Shape

Unit 4

Triangle Congruence

MODULE 7 Congruent Triangles and Polygons

(l) ©Houghton Mifflin Harcourt; (r) ©Compassionate Eye Foundation/Robert Kent/
Digital Vision/Getty Images

Build Conceptual Understanding   Connect Concepts and Skills   Apply and Practice

MODULE 8 Triangle Congruence Criteria

Unit

5

Relationships Within Triangles

MODULE 9 Properties of Triangles

MODULE 10 Triangle Inequalities

● Build Conceptual Understanding   ● Connect Concepts and Skills   ● Apply and Practice

Quadrilaterals, Polygons, and Triangle Similarity

MODULE 11 Quadrilaterals and Polygons

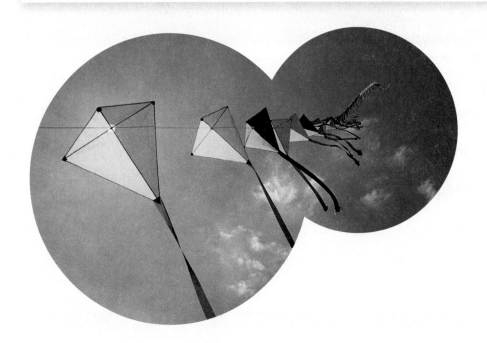

MODULE 12 Similarity

(l) ©davorana/Shutterstock; (r) ©Cameris/Shutterstock

Build Conceptual Understanding   Connect Concepts and Skills   Apply and Practice

Right Triangle Trigonometry

MODULE 13 Trigonometry with Right Triangles

MODULE 14 Trigonometry with All Triangles

(bc) ©Jul Miryash/Shutterstock; (br) ©Caia Images/Superstock

 Build Conceptual Understanding    Connect Concepts and Skills   Apply and Practice

©Houghton Mifflin Harcourt

Build Conceptual Understanding   Connect Concepts and Skills   Apply and Practice

Unit 10 Probability

©nattanan726/Shutterstock

MODULE 21 Conditional Probability and Independence of Events

○ Build Conceptual Understanding   ○ Connect Concepts and Skills   ○ Apply and Practice

STUDENT RESOURCES

Essentials of Geometry

Wildlife Conservationist

©Louise Murray/robertharding/Getty Images

Wildlife conservationists analyze data and maps to make inferences and decisions about endangered species. They must manage and protect a variety of environments to ensure they are conserved for the plants and animals that live there. In order to advocate for the conservation of endangered species habitats, they use data to educate the public.

STEM Task

A conservationist uses data to construct arguments about the status of the endangered North Atlantic right whale population.

Year	IDs	Population	Year	IDs	Population
2006	344	432	2012	370	502
2008	388	467	2014	361	502
2010	418	501	2016	304	490

Make inferences about the right whale population over time. Conduct research and use the data provided to justify your reasoning.

Learning Mindset

Perseverance Sustains Attention

©Jon Bilous/Shutterstock

How do you sustain attention to tasks? Whenever you approach a new assignment, it is important to prioritize tasks and to organize and monitor your progress. Putting off elements of the assignment can interfere with your learning and produce undesired results. Maintaining focus throughout the project deepens your understanding and yields a higher quality product. It's especially important to keep up with tasks when working collaboratively to ensure not only your own success, but the success of your team. Here are some questions you can ask yourself to help you sustain attention:

- Why is it important to complete my tasks completely and on time?

- What strategies am I using to stay on task when I work on my own?

- What strategies am I using to stay on task when I work with a team?

- What do I need to consider when prioritizing my tasks?

- How can I prioritize tasks when working with a team to help me complete my contributions on time?

Reflect

Q What strategies might a conservationist use to stay organized when collecting data over several years?

Q Imagine that you are a wildlife conservationist. Why is there a difference between the unique IDs and the presumed living population? How might a team use the strategies you identified to approach the task?

1 Geometry in the Plane

Module Performance Task: *Spies and Analysts*™

FIGHT WILDFIRES

How can we figure out what percentage of the fire is contained?

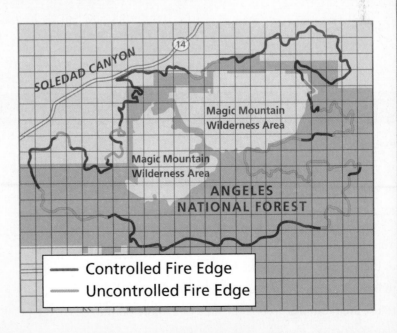

SOLEDAD CANYON

Magic Mountain Wilderness Area

Magic Mountain Wilderness Area

ANGELES NATIONAL FOREST

—— Controlled Fire Edge
—— Uncontrolled Fire Edge

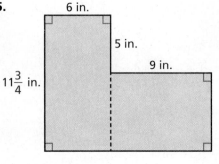

Are You Ready?

Complete these problems to review prior concepts and skills you will need for this module.

Areas of Triangles

Find the area of the triangle with the given base and height.

1. $b = 2$ cm and $h = 7.5$ cm

2. $b = 6\frac{3}{5}$ ft and $h = 7$ ft

3. $b = 3$ m and $h = 10\frac{1}{2}$ m

Areas of Composite Figures

Find the area. Round to the nearest tenth.

4.

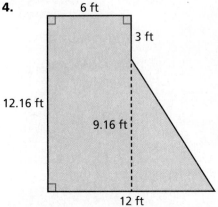

6 ft
3 ft
12.16 ft
9.16 ft
12 ft

5.

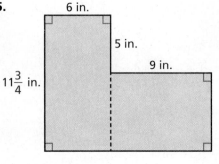

6 in.
5 in.
9 in.
$11\frac{3}{4}$ in.

Types of Angle Pairs

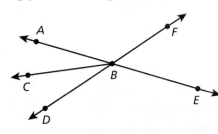

6. Name a pair of vertical angles.

7. Name a pair of adjacent angles.

8. If $m\angle ABD = 83°$, $m\angle ABC = (x + 10)°$, and $m\angle DBC = (4x - 12)°$, what is the measure of each angle?

Connecting Past and Present Learning

Previously, you learned:

• to use the area formula to find the area of triangles,

• to write the area formulas to find the area of composite figures, and

• to use angle relationships to find the measurement of angles.

In this module, you will learn:

• to understand the difference between undefined and defined terms,

• to use the distance formula to find the length of a line, and

• to use area formulas to find the area of a figure on the coordinate plane.

Points, Lines, and Planes

(I Can) copy and add segments.

Spark Your Learning

Geometry is the study of shapes, and it requires careful use of precise language. Many words that have a specific meaning in geometry have additional and sometimes related meanings that we use in everyday speech.

Complete Part A as a whole class. Then complete Parts B–D in small groups.

A. What mathematical terms are suggested by the photo and the situation it represents? Construct a definition for each term and use the picture to explain your reasoning.

B. Do the English meanings of these terms help you understand the mathematical meanings? What strategy and tool would you use to give an example where the English meaning of a term is helpful?

C. Give an example where the English meaning is not helpful.

D. Does your answer depend on the context in which you are using the term? Explain your reasoning.

Turn and Talk

- Discuss with your partner other words that have meanings that depend on the situation.
- Discuss how the meaning of *plane* is different in Geometry and English.

Build Understanding

Use Geometry Vocabulary

Most words, or terms, used in geometry are defined, but some concepts are so basic that it is impossible to write a definition that does not refer to the term being defined. These are called **undefined terms**.

Undefined Terms		
Term	**Figure**	**Ways to Name Figure**
A **point** names a location. A point has no dimension.	$\overset{C}{\bullet}$ $\overset{E}{\underset{D\,\bullet}{}}$	point C, point D, point E
A **line** names a straight path of points in a plane. A line has no width or thickness, and it continues forever in one dimension.	$\longleftrightarrow \ell$ $A \quad B$	line ℓ, $\overleftrightarrow{AB}$ and $\overleftrightarrow{BA}$
A **plane** is a flat surface. A plane has no thickness and it extends forever in two dimensions.	B $\mathcal{R}$ A C	plane $\mathcal{R}$, plane ABC

Defined Terms		
Term	**Figure**	**Ways to Name Figure**
An **endpoint** is a point at an end of a segment or the starting point of a ray.	$A \qquad B$ $\bullet\!\!-\!\!\!-\!\!\!-\!\!\bullet$ $\bullet\!\!-\!\!\!-\!\!\!-\!\!\rightarrow$ F	The endpoints are A and B or F.
A **ray** is a part of a line that starts at an endpoint and extends forever in one direction.	$H \qquad I$ $\bullet\!\!-\!\!\!-\!\!\bullet\!\!-\!\!\rightarrow$	ray HI or $\overrightarrow{HI}$
A **line segment** is part of a line consisting of two endpoints and all points between them.	$A \qquad B$ $\bullet\!\!-\!\!\!-\!\!\!-\!\!\bullet$	$\overline{AB}$ or $\overline{BA}$

1 **A.** Draw a plane and label three points in the plane. Name the plane in two ways. How many points do you need to use to name a plane? Does the order of the points matter?

  B. Draw a ray with P as an endpoint. Write a name for the ray. How many points do you need to use to name a ray? Does the order of the points matter? Explain.

  C. Draw a line segment and a ray that lie on the same line and that share an endpoint. Explain how the rules for naming the two figures are different.

 Turn and Talk Describe a figure to your partner and have them draw the figure from your description. Did you get the expected results? Trade roles and do it again.

Copy Segments and Add Their Lengths

The **distance** between two points is a measure of the length of the shortest line segment that would connect them. Distance is not defined until a unit of measure has been chosen. Points are **collinear** if they lie on the same line. Points and lines are **coplanar** if they lie in the same plane.

A **postulate** is a statement that is accepted as true without proof. Congruency allows you to say segments have the same length without knowing the length.

Segment Addition Postulate
Assume that A, B, and C are collinear points. If B is between A and C, then $AB + BC = AC$. 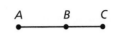

2 ▶ Use a compass and straightedge to copy $\overline{AB}$ and $\overline{CD}$. Then construct a line segment with length $AB + CD$.

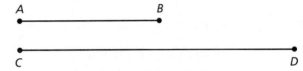

A. Use a straightedge to draw a line segment that is longer than $AB + CD$. Label point M at the left end of the segment.

B. Open the compass to length AB. Using the same compass setting, place the compass on point M and draw an arc. Label the intersection N. Compare AB and MN. How do you know this relationship is true?

C. Use the information in Parts A and B to explain how to add $\overline{CD}$ to $\overline{MN}$. Explain why the length of the resulting segment is equal to the sum of the lengths of $\overline{CD}$ and $\overline{MN}$.

D. Would the length of the resulting segment be the same or different if you started with a copy of $\overline{CD}$ instead of with a copy of $\overline{AB}$? Explain your reasoning.

 Turn and Talk Discuss with your partner how you could use a ruler to draw a segment with length $AB + CD$. Rank the accuracy of the two methods: using a ruler and using a compass and straightedge. Which method is better? Explain your reasoning.

Bisect a Segment to Find the Midpoint

Two segments that have the same length are **congruent**, and you can write a congruence statement using the symbol ≅. So if the segments $\overline{PQ}$ and $\overline{RS}$ are the same length, you can write $\overline{PQ} \cong \overline{RS}$.

The **tick marks** on $\overline{PQ}$ and $\overline{RS}$ indicate that the segments are congruent. Multiple tick marks may be used, but two segments must have the same number of tick marks to indicate that the segments are congruent.

A line segment can be bisected using a compass and straightedge to find the midpoint. To **bisect** a figure is to divide it into two congruent parts. The **midpoint** of a segment is the point that bisects the segment into two congruent segments.

3 Use a compass and straightedge to bisect a segment.

A. Draw $\overline{AB}$ on a piece a paper. Place your compass on the endpoint A. Open the compass to about $\frac{2}{3}$ the length of the segment. Draw an arc that starts above the line and continues below the line to form about half a circle.

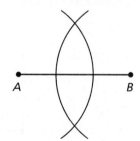

B. Do not change the compass setting. Place the compass on endpoint B. Draw an arc that intersects your first arc both above and below the line segment.

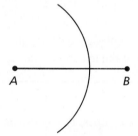

C. Connect the two points where the two arcs intersect each other. Label the point M where this segment intersects the original segment.

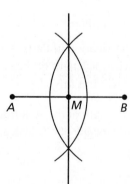

D. How can you verify that $\overline{MA} \cong \overline{MB}$? Explain your reasoning.

 Turn and Talk Describe a process to bisect a segment using paper folding.

Step It Out

Identify Points and Segments on the Coordinate Plane

Remember that points on the coordinate plane can be represented using an ordered pair (x, y) where x is the x-coordinate and y is the y-coordinate. To find the midpoint of a segment on the coordinate plane, you can use the Midpoint Formula.

Midpoint Formula

The midpoint M of $\overline{AB}$ with endpoints $A(x_1, y_1)$ and $B(x_2, y_2)$ is given by $M\left(\frac{x_1 + x_2}{2}, \frac{y_1 + y_2}{2}\right)$.

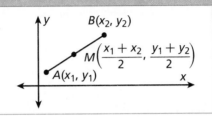

4 Given the points $A(-3, 2)$, $B(5, 2)$, $C(1, 1)$, and $D(1, 7)$, find the midpoint of $\overline{AB}$, $M_{\overline{AB}}$, and the midpoint of $\overline{CD}$, $M_{\overline{CD}}$. Do the segments intersect at one of the midpoints? Explain your reasoning.

Use the Midpoint Formula to calculate the coordinates of $M_{\overline{AB}}$.

$$M_{\overline{AB}} = \left(\frac{x_a + x_b}{2}, \frac{y_a + y_b}{2}\right)$$
$$= \left(\frac{-3 + 5}{2}, \frac{2 + 2}{2}\right)$$
$$= (1, 2)$$

Use the Midpoint Formula to calculate the coordinates of $M_{\overline{CD}}$.

$$M_{\overline{CD}} = \left(\frac{x_c + x_d}{2}, \frac{y_c + y_d}{2}\right)$$
$$= \left(\frac{1 + 1}{2}, \frac{1 + 7}{2}\right)$$
$$= (1, 4)$$

A. Why is the y-coordinate of the midpoint the same as the y-coordinate of both endpoints?

B. Why is the x-coordinate of the midpoint the same as the x-coordinate of both endpoints?

C. You can graph the segments to find the point where they intersect. Do the segments intersect at one of the midpoints? Explain your reasoning.

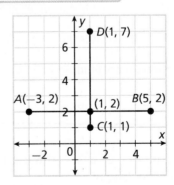

 Turn and Talk If $\overline{CD}$ has an endpoint $C(4, -6)$ and the midpoint is $M(-2, 6)$, what are the coordinates of the endpoint D? Explain how you found the endpoint D.

Check Understanding

1. Draw points A and B. Draw a line through them. What is a name of the line?

2. Given two segments, describe a method of drawing a segment with length equal to the sum of the lengths of the given segments.

3. Explain how to find the midpoint of a segment using a compass.

4. Suppose $\overline{AB}$ on the coordinate plane is horizontal and has length 4 units. If the coordinates of A are $(4, 6)$ and B is to its right, give the coordinates of B and of the midpoint of $\overline{AB}$.

On Your Own

5. Tell whether each term is *defined* or *undefined*.

   A. point   **C.** segment   **E.** plane

   B. line   **D.** ray   **F.** endpoint

Use the campus map to answer Problems 6–8.

6. Name three different rays in the figure.

7. Name three different points in the figure.

8. Name three different ways to name the plane.

9. Use a compass and straight edge to construct a segment with length $AB + CD$.

Use the figure to answer Problems 10 and 11.

10. If $AB = 49$ and $BC = 22$, what is the length AC?

11. If $AC = 62$ and $BC = 27$, what is the length AB?

12. Use the figure to solve for x. Find AB and BC.

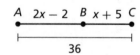

13. The length of $\overline{DF}$ is $(4x + 2)$ inches, with E as the midpoint. The length of $\overline{DE}$ is 17 inches. What is the value of x?

14. Use a ruler to draw a 4-inch long segment $\overline{MN}$. Use a compass and straightedge to locate the midpoint of $\overline{MN}$.

15. Point B lies along $\overline{AC}$ between points A and C. The length of $\overline{AC}$ is 38 centimeters. If $AB = 7x - 1$ and $BC = 4x + 6$, is B the midpoint of $\overline{AC}$? Explain your reasoning.

Use the figure to answer Problems 16–21. Assume integer coordinates.

16. Find the midpoint of $\overline{AB}$.

17. Find the midpoint of $\overline{HI}$.

18. Find the midpoint of $\overline{CD}$.

19. Do the segments $\overline{AB}$ and $\overline{CD}$ have the same length?

20. Do the segments $\overline{HI}$ and $\overline{CD}$ have the same length?

21. Do the segments $\overline{EF}$ and $\overline{HI}$ have the same length?

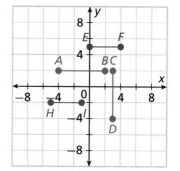

Find the midpoint M of a segment with the given endpoints.

22. $A(-4, 6)$ and $B(2, 8)$

23. $C(-4, 0)$ and $D(0, -10)$

24. $E(-5, -3)$ and $F(3, 7)$

25. $G(-9, 11)$ and $H(-13, 1)$

26. $J(-7, 3)$ and $K(2, -8)$

27. $L(-8, 11)$ and $N(-3, 12)$

28. The lacrosse player shown passes the ball to a team member who is directly in front of the center of the net and is directly below her in the diagram. If the team member catches the ball and then throws it to the center of the net, what is the total distance of the two throws?

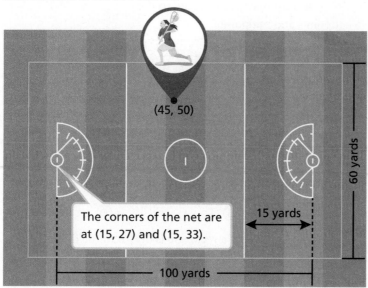

(45, 50)

The corners of the net are at (15, 27) and (15, 33).

15 yards

60 yards

100 yards

29. Two vertices of rectangle $ABCD$ are located at $A(-4, -2)$ and $B(5, -2)$. If the midpoint of $\overline{AD}$ is located 5 units down from A, what are the coordinates of the vertices C and D?

30. **Open Ended** Suppose $\overline{AB}$ has length 7 units and the coordinates of A are $(4, 6)$. Give coordinates for three possible locations for B and the midpoint of each of those possible segments.

31. (MP) **Use Structure** If $\overline{BC}$ has endpoints $B(-6, -2)$ and $C(3, -2)$, which quadrant does the midpoint lie in?

32. If the midpoint of a segment on the coordinate plane is the origin, can the endpoints be located in the same quadrant? Explain.

33. (MP) **Critique Reasoning** A teacher asked students to find the midpoint of $\overline{AB}$, with $A(-8, 7)$ and $B(2, -1)$. Describe and correct the error John made in finding the midpoint.

$$M_{\overline{AB}} = \left(\frac{-8 - 2}{2}, \frac{7 - (-1)}{2} \right)$$
$$= (-5, 4) \ \text{✗}$$

34. A city is planning to include a skate park in the renovation of a recreational facility. The skate park will include a bowl that runs the length of one end of the park. What are the coordinates of A and B, the top and bottom of the bowl?

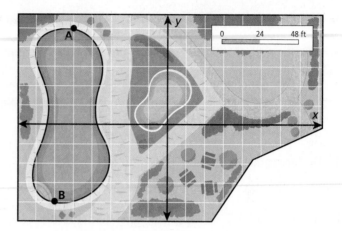

35. Open Ended Suppose the coordinates of one endpoint of $\overline{CD}$ are $C(1, 6)$. If the midpoint is 2 units from C, plot 4 possible locations for point D. Explain how you found those points.

36. Harrison's house is halfway between the library and town hall. If Harrison's house is at $(6, -2)$ on a coordinate plane and the library is at $(4, -9)$. What is the location of town hall?

37. (Open Middle™) Using the digits 1 to 9, at most one time each, fill in the boxes to create a line segment's two endpoints and midpoint.

Endpoints $\left(\boxed{}, \boxed{}\right)$ and $\left(\boxed{}, \boxed{}\right)$ Midpoint $\left(\boxed{}, \boxed{}\right)$

Spiral Review • Assessment Readiness

38. Liam goes to the movies with 5 friends. The movie costs $5.25 per person. They also bought 5 sodas at $2.75 each. How much did they spend at the movies?

Ⓐ $5.75

Ⓒ $26.25

Ⓑ $13.75

Ⓓ $40.00

39. What is the y-intercept of the graph of the equation $x + 2y = 2$?

Ⓐ $(0, 1)$

Ⓒ $(1, 0)$

Ⓑ $(0, 2)$

Ⓓ $(2, 0)$

40. Given the function $f(x) = 6(3x - 5)$, if $f(x) = 42$, what is x?

Ⓐ 3

Ⓒ 5

Ⓑ 4

Ⓓ 6

41. If a rectangle is drawn in the first quadrant and reflected over the y-axis, what quadrant is the new image in?

Ⓐ I

Ⓒ III

Ⓑ II

Ⓓ IV

 I'm in a Learning Mindset!

Did I manage my time effectively when constructing segments and determining their midpoints? What steps did I take to manage my time?

Define and Measure Angles

(I Can) **copy and measure angles.**

Spark Your Learning

Kimora is practicing for an in-game scenario. A teammate crosses the ball beyond the far post, leaving the goalie out of position and an empty net for Kimora.

Complete Part A as a whole class. Then complete Parts B–D in small groups.

A. What is a mathematical question you can ask about this situation? What information would you need to know to answer your question?

B. What would give you the most room for error? Should you consider lengths or angles? Explain your reasoning.

C. To answer your question, what strategy and tool would you use along with all the information you have? What answer do you get?

D. How does precision in language help you organize your thinking?

  Turn and Talk Predict how your answer would change for each of the following changes in the situation:
- Kimora was in the center of the field.
- Kimora was closer to the end-line.

Build Understanding

Draw and Name Angles

You can use the undefined terms point and line to define terms used with angles.

Defined Terms		
Term	**Figure**	**Names**
A **ray** is a part of a line that starts at an endpoint and extends forever in one direction.	$\bullet$—$\bullet$→ A B	$\overrightarrow{AB}$ or ray AB
An **angle** is formed by two line segments or rays that share the same endpoint.	A B C	$\angle ABC$ or $\angle B$
A **vertex** of an angle is the common endpoint of the two rays that form the angle.	A B C	The vertex is at B.
Adjacent angles are two angles in the same plane with a common vertex and a common side, but no common interior points.	A C B D	$\angle ABC$ and $\angle CBD$

1 ▶ A. Draw two rays that form an angle. Draw two rays that do not form an angle.

B. Draw and label adjacent angles ABC and CBD. Write all possible ways to name all three angles using the point names.

C. Draw and label angles ABC and DBE so that they share the vertex B but are not adjacent angles.

 Turn and Talk Describe a figure to your partner that has at least one angle and have them draw the figure from your description. Did you get the expected results? Trade roles and do it again.

Measure and Classify Angles

The measure of a segment is a description of its length. The measure of an angle is a description of the distance around a circular arc. A common measure for angles is degrees. One degree, written 1°, is $\frac{1}{360}$ of the way around the circular arc.

Angle Classification by Measure		
Name	**Measure**	**Example**
acute	$0° < m\angle A < 90°$	
right	$m\angle A = 90°$	
obtuse	$90° < m\angle A < 180°$	
straight	$m\angle A = 180°$	
reflex	The measure of the reflex angle of a given acute, right, or obtuse angle will be greater than 180° and less than 360°.	

2 ▶ **A.** Classify each angle as acute, right, obtuse, or straight.

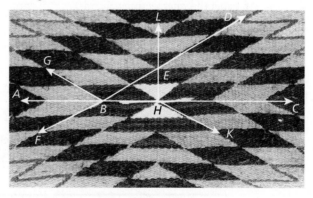

∠ABG   ∠DBC

∠ABD   ∠LHC

∠GBD   ∠ABF

∠DBF   ∠LHK

∠KHC   ∠ABC

B. Use a protractor to find the measure of each of the named angles. Did you classify each one correctly?

C. When can estimating an angle measure be useful in solving a problem?

> **Turn and Talk** Reflex angles are defined in terms of a given angle; they are considered the "other half" of an acute, right, or obtuse angle. Together, an angle and its reflex angle form a complete rotation, or a full angle of 360°.
>
> • What is the measure of the reflex angle of ∠LHC in the rug shown?
> • If the measure of an angle is $x°$, what is the measure of its reflex angle?

Step It Out

Copy and Bisect an Angle

You can use a compass and straightedge to copy and bisect angles. You can write a congruence statement about angles using the same symbol you used for segments: $\angle A \cong \angle B$.

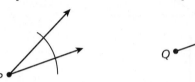

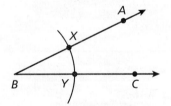

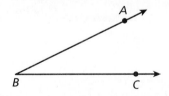

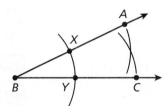

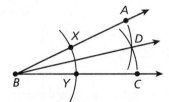

> **Connect to Vocabulary**
>
> To bisect a figure is to divide it into two congruent parts. The **angle bisector** of an angle is a ray that divides the angle into two congruent angles.

3 ▶ The steps of a construction using a compass and straightedge are shown.

Step 1

Step 2

Step 3

Step 4

Step 5

A. Describe what happens in each step.

B. What is the purpose of this construction?

The steps you can use to construct an angle bisector using a compass and straightedge are shown. Put the steps in order.

C. Place the point of the compass on vertex B. Draw an arc that intersects both sides of the angle. Label the intersections X and Y.

D. Place the point of the compass on X and draw an arc. Place the point of the compass on Y and draw an arc.

E. Draw an angle and label it $\angle ABC$.

F. Label the intersection of the arcs D. Use a straightedge to draw $\overrightarrow{BD}$.

You can measure each angle with a protractor to verify that $\angle ABD \cong \angle DBC$.

⬡ **Turn and Talk** Describe a process to bisect an angle using paper folding.

Analyze Angle Relationships

The arcs on $\angle T$ and $\angle W$ indicate that the angles are congruent. Multiple arcs may be used, but two angles must have the same number of arcs to indicate that the angles are congruent.

Angles may also have different relationships. Two angles are **supplementary** if the sum of their angle measures is equal to 180°. Two angles are **complementary** if the sum of their angle measures is equal to 90°.

Angle Addition Postulate

If P is in the interior of $\angle MNQ$, then
$m\angle MNQ = m\angle MNP + m\angle PNQ$.

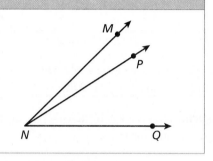

4 ▶ In the image, $m\angle ABC = 156°$. Find $m\angle ABD$ and $m\angle CBD$.

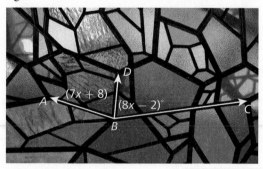

$$m\angle ABC = m\angle ABD + m\angle CBD$$

> **A.** What postulate can be used to find $m\angle ABC$?

$$156 = (7x + 8) + (8x - 2)$$

> **B.** What property justifies this step?

$$156 = 15x + 6$$

$$150 = 15x$$

$$10 = x$$

So, $m\angle ABD = 78°$ and $m\angle CBD = 78°$.

> **C.** How were these measures determined?

Turn and Talk Suppose $\angle ABC$ and $\angle CBD$ are adjacent complementary angles and $m\angle ABC = (3x + 11)°$ and $m\angle CBD = (6x - 2)°$.

What is the value of x? What are the measures of the angles?
Does the shared ray bisect the angle?

Check Understanding

1. Draw each figure.

   A. ray *CA*

   B. angle *ABC*; Identify the vertex.

2. Classify the angles below without using a protractor.

   A. 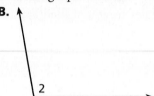   **B.**   **C.**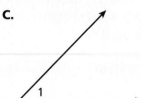

3. Use a protractor to draw a 42° angle. Label the angle *ABC*. Use a compass and straightedge to construct the angle bisector of ∠*ABC*.

4. ∠*CDE* and ∠*EDF* are supplementary angles. If m∠*CDE* = $(2x + 6)°$ and m∠*FDE* = $(x - 9)°$ what is the value of *x*?

On Your Own

Name each angle in three different ways.

5. 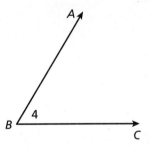   6. 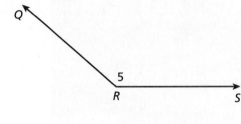   7.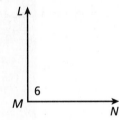

8. Draw two segments that intersect to form an angle.

9. Draw two rays that do not form an angle.

10. Draw and label adjacent angles *ABC* and *CBD*.

11. Draw and label angles *PQR* and *SQT* so that they share the vertex *Q* but are not adjacent angles. Name two other angles formed in your drawing.

Use a protractor to draw an angle with the given measure.

12. 79°   13. 125°   14. 185°

Use a compass and straightedge to construct an angle bisector.

15. 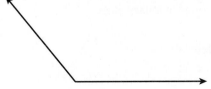   16.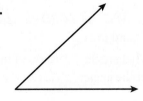

Use the protractor photo to find the measure of each of the following angles.

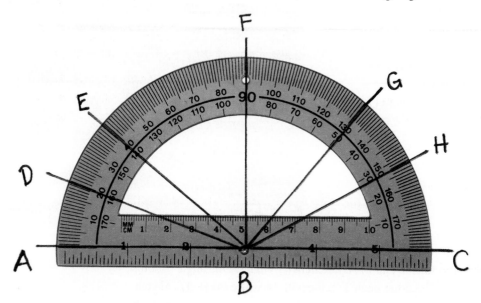

17. ∠ABD

18. ∠EBF

19. ∠GBC

20. ∠DBF

21. ∠EBG

22. ∠DBC

23. Find the measure of ∠ABD and ∠DBC given m∠ABC = 77°.

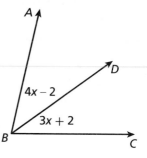

24. Find the measure of ∠ABD and ∠DBC given m∠ABC = 140°.

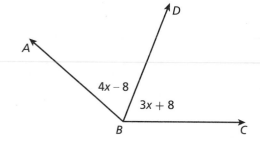

25. If ∠MNO and ∠QRS are complementary angles and m∠MNO is 63°, what is m∠QRS?

26. If ∠MNO and ∠QRS are supplementary angles and m∠MNO is 74°, what is m∠QRS?

27. (MP) **Use Structure** Angles P and Q are supplementary angles. If m∠P is 3 times m∠Q minus 4, what are the measures of the two angles?

28. (MP) **Reason** Use a compass to create a new angle with measure equal to m∠A − m∠B.

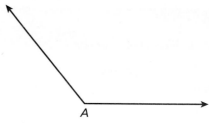

29. The Fan Bridge (or Merchant Square Bridge) is designed to open to allow boats to travel through the canal that it crosses. When it opens, each of the angles created by two adjacent sections is congruent. When m∠AFD = 60°, what are the measures of each of the other angles formed by adjacent sections? What is the measure of m∠AFE?

30. The measure of ∠ABC is 174° and $\vec{BD}$ bisects the angle into ∠ABD and ∠DBC. If ∠ABD measures $(7x - 10)°$, what is the value of x?

31. Main Street is a straight road that runs through the center of town. Sycamore Street intersects Main Street to form a pair of supplementary angles. One angle is obtuse with measure $(9x - 5)°$. The other angle is acute with measure $(4x + 3)°$. Sketch the roads. What are the measures of the given angles Sycamore Street forms with Main Street?

Spiral Review • Assessment Readiness

32. Solve the equation $x - 7 = 4(x + 5)$.

Ⓐ $x = -9$

Ⓑ $x = -7$

Ⓒ $x = 7$

Ⓓ $x = 9$

33. A proposed structure shaped as a right triangle will have side lengths of 50 yards and 120 yards. The hypotenuse length will be 130 yards. What is the area of the triangle?

Ⓐ 3000 yd²   Ⓒ 6000 yd²

Ⓑ 3250 yd²   Ⓓ 6500 yd²

34. Match the segment described on the left with its midpoint on the right.

Segment Endpoints	Midpoint
A. $G(4, 7)$ and $H(3, -9)$	**1.** $(2.5, -2)$
B. $J(4, 7)$ and $K(-3, 9)$	**2.** $(0.5, 8)$
C. $L(-4, -7)$ and $M(9, 3)$	**3.** $(-0.5, 1)$
D. $N(-4, -7)$ and $P(3, 9)$	**4.** $(3.5, -1)$

 I'm in a Learning Mindset!

When I analyze angle relationships, what strategies do I use to persevere through difficulties when the diagrams get more complex?

Polygons and Other Figures in the Plane

(I Can) **identify and measure a polygon.**

Spark Your Learning

Researchers who study demographics often use census data about the United States when studying an area. One important factor of a location is *population density*, or the number of people per unit of area. Staten Island and Manhattan, two boroughs of New York City, are compared below.

Staten Island is approximately 7.3 miles wide and 13.9 miles long.

Manhattan is approximately 2.3 miles wide and 13.4 miles long.

Complete Part A as a whole class. Then complete Parts B–D in small groups.

A. What is a mathematical question you can ask about this situation? What information would you need to know to answer your question?

B. How could geometric shapes play a role in this situation? How could someone comparing the two boroughs use geometric shapes?

C. To answer your question, what strategy and tool would you use along with all the information you have? What answer do you get?

D. How could the information you found be applied to a real-world scenario about the two regions? Why is this an important comparison?

Turn and Talk How do you think your answer would change if you chose different geometric shapes to model the boroughs? Is there only one correct way to create a model? How could you make your estimation more accurate?

©Planet Observer/Universal Images Group/Getty Images

Build Understanding

Understand the Definition of a Polygon

The definition of a polygon varies across the field of mathematics. In this course, we define a **polygon** as a closed plane figure formed by three or more line segments such that each segment intersects exactly two other segments only at their endpoints; no two segments with a common endpoint are collinear. Other definitions of a polygon may allow lines to intersect or allow two polygons to be called a polygon. A **nonpolygon** is a geometric object that does not meet the definition of a polygon.

 A. Determine whether each figure is a polygon.

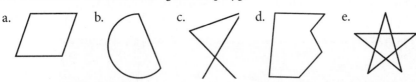

a. b. c. d. e.

B. Explain your reasoning for each figure.

Classify Polygons by the Number of Sides

Polygons can be classified according to the number of sides in the figure.

Name	Triangle	Quadrilateral	Pentagon	Hexagon	*n*-gon
Number of Sides	3	4	5	6	*n*

You may also see a polygon described as an ***n*-gon**, where *n* is the number of sides in the figure. For example, a polygon with nine sides may be called a 9-gon.

Polygons are named by listing the vertices in order moving either clockwise or counterclockwise around the figure. The sample quadrilateral can be named many different ways, including *ABCD*, *BCDA*, and *ADCB*, but it cannot be named *ABDC*.

2 Draw the polygons described below. Then classify the polygon and name it using the vertices.

A. a polygon with five vertices

B. a polygon with four sides of different lengths

C. a polygon with six sides of equal length

 Turn and Talk Secretly draw a polygon, then describe and ask your partner to draw the polygon. Does each person's drawing look the same? Why or why not? Trade roles and try the exercise again.

Step It Out

Construct Regular Polygons

A polygon is a **regular polygon** when all the sides and angles of the polygon are congruent.

The steps for constructing a regular hexagon using a ruler and compass are shown.

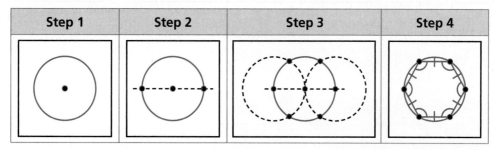

Step 1	Step 2	Step 3	Step 4

A. Describe what happens in each step.

B. What is the purpose of this construction? Do you achieve the same result if the points are not evenly spaced?

C. What is the purpose of the tick mark on each side and the arc on each angle in Step 4?

 Turn and Talk How could you change the construction to create a regular triangle inscribed in the circle?

Model to Estimate Area and Perimeter

The **area** of a geometric figure is the surface contained within the boundaries of a two-dimensional object such as a **triangle**, **rectangle**, or **trapezoid**. The perimeter of a two-dimensional shape is the distance all the way around the figure, found by adding all the side lengths. The table below reviews common area formulas.

Polygon	Triangle	Rectangle	Trapezoid
Figure	height h, base b	width w, length ℓ	b_1, h, b_2
Area Formula	$A = \frac{1}{2}bh$	$A = lw$	$A = h\left(\dfrac{b_1 + b_2}{2}\right)$

If a figure on a plane is more complex, it can often be divided into the basic shapes shown in the table. You can then calculate the area of each individual shape.

Area Addition Postulate

If a figure is composed of two or more shapes, the area of the figure is the sum of the areas of the individual shapes.

Population density is the measurement of population over a certain area. You can calculate population density by dividing the population by the area of the region.

4 Scientists tracking an endangered bird species need to estimate the area of a small island that will be a sanctuary. The current bird population is 1,058. To determine if the population is increasing, they need to relate the current bird population to the area of the island.

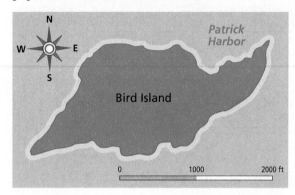

A. Choose one or more shapes to model the island.

B. Find the area of each individual shape. Then, using the Area Addition Postulate, find the total approximate area of the island.

C. Compare your solution to the one shown. Which estimate appears more accurate? Why?

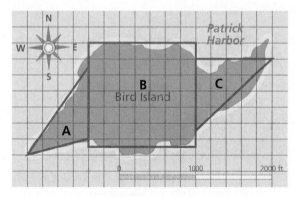

D. The population density of endangered birds on the island gives the number of birds per square foot. What do the units of the population density indicate about how to calculate it?

E. If the population of endangered birds on the island is 1058, use the area you calculated in Part B to find the approximate population density of endangered birds on the island.

 Turn and Talk Would you use the same shapes to approximate the island if you were measuring perimeter instead of area? If not, what changes would you make?

Prove the Pythagorean Theorem

Recall that the Pythagorean Theorem, $a^2 + b^2 = c^2$, can be used to find unknown side lengths or the hypotenuse length of any right triangle.

Pythagorean Theorem

In a right triangle with legs a and b and hypotenuse c, the square of the length of the hypotenuse is equal to the sum of the squares of the lengths of the legs.

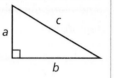

$a^2 + b^2 = c^2$

5 ▶ The figure shows right triangle ABC, which has been copied four times to make the shape of a square with vertices A, B, F, and E.

Notice the placement of the four triangles also creates a centrally located square.

Follow the steps below to examine why the Pythagorean Theorem applies to any right triangle.

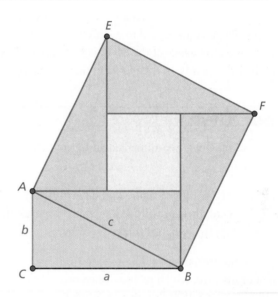

Write an equation to describe the area of square $ABFE$.

$A = lw$

$A = c \cdot c = c^2$

> **A.** Why does this describe the area of square $ABFE$?

We can break the area of the square into the area of the individual shapes that make up the square.

Area of the square = 4(area of triangle ABC) + area of central square

$c^2 = 4\left(\frac{1}{2}bh\right)_{\text{triangle}} + (lw)_{\text{square}}$

$c^2 = 4\left(\frac{1}{2}ab\right) + (a-b)(a-b)$

> **B.** Why does this describe the area of the smaller central square?

$c^2 = 2ab + a^2 - 2ab + b^2$

> **C.** Explain how you obtain this trinomial from the product $(a-b)(a-b)$.

Simplify the equation to $c^2 = a^2 + b^2$.

 Turn and Talk What formula results if $b > a$? What formula results if $b = a$? How do you know the four triangles meet at right angles to form square $ABFE$.

Check Understanding

1. **(MP) Construct Arguments** Draw a figure that is a polygon, a figure that is not a polygon, and a figure that is a polygon under some but not all definitions of polygon. Explain your reasoning.

2. Classify and name the polygon. Is it a regular polygon? Justify your answer.

3. Draw a regular polygon with 9 vertices. Label the vertices and classify the polygon.

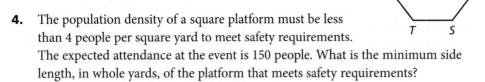

4. The population density of a square platform must be less than 4 people per square yard to meet safety requirements. The expected attendance at the event is 150 people. What is the minimum side length, in whole yards, of the platform that meets safety requirements?

On Your Own

5. Give an example of a two-dimensional figure that is not a polygon. Justify your answer.

6. Kayla examined the given figure and determined it was a regular hexagon because all the angles are congruent. Did Kayla classify the figure correctly? Why?

7. Jason used the formula $A = h\left(\frac{b_1 + b_2}{2}\right)$ to find the area of his yard, which he has drawn on a coordinate plane. Will this give an accurate result? If not, what method would give the correct area?

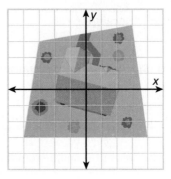

8. Can the formula used to find the area of a trapezoid be used to find areas of parallelograms? What about to find areas of triangles? Use the formulas for the areas of parallelograms and triangles to justify your answer.

Determine if each statement provides enough information to find the value. If yes, find the value.

9. the area of a triangle with a hypotenuse of 5 ft

10. the perimeter of a regular pentagon with a side length of 3 m

11. the width of a rectangle with an area of 24 in² and a length of 6 in.

12. the side length of a square with an area of 64 ft²

Name each polygon three different ways.

13.
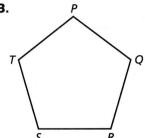

14.
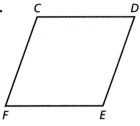

15.
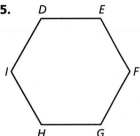

16. The equation used to find the area of a geometric figure is shown. Draw a figure that matches the formula.

$$A = 5 \cdot \left(\frac{1}{2}\right)(6)(4)$$

17. (MP) **Model with Mathematics** Quinn is coating the sides of her tent in a water repellant spray to prepare for an upcoming camping trip. Each can of spray lists the approximate square footage of fabric it will cover, but she isn't sure of the area of the tent's surface. Approximate the surface area by modeling each side using geometric figures. Assume that the tent has a square base.

18. A rectangular pool that is fifteen feet wide and twenty feet long is surrounded by a deck that is four feet wide. What is the area of the surface of the deck?

19. (MP) **Use Repeated Reasoning** There are two homeroom classes at Whiteford High School. The plans below show the layouts for Ms. Chang's and Mr. Edwards's classrooms.

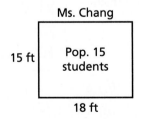

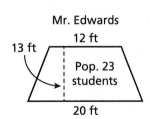

A. Which classroom has a greater population density? Explain.

B. Use the population and area to determine how many square feet of classroom space each student has in Ms. Chang's room.

C. How many students should be added to the classroom with a lower population density in order to make the population density of the two classrooms approximately equal?

20. Science A wildlife preserve aims to keep the population density of large mammals at a natural balance. In order to help determine what the relative and total population density of a preserve should be, a researcher is looking at populations in a large wild area covering about 9000 square miles. Compare the population densities of the different mammals. What conjectures do you have about why some populations are denser than others?

Animal Preserve Population

Black bears: 2500   Grizzly bears: 600

Caribou: 2200   Moose: 1500

Dall sheep: 1700   Wolves: 65

21. Open Ended Create a population density problem that can be solved by modeling an area. Show two different methods of choosing shapes to model the area. Then calculate the area from each model. Compare the two solutions.

Spiral Review • Assessment Readiness

22. Which figure represents ∠AEF?

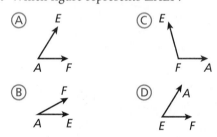

Ⓐ E ... A F

Ⓒ E ... F A

Ⓑ F ... A E

Ⓓ A ... E F

23. Point (0.5, 3) is the midpoint of which set of ordered pairs?

Ⓐ $(-4, -4), (5, -3.5)$

Ⓑ $(1, 3.5), (-2, 4)$

Ⓒ $(2, 9), (-1, -3)$

Ⓓ $(8, 0.5), (7, -3.5)$

24. Which sets of angles are supplementary angles? Select all that apply.

Ⓐ $60°, 30°$ Ⓓ $50°, 130°$

Ⓑ $30°, 150°$ Ⓔ $50°, 40°$

Ⓒ $60°, 60°$ Ⓕ $130°, 130°$

25. A sketch of a section of tempered glass to be used for a shelf is shown. Which expression represents the length of x?

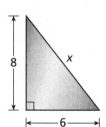

Ⓐ $(6 + 8)^2$ Ⓒ $6^2 - 8^2$

Ⓑ $8^2 + 6^2$ Ⓓ $\sqrt{6^2 + 8^2}$

I'm in a Learning Mindset!

Do my methods for estimating area give me results that have acceptable levels of accuracy? What evidence supports that claim?

Apply the Distance Formula

(I Can) measure the distance between two points on the coordinate plane.

Spark Your Learning

A city has recently redrawn their city map. There are city councilors that represent different areas within the city. The new city map is shown below.

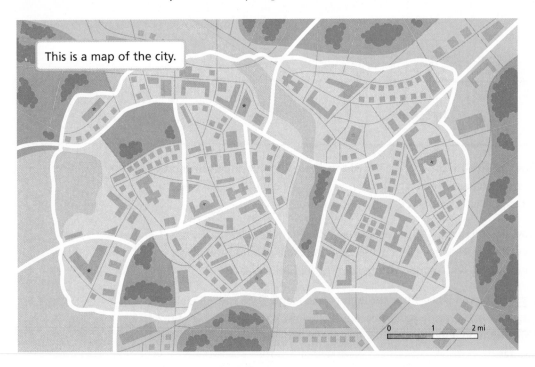

This is a map of the city.

0   1   2 mi

Complete Part A as a whole class. Then complete Parts B–D in small groups.

A. What is a mathematical question you can ask about this situation? What information would you need to know to answer your question?

B. How do you ensure the entire city is evenly represented?

C. What strategy and tool would you use to determine how to divide the city? In what ways could you divide the city? Why?

D. How can you compute the area of each region you drew within the city?

 Turn and Talk Compare the perimeters of each region of the city. Are the perimeters all the same? Does it make sense for the perimeters to be equal as well as the areas?

Build Understanding

Find Area on the Coordinate Plane

When you calculate the area of a composite figure on a coordinate plane, you can often split the figure into simple shapes with horizontal and vertical sides to make it easier to calculate the individual areas.

1 ▸ Find the area of parallelogram *PQRS*.

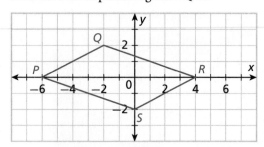

A. How can you use the coordinates of the vertices to find the horizontal distance between *P* and *R*? How can you use the coordinates to find the vertical distance between *Q* and *S*? What are those distances?

B. How can you divide the parallelogram into shapes that allow you to calculate the total area of the parallelogram using the distances you found in Part A? Describe your reasoning. Find the area.

C. Copy the figure. Draw a line through points *P* and *Q*. Suppose $\overline{PQ}$ moves along that line. Draw a parallelogram that shows a possible result of this transformation. Find the area. Compare the two areas and describe your findings.

D. Copy the figure. Draw a line through points *Q* and *R*. Suppose $\overline{QR}$ moves along that line. Do you think the result would be the same as when you moved $\overline{PQ}$? Why or why not?

E. The parallelogram in the figure below has a similar shape to parallelogram *PQRS*. Can you use the same strategy to calculate the area of this parallelogram as you did for parallelogram *PQRS*? What makes this orientation easier or more difficult to calculate the area?

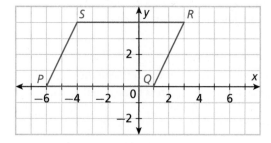

 Turn and Talk Suppose *S* is moved from $(0, -2)$ to $(0, -4)$. What changes? What process can you use to find the area?

Step It Out

Find Length on the Coordinate Plane

Previously you've used the Pythagorean Theorem to calculate the distance between two points on the coordinate plane. The **Distance Formula** is a variation of the Pythagorean Theorem that can be easily applied when working with coordinates to calculate the distance between points on a coordinate plane.

Distance Formula

The distance between two points (x_1, y_1) and (x_2, y_2) on the coordinate plane is $\sqrt{(x_2 - x_1)^2 + (y_2 - y_1)^2}$.

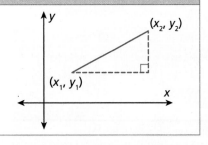

The Distance Formula can be derived using a right triangle where the hypotenuse represents the segment and vertical and horizontal legs are drawn. Substitute expressions for the lengths of the legs into the Pythagorean Theorem.

$$a^2 + b^2 = c^2 \qquad\qquad \text{Pythagorean Theorem}$$

$$(x_2 - x_1)^2 + (y_2 - y_1)^2 = c^2 \qquad\qquad \text{Substitute coordinates.}$$

$$\sqrt{(x_2 - x_1)^2 + (y_2 - y_1)^2} = c \qquad\qquad \text{Distance Formula}$$

2 ▶ Calculate the perimeter of the triangle, rounded to the nearest hundredth.

A. Identify the coordinates of the vertices.

B. The calculation for *AB* is shown. Calculate the length of the each side.

$A(0, 5)$ and $B(5, -5)$ Points

$\sqrt{(x_2 - x_1)^2 + (y_2 - y_1)^2}$ Distance Formula

$= \sqrt{(5 - 0)^2 + (-5 - 5)^2}$ Substitute coordinates for *A* and *B*.

$= \sqrt{(5)^2 + (-10)^2}$ Simplify.

$= \sqrt{125} \approx 11.18$ Simplify.

C. Calculate the sum of the lengths to find the perimeter.

 Turn and Talk What happens to the perimeter if you move the figure on the coordinate plane? What happens to the perimeter if you move one side along the line that contains it? How does that compare to your findings about the area from the previous task?

Model Area on the Coordinate Plane

 A group of scientists are observing a lake in order to assess the effects of recent high temperatures on the water level. To do this, they can compare two aerial photos and estimate the loss of lake area. The most recent photo of the lake is shown.

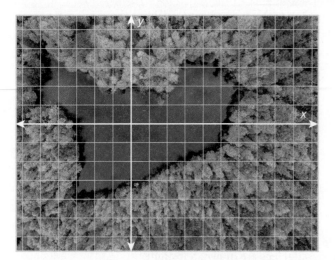

A. Choose one or more shapes to model the area of the lake.

B. Count or use the distance formula to calculate the lengths needed to find the areas of each shape you chose to model the lake. Then add the areas to estimate the total area.

C. Compare your solution to the one below. Which estimate do you think is more accurate? Is there only one solution to estimate an area? Justify your answer.

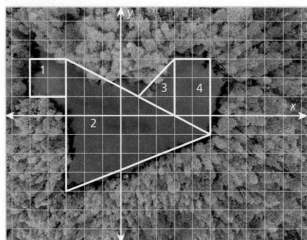

1: $A = lw = (2)(2) = 4$

2: $A = \frac{1}{2}bh = \frac{1}{2}(7)(8) = 28$

3: $A = \frac{1}{2}bh = \frac{1}{2}(3)(2) = 3$

4: $A = \frac{1}{2}(b_1 + b_2)h = \frac{1}{2}(3 + 4)(2) = 7$

Total: $4 + 28 + 3 + 7 = 42$

One estimate of the area is 42 square units.

D. How could you revise your model to make the area estimate more accurate? Discuss the challenges of obtaining a more accurate estimate.

> **Turn and Talk** What shapes would you use to estimate the perimeter of the lake? Can you use the sum of the perimeters of the individual shapes as an estimate of the perimeter of the lake?

Check Understanding

1. Find the area of the parallelogram.

2. Calculate the perimeter of the parallelogram. Round to the nearest hundredth.

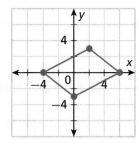

3. Kyle states he can find the distance between two points on the coordinate plane by creating a triangle and using the Pythagorean Theorem. Ava states she can find the distance between the two points using only the coordinates of each point and the Distance Formula. Which student is correct? Explain your reasoning.

4. **(MP) Model with Mathematics** Meg walks to school and work each day and wants to track how far she walks each day. In the morning, Meg walks 7 blocks due east to school. After school, she walks 2 blocks north then 4 blocks west to reach work. She walks straight home from work. How far does she walk in all?

On Your Own

Are the areas of the two parallelograms equal? Explain.

5.

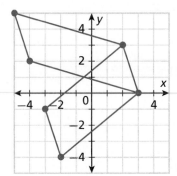

6.

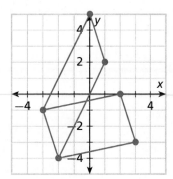

7. Describe a change you could make to a geometric figure so that the perimeter would change but the area would remain the same.

8. Use the figure shown.

   A. Which segments are congruent?

   B. What are the lengths of the congruent segments?

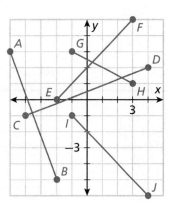

Draw a figure on the coordinate plane that matches the given description. Then calculate the perimeter.

9. an isosceles right triangle with endpoints of one leg at $(0, 0)$ and $(5, 0)$

10. a triangle that contains the vertices $(-2, -1)$, $(4, 3)$, and $(-3, 3)$.

Find the perimeter and area of the described figure.

11. a polygon with vertices $(-5, -3.5)$, $(0, -2)$, $(2.5, 4)$, and $(-1, 6)$

12. a polygon with vertices $(-10, -4)$, $(-2, 1)$, and $(-5, 4)$

13. a polygon with vertices $(-2, -6)$, $(0, -2)$, $(1, 3)$, $(-1, 3)$ and $(-2, 1)$

14. (MP) **Critique Reasoning** Braden is trying to find the length of the given line segment to the nearest tenth of a unit. Is his work accurate? If not, identify and explain the error. Then show the correct work and result.

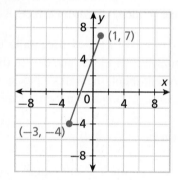

Distance Formula $\sqrt{(x_2 - x_1)^2 + (y_2 - y_1)^2}$

Step 1 $\sqrt{(-3 - (-4))^2 + (1 - 7)^2}$

Step 2 $\sqrt{(1)^2 + (-6)^2}$

Step 3 $\sqrt{1 + 36}$

Step 4 $\sqrt{37} \approx 6.1$

Find the area of each figure.

15.

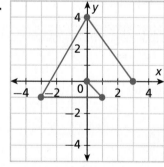

16.

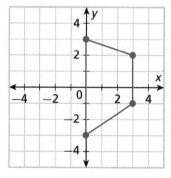

17.

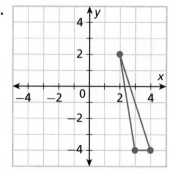

18.

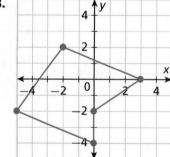

19. Sam is landscaping the area around a backyard pool. He has 150 feet of fencing to enclose the area and will be using landscape rock to cover the enclosed area around the pool. Sam's sketch of the situation is shown. Each unit represents 10 feet.

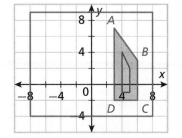

   A. Does Sam have the right amount of fencing? How much extra does he have or how much more does he need?

   B. How many square feet of rock should he purchase?

   C. Sam's client is considering moving B and C 20 feet to the right. What are the new coordinates of B and C? What is the perimeter of the expanded fenced area ABCD?

Find the perimeter of each figure.

20.

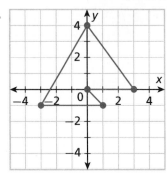

21.

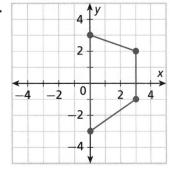

22. A city planner designs a trail through a new green space. On the plan, the trail begins at $(-4, -0.5)$ and ends at $(5, 1.75)$. The trail has 3 straight segments with endpoints at $(-4, -0.5)$, $(0, 0)$, $(3, 1)$, and $(5, 1.75)$. The city would like to use the trail for an upcoming 10K race. If each unit on the plan represents 1 km, will the trail qualify for a 10K race? Justify your reasoning.

23. Aliya is viewing a sign located at the Ferris wheel. She sees the locations of three picnic areas labeled on the map. She wants to eat lunch at the closest picnic area. Which area should she choose?

24. An orchard needs to estimate their crops for next spring. Approximate the area of the region containing orange trees. The roads separate the orchards and each unit represents 50 feet.

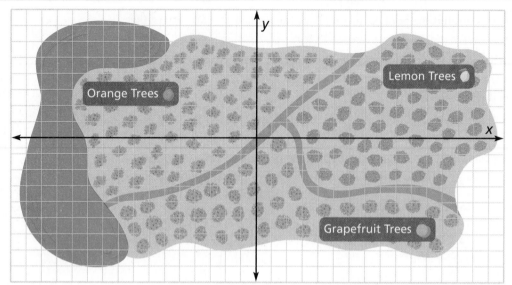

25. (Open Middle™) Using the digits 1 to 9, at most one time each, fill in the boxes to make coordinates for a triangle's vertices with the greatest possible area.

Spiral Review • Assessment Readiness

26. Which sets of angles are complementary angles? Select all that apply.

(A) 10°, 170° (D) 70°, 20°

(B) 55°, 45° (E) 40°, 50°

(C) 65°, 25° (F) 120°, 60°

27. To start to solve the equation $9x + 3 = 3x$, Mohammed writes $9x - 3x + 3 = 3x - 3x$. Which property of equality did he use?

(A) Subtraction (C) Multiplication

(B) Division (D) Addition

28. Determine whether each figure is a polygon.

	A.	B.	C.	D.
Polygon	?	?	?	?
Nonpolygon	?	?	?	?

 I'm in a Learning Mindset!

How did an initial failure with estimating area lead to learning growth when determining more exact areas of figures on the coordinate plane?

Review

Segment Addition

Segment Addition Postulate: If points A, B, and C are collinear and B is between A and C, then $AB + BC = AC$.

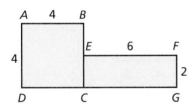

$$AB + BC = AC$$
$$2x - 5 + 3x + 6 = 46$$
$$5x + 1 = 46$$
$$5x = 45$$
$$x = 9$$

$AB = 2 \cdot 9 - 5 = 13$ and $BC = 3 \cdot 9 + 6 = 33$.

Angle Addition

Angle Addition Postulate: If D is in the interior of $\angle ABC$, then $\text{m}\angle ABC = \text{m}\angle ABD + \text{m}\angle CBD$.

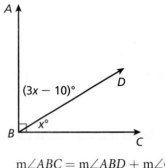

$$\text{m}\angle ABC = \text{m}\angle ABD + \text{m}\angle CBD$$
$$90 = (3x - 10) + x$$
$$90 = 4x - 10$$
$$25 = x$$

$\text{m}\angle ABD = 3 \cdot 25 - 10 = 65°$ and $\text{m}\angle CBD = 25°$.

Area

Area Addition Postulate: If a figure is formed by two or more shapes that do not overlap, the area of the figure is the sum of the areas of the individual shapes.

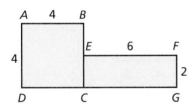

$$\text{Area} = ABCD + EFGC$$
$$= 4 \cdot 4 + 6 \cdot 2$$
$$= 16 + 12$$
$$= 28 \text{ square units}$$

Perimeter

The Distance Formula can be used to find lengths on the coordinate plane.

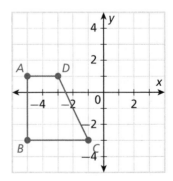

$$DC = \sqrt{(x_2 - x_1)^2 + (y_2 - y_1)^2}$$
$$= \sqrt{\left(-1 - (-3)\right)^2 + \left((-3) - 1\right)^2}$$
$$= \sqrt{20} \approx 4.5$$

Perimeter $\approx 2 + 4 + 4 + 4.5 = 14.5$ units

Vocabulary

Choose the correct term from the box to complete each sentence.

1. A(n) ___?___ is a(n) ___?___; it is a basic figure that is not defined in terms of other figures.

2. The ___?___ of a segment divides the segment into two congruent segments.

3. A polygon with *n* sides is called a(n) ___?___.

4. A(n) angle ___?___ divides an angle into two congruent parts.

5. Points that lie on the same line are ___?___.

6. The common endpoint of the sides of an angle is the ___?___.

Concepts and Skills

7. Sam lives exactly halfway between his friends, Danny and Leo. Danny's house is located at the point $(-4, 4)$ and Leo lives at the point $(9, -8)$. At what point is Sam's house located?

8. Two angles are supplementary. The measure of $\angle ABD$ is $(2x - 9)°$ and the measure of $\angle CBD$ is $(4x + 12)°$. What are the measurements of the two angles?

9. On July 4, 2017, the United States of America had a population of 325.7 million people. The total land area of the United States is 3,535,932 square miles. What was the population density of the United States on July 4, 2017?

Find the area of the figure.

10.

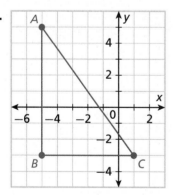

11.

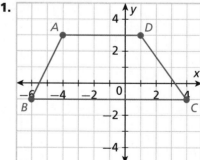

12. (MP) **Use Tools** Liam is putting up fence around a garden. He has poles located at $A(7, 7)$, $B(16, 7)$, $C(2, 2)$, and $D(16, 2)$. Each unit on his coordinate grid represents 1 foot. How many feet of fencing does he need to fence in the garden? Round to the nearest foot. State what strategy and tool you will use to answer the question, explain your choice, and then find the answer.

Tools for Reasoning and Proof

Module Performance Task: Focus on STEM

Scientific Reasoning

The image above shows a geoid model of Earth, which depicts gravitational anomalies at the surface. Scientists often display quantitative data through pseudocolor images, where information is visualized by mapping a function's magnitude to a specific color.

The graph below shows the relationship between mass (in kilograms) and weight (in newtons) as measured at the Amundson-Scott South Pole Station.

Effect of Gravity

Weight (N) vs *Mass (kg)*

A. Form a conjecture from the data. Use evidence to explain your reasoning.

B. Write a conditional statement, an if-then statement, to test your conjecture.

C. If additional data supports your conjecture, are you proven correct? Explain.

D. A measurement taken at Mount Nevado Huascaran in Peru shows a mass of 10 kilograms has a weight of 97.6 N. Does this prove your conjecture wrong? How can you refine your conjecture to account for this data?

Are You Ready?

Complete these problems to review prior concepts and skills you will need for this module.

Justify Steps for Solving Equations

Solve the equation. Justify each step of the solution.

1. $4x + 7 = 39$

2. $\frac{5}{8}t = 2\frac{1}{2}$

3. $6m - 11 = 2m + 13$

4. $0.4(c - 2) = -1.6$

The Pythagorean Theorem and Its Converse

Find the missing side length of the right triangle.

5. $a = 5, b = 12, c = ?$

6. $a = 24, b = 7, c = ?$

7. $a = 6, b = ?, c = 10$

8. $a = ?, b = 15, c = 17$

Use the Converse of the Pythagorean Theorem to determine if the triangle is a right triangle.

9. $a = 8, b = 6, c = 10$

10. $a = 2, b = 7, c = 8$

Angle Relationships in Triangles

11. A triangle has angles that measure 40° and 80°. What is the measure of the third angle of the triangle?

12. The three angle measures of a triangle are $(2x)°$, $(x + 5)°$, and $(5x - 25)°$. Solve for x.

13. The three angle measures of a triangle are $(x - 5)°$, $(x + 30)°$, and $(2x - 5)°$. Solve for x.

14. A triangle has angles that measure 35° and 95°. What is the measure of the opposite exterior angle?

Connecting Past and Present Learning

Previously, you learned:
- to determine horizontal and vertical lengths on the coordinate plane,
- to measure and classify angles, and
- to classify polygons by the number of sides.

In this module, you will learn:
- to add the lengths of segments and show segments are congruent,
- to show that angles are congruent, and
- to prove that statements are true.

Write Conditional Statements

(I Can) write conditional statements and related conditional statements.

Spark Your Learning

Clara meets with friends at a public park. They notice another group being issued a fine and check the posted rules and regulations.

Complete Part A as a whole class. Then complete Parts B–D in small groups.

    A. What is a mathematical question you can ask about this situation? What information would you need to know to answer your question?

    B. How can you rewrite each rule as an if-then statement? Is each statement still true if you swap the words in the "if" part with the words in the "then" part? Explain your reasoning.

    C. To answer your question, what strategy and tool would you use along with all the information you have? What answer do you get?

    D. How could you rewrite one of the statements using the word "not" either once or twice to make a new true statement? Explain your reasoning.

     Turn and Talk How would your answer change if the group was fined $100?

Build Understanding

Make Sketches From Descriptions

In this course, you will use geometric reasoning to write proofs. As a starting point, you will use some postulates that are so basic that you cannot prove them.

Often, you will see the phrases "there exists" and "exactly one," such as "There exists an acute triangle that is isosceles" or "There is exactly one solution to the equation $x + 4 = 9$." "There exists" means that there is at least one, but there may be many more than one. "Exactly one" means there is only one.

> **Connect to Vocabulary**
>
> A postulate is a statement that is accepted as true without proof. A **counterexample** is an example that proves that a conjecture or statement is false.

> **Postulates of Geometry**
>
> - Through any two points, there is exactly one line.
> - Through any three noncollinear points, there is exactly one plane containing them.
> - If two points lie in a plane, the line containing them also lies in the plane.
> - If two lines intersect, they intersect in exactly one point.
> - If two planes intersect, then they intersect in exactly one line.

1 A. Draw a sketch that demonstrates that through any two points, there is exactly one line.

B. Can you find a counterexample of the statement? If so, draw a sketch of the counterexample.

C. What do your findings in Parts A and B suggest about the statement?

D. Draw a sketch that demonstrates that if two lines intersect, they intersect in exactly one point.

E. Can you find a counterexample of the statement? If so, draw a sketch of the counterexample.

F. What do your findings in Parts D and E suggest about the statement?

G. Draw sketches that demonstrate that through any three noncollinear points, there is exactly one plane containing them, if two points lie in a plane, the line containing them also lies in the plane, and if two planes intersect, then they intersect in exactly one line.

H. Can you find a counterexample of each statement in Part G? If so, draw a sketch of the counterexample.

I. What do your findings in Parts G and H suggest about the statements?

 Turn and Talk Think of a mathematical statement about numbers that is not always true. Show that it is not true by finding a counterexample.

Write Related Conditional Statements

A **conjecture** is a statement that is believed to be true. A **conditional statement** is a statement that can be written in the form "if p, then q," where p is the hypothesis of the statement and q is the conclusion.

There are three statements that are related to a conditional statement. These are the **converse**, **inverse**, and **contrapositive** of a conditional statement.

Conditional Statements		
Statement	**Definition**	**Symbols**
Conditional Statement	A statement that can be written in the form "if p, then q," where p is the hypothesis and q is the conclusion.	If p, then q.
Converse	A statement formed by exchanging the hypothesis and conclusion of a conditional statement.	If q, then p.
Inverse	A statement formed by negating the hypothesis and conclusion of a conditional statement.	If not p, then not q.
Contrapositive	A statement formed by both exchanging and negating the hypothesis and conclusion of a conditional statement.	If not q, then not p.

A conditional statement and its contrapositive are either both true or both false. The converse of a conditional statement and the inverse of a conditional statement are also either both true or both false.

2 Use the following conjecture for this task.

> The product of two real numbers is a negative number when exactly one of the factors is a negative number.

A. Identify the hypothesis and conclusion in the conjecture.

B. Write the conjecture in the form "if p, then q."

C. Write the converse of the statement. Is the converse a true statement? Explain.

D. Write the inverse of the statement. Is the inverse a true statement?

E. Write the contrapositive of the statement. Is the contrapositive a true statement?

 Turn and Talk Write a true conditional statement. Show that the contrapositive of the statement is also true.

Step It Out

Write Definitions as Biconditional Statements

If a conditional statement and its converse are both true, they can be combined into a single **biconditional statement**. A biconditional statement is a statement that can be written in the form "*p* if and only if *q*," where *p* is the hypothesis and *q* is the conclusion. Biconditional statements can be used to write **definitions**.

> **Connect to Vocabulary**
>
> You have used definitions to understand the meanings of new words. In mathematics, a **definition** is a statement that describes a mathematical object and can be written as a true biconditional statement.

 3 Write the given definition as a biconditional statement.

> Midpoint of a line segment: the point that divides the segment into two congruent segments

Let *p* be "a point is a midpoint of a line segment." Let *q* be "the point divides a segment into two congruent segments."

A. Does it matter which statement is used for *p* and for *q* in a biconditional statement?

The definition of a midpoint of a line segment, written as a biconditional statement, is: A point is a midpoint of a line segment if and only if the point divides the segment into two congruent segments.

B. What other way can you write the biconditional statement?

C. Write the definition of an acute angle as a biconditional statement.

> **Turn and Talk** Write the definition of a mathematical term you know as a biconditional statement.

Apply Conditional Statements in the Real World

 4 A store creates a banner with its new advertising slogan.

Match each related statement to the type of statement it is.

Type	Statement
A. Converse	**1.** If you did not buy it from us, then you did not buy the best.
B. Inverse	**2.** If you did not buy the best, then you did not buy it from us.
C. Contrapositive	**3.** If you bought the best, then you bought it from us.

> **Turn and Talk** Why would an advertiser choose to use the contrapositive of a conditional statement? Explain.

Check Understanding

1. **(MP) Reason** Draw a sketch that demonstrates this statement. Is it possible to find a counterexample? If so, draw a sketch of the counterexample.

   > Two distinct lines that intersect will intersect at exactly one point.

2. Write the statement "Yesterday was Monday, so today is Tuesday." in if-then form. Write the converse, inverse, and contrapositive of the statement.

3. Write the definition of a right angle as a biconditional statement.

4. A pizza chain has a slogan "Your pizza will be made right, or your next one is free." Write this slogan in if-then form.

On Your Own

Draw a sketch that demonstrates each statement. Determine if it is possible to find a counterexample. If possible, draw a sketch of the counterexample.

5. Given three points, there is only one plane that contains them.

6. Through a point not on a line, there is exactly one line that does not intersect the given line.

Write the conditional statement in if-then form.

7. $4x + 7 = 15$ when $x = 2$.

8. Today is Thursday, so tomorrow is Friday.

9. The sum of the measures of two supplementary angles is 180 degrees.

Write the conditional statement, the converse, the inverse, and the contrapositive of the statement.

10. $2t + 3 = 13$ when $t = 5$.

11. The dog gets a treat when it performs the trick.

12. An isosceles triangle has two sides with the same length.

Write the definition as a biconditional statement.

13. A scalene triangle is a triangle with three sides with different lengths.

14. A square is a rectangle with four sides that are the same length.

15. Perpendicular lines are lines that intersect at a 90° angle.

16. **(MP) Reason** Write the statement as an if-then statement. Write the converse of this statement. Is the converse a true statement? Explain.

    The sum of two positive numbers is a positive number.

Give a counterexample for each conclusion.

17. The difference of two negative numbers is always negative.

18. A number times a greater number is always greater than the number.

19. **Open Ended** Write a conditional statement that is not true, but the inverse of the statement is true.

20. Can the statement be written as a biconditional statement? If so, write the statement as a biconditional statement. If not, explain why not.

> The *y*-intercept of a line is the point where the line intersects the *y*-axis.

21. A painting company has its slogan on a van. Write this statement as an if-then statement, then find the converse, inverse, and contrapositive of the statement.

22. Consider the statement "If you bought a ticket to a concert, then you attended the concert." Find the converse, inverse, and contrapositive of the statement. Is the converse of the statement true? Explain your reasoning.

Spiral Review • Assessment Readiness

23. The tip of a toy arrowhead shaped as an isosceles right triangle is sketched on a graph. The endpoints of one leg are (0, 0) and (0, 10). What is the length of the longest side of the tip?

   Ⓐ $10\sqrt{2}$ units   Ⓒ $20\sqrt{2}$ units

   Ⓑ 100 units   Ⓓ 200 units

24. A polygon has five sides. What type of polygon is it?

   Ⓐ quadrilateral

   Ⓑ pentagon

   Ⓒ hexagon

   Ⓓ octagon

25. For $8(-2x + 1) - 10 = -6$, match each step in the solution with the its justification.

Step	Justification
A. $8(-2x + 1) - 10 = -6$	**1.** Combine constants.
B. $-16x + 8 - 10 = -6$	**2.** Addition Property of Equality
C. $-16x - 2 = -6$	**3.** Given equation
D. $-16x = -4$	**4.** Division Property of Equality
E. $x = 0.25$	**5.** Distributive Property

 I'm in a Learning Mindset!

What strategies can I use to concentrate when writing the related statements of conditional statements?

Use Inductive and Deductive Reasoning

use inductive and deductive reasoning to justify conjectures.

Spark Your Learning

Felicia is packing a variety of items to show in a craft fair booth.

Complete Part A as a whole class. Then complete Parts B–C in small groups.

A. What is a mathematical question you can ask about this situation?
What information would you need to know to answer your question?

B. To answer your question, what strategy and tool would you use
along with all the information you have? What answer do you get?

C. After the fair, how will Felicia know whether she prepared well for the fair?
What might Felicia learn that could affect her preparation for the next fair?

Turn and Talk Suppose that the craft fair went very well and that Felicia plans on
returning to the same craft fair in three months. What considerations would cause
Felicia to prepare differently?

Build Understanding

Compare Inductive and Deductive Reasoning

Inductive reasoning and deductive reasoning are two processes that are used to determine if a statement is true.

Inductive reasoning is the process of reasoning that a rule or a statement may be true by looking at specific cases.

Deductive reasoning is the process of using logic to draw conclusions. Deductive reasoning uses facts, definitions, postulates, theorems, and logic to *prove* a statement is true for all cases.

 Rebecca is shopping for a new phone. She is reading reviews of a brand of phone on a website.

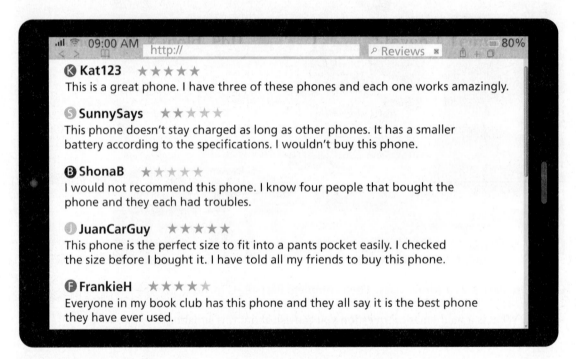

K Kat123 ★★★★★
This is a great phone. I have three of these phones and each one works amazingly.

S SunnySays ★★★★★
This phone doesn't stay charged as long as other phones. It has a smaller battery according to the specifications. I wouldn't buy this phone.

B ShonaB ★★★★★
I would not recommend this phone. I know four people that bought the phone and they each had troubles.

J JuanCarGuy ★★★★★
This phone is the perfect size to fit into a pants pocket easily. I checked the size before I bought it. I have told all my friends to buy this phone.

F FrankieH ★★★★★
Everyone in my book club has this phone and they all say it is the best phone they have ever used.

A. Which reviews use inductive reasoning? Which reviews use deductive reasoning? Explain your reasoning.

B. Does the use of inductive reasoning or deductive reasoning indicate a positive review or a negative review? Explain your reasoning.

C. Write your own review of a phone using inductive reasoning. Explain why your review uses inductive reasoning.

D. Write your own review of a phone using deductive reasoning. Explain why your review uses deductive reasoning.

 Turn and Talk Do you think Rebecca should buy this phone based on the reviews? Explain your reasoning.

Step It Out

Apply Properties of Equality

When you solve an algebraic equation, you are using deductive reasoning. As you solve an equation, you can state the rule or property that justifies each of the steps in the solution process.

Properties of equality are rules that describe ways that you can change both sides of an equation in the same way and have the equality remain true. These properties allow you to add, subtract, multiply, or divide both sides of an equation by the same quantity in the process of solving an equation.

Properties of Equality	
Property	**Symbols**
Addition Property of Equality	If $a = b$, then $a + c = b + c$.
Subtraction Property of Equality	If $a = b$, then $a - c = b - c$.
Multiplication Property of Equality	If $a = b$, then $ac = bc$.
Division Property of Equality	If $a = b$, and $c \neq 0$, then $\frac{a}{c} = \frac{b}{c}$.

2 ▶ Use algebra and deductive reasoning to justify the statement.

If $3x + 8 = -x$, then $x = -2$.

$3x + 8 = -x$	Given
$3x + 8 + x = -x + x$	_____?_____
$4x + 8 = 0$	Simplify.
$4x + 8 - 8 = 0 - 8$	_____?_____
$4x = -8$	Simplify.
$\dfrac{4x}{4} = \dfrac{-8}{4}$	_____?_____
$x = -2$	Simplify.

A. What property of equality is being used here? Why is this step needed?

B. What property of equality is being used here? Why is this step needed?

C. What property of equality is being used here? Why is this step needed?

D. Based on the statements of the properties of equality in the table, what are the values of a, b, and c for the property of equality used in this step?

Turn and Talk

- Use algebra and deductive reasoning to justify the statement. Be sure to name a property of equality when you use one.

  If $\frac{1}{4}z - \frac{3}{4} = 1$, then $z = 7$.

- Write an if-then statement for the equation $\frac{1}{4}z + \frac{3}{4} = 1$. What steps and justifications change in the solution?

Write a Two-Column Proof

A **theorem** is a statement you can prove is true, using a series of logical steps. A **proof** is an argument that uses true statements and logic to arrive at a conclusion. Once you prove that a statement or theorem is true, you can use it in later proofs.

There are different formats for proofs. A common format is a **two-column proof** listing statements in the first column and reasons in the second column. The first column contains numbered mathematical statements about the given information. It also contains the results of applying definitions, postulates, and established theorems to statements that have already been made. The second column gives the reason that the corresponding statement is true. When you provide justifications for the steps you take when solving an equation, you are essentially writing a two-column proof.

Statements	Reasons
1. $3(x + 1) = 15$	**1.** Given equation
2. $3x + 3 = 15$	**2.** Distributive Property
3. $3x = 12$	**3.** Subtraction Property of Equality
4. $x = 4$	**4.** Division Property of Equality

In Geometry, you will write proofs of theorems which are intended to prove that something is true in every case, as in the task below. You will also write proofs where you are proving something about a specific situation.

3 Write a two-column proof to prove that a midpoint divides a segment so that the length of the whole segment is two times the length of each part.

Given: M is the midpoint of $\overline{AB}$.

Prove: $AB = 2 \cdot AM$

Statements	Reasons
1. M is the midpoint of $\overline{AB}$.	**1.** Given
2. $AM = MB$	**2.** Definition of ___?___
3. $AB = AM + MB$	**3.** Segment Addition Postulate
4. $AB = AM + AM$	**4.** ___?___ Property
5. $AB = 2 \cdot AM$	**5.** Simplify.

A. Is this the definition of midpoint or the definition of line segment? How do you know?

B. Is this the Substitution Property or the Transitive Property of Equality? How do you know?

 Turn and Talk How can you decide what the order of statements in a two-column proof should be?

Check Understanding

1. **(MP) Reason** Explain why the given conclusion uses inductive reasoning.

   For the sequence 5, 10, 15, 20, … , the next term is 25 because the previous terms are multiples of 5.

2. Is proving the Midpoint Formula an example of inductive reasoning or deductive reasoning? Explain.

3. You are given that $\overline{ST}$ has length 23. Prove that $t = 7$ by copying and completing the two-column proof.

   Given: $ST = 23$

   Prove: $t = 7$

   $4t - 5$ T

   S

Statements	Reasons
1. $4t - 5 = 23$	**1.** Given
2. $4t - 5 + 5 = 23 + 5$	**2.** ___?___
3. $4t = 28$	**3.** Simplify.
4. $\dfrac{4t}{4} = \dfrac{28}{4}$	**4.** ___?___
5. $t = 7$	**5.** Simplify.

On Your Own

Explain why the given conclusion uses inductive reasoning.

4. It always snows on my birthday.

5. The next term in the pattern 4, 8, 12, … is 16.

6. Justin wears a white shirt four days in a row, so Justin only has white shirts.

7. Antonia made a list of her soccer team's game results. Antonia's soccer team wins when they score 3 or more goals.

8. $15 + 17 = 32$, $8 + 4 = 12$, and $2 + 7 = 9$, so the sum of two positive integers is a positive integer.

9. Janet is working on a puzzle that includes the following.

   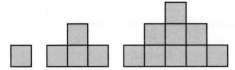

   She decides that this will be the next image.

   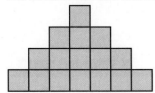

SOCCER RESULTS

5	4
2	4
3	2
3	1
0	2
4	3
5	2

In Problems 10–15, decide if inductive reasoning or deductive reasoning is used to make the conjecture. Explain your reasoning.

10. Each time Jose went to the store this week, he bought a bag of apples.
If Jose is going to the store today, you can conclude that he will buy a bag of apples.

11. All right angles measure 90°. ∠ABC is a right angle, so m∠ABC is 90°.

12. All mammals are warm-blooded animals.
If an otter is a mammal, you can say that it is a warm-blooded animal.

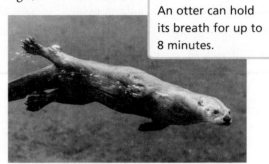

An otter can hold its breath for up to 8 minutes.

13. Cindy rolls a number cube six times and the result is an even number each time. You can conclude that she will roll an even number the next time she rolls the number cube.

14. A scalene triangle has three sides with different lengths.
If triangle *XYZ* is a scalene triangle, it has three sides with different lengths.

15. Tammy goes bowling and her scores were 122, 138, and 117.
When Tammy goes bowling the next time, she will get a score of over 100 points.

16. Consider the following pattern.

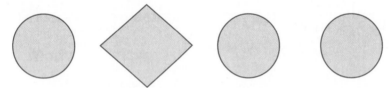

A. Assume that the pattern continues using just these two shapes. Describe how the pattern might continue. Did you use inductive or deductive reasoning?

B. Describe another way that the pattern might continue.

Use deductive reasoning to write a conclusion.

17. If two distinct lines intersect, they intersect at one point.
Line *m* and line *n* intersect.

18. If a person is over 48 inches tall, they can ride the roller coaster.
Emma is over 48 inches tall.

19. If an integer is not divisible by 2, then it is an odd number.
17 is not divisible by 2.

20. If the measure of an angle is greater than 90° and less than 180°, then it is an obtuse angle.
The measure of an angle is 120°.

21. If a number is divisible by 6, then it is divisible by 2.
54 is divisible by 6.

22. If Victoria has less than $50, she does not go to the movies.
Victoria has $35.

Write the statement as an if-then statement.

23. $x - 7 = 22$; $x = 29$

24. $t + 4 = 17$; $t = 13$

25. $3a + 4 = 10$; $a = 2$

26. $2m - 7 = 25$; $m = 16$

27. $x = 7$; $2x - 13 = 1$

28. $r = -2$; $6 - 2r = 10$

29. $n = 12$; $n - 20 = -8$

30. $b = 0$; $4b - 9 = -9$

(MP) **Reason** **For Problems 31–37, select the word that makes the statement true.**

31. If a triangle has an obtuse angle it (must, may, cannot) be an acute triangle.

32. If one endpoint of a segment is on a line so that two angles are formed, then the two angles formed (must, may, cannot) be supplementary.

33. If the sun is shining this morning, then it (must, may, cannot) rain this afternoon.

34. Acadia National Park is in Maine. Joshua lives in Maine. So Joshua (must have, may have, never) visited Acadia National Park.

35. If a number is even, then it (must, may, cannot) be a whole number.

36. A quadrilateral (always, sometimes, never) has congruent sides.

37. If a is 0, then ab is (always, sometimes, never) equal to 0.

Write a two-column proof that the solution to the equation is true.

38. $y - 23 = 7$; $y = 30$

39. $n + 14 = 19$; $n = 5$

40. $3a + 7 = 16$; $a = 3$

41. $2r - 11 = 1$; $r = 6$

Write a two-column proof of the statement. Include Given and Prove statements.

42. If M is between A and B and $AM = \frac{1}{2} \cdot AB$, then M is the midpoint of $\overline{AB}$.

43. If $\overrightarrow{EG}$ is the angle bisector of $\angle DEF$, then m$\angle DEF = 2 \cdot$ m$\angle DEG$.

In Problems 44–47, determine whether the statement is true based on the true statements.

- If Jin goes to the library, she will only borrow books.
- If Jayden goes to the library, he will only borrow movies.
- If Jin goes to the library, then she doesn't have a softball game that day.
- Jin and Jayden are at the library.

44. Jin borrowed a book.

45. Jayden borrowed a book.

46. Jin had a softball game.

47. Jayden borrowed a movie.

48. (MP) **Construct Arguments** Jerome states that if a line segment is 23 units long, and part of the segment is 9 units long, then the rest of the segment is 14 units long. What postulates allow Jerome to make this conclusion?

49. Marita claims that the sum of three consecutive counting numbers is three times the second number. Prove that this conjecture is true.

   A. Let the second number be *n*. Write expressions for the first and third numbers using *n*.

   B. Find the sum of the three numbers.

   C. Explain why your result proves the conjecture.

   D. Is Marita's claim true for negative numbers? Explain your reasoning.

50. Open Ended Write a true statement. Use deductive reasoning to explain why the statement is true.

51. A rectangle with four congruent sides is a square. What conclusion can you make about rectangle *JKLM* based on the sides? rectangle *WXYZ*?

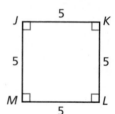
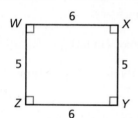

52. Open Ended Write a math problem that uses the Segment Addition Postulate, the Addition Property of Equality, and the Division Property of Equality to find the length of a segment.

Spiral Review • Assessment Readiness

53. What is the length of $\overline{BD}$?

   (A) $\sqrt{14}$ units

   (B) $\sqrt{34}$ units

   (C) 8 units

   (D) 15 units

54. A fenced-in area for riding horses has six sides. What is the name of this shape?

   (A) quadrilateral

   (B) pentagon

   (C) hexagon

   (D) octagon

55. The _____ of a statement is formed by negating the hypothesis and conclusion of a conditional statement.

   (A) inverse

   (C) contrapositive

   (B) converse

   (D) biconditional

56. On a number line, point *X* is located at 8 and point *Z* is located at 44. Point *Y* is between *X* and *Z* where $XY = 14$ units. What is *YZ*?

   (A) 32 units

   (B) 22 units

   (C) 20 units

   (D) 18 units

 I'm in a Learning Mindset!

When a proof requires many steps, what strategies can I use to stay focused when writing each step and reason in the correct, logical sequence?

Write Proofs about Segments

(I Can) **use properties of segments to show congruence.**

Spark Your Learning

Brianna and Carl make several stops on their walk home from school. They use an app to keep track of their distance for only one portion of their trip.

Complete Part A as a whole class. Then complete Parts B–D in small groups.

  A. What is a mathematical question you can ask about this situation? What information would you need to know to answer your question?

  B. What relationship(s) are involved in this situation? What postulate(s) or theorem(s) are involved in this situation? How do you know?

  C. To answer your question, what strategy and tool would you use along with all the information you have? What answer do you get?

  D. Does your answer make sense in the context of the situation? Justify your reasoning with relationship(s), postulate(s), or theorem(s).

> **Turn and Talk** Is the grocery store the midpoint between the soccer field and their home? Explain your reasoning.

Build Understanding

Investigate Properties of Congruence

Remember that two segments are congruent if the lengths of each segment are equal.

The table below shows how the properties of congruence are applied to segments.

Properties of Segment Congruence	
Property	**Example**
Reflexive	$\overline{AB} \cong \overline{AB}$
Symmetric	If $\overline{AB} \cong \overline{CD}$, then $\overline{CD} \cong \overline{AB}$.
Transitive	If $\overline{AB} \cong \overline{CD}$ and $\overline{CD} \cong \overline{EF}$, then $\overline{AB} \cong \overline{EF}$.

1 The climbing structure shown is made using rope segments.

A. Why would you expect some rope segments to be congruent?

B. How can you determine if $\overline{TV}$ is congruent to $\overline{WX}$ if you know that $\overline{WX} \cong \overline{TV}$?

C. How can you determine if $\overline{GH}$ is congruent to $\overline{LM}$ if you know that $\overline{GH} \cong \overline{JK}$ and $\overline{JK} \cong \overline{LM}$?

D. What does the Reflexive Property of Congruence tell you about each rope segment?

 Turn and Talk If a rope segment $\overline{NP}$ is congruent to $\overline{LM}$ in Part C, how can you show that $\overline{NP}$ is congruent to $\overline{JK}$ or $\overline{GH}$?

Step It Out

Use Segment Congruence in a Real-World Problem

2 Jessica is constructing a bookshelf for her bedroom. The instructions show a diagram of the completed bookshelf. The boards used to construct the bookshelf are represented by $\overline{AB}$, $\overline{BE}$, $\overline{EG}$, $\overline{AG}$, $\overline{CH}$, $\overline{DK}$, and $\overline{FJ}$.

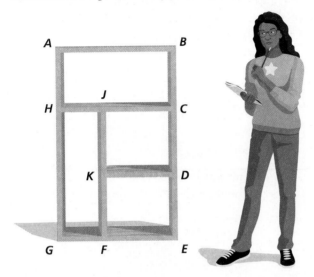

A. Jessica wants to organize the boards into groups of congruent boards before she starts working. She sets aside the boards represented by $\overline{AB}$, $\overline{AG}$, and $\overline{DK}$. Which boards appear to be congruent to these segments?

 Turn and Talk Why might Jessica want to work on groups of congruent boards at the same time?

Use the Segment Addition Postulate

3 The length of $\overline{AC}$ is 24. Prove that $\overline{AB} \cong \overline{BC}$.

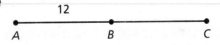

Statements	Reasons
1. $AC = 24$, $AB = 12$	**1.** Given
2. $AB + BC = AC$	**2.** ___?___
3. $12 + BC = 24$	**3.** Substitution
4. $BC = 24 - 12$	**4.** ___?___
5. $BC = 12$	**5.** Simplify.
6. $\overline{AB} \cong \overline{BC}$	**6.** Definition of congruent segments

A. What allows you to write $AB + BC = AC$?

B. What allows you to write $BC = 24 - 12$?

C. Which statements allow you to use this reason?

 Turn and Talk Are all segments of length 12 centimeters congruent? Explain.

Prove Segment Congruence

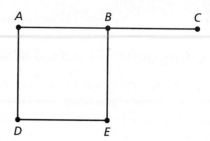

4 **Given:** *ABED* is a square.

$$\overline{AB} \cong \overline{BC}$$

Prove: $\overline{DE} \cong \overline{BC}$

A. Write the statements in the correct order.

> $\overline{AB} \cong \overline{DE}$

> $\overline{DE} \cong \overline{BC}$

> $AB = DE$

> *ABED* is a square.

> $\overline{AB} \cong \overline{BC}$

B. Write the reasons in the correct order.

> Given

> All sides of a square are equal in length.

> Transitive Property of Congruence

> Given

> Definition of congruent segments

 Turn and Talk What parts of the proof would need to change if *ABED* were a rectangle instead of a square? Explain.

Apply Algebra to Ensure Segment Congruence

5 What value of *x* will make $\overline{LM} \cong \overline{MN}$.

$7x - 17$ $2x + 53$

L M N

$$7x - 17 = 2x + 53$$

$$7x - 17 - 2x = 2x - 2x + 53$$

> **A.** Why do you set $7x - 17$ equal to $2x + 53$?

$$5x - 17 = 53$$

$$5x - 17 + \underline{\quad ? \quad} = 53 + \underline{\quad ? \quad}$$

$$5x = \underline{\quad ? \quad}$$

> **B.** Complete the solution to the equation.

$$\frac{5x}{5} = \frac{?}{5}$$

$$x = \underline{\quad ? \quad}$$

 Turn and Talk How would you write an expression for the length of $\overline{LN}$?

Check Understanding

1. You know that $\overline{PQ} \cong \overline{ST}$ and that $\overline{XY} \cong \overline{ST}$. What can you conclude about $\overline{PQ}$ and $\overline{XY}$?

2. The floor design for a new hotel is shown in the figure. The design involves a rectangle, *DEGF*, joined with an isosceles triangle, *ABC*. The triangular portion of the floor design is centered where it meets the rectangular portion so that points *B* and *C* are the midpoints of $\overline{DC}$ and $\overline{BE}$, respectively. Which outside edges of the floor design are congruent?

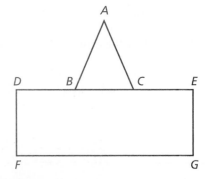

3. Suppose $VW = 4$ and $WX = 5$. What must be true about *V*, *W*, and *X* to conclude that $VX = 9$?

4. In the figure, *DEGF* is a rectangle, $\overline{DB} \cong \overline{CE}$, and $FG = 3BC$. Write the correct statements to complete the proof to show that $\overline{BC} \cong \overline{DB}$.

Statements	Reasons
1. $\overline{DB} \cong \overline{CE}$	1. Given
2. ___?___	2. Definition of congruent segments
3. $DE = DB + BC + CE$	3. Segment Addition Postulate
4. ___?___	4. Substitution
5. ___?___	5. Opposite sides of a rectangle have equal length.
6. $FG = DB + BC + DB$	6. Substitution
7. ___?___	7. Given
8. $3BC = DB + BC + DB$	8. Substitution
9. $BC = DB$	9. Simplify.
10. ___?___	10. Definition of congruent segments

5. If $AB = 3x - 12$ and $CD = 44 - x$, what value of *x* will make $\overline{AB} \cong \overline{CD}$?

On Your Own

Match the statement with the property of congruence that makes the statement true.

A. Reflexive Property   **B.** Symmetric Property   **C.** Transitive Property

6. $\overline{BC} \cong \overline{FG}$, so $\overline{FG} \cong \overline{BC}$.

7. $\overline{PQ} \cong \overline{PQ}$

8. $\overline{AB} \cong \overline{CD}$ and $\overline{CD} \cong \overline{EF}$, so $\overline{AB} \cong \overline{EF}$.

9. $\overline{CD} \cong \overline{CD}$

10. $\overline{LM} \cong \overline{NO}$ and $\overline{NO} \cong \overline{PQ}$, so $\overline{LM} \cong \overline{PQ}$.

11. $\overline{WX} \cong \overline{YZ}$, so $\overline{YZ} \cong \overline{WX}$.

Use the Segment Addition Postulate to find the missing length if the given points are collinear and appear in alphabetical order.

12. $AB = 7$, $AC = 15$, $BC = ?$

13. $XY = 11$, $XZ = 13$, $YZ = ?$

14. $JK = 8$, $KL = 10$, $JL = ?$

15. $FG = 15$, $GH = 12$, $FH = ?$

A, B, and C are collinear and B is between A and C. Use the Segment Addition Postulate to determine if $\overline{AB} \cong \overline{BC}$.

16. $AB = 8$, $AC = 18$

17. $AC = 18$, $BC = 9$

18. $AB = 12$, $AC = 24$

19. $BC = 15$, $AC = 20$

List the groups of segments in the figure that appear to be congruent.

20.

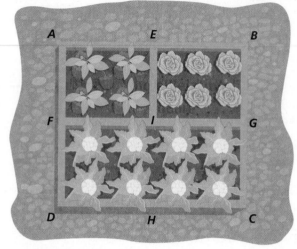

21.

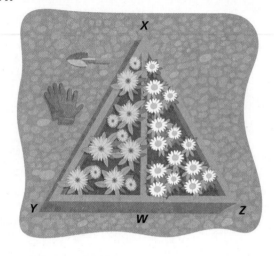

22. Point S lies on $\overline{RT}$. The length of $\overline{RS}$ is 25 units. The length of $\overline{RT}$ is 50 units. Is $\overline{RS}$ congruent to $\overline{ST}$? Explain.

23. Triangle DEF is an equilateral triangle. $\overline{FG} \cong \overline{DE}$. Write a two-column proof that proves that $\overline{EF} \cong \overline{FG}$.

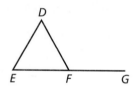

24. Write a two-column proof.
Given: $AB = CD$
Prove: $AC = BD$

25. **(MP) Reason** Raul is building a table from the kit. The instructions include a diagram of the finished table. Which pieces of the frame appear to be congruent?

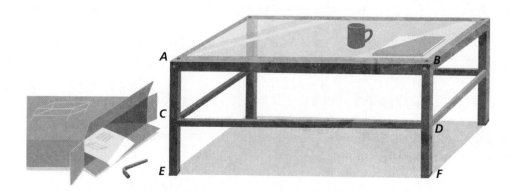

Solve for *x*.

26. $\overline{BD}$ has a point *C* between points *B* and *D*. $BC = 7x - 4$, $CD = 3x + 1$, and $BD = 9x$.

27. $\overline{XZ}$ has a point *Y* between points *X* and *Z*. $XY = 17$, $YZ = 4x + 9$, and $XZ = 11x - 9$.

28. $\overline{LN}$ has a point *M* between points *L* and *N*. $LM = x + 13$, $NM = 2x + 1$, and $LN = 6x - 7$.

29. $\overline{FH}$ has a point *G* between points *F* and *H*. $\overline{FG} \cong \overline{GH}$, $FG = 8x - 7$, and $FH = 13x - 2$.

30. $\overline{JL}$ has a point *K* between points *J* and *L*. $\overline{JK} \cong \overline{KL}$, $KL = 2x - 1$, and $JL = 5x - 12$.

31. $\overline{PR}$ has a point *Q* between points *P* and *R*. $\overline{PQ} \cong \overline{QR}$, $PQ = x + 1$, and $PR = 3x - 13$.

32. Find the length of segment *GI*, if $GJ = 64$ centimeters.

33. Find the length of segment *WY*, if $WZ = 128$ feet and segment *WX* is congruent to segment *YZ*.

34. **Open Ended** Write a problem with three points on a segment that uses the Segment Addition Postulate to solve.

35. (MP) **Model with Mathematics** The distance from the convention center to the airport is 16 miles. A restaurant lies on a line segment drawn from the convention center to the airport. The restaurant is 4 miles from the airport. Sketch the situation. How far is the restaurant from the convention center?

36. **STEM** An engineering student creates a model of a bridge for a project. The photo shows the student's model. The student intends that $\overline{AB} \cong \overline{CD}$ and $\overline{DF} \cong \overline{GH}$. What additional information would you need to know to determine that $\overline{AB} \cong \overline{DF}$?

37. Find the value of a that makes $\overline{XY} \cong \overline{YZ}$. What are the lengths of $\overline{XY}$, $\overline{YZ}$, and $\overline{XZ}$?

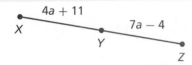

38. Find the value of n when $AC = 48$. What are the lengths of $\overline{AB}$ and $\overline{BC}$? Is $\overline{AB} \cong \overline{BC}$?

Spiral Review • Assessment Readiness

39. What is the missing operation that completes the proof?

If $6x + 8 = 74$, then $x = 11$.

Statements	Reasons
$6x + 8 = 74$	Given
$6x = 66$	_____ Property of Equality
$x = 11$	Division Property of Equality

(A) Addition (C) Subtraction

(B) Multiplication (D) Division

40. Find the measures of $\angle FGI$ and $\angle IGH$ given $m\angle FGH = 128°$.

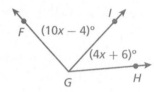

(A) $86°, 42°$

(B) $74\frac{6}{7}°, 53\frac{1}{7}°$

(C) $94°, 34°$

(D) $76\frac{1}{7}°, 51\frac{6}{7}°$

41. Consider the conditional statement: "*If a member of the track team is a sprinter, then they are a fast runner.*" Identify the type of related statement with the conditional.

Related Statement	Converse	Inverse	Contrapositive
A. If a member of the track team is not a fast runner, then they are not a sprinter.	?	?	?
B. If a member of the track team is a fast runner, then they are a sprinter.	?	?	?
C. If a member of the track team is not a sprinter, then they are not a fast runner.	?	?	?

🔷 **I'm in a Learning Mindset!**

Is my understanding of proofs using segments improving? Are there any adjustments I need to make to enhance my learning?

Write Proofs about Angles

(I Can) **prove theorems about angles.**

Spark Your Learning

Heavy cargo is raised by a hydraulic scissor lift table to be loaded into an airplane. The scissor legs move along the base track from a horizontal to a vertical position, raising the platform to the desired height.

Complete Part A as a whole class. Then complete Parts B–D in small groups.

- **A.** What is a mathematical question you can ask about the scissor legs as they move? What information would you need to know to answer your question?

- **B.** What reasonable assumptions can you make? What shapes can you use to model the scissor legs? What do you know about the parts of these shapes?

- **C.** To answer your question, what strategy and tool would you use along with all the information you have? What answer do you get?

- **D.** Does your answer make sense in the context of the situation? Explain why or why not.

Turn and Talk Describe what would happen in the following scenarios.
- The scissor legs were not straight.
- The pair of scissor legs on one side of the platform were not in the same position as the pair on the other side.

Build Understanding

Analyze Congruence and Equal Measure in a Proof

Two angles are congruent if and only if the angles have the same measure. Recall the properties of congruence for segments that you learned previously. These properties of congruence are also true for angles.

Properties of Angle Congruence	
Property	**Words**
Reflexive	$\angle A \cong \angle A$
Symmetric	If $\angle A \cong \angle B$, then $\angle B \cong \angle A$.
Transitive	If $\angle A \cong \angle B$ and $\angle B \cong \angle C$, then $\angle A \cong \angle C$.

Right Angle Congruence Theorem
All right angles are congruent.

1 Consider the following proof of the Right Angle Congruence Theorem.

Given: $\angle A$ and $\angle B$ are right angles.

Prove: $\angle A \cong \angle B$

Statements	Reasons
1. $\angle A$ and $\angle B$ are right angles.	1. Given
2. $m\angle A = 90°$ $m\angle B = 90°$	2. Definition of Right Angle
3. $m\angle A = m\angle B$	3. ___?___
4. $\angle A \cong \angle B$	4. Definition of Congruent Angles

A. In Step 3 of the proof, the measures of $\angle A$ and $\angle B$ are shown to be equal. What is the property that justifies this step?

B. Why would the definition of right angles be used in Step 2?

C. Why is it correct to apply the definition of congruent angles in Step 4? Explain your reasoning.

D. What is a reason for using the angle names, then switching to angle measures, and then switching back to the angle names?

Turn and Talk You proved the Right Angle Congruence Theorem in Task 1. Describe why you no longer have to state the definition and angle measures of right angles when proving any theorems that contain right angles, such as any theorem involving rectangles or right triangles.

Step It Out

Justify Each Step in a Solution

2 Use algebraic properties of equality to justify the steps.

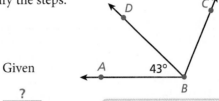

If m∠ABC = 114°, find m∠DBC.

m∠ABC = 114°	Given
m∠ABD + m∠DBC = m∠ABC	**?**
43° + m∠DBC = 114°	Substitution
m∠DBC = 71°	**?**

A. What property justifies m∠ABD + m∠DBC = m∠ABC?

B. What property justifies m∠DBC = 71°?

C. How is proving this specific case different from proving the general case of a theorem?

 Turn and Talk Write the problem in this task as an if-then statement.

Prove the Congruent Supplements Theorem

Congruent Supplements Theorem

If two angles are supplements of the same angle, or congruent angles, then the two angles are congruent.

3 Prove the Congruent Supplements Theorem.

Given: ∠1 and ∠2 are supplementary.
∠2 and ∠3 are supplementary.

Prove: ∠1 ≅ ∠3

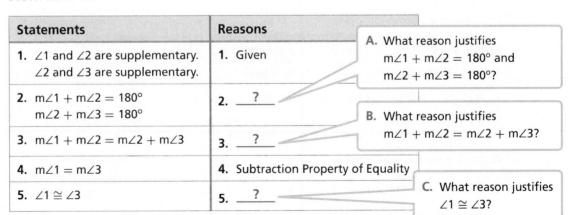

Statements	Reasons
1. ∠1 and ∠2 are supplementary. ∠2 and ∠3 are supplementary.	1. Given
2. m∠1 + m∠2 = 180° m∠2 + m∠3 = 180°	2. **?**
3. m∠1 + m∠2 = m∠2 + m∠3	3. **?**
4. m∠1 = m∠3	4. Subtraction Property of Equality
5. ∠1 ≅ ∠3	5. **?**

A. What reason justifies m∠1 + m∠2 = 180° and m∠2 + m∠3 = 180°?

B. What reason justifies m∠1 + m∠2 = m∠2 + m∠3?

C. What reason justifies ∠1 ≅ ∠3?

 Turn and Talk Describe how to use the proof of the Congruent Supplements Theorem as a model for a proof of the Congruent Complements Theorem.

Prove Theorems about Angles

Linear Pairs Theorem

If two angles form a linear pair, then they are supplementary.

∠1 and ∠2 are a linear pair,
so m∠1 + m∠2 = 180°.

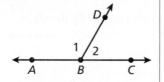

Vertical Angles Theorem

Vertical angles are always congruent.
∠1 and ∠3 are vertical angles so ∠1 ≅ ∠3.
∠2 and ∠4 are vertical angles so ∠2 ≅ ∠4.

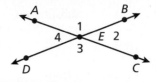

4 ▶ Prove the Linear Pairs Theorem.

Given: ∠1 and ∠2 form a linear pair.

Prove: ∠1 and ∠2 are supplementary.

Statements	Reasons
1. ∠1 and ∠2 form a linear pair.	**1.** Given
2. $\overrightarrow{BA}$ and $\overrightarrow{BC}$ are opposite rays.	**2.** ___?___
3. m∠ABC = 180°	**3.** Definition of straight angle
4. m∠1 + m∠2 = m∠ABC	**4.** ___?___
5. m∠1 + m∠2 = 180°	**5.** Transitive Property
6. ∠1 and ∠2 are supplementary.	**5.** Definition of supplementary angles

A. What property justifies $\overrightarrow{BA}$ and $\overrightarrow{BC}$ being opposite rays?

B. What property justifies m∠1 + m∠2 = m∠ABC?

5 ▶ Prove the Vertical Angles Theorem.

Given: ∠1 and ∠3 are vertical angles.

Prove: ∠1 ≅ ∠3

Statements	Reasons
1. ∠1 and ∠3 are vertical angles.	**1.** Given
2. m∠AEC = 180°; m∠DEB = 180°	**2.** Definition of straight angle
3. m∠1 + m∠2 = 180° m∠2 + m∠3 = 180°	**3.** Angle Addition Postulate
4. m∠1 + m∠2 = m∠2 + m∠3	**4.** ___?___
5. m∠1 = m∠3	**5.** ___?___
6. ∠1 ≅ ∠3	**6.** Definition of congruent angles

A. What property justifies m∠1 + m∠2 = m∠2 + m∠3?

B. What property justifies m∠1 = m∠3?

 Turn and Talk In Task 5, why is the final step of the proof needed?

Check Understanding

1. **(MP)** **Attend to Precision** Are ∠1 and ∠2 congruent? Explain your reasoning.

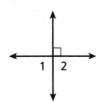

2. Find m∠ABC, if m∠ABD = 120°.

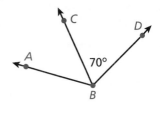

3. If ∠X ≅ ∠Y and ∠Y ≅ ∠Z, what can you conclude about the relationship between ∠X and ∠Z?

On Your Own

Match each statement with the property of congruence that makes the statement true.

4. ∠C ≅ ∠D, so ∠D ≅ ∠C.

5. ∠L ≅ ∠M and ∠M ≅ ∠N, so ∠L ≅ ∠N.

6. ∠BCD ≅ ∠BCD

7. ∠XYZ ≅ ∠RST and ∠RST ≅ ∠ABC, so ∠XYZ ≅ ∠ABC.

8. ∠Q ≅ ∠Q

9. ∠JKL ≅ ∠FGH, so ∠FGH ≅ ∠JKL.

A. Reflexive Property
B. Symmetric Property
C. Transitive Property

Find the measure of each angle.

10. ∠1 and ∠2 form a linear pair and m∠2 = 52°.

11. ∠1 and ∠2 are supplementary, ∠2 and ∠3 are supplementary, and m∠2 = 32°.

12. ∠1 and ∠2 are vertical angles and m∠1 = 44°.

13. ∠1 and ∠2 form a linear pair and m∠1 = 132°.

14. ∠1 and ∠2 are supplementary, ∠2 and ∠3 are supplementary, and m∠2 = 85°.

15. ∠1 and ∠2 are vertical angles and m∠2 = 103°.

16. A section of fencing has four angles that are labeled as shown. Which angle is a vertical angle to ∠4? Which angles form linear pairs with ∠4?

17. (MP) **Construct Arguments** Prove the measure of angle *AEC* is equal to twice the measure of angle *FEB*.

18. (MP) **Reason** What is the converse of the Linear Pair Theorem? Is this a true statement? Explain your reasoning.

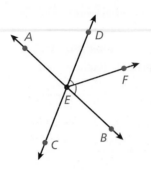

19. Write a two-column proof.

Given: $\angle 1 \cong \angle 2$; $\angle 2$ is a complement of $\angle 3$.

Prove: $\angle 1$ is a complement of $\angle 3$.

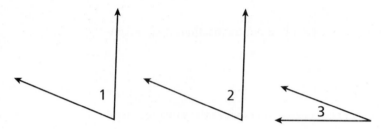

In Problems 20–28, find the value of *x*.

20. $\angle 1$ and $\angle 2$ are vertical angles. $m\angle 1 = 40°$ and $m\angle 2 = (7x + 5)°$.

21. $\angle 1$ and $\angle 2$ are a linear pair. $m\angle 1 = (11x + 6)°$ and $m\angle 2 = 75°$.

22. $\angle 1$ and $\angle 2$ are supplementary. $\angle 2$ and $\angle 3$ are supplementary. $m\angle 1 = (4x)°$ and $m\angle 3 = (x + 48)°$.

23. $\angle 1$ and $\angle 2$ are vertical angles. $m\angle 1 = (7x - 8)°$ and $m\angle 2 = (5x + 34)°$.

24. $\angle 1$ and $\angle 2$ are supplementary. $\angle 2$ and $\angle 3$ are supplementary. $m\angle 1 = (12x + 17)°$ and $m\angle 3 = (23x - 5)°$.

25. $\angle 1$ and $\angle 2$ are a linear pair. $m\angle 1 = (4x + 17)°$ and $m\angle 2 = (11x - 17)°$.

26. $\angle 1$ and $\angle 2$ are vertical angles. $m\angle 1 = (9x - 13)°$ and $m\angle 2 = (6x + 38)°$.

27. $\angle 1$ and $\angle 2$ are a linear pair. $m\angle 1 = (18x + 43)°$ and $m\angle 2 = (31x - 10)°$.

28. $\angle 1$ and $\angle 2$ are vertical angles. $\angle 2$ and $\angle 3$ are supplementary. $m\angle 1 = (2x - 13)°$ and $m\angle 3 = (4x + 1)°$.

29. Which angles are congruent to each other in the figure if you know that angle 1 is congruent to angle 5? Explain your reasoning.

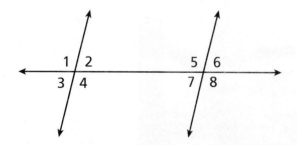

30. STEM Engineers design structures to support the weight of the structure itself and other forces that might be applied to the structure. The diagram shows the internal support structure of the Statue of Liberty. Four angles are labeled in the diagram. What is the measure of ∠1, ∠2, and ∠3? Justify your reasoning for each measure.

31. How many pairs of vertical angles are shown in the drawing? List the pairs of angles.

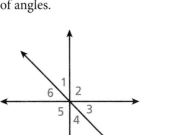

32. ∠HEF and ∠DEH are complementary angles. What is the measure of ∠HEG?

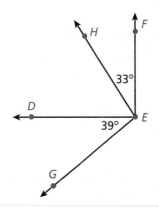

33. The lines through $\overline{AD}$ and $\overline{BE}$ intersect at point F. Complete the proof that m∠AFE = m∠BFC + m∠CFD.

Statements	Reasons
1. ∠AFE and ∠BFD are vertical angles.	**1.**
2.	**2.** Vertical Angles Theorem
3. m∠AFE = m∠BFD	**3.**
4.	**4.** Angle Addition Postulate
5. m∠AFE = m∠BFC + m∠CFD	**5.**

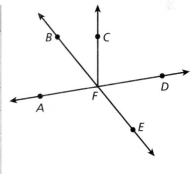

34. Find the measures of ∠1, ∠2, and ∠3. Justify your reasoning for the measure of each angle.

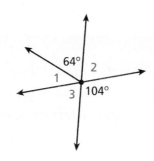

(t) ©Helene Roche Photography/Alamy

35. The figure shows a map of five streets that meet at Winthrop Circle. The measure of the angle formed by Mea Road and Hawk Lane is 130°. The measure of the angle formed by East Avenue and Hawk Lane is 148°. Tulip Street bisects the angle formed by Mea Road and Hawk Lane. Summer Drive bisects the angle formed by East Avenue and Hawk Lane. What is the measure of the angle formed by Tulip Street and Summer Drive? Explain your reasoning.

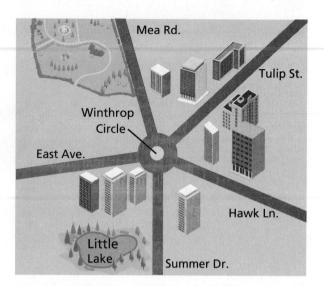

36. Open Ended Write a math problem that can be solved using the Congruent Supplements Theorem.

37. A rhombus is a quadrilateral with four sides of equal length. Draw a rhombus. Use a compass and straightedge to bisect one of the angles in the rhombus. What do you notice? Confirm your conjecture using at least two additional rhombuses.

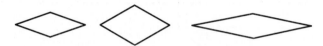

Spiral Review • Assessment Readiness

38. Two braces support a table top. Which pair(s) of angles are vertical angles? Select all that apply.

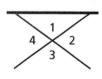

Ⓐ ∠1, ∠3   Ⓒ ∠2, ∠3

Ⓑ ∠3, ∠4   Ⓓ ∠2, ∠4

39. Write the statement as an if-then statement.

$5x - 7 = 8; x = 3$

Ⓐ If $x = 3$, then $5x = 15$.

Ⓑ If $x = 3$, then $5x - 7 = 8$.

Ⓒ If $5x - 7 = 8$, then $5x = 1$.

Ⓓ If $5x - 7 = 8$, then $x = 3$.

40. Match each statement with the property of congruence that makes it true.

Statement

1. $\overline{RS} \cong \overline{TU}$, so $\overline{TU} \cong \overline{RS}$.

2. $\overline{UV} \cong \overline{WX}$ and $\overline{WX} \cong \overline{YZ}$, so $\overline{UV} \cong \overline{YZ}$.

3. $\overline{CD} \cong \overline{CD}$

Property

A. Reflexive Property

B. Symmetric Property

C. Transitive Property

 I'm in a Learning Mindset!

When I prove and utilize theorems about angles in group settings, what strategies do I use to stay on task while working with my peers?

Conditional Statements

A rectangle that has four equal sides is a square.

Conditional Statement If a rectangle has four equal sides, then it is a square.

Converse If a rectangle is a square, then it has four equal sides.

Inverse If a rectangle does not have four equal sides, then it is not a square.

Contrapositive If a rectangle is not a square, then it does not have four equal sides.

Inductive and Deductive Reasoning

Inductive Reasoning Helen measured the sides of five squares and noticed that all sides are the same length. Helen concludes that all squares have four sides that are the same length.

Deductive Reasoning A rectangle with four equal sides is a square.

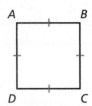

Rectangle *ABCD* is a square.

Segments

$\overline{JK}$ has a midpoint at *L*.

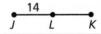

Because *L* is the midpoint of $\overline{JK}$, $JL = LK$.

Because the lengths of the segments are equal, the segments are congruent.

So, $\overline{JL} \cong \overline{LK}$.

Figure *ABCD* is a square.

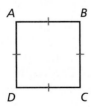

Because the figure is a square, all sides have the same length. So, $\overline{AB} \cong \overline{BC} \cong \overline{CD} \cong \overline{DA}$.

Angles

Figure *ABCD* is a square.

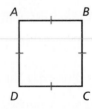

Each angle in square *ABCD* is a right angle, so each angle measures 90°. Each angle has the same measure, so each angle is congruent.

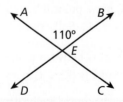

$\angle AEB$ and $\angle DEC$ are vertical angles, so they are congruent. So, m$\angle DEC = 110°$.

$\angle AEB$ and $\angle AED$ form a linear pair, so they are supplementary. So, m$\angle AED = 70°$.

$\angle AED$ and $\angle BEC$ are vertical angles, so they are congruent. So, m$\angle BEC = 70°$.

Vocabulary

Choose the correct term from the box to complete each sentence.

1. A two-column proof is an example of ___?___.

2. A ___?___, is a pair of adjacent angles whose noncommon sides are opposite rays.

3. The statement "If a number is divisible by 2, then it is even" is an example of a ___?___.

4. A statement formed by both exchanging and negating the hypothesis and conclusion of a conditional statement is the ___?___.

Concepts and Skills

Write the definition of the term as a biconditional statement.

5. obtuse angle

6. pentagon

7. Write the statement "Monday is a weekday" in if-then form. Then write the converse, inverse, and contrapositive of the statement.

8. A triangle with three acute angles is an acute triangle. Triangle *RST* has three acute angles. Use deductive reasoning to write a conclusion.

In Problems 9 and 10, decide if inductive reasoning or deductive reasoning is used to reach the conclusion. Explain your reasoning.

9. All acute angles measure less than 90°.

$\angle LMN$ is an acute angle, so $\angle LMN$ has a measure less than 90°.

10. (MP) **Use Tools** Every day last week, Sally had a turkey sandwich for lunch.

Sally will have a turkey sandwich for lunch today. State what strategy and tool you will use to determine which type of reasoning is used, explain your choice, and then find the answer.

11. Segment *AC* has a point *B* between points *A* and *C*. $AB = 4x + 2$, $BC = 3x - 1$, and $AC = 9x - 11$. Solve for *x*.

12. $\overline{PR}$ had a point *Q* between points *P* and *R*. The length of $\overline{QR}$ is 15 units. The length of $\overline{PR}$ is 32 units. Is $\overline{PQ} \cong \overline{QR}$? Explain.

Find the measure of each angle.

13. $\angle 1$ and $\angle 2$ are vertical angles. $m\angle 1 = 66°$.

14. $\angle 1$ and $\angle 2$ are supplementary. $\angle 2$ and $\angle 3$ are supplementary. $m\angle 1 = 133°$.

Parallel and Perpendicular Lines

Textile Engineer

Textile engineers design and develop the processes, equipment, and procedures that create fabric materials. They design versatile materials that must be strong and light. Using the properties of parallel lines, textile engineers can create woven carbon fiber that is commonly used in a wide variety of industries, including medicine, automotive, sports, and aerospace.

STEM Task

A triaxial woven carbon fiber provides a lot of strength while remaining lightweight. The fiber has an area density of only 75 kg/m^2.

The frame of a drone is made from the fiber. One section of the frame is 150 mm × 20 mm.

What mass does the section add to the drone?

Learning Mindset

Strategic Help-Seeking Identifies Sources of Help

How do you identify sources of help? It is important to determine your external support systems and the situations in which they are used. Your learning community may offer a list of potential resources that you can easily reference. Creating your own tracker of useful resources will enable you to find the information you need quickly. Here are some questions you can ask yourself as you identify different sources of help:

- What resources are available to help me understand the concept of parallel and perpendicular lines? What type of resource would be helpful?

- Does my learning community offer a list of potential resources? How can I organize the resources that are available to me?

- Would it be helpful to seek out a peer or mentor? Who can support me in learning about coordinate proofs?

- What can I contribute to my learning community regarding these concepts? How can I let others know I am available to support them?

Reflect

Q What resources have you used in the past? Why were they helpful to you? Ask a peer about resources they have used and exchange your experiences.

Q As a textile engineer, what are some other calculations you might need to make? How would you determine the sources of information needed to make these calculations? How could you organize the resources that you find helpful?

3 Lines and Transversals

Module Performance Task: Focus on STEM

Geometry of Truss Bridges

Truss bridges are one of the oldest types of modern bridges. The bridges are composed of trusses, which are beams, called struts, which connect together to form triangular shapes for strength. The triangular shapes contract to handle heavy weights and expand during extreme weather conditions.

A. Identify two parallel struts in the diagram. How can an engineer ensure that the struts are parallel during construction? Explain your reasoning.

B. Identify two perpendicular struts in the diagram. How can an engineer ensure that the struts are perpendicular during construction? Explain your reasoning.

C. Use a transversal to identify a pair of congruent angles and a pair of supplementary angles. Explain how you determined your answer.

D. Would an engineer use parallel lines to ensure angles are congruent, or congruent angles to ensure lines are parallel? Explain your reasoning.

(t), (b) ©Sherman Cahal/Shutterstock

Are You Ready?

Complete these problems to review prior concepts and skills you will need for this module.

Solve Multi-Step Equations

Solve each equation.

1. $5t - 7 = -23 - 3t$

2. $6(z + 4) = 10z + 12$

3. $8m + 1 = 3m - 4$

4. $5(w - 7) = w + 9$

5. $-2(3x + 8) + 4 = x + 9$

6. $4r + 6 = 6r - 6$

7. $5(2n + 3) = 15 - n$

8. $-3(4 - y) + 5 = y + 1$

Types of Angle Pairs

Given that $\angle 1 = 25°$, find each missing measure.

9. $\angle 2$

10. $\angle 3$

11. $\angle 4$

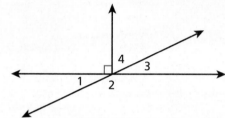

Parallel Lines Cut by a Transversal

Two parallel lines are cut by a transversal.
Find the measure of each angle.

12. $\angle 5$

13. $\angle 6$

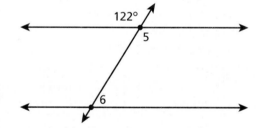

Connecting Past and Present Learning

Previously, you learned:

- to find missing side lengths in right triangles,
- to determine if two angles are congruent, and
- to determine if two angles are supplementary.

In this module, you will learn:

- to determine if angles formed by a transversal are congruent or supplementary,
- to construct parallel and perpendicular lines, and
- to prove or disprove if two lines are parallel or perpendicular.

Parallel Lines Crossed by a Transversal

(I Can) determine the relationship between angle pairs formed by a transversal crossing parallel lines.

Spark Your Learning

Leon has a Z-shaped shelf unit.

Complete Part A as a whole class. Then complete Parts B–D in small groups.

A. What question can you ask about the design of the shelf unit?

B. To answer your question, what strategy and tool would you use along with all the information you have? What answer do you get?

C. Why do you think the sides of the shelf unit are designed this way?

D. What is another design for the side supports of the shelf that will not affect the position of the shelves in the image?

 Turn and Talk What happens if the design of the shelf unit changes as described below?

- The acute angles between the shelves and the side supports remain congruent, but become smaller?
- One of the acute angles between the shelves and the side supports becomes larger than the other?

Build Understanding

Explore Angle Pairs Formed by Transversals

A **transversal** is a line that intersects two or more coplanar lines at different points. In the diagram, line *t* is the transversal.

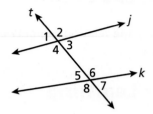

When a transversal intersects two lines, several angles are formed. These angles are related in different ways.

Angles that are on the same side of the transversal are consecutive angles.
Angles that are on opposite side of the transversal are alternate angles.

Angles that are on the outside of two lines are exterior angles.
Angles that are on the inside of the two lines are interior angles.

Angle Pair Relationships When Lines are Cut by a Transversal	
Term	**Examples**
Corresponding angles lie on the same side of the transversal and on the same sides of the intersecting lines.	∠1 and ∠5, ∠2 and ∠6 ∠3 and ∠7, ∠4 and ∠8
Alternate interior angles are nonadjacent angles that lie on opposite sides of the transversal between the intersected lines.	∠3 and ∠5 ∠4 and ∠6
Consecutive interior angles lie on the same side of the transversal between the intersected lines.	∠3 and ∠6 ∠4 and ∠5
Alternate exterior angles lie on opposite sides of the transversal outside the intersected lines.	∠1 and ∠7 ∠2 and ∠8
Consecutive exterior angles lie on the same side of the transversal outside the intersected lines.	∠1 and ∠8 ∠2 and ∠7

1 **A.** Draw two lines intersected by a transversal. Label the lines and number the angles formed.

   B. Give one example for each of the following types of angle pairs: corresponding angles, alternate exterior angles, alternate interior angles, consecutive exterior angles, and consecutive interior angles.

   C. Are any pairs of angles in your diagram congruent? Are any pairs of angles supplementary? Explain your reasoning.

Turn and Talk What do you think will happen with the angle relationships if the two lines crossed by the transversal are parallel?

Investigate Transversals and Parallel Lines

Parallel lines are any lines in the same plane that do not intersect.

Transversals intersecting parallel lines occur in real-world situations. For example, consider the paths across this university campus.

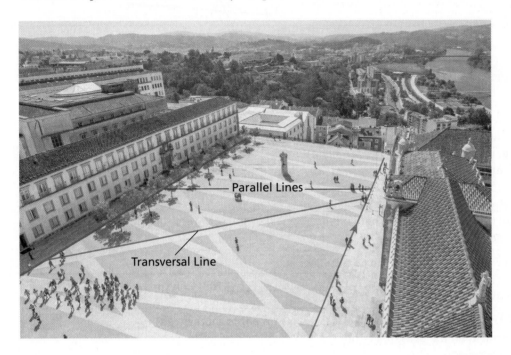

When a transversal intersects two parallel lines, there are relationships between the pairs of angles formed.

2 ▶ Two parallel lines *m* and *n* are intersected by a transversal *t*.

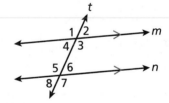

A. Trace the diagram onto tracing paper. Slide the tracing paper so that ∠5 on the tracing paper is positioned over ∠1. What do you notice?

B. Use the tracing-paper method to compare the angle measures of all of the corresponding angle pairs. What appears to be true about the corresponding angles?

C. Use tracing paper to compare the measures of alternate interior angle pairs and alternate exterior angle pairs. What do you notice about the measures of the pairs of angles?

D. Use tracing paper to compare the measures of consecutive interior angle pairs and consecutive exterior angle pairs. What do you notice about the measures of the pairs of angles?

 Turn and Talk Compare your drawings in Task 1 and Task 2. Do you think these angle pair relationships will change if the lines are not parallel? Explain.

Prove Relationships Between Angle Pairs Formed by Parallel Lines and a Transversal

When two parallel lines are intersected by a transversal, every angle formed is either congruent or supplementary to a given angle. Many of these relationships are described in the following table.

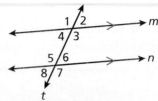

Angle Pair Relationships When Parallel Lines are Cut by a Transversal	
Postulate or Theorem	**Examples**
Corresponding Angles Postulate If two parallel lines are cut by a transversal, then the resulting corresponding angles are congruent.	$\angle 1 \cong \angle 5$ $\angle 2 \cong \angle 6$ $\angle 3 \cong \angle 7$ $\angle 4 \cong \angle 8$
Alternate Interior Angles Theorem If two parallel lines are cut by a transversal, then the pairs of alternate interior angles are congruent.	$\angle 3 \cong \angle 5$ $\angle 4 \cong \angle 6$
Consecutive Interior Angles Theorem If two parallel lines are cut by a transversal, then the pairs of consecutive interior angles are supplementary.	$m\angle 3 + m\angle 6 = 180°$ $m\angle 4 + m\angle 5 = 180°$
Alternate Exterior Angles Theorem If two parallel lines are cut by a transversal, then the pairs of alternate exterior angles are congruent.	$\angle 1 \cong \angle 7$ $\angle 2 \cong \angle 8$
Consecutive Exterior Angles Theorem If two parallel lines are cut by a transversal, then the pairs of consecutive exterior angles are supplementary.	$m\angle 1 + m\angle 8 = 180°$ $m\angle 2 + m\angle 7 = 180°$

A **flow proof** uses boxes and arrows to show the structure of a logical argument. The justification for each step is written below the box.

3 **A.** Which pair of angles are alternate interior angles?

B. What are the justifications for each step in the flow proof below?

Prove the Alternate Interior Angles Theorem.

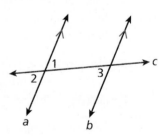

Given: $a \parallel b$

Prove: $\angle 1 \cong \angle 3$

$a \parallel b$	→	$\angle 1 \cong \angle 2$	→	$\angle 2 \cong \angle 3$	→	$\angle 1 \cong \angle 3$
?		?		?		?

 Turn and Talk Suppose any one of the theorems in the list above could instead be a postulate used to prove the other theorems. Which angle pair relationship should be a postulate? Explain your reasoning.

Step It Out

Use Parallel Lines to Determine Angle Measures

4 In 1791, Pierre Charles L'Enfant designed a plan for Washington, D.C. His plan included a grid of streets with avenues running diagonally across the grid.

Look at the map of a section of Washington, D.C. 12th St. NW and 10th St. are parallel. They are intersected by Pennsylvania Avenue.

Find the measures of ∠1 and ∠2.

m∠1 = 70° ⟵ Explain how you can find this measure.

m∠2 = 110°

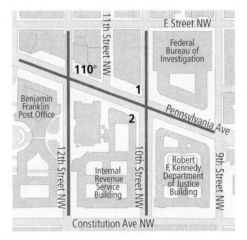

5 The highlighted streets in Washington, D.C. form two trapezoids with a common side. The vertical streets are parallel and the horizontal streets are parallel.

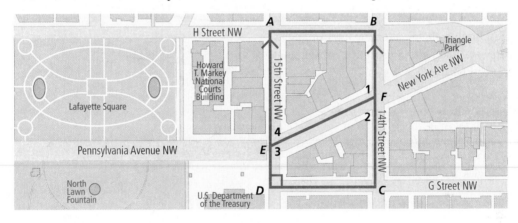

Prove that the sum of the angle measures of the trapezoid is 360°.

Given: $\overline{AD} \parallel \overline{BC}$, ∠D is a right angle.

Prove: m∠2 + m∠3 + m∠C + m∠D = 360°

Statements	Reasons	
1. $\overline{AD} \parallel \overline{BC}$	**1.** Given	**A.** What is the reason Statement 2 is true?
2. m∠2 + m∠3 = 180°	**2.** ___?___	
3. m∠C + m∠D = 180°	**3.** ___?___	**B.** Is Statement 3 true for the same reason?
4. m∠2 + m∠3 + m∠C + m∠D = 180° + 180°	**4.** Substitution Property of Equality	
5. m∠2 + m∠3 + m∠C + m∠D = 360°	**5.** Simplify.	

 Turn and Talk If m∠1 = (7n − 2)° and m∠4 = (4n + 6)°, find the values of n, m∠1, and m∠4.

Check Understanding

Use the diagram for Problems 1–3.

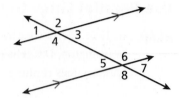

1. Give one example for each of the following types of angle pairs: corresponding angles, alternate exterior angles, alternate interior angles, consecutive exterior angles, and consecutive interior angles.

2. Which angles are congruent to ∠3?

3. Use the diagram to explain how you could use the Consecutive Interior Angles Theorem and a linear pair of angles to prove the Alternate Interior Angles Theorem.

4. Megan is making a wood model of each letter of the alphabet. She drew a sketch of the letter N. The vertical sides of the N are parallel. What is the value of *x*?

$(2x)°$ $24°$

On Your Own

5. **(MP) Attend to Precision** List all of the pairs of corresponding angles, alternate interior angles, alternate exterior angle, consecutive interior angles, and consecutive exterior angles.

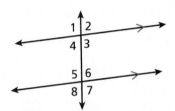

For Problems 6–11, use the diagram shown.

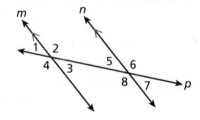

6. Which angles are congruent to ∠2?

7. Which angles are supplementary to ∠7?

8. Which postulate or theorem justifies that ∠1 is congruent to ∠5?

9. Which postulate or theorem justifies that ∠4 is supplementary to ∠7?

10. Which postulate or theorem justifies that ∠3 is congruent to ∠5?

11. Which postulate or theorem justifies that ∠2 is supplementary to ∠5?

12. **Open Ended** Draw a pair of parallel lines intersected by a transversal. Label the angles. Choose one of the angles and list the angles congruent and supplementary to that angle.

13. **Science** Venation is the pattern of the veins in a leaf. Some leaves have parallel venation. Find the measure of the angles in the photo of the leaf.

14. **(MP) Construct Arguments** Prove the Consecutive Exterior Angles Theorem.

15. (MP) **Reason** Let the fact that consecutive interior angles are supplementary be a postulate. Use this postulate to prove the relationship between corresponding angles as a Corresponding Angles Theorem.

Find the value of x.

16.

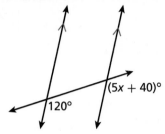

$(5x + 40)°$

$120°$

17.

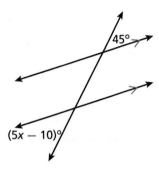

$45°$

$(5x - 10)°$

18.

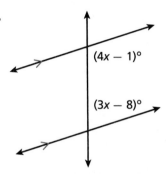

$(4x - 1)°$

$(3x - 8)°$

19.

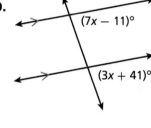

$(7x - 11)°$

$(3x + 41)°$

20.

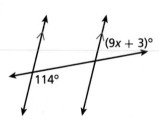

$(9x + 3)°$

$114°$

21.

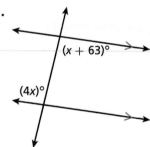

$(x + 63)°$

$(4x)°$

22. (MP) **Construct Arguments** Prove the Alternate Exterior Angles Theorem.

23. STEM An engineer is designing a railing for a staircase.

A. Which angle is congruent is to $\angle 4$?

B. Which postulate or theorem did you use to determine the congruent angle?

C. Suppose that the measure of $\angle 4$ is 75°. What are the measures of the other angles?

24. (MP) **Construct Arguments** Prove the Consecutive Interior Angles Theorem.

Use the diagram for Problems 25 and 26.

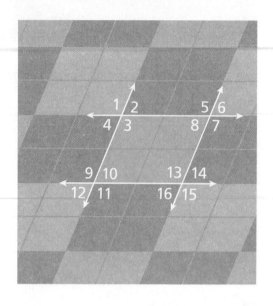

25. Two parallel lines are intersected by a transversal. ∠3 and ∠9 are alternate interior angles. The measure of ∠3 is $(4m + 1)°$. The measure of ∠9 is $(187 - 2m)°$. What is the measure of each angle?

26. Two parallel lines are intersected by a transversal. ∠12 and ∠15 are consecutive exterior angles. The measure of ∠12 is $(14a + 17)°$ and the measure of ∠15 is $(26a + 43)°$. What is the measure of each angle?

27. Line a is parallel to line b. Line x is parallel to line y. Prove that ∠2 and ∠13 are supplementary angles.

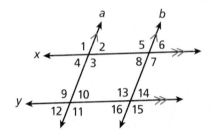

Spiral Review • Assessment Readiness

28. The length of a piece of wood represented by $\overline{RT}$ is 65 inches. Suppose you cut the wood at some point S so that $RS = 4b + 7$ and $ST = 7b - 8$. What is RS?

   Ⓐ 6 inches

   Ⓑ 31 inches

   Ⓒ 34 inches

   Ⓓ 65 inches

29. Segment AB has endpoints at $A(4, 1)$ and $B(6, -2)$. What is the slope of the segment?

   Ⓐ $-\frac{3}{2}$ Ⓒ $\frac{2}{3}$

   Ⓑ $-\frac{2}{3}$ Ⓓ $\frac{3}{2}$

30. ∠1 and ∠2 are vertical angles. $m∠2 = 122°$ and $m∠1 = (4z - 10)°$. What is z?

   Ⓐ 10   Ⓒ 122

   Ⓑ 33   Ⓓ 132

31. If a conditional statement is given by "If a number is a whole number, then it is an integer," then its _____ statement is "If a number is an integer, then it is a whole number."

   Ⓐ inverse

   Ⓑ definition

   Ⓒ contrapositive

   Ⓓ converse

I'm in a Learning Mindset!

What resources are available for me to understand the relationship between angle pairs formed by transversals and parallel lines?

Prove Lines Are Parallel

(I Can) ensure that two lines are parallel by construction.

Spark Your Learning

Look at the optical illusion, known as the Café Wall Illusion.

Complete Part A as a whole class. Then complete Parts B–D in small groups.

A. What is a question you can ask about the optical illusion? What information would you need to know to answer your question?

B. Focus on two or three rows of the illusion. How does this help you answer your question?

C. To answer your question, what strategy and tool would you use along with all the information you have? What answer do you get?

D. How can you use tools to verify your answer?

Turn and Talk

- Suppose all of the black squares are changed to white. How do you think changing the color would change the illusion? Explain your reasoning.
- Does turning the image so that the stripes are vertical change the illusion? What difference do you see, if any?

©Iconsinternational.Com/Alamy

Build Understanding

Construct Parallel Lines

You can use the Parallel Postulate to construct a pair of parallel lines.

> **Parallel Postulate**
>
> For point *P* not on line *l*, there is exactly one line parallel to *l* through point *P*.

1 Use a compass and a straightedge to construct parallel lines. This construction involves copying an angle.

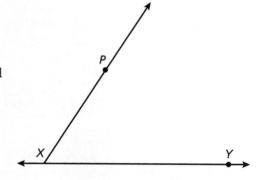

A. Draw a line and a point *P* not on the line. Draw and label points *X* and *Y* on the line. Use a straightedge to draw $\overrightarrow{XP}$. Explain why *P* must not lie on $\overleftrightarrow{XY}$.

B. Use a compass to copy ∠*PXY* at point *P*. Draw point *Z*. Draw a straight line through points *P* and *Z*. Why is $\overleftrightarrow{XY}$ parallel to $\overleftrightarrow{PZ}$?

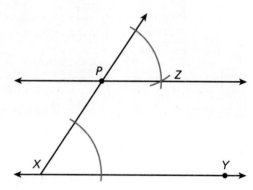

C. What is true about the corresponding angles? What would be true about $\overleftrightarrow{XY}$ and $\overleftrightarrow{PZ}$ if the corresponding angles did not have this relationship?

D. How is the Parallel Postulate used in this construction?

Turn and Talk How would the construction steps be different, if at all, if you drew $\overrightarrow{YP}$ instead of $\overrightarrow{XP}$?

Converses of the Parallel Lines Theorems

Recall that the converse of a conditional statement is formed by exchanging the hypothesis and conclusion of the statement. The converse of a statement in the form "If *p*, then *q*" is "If *q*, then *p*."

Conditional statement: If $x + 4 = 6$, then $x = 2$.

Converse: If $x = 2$, then $x + 4 = 6$.

The parallel lines postulates and theorems you learned previously have true converses. These converses are listed below along with an example from the diagram.

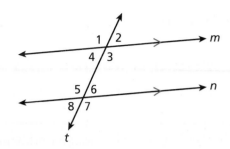

Converses of Parallel Lines Postulates and Theorems	
Postulate or Theorem	**Example**
Converse of the Corresponding Angles Postulate If two lines are cut by a transversal so that corresponding angles are congruent, then the lines are parallel.	If $\angle 1 \cong \angle 5$, then $m \parallel n$.
Converse of the Alternate Interior Angles Theorem If two lines are cut by a transversal so that alternate interior angles are congruent, then the lines are parallel.	If $\angle 4 \cong \angle 6$, then $m \parallel n$.
Converse of the Alternate Exterior Angles Theorem If two lines are cut by a transversal so that alternate exterior angles are congruent, then the lines are parallel.	If $\angle 1 \cong \angle 7$, then $m \parallel n$.
Converse of the Consecutive Interior Angles Theorem If two lines are cut by a transversal so the consecutive interior angles are supplementary, then the lines are parallel.	If $\angle 3$ and $\angle 6$ are supplementary, then $m \parallel n$.
Converse of the Consecutive Exterior Angles Theorem If two lines are cut by a transversal so the consecutive exterior angles are supplementary, then the lines are parallel.	If $\angle 1$ and $\angle 8$ are supplementary, then $m \parallel n$.

2 In the photo, $\angle 2 \cong \angle 6$.

A. What theorem or postulate can you use to show that line j and line k are parallel?

B. How can you use a different theorem or postulate to show that line j and line k are parallel?

Turn and Talk Are converses of conditional statements always true? Give an example that supports your answer.

Step It Out

Prove Whether or Not Two Lines Are Parallel

You can use the converses of the parallel line postulates and theorems to prove whether or not two lines are parallel.

3 Belinda is tiling a floor using quadrilateral tiles. Regardless of the color, the central tiles are identical. She knows that $\angle 1 \cong \angle 2$. She wants to prove $l \parallel m$.

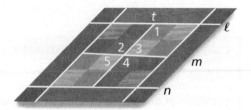

Given: $\angle 1 \cong \angle 2$

Prove: $l \parallel m$

Statements	Reasons
1. $\angle 1 \cong \angle 2$	**1.** Given
2. $\angle 2 \cong \angle 4$	**2.** ___?___
3. $\angle 1 \cong \angle 4$	**3.** ___?___
4. $l \parallel m$	**4.** ___?___

A. What reason justifies $\angle 2 \cong \angle 4$?

B. What reason justifies $\angle 1 \cong \angle 4$?

C. What reason justifies $l \parallel m$?

 Turn and Talk What theorem can you use to prove $l \parallel m$ using fewer steps?

4 Are Oak Avenue and Pearl Street parallel? Write a proof that justifies your conclusion.

A. What information are you given in the diagram? Use this to write the Given statement.

B. What is the Prove statement?

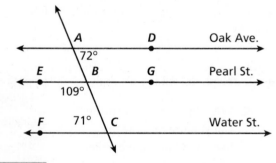

Statements	Reasons
1. ___?___	**1.** Given
2. $m\angle ABE = 71°$	**2.** ___?___
3. ___?___	**3.** ___?___

C. What theorem justifies $m\angle ABE = 71°$?

D. What reason completes the proof?

E. What conclusion can you make?

 Turn and Talk Why is it not always valid to model a road with a line or a line segment?

Transitive Property of Parallel Lines

The Transitive Property can be applied to parallel lines.

Transitive Property of Parallel Lines	
If two lines are parallel to the same line, then they are parallel to each other.	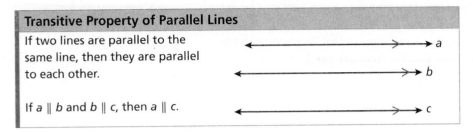
If $a \parallel b$ and $b \parallel c$, then $a \parallel c$.	

5 ▶ A drawing of a subway system shows the different levels used to reach the subway platforms. Level 1 is line p, level 2 is line q, and level 3 is line r. Prove that Level 2 and level 3 are parallel.

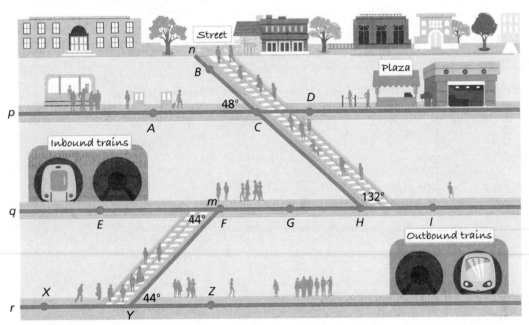

Statements	Reasons
1. $m\angle ACB = 48°$, $m\angle CHI = 132°$	1. Given
2. $m\angle DCH = 48°$	2. ___?___ **A.** What property justifies $m\angle DCH = 48°$?
3. $48° + 132° = 180°$	3. Addition
4. $m\angle DCH + m\angle CHI = 180°$	4. Substitution Property of Equality
5. $\angle DCH$ and $\angle CHI$ are supplementary.	5. Definition of supplementary angles
6. $p \parallel q$	6. ___?___ **B.** What property justifies $p \parallel q$?
7. $m\angle EFY = 44°$, $m\angle FYZ = 44°$	7. Given
8. $\angle EFY \cong \angle FYZ$	8. Definition of congruent angles
9. $p \parallel r$	9. ___?___ **C.** What property justifies $p \parallel r$?
10. $q \parallel r$	10. ___?___ **D.** What allows you to write $q \parallel r$?

Check Understanding

1. Draw line *k* and point *P* that is not on line *k*. How many lines can be drawn through *P* that are parallel to line *k*? How do you know?

In Problems 2–5, name a postulate or theorem that can be used with the given information to prove that the lines are parallel.

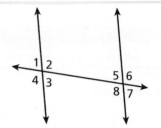

2. ∠3 ≅ ∠7

3. ∠3 ≅ ∠5

4. ∠2 and ∠5 are supplementary

5. ∠1 ≅ ∠7

6. Is line *m* parallel to line *n*? Explain your reasoning.

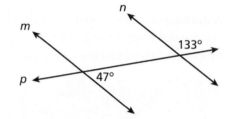

On Your Own

Determine if there is enough information to show that line *a* is parallel to line *b*. If there is, tell which postulate or theorem you would use.

7.

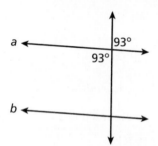

8.

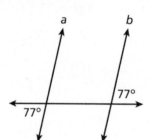

9.

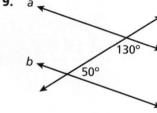

10. Which sides of *QRST* are parallel if you know that ∠1 ≅ ∠2?

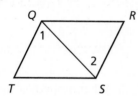

11. **(MP) Construct Arguments** Fill in the missing steps of the proof of the Converse of the Alternate Interior Angles Theorem.

Given: ∠1 ≅ ∠2

Prove: *a* ∥ *b*

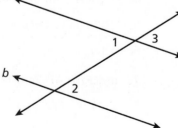

Statements	Reasons
1. ∠1 ≅ ∠2	1. Given
2. ___?___	2. Vertical Angles Theorem
3. *a* ∥ *b*	3. ___?___

Find the value of x that makes $p \parallel q$.

12.

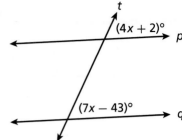

$(4x + 2)°$ p

$(7x - 43)°$ q

13.

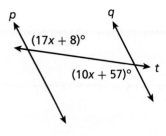

$(17x + 8)°$

$(10x + 57)°$ t

14.

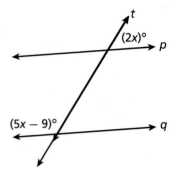

$(2x)°$ p

$(5x - 9)°$ q

15.

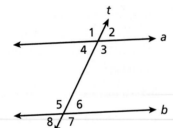

p q

t $63°$ $(9x + 36)°$

Use the diagram to write each two column proof.

16. Prove the Converse of the Alternate Exterior Angles Theorem.

Given: $\angle 1 \cong \angle 7$

Prove: $a \parallel b$

17. Prove the Converse of the Consecutive Interior Angles Theorem.

Given: $\angle 4$ and $\angle 5$ are supplementary.

Prove: $a \parallel b$

18. Each lane in the swimming pool is parallel to the lane to its right. Explain why the left side of the pool is parallel to the right side of the pool.

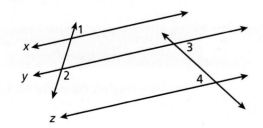

19. (MP) **Use Tools** Use a straightedge and a protractor to construct three parallel lines. Explain how you know that all three lines are parallel.

20. Write a two column proof to show that line x and line z are parallel.

Given: $\angle 1$ and $\angle 2$ are supplementary. $\angle 3 \cong \angle 4$

Prove: $x \parallel z$

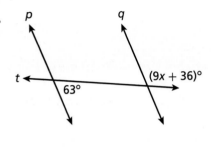

21. A marching band is performing at halftime of a football game. A section of their formation is shaped as shown.

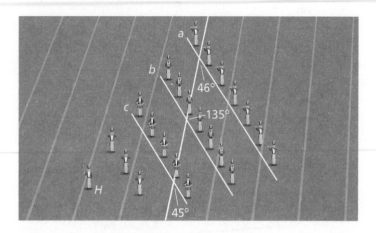

A. Which pairs of lines of marchers are parallel? Explain how you know these lines are parallel.

B. Are there any lines that are not parallel with the others? Explain your reasoning.

Spiral Review • Assessment Readiness

22. $\overline{AC}$ represents the width of a banner. The length of $\overline{AC}$ is 72 inches. Point B is the midpoint of $\overline{AC}$. What is the length of $\overline{AB}$ in inches?

(A) 36 inches   (C) 72 inches

(B) 48 inches   (D) 144 inches

23. $\angle 1$ and $\angle 2$ form a linear pair. $m\angle 1 = (5x + 7)^{\circ}$ and $m\angle 2 = (8x + 4)^{\circ}$. What is $m\angle 1$?

(A) 72°   (C) 130°

(B) 108°   (D) 167°

24. Match each pair of angles on the left with the correct description on the right.

Angle pair	Description
A. $\angle 1$ and $\angle 7$	**1.** Consecutive interior angles
B. $\angle 3$ and $\angle 6$	**2.** Alternate exterior angles
C. $\angle 4$ and $\angle 8$	**3.** Alternate interior Angles
D. $\angle 4$ and $\angle 6$	**4.** Corresponding angles

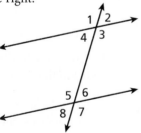

I'm in a Learning Mindset!

Who can support me while learning about proving that lines are parallel?

Prove Lines Are Perpendicular

(I Can) ensure that a line is a perpendicular bisector of a segment
by construction.

Spark Your Learning

A city is designing a park that is shaped like a triangle.

Complete Part A as an entire class. Then complete Parts B–D in small groups.

   A. What geometric question can you ask about the design of the park?
      What information do you need to answer your question?

   B. What information about relationships between geometric figures in the park
      does the diagram *not* give?

   C. To answer your question, what strategy and tool would you use along
      with all the information you have? What answer do you get?

   D. What other relationships do you see among the paths in the park? Explain.

Turn and Talk

   • Predict whether the paths would remain perpendicular if the path parallel
     to a side of the park were moved closer to that side.

   • Would you be able to determine anything about whether the paths were
     perpendicular if you knew that the paths intersecting sides of the park
     each intersected the midpoint of the side?

Build Understanding

Prove the Perpendicular Bisector Theorem

Perpendicular lines intersect at 90° angles. A **perpendicular bisector** of a segment is a line perpendicular to the segment at the midpoint of the segment.

Perpendicular Bisector Theorem
In a plane, if a point is on the perpendicular bisector of a segment, then it is equidistant from the endpoints of the segment.

In the diagram, $\overleftrightarrow{CD}$ is a perpendicular bisector of $\overline{AB}$. Each triangle is formed by the reflection of a segment over $\overleftrightarrow{CD}$, so $AE = BE$, $AF = BF$, and $AG = BG$. Each point on $\overleftrightarrow{CD}$ is the same distance from the endpoints A and B.

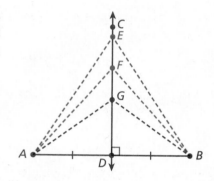

1 ▶ Prove the Perpendicular Bisector Theorem.

Given: $\overleftrightarrow{CD}$ is a perpendicular bisector of $\overline{AB}$.
Prove: $AC = BC$

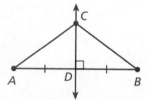

Statements	Reasons
1. $\overleftrightarrow{CD}$ is a perpendicular bisector of $\overline{AB}$.	1. Given
2. $AD = BD$	2. Definition of perpendicular bisector
3. $m\angle ADC = m\angle BDC = 90°$	3. Definition of perpendicular bisector
4. $CD = CD$	4. ___?___ **A.** What property justifies Step 4?
5. $\triangle ADC$ and $\triangle BDC$ are right triangles.	5. Definition of right triangle
6. $(AC)^2 = (AD)^2 + (CD)^2$ $(BC)^2 = (DB)^2 + (CD)^2$	6. ___?___ **B.** What theorem justifies Step 6?
7. $(BC)^2 = (AD)^2 + (CD)^2$	7. Substitution Property
8. $(AC)^2 = (BC)^2$ **C.** Which steps combined to create Statement 7?	8. ___?___ **D.** What property justifies Step 8?
9. $AC = BC$	9. If $x^2 = y^2$ and x and y are both nonnegative, then $x = y$.

 Turn and Talk What type of triangle is $\triangle ACB$ in the proof of the Perpendicular Bisector Theorem? Explain your reasoning.

Prove the Converse of the Perpendicular Bisector Theorem

The Converse of the Perpendicular Bisector Theorem is true.

Converse of the Perpendicular Bisector Theorem
If a point is equidistant from the endpoints of a segment, then it lies on the perpendicular bisector of the segment. If $CA = CB$, then $\overleftrightarrow{CD}$ is perpendicular to $\overline{AB}$, and $\overleftrightarrow{CD}$ bisects $\overline{AB}$. 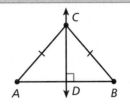

To prove this Converse, you may need to add a perpendicular line or segment into a given figure. You can do this because of the Perpendicular Postulate.

Perpendicular Postulate
If there is a line and a point that is not on the line, there is exactly one line through the point that is perpendicular to the given line.

2 Prove the Converse of the Perpendicular Bisector Theorem.

Given: $CA = CB$

Prove: C lies on the perpendicular bisector of $\overline{AB}$.

A figure for the given information would have $\overline{CA}$ and $\overline{CB}$ drawn and labeled congruent. Draw $\overline{AB}$ and draw a line through C that crosses $\overline{AB}$ at a point D such that $\overleftrightarrow{CD}$ is perpendicular to $\overline{AB}$. (See the Perpendicular Postulate above.)

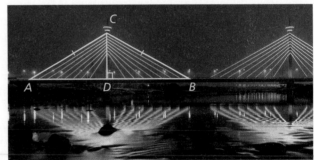

A. What do you know about $\triangle ACD$ and $\triangle BCD$?

B. How can you use the Pythagorean Theorem to describe the relationship of the side lengths of $\triangle ACD$ and $\triangle BCD$?

C. What is true about $(CA)^2$ and $(CB)^2$? How do you know?

D. What equation can you write using the information that $(CA)^2 = (CB)^2$? How do you know this is true?

E. When you simplify the equation from Part D, you find that $AD = BD$. Explain how that relationship completes the proof.

Turn and Talk Why can you draw the extra lines on the diagram as part of the proof?

Step It Out

Construct Perpendicular Bisectors and Lines

3 The steps below show the construction of the perpendicular bisector of a segment.

Use a compass to draw an arc centered at X such that the radius of the arc is greater than $\frac{1}{2}$ XY.

Without changing the compass setting, draw an arc centered at Y.

Use a straightedge to draw a line through the two points where the arcs intersect.

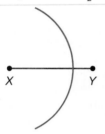
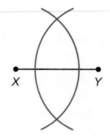
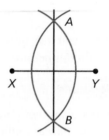

A. Justify the construction using the Perpendicular Bisector Theorem or its Converse.

B. These construction steps are also used to construct the midpoint of a segment. Explain why the midpoint is also on the perpendicular bisector of the segment.

4 Use a compass and a straightedge to construct a line perpendicular to a line through a point.

Place the compass on P. Draw an arc that intersects line m at two points. Label the intersections A and B.

Draw an arc centered at A below line m. Use the same compass setting to draw an arc centered at B that intersects the arc centered at A.

Use a straightedge to draw a line through point P and the point below m where the arcs intersect.

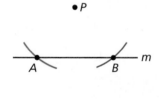
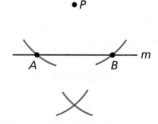
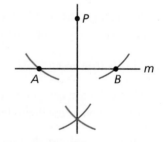

A. Are points A and B equidistant from point P?

B. Justify the construction using the Perpendicular Bisector Theorem or its Converse.

Turn and Talk Describe how you can use perpendicular segments drawn from one line to another to determine whether the lines are parallel.

Use Theorems About Right Angles

Perpendicular Transversal Theorem

If a line is perpendicular to one of two parallel lines, then it is perpendicular to the other line as well.
If $m \parallel n$ and $t \perp m$, then $t \perp n$.

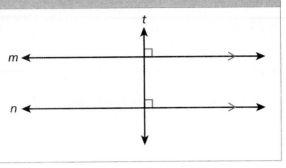

5 Find the length of the bridge supports indicated by $\overline{PQ}$ and $\overline{RQ}$. The measurements are in feet.

A. How do you know that line t is perpendicular to line n?

Given: $PS = RS$

Find the value of x.
$$PQ = RQ$$

B. Why can you write this equation?

$$8x + 31 = 12x - 5$$
$$36 = 4x$$
$$9 = x$$

Determine PQ and RQ.
$$PQ = 8x + 31$$

C. Why do you only need to calculate PQ and not also RQ?

$$PQ = 8(9) + 31$$
$$PQ = 72 + 31 = 103$$

The bridge supports are each 103 feet long.

 Turn and Talk How would your answer change if you calculated RQ instead of PQ?

Check Understanding

1. How can you construct a perpendicular bisector of a segment *RS* by folding a piece of paper?

2. In the figure, is $\overline{BD}$ perpendicular to $\overline{AC}$? Explain why or why not.

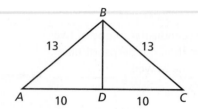

Find the value of the variable. Explain your reasoning.

3.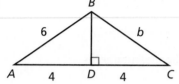

4.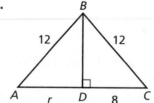

On Your Own

Decide if there is enough information to conclude that *P* lies on the perpendicular bisector of $\overline{QR}$.

5.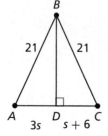

6.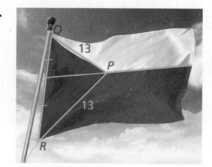

7. (MP) **Use Tools** Draw a segment. Construct the perpendicular bisector.

Find the value of the variable.

8.

9.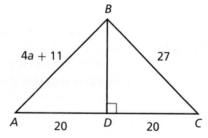

10.

11.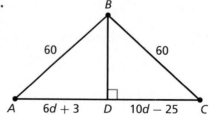

12. Is line t perpendicular to line j? Explain how you know.

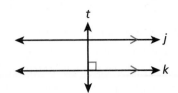

13. (MP) **Construct Arguments** If $AC = BC$ and $AD = BD$, prove $\overleftrightarrow{CD} \perp \overline{AB}$.

Given: $AC = BC$ and $AD = BD$

Prove: $\overleftrightarrow{CD} \perp \overline{AB}$

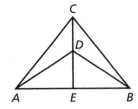

Use the diagram to find the lengths. $\overline{BF}$ is the perpendicular bisector of $\overline{AC}$. $\overline{EC}$ is the perpendicular bisector of $\overline{BD}$.

14. Suppose $AC = 24$. What is the length of $\overline{FC}$?

15. Suppose $BD = 30$. What is the length of $\overline{AB}$?

16. Suppose $ED = 11$. What is the length of $\overline{BE}$?

17. Suppose $AB = 14$. What is the length of $\overline{BD}$?

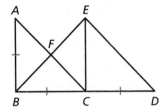

18. Construct a diameter and the center of a circle.

  A. Draw a circle. Use a straightedge to draw a segment that intersects the circle in two points. Label the intersections with the circle A and B.

  B. Use a compass to draw a perpendicular bisector of $\overline{AB}$. How do you know that the perpendicular bisector of $\overline{AB}$ is a diameter of the circle?

  C. Use a compass to draw a perpendicular bisector of the diameter of the circle. How do you know that the point of intersection of this perpendicular bisector and the diameter of the circle is the center of the circle?

  D. Is it possible for a point to be the center of a circle, but not be on the perpendicular bisector of a chord? Explain your reasoning.

19. Prove the Perpendicular Transversal Theorem.

  Given: $a \perp t$ and $a \parallel b$

  Prove: $b \perp t$

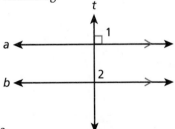

In 20–24, consider the possible design variations in the pattern shown. In the figure, $XY = ZY$ and $XW = ZW$.

20. Suppose $m\angle 3 = 48°$. What is $m\angle 1$?

21. Suppose $WZ = 5$ and $XZ = 8$. What is WY?

22. Find $m\angle 1 + m\angle 2$.

23. Suppose $WY = 15$ and $XZ = 16$. What is WZ?

24. Suppose $m\angle 4 = 51°$. What is $m\angle 1$?

25. STEM A water molecule has two hydrogen atoms and one oxygen atom. The distance between each hydrogen atom and the oxygen atom is the same. Do you have enough information to determine if the oxygen atom lies on the perpendicular bisector of a segment between the two hydrogen atoms? Explain your reasoning.

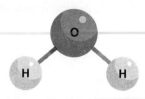

26. If $m \perp p$ and $n \perp p$, show that $m \parallel n$.

   Given: $m \perp p$ and $n \perp p$

   Prove: $m \parallel n$

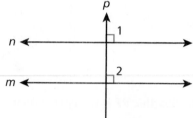

27. Two lines intersect to form a linear pair of congruent angles. The measure of one angle is $(15w + 15)°$. The measure of the other angle is $\left(\frac{25v}{2}\right)°$. Find the values of w and v. Explain your reasoning.

28. Music The valve pistons on a trumpet are all perpendicular to the lead pipe. Explain why the valve pistons must be parallel to each other.

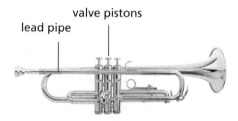

lead pipe   valve pistons

Spiral Review • Assessment Readiness

29. What is the slope of a line that passes through $(-4, 7)$ and $(2, -5)$?

   (A) 2   (C) $-\frac{1}{2}$

   (B) $\frac{1}{2}$ (D) -2

30. Which angle(s) are congruent to $\angle 3$? Select all that apply.

   (A) $\angle 1$

   (B) $\angle 2$

   (C) $\angle 4$

   (D) $\angle 5$

   (E) $\angle 6$

   (F) $\angle 7$

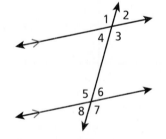

31. _____?_____ angles are nonadjacent angles that lie on opposite sides of the transversal between the intersected lines.

   (A) Alternate exterior

   (B) Alternate interior

   (C) Consecutive interior

   (D) Consecutive exterior

32. $\angle 1$ and $\angle 2$ are supplementary angles. $m\angle 1 = (6y + 7)°$ and $m\angle 2 = (9y - 7)°$. What is y?

   (A) 12   (C) 79

   (B) 16   (D) 101

🔲 **I'm in a Learning Mindset!**

What can I contribute to my learning community to prove that intersecting lines are perpendicular?

Angle Pairs Formed
by Parallel Lines and a Transversal

Two paths at a park are parallel. These paths are crossed by another path as shown.

Using the Corresponding Angles Postulate, Alternate Interior Angles Theorem, Alternate Exterior Angles Theorem, Consecutive Interior Angles Theorem, and Consecutive Exterior Angles Theorem, we know the following relationships:

$\angle 1$ is congruent to $\angle 4$, $\angle 5$, and $\angle 8$.

$\angle 1$ is supplementary to $\angle 2$, $\angle 3$, $\angle 6$, and $\angle 7$.

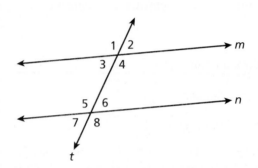

Parallel Lines

Andrea studied another section of the park. She wanted to know if the North Trail and South Trail are parallel. She measured the angles formed by a trail that crosses them.

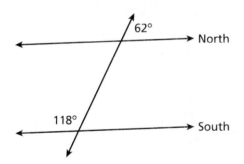

She uses the fact that the vertical angle of the 62° angle also measures 62°.

Because $62° + 118° = 180°$, she can use the Converse of the Consecutive Interior Angles Theorem to show that the North Trail and South Trail are parallel.

Perpendicular Lines

The park plans to build another trail to connect to the East Trail. The trail should be a perpendicular bisector of the East Trail.

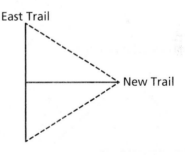

The park measures the distances from the end of New Trail to the ends of East Trail and find they are equal. New Trail also bisects East Trail.

The park knows New Trail is a perpendicular bisector by Converse of the Perpendicular Bisector Theorem.

Vocabulary

Choose the correct term from the box to complete each sentence.

1. A(n) ___?___ is a line that intersects two coplanar lines at two distinct points.

2. ___?___ lines are lines in the same plane that do not intersect.

3. Two lines are ___?___ if they intersect to form 90° angles.

Concepts and Skills

Given that $m \parallel n$, identify an example of each angle pair and explain if they are supplementary or congruent.

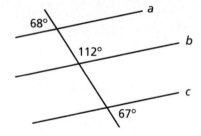

4. Corresponding angles

5. Consecutive interior angles

6. Alternate interior angles

7. Alternate exterior angles

8. Two parallel lines are intersected by a transversal. Two angles, $\angle 1$ and $\angle 2$, are consecutive interior angles. The measure of $\angle 1$ is $(7t - 4)°$. The measure of $\angle 2$ is $(t + 24)°$. What is the measure of each angle?

9. Determine if each set of lines is parallel or not. Justify your reasoning.

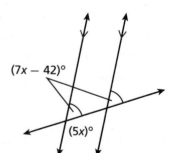

Find the value of the variable.

10.

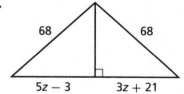

11.

12. $\overline{LM}$ is a perpendicular bisector of $\overline{NP}$. The length of $\overline{LN}$ is $12w + 7$, and the length of $\overline{LP}$ is $15w - 5$. What is the length of $\overline{LN}$?

13. **(MP) Use Tools** $\overline{AB}$ is a perpendicular bisector of $\overline{CD}$. The length of $\overline{AD}$ is $7h + 11$, and the length of $\overline{AC}$ is $15h + 3$. What is the value of h? State what strategy and tool you will use to answer the question, explain your choice, and then find the answer.

Lines on the Coordinate Plane

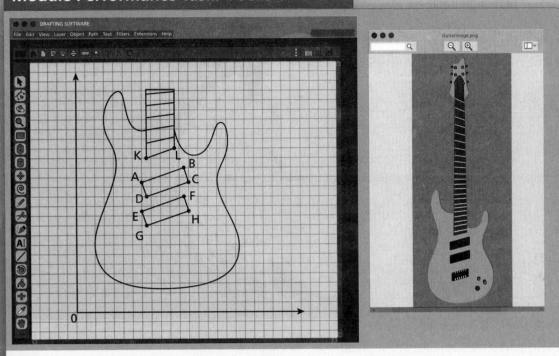

Pickup Placement in Acoustic Design

Electric guitars contain pickups, which create a magnetic field. The movement of the strings create deviations in the magnetic field, and these deviations are converted to reproduce the sound of the strings.

The placement of the pickups affects the tone of the guitar, so the holes for the pickups in the body must be planned into the design of the guitar. The designer wants the pickups to be parallel to the last fret. The body is designed using Computer Aided Drafting software and designates the coordinates of the cutout *ABCD* at *A*(14, 27), *B*(23, 30), *C*(24, 27), and *D*(15, 24). The end points of the last fret are *K*(15, 32) and *L*(21, 34).

A. Prove that the last fret of the guitar is parallel to the cutout of the pickup *ABCD*.

B. What relationships do you notice between the other segments of the cutout and the last fret of the guitar? Justify your statement.

C. The cutout *EFGH* needs to be in the same orientation as *ABCD*. Point *E* must be located 6 cm directly below *A*. What are the coordinates of cutout *EFGH*, given that 1 unit is equivalent to 1 cm?

D. Another fret has end points at *M*(15, 40) and *N*(21, 41). Is this fret parallel to the cutout of pickup *ABCD*? Explain your reasoning.

Are You Ready?

Complete these problems to review prior concepts and skills you will need for this module.

Slopes of Lines

Find the slope of each line given two points on the line.

1. $(2, 3)$ and $(4, 9)$

2. $(-4, -1)$ and $(4, 1)$

3. $(0, 2)$ and $(12, -1)$

4. $(3, 7)$ and $(8, 7)$

5. $(1, 4)$ and $(5, 8)$

6. $(-3, -7)$ and $(-1, -15)$

Point-Slope Form

Write an equation in point-slope form for each line given its slope and a point on the line.

7. -2 and $(0, 1)$

8. $\frac{4}{3}$ and $(3, -1)$

9. $\frac{1}{6}$ and $(2, 1)$

10. $-\frac{3}{2}$ and $(-2, -2)$

11. 5 and $(-6, 2)$

12. -4 and $(7, -1)$

Distance and Midpoint Formulas

Find the length and the midpoint of a segment with the endpoints A and B. Round to the nearest hundredth.

13. $A(0, 0)$
$B(6, 10)$

14. $A(-4, -6)$
$B(5, 12)$

15. $A(1, 5)$
$B(7, 12)$

16. $A(-11, -9)$
$B(-2, -5)$

Connecting Past and Present Learning

Previously, you learned:

• to find the slope of a line given two points,

• to prove if lines are parallel or perpendicular using angle pairs, and

• to write equations for lines on the coordinate plane.

In this module, you will learn:

• to write equations for parallel and perpendicular lines,

• to determine if two lines are parallel or perpendicular based on their slope, and

• to write coordinate proofs.

Slope and Equations of Parallel Lines

(I Can) find the equation of a line that is parallel to a given line.

Spark Your Learning

A city is building a parking lot and needs to plan the spacing of each parking space.

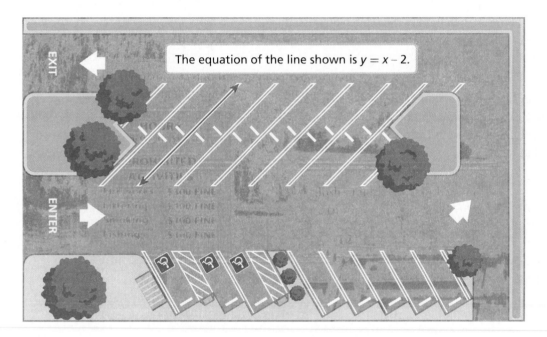

The equation of the line shown is $y = x - 2$.

Complete Part A as a whole class. Then complete Parts B–D in small groups.

A. What is a mathematical question that you can ask about this situation? What information would you need to know to answer your question?

B. What mathematical facts about the parking space lines do you already know? What form for an equation of a line on a coordinate plane could be helpful?

C. To answer your question, what strategy and tool would you use along with all the information you have? What answer do you get?

D. Suppose you extend the lines to the x-axis to find the x-intercepts. How would this help you check your answer for Part C?

 Turn and Talk Could you determine the perpendicular distance between two of these lines if you knew the horizontal distance between two lines? What might those steps look like if so?

Build Understanding

Investigate Properties of Parallel Lines

The **slope** m of a nonvertical line is the ratio of the vertical change (the *rise*) to the horizontal change (the *run*) between any two points on the line. For the line shown, $m = \frac{\text{rise}}{\text{run}} = \frac{y_2 - y_1}{x_2 - x_1}$, where (x_1, y_1) and (x_2, y_2) are two points on the line. The subscript notation indicates whether each value in the ratio is the x- or y-coordinate of the first point or the second point.

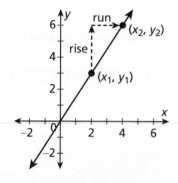

Recall that parallel lines are two lines in the same plane that do not intersect. There is a special relationship between the slopes of any two parallel lines.

1 The coordinates of two points on each line are given. Indicate which of the points you chose as the first point and which is the second point.

$A(6, 4)$, $B(7, 3)$, where A is (x_1, y_1) and B is (x_2, y_2)

$C(1, 3)$, $D(3, 1)$, where C is (x_1, y_1) and D is (x_2, y_2)

Find the slopes of $\overleftrightarrow{AB}$ and $\overrightarrow{CD}$.

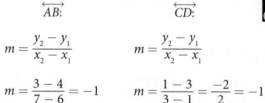

$\overleftrightarrow{AB}$:	$\overrightarrow{CD}$:
$m = \dfrac{y_2 - y_1}{x_2 - x_1}$	$m = \dfrac{y_2 - y_1}{x_2 - x_1}$
$m = \dfrac{3 - 4}{7 - 6} = -1$	$m = \dfrac{1 - 3}{3 - 1} = \dfrac{-2}{2} = -1$

A. Does it matter which point is chosen as the first point and which is the second point? If the assignment of the first point and second point are interchanged, does it change the slope of $\overleftrightarrow{AB}$? Explain.

B. How can you graphically confirm the slopes should be negative?

C. What do you observe about the slopes of the parallel lines?

D. What do you predict the outcome would be if we highlighted a third parallel line in the figure and then calculated the slope of that line? Why?

 Turn and Talk Would the results of Task 1 be different if different points from each line had been used in the slope equation? Why or why not?

Identify Parallel Segments

Slope Criteria of Parallel Lines
Two nonvertical lines are parallel if and only if they have the same slope.

A line segment is a section of a line that is contained within the line. The equation of the line segment is the same equation of the line that contains it, except limitations on the domain are given for the segment. The limitations describe the endpoints of the segments.

Parallel segments, like parallel lines, have equal slopes and do not intersect.

2 ▸ A parallelogram is a four-sided shape (or quadrilateral) with two pairs of parallel, opposite sides. You can determine if a shape shown on a coordinate plane is a parallelogram by examining the slopes of each of its sides.

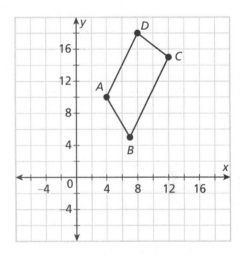

The coordinates of the vertices of the figure shown are.

$A(4, 10)$, $B(7, 5)$, $C(12, 15)$, $D(8, 18)$

A. Why do you need the coordinate points to determine the slopes?

B. What should be true about the slopes of any parallel sides?

Using the slope formula $m = \frac{y_2 - y_1}{x_2 - y_1}$, the slopes of each segment are:

$\overline{AB}$:

$m = \dfrac{5 - 10}{7 - 4} = \dfrac{-5}{3}$

$m = -\dfrac{5}{3}$

$\overline{BC}$:

$m = \dfrac{15 - 5}{12 - 7} = \dfrac{10}{5}$

$m = 2$

$\overline{CD}$:

$m = \dfrac{18 - 15}{8 - 12} = \dfrac{3}{-4}$

$m = -\dfrac{3}{4}$

$\overline{DA}$:

$m = \dfrac{10 - 18}{4 - 8} = \dfrac{-8}{-4}$

$m = 2$

C. Which segments are parallel? How can you classify the shape using this information?

D. Examine the lengths of $\overline{DA}$ and $\overline{BC}$. Is it necessary that the two segments be of equal length or be located near each other on the coordinate plane to be parallel?

 Turn and Talk How can you change one point on the figure to create a parallelogram?

Prove the Slope Criteria of Parallel Lines

A **coordinate proof** is a style of proof where generalized coordinates are used to prove a geometric theorem. You can assign variables to one or more points and then prove the geometric theorem applies to any points on the coordinate plane.

3 **Given:** $p \parallel q$, neither line is vertical or horizontal

Prove: $m_p = m_q$

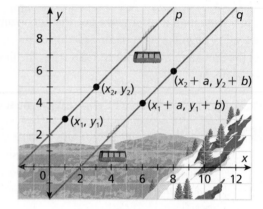

Choose two points from each line.
The points identified on the parallel lines are labeled to represent that the points on line q are a translation of the points on line p. Recall that if any lines are parallel, one can be mapped to the other by a translation.

Find the slopes.
The slopes of line p and line q are calculated using the slope formula, $m = \frac{y_2 - y_1}{x_2 - x_1}$, and the x-and y-coordinates of each point.

Line p:

$$m_p = \frac{y_2 - y_1}{x_2 - x_1}$$

Line q:

$$m_q = \frac{\left(y_2 + b\right) - \left(y_1 + b\right)}{\left(x_2 + a\right) - \left(x_1 + a\right)}$$

$$m_q = \frac{y_2 + b - y_1 - b}{x_2 + a - x_1 - a}$$

$$m_q = \frac{y_2 - y_1}{x_2 - x_1}$$

Substitute.
Using substitution, we can see that $m_p = m_q$ for any pair of parallel lines.

A. For line q, explain the meaning of a and b. What do they represent?

B. In your own words, how does the fact that any line parallel to another line is a translation of that line help you prove the slopes of the two lines are the same?

C. Would the outcome of the proof change if we had used lines with a negative slope to choose generic points?

 Turn and Talk The given information specified that the lines were not vertical or horizontal. What would happen in the calculations of the slopes in the proof if the lines were either vertical or horizontal?

Step It Out

Write Equations of Parallel Lines

When given the equation of a line, you can find the slope by rearranging the equation into slope-intercept form, $y = mx + b$, where m is the slope and b is the y-intercept.

4 ▶ Write an equation for a line parallel to $y = 0.25x - 5$ that passes through the point $(8, 5)$.

First, collect the given information.

$m = 0.25, x = 8, y = 5$ ◁── **A.** Where do you find the values of x and y?

The only unknown piece of information to write an equation in the form $y = mx + b$ is the y-intercept of the parallel line.

Use the slope-intercept form and substitute the given information.

$y = mx + b$

$5 = (0.25)8 + b$

$5 = 2 + b$

$b = 3$ ◁── **B.** What does this value of b tell you?

Replace the values for m and b back into the general slope-intercept form.

$y = mx + b$

$y = 0.25x + 3$ ◁── **C.** Why do we substitute the values back into the slope-intercept form?

The equation for a line parallel to $y = 0.25x - 5$ that passes through the point $(8, 5)$ is $y = 0.25x + 3$.

Write Equations of Parallel, Horizontal, and Vertical Lines

Remember that horizontal lines have a slope of 0, and vertical lines have an undefined slope.

The equation $y = 3$ can be written in slope-intercept form as $y = 0x + 3$ since the slope of a horizontal line is 0. However, $x = -1$ cannot be written in slope-intercept form since the slope is undefined.

The equation for a horizontal line that passes through the point (a, b) is $y = b$.

The equation for a vertical line that passes through the point (a, b) is $x = a$.

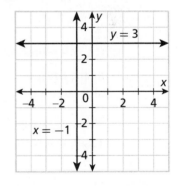

5 ▶ Write an equation for a line parallel to $y = -5$ that passes through $(3, 6)$ and an equation for a line parallel to $x = 4$ that passes through the point $(-1, 2)$.

Parallel to:	Passes through:	Equation
$y = -5$	$(3, 6)$	$y = 6$
$x = 4$	$(-1, 2)$	$x = -1$

A. How do you know these two lines have the same slope?

B. Why are the slopes of $x = 4$ and $x = -1$ undefined?

Apply the Slope Criteria for Parallel Lines

When solving a problem involving equations of parallel lines, first determine how to use the given information to find the answer. For example, you may need to find the slope of a given line, and then use the slope to write an equation for a parallel line through a given point.

6 A landscape designer is planning parallel walking paths through a large rectangular garden. The figure shows the centerline of two paths. A fountain on the other side of the garden will be located along the centerline of a third parallel path. What equation represents the centerline of the third path?

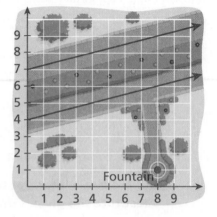

Find the slope of a given line.

The given parallel lines have the same slope. Choose either to determine the slope for the unknown equation.

$$m = \frac{\text{rise}}{\text{run}} = \frac{1}{4}$$

A. Why might you count rise and run here versus using the slope formula?

Determine the point through which the line must pass.

The fountain is located at $(8, 1)$.

Find the *y*-intercept of the unknown line.

$y = mx + b$

$1 = \frac{1}{4}(8) + b$

$1 = 2 + b$

$b = -1$

B. How can finding the *y*-intercept help to graph the line on the coordinate plane?

Write the equation of the line.

Write the equation for the third path using the same slope as the given parallel lines and the *y*-intercept calculated in the previous step.

C. What is the equation for the path parallel to the paths shown in the figure that passes through the point $(8, 1)$?

Turn and Talk How would you find the slope of a line given in standard form? Write the slope of $Ax + By = C$ in terms of A, B, and C.

Check Understanding

1. Can you write an equation for a line parallel to a given line that passes through exactly one point on the given line? Explain.

2. Which two equations could describe two parallel sides of a quadrilateral? Explain your reasoning.

   A. $3x + y = -5$ from $x = 0$ to $x = 5$

   B. $y = \frac{1}{3}(21 - 9x)$ from $x = -1$ to $x = 2$

   C. $y = 3x + 2.5$ from $x = -10$ to $x = -3$

3. Points (x_1, y_1) and (x_2, y_2) lie on line u. Points $(x_1 + 2, y_1 - 1)$ and $(x_2 + 2, y_2 - 1)$ lie on line v. Are lines u and v parallel? Justify your reasoning.

4. Write an equation for a line that passes through $(0, 0)$ and is parallel to a line that passes through $(-5, 3)$ and $(2, 1)$.

5. Are the lines $y = \frac{1}{2}$ and $x = \frac{1}{2}$ parallel? Justify your answer.

6. On a map, Padma's house is located at $(0, 2)$ on a street modeled by the equation $y = 2x + 2$. Each unit on the map represents one block. Padma leaves her house, walks four blocks east, then turns and walks one block north. She continues walking parallel to her street. What equation models her new path?

On Your Own

In Problems 7–9, use the graph to find the unknown slope.

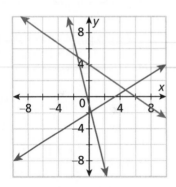

7. A line is parallel to the line with a y-intercept of -2. What is its slope?

8. A line is parallel to the line with a y-intercept of 4. What is its slope?

9. A line is parallel to the line with a y-intercept of -1. What is its slope?

Graph the pairs of parallel segments on a coordinate plane. Connect the endpoints of the segments to create a quadrilateral.

10. $y = \frac{4}{5}x - 1.5$ from $x = 2$ to $x = 6$ $y = \frac{4}{5}x + 3$ from $x = 0$ to $x = 3$

11. $y = 3x$ from $x = -1.5$ to $x = 3$ $y = 3x - 5$ from $x = 1$ to $x = 3$

For Problems 12–15, determine if the two lines are parallel.

12. Line m passes through points $(1, 5)$ and $(3.5, 7)$. Line n passes through points $(4, 7)$ and $(7.5, 10)$.

13. Line a passes through points $(2, -3)$ and $(6, 9)$. Line b passes through points $(0, 9)$ and $(2, 3)$.

14. Line p passes through points $(4, 1)$ and $(8, 3)$. Line q passes through points $(-8, 1)$ and $(4, 7)$.

15. Line j passes through points $(-3, 0)$ and $(2, 4)$. Line k passes through points $(1, -9)$ and $(9, 1)$.

16. **(MP)** **Use Repeated Reasoning** Eva is asked to create a blueprint of a tabletop before the prototype is produced. The tabletop is in the shape of a parallelogram, which is a quadrilateral with two pairs of parallel sides. She graphs the following segments.

Length 1: $y = 5$ from $x = -1$ to $x = 4$

Length 2: $y = 10$ from $x = -1$ to $x = 4$

Width 1: $x = -1$ from $y = 5$ to $y = 10$

Width 2: $x = 4$ from $y = 5$ to $y = 10$

Is Eva's graph a parallelogram? Discuss the slopes in your justification.

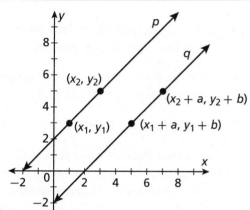

17. Put the reasons of the proof that parallel lines have the same slope in the correct order.

Given: $p \parallel q$

Prove: $m_p = m_q$

Statements	Reasons
1. Lines p and q are parallel.	?
2. If a point on line p is (x, y), any point on line q is $(x + a, y + b)$, where a and b are constants.	?
3. $m_p = \dfrac{y_2 - y_1}{x_2 - x_1}$, $m_q = \dfrac{(y_2 + b) - (y_1 + b)}{(x_2 + a) - (x_1 + a)}$	?
4. $m_q = \dfrac{(y_2 + b) - (y_1 + b)}{(x_2 + a) - (x_1 + a)} = \dfrac{y_2 - y_1}{x_2 - x_1}$	?
5. $m_p = m_q$	?

A. Any parallel lines can be mapped to each other by a translation.

B. slope $m = \dfrac{y_2 - y_1}{x_2 - x_1}$

C. Given

D. Substitution Property of Equality

E. Combine like terms.

Find the equation for each line.

18. Line n passes through $(-4, -1.5)$ and is parallel to a line that passes through $(0, 2)$ and $(5, 4)$.

19. Line f passes through $\left(\frac{1}{4}, 0\right)$ and is parallel to a line that passes through $(7, -3)$ and $(-10, -2)$.

20. Line j passes through $(15, 13)$ and is parallel to a line that passes through $(-0.5, 1)$ and $(11.5, 9)$.

Find the equation for the line parallel to the given line and passing through the given point.

21. $y = -\frac{1}{3}x + 7$; $(-2, 5.5)$

22. $y = \frac{4}{5}x - 1$; $(0, 6)$

23. $-2x + y = -8$; $(11, 0)$

24. $3y = -12x + 4$; $(1, 1)$

25. $x = y$; $(1.25, 3)$

26. $y = mx + b$; (x_1, y_1)

27. Open Ended A line passes through $(0, -1)$ and $(5, 10)$. Write the equation of any line parallel to that line, and provide a point other than the y-intercept through which the line passes. Show your work and explain the steps used to find a point along the parallel line.

Identify the slope of each given line. Write an equation for the line parallel to the given line passing through the given point.

28. $x = -3$; $(2, 0)$

29. $x = 5$; $(1.4, 8)$

30. $y = -10$; $(0, 0)$

31. $y = \frac{2}{3}$; $(-4, 3)$

32. $x = 0$; $(20, 14)$

33. $y = 8.5$; $\left(1, \frac{3}{5}\right)$

34. STEM An engineer has a sketch of a U-shaped bracket to be manufactured. Before manufacturing, the part is modeled using computer-aided design (CAD) software, which then tells a machine how to cut the part. One leg and the bottom of the bracket have been modeled using line segments. The legs must be parallel and the same length. Write the equation and domain limitation of the segment that represents the missing leg, and draw the segment.

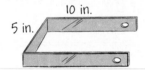

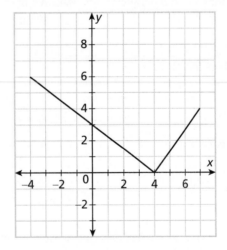

35. Use the figure to answer Parts A–C.

A. Are lines a and b parallel? Use the slopes to justify your answer.

B. If so, write the equation to a third parallel line. If not, find the equation for line a.

C. Suppose line b passed through $(0, -2)$ and $(6, -4)$. How would your answer to Part A change?

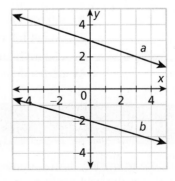

36. (MP) **Critique Reasoning** Consider the statement "Two lines in a coordinate plane are parallel if and only if the slopes of the lines are m and m, where m is any real number." Is this statement true or false? Explain your reasoning.

37. A city is planning to add a light rail track and a community walking path alongside an existing train line track. The current rail bed and track are shown in the diagram. The light rail track and the walking path will be on opposite sides of the existing train line track. The city engineer has determined that the walking path will pass through the point (200, 110.9) and the light rail track will pass through (100, 82). What lines do the centers of the light rail track and the community walking path follow?

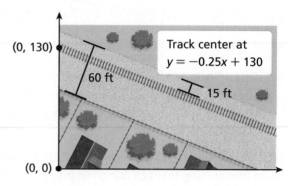

38. (Open Middle™) Using the digits 1 to 9, at most one time each, fill in the boxes to create linear equations for two lines that are parallel.

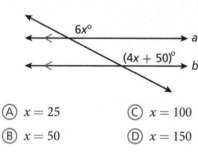

Spiral Review • Assessment Readiness

39. What value of x makes lines a and b parallel?

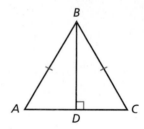

Ⓐ $x = 25$ Ⓒ $x = 100$

Ⓑ $x = 50$ Ⓓ $x = 150$

40. $\overline{AB}$ is 13 inches long. $\overline{BD}$ is 12 inches long. What is the length of $\overline{AD}$?

Ⓐ 25 in.   Ⓒ 10 in.

Ⓑ 15 in.   Ⓓ 5 in.

41. Match the name on the left with its correct description on the right.

A. parallel lines   **1.** intersect at a 90° angle

B. perpendicular lines   **2.** do not intersect

C. transversal   **3.** intersects two lines at two different points

D. perpendicular bisector   **4.** perpendicular to a segment at the midpoint

 I'm in a Learning Mindset!

What can I contribute to my learning community regarding how to use parallel lines to solve real-world problems?

Slope and Equations of Perpendicular Lines

(I Can) use slope to write the equation of a line that is perpendicular to a given line.

Spark Your Learning

Windmills have evenly-spaced blades to maximize capturing wind energy and to maintain balance while the blades are turning.

The angles between the blades are all congruent.

An equation for one of the blades is $y = \frac{2}{3}x$.

Complete Part A as a whole class. Then complete Parts B–D in small groups.

A. What is a mathematical question you can ask about this windmill? What information would you need to know to investigate your question?

B. Lines representing the blades would have what kind of relationship? Explain how you know.

C. Would the same relationship between the lines be true for a windmill with six blades? How do you know?

D. To answer your question, what strategy and tool would you use along with all the information you have? What answer do you get?

Turn and Talk Suppose you know that each of the four blades is 32 feet long. What can you determine about the center point of all four blades by using the Perpendicular Bisector Theorem or its converse?

©Neirfy/Shutterstock

Build Understanding

Investigate Properties of Perpendicular Lines and Segments

Perpendicular lines are two lines in the same plane that intersect to form 90° angles. When given the equations of two lines, you can determine if they are perpendicular by examining the slopes of the lines.

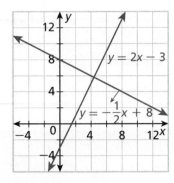

The figure shows a pair of perpendicular lines, along with the equation of each line. The slopes of the lines are 2 and $-\frac{1}{2}$. Do those slopes appear to have any special relationship? You will examine another case in Task 1 below.

 A. Examine the figure on the coordinate plane. Copy the table and write the slope for each line or segment.

Name	Slope
$\overleftrightarrow{AD}$	?
$\overline{AB}$	?
$\overline{BC}$	?
$\overline{CD}$	?

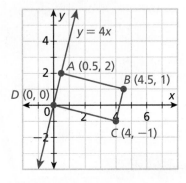

B. What do you notice about the slopes of $\overleftrightarrow{AD}$ and $\overline{BC}$? What do you notice about the slopes of $\overline{AB}$ and $\overline{CD}$? Is there a general relationship between the two slope values?

C. Think about the general relationship you found between the slopes of the perpendicular lines. How could you use this relationship to determine if two lines are perpendicular when presented with the equations of the lines?

D. Suppose you have the set of lines $y = 3x - 0.5$, $x + 3y = 6$, and $y = x + 3$. Which lines, if any, are perpendicular? How do you know? If any are perpendicular, graph them on a coordinate plane.

> **Turn and Talk** What is an equation of a line perpendicular to $x = -4$? How many lines fit this description? How can you use the slopes of the lines to support your answer?

Prove the Slope Criteria for Perpendicular Lines Theorem

In Task 1, you discovered lines with a slope of 4 are perpendicular to lines with a slope of $-\frac{1}{4}$. In general, the slopes of perpendicular lines are opposite reciprocals. Notice that the product of any pair of opposite reciprocals is -1. So, $4 \cdot \left(-\frac{1}{4}\right) = -1$.

> **Slope Criteria for Perpendicular Lines**
>
> The product of the slopes m of any two nonvertical perpendicular lines is -1.
> $$m_1 \cdot m_2 = -1$$

2 **Given:** Nonvertical lines p and q are perpendicular.

Prove: The product of their slopes is -1.

The quilt shown includes triangles you can use to verify the slope criteria. Mark the point (a, b) along line p. Draw a line from the point to the x-axis to create a right triangle.

For line p, the slope is $\frac{b}{a}$.

The quilt shows a rotation of the triangle by $90°$ about the origin. The image is a right triangle with the hypotenuse on top of line q. The coordinate where the triangle intersects line q is $(-b, a)$. The slope of line q is $\frac{a}{-b} = -\frac{a}{b}$.

Show that the product of the slopes of lines p and q is -1.

$$\left(\text{slope of line } p\right) \cdot \left(\text{slope of line } q\right) = -1$$
$$\frac{b}{a} \cdot \left(-\frac{a}{b}\right) \overset{?}{=} -1$$
$$-\frac{ab}{ab} = -1 \checkmark$$

So, if two lines are perpendicular, the product of their slopes must be -1.

A. How do you know the triangle created by the image after the rotation is a right triangle with the same side lengths as the preimage?

B. Is the following statement always true? "If two lines are perpendicular and one line has a negative slope, the other must have a positive slope." Why?

C. Does the theorem apply when one of the lines is vertical? Why or why not?

> **Turn and Talk** In the proof, what could change if you started with a line that has a negative slope? Will the proof still be valid?

Step It Out

Write Equations of Perpendicular Lines

3 ▸ Write an equation of the line perpendicular to $\overline{AB}$ that passes through $(-1, -1)$.

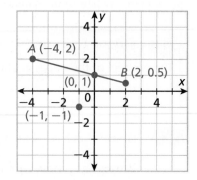

First, identify two points on the given segment.

$(-4, 2)$ and $(0, 1)$

Find the slope of $\overline{AB}$.

$m = \dfrac{\text{rise}}{\text{run}} = -\dfrac{1}{4}$ ◁ **A. How was the slope calculated?**

Find the slope of the perpendicular line.

The slope of $\overline{AB}$ is $-\dfrac{1}{4}$, so the slope of a perpendicular line is 4. ◁ **B. Why is the slope of the perpendicular line 4?**

Write the equation of the perpendicular line.

Use $(-1, -1)$ and the slope-intercept form to find b.

$y = mx + b$

$-1 = 4(-1) + b$

$-1 = -4 + b$, or $b = 3$

The equation of the line is $y = 4x + 3$.

Finally, substitute the slope and the calculated value of b back into slope-intercept form.

$y = mx + b$

$y = 4x + 3$ ◁ **C. Why do you substitute these values back into the general slope-intercept form of a line?**

Turn and Talk Explain how the equation would change if the perpendicular line passed through the point $(2, 2)$ instead.

---

4 ▸ Vertical and horizontal lines are a special case of perpendicular lines. Write an equation for the line perpendicular to $y = -3$ that passes through the point $(5, 7)$.

Two methods of finding the equation of the line are shown.

$y = -3$, or $y = 0x - 3$, so $m = 0$	$y = -3$
The opposite reciprocal slope of $m = 0$ is $m = -\dfrac{1}{0}$, which is undefined. Therefore, the answer must be a vertical line.	I know the line $y = -3$ is a horizontal line. I know that vertical lines are perpendicular to horizontal lines, so the answer must be a vertical line. The x-coordinate given in the problem is 5. Therefore the line perpendicular to $y = -3$ that passes through point $(5, 7)$ is the vertical line $x = 5$.
$x = a$ is the vertical line that passes through (a, b), so the line perpendicular to $y = -3$ that passes through the point $(5, 7)$ is $x = 5$.	

A. What are the coordinates of the point where the two lines intersect?

B. Explain why the vertical line passes through the x-coordinate given in the problem.

Apply the Criteria for Slopes of Perpendicular Lines

When solving a problem involving equations of perpendicular lines, first determine how to use the given information to find the answer. For example, you may need to find the slope of a given line, and then use the slope to write an equation for a perpendicular line through a given point.

5 A ship in distress is located at the point shown on the grid. The quickest way to reach the shoreline is to direct the ship along a line perpendicular to the shore. What is the equation of the line the navigator must use to sail the ship perpendicular to the shoreline from their current location?

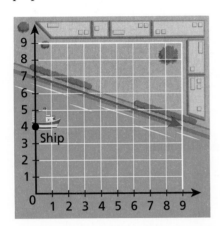

Write an equation for the shoreline.

The line has a slope of $-\frac{1}{3}$, and the y-intercept is 7.

$$y = -\frac{1}{3}x + 7$$

> **A.** How do you know this is the slope?

Find the slope of the line the captain will follow.

The line the captain will follow has a slope of 3, the opposite reciprocal of $-\frac{1}{3}$.

> **B.** Why must you find the slope before you can write the equation?

Write the equation of the perpendicular line the ship will follow.

The ship is located at $(0, 4)$, so the perpendicular line should pass through this point. This point lies on the y-axis, so the y-intercept is 4. The equation of the line the ship will follow is $y = 3x + 4$.

> **C.** How would this step be different if the given point was not the y-intercept?

 Turn and Talk At what point would the two lines intersect? What are two different methods you can use to find the solution?

Check Understanding

1. Find the slopes of the line and a line perpendicular to $y = -x + 20$.

2. If k is a constant, is the line $y = mx + k$ perpendicular to the line $y = -mx + k$? Explain your reasoning.

3. What is the equation of a line perpendicular to $y = \frac{1}{3}x - 9$ that passes through the point $(0, 1)$?

4. Write an equation for a line perpendicular to $y = 7$ that passes through the point $(2, 13)$.

5. On a map, Peach Street is modeled by the equation $4x - y = 7$. Apple Street is perpendicular to Peach Street and passes through the point $(12, 2)$. Find the equation that models Apple Street.

On Your Own

Write the equation of a line perpendicular to the line that passes through the given point.

6. $y = 2$
   $(1, -3)$

7. $y = -x + 20$
   $(-4, 2)$

8. $y = -5x - \frac{4}{3}$
   $(6, -4)$

9. $3x - 2y = 10$
   $(7, 5)$

10. $\frac{1}{2}y - 8x + 3 = 0$
    $(-8, 0)$

11. $12x = 33$
    $(0, 0)$

For Problems 12–18, determine whether each statement is *always*, *sometimes*, or *never* true.

12. A line with slope $\frac{a}{b}$ and a line with slope $-\frac{b}{a}$, where $a \neq 0$ and $b \neq 0$, are perpendicular.

13. Two perpendicular lines in the same plane intersect just once.

14. The line $y = c$, where c is a constant, is perpendicular to the line $y = x$.

15. A line perpendicular to another line has an undefined slope.

16. The sum of the slopes of perpendicular lines is 0.

17. Two lines are both parallel and perpendicular.

18. If two lines are perpendicular, exactly one of the lines has a negative slope.

19. The endpoints of one side of square $PQRS$ are at $P(1, 1)$ and $Q(3, 4)$.

    A. What is the equation for the line that contains $\overline{QR}$?

    B. What is the equation for the line that contains $\overline{SP}$?

    C. Are $\overline{PQ}$ and $\overline{QR}$ parallel or perpendicular? Write an equation using their slopes that proves your choice.

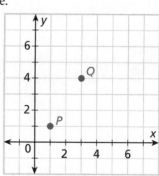

20. Consider the line segments in the graph.

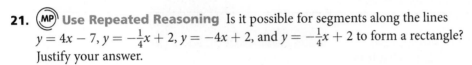

  A. Are any of the line segments perpendicular? Justify your answer.

  B. Write equations for the line containing $\overline{AB}$ and a line perpendicular to that line that passes through point $(8, -27)$.

  C. Write equations for the line containing $\overline{CD}$ and a line perpendicular to that line that passes through point $(-9, -10)$.

  D. Write equations for the line containing $\overline{EF}$ and a line perpendicular to that line that passes through point $(15, 0)$.

  E. Where could you place point G so that $\overline{FG}$ is perpendicular to $\overline{CD}$?

21. (MP) **Use Repeated Reasoning** Is it possible for segments along the lines $y = 4x - 7$, $y = -\frac{1}{4}x + 2$, $y = -4x + 2$, and $y = -\frac{1}{4}x + 2$ to form a rectangle? Justify your answer.

22. (MP) **Construct Arguments** Check Michael's work for errors. He wants to write an equation of the line perpendicular to $6x + 8y = -4$ that passes through the point $(-2, 6)$ but isn't sure if he's made any mistakes.

Step 1	Step 2	Step 3
$-4 = 6x + 8y$	$y = mx + b$	$y = mx + b$
$y = -\frac{3}{4}x - \frac{1}{2}$	$6 = -\frac{4}{3}(-2) + b$	$y = -\frac{4}{3}x + \frac{10}{3}$
	$b = \frac{10}{3}$	

  A. In which step(s) does Michael make an error, if any? Describe the error(s).

  B. If there are any errors, correct them and write the correct equation.

23. The converse of the Slope Criteria for Perpendicular Lines Theorem states, "If the slopes of two lines are opposite reciprocals, the two lines are perpendicular." Write a proof for the Converse of the Slope Criteria for Perpendicular Lines Theorem.

24. A helicopter landing pad is often a large circle marked with an "H". In a scale drawing of the ship's landing pad, the segment of $x = -5$ from $y = -2$ to $y = 6$ represents the vertical left leg of the H. The horizontal leg bisects both vertical legs and is 6 units long. What segment equations represent the middle leg and the right leg of the H?

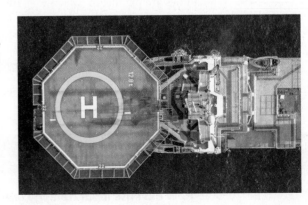

25. **(MP)** **Use Repeated Reasoning** Ivis walks home from school, but today she takes a detour due to construction. Her school is located on a horizontal street at the point $(0, 2)$. Each unit on the coordinate plane represents one block. She walks 3 blocks due south, 2 blocks east, 1 block north, and 2 more blocks east. Her house is located on a vertical street that passes through this point. Find the equation of the line that models her street.

26. A trail through a national park is being extended to include side paths to different natural features. The planners would like to add a perpendicular path that leads to a banyan tree, a unique type of tree that grows new roots from the canopy down to the ground. The trail and tree are modeled on the coordinate plane.

Banyan Tree

A. What are the slopes of the current trail and the new perpendicular path?

B. What is the equation for the line that contains the new path to the tree?

C. A trail marker will be placed where the trail and path intersect. What is the location of the marker?

D. The planners want to add another side path leading to a small waterfall. This path will be parallel to the path to the banyan tree. Is the path to the waterfall perpendicular to the trail as well? Explain.

27. **(Open Middle™)** Using the digits 1 to 9, at most one time each, fill in the boxes to create equations for two lines that are perpendicular.

$$y = \frac{\square}{\square}x + \square; \quad \square x + \square y = \square$$

Spiral Review • Assessment Readiness

28. When two lines are cut by a transversal, and corresponding angles are congruent, the two lines are ___?___.

(A) perpendicular   (C) congruent

(B) parallel   (D) complementary

29. Which lines are parallel to $5y = -x + 10$? Select all that apply.

(A) $y = -5x + 2$ (D) $-5y - 5x = 2$

(B) $-x - 3 = 5y$ (E) $2x = -10y + 2$

(C) $2y = 10x - 9$ (F) $y = 2x + 5$

30. Any point on a perpendicular bisector of a segment is ___?___ from the endpoints of that segment.

(A) equilateral   (C) perpendicular

(B) parallel   (D) equidistant

31. What is the length of the line segment with endpoints $A(-1, 2)$ and $B(-7, 4)$?

(A) $3\sqrt{5}$ (C) $2\sqrt{10}$

(B) 6.5   (D) 5.5

 I'm in a Learning Mindset!

How did I use input from my group members to solve the Spark Your Learning Task from the beginning of the lesson?

Write a Coordinate Proof

(I Can) use the Distance Formula to show congruence on the coordinate plane.

Spark Your Learning

A state park has two hiking trails to an extinct volcano dome. One trail travels around the north side of the volcano dome, and the other trail travels around the south side.

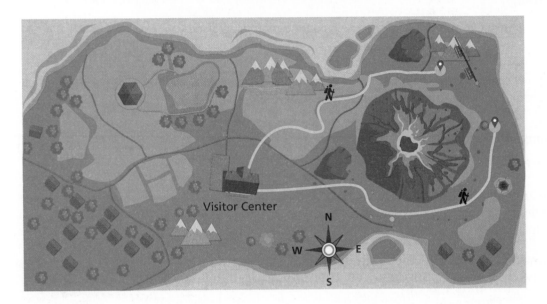

Complete Part A as a whole class. Then complete Parts B–D in small groups.

A. What is a mathematical question you can ask about this situation? What information would you need to know to answer your question?

B. What tools can you use to answer the question? How can you use them to make an estimate?

C. How would you use the information in the diagram and the additional information your teacher gave you to answer your question? What is the answer?

D. Can you think of any ways to find a more precise answer?

 Turn and Talk Predict how your answer would change for each of the following changes in the situation:
- The trails are straight lines.
- The trails have hills or other elevation changes not mapped.
- The scale is 5 miles per unit.

Build Understanding

Prove the Distance Formula

The Pythagorean Theorem states that $c^2 = a^2 + b^2$, where a and b are the lengths of the legs of a right triangle and c is the length of the hypotenuse. You can use the Distance Formula to apply the Pythagorean Theorem to find the distance between points on the coordinate plane.

Distance Formula

The distance between two points (x_1, y_1) and (x_2, y_2) on the coordinate plane is given by $\sqrt{(x_2 - x_1)^2 + (y_2 - y_1)^2}$.

A coordinate proof is one that uses both coordinate geometry and algebra. You can use a coordinate proof to place a figure on the coordinate plane to prove the Distance Formula.

1   **Given:** $P(x_1, y_1)$ and $Q(x_2, y_2)$, $x_1 \neq x_2$ and $y_1 \neq y_2$
Prove: $PQ = \sqrt{(x_2 - x_1)^2 + (y_2 - y_1)^2}$

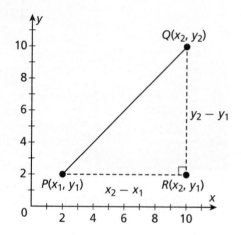

Begin by finding the length of each side of the right triangle by using the coordinates of each vertex.

The length of $\overline{PR}$ is the difference of the x-coordinates of the two endpoints: $PR = x_2 - x_1$.

The length of $\overline{QR}$ is the difference of the y-coordinates of the two endpoints: $QR = y_2 - y_1$.

The length of the hypotenuse of the triangle is PQ.

Write the Pythagorean Theorem and then substitute the lengths in terms of the coordinates.

$$c^2 = a^2 + b^2$$

$$PQ^2 = PR^2 + QR^2$$

$$PQ^2 = (x_2 - x_1)^2 + (y_2 - y_1)^2$$

$$PQ = \sqrt{(x_2 - x_1)^2 + (y_2 - y_1)^2}$$

Therefore, for any two points on the coordinate plane, the distance between the points is given by $\sqrt{(x_2 - x_1)^2 + (y_2 - y_1)^2}$.

A. How do you know $\triangle PQR$ is a right triangle?

B. Suppose the triangle is drawn in a different quadrant, and $x_2 - x_1$ is a negative number. Is the proof still valid? Why or why not?

Turn and Talk How can you find the distance between two points on the coordinate plane if you forget the Distance Formula?

124

Prove the Midpoint Formula

Recall that the coordinates of the midpoint of a segment are the averages of the x-coordinates and of the y-coordinates of the endpoints.

The coordinates of the midpoint of $\overline{AB}$, shown in the figure, are found using the Midpoint Formula.

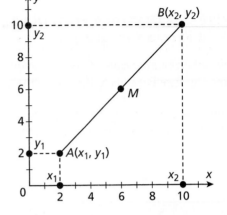

Midpoint Formula

The midpoint of the segment between any points (x_1, y_1) and (x_2, y_2) is $M\left(\frac{x_2 + x_1}{2}, \frac{y_2 + y_1}{2}\right)$.

2 ▶ Prove the Midpoint Formula.

Given: $A(x_1, y_1)$ and $B(x_2, y_2)$

Prove: The midpoint of $\overline{AB}$ is $M\left(\frac{x_2 + x_1}{2}, \frac{y_2 + y_1}{2}\right)$.

The horizontal distance from A to B is $x_2 - x_1$.

If M is halfway between A and B, the distance from A to M is half the distance from A to B. The horizontal distance between A and M is $\frac{x_2 - x_1}{2}$.

To find the x-coordinate of point M, add the horizontal distance from the origin to A to the horizontal distance from A to M.

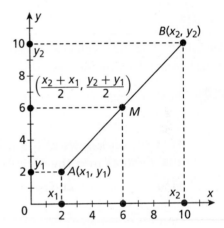

x-coordinate of M: $\quad x_1 + \dfrac{x_2 - x_1}{2} \qquad$ The horizontal distance from the origin to A added to the horizontal distance from A to M

$\dfrac{2x_1}{2} + \dfrac{x_2 - x_1}{2} \qquad$ Find a common denominator.

$\dfrac{2x_1 + x_2 - x_1}{2} \qquad$ Add the fractions.

$\dfrac{x_1 + x_2}{2} \qquad$ Combine like terms.

A. Show the steps to find the y-coordinate of M.

B. Suppose $x_1 = x_2$ or $y_1 = y_2$. Would the Midpoint Formula still apply? What would change?

C. Could you find the x-coordinate of M by subtracting the horizontal distance between A to M from the x-coordinate of B, rather than adding it to the x-coordinate of A? Why?

 Turn and Talk Suppose you used the Midpoint Formula to calculate the distance between $(-2, 5)$ and $(5, -8)$, and then measured the distance with a ruler to verify. Would that be sufficient to prove the Midpoint Formula? Why or why not?

Step It Out

Use the Distance Formula to Find Segment Length and Prove Congruence

Recall that a line segment is a portion of a line bounded by two endpoints. You can use the Distance Formula to determine the length of a line segment on the coordinate plane.

Sometimes a line segment will be the side of a figure. So, you find the distance between the vertices of the figure. The triangle with vertices $A(-2, -2)$, $B(3, 6)$, and $C(8, -2)$ has two congruent sides.

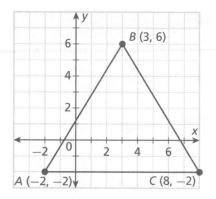

AB: $\sqrt{(3 - (-2))^2 + (6 - (-2))^2} = \sqrt{89}$

BC: $\sqrt{(8 - 3)^2 + (-2 - 6)^2} = \sqrt{89}$

CA: $\sqrt{(8 - (-2))^2 + (-2 - (-2))^2} = \sqrt{100}$

You can also find the length of a segment of a line using the equation of the line and the x-coordinates of the endpoints.

3 ▸ Find the length of the segment of the line $y = 3x - 6$ from $x = -3$ to $x = 4$.

Find the endpoints of the line segment by substituting the x values into the equation.

Line	Endpoint 1 (when x = −3)	Endpoint 2 (when x = 4)
$y = 3x - 6$	$y = 3(-3) - 6 = -15$	$y = 3(4) - 6 = 6$
	Endpoint 1: $(-3, -15)$	Endpoint 2: $(4, 6)$

Use the Distance Formula to find the distance between the endpoints.

$$\text{Distance between Points 1 and 2} = \sqrt{(x_2 - x_1)^2 + (y_2 - y_1)^2}$$
$$= \sqrt{(4 - (-3))^2 + (6 - (-15))^2}$$
$$= \sqrt{(7)^2 + (21)^2} = \sqrt{49 + 441}$$
$$= \sqrt{490} = 7\sqrt{10}$$

The length of the segment of the line $y = 3x - 6$ from $x = -3$ to $x = 4$ is $7\sqrt{10}$.

A. Find the length of the segment of the line $y = 2x + 8$ from $x = -8$ to $x = 2$.

B. In the first step, why do you substitute the given x-values into the equation?

C. In the Distance Formula, is the answer different if you use $(y_2 - y_1)^2 + (x_2 - x_1)^2$ under the radical instead?

Turn and Talk Is the length of the segment of the line $y = 3x - 6$ from $x = -3$ to $x = 4$ the same as the length of the segment of the line $y = 2x + 8$ from $x = -8$ to $x = 2$? Why or why not?

Apply the Distance Formula to a Real-World Problem

4 A ship is traveling along the line $y = 1.5x + 20$ from a port located at $x = 0$ to an anchor point along the same line 30 nautical miles horizontally from the port. One unit represents one nautical mile. Approximately how far does the ship travel? What point represents half the distance traveled?

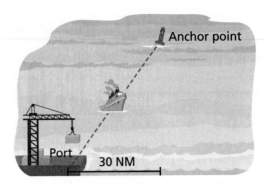

Anchor point

Port

30 NM

Determine the coordinates of the line segment described in the problem.

Starting Point

$y = 1.5x + 20; x = 0$

$y = 1.5(0) + 20 = 20$

$(0, 20)$

Ending Point

$y = 1.5x + 20; x = 30$

$y = 1.5(30) + 20 = 65$

$(30, 65)$

> **A.** What clue tells us the ending point is at $x = 30$?

Determine the distance between the coordinates using the Distance Formula.

$\sqrt{(x_2 - x_1)^2 + (y_2 - y_1)^2}$

$\sqrt{(30 - 0)^2 + (65 - 20)^2}$

$\sqrt{(30)^2 + (45)^2}$

$\sqrt{900 + 2025} = \sqrt{2925} \approx 54.1$

> **B.** How can an approximate answer be helpful in real-world problems?

The boat travels approximately 54.1 nautical miles.

Determine the halfway point between the coordinates using the Midpoint Formula.

$M\left(\dfrac{x_2 + x_1}{2}, \dfrac{y_2 + y_1}{2}\right)$

$M\left(\dfrac{30 + 0}{2}, \dfrac{65 + 20}{2}\right) = \left(\dfrac{30}{2}, \dfrac{85}{2}\right)$

$M(15, 42.5)$

The midpoint is $(15, 42.5)$.

> **C.** How could you find the location when the boat has traveled one-fourth the total distance?

Turn and Talk A second ship travels along the line $y = 2x + 25$ from $x = 5$ to $x = 32$. Which ship travels a longer distance? Explain your reasoning.

Check Understanding

1. How is the Distance Formula related to the Pythagorean Theorem?

2. In your own words, explain how averaging the x-coordinates and averaging the y-coordinates of the endpoints of a line segment provide the coordinates of the midpoint of the segment.

3. What is the length of the segment $y = 2.5x + 10$ from $x = 0$ to $x = 16$?

4. A triangle has vertices $(2, -3)$, $(-2, 1)$, and $(1, 2)$. Are any of the sides congruent?

5. A straight jogging path runs from $(-6, -9)$ to $(5, 4)$ on the map of the city park. Each unit on the map represents half of a mile. Approximately how long is the jogging path?

On Your Own

6. **(MP) Reason** When using the Pythagorean Theorem to prove that the distance between two points on the coordinate plane is given by $\sqrt{(x_2 - x_1)^2 + (y_2 - y_1)^2}$, why do you assume $x_1 \neq x_2$ and $y_1 \neq y_2$?

7. **(MP) Construct Arguments** Given that endpoints of a segment are (x_1, y_1) and (x_2, y_2), explain why the x-coordinate of the midpoint of the segment is $\left(\dfrac{x_1 + x_2}{2}\right)$ rather than $\left(\dfrac{x_2 - x_1}{2}\right)$.

Determine whether $\overline{AB}$ is congruent to $\overline{CD}$. Justify your answer.

8. $A(-2, -6)$, $B(7, 12)$
   $C(-9, -12)$, $D(2, 3)$

9. $A(-4.5, 2.5)$, $B(10.5, 22.5)$
   $C(0, 0)$, $D(15, 20)$

10. $A(20, 3)$, $B(18, 7)$
    $C(-19, -4)$, $D(-15, -6)$

11. $A(4, 11)$, $B(1, 1)$
    $C(-3, -3)$, $D(-5, -12)$

12. $A(1, 7)$, $B(3, -5)$
    $C(2, 2)$, $D(14, 0)$

13. $A(-8, -2)$, $B(-5, 1)$
    $C(11, 3)$, $D(14, 6)$

14.

15.

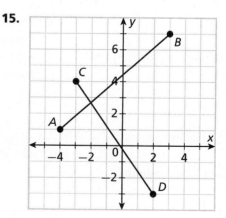

Use the figure for Problems 16–19.

16. Find the length and midpoint of $\overline{AB}$.

17. Find the length and midpoint of $\overline{BC}$.

18. Find the length and midpoint of $\overline{CA}$.

19. An *equilateral triangle* has three sides of equal length. If you form a triangle with vertices A, B, and C, is it an equilateral triangle? Explain your reasoning.

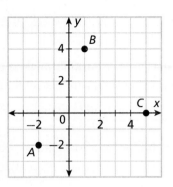

20. **Open Ended** Write a real-world problem that can be solved using the Midpoint Formula. Then solve the problem and justify your results.

21. **Health and Fitness** Amy is training for a race by running laps around her school gym. To estimate the distance of each lap, she calculates the perimeter of the gym, which has vertices of $W(-4, -3)$, $X(-2, 1)$, $Y(5, 5)$, and $Z(3, -1)$ on the school map.

    A. Approximately how many feet are in one lap around the gym if each unit on the map represents 50 feet? Round to the nearest foot.

    B. There are 5280 feet in a mile. Approximately how many full laps must she run to train for 3 miles?

22. A triangle has the vertices $(-4, -3)$, $(-1, 0)$, and $(-3, 2)$. Is it the same size as a triangle with the vertices $(4, 1)$, $(9, 2)$, and $(7, 4)$? Explain.

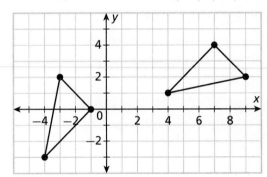

23. A trolley around a botanical garden needs a new schedule for the tourist season. A transportation planner plots the main station at the origin, and the first and second stops on the map, where each unit represents 0.5 mile.

    A. Determine the distance the trolley travels between the station and the first stop. If it leaves the station at 9:15 a.m. and travels at a rate of 15 mi/h, what time will the trolley reach the first stop?

    B. How far will the trolley travel from the first stop to the second stop?

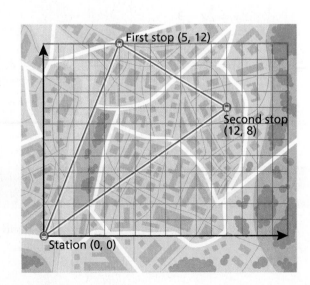

24. (MP) **Model with Mathematics** A car travels 26 miles down a straight road, starting at the origin. The final location of the car is the $(10, y_2)$.

A. Use the Distance Formula to write and solve an equation to find the final y-coordinate of the car. Show your work.

B. What is the midpoint of the path of the car?

25. A wooden bridge has a triangular support system. One support has the vertices $P(-1, 3)$, $Q(1, -2)$, and $R(-3, -2)$.

A. Which legs of the triangle are congruent?

B. If each unit on the coordinate plane represents 2 ft, how many whole triangular supports can be constructed with 100 ft of lumber?

Spiral Review • Assessment Readiness

26. Which line is perpendicular to $x = -5$ and passes through $(1, 6)$?

(A) $x = 1$ (C) $x = 5$

(B) $y = 6$ (D) $y = -5$

27. If (x, y) represents the point $(2, 4)$, what represents the point $(5, 6)$?

(A) $(x - 3, y + 2)$ (C) $(x + 2, y + 3)$

(B) $(x - 2, y - 3)$ (D) $(x + 3, y + 2)$

28. For each set of linear equations, determine if the lines are parallel, perpendicular, or neither.

Equations	Parallel	Perpendicular	Neither
A. $y = \frac{2}{5}x + 3$ $y = \frac{5}{2}x - 3$	?	?	?
B. $y = x - 2.5$ $y = -x + 9$	?	?	?
C. $y = 2x$ $y = 2x - 10$	?	?	?

 I'm in a Learning Mindset!

What resources are available to help me understand writing a coordinate proof?

Review

The Distance Formula

Two races through the city are shown. Race A follows the path $y = 2x - 4$ from $x = -1$ to $x = 4$. Race B follows the path $y = -0.25x - 2$ from $x = -6$ to $x = 5$. Are the races the same length?

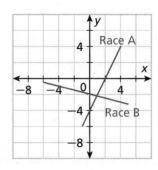

Find the coordinates of the endpoints.

Race A:

$y = 2x - 4$

$y = 2(-1) - 4 = -6 \rightarrow (-1, -6)$

$y = 2(4) - 4 = 4 \rightarrow (4, 4)$

Race B:

$y = -0.25x - 2$

$y = -0.25(-6) - 2 = -0.5 \rightarrow (-6, -0.5)$

$y = -0.25(5) - 2 = -3.25 \rightarrow (5, -3.25)$

Use the Distance Formula with the endpoint coordinates of each segment to determine the length of each race.

Race A:

$\sqrt{(x_2 - x_1)^2 + (y_2 - y_1)^2}$

$\sqrt{(4 - (-1))^2 + (4 - (-6))^2} = \sqrt{125}$

Race B:

$\sqrt{(x_2 - x_1)^2 + (y_2 - y_1)^2}$

$\sqrt{(5 - (-6))^2 + (-3.25 - (-0.5))^2} = \sqrt{128.5625}$

The segments are not congruent. Race B is the longer race because $\sqrt{128.5625} > \sqrt{125}$.

Parallel Lines

A major roadway runs parallel to Race A and passes through the point $(1, 1)$. What is the equation of the parallel road?

Parallel lines have equal slopes.

Race A: $y = 2x - 4$

Parallel Road: $y = 2x + b$

> $y = mx + b$, where m is the slope

Use slope-intercept form and the point through which the road passes to find the missing y-intercept.

$y = mx + b$

$1 = 2(1) + b$

$-1 = b$

Write the equation of the parallel line using the slope and y-intercept. The equation that describes the parallel road is $y = 2x - 1$.

Perpendicular Lines

A city walking path is perpendicular to Race A and passes through the point $(4, 2)$. What is the equation of the path?

Perpendicular lines have opposite reciprocal slopes.

Race A: $y = 2x - 4$.

Path: $y = -\dfrac{1}{2}x + b$

> m and $-\dfrac{1}{m}$ are opposite reciprocals.

Use slope-intercept form and the point through which the path passes to find the missing y-intercept.

$y = mx + b$

$2 = -\dfrac{1}{2}(2) + b$

$3 = b$

Write the equation of the perpendicular path using the slope and y-intercept. The equation that models the path is $y = -\dfrac{1}{2}x + 3$.

Vocabulary

Choose the correct term from the box to complete each sentence.

1. __?__ never intersect and have equal slopes.

2. Formulas with __?__ use small numbers on the lower right corner of variables to help identify different parts of the equation.

3. __?__ intersect at 90° angles and have opposite reciprocal slopes.

4. A __?__ uses geometry and algebra to show each step of a mathematical conclusion.

Concepts and Skills

Write an equation for a line parallel to and a line perpendicular to the given line.

5. $y = 4x - 5$

6. $3x - y = 9$

7. $y = -2x + 5$

8. $4x + 5y = 2$

9. $y = \frac{3}{4}x - 8$

10. $-6x + 2y = -7$

Write an equation for a line parallel and a line perpendicular to the given line that passes through the given point.

11. $2x + 3y = 6; (-2, -6)$

12. $-4y + x + 12 = 0; (5, 3)$

13. $y = -4x + 6; (1, 1)$

14. $y = \frac{1}{3}x - 5; (-4, 2)$

15. (MP) **Use Tools** A landscape architect is designing a water feature for a botanical garden. The current path follows the line $y = -3x + 1$. The water feature will be located at $(7, -4)$. Write an equation for a path that will run to the water feature and is perpendicular to the current path. State what strategy and tool you will use to answer the question, explain your choice, and then find the answer.

16. Justify each step of the proof for the Distance Formula.

A.	$\triangle PQR$ is a right triangle.
B.	$c^2 = a^2 + b^2$
C.	$PQ^2 = (x_2 - x_1)^2 + (y_2 - y_1)^2$
D.	$PQ = \sqrt{(x_2 - x_1)^2 + (y_2 - y_1)^2}$

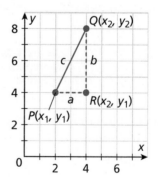

17. Are the segments $y = 4x + 9$ from $x = 0$ to $x = 5$ and $y = -0.5x - 2$ from $x = -3$ to $x = 1$ congruent segments? Explain using the Distance Formula.

18. A triangle has vertices $A(10, -2)$, $B(14, 1)$, and $C(14, -4)$. Classify the triangle and justify your answer.

Transformations

Pulmonologist

A pulmonologist is a physician that specializes in diagnosing and treating illnesses of the lungs. Some lung diseases and conditions are asthma, pneumonia, tuberculosis, and emphysema. Pulmonologists use various tools and models to understand how the lungs develop and operate.

STEM Task

Lung morphogenesis is an iterative process of sequential branching. Each branch is divided into two smaller parts, compartmentalizing the lung into self-similar sections.

Describe how the lung structure develops using transformations. Explain your reasoning.

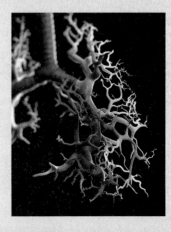

Learning Mindset

Challenge Seeking Defines Own Challenges

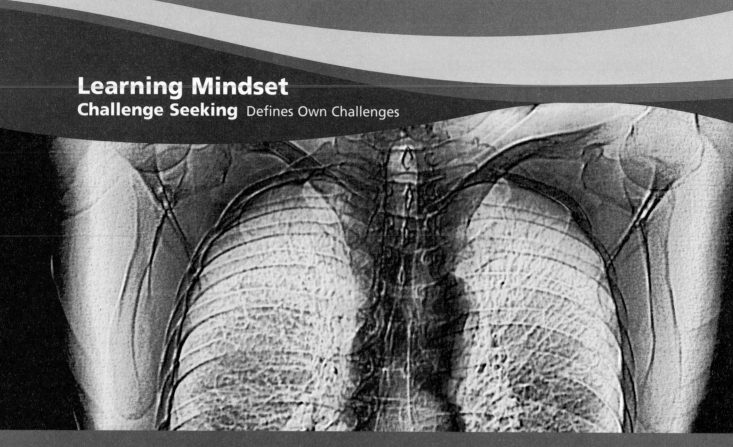

How do you seek challenges? The challenges you face help you develop and grow into the person you want to be. Defining your own challenges helps you to take ownership of your own development. The goals we set should stretch our capabilities, but still be within reach. Here are some questions you can ask yourself when thinking about challenging yourself:

- What do I want to be like? How can I set goals for myself to grow in this direction?

- What goals have I set for myself? Will my goals cause me to stretch my abilities and grow?

- What can I do if a challenge is too simple or difficult? How can I redefine my goals to make them more manageable?

- How do I proactively seek out additional learning opportunities? What resources do I use to seek out additional learning opportunities?

- What benefit is there to creating my own learning path? Why is it important to take ownership of my own development?

Reflect

Q Think of a time when have you defined your own challenge. How did you benefit from that experience? How was it different from having somebody else set your goals?

Q As a pulmonologist, why would you continue to challenge yourself to learn more? How would you benefit, and how would your community benefit?

Module Performance Task: *Spies and Analysts*™

The High Flying TYPE

How do skytypers write messages?

Are You Ready?

Complete these problems to review prior concepts and skills you will need for this module.

Translate Figures in the Coordinate Plane

The coordinates of a triangle are $(2, 7)$, $(5, -3)$, and $(-1, -1)$. Find the coordinates of the image after translating by the rule.

1. $(x, y) \rightarrow (x + 1, y - 2)$

2. $(x, y) \rightarrow (x - 3, y - 1)$

3. $(x, y) \rightarrow (x - 4, y + 2)$

4. $(x, y) \rightarrow (x + 3, y + 6)$

Rotate Figures in the Coordinate Plane

5. The coordinates of a triangle are $(-2, -1)$, $(1, 6)$, and $(3, -2)$. Find the coordinates of the image after rotating the triangle 180° about the origin.

6. The coordinates of a quadrilateral are $(-4, 0)$, $(1, 5)$, $(2, -3)$, and $(-3, -1)$. Find the coordinates of the image after rotating the quadrilateral 270° counterclockwise about the origin.

7. The coordinates of a quadrilateral are $(2, 5)$, $(6, 1)$, $(1, -3)$, and $(-1, -1)$. Find the coordinates of the image after rotating the quadrilateral 90° counterclockwise about the origin.

Reflect Figures in the Coordinate Plane

8. The coordinates of a triangle are $(6, -4)$, $(2, 0)$, and $(4, 4)$. Find the coordinates of the image after reflecting the triangle across the y-axis.

9. The coordinates of a triangle are $(-3, -1)$, $(2, -7)$, and $(5, -3)$. Find the coordinates of the image after reflecting the triangle across the x-axis.

10. The coordinates of a rectangle are $(-2, 6)$, $(-2, -3)$, $(3, 6)$, and $(3, -3)$. Find the coordinates of the image after reflecting the rectangle across the y-axis.

11. The coordinates of a rectangle are $(-5, 1)$, $(-5, -7)$, $(2, 1)$, and $(2, -7)$. Find the coordinates of the image after reflecting the rectangle across the x-axis.

Connecting Past and Present Learning

Previously, you learned:

• to graph points in the coordinate plane and

• to transform figures in the coordinate plane.

In this module, you will learn:

• to define transformations as functions and

• to describe symmetries of figures based on transformations.

Define and Apply Translations

(I Can) **translate figures in the plane.**

Spark Your Learning

Ya'ara is designing a kitchen, and her client has chosen the tiles shown.

Complete Part A as a whole class. Then complete Parts B–D in small groups.

A. What is a geometric question you can ask about the situation?
What information do you need in order to answer your question?

B. Once the pattern is started, describe how the position of the next tile
is determined.

C. To answer your question, what strategy and tool would you use along
with all the information you have? What answer do you get?

D. This pattern is being used on a surface in a kitchen. Why is it important
for all of the tiles to have the same orientation?

 Turn and Talk The pattern created by the tiles is called a tessellation. Where are
tessellating patterns commonly used? What makes them useful in these situations?

Build Understanding

Properties of Translations

A **transformation** is a function that changes the position, size, or shape of a figure or graph. A transformation maps a **preimage** determined by set of points in the plane to a corresponding set of points called the **image**.

An **isometry** or **rigid motion** is a transformation that does not change the size or shape of a figure. The properties of rigid motions are listed below.

Properties of Rigid Motions
• Rigid motions preserve distance.
• Rigid motions preserve angle measures.
• Rigid motions preserve collinearity.
• Rigid motions preserve betweenness.

One type of rigid motion is a translation, or slide. A **translation** is a transformation that maps every point of a figure or graph the same distance in the same direction. A translation is a rigid motion.

A **vector** is a quantity that has both direction and magnitude (or length). A vector has an initial point and a terminal point. You can use a vector to describe the distance and direction of a translation.

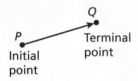

You can use the notation $T_{\vec{v}}(A) = A'$ to identify a translation of point A to A' along the vector v or $\overrightarrow{v}$ as shown below.

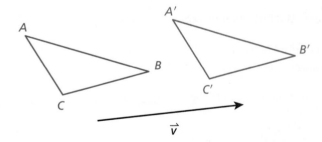

1 ▶ Confirm the properties of rigid motions under translations.

    A. Copy $\triangle ABC$ and $\triangle A'B'C'$ above. What is the relationship between the lengths of corresponding sides of the triangles?

    B. What is the relationship between the measures of corresponding angles in the triangles?

    C. Are the corresponding sides of the triangles parallel? Justify your answer.

    D. What is the distance between corresponding vertices?

 Turn and Talk What would happen if you translated $A'B'C'$ by the vector v?

Construct a Translation

In the context of transformations, the orientation of a figure means the order of the vertices around the figure. A translation preserves the orientation of the shape because it does not change the order of the vertices.

In the figures below, *ABC* and *A'B'C'* have the same orientation, but *ABC* and *A"B"C"* do not have the same orientation.

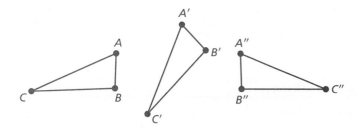

2 ▸ Construct a translation of quadrilateral *CDEF* using vector *XY*.

Step 1 Set a compass to the distance from *X* to *Y*.

Step 2 Place the point of the compass on *C* and make an arc. Repeat this step for each of the other vertices.

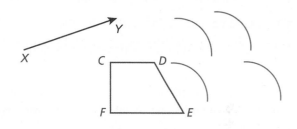

A. In Step 2, how do you know to make an arc above and to the right of each vertex?

Step 3 Open your compass to the distance from *X* to *C*. Slide the compass point up the vector until the compass point is at point *Y*. Draw an arc from point *Y* so that it intersects the first arc.

Step 4 Repeat Step 3 for the other vertices.

Step 5 Use a straightedge to connect the points where the arcs intersect.

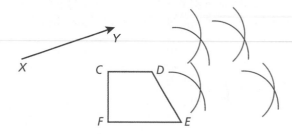

B. Are $\overline{CC'}$, $\overline{DD'}$, $\overline{EE'}$, and $\overline{FF'}$ parallel, perpendicular, or neither. Describe how you can use lined paper to check that your answer is reasonable.

C. How do you know that the distances *CC'*, *DD'*, *EE'*, and *FF'* are all equal to *XY*?

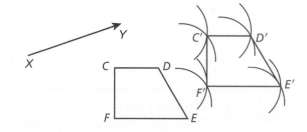

 Turn and Talk Identify parallel lines cut by a transversal within your figure. Then, identify the corresponding angles. Use translations to justify the Corresponding Angles Postulate.

Step It Out

Translate in a Coordinate Plane

When translating a figure in a coordinate plane, you can write the translation vector in **component form** $\langle a, b \rangle$ where a is the horizontal change and b is the vertical change. The component form of $\overrightarrow{ST}$ in the diagram is $\langle 4, -3 \rangle$.

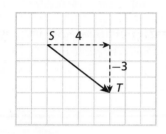

The horizontal change a and the vertical change b can be used to write a rule for a translation in the coordinate plane.

Rules for Translations on a Coordinate Plane	
Translation a units to the right, or positive direction	$(x, y) \rightarrow (x + a, y)$
Translation a units to the left, or negative direction	$(x, y) \rightarrow (x - a, y)$
Translation b units up, or positive direction	$(x, y) \rightarrow (x, y + b)$
Translation b units down, or negative direction	$(x, y) \rightarrow (x, y - b)$

The rules for translations can be combined. For example, when a figure is translated a units to the left and b units down, the rule for the translation is $(x, y) \rightarrow (x - a, y - b)$.

3 Draw the preimage and image of the polygon with vertices $A(0, 6)$, $B(4, 8)$, $C(4, 4)$, and $D(0, 2)$ translated using the vector $\langle 4, -2 \rangle$.

Preimage	Image
$A(0, 6)$	$A'(4, 4)$
$B(4, 8)$	$B'(8, 6)$
$C(4, 4)$	$C'(8, 2)$
$D(0, 2)$	$D'(4, 0)$

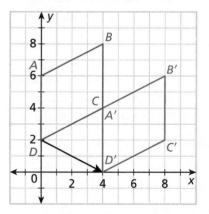

A. What coordinate rule is used to determine the image coordinates?

B. What transformation function could be used to describe the translation of a point P on the polygon, using the component form of the vector?

 Turn and Talk How is a vector different from a ray? How is a vector different from a line segment? Is it always possible to write a vector using its horizontal and vertical components? When and why would you want to use the component form of a vector?

Identify a Translation Vector

4 ▶ **A.** Match the correct image with the correct table. Justify your answer.

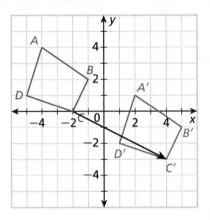

Preimage coordinates (x, y)	Image $\langle 6, -3 \rangle$
$A(-4, 4)$	$A'(2, 1)$
$B(-1, 2)$	$B'(5, -1)$
$C(-2, 0)$	$C'(4, -3)$
$D(-5, 1)$	$D'(1, -2)$

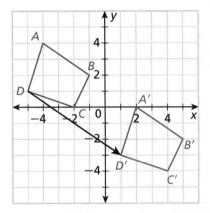

Preimage coordinates (x, y)	Image $\langle 6, -4 \rangle$
$A(-4, 4)$	$A'(2, 0)$
$B(-1, 2)$	$B'(5, -2)$
$C(-2, 0)$	$C'(4, -4)$
$D(-5, 1)$	$D'(1, -3)$

The table shows a translation of $ABCD$ to $A'B'C'D'$.

Preimage coordinates (x, y)	Image $\langle ?, ? \rangle$
$A(-4, 4)$	$A'(-6, 9)$
$B(-1, 2)$	$B'(-3, 7)$
$C(-2, 0)$	$C'(-4, 5)$
$D(-5, 1)$	$D'(-7, 6)$

B. What vector maps $ABCD$ to $A'B'C'D'$?

 Turn and Talk Can you invert a translation? How can you identify the translation? Is it a translation if every point is mapped to itself?

Check Understanding

1. Quadrilateral *DEFG* is translated using $\overrightarrow{AB}$. The magnitude of $\overrightarrow{AB}$ is 26 mm. What is the distance between *E* and *E'*?

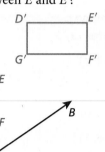

2. Copy $\triangle ABC$ shown below. Then translate the triangle using $\overrightarrow{XY}$.

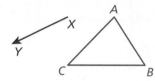

3. Draw a polygon with vertices $A(6, 7)$, $B(8, 4)$, $C(5, 2)$, and $D(2, 3)$. Then draw its image after a translation by the vector $\langle -4, -2 \rangle$. Write a coordinate rule for the translation.

Each table gives the coordinates of the vertices of a figure and its image after a translation. Give the component form of a vector that maps $\triangle PQR$ to $\triangle P'Q'R'$.

4.

$\triangle PQR$	$\triangle P'Q'R'$
$P(-3, 2)$	$P'(3, -1)$
$Q(1, 3)$	$Q'(7, 0)$
$R(-2, -1)$	$R'(4, -4)$

5.

$\triangle PQR$	$\triangle P'Q'R'$
$P(1, 2)$	$P'(-4, 3)$
$Q(5, 2)$	$Q'(0, 3)$
$R(8, -1)$	$R'(3, 0)$

On Your Own

F'G'H'J' is the image of *FGHJ* after a translation along $\overrightarrow{ST}$. Determine whether each statement is *always*, *sometimes*, or *never* true.

6. $\angle F \cong \angle G'$

7. $HH' = GG'$

8. $HJ = H'J'$

9. *A'B'C'* is the image of *ABC* after a translation in the coordinate plane. Write a coordinate rule for the translation.

Preimage coordinates	Image coordinates
$A(-6, 4)$	$A'(-8, 12)$
$B(5, 9)$	$B'(3, 17)$
$C(3, 0)$	$C'(1, 8)$

Draw the figure with the given vertices. Then draw its image after a translation by the given vector.

10. $A(-1, 5)$, $B(-1, -1)$, $C(-6, 2)$; vector $\langle 4, 2 \rangle$

11. $A(2, 7)$, $B(4, 6)$, $C(4, 3)$, $D(-1, 5)$; vector $\langle 5, -3 \rangle$

12. $A(-1, 5)$, $B(5, 5)$, $C(5, 3)$, $D(-1, 3)$; vector $\langle 1, 4 \rangle$

Match each set of coordinates for a preimage with the coordinates of its image after applying the vector $\langle -4, 4 \rangle$.

13. $X(-6, 2), Y(-1, -1), Z(-1, 5)$

14. $W(9, 5), X(4, 7), Y(3, 2), Z(1, 7)$

15. $X(-4, -2), Y(-1, -2), Z(-1, 5)$

16. $W(4, 9), X(3, 2), Y(6, 9), Z(6, 2)$

A. $W'(0, 13), X'(-1, 6), Y'(2, 13), Z'(2, 6)$

B. $X'(-8, 2), Y'(-5, 2), Z'(-5, 9)$

C. $X'(-10, 6), Y'(-5, 3), Z'(-5, 9)$

D. $W'(5, 9), X'(0, 11), Y'(-1, 6), Z'(-3, 11)$

Specify the component form of the vector that maps each figure to its image.

17.

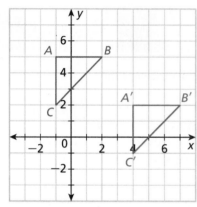

18.

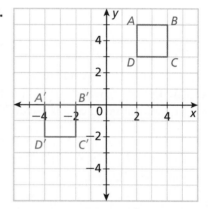

19. Part of a fabric pattern is shown. When the pattern is translated so that the left edge touches the right edge or so that the top edge touches the bottom edge, the pattern continues. Describe the vectors that can be used to map A to each of the points B, C, and D. Explain your reasoning.

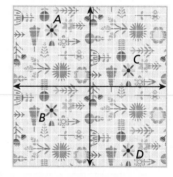

20. **(MP) Reason** Mark, Josh, and Will are standing in a classroom in different spots. They each draw a map of the classroom on a coordinate plane. Each student marks where the other students are standing, and places himself at the origin. Point M represents Mark, point J represents Josh, and point W represents Will. Does a translation map graph A onto graph B? graph A onto graph C? Two of the graphs are correct. Which graph is incorrect? How do you know?

A

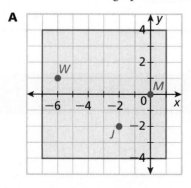

B

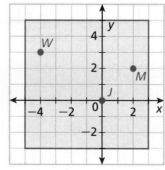

C

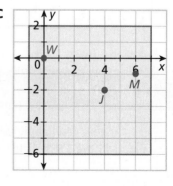

21. Mr. Smith wants to tile a wall in his bathroom. The wall is 5 feet long × 6 feet tall. He is using black and white tiles to create a checkerboard pattern. Each tile measures 6 inches by 3 inches. Will he use the same number of black and white tiles to make a checkerboard pattern? If so how many of each will he use?

22. The cyclist is riding her bicycle through a city. She starts by riding 6 blocks south, then 3 blocks west, then 2 blocks south, and lastly 4 blocks west. What vector describes the position of the cyclist from her starting position to her final destination? Let 1 unit represent 1 block.

23. (MP) **Critique Reasoning** A student is trying to identify the vector that maps the preimage $P(1, 4)$, $Q(4, 1)$, and $R(-2, -1)$ to the image $P'(4, 1)$, $Q'(7, -2)$, and $R'(1, -4)$. The student says that it is vector $\langle -3, -3 \rangle$. Explain the error.

24. (MP) **Use Structure** Find the vertices of the preimage of a figure if the image coordinates are $A'(2, 6)$, $B'(8, 8)$, $C'(8, 4)$ and $D'(4, 2)$ and the preimage is translated using the translation function $T_{\langle 4, -4 \rangle}$.

Spiral Review • Assessment Readiness

25. Find the distance between $(4, 6)$ and $(3, 2)$.

Ⓐ 4.1

Ⓑ 7.1

Ⓒ 8.2

Ⓓ 16.3

26. Find the equation of a line that is perpendicular to the line $y = -6x + 5$ that passes through $(-3, 2)$.

Ⓐ $y = -6x - 16$ Ⓒ $y = \frac{1}{6}x + \frac{5}{2}$

Ⓑ $y = -\frac{1}{6}x + \frac{5}{2}$ Ⓓ $y = 6x + 5$

27. For each angle, identify its classification.

Angle	Acute	Right	Obtuse	Straight
A. $m\angle C = 90°$	?	?	?	?
B. $90° < m\angle D < 180°$	?	?	?	?
C. $m\angle F < 90°$	?	?	?	?

 I'm in a Learning Mindset!

How can I apply what I have learned about translations to careers in the STEM field?

Define and Apply Rotations

(I Can) **rotate figures in the plane.**

Spark Your Learning

Here is an unfamiliar map of the world.

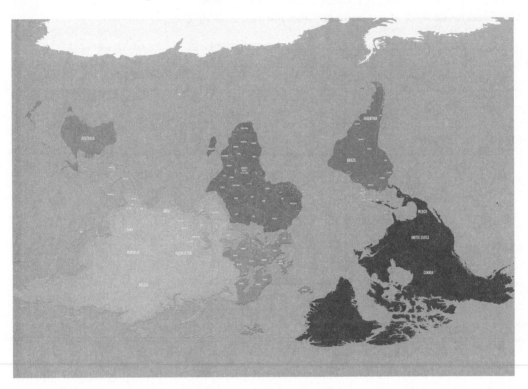

Complete Part A as a whole class. Then complete Parts B–D in small groups.

A. What is a geometric question you can ask about this map? Is there additional information you would need to know in order to answer your question?

B. What are some reasons that you might use a map that looks like this?

C. If you took a map that looks more familiar, and tried to match the country positions, what kind of transformation could you use? To answer your question in Part A, what strategy and tool would you use along with all the information you have? What answer do you get?

D. What are the clues that make it clear that this map is shown in the intended position?

> **Turn and Talk** Why do you think that someone might want to use the map that has been turned in this way?

Build Understanding

Explore Rotations as Rigid Motions

In order to be included as a type of rigid motion, a rotation (or turn) must meet all of the criteria for rigid motions described in the previous lesson.

1 ▶ Use a geometry drawing tool to investigate a rotation.

Draw △*DEF* and point *C* not on the triangle. Mark *C* as the center. Select △*DEF* and rotate it 75° about point *C*. Label the image △*D'E'F'*.

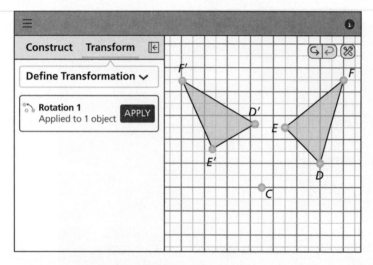

A. Does this transformation meet all of the properties of a rigid motion? Does this transformation preserve orientation? Explain your reasoning.

B. Measure ∠*DCD'*, ∠*ECE'*, and ∠*FCF'*. Explain why these angles have the same measure.

C. Measure the distance from *C* to *D* and from *C* to *D'*. What do you notice? Does this relationship remain true as you move point *C*?

 Turn and Talk Suppose you rotate a copy of the triangle, are you rotating the whole plane or just the figure? Why is it enough to find the image of the vertices and then claim that the entire figure has been rotated?

Construct a Rotation

A **rotation** is a rigid motion that turns a figure through an **angle of rotation** about a point *P*, such that each point and its image are the same distance from *P*. All the angles with vertex *P* formed by a point and its image are congruent. The point *P* is called the **center of rotation**.

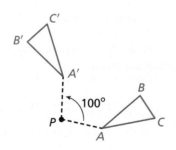

A rotation is a function that takes points in the plane as inputs. The function notation $R_{P,\theta}(A) = A'$ can be used for a rotation by angle θ with center *P* where point *A'* is the image of *A*. The diagram shows △*ABC* rotated 100° counterclockwise about point *P*.

When rotating about a given point, a figure can rotate counterclockwise or clockwise. When no direction is specified, you can assume a counterclockwise rotation. Also, a counterclockwise rotation of $x°$ is the same as a clockwise rotation of $(360 - x)°$.

2   Rotate $\triangle ABC$ about point P by the reference angle K.

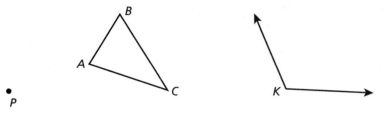

A. Draw a segment from point P to each vertex. Then construct an angle congruent to $\angle K$ with P as the vertex and C on one ray of the angle. What point will lie on the segment drawn?

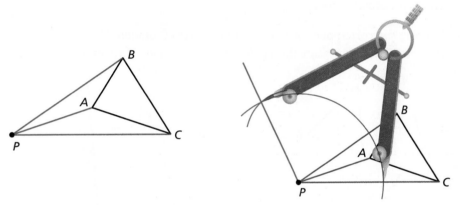

B. Use a compass to find the distance from point P to each vertex. Mark each distance on the corresponding ray. Then connect the images of the vertices. Explain how you know that $\triangle ABC \cong \triangle A'B'C'$.

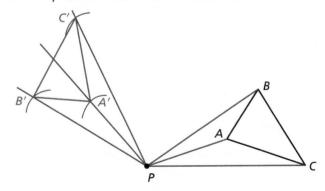

C. Construct circles with center P and with radius AP, radius BP, and radius CP. What do you notice about the circles?

D. How can tracing paper be used to check the construction?

E. Suppose you do not have a compass. Explain how to rotate $\triangle ABC$ about point P by the reference angle K using only a protractor and a ruler.

 Turn and Talk How does the construction of a triangle use the properties of a rotation to produce an accurate image?

Step It Out

Identify Parameters of a Rotation

When a figure is rotated, every point is moved along a circle centered at the center of rotation. This means that the points are equidistant from the center, and you can use this fact to find the center of rotation given the preimage and image of a rotation.

 Find the center of rotation and the angle of rotation that maps △ABC onto △A'B'C'.

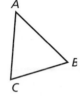

Step 1 Draw a line segment between two sets of corresponding points. Then draw the perpendicular bisectors of these segments.

Step 2 Locate the intersection of the two perpendicular bisectors. This is the center of rotation.

Step 3 Connect two corresponding vertices to the center of rotation. Use your protractor to measure this angle, which is the angle of rotation.

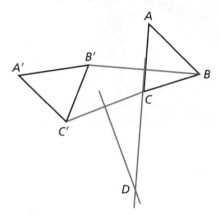 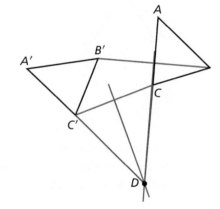

A. What point represents the center of rotation? What angle represents the angle of rotation?

B. Suppose a circle with radius AD is drawn with the compass point on D. Name another point that lies on the circle.

Rotations in a Coordinate Plane

For certain rotations in the coordinate plane, there are simple rules you can use to calculate the coordinates of the image for a given preimage point.

The table summarizes the rules for counterclockwise rotations in the coordinate plane.

Rules for Counterclockwise Rotations About the Origin	
90° rotation	$(x, y) \rightarrow (-y, x)$
180° rotation	$(x, y) \rightarrow (-x, -y)$
270° rotation	$(x, y) \rightarrow (y, -x)$
360° rotation	$(x, y) \rightarrow (x, y)$

4 ▸ Which graph shows a 180° rotation of *ABCD*? Explain your reasoning.

A.

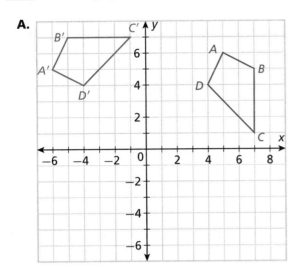

B.

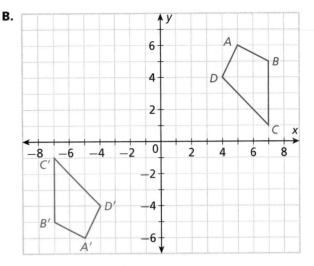

> **Turn and Talk** How would the rules for the rotation of an image change if the center of rotation is no longer (0, 0)?

Rotate a Figure Onto Itself

Regular polygons can be rotated so that the image of the figure looks exactly like the preimage. The angles of rotation that map a regular polygon to itself depend on the number of sides of the polygon. A rotation of 360° will always map a figure to itself. The other angles of rotation that will map a regular *n*-gon onto itself are multiples of $\frac{360}{n}$.

5 ▸ What is the smallest angle of rotation less than or equal to 360° that will map the glass tile onto itself?

A. Equilateral triangle

$$\frac{360°}{3} = 120°$$

A. What are all the rotations that map the triangle onto itself?

B. Square

$$\frac{360°}{4} = 90°$$

B. What are all the rotations that map the square onto itself?

> **Turn and Talk** Draw a polygon that is not regular that can be rotated so that it maps to itself. Identify the angles of rotation that will map the figure to itself.

Check Understanding

In Problems 1–3, use △PQR, point M, and ∠Z.

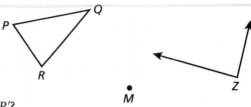

1. Copy △PQR and rotate it about point M by the reference angle Z.

2. After a rotation of △PQR to △P′Q′R′ about point M, what should be true about ∠PMP′, ∠QMQ′, and ∠RMR′?

3. After a rotation of △PQR to △P′Q′R′ about point M, where will the perpendicular bisectors of $\overline{RR'}$ and $\overline{QQ'}$ intersect?

Draw the image of the figure under the given rotation.

4. counterclockwise 90°

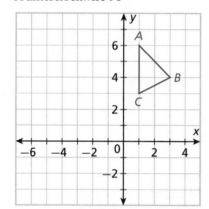

5. counterclockwise 270°

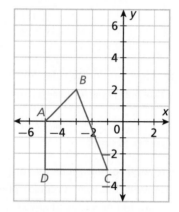

6. Sketch a polygon that will map to itself after a rotation of 60°.

On Your Own

A rotation about point N maps △FGH to △F′G′H′. Tell whether the statement about the rotation is *always*, *sometimes*, or *never* true. Explain your reasoning.

7. △FGH ≅ △F′G′H′

8. NH = NH′

9. ∠GHF ≅ ∠HFG

10. Copy WXYZ and point Q. Rotate WXYZ about point Q using the measure of ∠WZY in the quadrilateral as the angle of rotation.

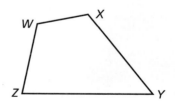

11. (MP) **Critique Reasoning** Rocco drew the image of △LMN after a rotation of 104°. His work is shown at the right. Did Rocco rotate △LMN correctly? Explain why or why not.

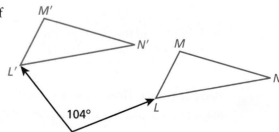

In Problems 12 and 13, copy each set of figures which show the image after a rotation and its preimage. Find the angle of rotation and the center of rotation using a compass, a straightedge, and a protractor.

12.

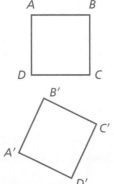

13.

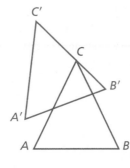

14. (MP) **Critique Reasoning** Mehta said that since all points turn about the center of rotation by the same angle, all points move the same distance under a rotation. Do you agree with Mehta's statement? Why or why not?

In Problems 15–17, draw the preimage and image of each polygon under the given rotation.

15. Polygon $A(2, 5)$, $B(5, 4)$, $C(5, 2)$, $D(1, 2)$; counterclockwise $180°$

16. Polygon $A(2, 7)$, $B(4, 6)$, $C(4, 3)$, $D(-1, 5)$; counterclockwise $270°$

17. Rectangle $A(-1, 5)$, $B(5, 5)$, $C(5, 3)$, $D(-1, 3)$; clockwise $90°$

18. Triangle ABC has vertices $A(-2, 2)$, $B(-7, 2)$, and $C(-6, 5)$. The triangle is rotated $270°$ about the origin. Will the coordinates of the vertices of the image of the triangle have positive or negative x-coordinates? Explain your reasoning.

19. (MP) **Use Repeated Reasoning** Given a preimage triangle with vertices $A(7, -5)$, $B(6, -9)$, and $C(3, -6)$, rotate the triangle $1350°$ counterclockwise about the origin. What are the coordinates of the vertices of the image?

Describe any rotations less than or equal to $360°$ that map the polygon onto itself.

20. Regular pentagon

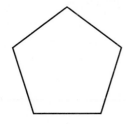

21. Regular octagon

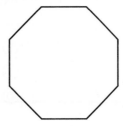

22. **History** The first Ferris wheel was invented in 1893. It had 36 cars that were equally spaced around the circumference of the wheel. The wheel rotates so that the car at the bottom of the ride is replaced by the next car. By how many degrees does the wheel rotate between consecutive cars?

23. The 12-sided polygon shown is regular. Suppose the polygon is rotated counterclockwise about its center so that $\overline{AB}$ maps onto $\overline{FG}$. What is the angle of rotation?

24. (MP) **Use Repeated Reasoning** Oliver was walking from his house to the grocery store. He started walking at 4:12 pm and arrived at the grocery store at 4:25 pm. Through what angle of rotation did the minute hand turn?

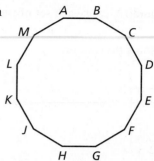

In Problems 25 and 26, the Skylon Tower, in Niagara Falls, Canada, has a revolving restaurant 775 feet above the falls. The restaurant makes a complete revolution once every hour.

25. While a visitor was at the tower, the restaurant rotated through 135°. How long was the visitor in the tower?

26. A visitor was in the tower for 40 minutes. How many degrees did the restaurant rotate?

27. Open Ended Describe a rotation using function notation. Give the coordinates of the image of point $P(2, 3)$ after your rotation.

Spiral Review • Assessment Readiness

28. Find the distance between $(6, 7)$ and $(3, -12)$.

(A) 9.25

(B) 10.8

(C) 12.6

(D) 19.2

29. If you reflect the point $(6, 2)$ across the x-axis, in which quadrant is the new point located?

(A) I

(B) II

(C) III

(D) IV

30. Find the equation of a line that is perpendicular to the line that passes through points $(4, 6)$ and $(-2, 3)$.

(A) $y = -\frac{1}{2}x - 8$

(B) $y = \frac{1}{2}x + 8$

(C) $y = -2x - 8$

(D) $y = 2x + 8$

31. Find the image of $(3, -2)$ after you translate the point using the vector $\langle 4, -2 \rangle$.

(A) $(7, -4)$

(B) $(-7, -4)$

(C) $(7, 4)$

(D) $(-7, 4)$

I'm in a Learning Mindset!

How do I know that the tasks about rotations are the right level of challenge for me?

Keep Going to ▷ Journal and Practice Workbook

Define and Apply Reflections

(I Can) **reflect figures in the plane.**

Spark Your Learning

Magid was working in the art studio and created the image below.

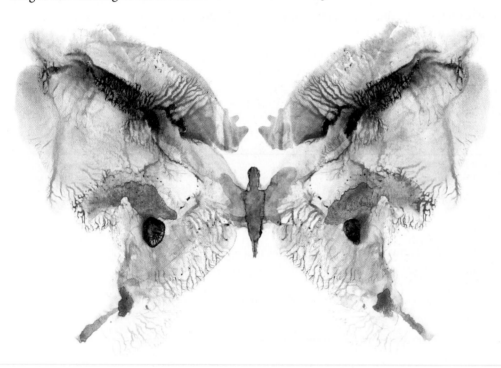

Complete Part A as a whole class. Then complete Parts B–D in small groups.

   A. What is a geometric question you can ask about this image? What
information would you need to know to answer your question?

   B. How do you think the image was created?

   C. To answer your question, what strategy and tool would you use
along with all the information you have? What answer do you get?

   D. How do you know that a translation or a rotation was not used to
create the image shown?

   Turn and Talk How can you use a mirror to create an image and its
reflection in the same plane? How is this different from the reflection
you see when you look at yourself in the mirror?

Build Understanding

Explore Reflections as Rigid Motions

In order for a transformation to be considered a rigid motion, it must meet all of the criteria for rigid motions.

 Use tracing paper to reflect an image across a line.

Draw and label a line p on tracing paper. Then draw and label a quadrilateral *DEFG* with vertex *D* on line p. Fold the tracing paper along line p. Trace the quadrilateral. Then unfold the paper and label the new image *D'E'F'G'*.

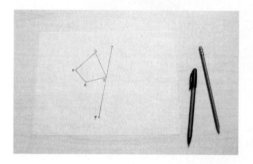  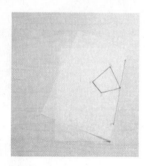

A. Does the transformation meet all of the properties of a rigid motion? Does the transformation preserve orientation? Explain your reasoning.

B. Draw line segments to connect the corresponding vertices of the two quadrilaterals. Use a protractor to measure the angles formed by each line segment and line p. What do you notice?

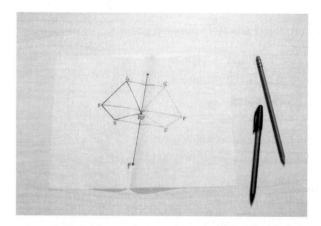

C. Using a ruler, measure each segment that connects corresponding vertices. Then measure the part of the segment that connects each vertex to line p. How is line p related to $\overline{EE'}$, $\overline{FF'}$, and $\overline{GG'}$?

> **Turn and Talk** How would you map the image back to the preimage? Is it possible to do this without using a reflection?

Construct a Reflection

A **reflection** is a transformation across a line, called the
line of reflection, such that the line of reflection is the
perpendicular bisector of each segment joining each
point and its image. If a point is on the line of reflection,
the point is mapped to itself.

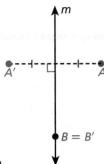

The function notation $r_m(A) = A'$ can be used for a reflection
across line m where point A' is the image of A.

2 ▶ Use a compass and straightedge to reflect △ABC across line p.

Construct a perpendicular line from vertex A to line p. Use a compass to measure
the distance from vertex A to line p along this line. Copy this segment onto the
perpendicular line so that one endpoint is on line p. Label the intersection as A'.

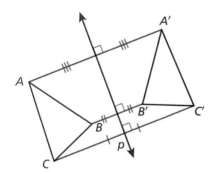

A. Explain how you know that point A' is a reflection of point A.

B. Repeat the process to find reflections of vertex B and vertex C. Use a straightedge
to connect A', B', and C'. Is △ABC ≅ △A'B'C'? Explain why or why not.

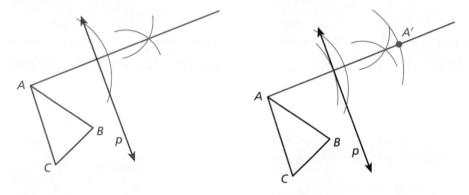

C. Suppose vertex C is reflected first instead of vertex A. Will the resulting image
be the same? Explain.

 Turn and Talk Explain how the construction results in the point and its image
being the same distance from the line of reflection.

Step It Out

Identify a Line of Reflection

If you are given a preimage and its image after a reflection, you can locate the line of reflection by finding the perpendicular bisector of segments connecting corresponding vertices.

3 The photo shows the reflection of a bird. The steps for drawing the line of reflection are out of order. Place them in the correct order. Explain each step.

A.

B.

C.

D.

 Turn and Talk Suppose Ellie has a ruler, but she does not have a compass. Explain how she can find the line of reflection in the photo using two pairs of corresponding points on the preimage and image.

Reflections in a Coordinate Plane

For certain lines in a coordinate plane, there are simple rules you can use to calculate the coordinates of the image for a given preimage point.

The table summarizes the rules for reflections in the coordinate plane.

Rules for Reflection in a Coordinate Plane	
Reflection across the x-axis	$(x, y) \rightarrow (x, -y)$
Reflection across the y-axis	$(x, y) \rightarrow (-x, y)$
Reflection across the line $y = x$	$(x, y) \rightarrow (y, x)$
Reflection across the line $y = -x$	$(x, y) \rightarrow (-y, -x)$

4 Which graph shows the correct image of △ABC reflected across the line $y = -x$? Explain how you know.

A.

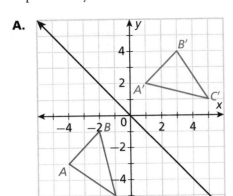

B.

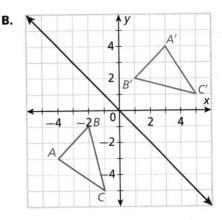

> **Turn and Talk** How would the rules for reflecting a figure in a coordinate plane change if the line of reflection did not pass through the origin but instead was parallel to one of the four types of lines in the table of reflection rules?

Perform Multiple Transformations

Transformations can be applied one after another in a sequence where you use the image of the first transformation as the preimage for the next transformation.

Pairs of reflections can be used to generate translations and rotations.

5 Reflect △ABC across the line $x = 5$. Then reflect its image across the y-axis.

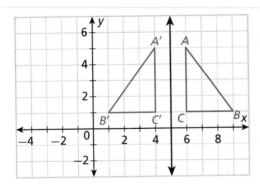
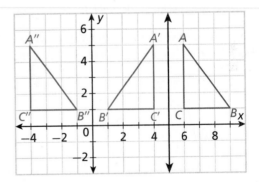

A. Describe one transformation that maps △ABC to △A″B″C″.

B. What kind of transformation is the result of reflecting a figure across a line and then reflecting its image across a line parallel to the first line of reflection?

> **Turn and Talk** Draw a triangle in a coordinate plane. Reflect the triangle across the x-axis, and then reflect its image across the y-axis. Describe one transformation that maps the resulting image to the original triangle.

Check Understanding

1. Use the figure and the line of reflection.

   A. Copy the figure and the line of reflection. Use a compass and a straightedge to construct the reflection of the figure across the line.

   B. Use a straightedge to connect each vertex of the preimage with its corresponding image. What should be true about the segments?

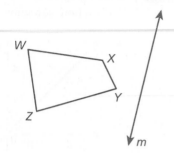

In each diagram, $\triangle A'B'C'$ is the image of $\triangle ABC$ after a reflection. Copy the triangles and draw the line of reflection.

2.

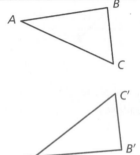

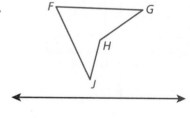

3.

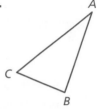

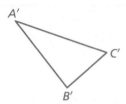

In a coordinate plane, quadrilateral $PQRS$ has vertices $P(0, 7)$, $Q(4, 6)$, $R(2, 3)$, and $S(-1, 3)$. Find the coordinates of the vertices of the image after each reflection.

4. Reflection across the x-axis

5. Reflection across the line $y = x$

On Your Own

6. Quadrilateral $K'L'M'N'$ is the image of $KLMN$ after a reflection across line q. If vertex M lies on line q, then what is true about point M and its image M'?

Copy each figure and the line of reflection. Use a compass and a straightedge to construct the reflection across the line. Label the vertices of the image.

7.

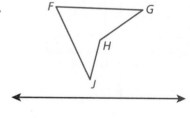

8.

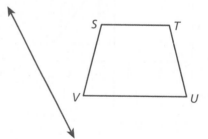

9. A trail designer is planning two trails that connect campsites A and B to a point on the river. She wants the total length of the trails to be as short as possible.

   A. Copy the points and the line. Find the image of point B after a reflection across the line. Label the point B'.

   B. Draw $\overline{AB'}$. Find the intersection of $\overline{AB'}$ and the line of reflection. Label this point X. Then draw $\overline{BX}$.

   C. What is the shortest distance between point A and point B'? Use your answer, along with the fact that $\overline{BX} \cong \overline{B'X}$, to explain why $AX + BX$ is least when X is in this position.

River

Each diagram of a hole at a miniature golf course shows the starting position for a ball and the hole. Draw a diagram for the path of a ball that will reach the hole in one shot.

10.

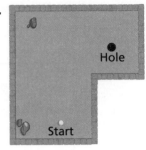

11.

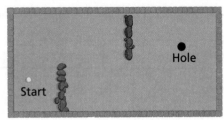

In each diagram, the red figure is the image of the blue figure after a reflection. Copy the figures and draw the line of reflection.

12.

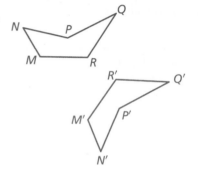

13.

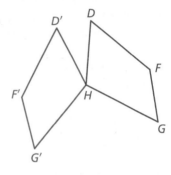

Find the images of the points in the pattern after the given reflection.

14. $A\left(\frac{5}{2}, \frac{5}{2}\right), B(4, 0), C\left(\frac{1}{2}, 3\right)$
reflected across $y = -x$

15. $A(-1, 1), B(2, 3), C(-2, -2)$
reflected across the y-axis

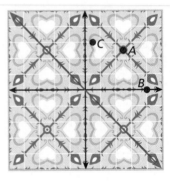

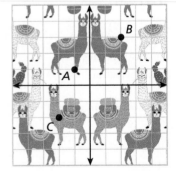

In the diagram, $\triangle ABC \cong \triangle PQR$.

16. Describe one transformation that maps $\triangle ABC$ to $\triangle PQR$.

17. Describe two reflections that map $\triangle ABC$ to $\triangle PQR$.

18. Reflect $\triangle ABC$ across the line $y = x$. Describe how to map the image to $\triangle PQR$.

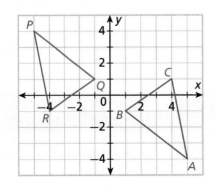

19. 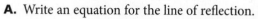 **Reason** In the diagram, $\triangle A'B'C'$ is the image of $\triangle ABC$ after a reflection.

   A. Write an equation for the line of reflection.

   B. Explain how you can use the equation of the line of reflection to determine the slope of $\overline{AA'}$. Then find the slope of $\overline{AA'}$.

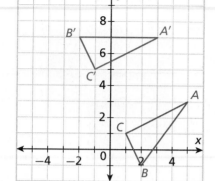

20. Suppose a reflection is described by the function $r_{y=2x}(A) = A'$.

   A. What does $y = 2x$ represent?

   B. Find $r_{y=2x}(P(0, 4))$.

   C. Find $r_{y=2x}(Q(1, 2))$.

21. (MP) **Critique Reasoning** A student reflects triangle $A(-2, 6)$, $B(5, 5)$, $C(5, 3)$ across $y = -2$ and says the image is $A'(-2, -6)$, $B'(5, -5)$, $C'(5, -3)$. Explain the student's error. Then give the correct coordinates for $\triangle A'B'C'$.

22. (Open Middle™) Using the digits 1 to 9, no more than one time each, fill in the blanks to make a true statement.

   _____?_____ reflections across the x-axis and/or the y-axis is the same as ___?___ 90° counterclockwise rotations about the origin.

Spiral Review • Assessment Readiness

23. Point $A(9, 4)$ is translated using the vector $\langle -6, -3 \rangle$. What is the image of the translated point?

   (A) $(3, 1)$ (C) $(7, 3)$

   (B) $(3, 7)$ (D) $(12, 4)$

24. Which of the following have a distance greater than or equal to 5.9? Select all that apply.

   (A) $A(-3, 4)$ and $B(8, -3)$

   (B) $C(3, 4)$ and $D(1, 1)$

   (C) $C(3, 4)$ and $E(1, -4)$

   (D) $G(9, 4)$ and $H(8, -3)$

   (E) $I(-9, 3)$ and $J(0, 4)$

25. A rotation maps $(4, 9)$ onto $(4, 9)$. What is the angle of rotation?

   (A) 90°   (C) 270°

   (B) 180°   (D) 360°

26. The square is rotated about its center. Which of the following rotations will not map the square onto itself?

   (A) 90°   (C) 270°

   (B) 135°   (D) 360°

I'm in a Learning Mindset!

How can I use reflections in my career of choice?

Define and Apply Symmetry

(I Can) identify symmetry in figures.

Spark Your Learning

While visiting a museum, Rose saw this piece of art. It inspired her to create a piece of art just like it.

Complete Part A as a whole class. Then complete Parts B–D in small groups.

A. What is a geometric question you can ask about this situation? What information would you need to know to answer your question?

B. To answer your question, what strategy and tool would you use along with all the information you have? What answer do you get?

C. What transformations do you see in the art? Describe them.

D. What tools do you think would be useful in creating this type of art?

 Turn and Talk How can you create your own circle art? How would you make sure it is symmetric?

©devi/Alamy

Build Understanding

Explore Line Symmetry

A figure has **symmetry** if there is a transformation that maps the figure to itself.

A figure has **line symmetry** if it can be reflected over a line so that the image coincides with the preimage. That line is called a **line of symmetry**. A line of symmetry divides a plane figure into two congruent, reflected halves. Two examples are shown.

1 line of symmetry

4 lines of symmetry

If a figure can be folded along a straight line so that one half of the figure exactly matches the other, the figure has line symmetry. The crease is the line of symmetry.

1 ▶ **A.** How many lines of symmetry does each figure have? Draw other polygons with four sides or five sides that have the same number of lines of symmetry.

 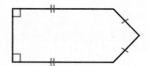

B. How many lines of symmetry does each figure have? Draw a polygon with an odd number of sides and a polygon with an even number of sides. Determine the number of lines of symmetry of each polygon.

C. How does a line of symmetry intersect a polygon with an odd number of sides?

D. Draw a figure with many lines of symmetry. How many lines of symmetry does your figure have?

E. Does a figure exist that has an infinite number of lines of symmetry?

 Turn and Talk You determined that a rectangle has only 2 lines of symmetry. Is it possible for a rectangle to have 4 lines of symmetry? Explain why or why not. Use diagrams to support your answer.

Explore Rotational Symmetry

A figure that can be rotated about its center by an angle of 180° or less so that the image coincides with the preimage has **rotational symmetry**. The **angle of rotational symmetry** is the smallest angle of rotation that maps a figure to itself.

A figure with rotational symmetry does not necessarily have line symmetry, but if it does, the intersection of the lines of symmetry is the center of rotational symmetry.

This flower has 3 lines of symmetry. It can be rotated twice to show rotational symmetry.

3 lines of symmetry
$360° \div 3 = 120°$

Rotate the flower 120°.

Rotate the flower again.
$120° + 120° = 240°$

To find the smallest angle of rotation, divide 360° by the number of lines of symmetry. Any additional angles of rotation will be multiples of the smallest angle.

2 ▶ Draw a square. Trace it onto tracing paper. Hold the center of the traced figure against the original figure with your pencil. Rotate the traced figure counterclockwise until it coincides again with the original figure beneath it.

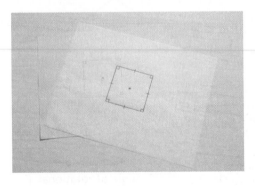

A. By how many degrees did you rotate the figure? What are all of the angles of rotation up to and including 360°?

B. Draw the lines of symmetry of the original figure. How many lines of symmetry does it have? Describe how the lines of symmetry can be used to determine the angle of rotational symmetry.

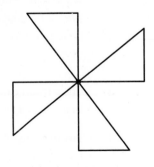

C. Repeat the procedure to find all of the angles of rotation up to and including 360° of the figure at the right. Are lines of symmetry helpful in this case? Explain.

> **Turn and Talk** Why can't an angle of rotational symmetry be 0°? Why can't it be greater than 180°?

Step It Out

Describe Symmetry in Regular Polygons

Recall that a regular polygon is a polygon that is both equilateral and equiangular.

The table shows the types of symmetry in some regular polygons.

Regular polygon	Sides	Lines of symmetry	Angle of rotational symmetry	Image
Equilateral triangle	3	3	120°	
Square	4	4	90°	
Pentagon	5	5	72°	

3 What are the lines of symmetry and the angle of rotational symmetry for a regular hexagon?

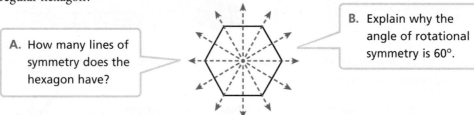

A. How many lines of symmetry does the hexagon have?

B. Explain why the angle of rotational symmetry is 60°.

C. Consider a regular decagon. How many lines of symmetry does it have? What is its angle of rotational symmetry?

D. Consider a regular polygon with n sides. How many lines of symmetry does it have? Write an expression for its angle of rotational symmetry in terms of n.

 Turn and Talk When you draw all of the lines of symmetry of a regular polygon, what kind of shapes are you creating? Can each piece be rotated onto its adjacent piece? Explain why or why not.

Use Symmetry in a Coordinate Plane

4 ▶ The *x*-axis and the *y*-axis are lines of symmetry of an image. Use the lines of symmetry to draw the entire image.

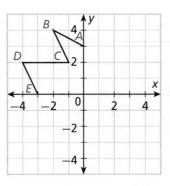

Reflect the part of the image shown across the *x*-axis.

$(x, y) \rightarrow (x, -y)$

$A(0, 3) \rightarrow J(0, -3)$

$B(-2, 4) \rightarrow H(-2, -4)$

$C(-1, 2) \rightarrow G(-1, -2)$

$D(-4, 2) \rightarrow F(-4, -2)$

A. Why is point *E* not included in the list of reflected points?

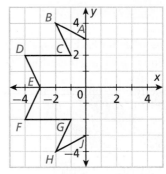

Reflect the new image across the *y*-axis.

$B(-2, 4) \rightarrow B'(2, 4)$

$C(-1, 2) \rightarrow C'(1, 2)$

$D(-4, 2) \rightarrow D'(4, 2)$

$E(-3, 0) \rightarrow E'(3, 0)$

$F(-4, -2) \rightarrow F'(4, -2)$

$G(-1, -2) \rightarrow G'(1, -2)$

$H(-2, -4) \rightarrow H'(2, -4)$

B. How do the coordinates change when a point is reflected across the *y*-axis?

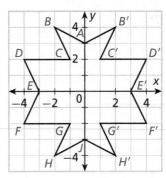

C. Suppose the original image was reflected across the *y*-axis first, and then the image was reflected across the *x*-axis. Would the resulting image be the same? Explain why or why not.

D. Describe any rotational symmetry in the final image.

E. Explain why the final image could not be created using only rotations of the original image.

 Turn and Talk Change the location of one vertex in the original image so that the final image can be obtained using only rotations.

Check Understanding

Determine whether each image has line symmetry. If so, how many lines of symmetry?

1.

2.

Determine whether each square nautical flag has rotational symmetry. If so, describe the rotations up to and including 360° that map the flag to itself.

3.

4.

5. How many lines of symmetry does a regular nonagon have? What is its angle of rotational symmetry?

6. In a coordinate plane, polygon *ABCDEF* has one line of symmetry which is $y = x$. Given the coordinates of the vertices $A(3, 3)$, $B(3, 0)$, $C(1, -3)$, $D(-3, -3)$, what are the coordinates of vertices E and F?

On Your Own

In Problems 7–9, determine whether each figure has line symmetry. If so, copy the shape and draw all the lines of symmetry.

7.

8.

9.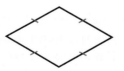

10. **(MP)** **Reason** Why is the diagonal of a rectangle not a line of symmetry?

Determine whether each figure has rotational symmetry. If so, describe the rotations up to and including 360° that map the figure to itself.

11.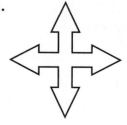

12.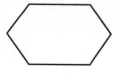

13.

14. **(MP) Critique Reasoning** Donna correctly states that the measure of an interior angle of a square is 90°, and the angle of rotational symmetry of the square is 90°. Then she states that the angle of rotational symmetry of an equilateral triangle is 60° because the measure of an interior angle is 60°. Explain her error.

15. What must be true for the snowflake shown at the right to have rotational symmetry?

16. **(MP) Use Structure** Point symmetry is when every part of a figure has a matching part and is the same distance from the central point but in the opposite direction. Name a polygon that has point symmetry.

17. **Open Ended** Draw a polygon with more than four sides that has exactly two lines of symmetry and an angle of rotation of 180°.

18. Compare the line symmetry and rotational symmetry of a rectangle and an ellipse.

Use the given information about a regular polygon to determine how many sides the polygon has.

19. This polygon has exactly 7 lines of symmetry.

20. This polygon has exactly 20 lines of symmetry.

21. The angle of rotational symmetry for this polygon is 30°.

22. The angle of rotational symmetry for this polygon is 18°.

In Problems 23–26, octagon *ABCDEFGH* is a regular octagon with its center at point *P*. Determine whether each statement about the octagon is true or false.

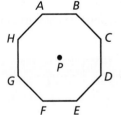

23. $\overleftrightarrow{HD}$ is a line of symmetry.

24. $\overline{BC}$ maps onto $\overline{EF}$ by a clockwise rotation about point *P* of 90°.

25. $\overleftrightarrow{FC}$ is a line of symmetry.

26. A clockwise rotation of 315° about point *P* maps the octagon onto itself.

27. A figure has a 90° angle of rotational symmetry about the origin. Part of the image is shown at the right.

   A. Draw the entire figure.

   B. Does the entire figure have line symmetry?

   C. Can any parts of the entire figure be determined using only reflections? Explain.

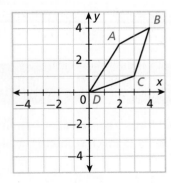

Describe any symmetry you see in each object found in nature.

28.

29.

30.

31.

32. (Open Middle™) Using the digits 1 to 9, at most one time each, create 4 ordered pairs to represent the vertices of a quadrilateral that has rotational symmetry and has 4 lines of symmetry.

Spiral Review • Assessment Readiness

33. Given the preimage $A(3, 3)$, $B(3, -1)$, and $C(6, 3)$, reflect the image across $y = -x$. What are the coordinates of the image?

Ⓐ $A'(1, -3)$, $B'(-3, -3)$, $C'(-3, 6)$

Ⓑ $A'(-3, 3)$, $B'(-3, -1)$, $C'(-6, -3)$

Ⓒ $A'(-3, -3)$, $B'(1, -3)$, $C'(-3, -6)$

Ⓓ $A'(-3, 6)$, $B'(1, -3)$, $C'(-3, -3)$

34. Which of the following is not a property of a rigid motion?

Ⓐ preserves angle measures

Ⓑ preserves orientation

Ⓒ preserves distance

Ⓓ preserves collinearity

35. Match the coordinate notation with the description of the transformation in the coordinate plane.

Coordinate notation	Description of transformation
A. $(x, y) \rightarrow (x, y - 1)$	**1.** a rotation of 90° about the origin
B. $(x, y) \rightarrow (-y, x)$	**2.** a translation of 1 unit to the left
C. $(x, y) \rightarrow (x, -y)$	**3.** a translation 1 unit down
D. $(x, y) \rightarrow (x - 1, y)$	**4.** a reflection across the x-axis

  I'm in a Learning Mindset!

What have I learned about symmetry and how can I make sure that the tasks in this lesson are challenging enough for me?

Review

Translations

Ralph is redesigning his living room. He moved a table as shown.

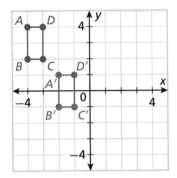

The horizontal change from $(-4, 4)$ to $(-2, 1)$ is $-2-(-4) = 2$.

The vertical change from $(-4, 4)$ to the $(-2, 1)$ is $1 - 4 = -3$.

The vector that represents the movement of the table is $\langle 2, -3 \rangle$.

Rotations

Ralph wants to rotate a triangular table 90° counterclockwise around the center of the room.

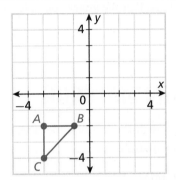

The rotated image of (x, y) is $(-y, x)$.

The new coordinates of the table are below.

$A(-3, -2) \rightarrow A'(2, -3)$

$B(-1, -2) \rightarrow B'(2, -1)$

$C(-3, -4) \rightarrow C'(4, -3)$

Reflections

Ralph has a cabinet against a wall that he wants to reflect to the other side of the room.

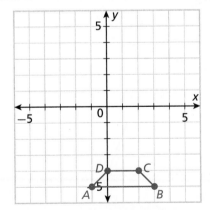

Reflect the cabinet across the x-axis. The new coordinates of the cabinet are below.

$A(-1, -5) \rightarrow A'(-1, 5)$

$B(3, -5) \rightarrow B'(3, 5)$

$C(2, -4) \rightarrow C'(2, 4)$

$D(0, -4) \rightarrow D'(0, 4)$

Symmetry

Ralph has an octagonal table. The shape of the table is a regular octagon.

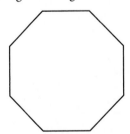

He wants to know what angles he can rotate the table and have it match his original position.

He finds that the angle of rotational symmetry of the table is 45°.

He can rotate the table 45°, 90°, 135°, 180°, 225°, 270°, 315°, and 360°.

Vocabulary

Choose the correct term from the box to complete each sentence.

1. A transformation about a point P such that each point and its image are the same distance from P is a ___?___.

2. A ___?___ is a change is the position, size, or shape of a figure or graph.

3. A figure has ___?___ if it can be rotated about a point by an angle less than 360° so that the image coincides with the preimage.

4. A ___?___ is a transformation across a line such that the line is the perpendicular bisector of each segment joining each point and its image.

Concepts and Skills

Draw the image of the figure under the given transformation.

5. 180° rotation

6. reflection across the x-axis

7. $(x, y) \rightarrow (x - 4, y + 1)$

8. reflection across the y-axis

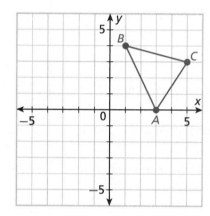

Copy the figure. Identify and describe the number of lines of symmetry for the figure. List the angles of rotation for the figures that have rotational symmetry.

9.

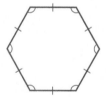

10.

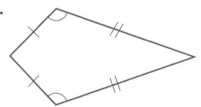

11.

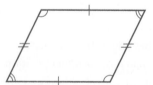

12.

13. (MP) **Use Tools** A carnival ride operates by rotating cars around a central axis. The coordinates of three points on one of the cars at the start of the ride are $A(3, -8)$, $B(5, -12)$, and $C(1, -12)$. What are the coordinates of three points on the car after it has rotated counterclockwise 180°? State what strategy and tool you will use to answer the question, explain your choice, and then find the answer.

6

Transformations that Change Size and Shape

Module Performance Task: Focus on STEM

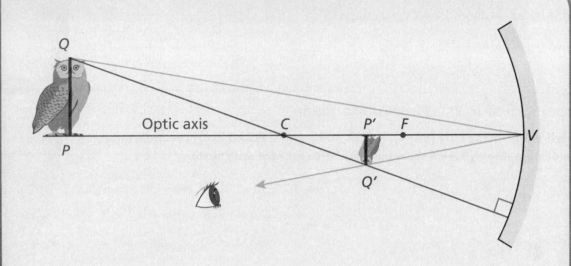

Geometric Optics

Geometric optics is one of two major modeling techniques for describing the propagation of light. The model is based on the underlying assumption that light travels in a straight line through a homogenous medium as a ray.

The diagram above shows a concave, spherical mirror with center C and an object represented by segment QP. The focal point of the mirror is located at point F and the vertex of the mirror, V, is located at the intersection of the optic axis and the mirror.

The location of the reflected image can be located using a process called ray tracing. The law of reflection states that the measure of the angle formed by the ray and the optic axis is equal to the measure of the angle formed by the reflected ray and the optic axis. Using this law, and the fact that a ray from the object through the center C is reflected back onto itself, you can determine the location of the image.

A. Describe how to locate the image $\overline{Q'P'}$ using a sequence of transformations.

B. Use a compass and straight edge to construct the image $\overline{Q'P'}$ when the location of $\overline{QP}$ is beyond C (as shown here), at C, between C and F, at F, and between F and V.

C. Compare the the images created from each of the locations of $\overline{QP}$ in Part B.

D. Repeat for a convex, spherical mirror. Explain any differences or similarities between the two mirrors.

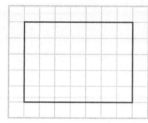

Are You Ready?

Complete these problems to review prior concepts and skills you will need for this module.

Scale Drawings

Consider the scale drawing.

1. Find the actual dimensions of the rectangle.

2. Find the actual area of the rectangle.

1 in.:6 ft

Dilate Figures in the Coordinate Plane

The vertices of a triangle are $(8, -4)$, $(0, 12)$, and $(-4, 4)$. Find the vertices of the image after a dilation using $(0, 0)$ as the center of dilation for each scale factor.

3. $\dfrac{1}{2}$

4. 2

5. $\dfrac{3}{2}$

6. $\dfrac{1}{4}$

Sequences of Transformations

7. A quadrilateral has vertices $(7, -2)$, $(1, 1)$, $(4, -3)$, and $(6, -4)$. Find the vertices of the image after reflecting the quadrilateral across the y-axis and then translating 2 units up and 3 units left.

8. A triangle has vertices $(4, -8)$, $(5, 1)$, and $(-1, 2)$. Find the vertices of the image after rotating the triangle 90° clockwise about the origin and then dilating by a scale factor of 2.

9. A line segment has endpoints $(-4, 9)$ and $(3, -2)$. Find the endpoints of the image after reflecting the segment across the x-axis, translating 4 units down, and then reflecting across the line $x = 4$.

Connecting Past and Present Learning

Previously, you learned:

- to apply rigid transformations,
- to create scale drawings, and
- to describe symmetries of figures.

In this module, you will learn:

- to dilate figures in the coordinate plane and
- to apply more than one transformation on a figure.

Define and Apply Dilations, Stretches, and Compressions

(I Can) dilate and stretch a figure and determine how a figure has been transformed.

Spark Your Learning

Jocelyn is researching what subjects adult learners choose to study. She found the charts below in a report about a survey of a group of adults taking classes at a university.

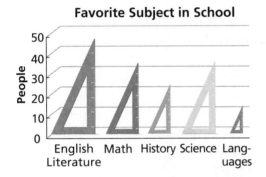

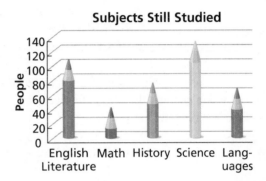

Complete Part A as a whole class. Then complete Parts B and C in small groups.

  A. What is a mathematical question you can ask about the charts and how they were made? What information would you need to know to answer your question?

  B. To answer your question, what strategy and tool would you use along with all the information you have? What answer do you get?

  C. Do these charts appear to accurately represent the survey data?

Turn and Talk Think about ways the data display might change.

  • Suggest a different way to present the data in one of the charts. Explain why your display would make the information easier to understand.
  • The totals in the two displays are different. What must be true if these represent a survey of the same group of adults?

Build Understanding

Investigate Transformations

Some transformations change the size and shape of a figure. Two nonrigid transformations are dilations and stretches.

A **dilation** changes the size of a figure by the same amount in all directions.

preimage

dilation by a factor greater than 1

dilation by a factor less than 1

A **stretch** changes the shape of a figure by a factor greater than 1 in one direction. A **compression** changes the shape of a figure by a factor greater than 0 and less than 1 in one direction.

preimage

vertical compression

horizontal stretch

1 Use a geometric drawing tool to draw $\triangle ABC$ with vertices $A(-2, 2)$, $B(2, 5)$, and $C(2, 2)$.

A. Transform $\triangle ABC$ using the rule $(x, y) \rightarrow (x - 2, y + 1)$. What kind of transformation is this?

B. Transform $\triangle ABC$ using the rule $(x, y) \rightarrow (3x, 3y)$. How does the figure change? Is this a rigid transformation?

C. Repeat Step B using the rule $(x, y) \rightarrow \left(\frac{1}{2}x, \frac{1}{2}y\right)$.

D. Repeat Step B using the rule $(x, y) \rightarrow (x, 2y)$.

> **Turn and Talk** Identify a real-world situation when each transformation would arise.

Explore Dilations

The **center of dilation** is the fixed point in the plane that does not change when the dilation is applied.
The center can be on the preimage or elsewhere on the plane.
When a dilation is applied to a point A, the image A' lies on the ray drawn from the center B through A.

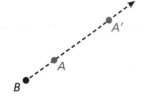

The **scale factor** k of a dilation is the ratio of the length of a segment on the image to the length of the corresponding segment on the preimage.
That is, $k = \frac{BA'}{BA}$. For example, if $k = 3$, then $BA' = 3BA$.

In function notation, the dilation with center B and scale factor k is written as $D_{B,k}(A) = A'$.

2 ▶ **A.** Use a compass and straightedge to construct a dilation with scale factor of 2.

Draw triangle PQR and a center of dilation C outside the triangle.

Draw a ray from the center of dilation through each vertex.

Set the compass to the distance CP. Then mark this distance along the ray CP from point P. Complete for vertices Q and R also.

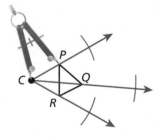

The intersections of the arcs and rays are the vertices of the image. Draw and label the image.

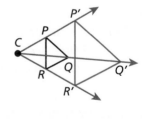

B. How are the ratios of the lengths of corresponding sides of the preimage and image related?

C. Do $\overline{PR}$ and $\overline{P'R'}$ appear to be parallel? How can you check?

 Turn and Talk Based on constructing the dilation of triangle PQR, Monica conjectured that for all dilations, corresponding sides of the image and preimage are parallel and the ratio of the length of a side of the image to the length of the corresponding side of the preimage is the scale factor. Consider dilating quadrilateral $CPQR$ in Task 2. Does this dilation support Monica's conjecture? If not, how would you modify her conjecture?

Step It Out

Use Properties of Dilations

Dilations share some of the properties with rigid motions, but they change lengths of corresponding segments.

Properties of Dilations
• preserve angle measure
• preserve collinearity
• preserve orientation
• map a segment to another segment whose length is the product of the scale factor and the length of the preimage
• map a line not passing through the center of the dilation to a parallel line and leave a line passing through the center unchanged

3 ▸ Images made with one-point perspective have one center point for the entire image. In the image shown, the backs of the buildings are drawn by creating dilations of the segments that determine the fronts of the buildings using a center point on the horizon.

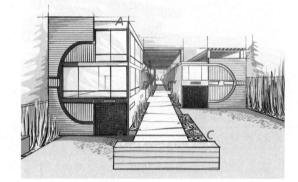

A. How was the center of the dilation found?

B. In the drawing $AB = 3$ in. $A'B' = 1$ in. $BC = 2$ in. $B'C' = \frac{2}{3}$ in. Find the scale factor.

 Turn and Talk If $ABCD$ is the preimage and $A'B'C'D'$ is the image, what would it take to turn $A'B'C'D'$ back into $ABCD$? Compare scale factors that will reduce an image to those that will enlarge an image.

Dilations, Stretches, and Compressions on the Coordinate Plane

The coordinate notation for dilations, stretches, and compressions are related. Each involves multiplying at least one of the coordinates by a scale factor k.

Transformation	Center at Origin
Dilation	$(x, y) \rightarrow (kx, ky)$
Vertical Stretch $(k > 1)$	$(x, y) \rightarrow (x, ky)$
Horizontal Stretch $(k > 1)$	$(x, y) \rightarrow (kx, y)$
Vertical Compression $(0 < k < 1)$	$(x, y) \rightarrow (x, ky)$
Horizontal Compression $(0 < k < 1)$	$(x, y) \rightarrow (kx, y)$

4 Draw a dilation with scale factor $\frac{1}{2}$ of quadrilateral $ABCD$ with vertices $A(-4, -2)$, $B(-6, -4)$, $C(-4, -6)$, and $D(-2, -4)$ centered at the origin.

Use the coordinate rule $(x, y) \rightarrow \left(\frac{1}{2}x, \frac{1}{2}y\right)$.

A. How do you know whether the image will be larger or smaller than the preimage?

Preimage	Image
$A(-4, -2)$	$(-2, -1)$
$B(-6, -4)$	$(-3, -2)$
$C(-4, -6)$	$(-2, -3)$
$D(-2, -4)$	$(-1, -2)$

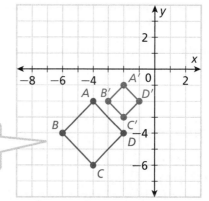

Plot and connect points to draw the dilation. Be sure to use prime notation for the image.

B. Which quadrilateral is the image?

 Turn and Talk How can you use the graph to check the dilation?

Predict the Effect of a Transformation Rule

5 Look at the coordinate points and predict what kind of transformation will happen in each case. Match the transformation in column A with the rule in column B.

A. Match the transformation in the left column with the rule in the right column.

1. Translation	A. $(x, y) \rightarrow (x, 3y)$
2. Dilation	B. $(x, y) \rightarrow (3x, y)$
3. Horizontal stretch	C. $(x, y) \rightarrow (x + 3, y)$
4. 270° Rotation	D. $(x, y) \rightarrow (x, 0.3y)$
5. Vertical stretch	E. $(x, y) \rightarrow (y, -x)$
6. Vertical compression	F. $(x, y) \rightarrow (3x, 3y)$

B. Is each transformation rigid or nonrigid?

 Turn and Talk
- Compare the transformation rules that result in rigid transformations and nonrigid transformations.
- Compare the results of applying rigid transformations and nonrigid transformations to a figure.

Check Understanding

1. What type of transformation is the result of applying the rule $(x, y) \rightarrow (2x, 2y)$?

Use the rule to transform the triangle with vertices $A(1, 4)$, $B(0, 1)$, and $C(-4, 0)$. Graph and label the image and the preimage.

2. $(x, y) \rightarrow (x, 3y)$

3. $(x, y) \rightarrow (2x, y)$

Name the transformation(s) used to map the blue figure to the red figure.

4.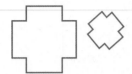

5.

On Your Own

6. **MP** **Critique Reasoning** Richard says that the rule $(x, y) \rightarrow (0.2x, y)$ describes a horizontal stretch because only the x-coordinates are affected by the rule. Is Richard correct? Why or why not?

7. Maya wants to figure out what sort of transformation was used to map the first picture to the second picture.

   A. Describe a method Maya could use to solve the problem.

   B. Why are the pictures given misleading?

   C. What kind of transformation was used?

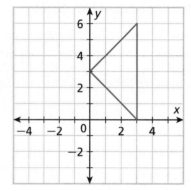

8. Figure $A'B'C'D'$ is a dilation of $ABCD$ with center of dilation B.

   A. What was the scale factor? Write a rule for the dilation.

   B. Which pairs of corresponding sides of the preimage and image are parallel? Which pairs overlap? Explain why this happens.

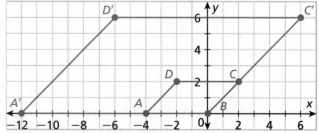

9. **MP** **Critique Reasoning** Bridget was constructing a dilation with scale $\frac{1}{2}$. She drew rays from the center through each vertex. Then she used a compass to find the distance from the center to each vertex, and then marked off that distance again along her rays. Then she connected the corresponding vertices. Did Bridget correctly construct the dilation? Why or why not?

For Problems 10–15, name the transformation(s) that the given rule produces.

10. $(x, y) \rightarrow (2x, 2y)$

11. $(x, y) \rightarrow (7x, y)$

12. $(x, y) \rightarrow \left(\frac{1}{4}x, \frac{1}{4}y\right)$

13. $(x, y) \rightarrow \left(x + 2, \frac{1}{2}y\right)$

14. $(x, y) \rightarrow (x, 1 - y)$

15. $(x, y) \rightarrow \left(2(x + 1), 2(y - 2)\right)$

16. Art Danica is studying perspective drawing in her art class. What kind of transformation did she use to create her drawing?

17. Open Ended Draw a $\triangle ABC$ on the coordinate plane. Then draw $D_{A, 0.5}(\triangle ABC)$. Describe the steps you took.

18. 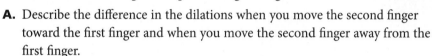 **Critique Reasoning** Joshua attempted to dilate a right triangle but his new triangle is not a right triangle. Could this be correct? Explain why or why not.

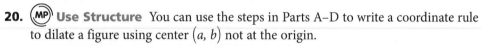

19. STEM Jeffrey is designing a dilation app for a touch-screen device. The app lets you place one finger on the center of the dilation and another finger on a point of a given figure.

A. Describe the difference in the dilations when you move the second finger toward the first finger and when you move the second finger away from the first finger.

B. Describe the difference in the dilations when the location of the center of dilation (where the first finger is placed) is on the figure and when it is not on the figure.

20. **Use Structure** You can use the steps in Parts A–D to write a coordinate rule to dilate a figure using center (a, b) not at the origin.

A. Write a rule that will translate a point (p, q) on the figure being dilated with center (a, b) so that the center is the origin $(0, 0)$.

B. Starting with your rule from Part A, write a rule that will dilate the figure by scale factor k.

C. Starting with your rule from Part B, write a rule that will translate the figure with the center at the origin so that the center is mapped back to its original location (a, b).

D. Draw a triangle and choose a center of dilation that is not the origin. Using scale factor 2, apply your rule from Part C to your triangle. Does your rule correctly dilate your figure?

21. Health and Fitness AJ wants to design a running track with two lanes. The lanes should be transformations of each other with the smaller one inside the larger one. Can AJ use a translation to draw one of the lanes from the other? Why or why not?

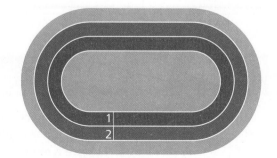

22. Kevin has a set of nesting dolls. He wants to draw a picture of them, and he wonders if he can use the same scale factor to reduce his first sketch to create the second as he would use to reduce the second sketch to create the third, etc. The heights of the dolls are 6 in., 4.5 in., 3.2 in., 2 in., and 1.25 in. Can Kevin use the same rule for each dilation?

23. Triangle ABC has vertices $A(-1, 1)$, $B(-3, -2)$, and $C(4, 1)$. For parts A–C, state whether each transformation preserves angle measure and distance.

A. $(x, y) \rightarrow (x - 4, y)$ **B.** $(x, y) \rightarrow (3x, y)$ **C.** $(x, y) \rightarrow (2x, 2y)$

D. Compare transformations that preserve angle measure and distance with ones that do not. Explain.

24. (Open Middle™) Using the integers -9 to 9, at most one time each, fill in the boxes two separate times so that the triangle with vertices at $(1, -3)$, $(2, 3)$, and $(-1, -2)$ has been dilated.

Image vertices: $\left(\boxed{}, \boxed{} \right)$, $\left(\boxed{}, \boxed{} \right)$, and $\left(\boxed{}, \boxed{} \right)$;

Dilation point: $\left(\boxed{}, \boxed{} \right)$; Scale factor: $\boxed{}$

Spiral Review • Assessment Readiness

25. How many lines of symmetry does an equilateral triangle have?

(A) 0   (C) 2

(B) 1   (D) 3

26. Which of the following are nonrigid transformations? Select all that apply.

(A) translation   (D) rotation

(B) compression   (E) reflection

(C) dilation   (F) stretch

27. Decide whether each pair of figures shows a reflection.

Reflection	?	?	?	?
No reflection	?	?	?	?

I'm in a Learning Mindset!

A photogrammetrist is someone who uses the science of making reliable measurements by the use of photographs and especially aerial photographs (as in surveying). If I were a photogrammetrist how would this lesson be helpful?

Apply Sequences of Transformations

(I Can) determine the effects of a sequence of transformations on a figure.

Spark Your Learning

Bryce has found animal tracks while hiking.

The tracks are every half foot.

Complete Part A as a whole class. Then complete Parts B–D in small groups.

A. What is a mathematical question you can ask about this situation? What information would you need to know to answer your question?

B. What transformation(s) are involved in this situation? How would you describe each transformation?

C. To answer your question, what strategy and tool would you use along with all the information you have? What answer do you get?

D. Does your answer make sense in the context of the situation? How do you know?

 Turn and Talk Will animal tracks always involve a reflection and a translation?

Build Understanding

Apply Two Rigid Motions to a Figure

You can apply a sequence of two or more transformation to a figure. When you do this, the image of the first transformation is the preimage for the second transformation, and so on.

1 Suppose you have two transformations to apply to a figure, but the order in which the transformations should be applied is not specified. It can be helpful to understand when the order in which you apply the transformations will affect the final image.

A. Describe the sequence of transformations used to map *ABC* to *A'B'C'* and to map *A'B'C'* to *A"B"C"*. Apply the translations in the other order. Does the order of applying the translations affect the final image? Explain your reasoning.

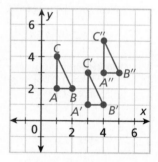

B. Make a conjecture: Can the order in which you apply two translations ever affect the final image? Explain your reasoning. Write a single transformation to justify your conjecture.

C. Describe the sequence of transformations used to map *DEF* to *D'E'F'* and to map *D'E'F'* to *D"E"F"*. Apply the transformations in the other order. Does the order of applying the transformations affect the final image? Explain your reasoning.

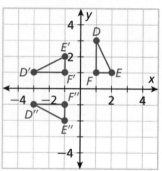

D. What are the possible sequences of two transformations including translations, rotations, and reflections that you might apply to a figure? Make and test predictions about when the order of two rigid transformations applied in a sequence affects the final image. Include translations, rotations, and reflections in your reasoning. You may want to use a geometric drawing tool to investigate the possibilities.

E. Make a conjecture about when the order of two rigid transformations applied in a sequence affects the final image. Include translations, rotations, and reflections in your reasoning.

Turn and Talk

- If you apply a sequence of three translations to a figure, will the order of the transformations matter? Explain your reasoning.

- If you apply a sequence of three reflections or three rotations with the same center, will the order of the transformations matter? Explain your reasoning.

Apply Transformations to Map an Image
Back to Its Preimage

Sometimes, you may need to map an image back to its preimage. While it can be helpful to have the sequence that was used in the original mapping, you may find a sequence using different transformations that accomplishes what you need.

 2 The graphs show a sequence of transformations.

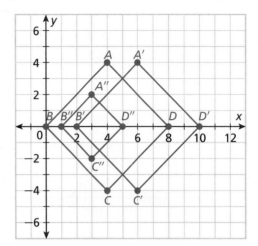

A. Describe the transformations used to map *ABCD* to *A'B'C'D'* and to map *A'B'C'D'* to *A"B"C"D"*. Describe two different sequences of transformations you could you use to map *A"B"C"D"* to *ABCD*.

B. Suppose the transformations in Part A included a horizontal stretch instead of a dilation. Predict how this would change the transformations used to map *A"B"C"D"* to *ABCD*.

C. Make a conjecture to describe a general rule for reversing the effect of a dilation, stretch, or compression.

D. Suppose you were given the image without labels appearing on the vertices. Describe two different sequences of transformations could you use to map *A"B"C"D"* to *ABCD* that include either a rotation or a reflection.

E. In the image below, the blue polygons are all congruent. Describe the transformations that could have been used to map A to B. Can you use the same transformations to map B to C and C to D? Predict what happens if you reverse the order of the transformations.

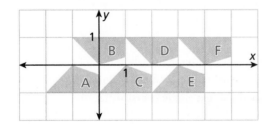

F. The pattern shown with Part E is called a *glide reflection*. How is this name related to the transformations used to create the pattern?

 Turn and Talk Make a conjecture about whether you can use a horizontal stretch to undo a vertical compression. Provide evidence to justify your conjecture.

Step It Out

Specify a Sequence of Transformations

3 ▶ Greg wants to create a T-shirt using an image he created for a poster. He plans to print the image on transfer paper and then iron it onto a shirt. The image on the shirt will be about one half the size of the original image. Greg uses the rough sketch below to figure out how to transform the figure to create the shirt.

Find a sequence of rigid motions that maps the original figure to the final image for the transfer. Give coordinate notation for the transformations you use.

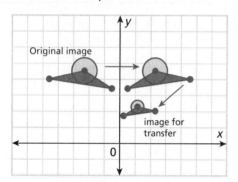

A. How do you know Greg used a reflection instead of a rotation or translation? Write a transformation to map the original image to the second image.

B. Is the third image a dilation, a stretch, or a compression? How do you know? What is the center of this transformation? What is the factor used for the transformation?

 Turn and Talk What is the final transformation that happens when the image is transferred to the shirt? Can the relationship between the original image and the image on the shirt be described using a single transformation?

Write a Composition of Functions

You can write a sequence of transformations as a function. The **composition** of several transformations is a new transformation that directly maps a preimage to the final image after each image is used as a preimage in the next transformation.

If each of the transformations included in a composition is a rigid motion, then the composition is also a rigid motion. If any nonrigid motion is included, then the composition may not be a rigid motion.

For example, consider the transformation rules $(x, y) \rightarrow (2x, 2y)$ and $(x, y) \rightarrow (y, x)$. The composition of these transformations is $(x, y) \rightarrow (2y, 2x)$.

A figure is transformed by a dilation centered at the origin with a scale factor of 2, and then a translation of 4 units to the right and 3 units down.

A. Write the sequence of transformations using coordinate notation for each transformation.

B. Which of the two transformations below represents the composition of transformations? Explain your reasoning.

$$(x, y) \rightarrow (2x + 4, 2y - 3) \qquad (x, y) \rightarrow \left(2(x + 4), 2(y - 3)\right)$$

 Turn and Talk On slips of paper, write coordinate rules for three different transformations including nonrigid transformations. Combine your rules with ones that your partner has written. Select two of the rules and write a composition of them. Then have your partner determine the rules you used in the composition.

In a **glide reflection**, a figure is translated then reflected across a line parallel to the translation vector. A glide reflection is a composition of a translation and reflection, and it is a rigid transformation.

Glide reflections are commutative: In a glide reflection, the resulting image is the same regardless of the order in which the transformations are performed.

5 The figure shows a glide reflection.

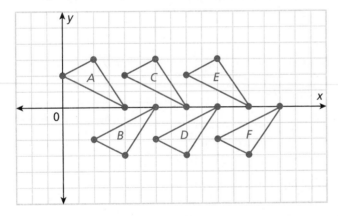

A. The functions that are used to map A to B are a translation by 2 units right and a reflection across the x-axis. Does the order matter for these transformations?

B. The glide reflection can be written as a composition of $(x, y) \rightarrow (x + 2, y)$ and $(x, y) \rightarrow (x, -y)$. The composition of these functions is $(x, y) \rightarrow (x + 2, -y)$. Notice that each of the transformations only affects one of the coordinates. Use this to justify your answer to Part A.

 Turn and Talk Name another pair of transformations that are commutative, meaning that the order in which you apply the transformations does not matter.

Check Understanding

Use the figure to the right for Problems 1–4.

1. Which figures are the result of a rotation being applied to triangle *A*?

2. Write a sequence of transformations to map triangle *A* to triangle *E*.

3. Write a sequence of transformations to map triangle *D* to triangle *A*.

4. Write a composition of functions that maps triangle *A* to triangle *C*.

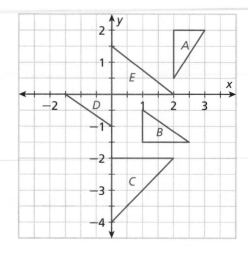

On Your Own

The figures given are congruent. Find a sequence of rigid motions that maps one figure to the other.

5. *BCDE*: $(6, 2), (8, 2), (6, 6), (-2, 6)$ to *FGHI*: $(2, -4), (4, -4), (2, -8), (-6, -8)$

6. *JKLM*: $(1, 8), (4, 4), (-2, -2), (-2, 6)$ to *OPQR*: $(5, -1), (1, -4), (-5, 2), (3, 2)$

Predict whether the order matters in the given transformations on *BCDE*. Check your prediction.

7. translate left 2 units and down 4 units; dilate by a factor of $\frac{1}{2}$ with center at the origin

8. dilate by factor of $\frac{1}{3}$; rotate 90° clockwise about the origin

9. (**MP**) **Critique Reasoning** Brett predicts that it doesn't matter whether he dilates rhombus *ABCD* first or rotates and translates it first and then dilates it. Provide evidence for or against his prediction.

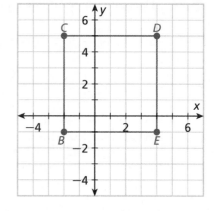

In Problems 10 and 11, write a composition of functions that will map Figure A to Figure B.

10.

11.

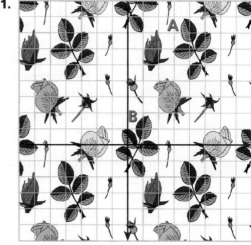

(l) ©Kiichytska Maryana/Shutterstock; (r) ©Natalya Danko/Alamy

12. Which sequence of transformations maps rectangle *ABCD* into quadrant 2?

    A. Reflect across *x*-axis; translate 8 units left; rotate clockwise 90°.

    B. Rotate clockwise 270°; reflect across *y*-axis; translate 6 units up.

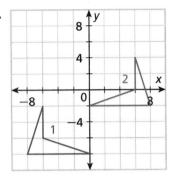

Apply the composition of transformations to triangle *ABC* with coordinates $A(-4, -2)$, $B(0, 3)$, and $C(-4, 3)$. Write the coordinates of the image.

13. $(x, y) \to (-4y - 2, 4x - 2)$

14. $(x, y) \to (-x, -3y)$

Write a sequence of transformations to map Figure 1 to Figure 2. Then write a sequence of transformations to map Figure 2 to Figure 1.

15.

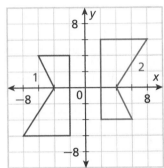

16.

17. Open Ended Deshaun has written a computer program that translates an image when a key is pressed. He wants to apply three transformations to move a triangle around a coordinate grid. He wants it to start in quadrant I and end up quadrant IV. Write a sequence of transformations that he could use.

In Problems 18–21, write a composition of transformations using the order of the sequence given.

18. *ABCD*, centered at the origin, is rotated 180° about the origin, and dilated by a factor of $\frac{1}{3}$.

19. *EFG*, centered at the origin, is reflected over the *x*-axis, rotated clockwise 90° about the origin, and translated down 4 units and to the right 1 unit.

20. *HIJ* is dilated by a factor of 4 with the origin as the center of dilation, reflected over the *y*-axis, and translated right 3 units and up 5 units.

21. *LMNO* is translated right 5 units and up 3 units, rotated counterclockwise 90°, and dilated by a factor of 0.5.

22. STEM Nakia is coding a computer game. She needs a character to jump up 2 units and right 1 unit, go down to the ground to duck under overhead objects, and then pivot around to face enemies. What transformations could she use to do this?

23. The coordinates of $\triangle ABC$ are $A(1, 1)$, $B(3, -6)$, and $C(5, 1)$.

    A. Is $\triangle ABC$ an equilateral triangle, an isosceles triangle, or a scalene triangle? Explain your reasoning.

    B. Apply a translation 6 units left and a dilation with the origin as the center of dilation, by a factor of $\frac{1}{2}$ to $\triangle ABC$. What are the coordinates of the vertices of the image?

    C. Is $\triangle A'B'C'$ the same type of triangle as you determined in Part A?

    D. Give an example of a sequence of transformations for which $\triangle ABC$ and its image $\triangle A'B'C'$ are different types of triangles.

24. DESIGN In the rug design, the shapes A and B are congruent.

  A. Find two sequences of rigid motions that map A to B using different types of transformations.

  B. Is the orientation of the figure affected by either sequence of transformations? Explain.

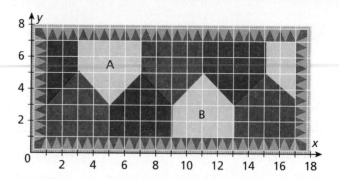

25. **MP** Use Structure Figure $L'M'N'$ has been transformed with function $(x, y) \rightarrow \left(\frac{1}{2}(-y + 4), \frac{1}{2}(x + 20)\right)$. What transformation will map it to the preimage LMN?

26. (**Open Middle™**) List three sequences of transformations that take preimage $STUVW$ to image $S'''T'''U'''V'''W'''$.

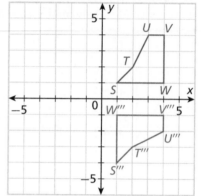

Spiral Review • Assessment Readiness

27. Which of the following will produce a dilation such that the sides on the image are 3 times as long as those on the preimage?

  (A) $(x, y) \rightarrow \left(\frac{1}{3}x, \frac{1}{3}y\right)$

  (B) $(x, y) \rightarrow (x + 3, y + 3)$

  (C) $(x, y) \rightarrow (3x, 3y)$

  (D) $(x, y) \rightarrow (x - 3, y - 3)$

28. How many lines of symmetry does the figure have?

  (A) 2

  (B) 3

  (C) 4

  (D) 8

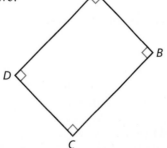

29. Which vector is applied in the translation with function notation $T_{\vec{v}}\left(A(2, 3)\right) = A'(3, -4)$?

  (A) $\langle 3, -4 \rangle$

  (B) $\langle 5, -1 \rangle$

  (C) $\langle 1, -7 \rangle$

  (D) $\langle 2, 3 \rangle$

30. In a reflection, which of the following is true?

  (A) The y-coordinate is always the opposite of the y-coordinate in the preimage.

  (B) A preimage is reflected across the perpendicular bisector to get the image.

  (C) Each point will be equally far away from the line of reflection.

  (D) The image and preimage are the same size and shape but a different orientation.

 I'm in a Learning Mindset!

How do I know whether a task is challenging enough for me?

Review

Dilations

Kimora drew a scale drawing and made sure of the following information.

- Angle measures are preserved.
- Side lengths are proportional.

Roche wanted to find the center and the scale factor.

- Identify corresponding points and connect them with a line. All three lines intersect at $(-3, 0)$.
- Compare the length of corresponding sides. The preimage to the image is related by the scale factor of $\frac{1}{3}$.

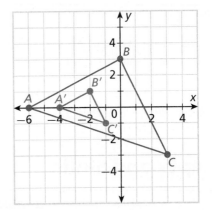

Sequences of Transformations

Write a sequence of transformation to that maps $\triangle ABC$ to $\triangle A'B'C'$.

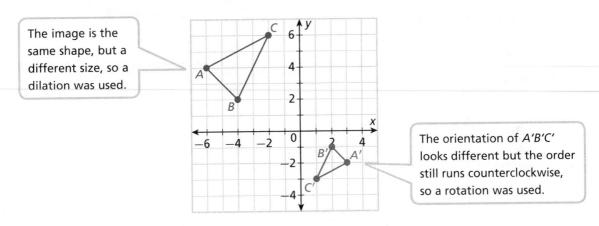

The image is the same shape, but a different size, so a dilation was used.

The orientation of $A'B'C'$ looks different but the order still runs counterclockwise, so a rotation was used.

Map $\triangle ABC$ to $\triangle A'B'C'$ with a clockwise rotation of $180°$ about the origin, followed by a dilation with a scale factor of $\frac{1}{2}$.

Vocabulary

Choose the correct term from the box to complete each sentence.

Vocabulary

center of dilation
dilation
rigid motion
scale factor

1. A ___?___ is a transformation that does not change the size or shape of a figure.

2. The ___?___ is the fixed point about which all other points are transformed in a dilation.

3. A ___?___ is a transformation that changes the size of a figure but does not change the shape.

4. The ratio of the lengths of corresponding sides in the image and the preimage of a dilation is the ___?___.

Concepts and Skills

5. **(MP) Use Tools** Describe how to construct the image of △ABC under a dilation with center C and scale factor 3. State what strategy and tool you will use to answer the question, explain your choice, and then find the answer.

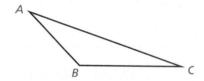

6. A dilation on the coordinate plane is shown.

   A. Explain why it is a dilation.

   B. Determine the coordinates of the center of dilation.

   C. Determine 2 possible scale factors.

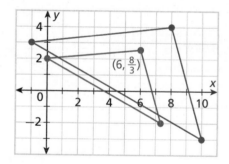

Find a sequence of transformations for the indicated mapping.

7.

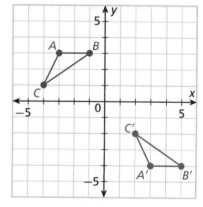

8.

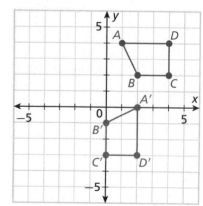

190

Architect

STEM
POWERING INGENUITY

Architects use their construction knowledge and drawing skills to design buildings. They work as part of a team to draw building schematics that are functional and aesthetically pleasing. They must work within the constraints of a project, including budgets, laws, and environmental impacts.

STEM Task

The Hearst Tower in New York was designed with a diagrid framing pattern composed of equilateral triangles on the sides and isosceles triangles on the corners. Each side of a triangle is formed by a steel beam.

How many of each length of steel beam are used to construct the frame of the tower?

Learning Mindset

Resilience Responds to Feedback

©Rafal Rodzoch/Calaimage/Getty Images

How can you give and respond to feedback appropriately? Do so with a mind to growth. It is important to be able to use feedback you receive from others to improve your learning. You also need to be able to give tips and help to others while they are learning. When giving feedback, mindset and tone are key. Here are some questions you can ask yourself to assess how you respond to and provide feedback:

- What feedback have I received? How is it meant to help me grow? How can I incorporate this feedback into my learning process?

- How did I acknowledge the feedback I received? Did I respond without being defensive?

- Did I administer feedback respectfully? What steps did I take to address the idea that was expressed instead of the person voicing the idea?

- Did I communicate effectively when providing feedback? How did I address any communication barriers?

Reflect

Q Think about a time when you received constructive feedback and responded positively. What was it about the feedback that made you respond positively? How does this shape the way you give feedback?

Q What are some possible types of feedback that an architect might encounter while designing a building such as the Hearst Tower? How would you respond to ensure the project was successful?

Congruent Triangles and Polygons

Module Performance Task: Focus on STEM

Image Stitching

Image stitching is the process of combining several overlapping images to create a larger image. It is used to create high-resolution satellite images and to stabilize shaky video recordings. The process identifies key features in a scene to align the photos before stitching them into one seamless image.

A. Select a group of images that would be ideal to stitch together. Explain your reasoning in terms of transformations and in terms of measures.

B. Describe an algorithm or procedure that can be used to select images that would be ideal to stitch together.

C. For the images you did not choose, why would they be less than ideal to stitch together? Explain your reasoning.

D. Describe how you would alter your algorithm or procedure to incorporate images that you identified as less than ideal.

Are You Ready?

Complete these problems to review prior concepts and skills you will need for this module.

Translate Figures in the Coordinate Plane

The coordinates of the vertices of a quadrilateral are $(-1, 2)$, $(2, 4)$, $(4, 3)$, and $(1, -1)$. Find the coordinates of the vertices of the image after translating by the given rule.

1. $(x, y) \rightarrow (x - 4, y + 1)$

2. $(x, y) \rightarrow (x + 2, y - 5)$

3. $(x, y) \rightarrow (x, y - 3)$

4. $(x, y) \rightarrow (x - 3, y - 2)$

Rotate Figures in the Coordinate Plane

The coordinates of the vertices of a triangle are $(-1, 1)$, $(3, -1)$, and $(-2, -4)$. Find the coordinates of the vertices of the image after performing the rotation about the origin.

5. 90° counterclockwise

6. 270° counterclockwise

7. 180°

Reflect Figures in the Coordinate Plane

The coordinates of the vertices of a quadrilateral are $(-2, 3)$, $(0, 4)$, $(4, 2)$, and $(-1, -1)$. Find the coordinates of the vertices of the image after performing the reflection across the given line.

8. x-axis

9. y-axis

Connecting Past and Present Learning

Previously, you learned:

• to transform figures in the coordinate plane,

• to determine unknown values using angle pairs, and

• to write proofs about segments and angles.

In this module, you will learn:

• to use transformations to prove if figures are congruent, and

• to use corresponding parts of congruent figures to determine unknown values.

Understand Congruent Figures

(I Can) determine whether figures are congruent.

Spark Your Learning

The architect chose to incorporate a wall of triangles as part of the design of this building.

Complete Part A as a whole class. Then complete Parts B–D in small groups.

A. What is a mathematical question you can ask about the exterior shapes of the building?

B. Describe a method you could use to answer your question.

C. To answer your question, what strategy and tool would you use along with all the information you have? What answer do you get?

D. Explain how the answer to your question is important in the design of a building like the one shown.

Turn and Talk How can the figures used in Parts B–D be transformed to map one onto the other? Describe each transformation and state whether each transformation is a rigid motion.

©Chris Hellier/age fotostock/Getty Images

Build Understanding

Transform Figures with Congruent Corresponding Parts

Two figures are **congruent** if and only if one can be obtained from the other by a sequence of rigid motions.

The definition of congruent figures above is written as a biconditional statement because it contains the phrase "if and only if." A true biconditional statement can be rewritten as a true conditional statement and its true converse.

Conditional statement: If a figure is obtained from another figure by a sequence of rigid motions, then the two figures are congruent.

Converse: If two figures are congruent, then one can be obtained from the other by a sequence of rigid motions.

1 **A.** In the figures *ABC* and *DEF*, all corresponding side lengths and angles are congruent. Trace *ABC* on a piece of tracing paper and trace *DEF* on a separate piece of tracing paper. How can you show that the figures are congruent according to the definition of congruent figures?

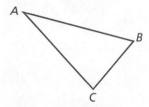
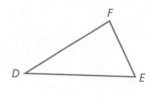

B. Arrange the two figures on a desk as shown above. Describe the transformation you can use to map point *A* to point *D*.

C. Describe the transformation you can use to map point *B* to point *E*.

D. Describe the transformation you can use to map point *C* to point *F*.

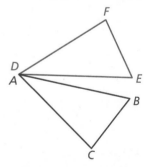
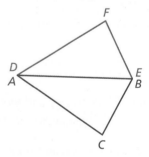

E. Complete the statements to verify that the image of ∠*B* is ∠*E*:

If two triangles are congruent, then their corresponding sides and angles map to each other.
Steps B–D showed that ___?___ through a sequence of rigid motions.
Based on △*ABC* ≅ △*DEF*, the image of ∠*B* is ___?___.

Turn and Talk Suppose a dilation is used to map a figure onto another figure. Are those figures congruent?

Use Corresponding Parts to Show Figures Are Congruent

Corresponding angles and **corresponding sides** are located in the same position for polygons with an equal number of sides. You can write a congruence statement for two figures by matching the congruent corresponding parts. In the statement $\triangle LMN \cong \triangle PQR$, $\overline{LM}$ corresponds and is congruent to $\overline{PQ}$, $\angle L$ corresponds and is congruent to $\angle P$, and so on.

> **Corresponding Parts of Congruent Figures are Congruent (CPCFC)**
>
> Corresponding pairs of sides and corresponding pairs of angles are congruent if and only if two figures are congruent.

This biconditional statement can be rewritten as a conditional statement and its converse.

Conditional statement: If two figures are congruent, then all pairs of corresponding sides and all pairs of corresponding angles are congruent.

Converse: If all pairs of corresponding sides and all pairs of corresponding angles of two figures are congruent, then the figures are congruent.

2 A tiled floor has the pattern shown. Determine whether $\triangle ABC$, $\triangle DEF$, and $\triangle KLM$ are congruent.

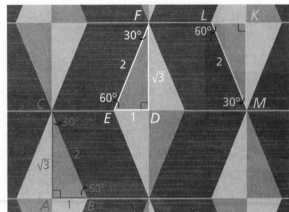

Use a table of corresponding parts.

$\triangle ABC$	$\triangle DEF$	$\triangle KLM$
$\overline{AB}$	$\overline{DE}$	$\overline{KL}$
$\overline{BC}$	$\overline{EF}$	$\overline{LM}$
$\overline{AC}$	$\overline{DF}$	$\overline{KM}$
$\angle A$	$\angle D$	$\angle K$
$\angle B$	$\angle E$	$\angle L$
$\angle C$	$\angle F$	$\angle M$

A. What information are you given about the lengths of the corresponding sides?

B. What information are you given about the measures of the corresponding angles?

C. Which triangles are congruent? How do you know?

D. Write a congruence statement for the congruent triangles. Is there more than one way to write the congruence statement? Explain.

E. Describe the transformations that map one of the highlighted triangles to the other two.

 Turn and Talk Is it possible to determine congruent corresponding parts of two figures given only a congruence statement, such as $GHJK \cong WXYZ$? Explain.

Step It Out

Apply the Third Angles Theorem

> **Third Angles Theorem**
>
> If two angles of one triangle are congruent to two angles of another triangle, then the third pair of angles are congruent.
>
> If $\angle A \cong \angle D$ and $\angle C \cong \angle F$, then $\angle B \cong \angle E$.

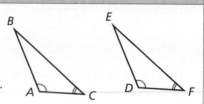

3 Determine whether the two triangles are congruent. If they are, write a congruence statement.

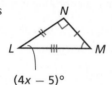 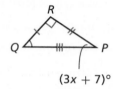

$(4x - 5)°$ $\qquad$ $(3x + 7)°$

The markings on the figure show that the following corresponding parts are congruent:

Sides: $\overline{LN} \cong \overline{PR}$, $\overline{NM} \cong \overline{RQ}$, $\overline{LM} \cong \overline{PQ}$

Angles: $\angle N \cong \angle R$, $\angle M \cong \angle Q$

By the Third Angles Theorem, $\angle L \cong \angle P$.

> **A.** Why can the Third Angles Theorem be used here?

All pairs of corresponding sides are congruent, and all pairs of corresponding angles are congruent, so $\triangle LMN \cong \triangle PQR$.

> **Turn and Talk** Congruent figures can be formed by many different rigid motions. What single rigid motion would map $\triangle LMN$ to $\triangle PQR$?

4 Find $m\angle L$ and $m\angle P$ in the triangles in Task 3.

$m\angle L = m\angle P$

> **A.** Why can you write this equation?

$4x - 5 = 3x + 7$

$x - 5 = 7$

$x = 12$

Find the measure of each angle.

$m\angle L = (4x - 5)° = \big(4(12) - 5\big)° = 43°$

So, $m\angle L = 43°$ and $m\angle P = 43°$.

> **B.** How do you know that $m\angle P = 43°$?

> **Turn and Talk** Does the rigid motion discussed in the previous Turn and Talk preserve the perimeter and area of the triangle? Explain.

198

Apply Properties of Congruent Figures

Patterns made of congruent figures are common in nature. These patterns can sometimes be adapted for industrial or safety uses.

5 Scientists have been able to use a difference between the skin of whales and sharks to develop a method that prevents bacteria growth. While whales can have barnacles, algae, and other sea creatures growing on their skin, sharks are not affected by such parasites because shark skin has a pattern of repeating congruent hexagons that does not allow parasites to stick.

Scientists copied this pattern to print an adhesive film that can be used on surfaces in hospitals and public restrooms to prevent bacteria from growing.

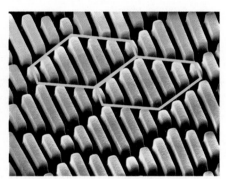

One way to generate the pattern of congruent hexagons is to use translations.

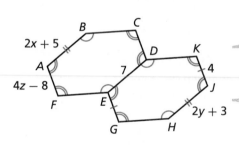

A. How can you state the congruence of the two hexagons after the translation?

B. Because $\overline{EG} \cong \overline{KJ}$, you know that $EG = 4$. What other two sides do you know have length 4?

Find the values of the variables in the congruent figures.

Solve for x.

$$AB = ED$$

$$2x + 5 = 7$$

$$2x + 5 - 5 = 7 - 5$$

$$2x = 2$$

$$\frac{2x}{2} = \frac{2}{2}$$

$$x = 1$$

Solve for y.

$$HJ = ED$$

$$2y + 3 = 7$$

$$2y + 3 - 3 = 7 - 3$$

$$2y = 4$$

$$\frac{2y}{2} = \frac{4}{2}$$

$$y = 2$$

C. Use a similar strategy to find the value of z.

Turn and Talk Can you map one hexagon onto the other by a reflection? What about a rotation? Give a congruence statement for each transformation if possible.

Check Understanding

1. 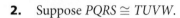 **Construct Arguments** How can you show two figures congruent?

2. Suppose $PQRS \cong TUVW$.

   A. Write a biconditional statement that describes the congruence relationship between $PQRS$ and $TUVW$.

   B. Describe a sequence of rigid motions that maps $PQRS$ to $TUVW$.

   C. List the corresponding congruent parts.

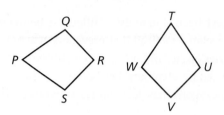

3. Find the measures of $\angle C$ and $\angle F$.

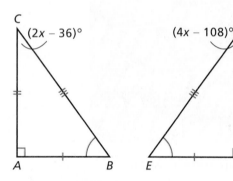

4. Find the value of the variable that results in congruent triangles.

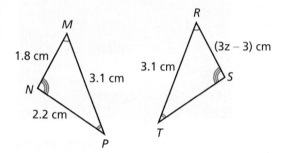

On Your Own

5. 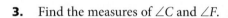 **Critique Reasoning** Chelsea says that the concept of rigid motion means two triangles cannot be congruent if any pair of corresponding parts is not congruent. Is Chelsea correct? Explain why or why not.

6. Describe a sequence of rigid motions that maps $\triangle MNP$ onto $\triangle MQR$ to show $\triangle MNP \cong \triangle MQR$.

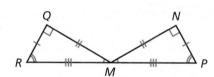

In Problems 7 and 8, use $\triangle ABC$ shown.

7. Suppose $\triangle ABC$ is reflected across the x-axis.

   A. What will be the measure of the image of $\angle ABC$?

   B. Which side(s) of the image of $\triangle ABC$ will have a length of 6 units?

8. Suppose $\triangle ABC$ is rotated $180°$ about the origin.

   A. What is an expression for the perimeter of the image of $\triangle ABC$?

   B. What is an expression for the area of the image of $\triangle ABC$?

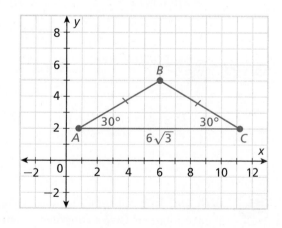

In Problems 9–12, describe a sequence of transformations you could use to prove that the figures are congruent. If there is no such sequence, explain why not.

9. Triangles *KLM* and *PQR*

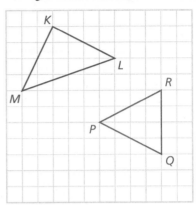

10. Pentagons *GHIJK* and *LMNOP*

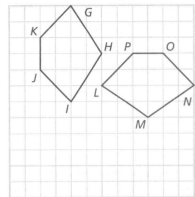

11. Squares *NOPQ* and *RSTU*

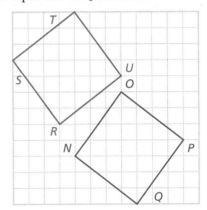

12. Hexagons *ABCDEF* and *UVWXYZ*

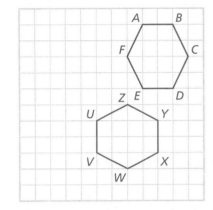

In Problems 13 and 14, use a ruler and protractor to measure the figures. Make a list of congruent corresponding parts. Determine if the figures are congruent.

13.

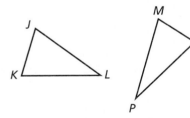

14.

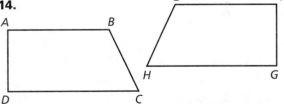

15. (MP) **Use Structure** Shamara is replacing the outlined pieces of glass. She needs to know whether the two shapes are congruent. How can she prove the shapes are congruent?

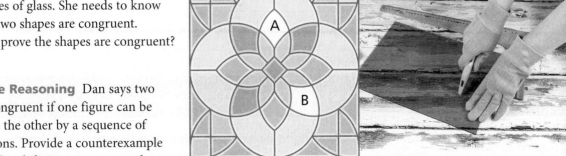

16. (MP) **Critique Reasoning** Dan says two figures are congruent if one figure can be mapped onto the other by a sequence of transformations. Provide a counterexample to show why his definition is not complete.

17. The illustration shows a square from a "Yankee Puzzle" quilt.

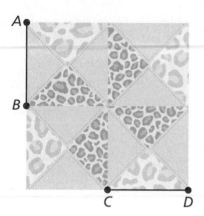

A. Use the idea of congruent shapes to describe the design of the quilt square.

B. Explain how the triangle with base $\overline{AB}$ can be transformed to the position of the triangle with base $\overline{CD}$.

C. Explain how you know $CD = AB$.

Spiral Review • Assessment Readiness

18. What are the coordinates of the image of $D(4, -1)$ after the composition of transformations $(x, y) \rightarrow (2y + 1, -x - 3)$?

Ⓐ $D'(-2, 9)$

Ⓑ $D'(9, -2)$

Ⓒ $D'(-1, -7)$

Ⓓ $D'(-7, -1)$

19. Are the given figures congruent? Explain.

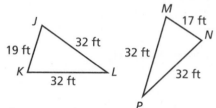

Ⓐ yes; by CPCFC

Ⓑ yes; The triangles have congruent angles.

Ⓒ no; $\overline{JK}$ and $\overline{MN}$ are not congruent.

Ⓓ no; $\overline{KL}$ and $\overline{MP}$ are not congruent.

20. For each type of transformation, identify whether it is a rigid motion or a nonrigid motion.

Transformation	Rigid Motion	Nonrigid Motion
A. Translation	?	?
B. Compression	?	?
C. Dilation	?	?
D. Rotation	?	?
E. Reflection	?	?
F. Stretch	?	?

 I'm in a Learning Mindset!

What steps am I taking to direct my own learning to understand congruent figures?

Corresponding Parts of Congruent Figures

(I Can) use congruent figures to solve problems.

Spark Your Learning

As part of a river festival, organizers plan to build a temporary bridge across a river.

Complete Part A as a whole class. Then complete Parts B–D in small groups.

A. What is a mathematical question you can ask about this situation? What information would you need to know to answer your question?

B. What measurements are involved in this situation? What do you know?

C. To answer your question, what strategy and tool would you use along with all the information you have? What answer do you get?

D. Does your answer make sense in the context of the situation? How do you know?

> **Turn and Talk** Predict how your answer would change for each of the following changes in the situation:
> - At a different point in the river, similar measurements are made, but angles *B* and *D* are obtuse and still congruent. If *AC* and *BC* do not change, what happens to *AB*?
> - At a different point in the river, similar measurements are made, but angles *B* and *D* are acute and still congruent. If *AC* and *BC* do not change, what happens to *AB*?

Build Understanding

Identify the Corresponding Congruent Parts of Congruent Figures

In this lesson you focus on the converse of Corresponding Parts of Congruent Figures are Congruent. If you know two figures are congruent, you can use CPCFC to conclude the sides and the angles of the figures are congruent.

Converse of CPCFC: If two figures are congruent, then all pairs of corresponding sides and all pairs of corresponding angles are congruent.

 Use the steps below to create and investigate congruent figures.

A. Fold a sheet of paper in half. Use a straightedge to draw a quadrilateral on the folded sheet. Then cut out the quadrilateral, cutting through both layers of paper. Label the quadrilaterals *ABCD* and *EFGH*. Use transformations to explain why the quadrilaterals are congruent.

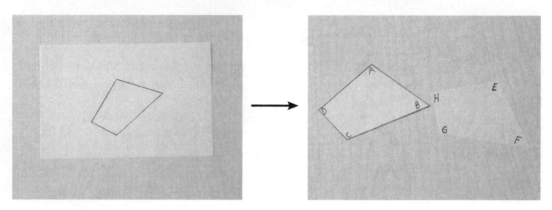

B. Write a congruence statement. Why is it better to start with a quadrilateral that has no symmetry or congruent sides?

C. List the corresponding sides of congruent quadrilaterals *JKLM* and *PQRS* below. What do you know about the corresponding side lengths? Justify your reasoning.

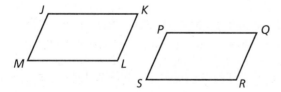

D. List the corresponding angles of the quadrilaterals above. What do you know about the corresponding angle measures? Justify your reasoning.

E. What can you conclude about the diagonals of the quadrilaterals?

 Turn and Talk
- Can you conclude that the quadrilaterals have the same perimeter? Explain.
- Can you conclude that the quadrilaterals have the same area? Explain.

Step It Out

Use Congruent Corresponding Parts

If you know that figures are congruent, you can use that information to solve problems using corresponding lengths and angles within the figures.

2 Find m∠S given that △HJK ≅ △RST.

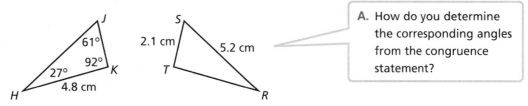

A. How do you determine the corresponding angles from the congruence statement?

Since △HJK ≅ △RST, ∠S ≅ ∠J. It is given that m∠J = 61°, so m∠S = 61°.

Turn and Talk For the triangles shown in Task 2, find m∠T and RT.

Prove a Geometric Relationship

When you need to prove relationships between two figures, one common strategy is to look for congruent figures and then use that congruence to prove corresponding segments or angles are congruent.

3 Write a two-column proof.

Given: △WXY ≅ △YZW

Prove: $\overline{XW} \parallel \overline{ZY}$

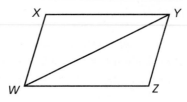

Statements	Reasons
1. △WXY ≅ △YZW	**1.** Given
2. ∠XWY ≅ ∠ZYW	**2.** Corresponding parts of congruent figures are congruent.
3. $\overline{XW} \parallel \overline{ZY}$	**3.** Converse of the Alternate Interior Angles Theorem

A. Explain how you know ∠XWY and ∠ZYW are corresponding angles.

B. What is the Converse of the Alternate Interior Angles Theorem?

Turn and Talk Use the proof in Task 3 as a template to prove $\overline{XY} \parallel \overline{ZW}$.

Check Understanding

1. 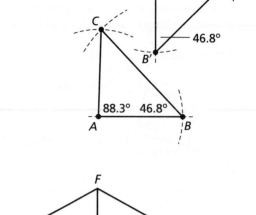 **Construct Arguments** Reggie claims the two figures shown are not congruent. Prove Reggie right or wrong.

In Problems 2 and 3, write the indicated proof.

2. **Given:** $PQTU \cong QRST$

   Prove: $\overline{QT}$ bisects $\overline{PR}$.

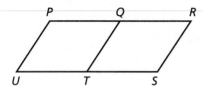

3. **Given:** $\triangle AFG \cong \triangle CAB$ and $\triangle DCG \cong \triangle CAB$

   Prove: $\overline{FG} \cong \overline{CG}$

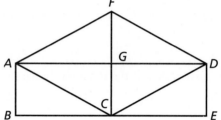

On Your Own

4. Write the indicated proof.

   Given: $\triangle ABC \cong \triangle ADC$

   Prove: $\overline{AC}$ bisects $\angle BAD$ and $\overline{AC}$ bisects $\angle BCD$

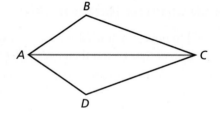

5. 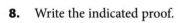 **Critique Reasoning** Madisyn says that if two triangles are congruent, their perimeters will always be the same. Is Madisyn right or wrong? Explain your reasoning.

6. If $\triangle ABC$ is a right triangle and $\triangle ABC \cong \triangle DEF$, is it possible for $\triangle DEF$ to not be a right triangle? Explain your reasoning.

7. $ABCD$ and $WXYZ$ are quadrilaterals.

   A. Use transformations to prove $ABCD \cong XWZY$.

   B. Use transformations to prove $\overline{AD} \cong \overline{XY}$.

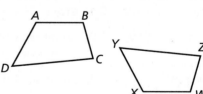

8. Write the indicated proof.

   Given: $\triangle SVT \cong \triangle SWT$

   Prove: $\overline{ST}$ bisects $\angle VSW$.

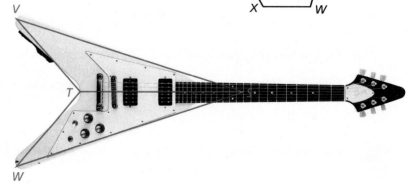

In Problems 9–12, explain how you know whether the figures are congruent. Then find the indicated measure, if possible.

9. w

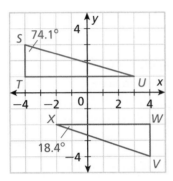

10. y

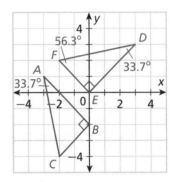

11. m∠V

12. m∠C

13. Which of the puzzle pieces could fit in the empty space? Explain how you know.

14. In the figure, △ABC ≅ △DEF.

   A. Find m∠D.

   B. Find AB.

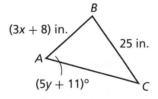 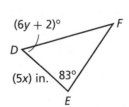

In Problems 15 and 16, write the indicated proof.

15. Given: △STU ≅ △VTU; $\overline{ST} \cong \overline{SV}$

   Prove: △STV is equilateral.

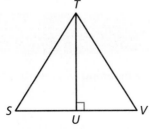

16. Given: △MNO and △QPR as marked

   Prove: △MNO ≅ △QPR

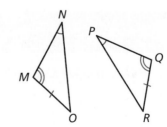

17. Gardening Marissa's design has multiple sections that should be identical, but she's not sure whether they are.

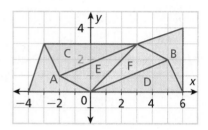

A. Prove that the figures A and B are congruent by mapping one to the other using transformations.

B. Will the same transformations as you used in Part A map figure C to figure D? If not, describe a different set of transformations you can use to prove C is congruent to D.

Spiral Review • Assessment Readiness

18. What value of the variable makes the figures congruent?

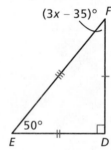 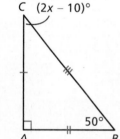

Ⓐ 90   Ⓒ 40

Ⓑ 50   Ⓓ 25

19. Which quadrant will the image of $P(2, 3)$ be in after this sequence of transformations: reflect across the x-axis and translate 5 units down?

Ⓐ Quadrant I

Ⓑ Quadrant II

Ⓒ Quadrant III

Ⓓ Quadrant IV

20. Match the rule on the left with the type of transformation on the right.

A. $(x, y) \rightarrow \left(\frac{1}{5}x, \frac{1}{5}y\right)$ **1.** Dilation

B. $(x, y) \rightarrow (x - 2, y + 5)$ **2.** Reflection

C. $(x, y) \rightarrow (y, -x)$ **3.** Rotation

D. $(x, y) \rightarrow (-x, y)$ **4.** Translation

I'm in a Learning Mindset!

How can I give and receive feedback about the meaning of congruent figures?

Use Rigid Motions to Prove Figures Are Congruent

(I Can) use rigid motions to show that figures are congruent.

Spark Your Learning

Phyl is teaching a workshop on making a fancy pie crust with a repeated design of hearts for the top of a cherry pie. Each serving of the pie should be identical.

Complete Part A as a whole class. Then complete Parts B–D in small groups.

A. What is a mathematical question you can ask about this situation? What information would you need to know to answer your question?

B. What assumptions must you make about the hearts to answer the question?

C. To answer your question, what strategy and tool would you use along with all the information you have? What answer do you get?

D. Does your answer make sense in the context of the situation? How do you know?

 Turn and Talk What if there had been a heart shape placed at the center of the pie top in addition to the shapes around the edge? How many identical servings could you make then?

Build Understanding

Determine Whether or Not Figures Are Congruent

Recall that two figures are congruent if and only if one can be obtained from the other by a sequence of rigid motions that may include reflections, translations, and rotations.

1 ▸ **A.** Use tracing paper to trace *ABCD*. Then move the tracing paper so that *ABCD* is mapped onto *EFGH*. Explain the translation used to map *ABCD* onto *EFGH*. How do you know that *ABCD* is congruent to *EFGH*?

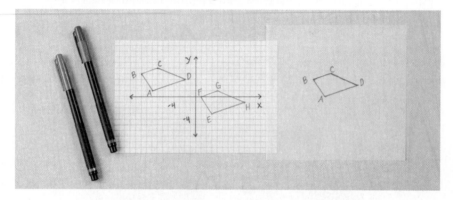

B. Trace *JKLM*. Flip the paper over and move it so *JKLM* is mapped onto *NPQR*. What transformation is used? Is *JKLM* congruent to *NPQR*? How do you know?

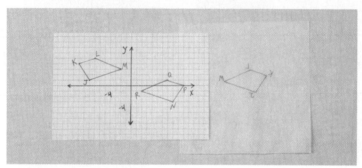

C. Is there a rigid transformation that maps *STUV* to *WXYZ*? Is *STUV* congruent to *WXYZ*? How do you know?

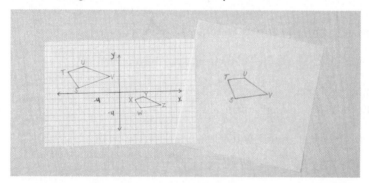

D. How do the sizes of the pairs of figures help determine if they are congruent?

 Turn and Talk Does changing the orientation of a figure affect its size and shape? Use the figures above to support your answer.

©Houghton Mifflin Harcourt

Step It Out

Find a Sequence of Rigid Motions

2 In the diagram, $JKLM \cong WXYZ$. Find a sequence of rigid motions that maps one figure onto the other.

Make a table of coordinates to look for a pattern.

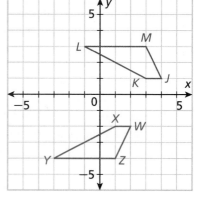

$J(4, 1)$	$W(2, -2)$
$K(3, 1)$	$X(1, -2)$
$L(-1, 3)$	$Y(-3, -4)$
$M(3, 3)$	$Z(1, -4)$

A. What type of transformation is suggested by the signs of the y-coordinates?

B. What is suggested by the differences between each pair of x- and y-coordinates?

Map $JKLM$ to $WXYZ$ with a reflection across the x-axis, followed by a translation.

Reflection: $(x, y) \rightarrow (x, -y)$

Translation: $(x, y) \rightarrow (x - 2, y - 1)$

 Turn and Talk What translation would you need to use if you wanted to translate $JKLM$ before applying the reflection across the x-axis?

3 In the diagram, $\triangle KLH \cong \triangle DGF$. Find a sequence of rigid motions that maps $\triangle DGF$ to $\triangle KLH$.

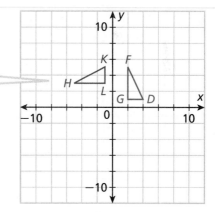

A. Based on the diagram, what transformations should be performed?

Two transformations that map DGF to KLH are shown.

Transformation 1: 90° rotation counterclockwise around the origin

Transformation 2: translation up 1 unit

B. The coordinate notation for each transformation is shown. Which notation describes Transformation 1? Which notation describes Transformation 2?

$(x, y) \rightarrow (x, y + 1)$

$(x, y) \rightarrow (-y, x)$

 Turn and Talk Describe a sequence of transformations that maps KLH to DGF.

Check Understanding

1. Suppose you are given this statement: If *ABCD* and *EFGH* are congruent, then *ABCD* can be mapped onto *EFGH* using a rotation and a translation. Determine whether or not this statement is true or false. Then explain your reasoning.

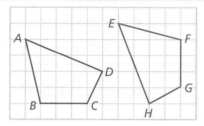

2. The figures shown are congruent. Find a sequence of transformations to map *PQRST* onto *DEFGH*. Give coordinate notation for the transformations you use.

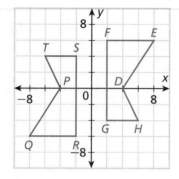

On Your Own

3. (MP) **Critique Reasoning** Marta says that given the statement *ABCD* ≅ *EFGH*, she can write all the side and angle congruence statements for the quadrilaterals without a diagram. Is Marta correct? Explain your answer.

In Problems 4–7, write a sequence of rigid motions that maps the first figure in the congruence statement to the second. Use coordinate notation to write the transformations.

4. *RSTU* ≅ *WXYZ*

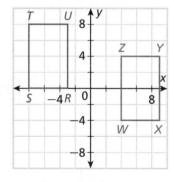

5. △*ABC* ≅ △*DEF*

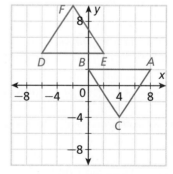

6. *DEFGH* ≅ *PQRST*

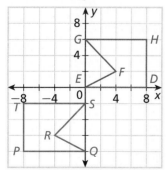

7. △*WXY* ≅ △*CED*

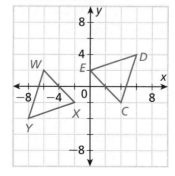

In Problems 8–11, use the definition of congruence to decide whether or not the two figures are congruent. Explain your answer using coordinate notation for any transformations you use.

8.

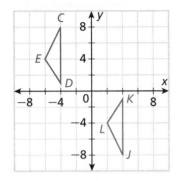

9.

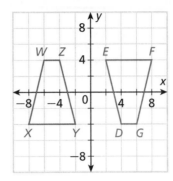

10.

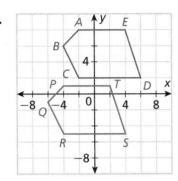

11.

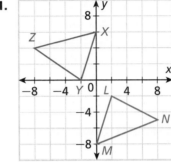

In Problems 12 and 13, describe the transformations that can be used to show that the shapes in each logo are congruent.

12.

13.

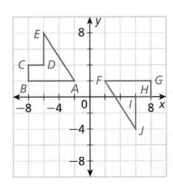

14. (MP) **Justify Reasoning** Two students are each trying to show the two figures are congruent. The first student maps *ABCDE* onto *FGHIJ* using a rotation of 180° about the origin, followed by a translation 4 units up. The second student uses the rule $(x, y) \rightarrow (-x, -y + 4)$. Are both students correct? If not, explain which student made an error and how to fix their work.

In Problems 15 and 16, find a sequence of transformations for the indicated mapping. Give coordinate notation for the transformations you use.

15. Map *PQRSTU* to *ABCDEF*.

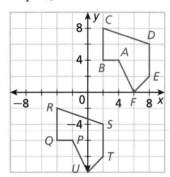

16. Map *DEF* to *KLM*.

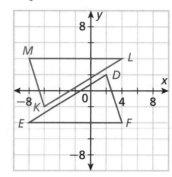

17. (Open Middle™) What is the fewest number of transformations needed to take preimage *ABCD* to image *A′B′C′D′*?

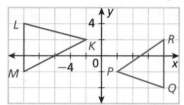

Spiral Review • Assessment Readiness

18. Given △*ABC* ≅ △*EDC*, which reason proves that ∠*A* ≅ ∠*E*?

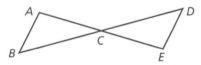

Ⓐ CPCFC

Ⓑ Alternate Interior Angles Theorem

Ⓒ Converse of the Alternate Interior Angles Theorem

Ⓓ Third Angles Theorem

19. What transformation will map *KLM* to *PQR*?

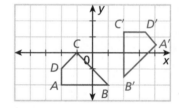

Ⓐ rotation   Ⓒ dilation

Ⓑ reflection   Ⓓ none of these

20. If △*GHK* ≅ △*STW*, which pairs of parts are congruent? Select all that apply.

Ⓐ $\overline{GH}$, $\overline{ST}$ Ⓒ $\overline{GK}$, $\overline{WT}$ Ⓔ ∠*GKH*, ∠*SWT*

Ⓑ ∠*GKH*, ∠*STW*   Ⓓ $\overline{KG}$, $\overline{WS}$ Ⓕ ∠*HGK*, ∠*STW*

 I'm in a Learning Mindset!

How can I make sure I understand every step of a proof and can give a reason for each step?

Review

Congruent Polygons

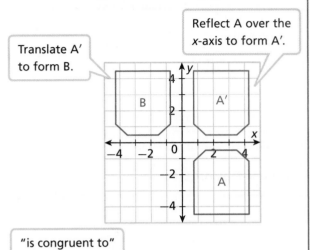

Translate A' to form B.

Reflect A over the x-axis to form A'.

"is congruent to"

Polygon A ≅ Polygon B because a series of rigid transformations can map Polygon A onto Polygon B.

Corresponding Parts of Congruent Triangles Are Congruent

The order gives the correspondence of points.

If △ABC ≅ △DEF, then all corresponding parts are congruent.

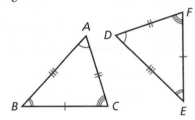

$\angle A \cong \angle D$	$\overline{BC} \cong \overline{EF}$
$\angle B \cong \angle E$	$\overline{CA} \cong \overline{FD}$
$\angle C \cong \angle F$	$\overline{AB} \cong \overline{DE}$

Using Congruence

Congruence can be used to find angle or side measures of figures. Given △ABC ≅ △DEF, determine m∠B.

$m\angle B = m\angle E$

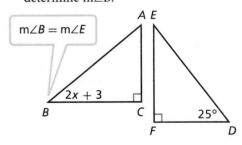

Triangle Sum Theorem

$m\angle D + m\angle E + m\angle F = 180$

$m\angle D + m\angle B + m\angle F = 180$

$25 + 2x + 3 + 90 = 180$

Substitution

$2x = 62$

$x = 31$

$m\angle B = 2x + 3 = 2(31) + 3 = 65$

Proofs

Congruence can be used to prove geometric relationships.

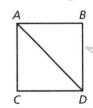

Reflect over $\overline{AD}$ or rotate around midpoint of $\overline{AD}$.

Given: Square ABDC; $\overline{AD}$ bisects ∠A and ∠D.

Prove △ABD ≅ △ACD

Statement	Reason
Square ABDC; $\overline{AD}$ bisects ∠A and ∠D.	Given
$\overline{AB} \cong \overline{CD} \cong \overline{AC} \cong \overline{BD}$	Definition of square
$\angle A \cong \angle B \cong \angle C \cong \angle D$	Right angles
$\angle BAD \cong \angle CDA \cong \angle CAD \cong \angle BDA$	Definition of bisection
$\triangle ABD \cong \triangle ACD$	CPCTC

Vocabulary

Choose the correct term from the box to complete each sentence.

1. A ___?___ is a transformation that does not change the size or shape of a figure.

2. Two figures that have the same size and shape are ___?___.

3. A ___?___ is a statement that can be written in the form "if p, then q."

4. A ___?___ is a statement that can be written in the form "p if and only if q."

Concepts and Skills

5. Given $\triangle JKL \cong \triangle PQR$, write congruency statements for all corresponding parts.

6. A triangle is translated, dilated, and rotated to map onto an image. Are the two figures congruent? Explain your reasoning.

7. You can show that $\triangle XYZ \cong \triangle X'Y'Z'$.

   A. Explain how to map $\triangle XYZ$ onto $\triangle X'Y'Z'$.

   B. Explain how to map $\triangle X'Y'Z$ onto $\triangle XYZ$.

   C. Explain how to map $\triangle X'Y'Z$ onto $\triangle XYZ$ with a different sequence of transformations.

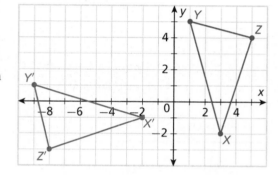

8. Write a proof.

   Given: $\triangle ABC \cong \triangle ADC$

   Prove: $BD = 2BC$

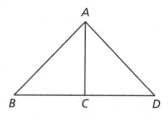

9. Parallelogram $PQRS$ has 2 pairs of opposite sides that are congruent and a diagonal.

   A. Identify 2 congruent triangles and write a congruence statement.

   B. Describe a rigid motion that demonstrates the congruency.

   C. What parts correspond to the diagonal? What property allows you to state that they are congruent?

   D. Write a formal proof to prove the congruency.

   E. (MP) **Use Tools** Determine PQ. State what strategy and tool you will use to answer the question, explain your choice, and then find the answer.

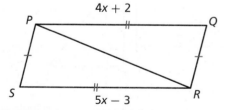

Triangle Congruence Criteria

Module Performance Task: Focus on STEM

Lunar Laser Ranging

During the Apollo missions to the moon, astronauts placed arrays of Cube Corner Retroreflectors (CCRs) on the lunar surface to use in future Lunar Laser Ranging (LLR) experiments.

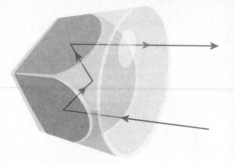

A CCR is created by cutting three perpendicular surfaces, similar to a corner you might see where two walls meet each other and the floor, within a circular pupil.

A. For the Apollo 15 mission, the CCRs were arranged in large rectangular panels. If the diameter of each CCR is 38 mm, estimate the surface area of a rectangular portion of the panel containing a 12 × 9 array of CCRs. Explain your reasoning.

B. A new retroreflector is scheduled to launch to the moon. Given that the diameter of this CCR is 100 mm, what is the total surface area of a similar 12 × 9 array of the new CCRs? How does this compare to the surface area of the array of 38 mm CCRs?

C. In the LLR experiment, the laser beam reflects off each surface of the corner before returning to Earth. Given the speed of light c and the time taken for the signal to travel to and return from the moon t, write an equation that represents the distance d between Earth and the moon.

D. Estimate the distance from Earth to the moon given $c \approx 3 \times 10^8$ m/s and $t \approx 2.6$ s. Then, research and compare your estimate to more exact values. Determine if your estimate was too high or too low. What might contribute to the difference in estimates?

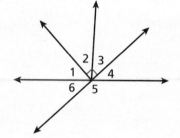

Are You Ready?

Complete these problems to review concepts and skills you will need for this module.

Types of Angle Pairs

Given that $m\angle 2 = m\angle 3$ and $m\angle 4 = 42°$, find each missing value.

1. $m\angle 2 + m\angle 3$

2. $m\angle 2$

3. $m\angle 3$

4. $m\angle 1$

5. $m\angle 6$

6. $m\angle 5$

The Pythagorean Theorem and Its Converse

Use the given diagram with the given information.

7. Find a, given $\triangle ABC$ is a right triangle, $c = 15$, and $b = 12$.

8. Find c, given $\triangle ABC$ is a right triangle, $a = 2$, and $b = 5$.

9. If $a = 10$, $b = 24$, and $c = 26$, is $\triangle ABC$ a right triangle?

10. If $a = 3$, $b = 4$, and $c = 6$, is $\triangle ABC$ a right triangle?

Congruent Figures

The coordinates of $\triangle ABC$ and $\triangle PQR$ are given. Determine whether the triangles are congruent. If so, provide a sequence of rigid motions that maps $\triangle ABC$ to $\triangle PQR$.

11. $A(0, 3)$, $B(2, 3)$, $C(2, 6)$;
    $P(6, 1)$, $Q(4, 1)$, $R(4, 4)$

12. $A(-5, 6)$, $B(-2, 5)$, $C(-6, 3)$;
    $P(5, 6)$, $Q(2, 5)$, $R(4, 3)$

13. $A(-2, -1)$, $B(0, -1)$, $C(-1, -3)$;
    $P(0, 1)$, $Q(6, 1)$, $R(3, 3)$

14. $A(4, 2)$, $B(4, 0)$, $C(0, 0)$;
    $P(-7, -2)$, $Q(-7, 0)$, $R(-3, 0)$

Connecting Past and Present Learning

Previously, you learned:

- to use angle pairs to determine unknown values,
- to find missing side lengths of right triangles using the Pythagorean Theorem, and
- to use transformations to determine whether two figures are congruent.

In this module, you will learn:

- to develop triangle congruency criteria from rigid transformations,
- to use triangle congruency criteria to solve problems, and
- to use triangle congruency criteria to prove relationships in geometric figures.

Develop ASA Triangle Congruence

(I Can) use ASA congruence criteria to prove that two triangles are congruent.

Spark Your Learning

Triangular road signs are used to alert drivers of upcoming roadway hazards.

Complete Part A as a whole class. Then complete Parts B–D in small groups.

A. What mathematical question can you ask about the two triangular signs? What information would you need to know to answer your question?

B. To answer your question, what strategy and tool would you use along with all the information you have? What answer do you get?

C. What can you conclude about the angles of each triangle? What can you conclude about the side lengths of each triangle?

D. How do you think your conclusion would apply to different triangles?

 Turn and Talk Think about what you already know about congruent triangles. What parts must be congruent? Can you think of various ways to check for congruency besides confirming all six corresponding parts of both triangles are congruent?

Build Understanding

Draw Triangles Given Two Angles and a Side

You have learned two ways to show that two figures are congruent.

- Show that the figure can be obtained from the other by a sequence of rigid motions.
- Show that all pairs of corresponding angles and corresponding sides are congruent.

However, there are special theorems you can apply to triangles to check for congruence without using these methods. These theorems depend on measures of certain sides and angles of the triangles. When applying these theorems, accurate measures must be used.

1 **A.** Use a ruler to draw a line segment 8 inches long. Label the endpoints *P* and *Q*.

B. Use a protractor to draw a 40° angle with segment *PQ* as one side and the vertex at point *P*.

C. Use a protractor to draw a 50° angle with segment *PQ* as one side and the vertex at point *Q*. Label the point where the two segments intersect as point *R*.

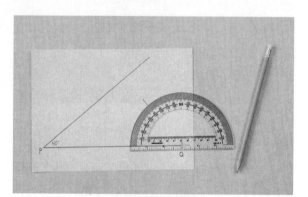

D. Find a partner and compare your triangles. Did you draw the same triangle? If not, is there a set of rigid transformations that maps your triangle to your partner's triangle? What can you conclude about the two triangles?

 Turn and Talk Based on your results, how can you decide whether two triangles are congruent without checking that all six pairs of corresponding sides and corresponding angles are congruent?

Justify ASA Triangle Congruence Using Transformations

In a triangle, the side connecting the vertices of two consecutive angles is called their **included side**. Given two side angle measures and the length of the included side, you can draw only one triangle. So, triangles with those measures are congruent.

Angle-Side-Angle (ASA) Triangle Congruence Theorem
If two angles and the included side of one triangle are congruent to two angles and the included side of another triangle, then the triangles are congruent. 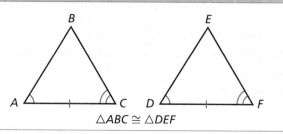 $\triangle ABC \cong \triangle DEF$

2 **A.** Use tracing paper to create two copies of your triangle from Task 1 as shown. Label the angles and side you know to be congruent. What can you do to show that these triangles are congruent?

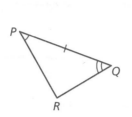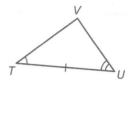

B. Start with a transformation that maps point P to point T. What transformation did you use? Is it a rigid transformation?

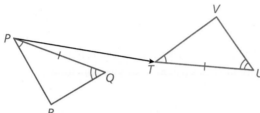

C. Now use a rotation to map point Q' to point U. What point is the center of rotation? What angle of rotation did you use?

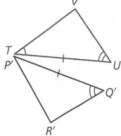

D. How do you know the image of point Q' is point U?

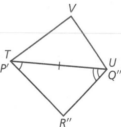

E. Finally, what rigid motion will map point R'' to point V?

F. Since $\angle P \cong \angle T$, $\angle Q \cong \angle U$, and $\overline{PQ} \cong \overline{TU}$, the image of $\overline{P'R''}$ lies on $\overline{TV}$ and the image of $\overline{Q''R''}$ lies along $\overline{VU}$. Point V is the only point that lies on both $\overline{TV}$ and $\overline{VU}$, and the image of point R'' must also lie on both $\overline{TV}$ and $\overline{VU}$. You can conclude that point V is the image of point R''. What else does this reasoning allow you to conclude? What is the sequence of rigid motions that maps $\triangle PQR$ to $\triangle TUV$?

 Turn and Talk Aliyah comments that this process works for any two triangles with two congruent angles, not necessarily only those with a congruent included side as well. Do you agree? Explain.

Module 8 • Lesson 8.1

Determine Whether or Not Triangles Are Congruent Using ASA Triangle Congruence

3 ▸ Use the ASA Triangle Congruence Theorem to determine whether the triangles are congruent.

Compare angle measures.

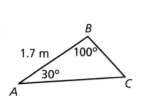
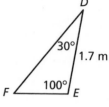

$m\angle A = m\angle D = 30°$

$m\angle B = m\angle E = 100°$

So, $\angle A \cong \angle D$ and $\angle B \cong \angle E$.

A. What other information is needed to prove that the triangles are congruent using the ASA Congruence Theorem?

B. Is $\overline{AB} \cong \overline{DE}$? How do you know?

C. Notice that the triangles have two pairs of congruent angles, and the included sides between each pair are also congruent. Can you conclude that $\triangle ABC \cong \triangle DEF$? Explain your reasoning.

Prove Triangles Are Congruent

You have been using two-column proofs to list statements and reasons to verify relationships and prove desired conclusions, such as proving triangles are congruent. You can also convey that reasoning in sentences to form a **paragraph proof**.

4 ▸ Write a paragraph proof that shows $\triangle XVY \cong \triangle WYV$.

Given: $\angle XVY \cong \angle WYV$ and $\angle XYV \cong \angle WVY$.

Prove: $\triangle XVY \cong \triangle WYV$

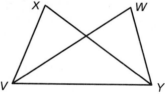

A. Draw the triangles as separate triangles and mark the given information on your diagram.

B. The proof is shown below. Why does the information about $\overline{VY}$, $\overline{VY} \cong \overline{VY}$, need to be included in the proof?

> In the diagram, two pairs of angles are congruent, $\angle XVY \cong \angle WYV$ and $\angle XYV \cong \angle WVY$. By the Reflexive Property of Congruence, the common side $\overline{VY}$ is congruent to itself, so $\overline{VY} \cong \overline{VY}$.
> So, $\triangle XVY \cong \triangle WYV$ by the ASA Triangle Congruence Theorem.
>
>

C. Suppose the two triangles don't share side $\overline{VY}$. What additional piece of information would you need to prove the triangles are congruent by the ASA Triangle Congruence Theorem?

D. Why is the order in a congruence statement so important? Is there ever a case where there is more than one possible order? Explain.

 Turn and Talk Explain how to turn the reasoning in the paragraph proof in Part B into a two-column format.

Step It Out

Apply the ASA Triangle Congruence Theorem

5 ▶ Kaylee is designing a kite to enter in a contest at the local park. Can she use the given information to conclude that the leading edges have the same length and the trailing edges have the same length?

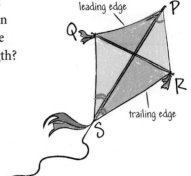

Determine the given information and what needs to be proved.

The diagram shows that $\angle QPS \cong \angle RPS$ and $\angle QSP \cong \angle RSP$.

It needs to be shown that the leading edges have the same length and the trailing edges have the same length.

Write a proof.

Given: $\angle QPS \cong \angle RPS$ and $\angle QSP \cong \angle RSP$.

Prove: $PQ = PR,\ QS = RS$

> **A.** How can you use triangle congruence to prove this statement?

Statements	Reasons
1. $\angle QPS \cong \angle RPS$	**1.** Given
2. $\angle QSP \cong \angle RSP$	**2.** Given
3. $\overline{PS} \cong \overline{PS}$	**3.** Reflexive Property of Congruence
4. $\triangle PQS \cong \triangle PRS$	**4.** ASA Triangle Congruence Theorem
5. $\overline{PQ} \cong \overline{PR},\ \overline{QS} \cong \overline{RS}$	**5.** Corresponding parts of congruent figures are congruent.
6. $PQ = PR,\ QS = RS$	**6.** Definition of congruent segments

B. In Statement 4, can a different congruence statement be written? If so, give an example.

C. In Statement 5, how do you know that $\overline{PQ}$ corresponds to $\overline{PR}$ and $\overline{QS}$ corresponds to $\overline{RS}$?

 Turn and Talk Could you still prove $\triangle PQS \cong \triangle PRS$ if the congruent angles are not marked in the figure, but instead you know $\overline{PS}$ bisects $\angle QPS$ and $\angle QSR$?

Check Understanding

1. What is one way you can determine if two triangles are congruent without checking all six pairs of corresponding angles and sides?

2. If two triangles have two pairs of congruent angles and a pair of congruent included sides, will a series of rigid transformations always map one triangle to the other? Explain.

3. Triangles *ABC* and *DEF* are being compared. In the triangles, m∠*A* = 45°, m∠*B* = 45°, m∠*D* = 45°, m∠*F* = 90°, and *AB* = *DE* = 1.5 cm. Are the two triangles congruent?

4. What must be true in order to use the ASA Triangle Congruence Theorem to prove that two triangles are congruent?

5. Two triangular pieces of artwork are hanging side by side. One is an equilateral triangle with a side length of 3 ft. The second is an equilateral triangle with a side length of 4 ft. Is it possible to prove the triangles are congruent using the ASA Triangle Congruence Theorem? Why or why not?

On Your Own

6. **(MP) Use Tools** Sara draws a triangle by first creating segment $\overline{AB}$ that is 2 in. long. She uses a protractor to draw a 20° angle with $\overline{AB}$ as one side and *B* as the vertex.

   Next, she draws a 50° angle with $\overline{AB}$ as one side and *A* as the vertex. Follow Sara's steps to create a triangle, labeling each vertex and angle. Is there a series of rigid transformations that would map your triangle to Sara's triangle? Justify your reasoning.

7. Describe a series of transformations that maps △*LMN* to △*XYZ*.

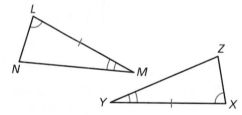

Determine if the triangles are congruent. Explain your reasoning.

8.

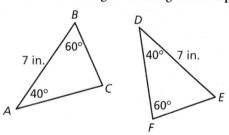

9.

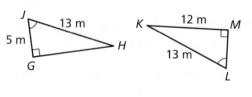

10.

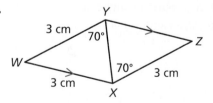

11.

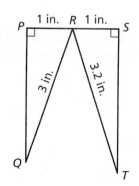

12. The figure shows figure *HJKL*. What additional information do you need to prove $\triangle HJL \cong \triangle KLJ$ by the ASA Triangle Congruence Theorem?

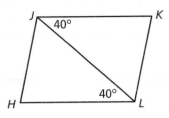

13. Copy and complete the proof.

Given: $\overline{WX}$ bisects $\angle YWZ$ and $\angle YXZ$.

Prove: $\triangle YWX \cong \triangle ZWX$

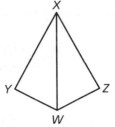

Statements	Reasons
1. $\overline{WX}$ bisects $\angle YWZ$ and ___?___.	1. Given
2. $\angle YWX \cong \angle ZWX$	2. Definition of angle bisector
3. $\angle YXW \cong \angle ZXW$	3. Definition of angle bisector
4. $\overline{XW} \cong \overline{XW}$	4. ___?___
5. ___?___	5. ___?___

In Problems 14–16, prove the triangles are congruent using either a two-column proof or a paragraph proof.

14. **Given:** $\overline{LM} \parallel \overline{PQ}$ and $\overline{LP} \parallel \overline{MQ}$.

Prove: $\triangle LMQ \cong \triangle QPL$

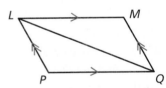

15. **Given:** $\overline{BD}$ is perpendicular to $\overline{AC}$, D is the midpoint of $\overline{AC}$, and $\angle A \cong \angle C$.

Prove: $\triangle ADB \cong \triangle CDB$

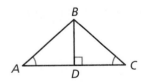

16. **Given:** $\overline{SQ}$ bisects $\overline{PT}$ and $\angle T \cong \angle P$.

Prove: $\triangle SRT \cong \triangle QRP$

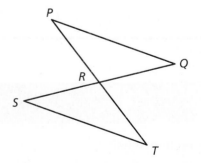

17. (MP) **Use Repeated Reasoning**
For what values of x and y is $\triangle ABD$ congruent to $\triangle ACD$?

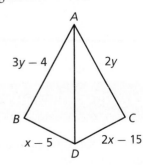

Determine if enough information is given to prove $\triangle LMN \cong \triangle LKN$ using the ASA Triangle Congruence Theorem. Explain your reasoning.

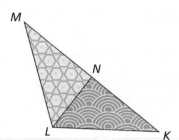

18. $\overline{LN} \perp \overline{MK}$

19. $\angle M \cong \angle K$

20. $\overline{LN}$ bisects $\overline{MK}$, $\overline{LN} \perp MK$

21. $\angle MNL \cong \angle KNL$, $\overline{LN}$ bisects $\angle MLK$

22. (MP) **Use Structure** Consider the diagram shown. Sometimes you can use triangle congruence to prove other relationships.

  A. Explain how you know the triangles are congruent by the ASA Congruence Theorem.

  B. Write a flow proof to show that $\overline{MN} \cong \overline{PQ}$.

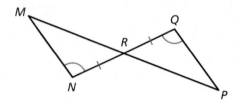

Spiral Review • Assessment Readiness

23. Which method can be used to prove two figures are congruent?

  (A) finding equivalent perimeters

  (B) rigid transformations

  (C) finding equivalent areas

  (D) counting vertices

24. If $\triangle PQR \cong \triangle XYZ$, which statements must be true? Select all that apply.

  (A) $\overline{RP} \cong \overline{ZX}$

  (B) $\angle QRP \cong \angle ZXY$

  (C) $\angle R \cong \angle Z$

  (D) $\overline{RP} \cong \overline{QR}$

  (E) $\overline{YX} \cong \overline{PQ}$

  (F) $\angle P \cong \angle Y$

25. Which function represents a rigid transformation?

  (A) $(x, y) \rightarrow (-x, -y)$

  (B) $(x, y) \rightarrow (2x, 2y)$

  (C) $(x, y) \rightarrow (x + y, y + x)$

  (D) $(x, y) \rightarrow \left(\dfrac{x}{2}, \dfrac{y}{2} \right)$

26. If quadrilateral $ABCD \cong$ quadrilateral $EFGH$, $m\angle BCD = (5x - 12)°$, and $m\angle FGH = (2x + 33)°$, what is the value of x?

  (A) 9

  (B) 11

  (C) 15

  (D) 45

Develop SAS Triangle Congruence

(I Can) use SAS congruence criteria to prove that two triangles are congruent.

Spark Your Learning

A triangular window must have precisely cut panes in order to fit together properly. In this window, the builder needed to cut all panes the same size and shape.

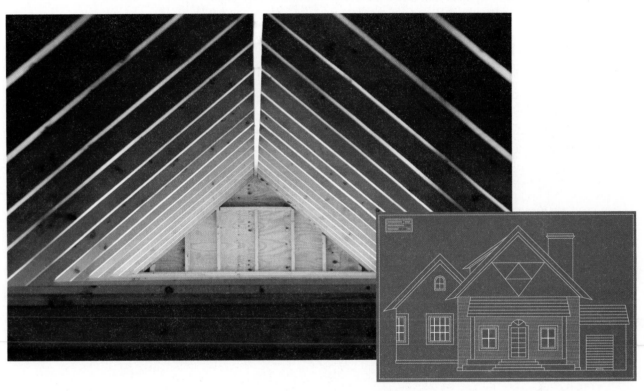

Complete Part A as a whole class. Then complete Parts B–D in small groups.

> **A.** What mathematical question can you ask about the triangles in the window? What kinds of information would you need to know to answer your question?
>
> **B.** State the facts you already know about triangle congruence.
>
> **C.** To answer your question, what strategy and tool would you use along with all the information you have? What answer do you get?
>
> **D.** How do you think your investigation and conclusion relates to other triangles?

 Turn and Talk Think about what you already know about triangle congruence. How can you combine what you already know with the information presented above to draw new conclusions about triangle congruence? Consider the given angle measures. How do you think that relates to your conclusion?

Build Understanding

Draw Triangles Given Two Sides and an Angle

In the previous lesson, you learned that two triangles are congruent if two pairs of corresponding angles and their included sides are congruent. The following steps explore a second way to check for triangle congruency.

 Use a ruler to draw a horizontal line. Use a protractor and a ruler to draw a 3-inch line segment that meets the horizontal line at a 45° angle.

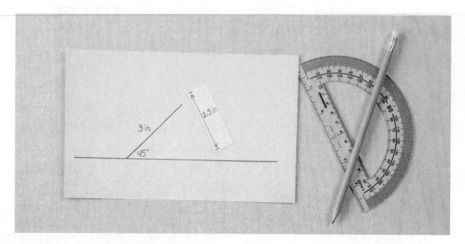

A. Use a thin strip of paper that is 2.5 inches long to complete the triangle. How many different triangles can you form? Draw each option you discover.

B. Now place the paper strip so that the angle between the 3-inch segment and 2.5-inch paper strip has a measure of 45°. With this arrangement, is there more than one way to complete the triangle? Why or why not?

 Turn and Talk If two triangles have two pairs of congruent corresponding sides and one pair of congruent corresponding angles, under what conditions can you conclude that the triangles must be congruent? Explain.

Justify SAS Triangle Congruence Using Transformations

Two sides of a triangle form an angle called the **included angle**. Given two side lengths and the measure of the included angle, you can draw only one triangle. So, two triangles with those measures are congruent.

Side-Angle-Side (SAS) Triangle Congruence Theorem
If two sides and the included angle of one triangle are congruent to two sides and the included angle of another triangle, then the triangles are congruent. 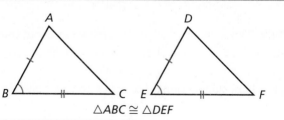

Because congruent figures can be mapped to one another using rigid transformations, we can justify SAS Triangle Congruence Theorem using transformations. Remember only rigid transformations such as reflections, translations, and rotations preserve the angle measurements and side lengths between the preimage and image.

2 **A.** Construct △LMN by copying ∠C, side $\overline{CA}$, and side $\overline{CB}$. How do the vertices of △LMN correspond to the vertices of △ABC?

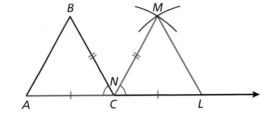

B. What transformation maps △LMN to △ABC? Is the transformation a rigid motion?

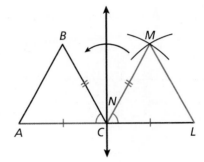

C. Can you conclude that △LMN ≅ △ABC? Explain your reasoning.

 Turn and Talk Trace △LMN and △ABC on a separate piece of paper. Cut out each triangle and place them on a desktop so $\overline{AC}$ and $\overline{LN}$ do not lie on the same line. Is it possible to use only one transformation to map △LMN to △ABC? If not, describe the sequence of transformations needed to map △LMN to △ABC.

Determine Whether or Not Triangles Are Congruent Using SAS Triangle Congruence

3 Use the SAS Triangle Congruence Theorem to determine whether the triangles are congruent.

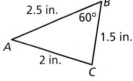

Compare side lengths.

$\overline{AB}$ corresponds to $\overline{DF}$ because $AB = DF = 2.5$ in.

$\overline{BC}$ corresponds to $\overline{FE}$ because $BC = FE = 1.5$ in.

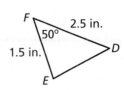

A. Why can you conclude that $\overline{AB} \cong \overline{DF}$ and $\overline{BC} \cong \overline{FE}$?

B. ∠B corresponds to ∠F because they are the included angles between the corresponding sides. Is ∠B ≅ ∠F?

C. Can the SAS Triangle Congruence Theorem be used to determine whether these triangles are congruent? Explain why or why not.

Step It Out

Apply SAS Triangle Congruence in a Real-World Context

You can use the SAS Triangle Congruence Theorem to prove triangles are congruent in real-world problems. You may need to determine if the given information meets the criteria for the SAS Triangle Congruence Theorem.

4 An engineer is building a prototype for a clothing rack. The cross bar is positioned so that $\overline{NP} \cong \overline{QP}$ along the congruent sides $\overline{MP}$ and $\overline{RP}$. Prove that the slanted supports $\overline{MQ}$ and $\overline{RN}$ are congruent.

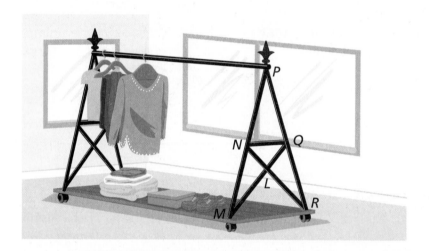

Collect the given information.

You know $\overline{MP} \cong \overline{RP}$ and $\overline{NP} \cong \overline{QP}$.

A. Why should the SAS Triangle Congruence Theorem be used to show congruent triangles?

Prove the unknown information.

The given information tells you about two sides of $\triangle MPQ$ and $\triangle RPN$, specifically that two sets of corresponding sides are congruent.

In both triangles, the included angle between those sides is $\angle P$. By the Reflexive Property of Congruence, $\angle P \cong \angle P$.

B. What is a congruence statement for the two triangles?

The triangles are congruent by the SAS Triangle Congruence Theorem.

Because all corresponding parts of congruent figures are congruent, $\overline{MQ} \cong \overline{RN}$.

C. What other information do you know about the triangles now that you know they are congruent?

 Turn and Talk Why is the ASA Triangle Congruence Theorem not the best choice for this problem?

Check Understanding

1. Kim draws a triangle with one 4 mm side, one 6 mm side, and a 25° included angle between those sides. If you follow the same steps as Kim to draw a triangle, is your triangle congruent to Kim's triangle? Explain.

2. Two triangles have two pairs of congruent sides and a congruent pair of included angles. Can you map one triangle to the other?

3. Explain the differences between the situations in which you would use the SAS Triangle Congruence Theorem versus the ASA Triangle Congruence Theorem.

4. $\overline{QS}$ is perpendicular to $\overline{RP}$, and $\overline{QS}$ is an angle bisector of $\angle PQR$. Can you prove $\triangle PQS \cong \triangle RQS$? Justify your answer.

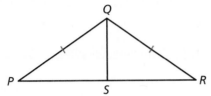

On Your Own

Determine if the triangles are congruent, not congruent, or if there is not enough information to determine. Explain your reasoning.

5.

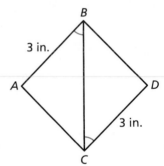

6.

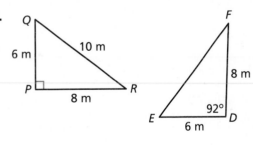

7.

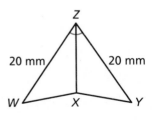

8.

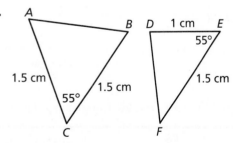

9. Two triangular road signs are mounted on the same post. They each have two pairs of 4-inch sides, and both have an included angle of 30°. Is it possible to prove the triangles are congruent? Explain.

10. **Open Ended** Two congruent triangles have one side that is twice the length of a second side, and a third side that is equal in length to one of the other sides. One angle is not congruent to the other two. Draw two congruent triangles that meet the description.

11. (MP) **Critique Reasoning** Zach creates the following proof to show △ACD is congruent to △ECB. Where did he make a mistake? Explain and correct his error.

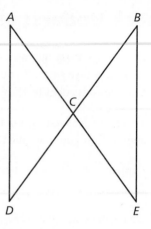

Given: $\overline{AD} \parallel \overline{BE}$ and $\overline{DB}$ bisects $\overline{AE}$.

Prove: △ACD ≅ △ECB

Statements	Reasons
1. $\overline{AD} \parallel \overline{BE}$	1. Given
2. $\overline{DB}$ bisects $\overline{AE}$.	2. Given
3. $\overline{AC} \cong \overline{CE}$	3. Definition of a bisector
4. ∠ACD ≅ ∠ECB	4. Vertical Angles Theorem
5. △ACD ≅ △ECB	5. ASA Triangle Congruence Theorem

12. In a regular polygon, all the sides have the same length and all the angles have the same measure. Copy and complete the proof.

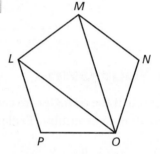

Given: Polygon *LMNOP* is a regular pentagon.

Prove: $\overline{LO} \cong \overline{MO}$

Statements	Reasons
1. *LMNOP* is a regular pentagon.	1. ___?___
2. *MN = LP, NO = PO*	2. Definition of regular polygon
3. $\overline{MN} \cong \overline{LP}, \overline{NO} \cong \overline{PO}$	3. Definition of congruence
4. ___?___	4. Definition of regular polygon
5. ∠P ≅ ∠N	5. ___?___
6. △LPO ≅ △MNO	6. ___?___
7. ___?___	7. Corresponding parts of congruent figures are congruent.

Write each proof using the SAS Triangle Congruence Theorem.

13. Given: $\overline{PQ} \parallel \overline{RS}, PQ = RS$

Prove: △PQS ≅ △RSQ

14. Given: $\overline{AC} \cong \overline{DE}, \overline{BC} \cong \overline{BD},$ ∠BCD ≅ ∠BDC

Prove: △ABC ≅ △EBD

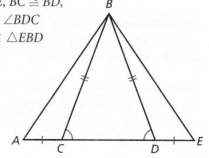

Find the value of the variable that results in congruent triangles.

15.

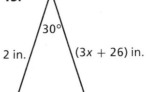

2 in.   30°   (3x + 26) in.   2 in.   (x + 10) in.   30°

16.

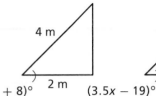

4 m   4 m

(2x + 8)°   2 m   (3.5x − 19)°   2 m

17. (MP) **Critique Reasoning** Ava claims she can use the SAS Congruence Theorem to prove two right triangles are congruent. Both triangles contain a 40° angle and a side that is 9 inches long. Is Ava correct? Is there a different theorem she could use if not? Justify your answer.

18. Refer to the figure to answer each question.

A. Explain why the triangles are congruent using any triangle congruence theorem.

B. Describe a sequence of transformations that maps one triangle to the other.

C. Write a congruence statement to relate the two triangles.

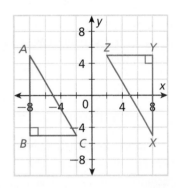

19. For a class project, students are sewing a quilt made of triangular pieces. Each piece must be congruent for the quilt pattern to fit together. To check the pattern pieces, a student carefully measures two different triangles. Triangle 1 has a longest side that is twice as long as the shortest side, with an included angle of 20°. Triangle 2 has an 8-inch side, a 4-inch side, and an included angle of 20°. Are the two triangles congruent? If not, what additional information would the student need to record to prove the triangles are congruent?

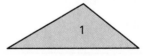

1

2

20. Anna and Sharon both construct a triangle. Anna begins by drawing a segment with a length of 3 inches. Starting from one vertex, she draws another segment with a length of 5 inches so that the two segments have an included angle of 35°. Sharon constructs her triangle by drawing a segment with a length of 5 inches, measuring a 35° angle, and drawing a ray from one vertex. Then she measures and terminates the ray at 3 inches. Do Anna and Sharon create congruent triangles? Explain.

21. (MP) **Construct Arguments** Explain in your own words why there is no SSA Triangle Congruence Theorem.

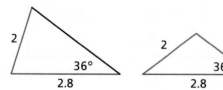

22. Explain what additional information you could use to prove two triangles are congruent when dealing with the ambiguous SSA case.

23. Assume that △ABC is an isosceles triangle with AB = AC. Use the SAS Triangle Congruence Theorem to show that the angle bisector of ∠A separates △ABC into two congruent triangles.

24. If both diagonals of the rectangle shown are the same length and bisect each other, explain how you know that $\overline{FG} \cong \overline{JH}$ and $\overline{FJ} \cong \overline{GH}$.

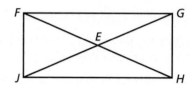

Spiral Review • Assessment Readiness

25. Triangle ABC is congruent to triangle PQR, where AB = 3.5 cm and BC = 4.2 cm. The measure of the included angle is 50°. The measure of ∠Q is $(3x - 10)°$. What is the value of x?

(A) 20   (C) 60

(B) 50   (D) 130

26. Is △LMN ≅ △XMY?

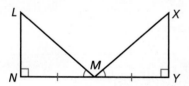

(A) Yes, all right triangles are congruent.

(B) Yes, by ASA Triangle Congruence.

(C) No, all three angles are not congruent.

(D) No, all three sides are not congruent.

27. In △DEF, $\overline{DG}$ bisects $\overline{EF}$ and $\overline{DG} \perp \overline{EF}$. What else do you know about the triangle?

(A) △DEF is scalene.   (C) $DE = 2 \cdot EF$

(B) DE = DF   (D) m∠EDF = 90°

28. A figure is transformed using the following coordinate rule. Which movements describe the transformations? Select all that apply.

$(x, y) \rightarrow (x + 2, -(y - 2))$

(A) translation two units to the left

(B) translation two units to the right

(C) translation two units up

(D) translation two units down

(E) reflection over the x-axis

(F) reflection over the y-axis

I'm in a Learning Mindset!

Did I administer feedback respectfully? How did I address the idea that was presented instead of the person who voiced the idea?

Develop SSS Triangle Congruence

(I Can) use SSS congruence criteria to prove that two triangles are congruent.

Spark Your Learning

A welder is making a wall sculpture of triangles made using standard lengths of metal pieces.

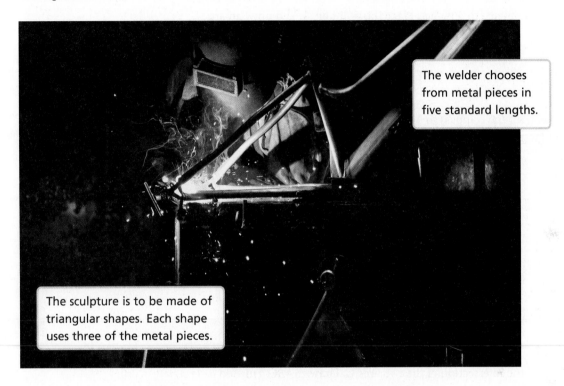

The welder chooses from metal pieces in five standard lengths.

The sculpture is to be made of triangular shapes. Each shape uses three of the metal pieces.

Complete Part A as a whole class. Then complete Parts B–D in small groups.

A. Suppose the welder uses the same three lengths for more than one triangle. What is a mathematical question you can ask about the situation?

B. Use tools and the additional information your teacher gives you to cut out strips of paper to match the metal pieces the welder uses. Build a triangle with those metal-piece lengths. Compare with your classmates' triangles. Does everyone's triangle look the same or different? Does this prove the answer to your question?

C. How does the construction of your triangle compare and contrast with the constructions of triangles from the previous lessons?

D. What do you know about congruent triangles and transformations you could use to check your theory?

 Turn and Talk Could you determine if two triangles are congruent knowing only two side lengths? Support your answer.

©Jan Sochor/Alamy

Build Understanding

Draw Triangles Given Three Side Lengths

Remember that two triangles are congruent only if a series of rigid transformations maps one triangle onto the other.

 A. Use a ruler to draw a horizontal line that is 2 inches long. Label the endpoints *A* and *B*.

B. Set a compass to 3 inches. Place the point on *A*, and draw an arc above the horizontal line.

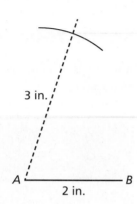

C. Next, set the compass to 4 inches. Place the point on *B*, and draw an arc that it intersects the first arc.

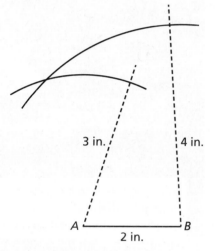

D. Label the intersection of the two arcs *C*. Draw △*ABC*. How do you know that the result is a triangle with side lengths of 2, 3, and 4 inches?

E. Draw a second horizontal 2 inch segment on your paper. Repeat steps B–D by drawing the arcs below the line. Is the resulting triangle congruent to the triangle you drew in part D?

F. Create a second triangle with side lengths 2, 3, and 4 inches. This time, begin with the 4-inch segment as the horizontal line. What is the relationship between the triangles? How do you know?

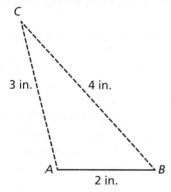

 Turn and Talk

- Do you expect that you would get another congruent triangle if you started the construction with the 3-inch side? Explain.
- What can you say about two triangles with 3 pairs of congruent sides if you do not know anything about the angles?

Justify and Use SSS Triangle Congruence

You can use three pairs of congruent sides to determine that two triangles are congruent.

Side-Side-Side (SSS) Triangle Congruence Theorem

If three sides of a triangle are congruent to three sides of another triangle, then the triangles are congruent.

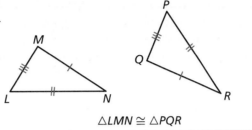

$\triangle LMN \cong \triangle PQR$

---

2 ▶ Use transformations to prove the SSS Triangle Congruence Theorem.

Let triangles LMN and PQR have congruent sides.

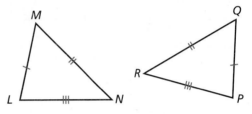

A. Translate $\triangle PQR$ along $\overrightarrow{PL}$ so that P lies on L. Then rotate $\triangle P'Q'R'$ counterclockwise about L with a rotation angle of $\angle Q'P'M$.

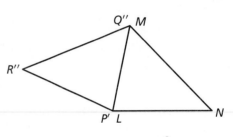

B. Reflect $\triangle P'Q''R''$ across $\overline{LM}$. Does this map R'' to N? Why or why not? Did the series of transformations prove the two triangles are congruent?

3 ▶ In the triangles shown, you know that $\overline{AB} \perp \overline{BC}$ and $\overline{DE} \perp \overline{EF}$.

A. Use the Pythagorean Theorem to find the lengths BC and DF. What allows you to use the Pythagorean Theorem to find these lengths?

B. Complete the statement: Three pairs of corresponding sides are congruent, so by the SSS Triangle Congruence Theorem, _____?_____.

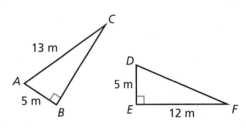

C. Why was the SSS Triangle Congruence Theorem used in this case? Could one of the other congruence theorems been applied instead?

 Turn and Talk The side lengths of one triangle are 5 inches, 3 inches, and 7 inches. The side lengths of another triangle are 5 cm, 3 cm, and 7 cm. Are the two triangles congruent?

Step It Out

Apply SSS Triangle Congruence in a Real-World Context

You can use the SSS Triangle Congruence Theorem to prove triangles are congruent in real-world problems.

4 ▶ Micah designs a pair of triangular beaded earrings for an art project. The numbers of beads on each side of the triangles are given. For what value of x can you use the SSS Triangle Congruence Theorem to prove the triangles are congruent?

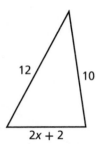 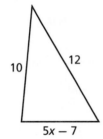 

Choose a strategy.
Each triangle has one side with length 10 cm and one side with length 12 cm. So two pairs of corresponding sides are congruent. In order for the triangles to be congruent by the SSS Triangle Congruence Theorem, the third pair of corresponding sides must also be congruent.

> **A.** Why choose the SSS Triangle Congruence Theorem to prove the triangles are congruent?

Write an equation.
If the third side of both triangles must be congruent, we can write an equation that shows the lengths of both sides are equal.

$$5x - 7 = 2x + 2$$

> **B.** Why are you able to write this equation?

Solve the equation.
Solve the equation to determine the value of x.

$$5x - 7 = 2x + 2$$

$$3x - 7 = 2$$

$$3x = 9$$

> **C.** What is the unknown side length in each triangle?

$$x = 3$$

Answer the question.
You can use the SSS Triangle Congruence Theorem to prove the two triangles are congruent when the value of x is 3.

 Turn and Talk What additional information would you have needed to prove the triangles are congruent by the SAS Triangle Congruence Theorem?

Check Understanding

1. Two triangles have side lengths of 3 inches, 4 inches, and 5 inches. Is it possible to draw two different triangles that meet this criteria? Justify your answer.

2. Describe a set of transformations that maps △ABC to △DEF.

3. What additional information is needed to use the SSS Triangle Congruence Theorem to provethat the triangles are congruent?

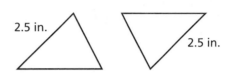

4. Triangles PQR and XYZ are equilateral triangles. The sides of △PQR are 5 inches long. One side of △XYZ is $(2x - 3)$ inches. What value of x makes the triangles congruent?

On Your Own

Use a compass and a ruler to construct two triangles with the given side lengths, and determine if they are congruent. Label each side.

5. 2 in., 3.5 in., 5 in.

6. 9.5 cm, 6 cm, 12 cm

In Problems 7–12, determine whether the triangles are *congruent, not congruent,* or if there is *not enough information.* Which triangle congruence theorem can be used? Explain your reasoning.

7.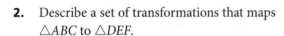

8.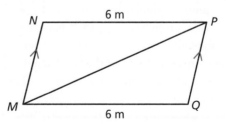

9.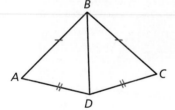

10.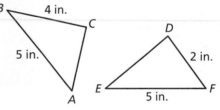

11.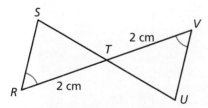

12.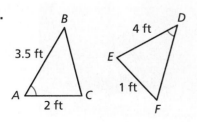

Identify a series of rigid transformations that maps △ABC onto △DEF.

13.

14.

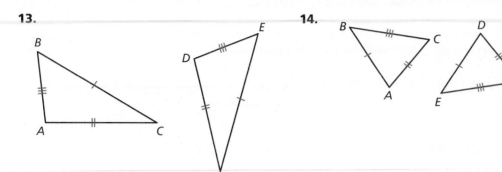

Find the values of *x* and *y* for which △ABC and △XYZ are congruent. Some problems may have more than one solution.

15. △ABC: side lengths of 5, 8, and *x*

△XYZ: side lengths of 5, 2*x*, and 4

16. △ABC: side lengths of 10, 10, and 2*x* − 1

△XYZ: side lengths of 10, 10, and 4*x* − 4

17. △ABC: side lengths of 2, *x* + 3, and *y* − 3

△XYZ: side lengths of 3*x* − 6, 6, and 2

18. △ABC: side lengths of 16, 20, and 4*x* − 8

△XYZ: side lengths of 20, 12, and 30 − 2*y*

19. △ABC: side lengths of 8, 6*y*, and *x*

△XYZ: side lengths of 18, 12, and 8

20. △ABC: side lengths of 3, *x* + *y*, and *x*

△XYZ: side lengths of 2, 3, and 3*x* − *y*

21. The Great Pyraminds of Giza are a set of ancient Egyptian structures large enough to be visible from space. Can you prove the front faces of the two pyramids are congruent triangles? Why or why not?

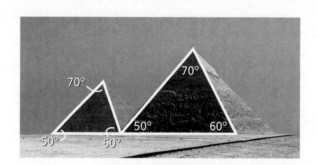

22. Sam is designing triangular metal braces to use while building a pergola for a patio. What value of the variables allows you to use the SSS Triangle Congruence Theorem to prove the two triangles are congruent? The sides using the same variable are corresponding.

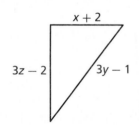

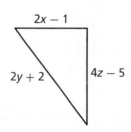

23. (MP) **Use Tools** Draw a 2-inch line segment labeled $\overline{DE}$ on your paper. Use a ruler and a compass to construct an equilateral triangle with $\overline{DE}$ as one of the sides. Then explain your construction.

24. Complete the proof.

Given: $\overline{AC} \cong \overline{AB}$, $\overline{AD} \cong \overline{AE}$, $\overline{BD} \cong \overline{CE}$

Prove: $\triangle BCD \cong \triangle CBE$

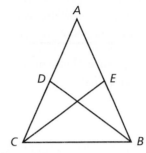

Statements	Reasons
1. $\overline{AC} \cong \overline{AB}$, $\overline{AD} \cong \overline{AE}$	1. Given
2. $AC = AB$, $AD = AE$	2. Definition of congruence
3. $AC = AD + DC$, $AB = AE + EB$	3. ___?___
4. $AD + DC = AE + EB$	4. ___?___ Property of Equality
5. $DC = EB$	5. ___?___ Property of Equality
6. ___?___	6. Definition of congruence
7. ___?___	7. Given
8. $\overline{BC} \cong \overline{CB}$	8. Reflexive Property of Congruence
9. $\triangle BCD \cong \triangle CBE$	9. SSS Triangle Congruence Theorem

25. STEM Any geostationary satellite orbits approximately 35,700 km above the surface of Earth at the equator and travels at the same rate as Earth's spin. Because of this, it will appear to be fixed in one spot in the sky to a viewer on the ground. Usually this type of satellite is used for communications, due to the constant signal available to the locations within the transmission range. Using the given information and the radius r of Earth, show that the distance the signal travels in each direction is congruent.

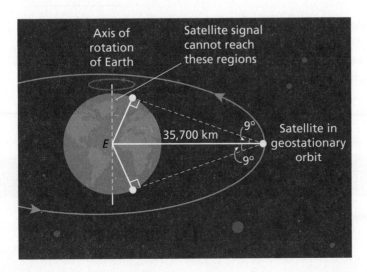

26. (MP) **Attend to Precision** Draw a 1.5-inch diameter circle with center *O*. Use a ruler and compass to construct a regular hexagon. Explain your construction.

27. (MP) **Critique Reasoning** Kevin draws two right triangles with angles of 45°, 45°, and 90°. He then creates a proof to show the two triangles are congruent using AAA criteria. Can you recreate the proof? Show the proof or describe why not.

28. Using the SSS Triangle Congruence Theorem and the Distance Formula, show that $\triangle PQR \cong \triangle XYZ$.

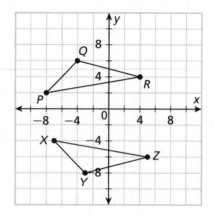

Spiral Review • Assessment Readiness

29. Which set of criteria cannot be used to prove any two non-right triangles are congruent?

   (A) Side-Angle-Side

   (B) Angle-Side-Angle

   (C) Side-Side-Angle

   (D) Side-Side-Side

30. Two right triangles each have a side that is 3 inches long and a hypotenuse that is 5 inches long. Can you prove the triangles are congruent?

   (A) Yes, all right triangles are congruent.

   (B) Yes, the Pythagorean theorem shows the pair of other legs are congruent.

   (C) No, the unknown leg could be any length.

   (D) No, not enough information is given to prove congruency.

31. Match the statement with the correct reason to show that $\triangle ABC \cong \triangle DCB$.

   A. $\overline{AC} \cong \overline{BD}$

   B. $\overline{AB} \cong \overline{CD}$

   C. $\angle ABC \cong \angle DCB$

   D. $\triangle ABC \cong \triangle DCB$

   1. Given
   2. SAS Triangle Congruence Theorem
   3. Alternate Interior Angles Theorem
   4. Given

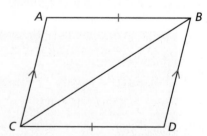

 I'm in a Learning Mindset!

How did I assert my own viewpoints and opinions when working with a group?

Develop AAS and HL Triangle Congruence

(I Can) use AAS and HL congruence criteria to determine if triangles are congruent.

Spark Your Learning

As part of a design challenge, a group is planning to paint a pattern of triangles on the wall.

Complete Part A as a whole class. Then complete Parts B–D in small groups.

A. What is a mathematical question you can ask about the image? What additional information would you need to answer your question?

B. What methods do you know to check for triangle congruence? Consider theorems and modeling.

C. To answer your question, what strategy and tool would you use along with all the information you have? What answer do you get?

D. Does your answer make sense in the context of the problem? Explain your reasoning.

Turn and Talk How does the information given in this case compare to the congruence criteria cases you have studied so far?

Build Understanding

Prove the AAS Triangle Congruence Theorem

The Angle-Angle-Side Triangle Congruence Theorem describes another set of three congruent corresponding pairs that you can use to prove two triangles are congruent.

> ### Angle-Angle-Side (AAS) Triangle Congruence Theorem
> If two angles and a non-included side of one triangle are congruent to the corresponding angles and non-included side of another triangle, then the triangles are congruent.

1 ▶ **A.** Look at the Given and Prove statements. What theorems do you know that can be used to prove the AAS Triangle Congruence Theorem?

Given: $\angle A \cong \angle X$, $\angle B \cong \angle Y$, $\overline{AC} \cong \overline{XZ}$

Prove: $\triangle ABC \cong \triangle XYZ$

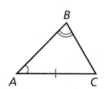 

Statements	Reasons
1. $\angle A \cong \angle X$ and $\angle B \cong \angle Y$	1. Given
2. $\overline{AC} \cong \overline{XZ}$	2. Given
3. $\angle C \cong \angle Z$	3. Third Angles Theorem
4. $\triangle ABC \cong \triangle XYZ$	4. ASA Triangle Congruence Theorem

B. Why is the final step proving the triangles are congruent using the ASA Triangle Congruence Theorem and not the AAS Triangle Congruence Theorem?

C. What previous information allows you to use the Third Angles Theorem in Line 2? What previous information allows you to use the ASA Triangle Congruence Theorem in Line 3?

D. Why doesn't the final step show the triangles are congruent by AAA criteria?

Turn and Talk
- What is another method you could use to prove the AAS Triangle Congruence Theorem?
- How is the proof of this theorem related to the proofs of the other congruence criteria theorems?

Explore SSA Triangle Congruence

The table shows a summary of the triangle congruence theorems you have studied.

Some Methods for Proving Triangles are Congruent		
Theorem	**Statement**	**Example**
ASA Triangle Congruence Theorem	If two angles and the included side of one triangle are congruent to two angles and the included side of another triangle, then the triangles are congruent.	
SAS Triangle Congruence Theorem	If two sides and the included angle of one triangle are congruent to two sides and the included angle of another triangle, then the triangles are congruent.	
SSS Triangle Congruence Theorem	If three sides of a triangle are congruent to three sides of another triangle, then the triangles are congruent.	
AAS Triangle Congruence Theorem	If two angles and a non-included side of one triangle are congruent to the corresponding angles and non-included side of another triangle, then the triangles are congruent.	

2 ▷ Another possible set of three congruent corresponding parts that might be used to prove triangles are congruent are adjacent sides and a non-included angle. Is there a Side-Side-Angle Triangle Congruence Theorem?

A. Draw a horizontal line. Use a ruler and protractor to draw a 3-inch line segment that meets your horizontal line at a 30° angle. Label the point where they meet as point *A* and the other endpoint as *B*.

B. Set a compass for 2 inches, and place the point of the compass on *B*. Draw an arc with a radius of 2 inches from point *B* through the horizontal line.

C. Label the points where it meets the horizontal line as point *C*, and draw a segment from *B* to each point to complete the triangles. Why is it possible to create more than one triangle?

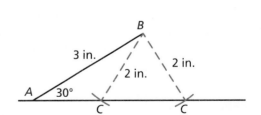

D. This construction creates two possible triangles. Can you use Side-Side-Angle criteria to prove two triangles are congruent? Why or why not?

 Turn and Talk How many triangles can you draw that have sides of length 2 inches and 3 inches and a non-included angle of 90°? Explain.

Step It Out

Prove the HL Triangle Congruence Theorem

In Task 2, you showed that Side-Side-Angle criteria are not sufficient to prove triangle congruence. Right triangles are a special case in which you can prove two right triangles are congruent using the hypotenuse and a leg of the triangle.

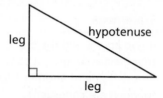

Hypotenuse-Leg (HL) Triangle Congruence Theorem

If the hypotenuse and a leg of a right triangle are congruent to the hypotenuse and a leg of another right triangle, then the right triangles are congruent.

3 ▸ Prove the HL Triangle Congruence Theorem.

Given: $\angle C$ and $\angle Z$ are right angles.
$\overline{AB} \cong \overline{XY}$ and $\overline{AC} \cong \overline{XZ}$.

Prove: $\triangle ABC \cong \triangle XYZ$

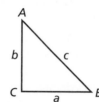 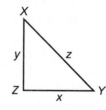

Since $\overline{AB} \cong \overline{XY}$, you know that $c = z$ and $c^2 = z^2$.

Since $\overline{AC} \cong \overline{XZ}$, you know that $b = y$ and $b^2 = y^2$.

> **A.** Why can you use the Pythagorean Theorem?

The triangles are right triangles, so $a^2 + b^2 = c^2$ and $x^2 + y^2 = z^2$.

$$c^2 = z^2$$
$$a^2 + b^2 = x^2 + y^2$$
$$a^2 + b^2 = x^2 + b^2$$
$$a^2 = x^2$$
$$a = x$$

> **B.** Why can you write this equation? What allows you to make the substitution in the second line?

All three pairs of corresponding sides are congruent, so by the SSS Triangle Congruence Theorem, $\triangle ABC \cong \triangle XYZ$.

> **C.** Why can't you use the HL Triangle Congruence Theorem in the proof?

 Turn and Talk

- What parts of the proof would not be valid if the triangles were not right triangles?
- Explain how you could use the SAS Triangle Congruence Theorem instead of the SSS Triangle Congruence Theorem in the proof.

Apply AAS and HL Triangle Congruence

4 ▶ Shar is planning her running route and needs to know if two triangular blocks are congruent. Determine whether the two blocks are congruent.

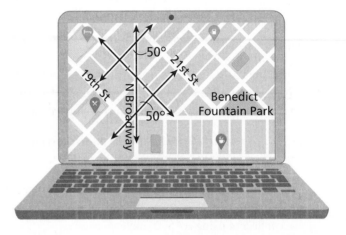

Examine the given information.
Notice the two blocks have corresponding 50° angles and congruent vertical angles.

> **A.** Explain why the intersection contains congruent angles.

Determine a possible congruence theorem.
There are two pairs of congruent angles, so consider AAS and ASA. The positions of the sides marked congruent mean that you should use the AAS Triangle Congruence Theorem.

> **B.** How does the position of the sides marked congruent tell you which theorem to use?

Answer the question.
The blocks have two pairs of corresponding congruent angles and a pair of corresponding congruent sides that are not included between the angles. The blocks are congruent by the AAS Triangle Congruence Theorem.

5 ▶ Shar is considering another possible running route. Are the routes shown congruent?

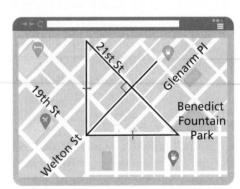

Examine the given information.
By the given information, we know the intersection of Welton Street and 21st Street creates two right angles.

> **A.** How do you know the measure of these angles?

Determine possible congruent sides.
The hypotenuses of the triangles are congruent.

> **B.** Why are these sides hypotenuses?

C. What side is shared by the two triangles? Is this shared side congruent?

Answer the question.
The triangles are congruent by the HL Triangle Congruence Theorem.

> **D.** What three congruent pairs are used to make this conclusion?

 Turn and Talk How are the HL criteria and the SSS criteria related?

Check Understanding

1. Compare the AAS Triangle Congruence Theorem to the ASA Triangle Congruence Theorem.

2. A triangle has side lengths of 2 inches and 3 inches and a non-included angle of 20° adjacent to the 3-inch side. Use a ruler and a protractor to draw the triangle or triangles that meet these criteria. Justify your answer.

3. In your own words, explain why the SSA criteria does prove congruence when the angle used in the theorem is a right angle.

4. What additional information must be known to prove the triangles are congruent using AAS Triangle Congruence?

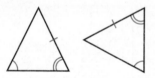

5. Can you prove that the two triangles are congruent? If so, explain how.

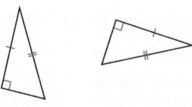

On Your Own

Is enough information given to prove the two triangles are congruent? If they are congruent, explain what triangle congruence criteria should be used.

6.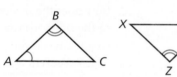

7.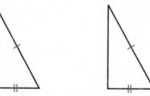

8.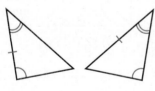

9.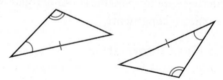

10.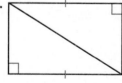

11.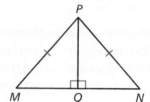

What value of x will make each pair of triangles congruent? Explain.

12.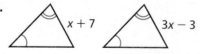
$x + 7$ $3x - 3$

13.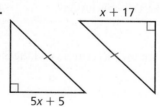
$x + 17$

$5x + 5$

Write a two-column proof to show the triangles are congruent.

14. **Given:** $\overline{JK} \parallel \overline{MN}$, and $\overline{JN}$ bisects $\overline{KM}$.

   Prove: $\triangle JKL \cong \triangle NML$

15. **Given:** $\angle A \cong \angle C$, and $\overline{DB}$ bisects $\angle ABC$.

   Prove: $\triangle ABD \cong \triangle CBD$

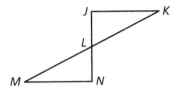

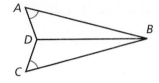

16. **Given:** $\overline{PT} \perp \overline{SQ}$, $\overline{ST} \cong \overline{PQ}$, and R is the midpoint of $\overline{PT}$.

   Prove: $\triangle PQR \cong \triangle TSR$

17. **Given:** $\angle E$ and $\angle C$ are right angles. $\overline{AE} \cong \overline{BC}$

   Prove: $\triangle ABC \cong \triangle BAE$

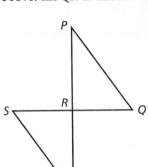

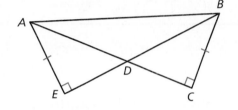

18. **Open Ended** Write a proof problem that would use the AAS Triangle Congruence Theorem. Provide a diagram with labels and list the Given and Prove statements. Explain how the AAS Theorem would be used in the proof.

19. An inspector needs to find the dimensions of a roof truss. The length of the bottom chord is 2.5 times the height of the truss. The length of the top chord is 21 ft, which includes a 5 ft overhang. The bottom chord and the king post are perpendicular. What are the lengths of the bottom chord and the king post? Round your final answers to the nearest foot.

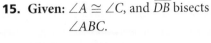

20. **(MP) Construct Arguments** Maya claims that if two right triangles share a hypotenuse, they must be congruent. Is Maya correct? Explain.

21. John is designing the base for a new sculpture to be placed in a city plaza. To determine how much material is needed for the border of the base, John needs to approximate the perimeter of the sculpture to plan its placement in the park. The figure represents the overhead view of the sculpture. Find the perimeter of the base for the new sculpture. Explain your steps.

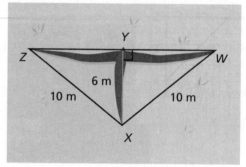

Spiral Review • Assessment Readiness

22. Decide whether this statement is true: Two triangles with two pairs of corresponding congruent angles and any one pair of corresponding congruent sides, included or not, are congruent.

Ⓐ always true
Ⓒ never true

Ⓑ sometimes true
Ⓓ can not be determined

23. The angles used to prove congruency in the SAS Triangle Congruence Theorem must be ___?___.

Ⓐ right angles

Ⓑ opposite a side being used in the theorem

Ⓒ acute angles

Ⓓ included angles

24. Which set of congruent parts does not guarantee congruence of triangles?

Ⓐ SSS

Ⓑ AAA

Ⓒ SAS

Ⓓ ASA

25. An equilateral triangle contains an interior angle of 60°. What is the sum of all three angles within the triangle?

Ⓐ 60°
Ⓒ 180°

Ⓑ 120°
Ⓓ 360°

 I'm in a Learning Mindset!

Did I communicate effectively? Did I respond non-defensively when questions were asked about the ideas I communicated?

ASA and AAS Triangle Congruence

Any two triangles with two pairs of congruent angles and a congruent included side are congruent by the Angle-Side-Angle (ASA) Triangle Congruence Theorem.

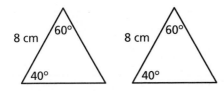

We also know by the Third Angles Theorem, that the missing angles are also congruent, so we could also say they are congruent by the Angle-Angle-Side (AAS) Triangle Congruence Theorem.

SAS Triangle Congruence

Any two triangles with two pairs of congruent sides and a congruent included angle are congruent by the Side-Angle-Side (SAS) Triangle Congruence Theorem.

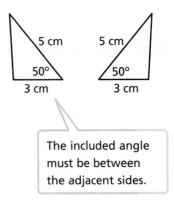

The included angle must be between the adjacent sides.

SSS Triangle Congruence

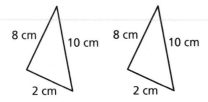

Only one possible triangle can be created when given all three side lengths. Therefore, any two triangles with three pairs of congruent sides must be congruent by the Side-Side-Side (SSS) Triangle Congruence Theorem.

HL Triangle Congruence

In right triangles, the third side is determined by the Pythagorean Theorem. Thus, any two right triangles with a congruent hypotenuse and leg are congruent by SSS or SAS.

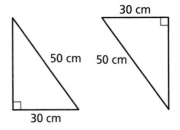

The two right triangles above have a congruent hypotenuse and a congruent leg. Therefore, they are congruent by the Hypotenuse-Leg (HL) Triangle Congruence Theorem.

Vocabulary

Choose the correct term from the box to complete each sentence.

1. When a transversal crosses two parallel lines, angles in the same position in each intersection are called __?__ and are congruent.

2. A(n) __?__ is formed by two adjacent sides of a triangle.

3. All corresponding parts of __?__ are congruent.

4. A(n) __?__ connects two consecutive angles in a triangle.

5. Two sides in the same position of two congruent triangles are called __?__.

Concepts and Skills

6. List all triangle congruence theorems and give an example of each.

7. What theorem relates the ASA and AAS triangle congruence theorems?

8. The HL Congruence Theorem is a specific case of what other theorem? Explain your reasoning.

9. (MP) **Use Tools** Explain why there is no Side-Side-Angle Triangle Congruence Theorem. State what strategy and tool you will use to answer the question, explain your choice, and then find the answer.

Determine the value of x that will make each pair of triangles congruent.

10.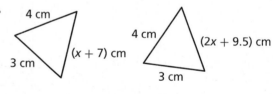

11.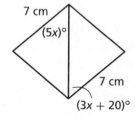

Write a proof to prove that the triangles in each pair are congruent.

12.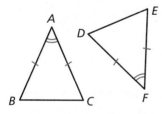

13.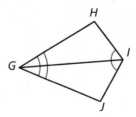

14.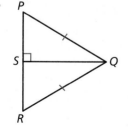

15.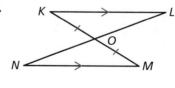

Relationships Within Triangles

Environmental Chemist

STEM
POWERING INGENUITY

Environmental chemists use their chemistry knowledge to study the impact of chemicals introduced into the land, water, and air. They work to develop and advocate for regulations that protect our natural resources. Harmful algal blooms (HABs) are becoming more prevalent in lakes worldwide, releasing harmful toxins that affect drinking water and recreational activities.

STEM Task

One factor that promotes undesired HAB growth is excess phosphorus. A mild HAB occurs at a biomass of 783. The goal for the Maumee River load is 40% of the current load, 2315. Is this a reasonable goal? Explain your reasoning.

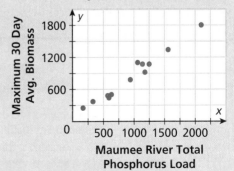

Western Lake Erie-Cyanobacteria Response

Learning Mindset

Challenge-Seeking Builds Confidence

How can you sustain your belief that success is possible? Whenever you approach a new topic, determine what you already know about it. Break down the task into smaller steps to allow yourself to slowly build your understanding in more manageable pieces. Remember that learning is a collaborative effort; help others build their confidence, and they will help you. Here are some questions you can ask yourself to build confidence in your ability to learn and improve:

- What are my strengths in working with triangles? How can I use prior knowledge to improve my understanding?

- What is my learning goal? How can I break that goal into smaller pieces? What can I accomplish today? What can I accomplish by the end of the week?

- How can I challenge myself to use what I'm learning in useful ways?

- Is there someone with whom I can exchange ideas to expand our knowledge of topics and build confidence for future successes?

Reflect

Q How have you strengthened your abilities in areas in which you once considered yourself weak? How does that experience affect how you approach new challenges?

Q If you were an environmental chemist, how might you take on more responsibilities as you continue to develop your career?

(t) ©Rashid Valitov/Shutterstock; (b) ©Thomas Warnack/picture-alliance/dpa/AP Images

Module Performance Task: *Spies and Analysts*™

The Grass Is Always Greener

How can we water all of the grass?

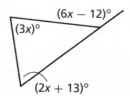

Are You Ready?

Complete these problems to review prior concepts and skills you will need for this module.

Slopes of Lines

Find the slope of the line that passes through each pair of points.

1. $(5, 1), (2, -1)$

2. $(-4, 3), (-2, -3)$

3. $(1, -6), (5, -1)$

4. $(3, 8), (7, 6)$

Angle Relationships in Triangles

Find the value of x.

5.

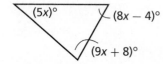

6.

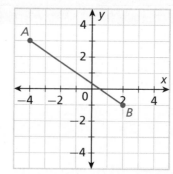

Distance and Midpoint Formulas

Find the length and midpoint of each line segment.

7.

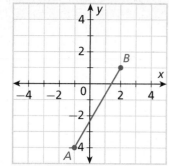

8.

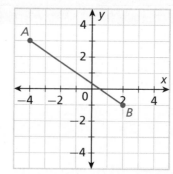

Connecting Past and Present Learning

Previously, you learned:

- to determine the midpoint of a line segment,
- to calculate unknown angle measures in triangles, and
- to construct perpendicular bisectors and angle bisectors.

In this module, you will learn:

- to determine the lengths of special segments within triangles,
- to locate points of concurrency within triangles, and
- to prove theorems about triangles.

Angle Relationships in Triangles

(I Can) prove theorems about triangle angles.

Spark Your Learning

As part of a dog agility competition, a dog must run up and down the ramp shown. The height of the ramp can be adjusted by changing the length of the chain attached to both sides of the ramp.

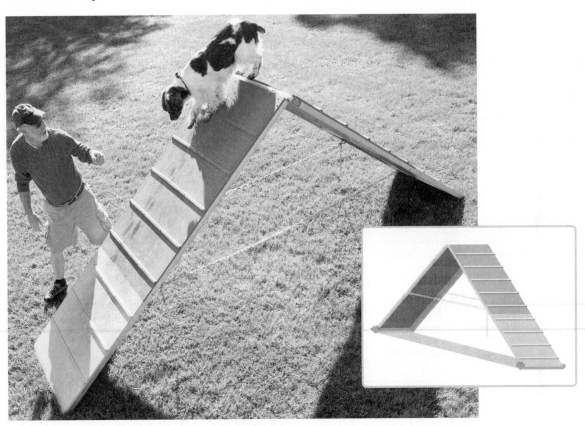

©Apple Tree House/Photodisc/Getty Images

Complete Part A as a whole class. Then complete Parts B and C in small groups.

   A. What is a geometric question you can ask about this ramp?

   B. To answer your question, what strategy and tool would you use along with all the information you have? What answer do you get?

   C. Does your answer make sense in the context of this situation? How do you know?

 Turn and Talk Suppose the chain is parallel to the ground. How is the triangle formed by the sides of the ramp and the ground related to the smaller triangle formed by the chain and the sides of the ramp?

Build Understanding

Prove the Triangle Sum Theorem

An **interior angle** is an angle formed by two sides of a polygon with a common vertex.

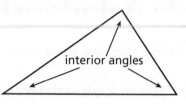

interior angles

An **auxiliary line** is a line drawn in a figure to aid in a proof. The word auxiliary means something that is helpful or gives assistance.

Triangle Sum Theorem
The sum of the measures of the interior angles of a triangle is 180°.

1 Prove the Triangle Sum Theorem.

A. Look at the diagram below. How is the auxiliary line *l* used in the proof? What do you know about each of the angles in the diagram?

B. What reason should be given for Step 2?

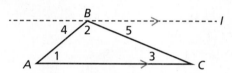

Given: △ABC

Prove: m∠1 + m∠2 + m∠3 = 180°

Statements	Reasons
1. Draw line *l* through point *B* parallel to $\overline{AC}$.	1. Parallel Postulate
2. ∠1 ≅ ∠4, ∠3 ≅ ∠5	2. ___?___
3. m∠1 = m∠4, m∠3 = m∠5	3. Definition of congruent angles
4. m∠4 + m∠2 + m∠5 = 180°	4. Angle Addition Postulate and definition of a straight angle
5. m∠1 + m∠2 + m∠3 = 180°	5. Substitution Property of Equality

 Turn and Talk How can the Triangle Sum Theorem help you solve problems?

Prove the Exterior Angle Theorem

An **exterior angle** is an angle formed by one side of a polygon and the extension of an adjacent side.

A **remote interior angle** is an interior angle that is not adjacent to the exterior angle.

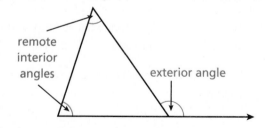

remote interior angles

exterior angle

You can find the relationship between exterior angles and interior angles as well.

Exterior Angle Theorem
The measure of an exterior angle of a triangle is equal to the sum of the measures of its remote interior angles.

2 ▶ Prove the Exterior Angle Theorem.

A. What do you know about the relationship between ∠3 and ∠4 from the diagram? What theorem(s) allow you to reach your conclusion?

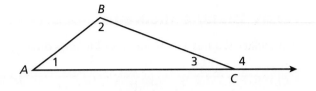

Given: ∠4 is an exterior angle of △ABC.

Prove: m∠4 = m∠1 + m∠2

Statements	Reasons
1. ∠4 and ∠3 are supplementary.	**1.** Linear Pairs Theorem
2. m∠4 + m∠3 = 180°	**2.** Definition of supplementary angles
3. m∠1 + m∠2 + m∠3 = 180°	**3.** Triangle Sum Theorem
4. m∠4 + m∠3 = m∠1 + m∠2 + m∠3	**4.** Substitution Property of Equality
5. m∠4 = m∠1 + m∠2	**5.** Subtraction Property of Equality

B. Describe how the Triangle Sum Theorem is being used to prove the Exterior Angle Theorem.

Prove the Isosceles Triangle Theorem

Recall that an **isosceles triangle** is a triangle with a least two congruent sides.

Isosceles Triangle Theorem
If two sides of a triangle are congruent, then the two angles opposite the congruent sides are congruent.

3 ▶ Prove the Isosceles Triangle Theorem.

A. $\overline{AD}$ is drawn so that it bisects ∠A. Explain why △ADB ≅ △ADC.

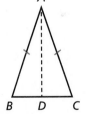

Given: $\overline{AB} \cong \overline{AC}$

Prove: ∠B ≅ ∠C

Statements	Reasons
1. $\overline{AB} \cong \overline{AC}$	**1.** Given
2. Draw $\overline{AD}$ so that it bisects ∠A.	**2.** An angle has one angle bisector.
3. ∠DAB ≅ ∠DAC	**3.** Definition of angle bisector
4. $\overline{AD} \cong \overline{AD}$	**4.** Reflexive Property of Congruence
5. △ADB ≅ △ADC	**5.** SAS Triangle Congruence Theorem
6. ∠B ≅ ∠C	**6.** CPCFC

B. The Isosceles Triangle Theorem can also be proven by drawing $\overline{AD}$ so that D is the midpoint of $\overline{BC}$. Explain the steps of this proof.

Step It Out

Apply Triangle Theorems

A **corollary** is a theorem whose proof follows directly from another theorem.

Corollary to the Triangle Sum Theorem
The two acute angles in a right triangle are complementary.

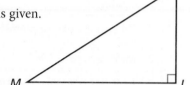

4   The proof for the Corollary to the Triangle Sum Theorem is given.

Given: $\triangle LMN$ is a right triangle.

Prove: $\angle M$ and $\angle N$ are complementary.

Statements	Reasons
1. $\triangle LMN$ is a right triangle.	1. Given
2. $m\angle L = 90°$	2. Definition of a right angle
3. $m\angle L + m\angle M + m\angle N = 180°$	3. ___?___
4. $90° + m\angle M + m\angle N = 180°$	4. Substitution Property of Equality
5. $m\angle M + m\angle N = 90°$	5. ___?___
6. $\angle M$ and $\angle N$ are complementary.	6. Definition of complementary angles

> **A.** What justifies the third statement?

> **B.** What justifies the fifth statement?

5   Find the value of the unknown angle measure.

$72° + 25° + x° = 180°$

$97° + x° = 180°$

$x° = 83°$

> What theorem was used to write this equation?

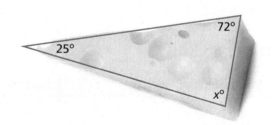

 Turn and Talk For each triangle, which theorem(s) do you apply to write an equation to find the value of the varaible?

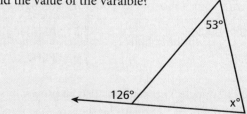

Check Understanding

1. If the interior angles of a triangle are congruent, what is the measure of each angle?

2. The measure of an exterior angle of a triangle is 54°. The measure of one of the remote interior angles is 33°. What is the measure of the other remote interior angle? What is the measure of the other angle of the triangle?

3. If an isosceles triangle has a right angle, what are the measures of the other interior angles?

Find the measure of the unknown interior angle.

4.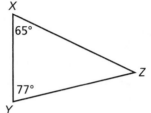

5.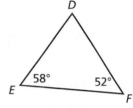

On Your Own

(MP) **Reason** In Problems 6–8, answer each question and explain your reasoning.

6. Is it possible for a triangle to have two obtuse angles?

7. Is it possible for an exterior angle of a triangle to be a right angle?

8. An isosceles triangle has an angle that measures 100°. Do you have enough information to determine the other two angles of the triangle?

9. Write a two-column proof of the converse of the Isosceles Triangle Theorem. If two angles of a triangle are congruent, the two sides opposite the angles are congruent.

   Given: $\angle B \cong \angle C$

   Prove: $\overline{AB} \cong \overline{AC}$

An asterism is a group of stars that is easier to recognize than a constellation. Find the value of *x* in each asterism.

10.

The Summer Triangle

11.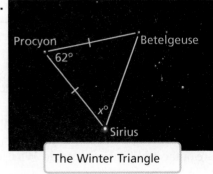

The Winter Triangle

Find the value of *x*.

12.

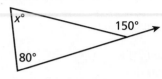

150°
x°
80°

13.

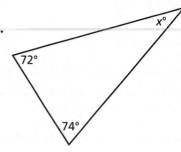

x°
72°
74°

14.

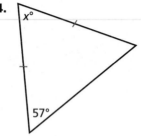

x°
57°

15.

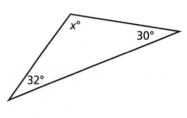

x°
40°   30°

16.

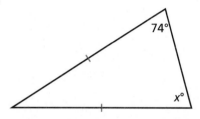

74°
x°

17.

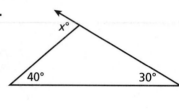

x°   30°
32°

18. (MP) **Critique Reasoning** A triangle has two angles that measure 82° and 44°. Jessica states that the measure of the exterior angle of the unknown angle is 126°. Tristan states that the measure of the exterior angle is 54°. Who is correct? Explain your reasoning.

19. Open Ended Write a problem that uses the Triangle Sum Theorem to find the value of a variable.

20. Two spotlights illuminate a stage as shown. Find the value of *x*, *y*, and *z*.

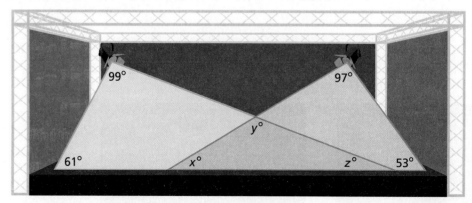

99°   97°
y°
61°   *x*°   *z*°   53°

21. Lily is cutting triangular shapes from fabric for a quilt she is making. One piece she cuts has an angle that measures 54°. The measure of one of the unknown angles is twice the measure of the other unknown angle. What are the measures of the unknown angles?

22. A person at T is observing a drone flying along $\overleftrightarrow{AC}$. The drone's path is parallel to a horizontal line at the person's eye level. At point A, the angle of elevation to the drone is 35°. After the drone has traveled 240 feet to point B, the angle of elevation is 70°. What is BT? Explain your reasoning.

23. (MP) **Reason** If you know the measure of an exterior angle of a triangle, can you determine the measures of the remote interior angles? Explain your reasoning.

24. Consider △XYZ shown. If m∠X is five times as great as m∠Y, find m∠X and m∠Y.

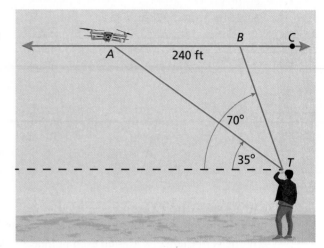

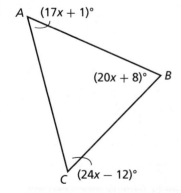

Find the measure of each interior angle of the triangle.

25.

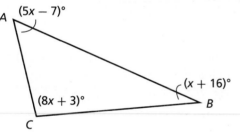

26.

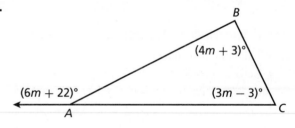

27.

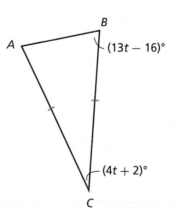

28.

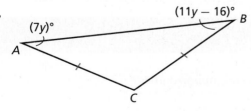

29.

30.

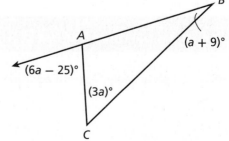

In Problems 31 and 32, find *MN*.

31.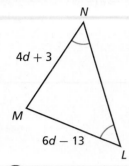

32.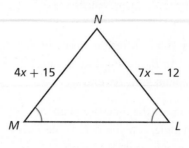

33. (MP) **Construct Arguments** In isosceles △*ABC*, ∠*B* and ∠*C* are the base angles. The measures of the interior angles are integers. How do you know that the measure of the vertex angle, ∠*A*, is an even number?

34. (Open Middle™) Using the integers from 1 to 9 at most one time each, fill in the boxes to give possible measures for the angles in the triangle.

m∠*KAB* = ⬚ ⬚ ⬚ °

m∠*ABC* = ⬚ ⬚ °

m∠*BCA* = ⬚ ⬚ °

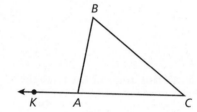

Spiral Review • Assessment Readiness

35. What value of *x* makes △*EDG* ≅ △*FDG* ?

Ⓐ 3

Ⓑ 5

Ⓒ 9

Ⓓ 26

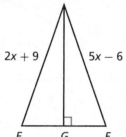

36. Rectangle *PQRS* is divided into two triangles by diagonal $\overline{PR}$. Which congruence statement is correct?

Ⓐ △*PRS* ≅ △*RPQ*

Ⓑ △*RSP* ≅ △*QRP*

Ⓒ △*PRS* ≅ △*QRP*

Ⓓ △*SPR* ≅ △*PQR*

37. Line *m* and line *n* are perpendicular. The slope of line *m* is 3. What is the slope of line *n*?

Ⓐ 3

Ⓒ $\frac{-1}{3}$

Ⓑ $\frac{1}{3}$

Ⓓ −3

38. Which theorem can be used most directly to show that △*ABC* ≅ △*DEF*?

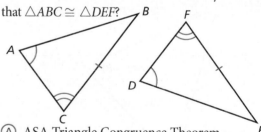

Ⓐ ASA Triangle Congruence Theorem

Ⓑ AAS Triangle Congruence Theorem

Ⓒ SAS Triangle Congruence Theorem

Ⓓ SSS Triangle Congruence Theorem

 I'm in a Learning Mindset!

How do I proactively seek out additional learning opportunities?

Perpendicular Bisectors in Triangles

(I Can) construct perpendicular bisectors and use the point of concurrency to circumscribe triangles with circles.

Spark Your Learning

A catering company that has food trucks in three locations wants to relocate its main office to a central location.

Complete Part A as a whole class. Then complete Parts B–D in small groups.

- **A.** What is a mathematical question you can ask about this situation? What information would you need to know to answer your question?

- **B.** How could you answer your question visually?

- **C.** To answer your question, what strategy and tool would you use along with all the information you have? What answer do you get?

- **D.** What is the answer to your question?

 Turn and Talk Can you think of any reasons that the new main office could not be built at the exact central location?

Build Understanding

Investigate Perpendicular Bisectors

A **perpendicular bisector** of a side of a triangle is a segment that is perpendicular to and bisects a side of a triangle.

1 ► Use a geometric drawing tool to draw a triangle. Construct the midpoint of each side of the triangle and a line perpendicular to each side through the midpoint.

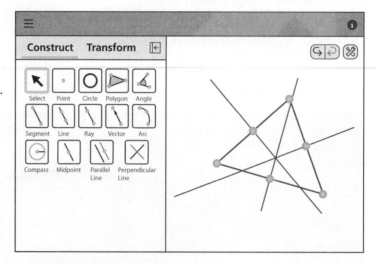

A. Move the vertices of the triangle. What is true about their perpendicular bisectors?

B. In what type of triangle is the intersection of the perpendicular bisectors inside the triangle? outside the triangle? on the triangle?

Prove that Perpendicular Bisectors Are Concurrent

In Task 1, the perpendicular bisectors of the sides of a triangle intersect in a point. **Concurrent lines** are three or more lines that intersect at one point. The **point of concurrency** is the point where concurrent lines intersect.

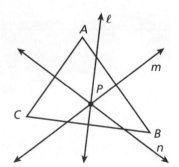

2 ► Prove that the perpendicular bisectors of a triangle are concurrent.

Given: Lines ℓ, m, and n are perpendicular bisectors of $\triangle ABC$.

Prove: Lines ℓ, m, and n are concurrent.

A. Why do you know line ℓ and line m intersect?

B. Explain how you know that lines ℓ, m, and n are concurrent in Step 6.

Statements	Reasons
1. Lines ℓ, m, and n are perpendicular bisectors of $\triangle ABC$.	1. Given
2. Let P be the intersection of m and ℓ.	2. Definition of intersecting lines
3. $PB = PC$; $PB = PA$	3. Perpendicular Bisector Theorem
4. $PA = PC$	4. Transitive Property of Equality
5. P is on line n.	5. Converse of Perpendicular Bisector Theorem
6. Lines ℓ, m, and n are concurrent.	6. ___?___

Prove the Circumcenter Theorem

The point of concurrency of the perpendicular bisectors of a triangle is called the **circumcenter of a triangle**.

A circle that contains all the vertices of a polygon is **circumscribed** about the polygon. A circle circumscribed about a polygon is called the **circumcircle** of the polygon.

Circumcenter Theorem

The perpendicular bisectors of the sides of a triangle intersect at a point that is equidistant from the vertices of the triangle.
$PA = PB = PC$

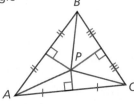

 Show that the distance from the circumcenter of the triangle to each vertex of the triangle is equal.

Given: Lines ℓ, m, and n are perpendicular bisectors of $\triangle ABC$.
 P is the circumcenter of $\triangle ABC$.

Prove: $PA = PB = PC$

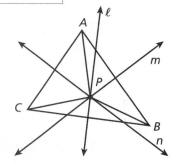

Statements	Reasons
1. Lines ℓ, m, and n are perpendicular bisectors of $\triangle ABC$.	1. Given
2. P is the circumcenter of $\triangle ABC$.	2. Given
3. P is on the perpendicular bisector of $\overline{AB}$, so $PA = PB$.	3. ___?___
4. P is on the perpendicular bisector of $\overline{BC}$, so $PB = PC$.	4. ___?___
5. $PA = PB = PC$	5. ___?___

A. What reasons should be given in Steps 3, 4, and 5? Should a step be included stating that P is on the perpendicular bisector of $\overline{AC}$? Why or why not?

B. Draw a triangle and construct the circumcenter. Using the circumcenter as the center and $\overline{AP}$ as the radius, construct a circle. Why is the point of concurrency of the perpendicular bisectors of a triangle called the circumcenter of the triangle?

C. The circumcenter of a triangle is used to draw a circle circumscribed about the triangle. If one side of the triangle is a diameter of the circumcircle, then how can you classify the triangle by its angles?

Turn and Talk Why is it only necessary to construct two perpendicular bisectors to circumscribe a triangle with a circle?

Step It Out

Use Circumcenters to Solve Problems

4 The diagram shows a bass player (point A), a drummer (point B), and a guitar player (point C) in a recording studio. Where should an overhead microphone be placed so that it is the same distance from each musician?

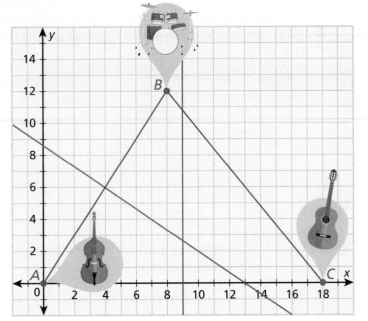

Find the perpendicular bisector of $\overline{AB}$.

midpoint of
$$\overline{AB} = \left(\frac{0+8}{2}, \frac{0+12}{2}\right) = (4, 6)$$
slope of $\overline{AB} = \frac{12-0}{8-0} = \frac{12}{8} = \frac{3}{2}$

The perpendicular bisector of $\overline{AB}$ is $y = -\frac{2}{3}x + \frac{26}{3}$.

A. How was this equation determined?

Find the perpendicular bisector of $\overline{AC}$.

The midpoint of $\overline{AC} = (9, 0)$.

B. How was this equation determined?

The perpendicular bisector of $\overline{AC}$ is $x = 9$.

Find the intersection of the perpendicular bisectors.

C. What are the coordinates of the circumcenter?

$y = -\frac{2}{3}x + \frac{26}{3}$ and $x = 9$ intersect at $y = -\frac{2}{3}(9) + \frac{26}{3} = \frac{8}{3}$.

> **Turn and Talk** Compare the processes of circumscribing a triangle with a circle on and off the coordinate plane.

5 The circumcenter of $\triangle ABC$ is P. Find the length of $\overline{PC}$.

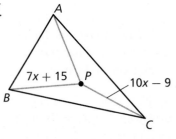

Solve for x.

$7x + 15 = 10x - 9$ ◁ Why is this equation true?

$15 = 3x - 9$

$24 = 3x$

$8 = x$

Substitute the value of x into the expression for PC.

$PC = 10(8) - 9 = 80 - 9 = 71$

The length of $\overline{PC}$ is 71.

Check Understanding

Copy each triangle. Construct the perpendicular bisectors of each side.

1.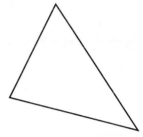

2.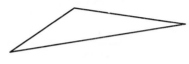

3. (MP) **Critique Reasoning** Alice states that the circumcenter of a triangle must be within the triangle. Nancy says that it is possible for the circumcenter to be outside of the triangle. Who is correct? Explain your reasoning.

4. Sketch a triangle on a coordinate plane with vertices at $(-1, 1)$, $(4, -2)$, and $(3, 3)$. Estimate the coordinates of the circumcenter of the triangle.

5. Point N is the circumcenter of $\triangle QPR$, $QN = 4x - 5$, and $RN = 2x + 3$. Is it possible to find the value of x? If so, explain how.

On Your Own

6. (MP) **Use Structure** Sketch three different right triangles. Find the circumcenter of each triangle. What do you notice about the circumcenter of each right triangle?

7. (MP) **Use Structure** Sketch three different obtuse triangles. Find the circumcenter of each triangle. What do you notice about the circumcenter of each obtuse triangle?

Copy each triangle. Construct the circumcircle of the triangle.

8.

9.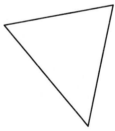

10.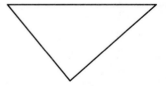

11.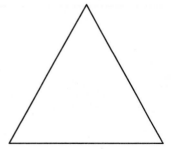

12. (MP) **Construct Arguments** Use a flow proof to prove the Circumcenter Theorem.

Given: Lines ℓ, m, and n are the perpendicular bisectors of $\overline{AB}$, $\overline{AC}$, and $\overline{BC}$. P is the intersection of ℓ, m, and n.

Prove: $PA = PB = PC$

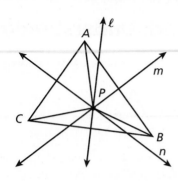

13. (MP) **Construct Arguments** Use geometry software to draw a circle. Draw a quadrilateral inside the circle so that all four vertices lie on the circle. What do you notice about the measures of the opposite angles in the quadrilateral?

14. A cell phone company plans to build a new tower that is the same distance from the three existing towers shown in the diagram. Copy the points and show where the new tower should be located.

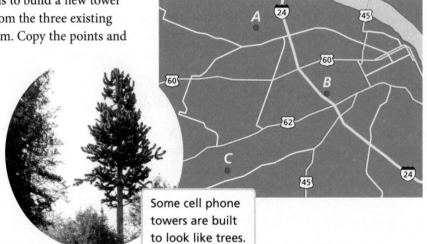

Some cell phone towers are built to look like trees.

Find the circumcenter of the triangle.

15.

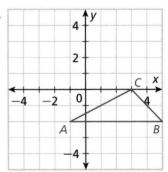

16.

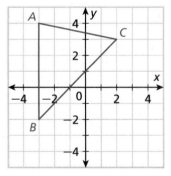

17.

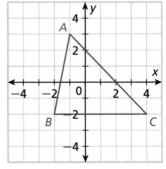

18.

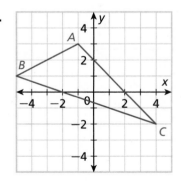

19. (MP) **Reason** Suppose you are finding the circumcenter of a triangle on a coordinate plane. Why might you want to find the perpendicular bisector of a horizontal or vertical side of the triangle first?

20. (MP) **Reason** When finding the circumcenter of a triangle on a coordinate plane, only two perpendicular bisectors are needed. Explain why. Then explain how the third perpendicular bisector can be used to check your answer.

The circumcenter P of $\triangle ABC$ on a coordinate plane is given. Find the unknown coordinate of the vertices of the triangle.

21. circumcenter: $P(3, 2)$; vertices: $A(1, 3)$, $B(4, ?)$, $C(5, 1)$

22. circumcenter: $P(-1, 3)$; vertices: $A(-4, 0)$, $B(-4, 6)$, and $C(?, 0)$

23. circumcenter: $P(2.5, 2)$; vertices: $A(7, ?)$, $B(-1, -1)$, and $C(-2, 1)$

The circumcenter of $\triangle ABC$ is P. Find the value of x.

24.

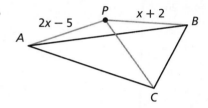

25.

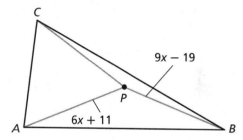

26.

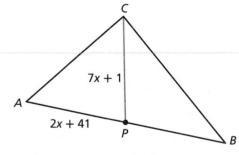

27.

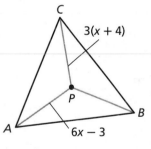

Use the diagram for Problems 28–31. $\overline{DE}$, $\overline{DF}$, and $\overline{DG}$ are the perpendicular bisectors of $\triangle ABC$. Use the given information to find the lengths. Note that the figure is not drawn to scale.

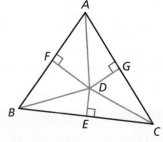

28. Given: $FD = 24$, $DA = 46$, $GC = 32$
Find: AC and DB

29. Given: $BD = 25$, $DE = 7$, $BC = 48$
Find: BE and DC

30. Given: $BC = 30$, $DC = 17$
Find: DE

31. Name a segment that is a radius of the circumcircle of $\triangle ABC$.

In the diagram, $\overline{PK}$, $\overline{PL}$, and $\overline{PM}$ are the perpendicular bisectors of sides $\overline{AB}$, $\overline{BC}$, and $\overline{AC}$, respectively. Tell whether the given statement is justified by the figure.

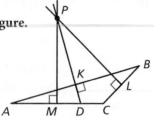

32. $AK = KB$ **33.** $PA = PB$ **34.** $PM = PL$

The circumcenter of $\triangle ABC$ is P. Find the length of $\overline{PA}$.

35.

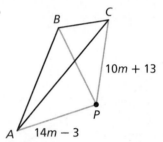

36.

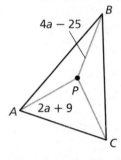

37.

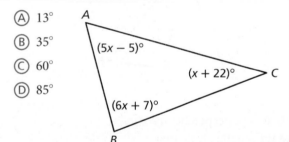

38.

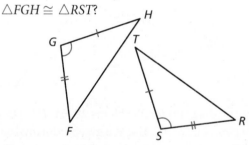

Spiral Review • Assessment Readiness

39. What is the measure of $\angle B$?

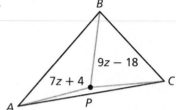

- Ⓐ 13°
- Ⓑ 35°
- Ⓒ 60°
- Ⓓ 85°

40. The measure of $\angle JKL$ is 88°, and $\angle JKL$ is bisected by $\overrightarrow{KM}$. What is the value of x if $m\angle JKM = (7x - 12)°$?

- Ⓐ 8   Ⓒ 44
- Ⓑ 14   Ⓓ 56

41. Which theorem can you use to show that $\triangle FGH \cong \triangle RST$?

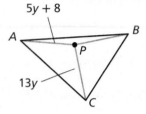

- Ⓐ ASA Triangle Congruence
- Ⓑ AAS Triangle Congruence
- Ⓒ SAS Triangle Congruence
- Ⓓ SSS Triangle Congruence

 I'm in a Learning Mindset!

What are my strengths when finding and using perpendicular bisectors?

Angle Bisectors in Triangles

(I Can) prove that angle bisectors are concurrent and inscribe circles in triangles.

Spark Your Learning

A group of friends are making scrapbooks. Maria wants to cut a circle out of a triangular piece of paper.

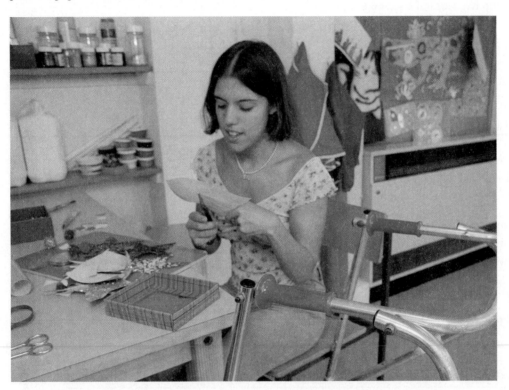

Complete Part A as a whole class. Then complete Parts B–D in small groups.

A. What is a geometric question you can ask about this situation? What information would you need to know to answer your question?

B. To answer your question, what strategy and tool would you use along with all the information you have? What answer do you get?

C. How should the edge of the circle relate to the sides of the triangle?

D. How can you check that the center of the circle is in the correct location?

 Turn and Talk Do you notice anything about the center of the circle that relates to the sides, vertices, or angles of the triangle?

Build Understanding

Prove the Angle Bisector Theorem

An **angle bisector** of a triangle is a ray that divides an angle into two congruent angles. You can find the relationship between an angle bisector and the sides of the angle it bisects.

Angle Bisector Theorem
If a point is on the bisector of an angle, then it is equidistant from the two sides of the angle.   If $\overrightarrow{PC}$ bisects $\angle APB$, $\overline{AC} \perp \overrightarrow{PA}$, and $\overline{BC} \perp \overrightarrow{PB}$, then $AC = BC$.

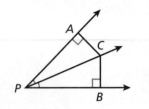

1. Prove the Angle Bisector Theorem.

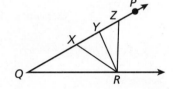

A. Many segments can be drawn from a point to a ray. In $\angle PQR$, which segment appears to represent the distance from point R to $\overrightarrow{QP}$? Explain your reasoning.

B. The theorem claims that $WX = WZ$. How can congruent triangles be used to show that $WX = WZ$? How can you show that the triangles are congruent if you know that $\angle XYW \cong \angle ZYW$?

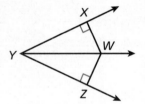

Given: $\overrightarrow{YW}$ bisects $\angle XYZ$, $\overline{WX} \perp \overrightarrow{YX}$, and $\overline{WZ} \perp \overrightarrow{YZ}$.

Prove: $WX = WZ$

Statements	Reasons
1. $\overrightarrow{YW}$ bisects $\angle XYZ$, $\overline{WX} \perp \overrightarrow{YX}$, and $\overline{WZ} \perp \overrightarrow{YZ}$.	**1.** Given
2. $\angle XYW \cong \angle ZYW$	**2.** Definition of angle bisector
3. $\angle WXY$ and $\angle WZY$ are right angles.	**3.** Definition of perpendicular lines
4. $\angle WXY \cong \angle WZY$	**4.** All right angles are congruent.
5. $\overline{YW} \cong \overline{YW}$	**5.** Reflexive Property of Congruence
6. $\triangle YXW \cong \triangle YZW$	**6.** AAS Triangle Congruence Theorem
7. $\overline{WX} \cong \overline{WZ}$	**7.** Corresponding parts of congruent figures are congruent.
8. $WX = WZ$	**8.** Definition of congruent segments

 Turn and Talk How is an angle bisector similar to a perpendicular bisector?

Prove the Converse of the Angle Bisector Theorem

The converse of the Angle Bisector Theorem is true as well.

Converse of the Angle Bisector Theorem

If a point in the interior of an angle is equidistant from the sides of the angle, then it is on the bisector of the angle.

If $\overline{AC} \perp \overrightarrow{PA}$, $\overline{BC} \perp \overrightarrow{PB}$, and $AC = BC$, then $\overrightarrow{PC}$ bisects $\angle APB$.

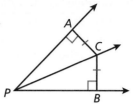

---

2 Prove the Converse of the Angle Bisector Theorem.

A. In the statement of the Converse of the Angle Bisector Theorem, why is it important to state that the point is in the interior of the angle?

B. What do you need to show before you can state that $\overrightarrow{YW}$ bisects $\angle XYZ$?

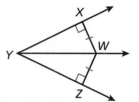

Given: $\overline{WX} \perp \overrightarrow{YX}$, $\overline{WZ} \perp \overrightarrow{YZ}$, and $WX = WZ$.

Prove: $\overrightarrow{YW}$ bisects $\angle XYZ$.

Statements	Reasons
1. $\overline{WX} \perp \overrightarrow{YX}$, $\overline{WZ} \perp \overrightarrow{YZ}$, and $WX = WZ$.	1. Given
2. $\overline{WX} \cong \overline{WZ}$	2. Definition of congruent segments
3. $\angle WXY$ and $\angle WZY$ are right angles.	3. Definition of perpendicular lines
4. $\triangle YXW$ and $\triangle YZW$ are right triangles.	4. Definition of a right triangle
5. $\overline{YW} \cong \overline{YW}$	5. Reflexive Property of Congruence
6. $\triangle YXW \cong \triangle YZW$	6. HL Triangle Congruence Theorem
7. $\angle XYW \cong \angle ZYW$	7. Corresponding parts of congruent figures are congruent.
8. $\overrightarrow{YW}$ bisects $\angle XYZ$.	8. Definition of angle bisector

C. Compare the proofs for the Angle Bisector Theorem and its converse. How are the proofs alike? How are they different?

 Turn and Talk Suppose $m\angle XYZ = 68°$ and $m\angle XYW = (3x + 7)°$. Do you have enough information to solve for x? Explain your reasoning.

Step It Out

Prove the Incenter Theorem

Recall that concurrent lines are three or more lines that intersect at one point, called the point of concurrency. An **angle bisector of a triangle** is a segment from a vertex of the triangle that divides that interior angle into two congruent angles. The point of concurrency of angle bisectors of a triangle is called the **incenter** of the triangle. You can show that the incenter is equidistant from the sides of the triangle.

Incenter Theorem

The angle bisectors of a triangle intersect at a point that is equidistant from the sides of the triangle.

If $\overline{AP}$, $\overline{BP}$, and $\overline{CP}$ are angle bisectors of $\triangle ABC$, then $PX = PY = PZ$.

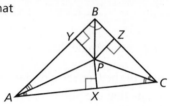

---

3 Prove the Incenter Theorem.

Given: Angle bisectors of $\angle A$, $\angle B$, and $\angle C$ in $\triangle ABC$.

Prove: The angle bisectors intersect at a point equidistant from $\overline{AB}$, $\overline{BC}$, and $\overline{AC}$.

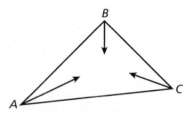

The bisectors of $\angle A$ and $\angle C$ intersect at point P. Perpendicular segments are drawn from point P so that $\overline{PX} \perp \overline{AC}$, $\overline{PY} \perp \overline{AB}$, and $\overline{PZ} \perp \overline{BC}$. So, $PX = PY$ and $PX = PZ$.

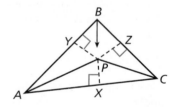

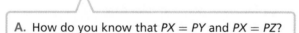

> **A.** How do you know that $PX = PY$ and $PX = PZ$?

Using the Transitive Property of Equality, $PY = PZ$. This means that P lies on the angle bisector of $\angle B$.

> **B.** How do you know that P lies the angle bisector of $\angle B$?

Because $PX = PY = PZ$, point P is equidistant from $\overline{AB}$, $\overline{BC}$, and $\overline{AC}$.

Use Properties of Angle Bisectors

A circle is inscribed in a triangle if each side of the triangle is tangent to the circle. In the figure, circle C is inscribed in $\triangle XYZ$. The center of the circle is the incenter of $\triangle XYZ$.

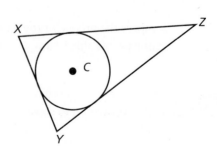

4 A circular tent will be set up for a graduation ceremony at a university. The tent will be located on a triangular section of land between a sculpture, a corner of the library building, and a gazebo.

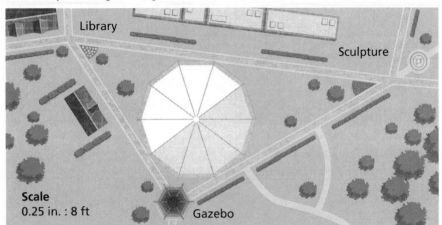

Reggie uses a scale drawing of the area to determine the largest circular tent that can be used. Reggie's steps are shown below.

Step 1 Draw the angle bisector of each angle.

> **A.** How can you construct an angle bisector using a compass and a straightedge?

Step 2 Find the incenter of the triangle. Using a compass, construct an inscribed circle.

> **B.** How is the radius of the circle determined?

Step 3 Use a ruler to measure the radius.

The radius is $\frac{5}{8}$, or 0.625, inch.

Step 4 Use the scale to determine the diameter of the largest possible circular tent that can be used.

$$\frac{0.25 \text{ in.}}{8 \text{ ft}} = \frac{0.625 \text{ in.}}{x \text{ ft}} \qquad \rightarrow \qquad x = 20$$

The largest circular tent that will fit has a radius of 20 feet.

 Turn and Talk Is it possible to use only two angle bisectors to find the incenter? Explain.

5 Point Z is the incenter of $\triangle PQR$. What is m$\angle QPZ$?

Use the Triangle Sum Theorem to write an equation.

$$\text{m}\angle QPR + \text{m}\angle PRQ + \text{m}\angle RQP = 180°$$

$$\text{m}\angle QPR + 2(13°) + 122° = 180°$$

$$\text{m}\angle QPR + 148° = 180°$$

$$\text{m}\angle QPR = 32°$$

> **A.** How do you know that m$\angle PRQ = 2(13°)$?

The measure of $\angle QPZ$ is half the measure of $\angle QPR$: m$\angle QPZ = \frac{1}{2}(32°) = 16°$.

> **B.** How do you know that the measure of $\angle QPZ$ is half the measure of $\angle QPR$?

Check Understanding

1. $\overline{BD}$ bisects $\angle ABC$. What is the value of x?

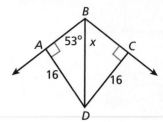

2. For what value of x does D lie on the bisector of $\angle ABC$?

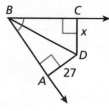

Point G is the incenter of $\triangle KLM$. Tell whether each statement can be determined from the given information.

3. $\overline{PG} \cong \overline{QG}$

4. $\overline{LG} \cong \overline{MG}$

5. $\angle QMG \cong \angle RMG$

6. $\angle PGK \cong \angle LGQ$

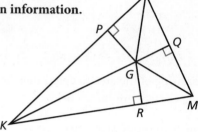

7. Copy the triangle. Construct the angle bisectors of each angle. Then label the incenter of the triangle.

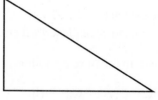

On Your Own

8. **(MP) Use Tools** Use a geometric drawing tool to draw a triangle. Construct angle bisectors of each angle.

A. Move the vertices of the triangle. What is true about the angle bisectors?

B. Is it possible to move the vertices in such a way that the intersection of the angle bisectors is outside the triangle? Explain.

Can you determine that $AQ = CQ$? Explain your reasoning.

9.

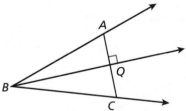

10.

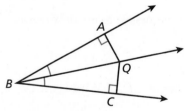

Can you determine that $\overrightarrow{BQ}$ bisects $\angle ABC$? Explain your reasoning.

11.

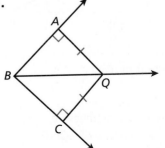

12.

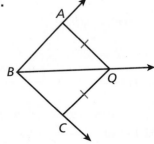

Copy the triangle. Then construct an inscribed circle for each triangle.

13.

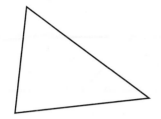

14.

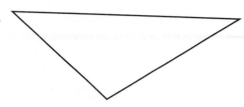

15. Open Ended Draw a triangle. Find the incenter of the triangle. Inscribe a circle in the triangle.

16. David is installing crown molding. The molding creates a triangular gap with the wall and the ceiling through which a circular tube, called conduit, will be run. The conduit will hold wires and cables.

    A. Copy the triangle in the diagram, which shows a cross section of the triangular space created by the molding. Draw an inscribed circle to represent the largest conduit that can be run through this space.

    B. Use a ruler and the dimensions given on the diagram to estimate the diameter of the largest conduit that will fit in the space.

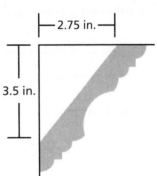

Find each measure.

17. m∠ABD

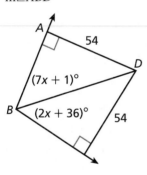

18. DC

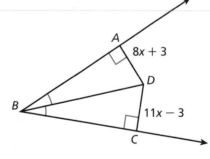

19. WZ

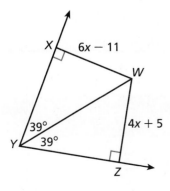

20. m∠XYW

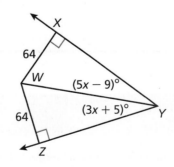

21. (MP) **Critique Reasoning** P and Q are the incenter and circumcenter of the triangle, but not necessarily in that order. Michael states that the incenter of the triangle is P and the circumcenter is Q. Eve states that the incenter of the triangle is Q and the circumcenter is P. Who is correct? Explain your reasoning.

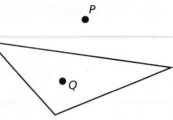

$\overline{AP}$ and $\overline{BP}$ are angle bisectors of $\triangle ABC$. Find each measure.

22. distance from P to $\overline{BC}$

23. m∠PAC

24. m∠QPB

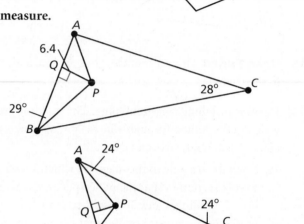

$\overline{AP}$ and $\overline{BP}$ are angle bisectors of $\triangle ABC$. Determine whether each statement is true or false.

25. P lies on the angle bisector of $\angle ACB$.

26. $\overline{PQ}$ is a perpendicular bisector of $\overline{AB}$.

Spiral Review • Assessment Readiness

27. What is the measure of $\angle ABD$?

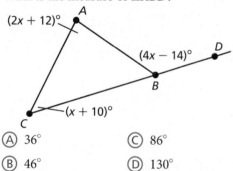

(A) $36°$ (C) $86°$

(B) $46°$ (D) $130°$

28. For what value of t is Y is the midpoint of $\overline{XZ}$?

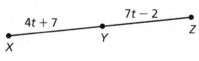

(A) $1\frac{2}{3}$ (C) 9

(B) 3 (D) 27

29. The circumcenter of $\triangle ABC$ is D. What is AD?

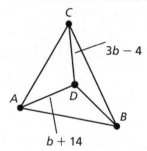

(A) 2 (C) 9

(B) 5 (D) 23

30. Which of the following set of statements does not allow you to conclude that $\triangle ABC \cong \triangle DEF$?

(A) $\angle A \cong \angle D$, $\angle B \cong \angle E$, $\overline{BC} \cong \overline{EF}$

(B) $\angle A \cong \angle D$, $\overline{AC} \cong \overline{DF}$, $\overline{AB} \cong \overline{DE}$

(C) $\overline{AB} \cong \overline{DE}$, $\overline{BC} \cong \overline{EF}$, $\overline{AC} \cong \overline{DF}$

(D) $\angle A \cong \angle D$, $\overline{AB} \cong \overline{DE}$, $\overline{BC} \cong \overline{EF}$

 I'm in a Learning Mindset!

How do my time-management skills impact decision-making?

Medians and Altitudes in Triangles

(I Can) construct medians and altitudes to find centroids and orthocenters.

Spark Your Learning

A city planner is creating an architectural model that shows the redevelopment plans for an area of the city. The model needs to include a miniature version of the sculpture shown.

Complete Part A as a whole class. Then complete Parts B–D in small groups.

A. What is a mathematical question you can ask about this sculpture?

B. To answer your question, what strategy and tool would you use along with all the information you have? What answer do you get?

C. Is it easier to balance the triangle on a pole that has a flat top like the one shown or on a pole that comes to a point like the tip of a pencil? Explain.

D. How do you think the shape of the triangle affects the location of the balance point of the triangle?

Turn and Talk Is it important that the triangle has an even thickness and density?

Build Understanding

Medians and the Centroid Theorem

A **median of a triangle** is a segment whose endpoints are a vertex of the triangle and the midpoint of the opposite side.

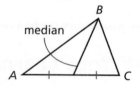

median

Every triangle has three distinct medians. The medians of a triangle are concurrent. The point of concurrency is called the **centroid** of the triangle.

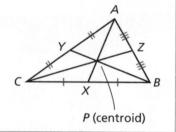

Centroid Theorem

The centroid of a triangle is located $\frac{2}{3}$ of the distance from each vertex to the midpoint of the opposite side.

$$AP = \frac{2}{3}AX \qquad BP = \frac{2}{3}BY \qquad CP = \frac{2}{3}CZ$$

P (centroid)

1 ▶ Use a geometric drawing tool to draw a triangle. Construct the midpoint of each side of the triangle. Then construct a line segment from each vertex to the midpoint of the opposite side.

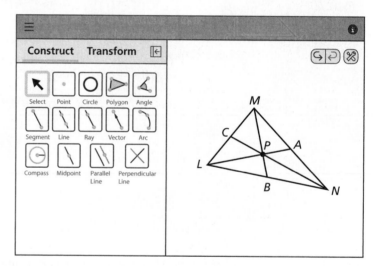

A. Move the vertices of the triangle. What is true about the medians?

B. Move the vertices to make acute, obtuse, and right triangles. Describe the location of the centroid in relation to the triangle.

C. Measure the distance from the centroid to the vertex and the centroid to the midpoint for one segment. What relationship do the lengths have? Is this true for each of the segments?

Turn and Talk

- What do you think might be true about the area of the triangles *MPN*, *MPL*, and *LPN*? What information would you need to justify this conjecture?
- How does the centroid of a triangle compare to the circumcenter and incenter?

Altitudes and the Orthocenter

An **altitude of a triangle** is a perpendicular segment from a vertex to the opposite side or to a line that contains the opposite side. An altitude can be inside, outside, or on the triangle.

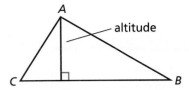

Every triangle has three altitudes. The altitudes of a triangle are concurrent. The point of concurrency is called the **orthocenter** of the triangle. The orthocenter can be inside, outside, or on the triangle.

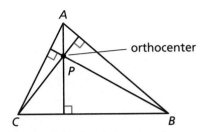

orthocenter

2 ▶ Copy △JKL. Construct an altitude at each vertex. In some cases, you may have to extend a side of the triangle to construct the altitude, as shown below.

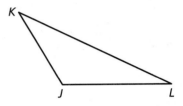 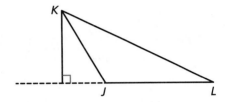

A. Do you think the orthocenter of △JKL will be inside, outside, or on the triangle?

B. Extend the altitudes and locate the orthocenter of the triangle. Where is the orthocenter located?

C. Construct additional triangles and orthocenters. Match the type of triangle on the left with the location of its orthocenter on the right.

Type of Triangle	Location of Orthocenter
A. Acute	**1.** Outside the triangle
B. Right	**2.** Inside the triangle
C. Obtuse	**3.** On the triangle

 Turn and Talk Suppose the orthocenter of △PQR occurs at a vertex of the triangle. What type of triangle is △PQR?

Step It Out

Find the Center of Gravity

3   A bicycle frame consists of two triangles. Describe the location of the center of gravity of each triangle given that $AH = BG = 13.8$ in. and $BF = DE = 18$ in.

If an object has a consistent density, then its center of gravity is its centroid.

Since point P is the centroid of $\triangle ABD$,
$AP = \frac{2}{3}AH = \frac{2}{3}(13.8) = 9.2$ inches

Since point Q is the centroid of $\triangle BCD$,
$BQ = \frac{2}{3}BF = \frac{2}{3}(18) = 12$ inches

So, the center of gravity of $\triangle ABD$ is 9.2 inches from A and B, and the center of gravity of $\triangle BCD$ is 12 inches from B and D.

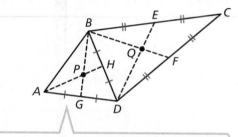

> Explain why P is the centroid of $\triangle ABD$, and why Q is the centroid $\triangle BCD$.

> **Turn and Talk**   Describe how you could modify the frame to lower its center of gravity to increase its stability.

Find the Orthocenter of a Triangle on the Coordinate Plane

4   Find the orthocenter of $\triangle PQR$ with vertices $P(1, 3)$, $Q(7, 9)$, and $R(9, 3)$.

Find the altitude from vertex Q.

Since the side opposite vertex Q is horizontal, the altitude will be vertical.

The altitude is a segment on the vertical line that passes through $(7, 9)$.

Find the altitude from vertex P.

The slope of the side opposite vertex P is -3.

> **A.** How do you know the slope is -3?

The slope of the line perpendicular to $\overline{QR}$ is $\frac{1}{3}$. Use this information to draw the altitude from P.

> **B.** How do you use this information to draw the altitude?

Locate the orthocenter.

The two altitudes intersect at $(7, 5)$.

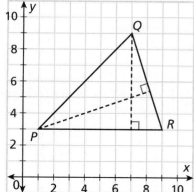

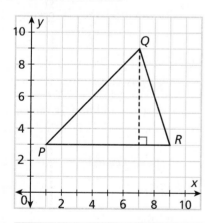

284

Check Understanding

1. Copy the triangle. Construct the medians and identify the centroid of the triangle.

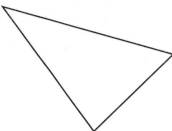

2. Copy the triangle. Construct the altitudes and identify the orthocenter of the triangle.

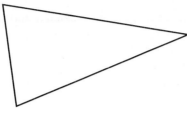

3. Suppose the orthocenter of △*PQR* occurs outside of the triangle. What type of triangle is △*PQR*?

4. Is it possible for the centroid and the orthocenter a triangle to be the same point? Explain.

5. In △*XYZ*, medians $\overline{XM}$ and $\overline{YN}$ intersect at *K*. If *XM* = 21, what is *XK*?

6. On a coordinate plane, △*ABC* has vertices *A*(0, 5), *B*(10, 0), and *C*(0, 0). What are the coordinates of the orthocenter of the triangle?

On Your Own

Copy each triangle and find its centroid.

7.

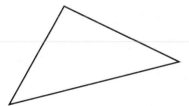

8.

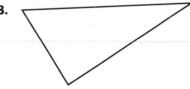

9. **STEM** In a cable-stayed bridge, cables are used to help support the weight of the bridge. The cables form triangles that are symmetric to each pylon. In the diagram, △*ABC*, △*ADF*, and △*AGH* are all symmetric about $\overleftrightarrow{AZ}$. Use the diagram to explain why the triangles formed by the cables all have the same centroid.

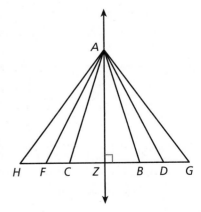

10. (MP) **Reason** The centroid of $\triangle ABC$ is located at $(4, 5)$.

   A. Choose one vertex and find the coordinates of the endpoints of the median from that vertex.

   B. Show that the Centroid Theorem is true for the median.

11. (MP) **Critique Reasoning** Joe draws a triangle and claims that the centroid of his triangle is outside of the triangle. Do you think this is possible? Explain your reasoning.

12. (MP) **Construct Arguments** Another term for the centroid of a triangle is the balancing point of a triangle. Why do you think this phrase is used to describe the centroid?

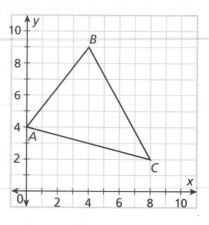

Copy each triangle and find its orthocenter. State whether the orthocenter is *inside*, *outside*, or *on* the triangle.

13.

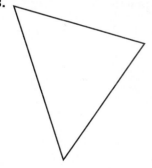

14.

15.

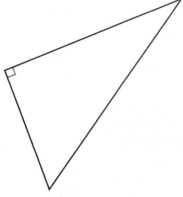

16.

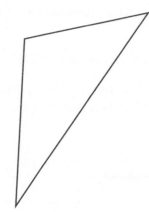

In Problems 17–22, find each measure.

17. AG if $AE = 15$

18. GF if $BF = 24$

19. CD if $CG = 34$

20. GE if $AG = 54$

21. BF if $GF = 12$

22. CG if $DG = 9$

23. (MP) **Reason** If you are given the distance from a vertex of a triangle to the centroid, can you determine the length of that median? Explain.

Point G is the centroid of $\triangle ABC$. Find the value of the variable.

24.

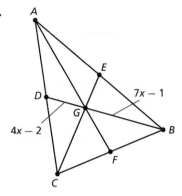

25.

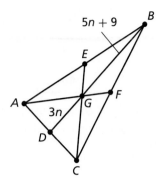

26.

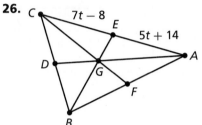

27.

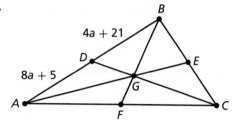

28.

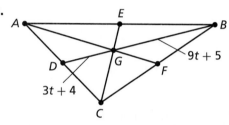

29.

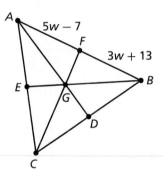

A map of a campground is drawn on a coordinate plane. The coordinates of three cabins are $A(0, 4)$, $B(10, 1)$, and $C(2, -5)$. Find the coordinates of each feature of the campground.

30. the main lodge, which is the midpoint of $\overline{AB}$

31. the fire pit, which is the midpoint of $\overline{AC}$

32. the archery range, which is the midpoint of $\overline{BC}$

33. the centroid of $\triangle ABC$

34. Open Ended Draw a triangle on a coordinate plane. Use the medians of the triangle to find the coordinates of the centroid of the triangle.

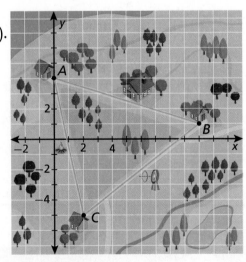

Find the centroid of each triangle with the given vertices.

35. $A(0, 4)$, $B(4, 7)$, $C(8, 1)$

36. $A(-2, 2)$, $B(0, -2)$, $C(5, 0)$

37. $A(-3, -3)$, $B(4, -4)$, $C(5, 4)$

38. $A(-5, -4)$, $B(-2, -1)$, $C(-5, -1)$

39. $A(-6, -7)$, $B(6, 2)$, $C(0, 5)$

40. $A(2, 4)$, $B(7, 2)$, $C(3, -3)$

Find the orthocenter of each triangle with the given vertices.

41. $A(11, 0), B(7, 4), C(5, -2)$

42. $A(12, 3), B(7, -2), C(1, 3)$

43. $A(-2, -1), B(2, 3), C(-4, 5)$

44. $A(-1, 1), B(3, 6), C(3, 1)$

45. $A(-1, 0), B(6, 7), C(4, 0)$

46. $A(5, 6), B(5, -2), C(-2, -1)$

47. Sergio is creating a pattern that he is going to use to cut out triangular pieces of wood. He draws his pattern on a coordinate plane. What are the coordinates of the orthocenter?

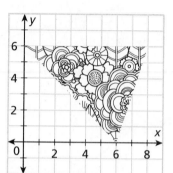

48. **Open Ended** Draw a triangle on a coordinate plane with an orthocenter that is is outside of the triangle. Draw a triangle on a coordinate plane with an orthocenter that is is on the triangle.

49. (**Open Middle**™) Using the digits 1 to 9, at most one time each, replace the boxes to create two triangles. One triangle should have an altitude x that is less than 5, and the other triangle should have an altitude y that is greater than 5.

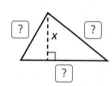 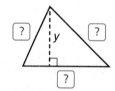

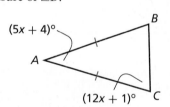

Spiral Review • Assessment Readiness

50. What is the measure of $\angle B$?

Ⓐ $6°$
Ⓑ $34°$
Ⓒ $73°$
Ⓓ $146°$

51. What is the midpoint M of $\overline{JK}$?

Ⓐ $M(0, 2)$
Ⓑ $M(1, 2)$
Ⓒ $M(2, 1)$
Ⓓ $M(2, 1.5)$

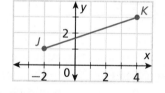

52. Determine whether the statement describes the incenter or circumcenter of a triangle.

Statement	Incenter	Circumcenter
A. This point is equidistant from the sides of the triangle.	?	?
B. This point is equidistant from the vertices of the triangle.	?	?

 I'm in a Learning Mindset!

How will I know when my goal is met successfully?

©mis-Tery/Shutterstock

The Triangle Midsegment Theorem

(I Can) construct midsegments and prove the Triangle Midsegment Theorem.

Spark Your Learning

The A-frame cabins at a camp have a second floor for sleeping.

Complete Part A as a whole class. Then complete Parts B–D in small groups.

A. What is a mathematical question you can ask about this situation? What information would you need to know to answer your question?

B. What should be true about the angles in the triangles formed by the floors and the roof?

C. To answer your question, what strategy and tool would you use along with all the information you have? What answer do you get?

D. What are some factors that determine the location of the second floor in relation to the the first floor?

> **Turn and Talk** What do you notice about the width of the second floor compared to the width of the first floor?

Build Understanding

Investigate Midsegments of a Triangle

A **midsegment of a triangle** is a segment that joins the midpoints of two sides of a triangle. Every triangle has three midsegments.

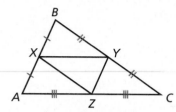

$\overline{XY}$, $\overline{YZ}$, and $\overline{ZX}$ are midsegments of $\triangle ABC$.

1 You can use a compass and straightedge to construct a midsegment of a triangle. Start by finding the midpoint of one side of the triangle.

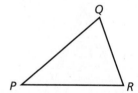 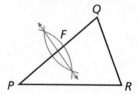

Then find the midpoint of another side, and connect the midpoints.

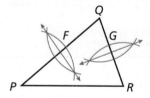 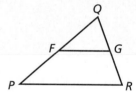

A. Explain why $\overline{FG}$ is a midsegment of $\triangle PQR$.

B. How can you construct the other two midsegments of the triangle?

C. Use a ruler to measure $\overline{FG}$ and $\overline{PR}$. How are the measures of the segments related?

D. Use a protractor to measure $\angle QFG$ and $\angle QPR$. What does this tell you about $\overline{FG}$ and $\overline{PR}$? Explain.

E. Make a conjecture about the midsegment of a triangle. Then construct the other two midsegments in the triangle and test your conjecture.

Turn and Talk

- Is it possible for the midsegments of a triangle to intersect in one point? Explain.
- The midsegments divide the original triangle into four smaller triangles. What appears to be true about these triangles? Justify your conjecture.

Step It Out

Use the Triangle Midsegment Theorem

> **Triangle Midsegment Theorem**
>
> The segment joining the midpoints of two sides of a triangle is parallel to the third side of the triangle, and its length is half of the length of that side.

2 ▶ The walking path connecting Holiday Street to Lakeview Avenue is a midsegment of the triangle formed by the roads. Verify that the midsegment is parallel to a side and half the length of that side.

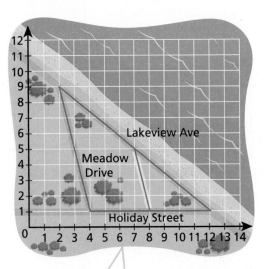

Compare slopes.

slope of Meadow Dr. $= \dfrac{9-1}{2-4} = \dfrac{8}{-2} = -4$

slope of path $= \dfrac{5-1}{7-8} = \dfrac{4}{-1} = -4$

The side and midsegment are parallel.

> **A.** How do you know that the side and midsegment of the triangle are parallel?

> **B.** How can you verify that the path is a midsegment of the triangle?

Compare lengths.

length of Meadow Dr. from $(2, 9)$ to $(4, 1) = \sqrt{(4-2)^2 + (1-9)^2}$

$$= \sqrt{68}$$
$$= 2\sqrt{17}$$

length of path $= \sqrt{(8-7)^2 + (1-5)^2} = \sqrt{17}$

The length of the midsegment is half the length of the side of the triangle.

3 ▶ What is the value of x?

$4x + 5 = \dfrac{1}{2}(34)$

$4x + 5 = 17$

$4x = 12$

$x = 3$

> Why is this equation true?

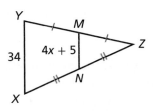

> **Turn and Talk** Suppose you know that m$\angle ZMN = 78°$ and m$\angle YXZ = 65°$. What is m$\angle Z$?

Check Understanding

Copy the triangle. Construct the midsegment parallel to the given side of the triangle.

1. $\overline{ST}$

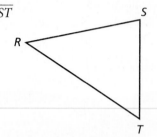

2. $\overline{EF}$

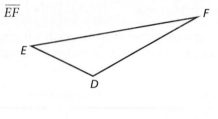

3. A triangle has vertices $F(-2, 3)$, $G(4, 3)$, and $H(2, -1)$. What are the endpoints of the midsegment that is parallel to $\overline{GH}$?

Find the value of x.

4.

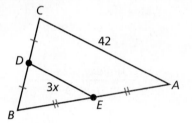

5.

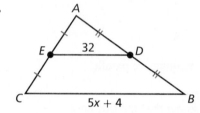

On Your Own

6. **(MP) Critique Reasoning** Henry claims that $\overline{MN}$ is a midsegment of $\triangle JKL$. Explain why this is not true.

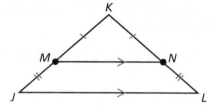

7. **(MP) Reason** Triangle PQR is an isosceles triangle.

A. Copy the triangle and construct the midsegments of the triangle.

B. What type of triangle is formed by the midsegments? Explain your reasoning.

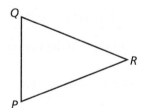

8. An example of a Sierpinski triangle is shown at the right. This triangle is a fractal formed by connecting the midpoints of a large triangle to form a smaller triangle. In the fractal, AC is 48. What is ST?

9. **(MP) Reason** $\triangle DEF$ is an equilateral triangle. The midsegments of $\triangle DEF$ form $\triangle ABC$. What type of triangle is $\triangle ABC$? Explain your reasoning.

In Problems 10–15, find each measure.

10. *CB*

11. *FE*

12. m∠*DFC*

13. *AE*

14. m∠*DFB*

15. *DF*

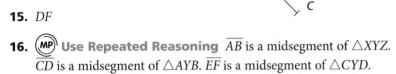

16. **Use Repeated Reasoning** $\overline{AB}$ is a midsegment of △*XYZ*. $\overline{CD}$ is a midsegment of △*AYB*. $\overline{EF}$ is a midsegment of △*CYD*.

   A. Copy and complete the table.

Midsegment	1	2	3
Length	___?___	___?___	___?___

   B. If this pattern continues, what will be the length of midsegment 8?

   C. Write an algebraic expression to represent the length of midsegment *n*. (*Hint:* Relate the pattern to powers of 2.)

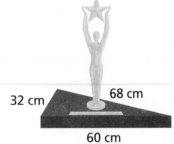

17. Sara is making a trophy for the winner of a math club contest. The base is a right triangle, and its dimensions are shown in the diagram. A midsegment is drawn so that it is parallel to the hypotenuse of the triangle. What is the perimeter of the smaller triangle that is formed? Is this triangle also a right triangle? Explain your reasoning.

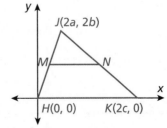

18. **Construct Arguments** Use coordinates to prove the Triangle Midsegment Theorem.

   A. *M* is the midpoint of $\overline{HJ}$. What are its coordinates?

   B. *N* is the midpoint of $\overline{JK}$. What are its coordinates?

   C. Find the slopes of $\overline{MN}$ and $\overline{HK}$. What can you conclude?

   D. Find *MN* and *HK*. What can you conclude?

The coordinates of the vertices of a triangle are given. Find the coordinates of the endpoints of the midsegment parallel to the given side of the triangle.

19. $A(-2, 5)$, $B(4, 9)$, $C(8, 3)$; $\overline{BC}$

20. $A(1, 1)$, $B(7, -1)$, $C(9, 3)$; $\overline{AB}$

21. $A(3, -1)$, $B(-3, -3)$, $C(-1, 5)$; $\overline{AC}$

22. $A(2, -3)$, $B(-4, -3)$, $C(4, 3)$; $\overline{AB}$

The vertices of $\triangle ABC$ are $A(3, -4)$, $B(-5, 2)$, and $C(5, 4)$. Verify that each segment is parallel to a side of the triangle and half the length of that side.

23. $\overline{LM}$ with endpoints $L(0, 3)$ and $M(4, 0)$

24. $\overline{MN}$ with endpoints $M(4, 0)$ and $N(-1, -1)$

Find the value of the variable.

25.

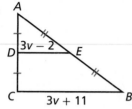

26.

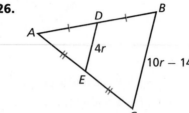

27.

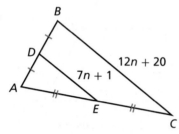

28.

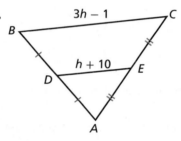

Spiral Review • Assessment Readiness

29. P is the centroid of $\triangle ABC$. What is the value of x?

   (A) 2

   (B) 17

   (C) 34

   (D) 51

30. Which of the following values of x make the inequality true? Select all that apply.

$$x + 5 > 17$$

   (A) $x = 5$ (C) $x = 12$

   (B) $x = 11$ (D) $x = 13$

   (E) $x = 17$

31. Match the segments of a triangle with the term for the point of concurrency of the segments.

Segments	Point of Concurrence
A. altitudes	**1.** centroid
B. medians	**2.** circumcenter
C. angle bisectors	**3.** orthocenter
D. perpendicular bisectors	**4.** incenter

 I'm in a Learning Mindset!

What is my plan for improving my performance with segments of triangles?

Triangle Sum Theorem

The sum of the measures of the interior angles of a triangle is 180°.

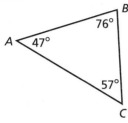

$$m\angle A + m\angle B + m\angle C = 47° + 76° + 57° = 180°$$

Perpendicular Bisectors

The perpendicular bisectors of a triangle are concurrent. The point of concurrency is called the circumcenter of the triangle.

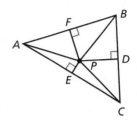

The circumcenter is equidistant from the vertices of the triangle.

$$PA = PB = PC$$

Angle Bisectors

The angle bisectors of a triangle are concurrent. The point of concurrency is called the incenter of the triangle.

The incenter is equidistant from the sides of the triangle.

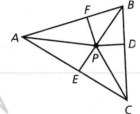

$$PA = PB = PC$$

Medians

The medians of a triangle are drawn from a vertex to the midpoint of the side opposite the vertex and are concurrent. The point of concurrency is called the centroid of the triangle.

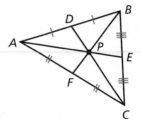

The centroid divides each median into a 2:3 ratio.

$$BP = \frac{2}{3}BF, \; AP = \frac{2}{3}AE, \; CP = \frac{2}{3}CD$$

Altitudes

The altitudes of a triangle are drawn from a vertex perpendicular to the side opposite the vertex and are concurrent. The point of concurrency is called the orthocenter of the triangle.

- Acute – inside triangle
- Right – on hypotenuse
- Obtuse – outside triangle

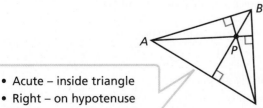

Midsegments

The midsegments are drawn from the midpoints of the sides of the triangle and are parallel to the third side.

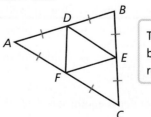

The triangle created by the midsegments represents a dilation.

$$AB = 2FE, \; BC = 2DF, \; AC = 2DE$$

$$\overline{AB} \parallel \overline{FE}, \; \overline{BC} \parallel \overline{DF}, \; \overline{CA} \parallel \overline{ED}$$

Vocabulary

Choose the correct term from the box to complete each sentence.

1. A(n) ___?___ is a segment whose endpoints are a vertex of the triangle and the midpoint of the opposite side.

2. An angle formed by one side of a polygon and an extension of an adjacent side is a(n) ___?___.

3. A(n) ___?___ is a perpendicular segment from a vertex to the line containing the opposite side.

4. Three or more lines that intersect at one point are ___?___ lines. The point of intersection is the ___?___.

Concepts and Skills

Determine each measure.

5. m∠B

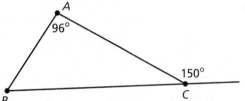

6. AB

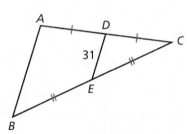

7. PD

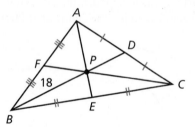

8. m∠ABC

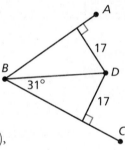

9. Determine the circumcenter of a triangle with vertices at $A(2, 4)$, $B(8, 2)$, and $C(4, -2)$.

10. A right triangle has an angle that measures 26°. What are the angle measures of all three angles of the triangle?

11. The coordinate of the vertices of a triangle are $X(1, 5)$, $Y(9, 3)$, and $Z(3, 1)$. Find the coordinates of the endpoints of the midsegment parallel to $\overline{XY}$.

12. **(MP) Use Tools** The coordinate of the vertices of a triangle are $J(-2, 4)$, $K(-1, -6)$, and $L(3, 2)$. Find the coordinates of the centroid of the triangle. State what strategy and tool you will use to answer the question, explain your choice, and then find the answer.

13. Explain why the circumcenter is equidistant to each vertex using properties of perpendicular bisectors.

14. Explain why the incenter is equidistant to each side using properties of angle bisectors.

15. What transformation maps a side of a triangle to the midsegment connecting the other two sides?

10 Triangle Inequalities

Robotic Scissor Lift

Triangles are commonly used in robotics to add stability and flexibility to the design. The control system of a robotic scissor lift uses an elastic belt to adjust the height of the lift.

A. The lengths of the metal bars, *AB* and *AC*, are 8 inches. What is the range of possible lengths of the rubber band? Explain your reasoning.

B. What type of triangle is formed by these components? Explain your reasoning.

C. At one setting, the length of the rubber band is 3 inches. At another setting, the length of the rubber band is 5 inches. At which setting is the measure of ∠A greater? Explain your reasoning.

D. How does the length of the rubber band affect the height of the scissor lift? Explain your reasoning.

Are You Ready?

Complete these problems to review prior concepts and skills you will need for this module.

Solve Two-Step Inequalities

Solve each inequality and graph the solution on a number line.

1. $3x - 5 > 10$

2. $4z + 7 \leq 23$

3. $7t - 4 \geq -32$

4. $-2b + 4 > 6$

5. $2x + 6 < 10$

6. $-5y - 4 \leq 11$

Draw Triangles with Given Conditions

Draw a triangle with the given measurements, if possible.

7. Side Lengths: 11, 15, 20

8. Side Lengths: 6, 9, 17

9. Angle Measures: 50°, 50°, 80°

10. Angle Measures: 30°, 50°, 90°

Solve Compound Inequalities

Solve each compound inequality and graph the solution on a number line.

11. $-4 < 3x - 1 < 8$

12. $2x + 5 < -1$ OR $2x - 5 \geq 3$

13. $5x + 3 \leq 8$ OR $4x + 1 \geq 17$

14. $-2 \leq 3x - 8$ AND $3x - 8 < 16$

15. $1 \leq 2x + 3 \leq 7$

16. $2x - 1 < -7$ AND $-3x + 9 < -3$

17. $5y - 16 \leq -1$ AND $3y + 4 > 13$

18. $-4x + 3 > 7$ OR $6x - 15 \geq 3$

Connecting Past and Present Learning

Previously, you learned:
- to write and solve inequalities that model geometric figures,
- to prove theorems about triangles, and
- to find the measure of an angle of a triangle using the other angle measures.

In this module, you will learn:
- to write inequalities comparing the side and angle measures within a triangle,
- to write inequalities comparing the side measures of two triangles, and
- to write inequalities comparing the angle measures of two triangles.

Inequalities Within a Triangle

(I Can) determine the relative sizes of angles and sides in a triangle.

Spark Your Learning

The map shows two paths through a ropes course, one orange and one purple.

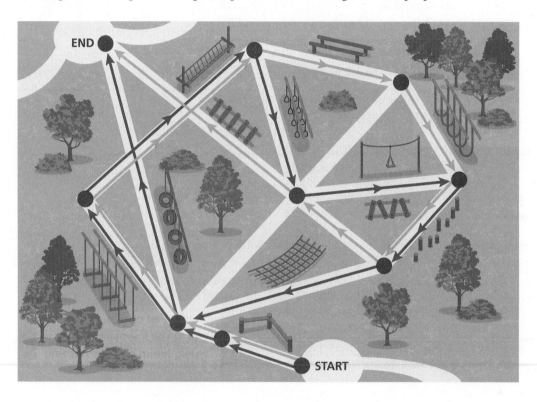

Complete Part A as a whole class. Then complete Parts B–D in small groups.

A. What is a mathematical question you can ask about this situation? What information would you need to know to answer your question?

B. What variable(s) are involved in this situation? What unit of measurement would you use for each variable?

C. To answer your question, what strategy and tool would you use along with all the information you have? What answer do you get?

D. Does your answer make sense in the context of the situation? How do you know?

 Turn and Talk Create a new path that is longer than any of the given paths. How do you know it is longer?

Build Understanding

Explore Triangle Inequalities

You have learned what combinations of angles are possible in a triangle and the relationships that exist among those angles. A relationship exists among the lengths of the sides of a triangle as well.

 A. In △*ABC*, *AB* = 3 inches and *BC* = 1.5 inches. To draw △*ABC*, first draw a segment that is 3 inches long with endpoints *A* and *B*.

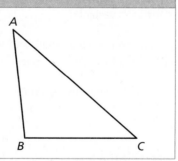

To determine all possible locations for vertex *C*, draw a circle centered at *B* with a radius of 1.5 inches.

How many triangles can be formed that have a side length of 3 inches and a side length of 1.5 inches?

B. Is it possible to place vertex *C* on the circle so that △*ABC* will have side lengths 1.5 inches, 3 inches, and 4 inches? Explain.

C. Is it possible to place vertex *C* on the circle so that *AC* will be greater than the sum of *AB* and *BC*? Explain.

D. Choose a placement for vertex *C* on the circle and draw the segments to form the triangle. Measure the side lengths and the angles. Where is the smallest angle in relation to the smallest side? Where is the largest angle in relation to the largest side?

 Turn and Talk Is it possible to place vertex *C* on the circle so that △*ABC* will be an isosceles triangle? Explain.

Use the Triangle Inequality Theorem

The relationship among the lengths of the sides of a triangle has been summarized in the following theorem.

Triangle Inequality Theorem
The sum of the lengths of any two sides of a triangle is greater than the length of the third side. $AB + BC > AC$ $BC + AC > AB$ $AC + AB > BC$ 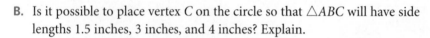

To be able to form a triangle, each of the three inequalities must be true. So, given three values, you can test to determine if they can be used as side lengths to form a triangle. To show that three values cannot be the side lengths of a triangle, you only need to show that one of the three triangle inequalities is false.

2 In an art class, Disha is designing a triangular picture frame using wooden strips of different lengths. Determine whether each set of wooden strips will form a triangle.

Set 1	Set 2
4 in., 5 in., 7 in.	3 in., 6 in., 11 in.

Compare the sum of each pair of possible side lengths to the third side length.

Set 1	Set 2
$4 + 5 > 7$	$3 + 6 \not> 11$
$5 + 7 > 4$	
$7 + 4 > 5$	

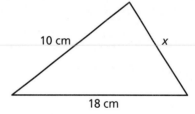

A. Explain why the wooden strips in Set 1 will form a triangle.

B. Why is only one inequality listed for Set 2?

C. What does the Triangle Inequality tell you about Set 2?

Turn and Talk In the same class, Arturo creates another design using three wooden strips with lengths 5 inches, 5 inches, and 5 inches. Does Arturo need to check all three inequalities to determine whether the design will form a triangle? Why?

3 Find the possible range of values for x in the triangle shown.

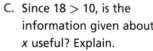

A. What is being compared in each of the inequalities below?

$10 + 18 > x$	$x + 10 > 18$	$x + 18 > 10$
$28 > x$	$x > 8$	$x > -8$

B. What information about the value of x is given in the first two inequalities?

C. Since $18 > 10$, is the information given about x useful? Explain.

Since the information in the third inequality is not useful, the range of values for x can be determined using the first two inequalities.

D. What is the range of values for x?

Turn and Talk Notice the range of values for x is between the sum of the two given side lengths and the difference of the two given side lengths. Is this relationship true for all triangles? Give examples to support your answer.

Step It Out

Use Side-Angle Relationships in Triangles

The side-angle relationships describe how the measures of the angles in a triangle are related to the side lengths of a triangle.

Side-Angle Relationships in Triangles

If one side of a triangle is longer than another side, then the angle opposite the longer side is larger than the angle opposite the shorter side.

$AC > BC$, so $m\angle B > m\angle A$.

If one angle of a triangle is larger than another angle, then the side opposite the larger angle is longer than the side opposite the smaller angle.

$m\angle D > m\angle F$, so $EF > DE$.

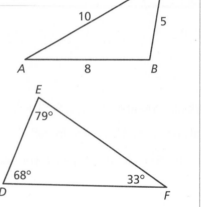

---

4 List the sides and angles in order from smallest to largest.

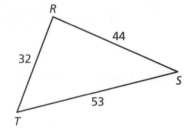

A. Why should the sides be listed in order from smallest to largest first, before listing the angles in order from smallest to largest?

Sides from smallest to largest: $\overline{RT}, \overline{RS}, \overline{ST}$

Angles from smallest to largest: $\angle S, \angle T, \angle R$

B. How do you know that $\angle S$ is the smallest angle?

C. How do you know that $\angle R$ is the largest angle?

5 List the sides and angles in order from smallest to largest.

A. What theorem is used to find the missing angle measure?

$m\angle G = 180° - (90° + 68°) = 22°$

Angles from smallest to largest: $\angle G, \angle F, \angle H$

Sides from smallest to largest: $\overline{FH}, \overline{GH}, \overline{FG}$

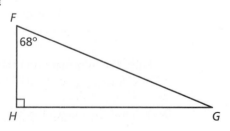

B. Why must the hypotenuse of a right triangle always be longer than either leg?

 Turn and Talk Suppose $\angle F$ and $\angle G$ have the same measure. What can you conclude about the sides opposite those angles?

Check Understanding

Use a compass and straightedge to decide whether each set of lengths can form a triangle. Explain your reasoning.

1. 7 cm, 9 cm, 18 cm

2. 2 in., 4 in., 5 in.

Determine whether a triangle can be formed with the given side lengths.

3. 3, 9, 11

4. 9, 12, 21

5. A triangle has sides with lengths 15, 23, and x. What is the range of possible values of x?

6. Name each angle in the triangle at the right. For each angle, name the side that is opposite that angle.

7. If you know the side lengths of a triangle, how can you determine which angle is the largest and which angle is the smallest?

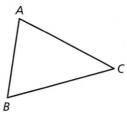

In Problems 8–10, use the given information about △ABC to list the sides and angles in order from smallest to largest.

8. m∠A = 60°, m∠B = 75°, m∠C = 45°

9. m∠A = 82°, m∠B = 48°, m∠C = 50°

10. AB = 14, BC = 26, AC = 20

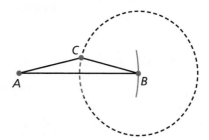

On Your Own

11. The construction below shows two possible triangles that can be formed when AB = 3 inches and BC = 1.5 inches. Describe what happens to the length of $\overline{AC}$ as point C moves counterclockwise around the circle toward point A.

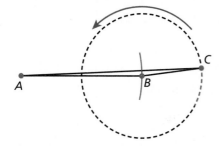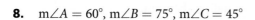

12. Jeannine is decorating pot holders with strips of fabric. She wants to make triangles using strips of fabric. Can she make a triangle with any of the following sets of strips of fabric? Explain your reasoning.

    A. 4 inches, 2 inches, and 5 inches

    B. 4 inches, 2 inches, and 1 inch

    C. 3 inches, 2 inches, and 5 inches

Use the two given side lengths of a triangle to describe the possible values for *x*, which represents the third side length.

13. 7, 13

14. 45, 44

15. 23, 14

16. 9, 15

17. STEM Nakia is an architect designing a house with a peaked roof. She is trying to decide what the limitations are on her design. If *AB* is 8 feet and $\triangle ABC$ will be isosceles, describe the possible lengths for *AC*.

18. Describe the values that are possible for the lengths of $\overline{BE}$, $\overline{CF}$, and $\overline{DE}$.

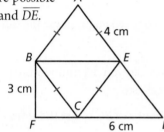

In Problems 19 and 20, use the diagram to prove the Triangle Inequality Theorem.

Given: $\triangle ABC$

Prove: (1) $AB + BC > AC$
(2) $AB + AC > BC$
(3) $AC + BC > AB$

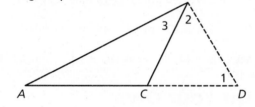

19. If the longest side of $\triangle ABC$ is $\overline{AB}$, why are (1) and (2) true?

20. Copy and complete the proof to prove (3) $AC + BC > AB$.

Statements	Reasons
1. ___?___	**1.** Given
2. Locate *D* on $\overrightarrow{AC}$ so that $BC = DC$.	**2.** Ruler Postulate
3. $AC + DC =$ ___?___	**3.** Segment Addition Postulate
4. $\angle 1 \cong \angle 2$	**4.** ___?___
5. $m\angle 1 = m\angle 2$	**5.** ___?___
6. $m\angle ABD = m\angle 2 +$ ___?___	**6.** Angle Addition Postulate
7. $m\angle ABD > m\angle 2$	**7.** Comparison Property of Inequality
8. $m\angle ABD > m\angle 1$	**8.** ___?___
9. $AD > AB$	**9.** ___?___
10. $AC + DC > AB$	**10.** ___?___
11. ___?___	**11.** Substitution

List the sides and angles in order from smallest to largest.

21.

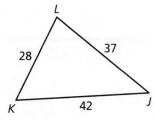

22.

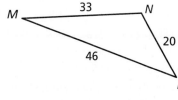

23.

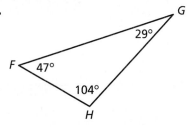

24.

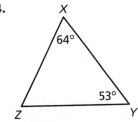

25. Navigation A large ship is sailing between three small islands. To do so, the ship must sail between two pairs of islands, avoiding sailing between a third pair. The safest route is to avoid the closest pair of islands. Which is the safest route for the ship?

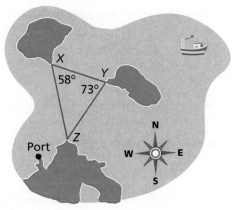

26. Three cell phone towers form △*PQR*. The measure of ∠*Q* is 10° less than the measure of ∠*P*. The measure of ∠*R* is 5° greater than the measure of ∠*Q*. Which two towers are closest together?

27. In any triangle *ABC*, suppose you know the lengths of $\overline{AB}$ and $\overline{BC}$, and suppose that *AB* > *BC*. If *x* is the length of the third side $\overline{AC}$, use the Triangle Inequality Theorem to show that *AB* − *BC* < *x* < *AB* + *BC*. That is, *x* must be between the difference and the sum of the other two side lengths.

Prove that the statements are true.

28. Given: △*ABC* ≅ △*DEF*

Prove: *d* + *e* > *c*

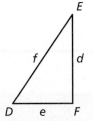

29. Given: △*ABC*

Prove: *AC* > *AB*

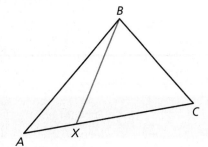

30. **Analyzing Cases** A hole on a golf course is a dogleg, meaning that it bends in the middle. A golfer will usually start by driving for the bend in the dogleg (from *A* to *B*), and then use a second shot to get the ball to the green (from *B* to *C*). Sandy believes she may be able to drive the ball far enough to reach the green in one shot, avoiding the bend (from *A* directly to *C*). Sandy knows she can accurately drive a distance of 250 yards. Should she attempt to drive for the green on her first shot? Explain.

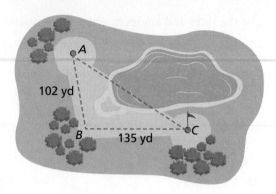

31. (Open Middle™) Fill in the boxes with possible measures for the three angles such that the measure of angle *A* is the greatest possible. Use each digit from 1 to 9 at most one time.

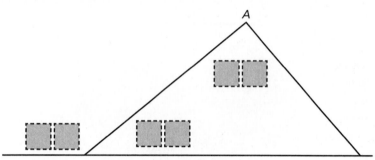

Spiral Review • Assessment Readiness

32. Find the length of $\overline{VW}$.

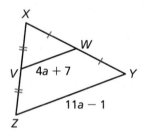

Ⓐ $\frac{8}{7}$

Ⓒ $\frac{81}{7}$

Ⓑ 5

Ⓓ 27

33. A triangle has angles that measure 46° and 76°. What is the measure of the third angle?

Ⓐ 14°

Ⓒ 58°

Ⓑ 44°

Ⓓ 122°

34. Find *GF* if *BF* = 45.

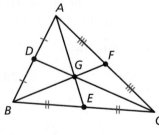

Ⓐ 15

Ⓒ 45

Ⓑ 30

Ⓓ 60

 I'm in a Learning Mindset!

Did I have any biases that affected my attempt to understand inequalities in one triangle? How did I address them?

Keep Going to▶ Journal and Practice Workbook

Inequalities Between Two Triangles

(I Can) determine the relative sizes of angles and sides in two triangles.

Spark Your Learning

A passenger, flying in a small plane, has two options of flights to get from the starting airport to the destination airport.

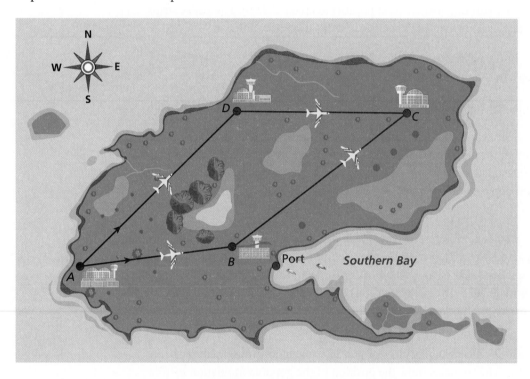

Complete Part A as a whole class. Then complete Parts B–D in small groups.

- **A.** What is a mathematical question you can ask about this situation? What information would you need to know to answer your question?

- **B.** What variable(s) are involved in this situation?

- **C.** To answer your question, what strategy and tool would you use along with all the information you have? What answer do you get?

- **D.** Does your answer make sense in the context of the situation? How do you know?

 Turn and Talk Predict how your answer would change if the measure of the angle in the left triangle was 39° and the measure of the angle in the right triangle was 36°.

Build Understanding

Explore Inequalities in Two Triangles

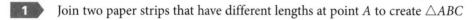

1 ▶ Join two paper strips that have different lengths at point *A* to create △*ABC*

    A. Move the paper strips so that ∠*A* is the largest angle in △*ABC*. Which side of the triangle is the longest?

    B. Move the paper strips so that ∠*A* is the smallest angle in △*ABC*. Which side of the triangle is the shortest?

Join another pair of paper strips at point *D* to create △*DEF*. The paper strips should be the same lengths as the paper strips used in △*ABC*.

    C. Adjust the paper strips so that ∠*A* is larger than ∠*D*. How are $\overline{BC}$ and $\overline{EF}$ related?

    D. Which corresponding parts in △*ABC* and △*DEF* are congruent? Explain.

    E. If you are given that two sides of a triangle are congruent to two sides of another triangle, and the included angle in the first triangle is larger than the included angle in the second triangle, what can you conclude about the sides opposite the included angles?

 Turn and Talk Suppose you are given that two sides of a triangle are congruent to two sides of another triangle, and the third side of the first triangle is longer than the third side of the second triangle. What can you conclude about the angles included between the two congruent sides? Use diagrams of the triangles to support your answer.

2 ▶ Two positions of a swinging circular gondola ride at an amusement park are shown. The triangles show the position of the gondola in relation to its starting point.

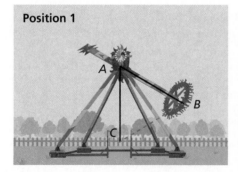

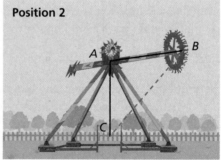

    A. Which corresponding sides of the triangles are congruent?

    B. The distance from *B* to *C* in Position 1 is less than the distance from *B* to *C* in Position 2. What can you conclude about the angles opposite these sides?

Step It Out

The Hinge Theorem and Its Converse

You have learned how to apply inequalities to relate the sides and angles in one triangle. The following theorems relate the sides and angles in two triangles.

Hinge Theorem

If two sides of one triangle are congruent to two sides of another triangle, and the included angle in the first triangle is larger than the included angle in the second triangle, then the third side of the first triangle is longer than the third side of the second triangle.

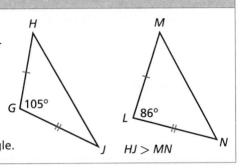

$HJ > MN$

Converse of the Hinge Theorem

If two sides of one triangle are congruent to two sides of another triangle, and the third side of the first triangle is longer than the third side of the second triangle, then the included angle in the first triangle is larger than the included angle in the second triangle.

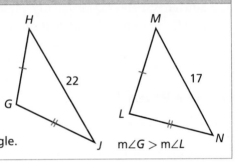

22   17

$m\angle G > m\angle L$

---

3 Compare DC and BC using the information given in the diagram.

Compare the sides and angles in $\triangle ADC$ and $\triangle ABC$.

$m\angle DAC > m\angle BAC$ $\overline{AD} \cong \overline{AB}$ $\overline{AC} \cong \overline{AC}$

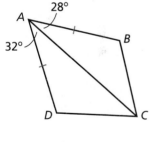

> **A.** How do you know that $m\angle DAC > m\angle BAC$?

> **B.** Why is this congruence statement listed?

By the Hinge Theorem, $DC > BC$. ◄

> **C.** Why can the Hinge Theorem be applied to compare DC and BC?

Turn and Talk The Hinge Theorem is also called the Side–Angle–Side Inequality Theorem. Explain why both names are appropriate for this theorem.

4 Find the range of possible values for x.

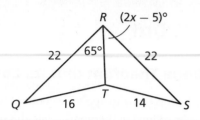

Compare the sides and angles in $\triangle QRT$ and $\triangle SRT$.

The Converse of the Hinge Theorem can be used to conclude that m$\angle SRT <$ m$\angle QRT$.

$2x - 5 < 65$ ← **A.** Why can the Converse of the
$2x < 70$ Hinge Theorem be applied
$x < 35$ to make this conclusion?

Find all positive values for m$\angle SRT$.

$2x - 5 > 0$ ← **B.** Why is this step necessary?
$2x > 5$
$x > 2.5$

The range of values for x is $2.5 < x < 35$.

 Turn and Talk Write a different variable expression to represent m$\angle SRT$ so that the value of the variable can be negative while the measure of the angle is positive.

Use the Hinge Theorem in a Proof

5 Use the Hinge Theorem to prove that $LM > NP$.

Given: $\overline{LN} \cong \overline{MP}$

Prove: $LM > NP$

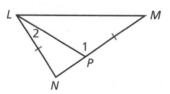

Statements	Reasons
1. $\overline{LN} \cong \overline{MP}$	**1.** Given
2. $\overline{LP} \cong \overline{LP}$	**2.** Reflexive Property of Congruence
3. $\angle 1$ is an exterior angle of $\triangle LPN$.	**3.** Definition of an exterior angle
4. m$\angle 1 =$ m$\angle 2 +$ m$\angle LNP$	**4.** Exterior Angle Theorem
5. m$\angle 2 +$ m$\angle LNP >$ m$\angle 2$	**5.** If $a = b + c$, where c is positive, then $a > b$.
6. m$\angle 1 >$ m$\angle 2$	**6.** Substitution
7. $LM > NP$	**7.** Hinge Theorem

A. Explain this property in words rather than in symbols.

B. Why can the Hinge Theorem be applied to make this conclusion?

Write an Indirect Proof

In an **indirect proof**, you begin by assuming that the conclusion is false. Then you show that this assumption leads to a contradiction. This type of proof is also called a proof by contradiction.

How to Write an Indirect Proof
Step 1: Identify the statement to be proven.
Step 2: Assume the opposite (negation) of that statement is true.
Step 3: Use direct reasoning until you reach a contradiction.
Step 4: Conclude that since the assumption is false, the original statement must be true.

6 ▶ Prove the Converse of the Hinge Theorem.

Given: $\overline{AB} \cong \overline{DE}$, $\overline{AC} \cong \overline{DF}$, $BC > EF$

Prove: $m\angle A > m\angle D$

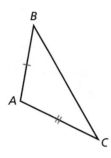
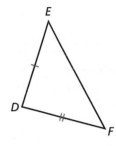

> **A.** Why do you want to make this assumption?

Assume $m\angle A \not> m\angle D$. So, either $m\angle A < m\angle D$ or $m\angle A = m\angle D$.

Check if each case is true.

Case 1

If $m\angle A < m\angle D$, then $BC < EF$ by the Hinge Theorem. This contradicts the given information that $BC > EF$. So, $m\angle A \not< m\angle D$.

> **B.** Why can you use SAS Triangle Congruence to show the triangles are congruent?

Case 2

If $m\angle A = m\angle D$, then $\angle A \cong \angle D$. So $\triangle ABC \cong \triangle DEF$ by SAS Triangle Congruence Theorem. Then $\overline{BC} \cong \overline{EF}$ by CPCTC, and $BC = EF$. This contradicts the given information that $BC > EF$. So, $m\angle A \neq m\angle D$.

The assumption $m\angle A \not> m\angle D$ is false. Therefore $m\angle A > m\angle D$.

 Turn and Talk Use the information below to write an indirect proof to show that a right triangle cannot have an obtuse angle.

Given: $\triangle RST$ is a triangle with right angle $\angle R$.

Prove: $\triangle RST$ does not have an obtuse angle.

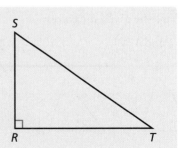

Check Understanding

1. Consider △ABC and △XYZ with $\overline{AB} \cong \overline{XY}$ and $\overline{AC} \cong \overline{XZ}$. If ∠A is smaller than ∠X, how are $\overline{BC}$ and $\overline{YZ}$ related?

2. Consider △ABC and △RST.

   If $\overline{AC}$ is shorter than $\overline{RT}$, what can you conclude about the angles opposite these sides?

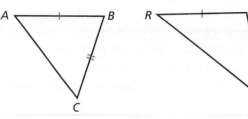

In Problems 3–6, use the triangles shown.

3. Compare m∠D and m∠G.

4. Compare BC and HJ.

5. Describe the restrictions on x.

6. Suppose the Hinge Theorem is being used to prove that EF is greater than HJ. What criteria need to be stated in the proof before the Hinge Theorem can be applied?

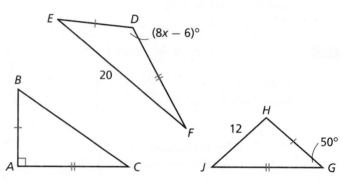

7. Explain why an indirect proof is called proof by contradiction.

On Your Own

8. Two positions of an open gate are shown. The triangles show the position of the gate in relation to its closed position. The distance from G to H in Position 1 is less than the distance from G to H in Position 2. What can you conclude about the angles opposite these sides?

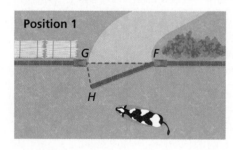

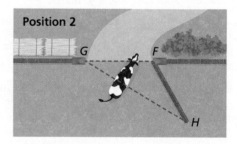

Compare the given measures.

9. ST and VW

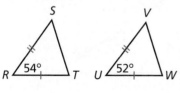

10. AB and BD

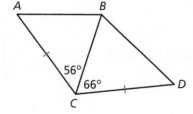

11. VW and CZ

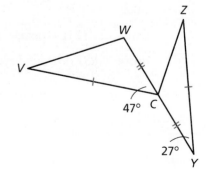

Compare the given measures.

12. m∠1 and m∠2

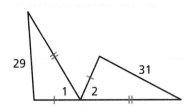

29

31

1 2

13. m∠L and m∠D

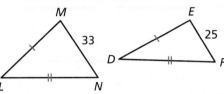

M

33

E

25

D

F

L

N

14. m∠1 and m∠2

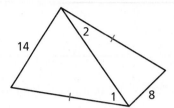

2

14

1   8

Use the Hinge Theorem and its converse to describe the restrictions on the value of the variable.

15.

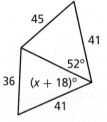

B (4x − 8) ft C

40°

30°

A

(2x + 12) ft

D

16.

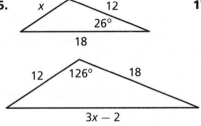

x   12

26°

18

12   126°   18

3x − 2

17.

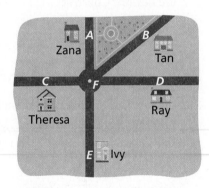

45

41

52°

36   (x + 18)°

41

18. Geography The road from A to E and the road from C and D are perpendicular and intersect at point F. Theresa's house is at C, 500 feet from the intersection. Ray's house is at D, 750 feet from the intersection. Ivy's house is at E, 750 feet from the intersection. Zana's house is at A, 500 feet from the intersection, and Tan's house is at B, 750 feet from F. Which distance is longer, the distance from Zana's house to Tan's house or the distance from Theresa's house to Ivy's house? Show how you know.

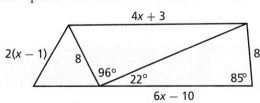

A
Zana
B
Tan
C   F   D
Theresa   Ray
E   Ivy

19. Two pairs of hikers leave the same camp heading in opposite directions. Each travels 2 miles, then changes direction and travels 1.2 miles. The first pair starts due east and then turns 50° toward north. The second pair starts due west and then turns 40° toward south. Which pair is farther from camp? Explain your reasoning.

20. **(MP) Critique Reasoning** Terrence says that $AB > CD$ by the Hinge Theorem. Is he right? Explain why or why not.

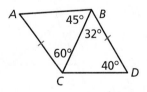

A   B
45°
32°
60°
40° D
C

21. The triangles at the right show the paths in a town's public square.

A. Write an inequality for the possible values of x.

B. If the triangle with the side length $2(x − 1)$ is equilateral, what is the value of x?

C. Using the value of x you found in Part B, what are the lengths of the sides represented by $4x + 3$ and $6x − 10$?

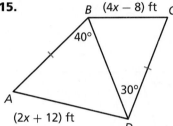

4x + 3

2(x − 1)   8

96°

22°

85°

8

6x − 10

22. Prove that ∠BCD > m∠ABC using the Converse of the Hinge Theorem.

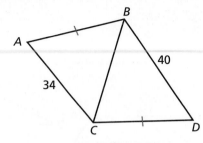

Given: $\overline{AB} \cong \overline{CD}$
Prove: ∠BCD > m∠ABC

23. Write an indirect proof to prove that two supplementary angles cannot both be obtuse angles.

Given: ∠1 and ∠2 are supplementary.

Prove: ∠1 and ∠2 cannot both be obtuse.

24. (MP) **Critique Reasoning** Tiffany says an indirect proof is less reliable than a direct proof because you have to start by assuming something. Is Tiffany right? Explain why or why not.

25. Open Ended Reginald is trying to design a stage riser as shown. *AC* must be equal to *CD* but the other lengths are flexible. Construct a set of triangles as shown that fit the requirements. Which side is longer, $\overline{AB}$ or $\overline{BD}$?

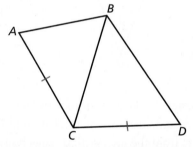

Spiral Review • Assessment Readiness

26. If a line joins a vertex of a triangle to the midpoint of the opposing side, bisecting it, it is the ____?____.

Ⓐ altitude

Ⓑ perpendicular bisector

Ⓒ angle bisector

Ⓓ median

27. In the picture shown, $\overline{DE}$ is which of the following?

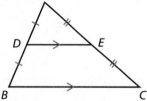

Ⓐ altitude

Ⓑ median

Ⓒ bisector

Ⓓ midsegment

28. If △ABC has sides 4 and 11 which of the following are possible measures for the length of the third side? Select all that apply.

Ⓐ 2   Ⓓ 9

Ⓑ 5   Ⓔ 11

Ⓒ 7.5   Ⓕ 15

29. Which angles are congruent to ∠1? Select all that apply.

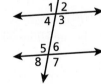

Ⓐ ∠2   Ⓓ ∠5

Ⓑ ∠3   Ⓔ ∠6

Ⓒ ∠4   Ⓕ ∠7

 I'm in a Learning Mindset!

How did I assert my own needs and viewpoints when learning about inequalities in two triangles?

Side-Angle Relationships

The sum of the interior angles of a triangle is 180°.

To determine the measure of ∠E, subtract the other angles from 180°.

m∠E = 180° − 84° − 67° = 29°

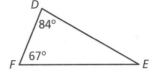

The angles in order greatest to least measure are ∠D, ∠F, ∠E.

If one angle of a triangle is larger than another angle, then the side opposite the larger angle is longer than the side opposite the smaller angle.

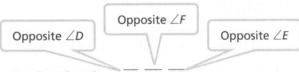

| Opposite ∠D | Opposite ∠F | Opposite ∠E |

So, the sides in order from greatest to least length are $\overline{EF}$, $\overline{DE}$, $\overline{DF}$.

Triangle Inequality Theorem

Not every combination of sides can be used to form a triangle.

| There is no point of intersection, so there is no triangle. | There are two points of intersection, so there is a triangle. | There is one point of intersection, so there is no triangle. |

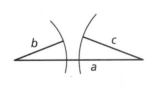

$a > b + c$

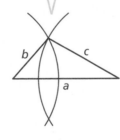

$a < b + c$

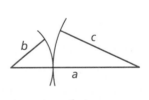

$a = b + c$

Hinge Theorem

When two triangles have two pairs of congruent sides but the included angles differ, then the sides opposite the included angle differ accordingly.

m∠YZX is greater than m∠WZX,

so YX is greater than WX.

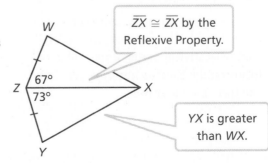

$\overline{ZX} \cong \overline{ZX}$ by the Reflexive Property.

YX is greater than WX.

Vocabulary

Choose the correct term from the box to complete each sentence.

1. A(n) ___?___ is a statement that has been proven.

2. The ___?___ is a statement formed by exchanging the hypothesis and conclusion of a condition statement.

3. A(n) ___?___ is a three-sided polygon.

4. A(n) ___?___ is a proof in which the statement to be proved is assumed to be false and a contradiction is shown.

5. A(n) ___?___ is a statement that compares two expressions by using one of the following signs: $>, <, \geq, \leq, \neq$.

Concepts and Skills

6. Explain why you can not create $\triangle ABC$ such that $AC \geq AB + BC$.

Determine whether a triangle can be formed with the given side lengths. Explain your reasoning.

7. 7 in., 2 in., 8 in.

8. 4 cm, 11 cm, 6 cm

9. 16 m, 10 m, 5 m

10. 23 ft, 16 ft, 38 ft

Find the range of possible values of x using the Triangle Inequality Theorem.

11.

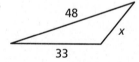

12.

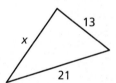

13. A. Compare BC and EF. Explain your reasoning.

   B. Compare $m\angle B$ and $m\angle E$. Explain your reasoning

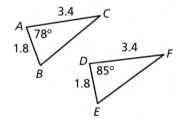

14. A. Compare $m\angle JGI$ and $m\angle HGI$. Explain your reasoning.

   B. **(MP) Use Tools** Write an indirect proof to prove that $\angle JGI$ is not congruent to $\angle HGI$. State what strategy and tool you will use to answer the question, explain your choice, and then find the answer.

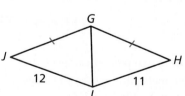

Quadrilaterals, Polygons, and Triangle Similarity

Digital Animator

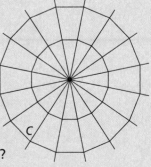
STEM
POWERING INGENUITY

Digital animators implement polygonal meshes to create models for graphics that are used in movies, video games, and other media. They need to communicate with clients to understand the requirements of a project, develop storyboards and 2-D models of the project, and work with the creative team to finalize designs.

©mofaez/Shutterstock

STEM Task

A client asks that circular regions be divided into polygonal regions that convey line and rotational symmetry. Because small angles cause problems in animation, the client asks that no angles be less than 7°.

What is the maximum possible angle measure for C?

What if no angle can be less than $x°$?

Learning Mindset
Resilience Adjusts to Change

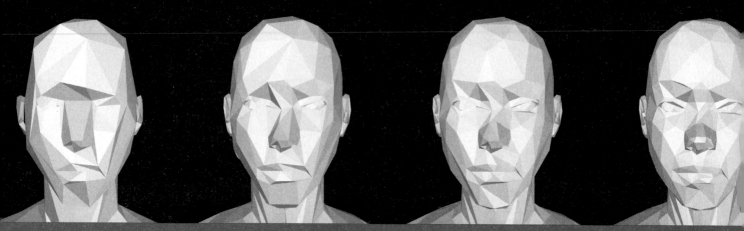

How do you respond to change? When any type of change occurs, it can be uncomfortable. Keep in mind that adapting to change yields growth. Having a plan to adjust to changes can build your confidence as you work through transitional periods. Here are some questions you can ask yourself to help you navigate and adjust to changes:

- Can the situation I am in be changed? Why or why not?

- If the situation can be changed, how am I going to change it? What reasons do I have for wanting the change?

- How am I devoting my energy to change my learning situation? Should I spend my energy on changing the situation or my approach?

- If the situation cannot be changed, how am I going to adapt to the new situation? How can I adjust? How will I grow?

- Who can I ask for advice about change? What questions can I ask?

©German Ovchinnikov/Alamy

Reflect

Q Think about a time when you had to deal with a big change. How did you approach the change? What was your mindset? What was the outcome, and how would you change your approach in the future?

Q As a digital animator, how would you adjust when the client changes the requirements of a project? What kind of response would be beneficial? How would this method help you in your career development?

Quadrilaterals and Polygons

Module Performance Task: Focus on STEM

4-Link Rear Suspension Systems

A parallel 4-link suspension system is used in both
street cars and race cars. This system is designed to
keep the rear axle centered while preventing it from
rotating. The position of the bars can be changed to
improve acceleration to meet the conditions that the
car will be driving in.

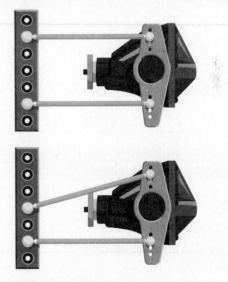

A. For street driving, the top and bottom bars are the
same length and the distance between the bolts
is equal on both front and rear. What type of
quadrilateral is formed? Explain your reasoning.

B. Keeping the bottom bar perpendicular to a
segment that passes between the front bolts,
what type of quadrilateral is formed? Explain
your reasoning.

C. For drag racing, you want to angle the bars so that, if they were extended,
they would intersect near the cars center of gravity. Keeping the bolt segments
vertical, what type of quadrilateral is formed? Explain your reasoning.

D. If the bars were extended, the location of the point of intersection
determines the cars acceleration. How can you determine where the
point of intersection is located?

Are You Ready?

Complete these problems to review prior concepts and skills you will need for this module.

Solve Multi-Step Equations

Solve each equation.

1. $5b + 7 = -3b + 39$

2. $7y + 15 = 10y + 21$

3. $5(t + 2) = 9t - 14$

4. $-3m + 1 = 4(m - 5)$

Congruent Figures

Can you perform a series of transformations on Figure 1 to create Figure 2? Explain your reasoning.

5.

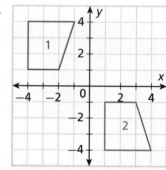

6.

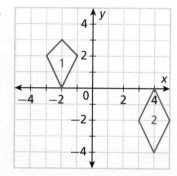

Parallel Lines Cut by a Transversal

Find the value of x.

7.

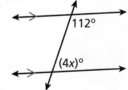

8.

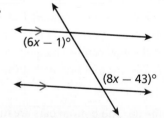

Connecting Past and Present Learning

Previously, you learned:

- to identify symmetries in figures,
- to determine if figures are congruent using transformations, and
- to use triangle congruence criteria to prove relationships.

In this module, you will learn:

- to classify a quadrilateral as a parallelogram, rectangle, rhombus, square, kite, or trapezoid,
- to use congruence criteria to prove properties of special quadrilaterals, and
- to use the properties of special quadrilaterals to determine unknown measures.

Properties of Parallelograms

(I Can) **prove and use properties of parallelograms.**

Spark Your Learning

Louisa is making a quilt using parallelograms.

Complete Part A as a whole class. Then complete Parts B–D in small groups.

A. What is a geometric question that you can ask about this situation?

B. Does it appear that the quadrilaterals are made from one piece of fabric? How are the fabric quadrilaterals made?

C. To answer your question, what strategy and tool would you use along with all the information you have? What answer do you get?

D. Does your answer make sense in the context of the situation? How do you know?

 Turn and Talk Do your results change if you use the longer diagonal of the quadrilateral to create triangles?

Build Understanding

Explore Quadrilaterals

Use a straightedge to draw three different quadrilaterals. Then draw a diagonal from one vertex of each quadrilateral. An example is shown.

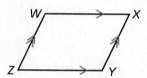

A. How many triangles are formed in each quadrilateral?

B. Use what you know about the Triangle Sum Theorem to find the sum of the measures of the interior angles in each quadrilateral. What is the sum?

 Turn and Talk Suppose you know that all four angles of a quadrilateral are congruent. What is the measure of each angle? Explain how you found your answer.

Explore Parallelograms

A **parallelogram** is a quadrilateral with both pairs of opposite sides parallel. The symbol $\square$ is used to write the name of a parallelogram. In $\square WXYZ$, $\overline{WZ}$ and $\overline{XY}$ are parallel, and $\overline{WX}$ and $\overline{ZY}$ are parallel.

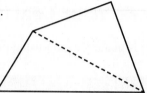

2 Use a geometric drawing tool to construct two pairs of parallel lines. The intersections of the lines create a parallelogram. Label the vertices of the parallelogram A, B, C, and D. Then show the measures of the interior angles and the side lengths of the parallelogram.

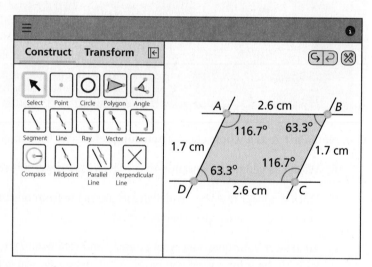

A. What do you notice about the side lengths?

B. What do you notice about the measures of the angles?

C. Drag one of the vertices to change the shape. Does the quadrilateral remain a parallelogram? How do you know?

D. Observe the side lengths and the angle measures of the parallelograms formed as you drag one of the vertices. Are your observations from Parts A and B the same for all of the parallelograms?

 Turn and Talk How could you use rotations to show that your observations in Parts A and B are true?

Theorems about Quadrilaterals and Parallelograms

The observations you made about quadrilaterals and parallelograms can be stated as theorems.

Quadrilateral Sum Theorem

The sum of the angle measures in a quadrilateral is 360°.

Opposite Sides of a Parallelogram Theorem

If a quadrilateral is a parallelogram, then its opposite sides are congruent.

Opposite Angles of a Parallelogram Theorem

If a quadrilateral is a parallelogram, then its opposite angles are congruent.

---

3 ▶ Prove that the opposite angles of a parallelogram are congruent.

Given: *ABCD* is a parallelogram.

Prove: $\angle A \cong \angle C$

A. How can the two triangles in the parallelogram be used to show that $\angle A \cong \angle C$?

Statements	Reasons
1. *ABCD* is a parallelogram.	1. Given
2. Draw $\overline{BD}$.	2. Through any two points, there is exactly one line.
3. $\overline{AB} \parallel \overline{DC}$, $\overline{AD} \parallel \overline{BC}$	3. Definition of parallelogram
4. $\angle 1 \cong \angle 4$, $\angle 2 \cong \angle 3$	4. Alternate Interior Angles Theorem
5. $\overline{DB} \cong \overline{DB}$	5. Reflexive Property of Congruence
6. $\triangle ABD \cong \triangle CDB$	6. ASA Triangle Congruence Theorem
7. $\angle A \cong \angle C$	7. Corresponding parts of congruent figures are congruent.

B. This proof shows only one result of the Opposite Angles of a Parallelogram Theorem. What else needs to be proven?

C. Explain how to show that $\angle B \cong \angle D$.

 Turn and Talk How can the proof shown, in Part A, be used to write a proof for the Opposite Sides of a Parallelogram Theorem?

Step It Out

Prove Diagonals Bisect Each Other

A **diagonal of a polygon** is a segment connecting two nonconsecutive vertices of a polygon.

Diagonals of a Parallelogram Theorem

If a quadrilateral is a parallelogram, then its diagonals bisect each other.

In *ABCD*, $\overline{AE} \cong \overline{CE}$ and $\overline{BE} \cong \overline{DE}$.

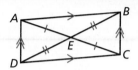

---

4 ▶ Prove that the diagonals of a parallelogram bisect each other.

Given: *ABCD* is a parallelogram.

Prove: $\overline{AE} \cong \overline{CE}$ and $\overline{BE} \cong \overline{DE}$

A. How are ∠2 and ∠3 related? How do you know?

B. How are ∠1 and ∠4 related? How do you know?

Statements	Reasons
1. *ABCD* is a parallelogram.	**1.** Given
2. $\overline{AB} \parallel \overline{DC}$	**2.** Definition of parallelogram
3. ∠1 ≅ ∠4, ∠2 ≅ ∠3	**3.** Alternate Interior Angles Theorem
4. $\overline{AB} \cong \overline{CD}$	**4.** Opposite Sides of a Parallelogram Theorem
5. △*ABE* ≅ △*CDE*	**5.** ASA Triangle Congruence Theorem
6. $\overline{AE} \cong \overline{CE}$ and $\overline{BE} \cong \overline{DE}$	**6.** Corresponding parts of congruent figures are congruent.

C. Is it possible to prove this theorem using a different triangle congruence theorem? Explain your reasoning.

D. Why do you think the Diagonals of a Parallelogram Theorem is presented after the Opposite Sides of a Parallelogram Theorem?

E. Suppose you stated $\overline{AD} \parallel \overline{BC}$ instead of $\overline{AB} \parallel \overline{DC}$ in Step 2. How does the proof change?

Turn and Talk Suppose you draw a quadrilateral with vertices $A(3, 2)$, $B(1, -2)$, $C(-3, -2)$, and $D(-1, 2)$ in the coordinate plane.
- Confirm that opposite sides are parallel, so *ABCD* is a parallelogram.
- What transformation carries parallelogram *ABCD* onto parallelogram *CDAB*? How does that transformation establish some of the properties of parallelograms discussed in this lesson?

Use Properties of Parallelograms

You can use the properties of parallelograms to find the unknown lengths and unknown angle measures of parallelograms.

5 ▶ A guitar has markers on the fret board that are shaped like parallelograms. Find BC and $m\angle B$ in the fret marker shown.

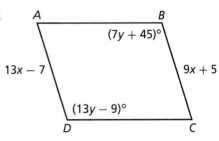

Find BC.

To find BC, first find the value of x.

$$\overline{AD} \cong \overline{BC}$$

A. What theorem allows you to conclude that $\overline{AD} \cong \overline{BC}$? Why can you apply this theorem?

$$AD = BC$$

$$13x - 7 = 9x + 5$$

$$4x = 12$$

$$x = 3$$

Next, substitute the value of x into the expression for BC.

$$BC = 9x + 5 = 9(3) + 5 = 32$$

The length of $\overline{BC}$ is 32.

Find m∠B.

To find $m\angle B$, first find the value of y.

$$\angle B \cong \angle D$$

B. What theorem allows you to conclude that $\angle B \cong \angle D$? Why can you apply this theorem?

$$m\angle B = m\angle D$$

$$7y + 45 = 13y - 9$$

$$54 = 6y$$

$$9 = y$$

Next, substitute the value of y into the expression for $m\angle B$.
$$m\angle B = (7y + 45)° = (7(9) + 45)° = 108°$$

The measure of $\angle B$ is 108°.

> **Turn and Talk** Do you have enough information to find AB and $m\angle A$? Explain your reasoning.

Check Understanding

1. You are given the measures of three of the angles of a quadrilateral. Explain how you can use the Quadrilateral Sum Theorem to find the measure of the fourth angle.

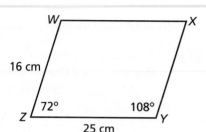

WXYZ is a parallelogram. Find each measure.

2. *WX*

3. *XY*

4. m∠*W*

5. m∠*X*

6. In parallelogram *KLMN*, diagonals $\overline{KM}$ and $\overline{NL}$ intersect at *V* and *KV* = 8. What is *MV*?

For Problems 7 and 8, ABCD is a parallelogram. Find the measure.

7. *AD*

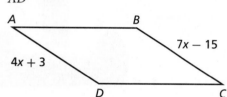

8. m∠*B*

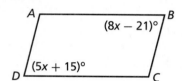

On Your Own

9. **(MP) Reason** Write a paragraph proof of the Quadrilateral Sum Theorem.

   Given: Quadrilateral *FGHJ*

   Prove: m∠*F* + m∠*G* + m∠*H* + m∠*J* = 360°

Find the measure of the unknown angle in each quadrilateral.

10.

11.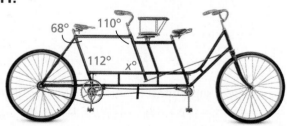

QRST is a parallelogram. QR = 2, RS = 4.1, SP = 2.5, and m∠RST = 76°. Find each measure.

12. *QT*

13. *PQ*

14. *QS*

15. m∠*TQR*

16. **(MP)** **Construct Arguments** Prove that the opposite sides of the parallelogram are congruent.

Given: $ABCD$ is a parallelogram.

Prove: $\overline{AB} \cong \overline{DC}$, $\overline{AD} \cong \overline{BC}$

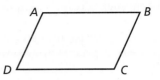

17. **(MP)** **Reason** Prove the Consecutive Angles of a Parallelogram Theorem, which is stated below.

> If a quadrilateral is a parallelogram, then its consecutive angles are supplementary.

Given: $ABCD$ is a parallelogram.

Prove: $\angle A$ is supplementary to $\angle B$,
$\angle B$ is supplementary to $\angle C$,
$\angle C$ is supplementary to $\angle D$, and
$\angle D$ is supplementary to $\angle A$.

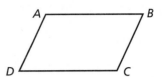

KLMN **is a parallelogram. Find each measure.**

18. KN

$9x - 6$

$7x + 2$

19. $m\angle K$

$(7x + 12)°$

$(4x + 3)°$

20. In parallelogram $EFGH$, diagonals $\overline{EG}$ and $\overline{FH}$ intersect at I.
$EI = 6s - 10$ and
$GI = 3s + 11$. What is GI?

WXYZ **is a parallelogram.** $WY = 4a - 6$,
$WP = a + 12$. **Find each measure.**

21. WZ

22. PY

23. $m\angle PYZ$

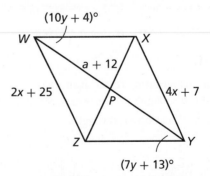

$(10y + 4)°$

$a + 12$

$2x + 25$

$4x + 7$

$(7y + 13)°$

24. Lindsey is designing a stained glass window using parallelograms. She draws a model before starting her work. In her model $BCGF$ and $CDHG$ are parallelograms, and $\overline{BC} \cong \overline{CD}$. Find all the segments that are congruent to $\overline{KG}$.

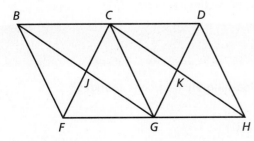

©Jasmin Merdan/Moment/Getty Images

For Problems 25 and 26, write a two-column proof.

25. **Given:** *ABCD* and *AXYZ* are parallelograms.

    Prove: $\angle C \cong \angle Y$

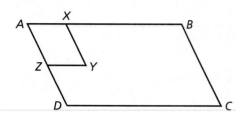

26. **Given:** *CDFE* and *FGIH* are parallelograms, and $\overline{EF} \cong \overline{FG}$.

    Prove: $\overline{CD} \cong \overline{HI}$

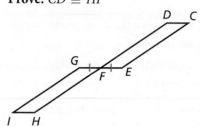

27. Prove that the three medians in a triangle are concurrent.

    Given: In $\triangle ABC$, $\overline{CD}$ and $\overline{BE}$ are medians that intersect at *G*.

    Prove: $\overline{AJ}$ is a median that also passes through *G*.

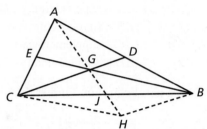

Spiral Review • Assessment Readiness

28. Which of the following sets of numbers can be the side lengths of a triangle? Select all that apply.

    (A) 4, 5, 10

    (B) 12, 15, 18

    (C) 7, 11, 17

    (D) 19, 21, 40

    (E) 13, 13, 25

    (F) 8, 10, 20

29. In $\triangle ABC$, $AB = 5$, $AC = 7$, and $m\angle A = 65°$. In $\triangle XYZ$, $XY = 5$ and $XZ = 7$. If $BC > YZ$, which of the following can be the measure of $\angle X$? Select all that apply.

    (A) 25°

    (B) 64°

    (C) 65°

    (D) 66°

    (E) 90°

    (F) 115°

30. The shaded parallelogram is created from two pairs of parallel lines. Match the statement on the left with its justification on the right.

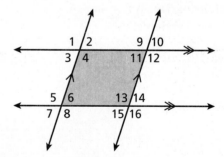

Statement	Justification
A. $\angle 4 \cong \angle 12$	**1.** Consecutive Interior Angles Theorem
B. $\angle 11 \cong \angle 14$	**2.** Consecutive Exterior Angles Theorem
C. $m\angle 12 + m\angle 14 = 180°$	**3.** Corresponding Angles Postulate
D. $m\angle 2 + m\angle 8 = 180°$	**4.** Alternate Interior Angles Theorem

 I'm in a Learning Mindset!

How am I directing my efforts when my learning environment changes?

Conditions for Parallelograms

(I Can) prove and use conditions for parallelograms.

Spark Your Learning

A vertical-lift door can be installed in a location where there is not enough space for a swing-out door.

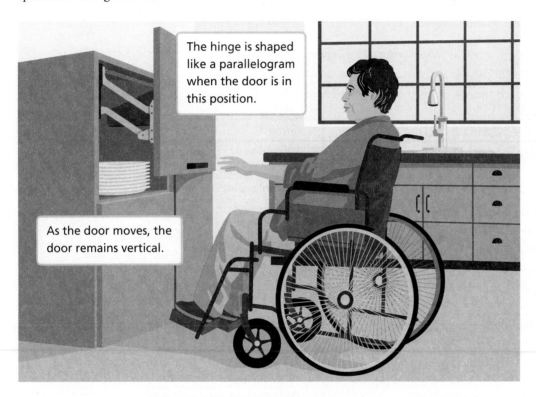

The hinge is shaped like a parallelogram when the door is in this position.

As the door moves, the door remains vertical.

Complete Part A as a whole class. Then complete Parts B–D in small groups.

- **A.** What is a geometric question you can ask about the door hinge in this situation?

- **B.** What information is needed in this situation?

- **C.** To answer your question, what strategy and tool would you use along with all the information you have? What answer do you get?

- **D.** Does your answer make sense in the context of the situation? How do you know?

 Turn and Talk What should be true about the angles and the sides of the hinge if it remains a parallelogram as it moves?

Build Understanding

Establish Parallelogram Criteria

You can use the definition of a parallelogram to show that a quadrilateral is a parallelogram. To do so, you need to show that both pairs of opposite sides are parallel. However, there are other criteria that guarantee a quadrilateral is a parallelogram.

1 ▶ The proof below verifies one of the criteria that can be used to show that a quadrilateral is a parallelogram.

The given information about the quadrilateral is marked on *ABCD*.

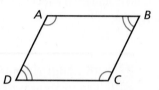

Statements	Reasons
1. $\angle A \cong \angle C$ and $\angle B \cong \angle D$	1. Given
2. $m\angle A = m\angle C$ and $m\angle B = m\angle D$	2. Definition of congruent angles
3. $m\angle A + m\angle B + m\angle C + m\angle D = 360°$	3. Quadrilateral Sum Theorem
4. $m\angle A + m\angle B + m\angle A + m\angle B = 360°$ $m\angle A + m\angle D + m\angle A + m\angle D = 360°$	4. Substitution
5. $2m\angle A + 2m\angle B = 360°$ $2m\angle A + 2m\angle D = 360°$	5. Combine like terms.
6. $m\angle A + m\angle B = 180°$ $m\angle A + m\angle D = 180°$	6. Division Property of Equality
7. $\angle A$ and $\angle B$ are supplementary. $\angle A$ and $\angle D$ are supplementary.	7. Definition of supplementary angles
8. $\overline{AD} \parallel \overline{BC}$, $\overline{AB} \parallel \overline{DC}$	8. Converse of the Consecutive Interior Angles Theorem
9. *ABCD* is a parallelogram.	9. Definition of parallelogram

A. What parallelogram criterion is being proved?

B. How is the criterion being proved related to one of the theorems in Lesson 11.1?

You have learned theorems about the properties of parallelograms. You can use the converses of these theorems to prove that a quadrilateral is a parallelogram.

Converse of the Opposite Sides of a Parallelogram Theorem
If both pairs of opposite sides of a quadrilateral are congruent, then the quadrilateral is a parallelogram.   If $\overline{AB} \cong \overline{DC}$ and $\overline{AD} \cong \overline{BC}$, then *ABCD* is a parallelogram. 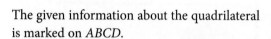

Converse of the Opposite Angles of a Parallelogram Theorem

If both pairs of opposite angles of a quadrilateral are congruent, then the quadrilateral is a parallelogram.

If $\angle A \cong \angle C$ and $\angle B \cong \angle D$, then $ABCD$ is a parallelogram.

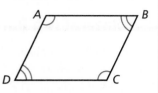

Converse of the Diagonals of a Parallelogram Theorem

If the diagonals of a quadrilateral bisect each other, then the quadrilateral is a parallelogram.

If $\overline{AE} \cong \overline{CE}$ and $\overline{BE} \cong \overline{DE}$, the $ABCD$ is a parallelogram.

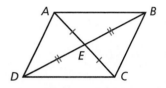

Opposite Sides Criteria for a Parallelogram Theorem

If a quadrilateral has one pair of opposite sides that are congruent and parallel, then the quadrilateral is a parallelogram.

If $\overline{AB} \cong \overline{DC}$ and $\overline{AB} \parallel \overline{DC}$, then $ABCD$ is a parallelogram.

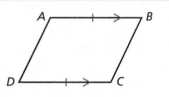

2 ▶ The lengths and slopes of two sides of quadrilateral $FGHJ$ are shown.

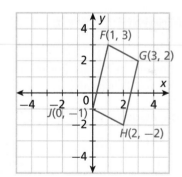

$$GH = \sqrt{(3-2)^2 + (2-(-2))^2} = \sqrt{17}$$

$$FJ = \sqrt{(1-0)^2 + (3-(-1))^2} = \sqrt{17}$$

$$\text{Slope of } \overline{GH} = \frac{2-(-2)}{3-2} = 4$$

$$\text{Slope of } \overline{FJ} = \frac{3-(-1)}{1-0} = 4$$

A. Do you have enough information to conclude that $FGHJ$ is a parallelogram? Explain.

B. What additional information is needed to apply the Converse of the Opposite Sides of a Parallelogram Theorem to show that $FGHJ$ is a parallelogram?

 Turn and Talk Use the definition of a parallelogram to show that $FGHJ$ is a parallelogram. What do you need to know about the quadrilateral?

Step It Out

Prove that a Quadrilateral Is a Parallelogram

3 ▶ You are asked to prove that if the diagonals of a quadrilateral bisect each other, then the quadrilateral is a parallelogram. The statements and reasons for the proof are shown, but they have been scrambled.

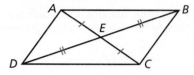

A. Write the statements in the correct order.

$\overline{AB} \cong \overline{CD}$, $\overline{AD} \cong \overline{CB}$

$\angle AEB \cong \angle CED$, $\angle AED \cong \angle CEB$

$ABCD$ is a parallelogram.

$\overline{AE} \cong \overline{CE}$, $\overline{DE} \cong \overline{BE}$

$\triangle AEB \cong \triangle CED$, $\triangle AED \cong \triangle CEB$

B. Write the reasons in the correct order.

SAS Triangle Congruence Theorem

Given

Corresponding parts of congruent figures are congruent.

If both pairs of opposite sides of a quadrilateral are congruent, then it is a parallelogram.

Vertical angles are congruent.

Use Parallelogram Criteria

4 ▶ The brackets that support an adjustable basketball hoop can be modeled by *KLMN*. For what values of *x* and *y* is *KLMN* a parallelogram?

Find the value of y.

$KL = NM$

$7y = 5y + 6$

$2y = 6$

$y = 3$

> **A.** Why are the lengths of the segments set equal to each other?

Find the value of x.

$KN = LM$

$x + 4 = 3x - 12$

$16 = 2x$

$8 = x$

> **B.** Why can this conclusion be made?

When $x = 8$ and $y = 3$, *KLMN* is a parallelogram.

 Turn and Talk Summarize the various methods you can use to prove that a quadrilateral is a parallelogram.

Check Understanding

For Problems 1–4, state the theorem that can be used to show that the quadrilateral is a parallelogram.

1.

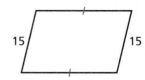

15   15

2.

3.

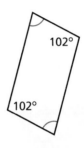

102°

102°

4.

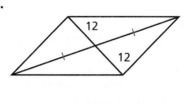

12

12

5. The slopes of the sides of *QRST* are shown below. Can you conclude that *QRST* is a parallelogram? Explain why or why not.

Slope of $\overline{QR} = -3$ Slope of $\overline{RS} = \frac{1}{2}$

Slope of $\overline{ST} = -3$ Slope of $\overline{TQ} = \frac{1}{2}$

Find the values of the variables that make the quadrilateral a parallelogram.

6.

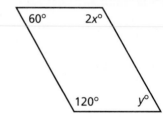

60°   2x°

120°   y°

7.

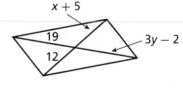

x + 5

19

3y − 2

12

On Your Own

8. Prove the Converse of Opposite Sides of a Parallelogram Theorem.

Given: $\overline{AD} \cong \overline{BC}$, $\overline{AB} \cong \overline{DC}$
Prove: *ABCD* is a parallelogram.

9. Prove that a quadrilateral with a pair of opposite sides that are parallel and congruent is a parallelogram.

Given: $\overline{AD} \cong \overline{BC}$, $\overline{AD} \parallel \overline{BC}$
Prove: *ABCD* is a parallelogram.

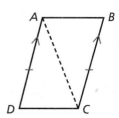

Determine whether the quadrilateral is a parallelogram. Justify your answer.

10.
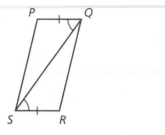

11.
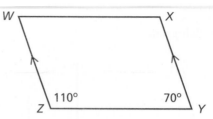

12.
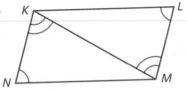

13.
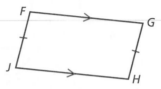

Part of a robotic arm is modeled by _PQRS_. Does each set of given information guarantee that _PQRS_ is a parallelogram?

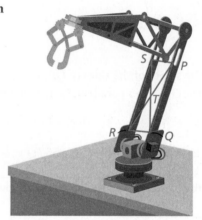

14. $\overline{PS} \cong \overline{PQ}$, $\overline{RS} \cong \overline{RQ}$

15. $\angle PST \cong \angle RQT$, $\overline{PS} \cong \overline{QR}$

16. $PT = 15$, $PR = 30$, $QT = ST = 23$

17. $\angle STR \cong \angle PTQ$, $\angle PTS \cong \angle QTR$

18. $\triangle PRS \cong \triangle RSQ$

19. $\triangle STR \cong \triangle QTP$

Determine whether the quadrilateral is a parallelogram. Explain your reasoning.

20.
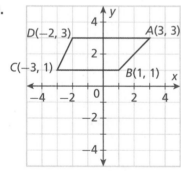

21.
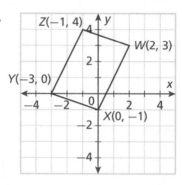

22.
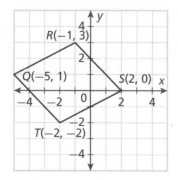

23.
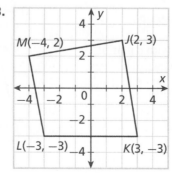

Find the values of the variables that make quadrilateral *ABCD* a parallelogram.

24.

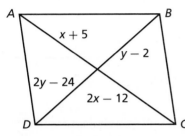

25.

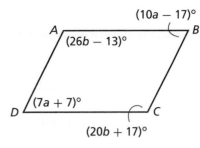

26.

27.

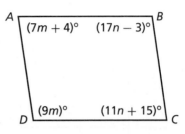

28. (MP) **Critique Reasoning** Ethan says that if you take a cardboard box apart to flatten it, the resulting shape is always a parallelogram. Jessica disagrees with him. Who is correct? Explain your reasoning.

29. Open Ended Draw a quadrilateral that you can prove is a parallelogram using the theorem that if opposite angles are congruent, the quadrilateral is a parallelogram. Find the angle measures.

30. (MP) **Construct Arguments** Explain why you know that a quadrilateral is a parallelogram if adjacent angles are supplementary.

Given: ∠A is supplementary to ∠B,
∠B is supplementary to ∠C,
∠C is supplementary to ∠D, and
∠D is supplementary to ∠A.
Prove: *ABCD* is a parallelogram.

31. (MP) **Construct Arguments** In △*ABC*, *M* is the midpoint of $\overline{AB}$.

A. Follow the steps below to form a quadrilateral. Is the quadrilateral a parallelogram? Explain your reasoning.
Step 1: Trace the triangle on a piece of tracing paper.
Step 2: Without moving the paper, place your pencil on the midpoint of $\overline{AB}$.
Step 3: Rotate the tracing paper 180°.

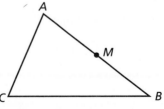

B. Describe any rotations and reflections that map the quadrilateral to itself.

C. Will all figures of this kind have this type of symmetry? Explain your reasoning.

32. Quadrilateral *ABCD* has vertices *A*(0, 6), *B*(7, 2), *C*(2, −1), and *D*(−5, 3). Use the Converse of the Diagonals of a Parallelogram Theorem to prove that *ABCD* is a parallelogram.

33. Quadrilateral *ABCD* represents the outdoor area of a dog boarding facility. An inner quadrilateral is formed by fencing that connects the midpoints of the sides of *ABCD*. Explain why quadrilateral *WXYZ* is a parallelogram.

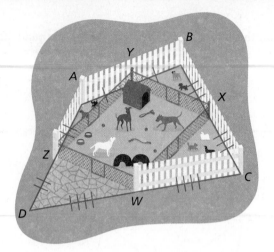

34. Describe three different ways that you can prove that *ABCD* is a parallelogram.

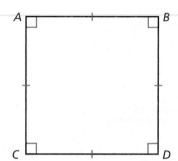

Spiral Review • Assessment Readiness

35. Which of the following sets of numbers can be the side lengths of a triangle? Select all that apply.

  Ⓐ 8, 9, 16   Ⓓ 3, 7, 11

  Ⓑ 7, 8, 15   Ⓔ 16, 18, 30

  Ⓒ 15, 15, 29

36. In $\triangle ABC$, $AB = 11$, $AC = 15$, and $m\angle A = 105°$. In $\triangle XYZ$, $XY = 15$ and $XZ = 11$. If $BC < YZ$, which of the following can be the measure of $\angle X$? Select all that apply.

  Ⓐ 75°   Ⓓ 105°

  Ⓑ 90°   Ⓔ 106°

  Ⓒ 104°   Ⓕ 135°

37. $\overline{MN}$ and $\overline{ST}$ are perpendicular. If the slope of $\overline{MN}$ is $\frac{2}{5}$, what is the slope of $\overline{ST}$?

  Ⓐ $-\frac{5}{2}$ Ⓒ $\frac{2}{5}$

  Ⓑ $-\frac{2}{5}$ Ⓓ $\frac{5}{2}$

38. *EFGH* is a parallelogram. Find the length of GH.

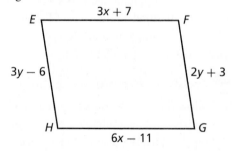

  Ⓐ 6   Ⓒ 21

  Ⓑ 9   Ⓓ 25

 I'm in a Learning Mindset!

How am I devoting my energy to learning what conditions make a quadrilateral a parallelogram?

Properties of Rectangles, Rhombuses, and Squares

(I Can) prove and use properties of squares, rectangles, and rhombuses.

Spark Your Learning

Patterns of tiles are commonly used to cover floors and walls.

Complete Part A as a whole class. Then complete Parts B–D in small groups.

A. What is a geometric question you can ask about the shapes that can be used to completely cover a flat surface?

B. Describe some different tile patterns you have seen. What properties of the patterns could you use to classify different patterns?

C. To answer your question, what strategy and tool would you use along with all the information you have? What answer do you get?

D. A shape can tessellate if you can completely cover the plane with congruent copies of it. Do you think that every possible quadrilateral should be able to tessellate? Provide evidence to support your reasoning.

 Turn and Talk Is the tile pattern shown a tessellation? Explain your reasoning.

Build Understanding

Special Parallelograms

There are three types of special parallelograms: rectangles, rhombuses, and squares.

A **rectangle** is a parallelogram with four right angles.

A **rhombus** is a parallelogram with four congruent sides.

A **square** is a parallelogram with four congruent sides and four right angles.

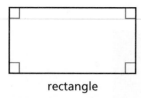
rectangle

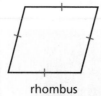
rhombus

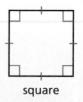
square

1 **A.** Use a geometry drawing tool to draw parallelogram *FGHJ* and its diagonals. Write the side lengths, the measures of the interior angles, the lengths of the diagonals, and the measure of ∠*FKJ*. Move vertex *F* so that the diagonals have the same length. What type of parallelogram results? How do you know?

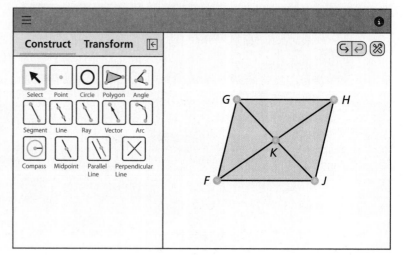

B. Move vertex *F* so that the diagonals are perpendicular. What type of parallelogram results? How do you know?

 Turn and Talk Make conjectures about the diagonals of a rectangle and the diagonals of a rhombus.

Diagonals of Special Parallelograms

You have learned that the diagonals of a parallelogram bisect each other. The diagonals of rectangles, rhombuses, and squares bisect each other because they are all parallelograms.

Diagonals of a Rectangle Theorem
If a parallelogram is a rectangle, then its diagonals are congruent. If *ABCD* is a rectangle, then $\overline{AC} \cong \overline{BD}$.

Diagonals of a Rhombus Theorem

If a parallelogram is a rhombus, then its diagonals are perpendicular.

If *ABCD* is a rhombus, then $\overline{AC} \perp \overline{BD}$.

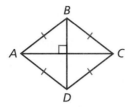

Diagonals of a Square Theorem

If a parallelogram is a square, then its diagonals are congruent and perpendicular.

If *ABCD* is a square, then $\overline{AC} \cong \overline{BD}$ and $\overline{AC} \perp \overline{BD}$.

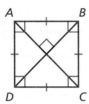

2 Consider the following conditional statements about squares.

- If a quadrilateral is a square, then it is a rectangle.
- If a quadrilateral is a square, then it is a rhombus.

By definition, a square is a parallelogram with four right angles.

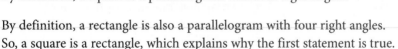

By definition, a rectangle is also a parallelogram with four right angles.
So, a square is a rectangle, which explains why the first statement is true.

A. Use definitions to explain why the second statement, "If a quadrilateral is a square, then it is a rhombus" is true.

B. Because a square is a rectangle and a rhombus, squares have the same properties as rectangles and rhombuses. Are the properties of the diagonals of a square the same as the properties of the diagonals of a rectangle and a rhombus? Explain.

 Turn and Talk List each type of quadrilateral—parallelogram, rectangle, rhombus, and square—for which the property always applies.

- All sides are congruent.
- All angles are congruent.
- The diagonals are congruent.
- The diagonals bisect each other.

Step It Out

Prove Diagonals of a Rectangle Are Congruent

3 Prove that the diagonals of a rectangle are congruent.

Given: *ABCD* is a rectangle.

Prove: $\overline{AC} \cong \overline{BD}$

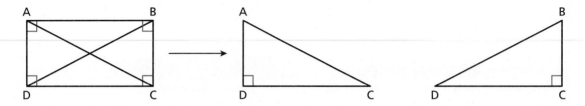

A. Why are both diagrams of the triangles helpful when writing the proof?

Statements	Reasons
1. *ABCD* is a rectangle.	**1.** Given
2. ∠*BCD* and ∠*ADC* are right angles.	**2.** Definition of rectangle
3. ∠*BCD* ≅ ∠*ADC*	**3.** All right angles are congruent.
4. *ABCD* is a parallelogram.	**4.** Definition of a rectangle
5. $\overline{AD} \cong \overline{BC}$	**5.** Opposite Sides of a Parallelogram Theorem
6. $\overline{DC} \cong \overline{DC}$	**6.** Reflexive Property of Congruence
7. △*ADC* ≅ △*BCD*	**7.** SAS Triangle Congruence Theorem
8. $\overline{AC} \cong \overline{BD}$	**8.** Corresponding parts of congruent figures are congruent.

B. The coordinate grid shows rectangle *ABCD*. Verify that the diagonals are congruent.

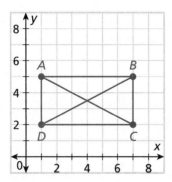

 Turn and Talk How would you show that the diagonals of a rhombus are perpendicular?

340

Use Properties of Squares, Rectangles, and Rhombuses

You can use the properties of squares, rectangles, and rhombuses to find the measures of sides, diagonals, and angles.

4 ▶ Cheryl is making a keychain that includes a rhombus trinket. In the rhombus, m∠XYZ = (5b − 10)°. Use rhombus WXYZ to find WZ and m∠XYZ.

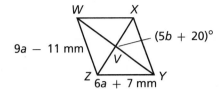

Find WZ.

Substitute the expressions for the lengths WZ and ZY and solve for a.

WZ = ZY

9a − 11 = 6a + 7

3a − 11 = 7

3a = 18

a = 6

> **A.** Why are you able to set WZ and ZY equal to each other?

Substitute 6 for a in the expression for WZ and simplify.

9a − 11 = 9(6) − 11 = 54 − 11 = 43

So, WZ = 43 mm.

Find m∠XYZ.

m∠XVY = 90°, so 5b + 20 = 90.

Solve for b.

5b + 20 = 90

5b = 70

b = 14

> **B.** How do you know that m∠XVY = 90°?

Substitute 14 for b to find m∠XYZ.

m∠XYZ = (5b − 10)°

5b − 10 = 5(14) − 10 = 70 − 10 = 60

m∠XYZ = 60°

 Turn and Talk Suppose you were told that quadrilateral WXYZ is a parallelogram but not a rhombus. Is it possible to find WZ and m∠XYZ using this given information? Explain.

Check Understanding

In Problems 1 and 2, *ABCD* is a parallelogram. Determine whether there is enough information to conclude that the *ABCD* is a rhombus. Explain your reasoning.

1.

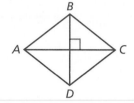

2.

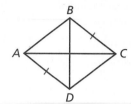

3. Explain why the following statement is true: If a quadrilateral is a square, then it is a parallelogram.

4. Rectangle *LMNQ* has diagonals $\overline{MQ}$ and $\overline{LN}$. Name two right triangles formed by the diagonals. Are the triangles congruent? Explain why or why not.

Find the value of the variable. Then give the lengths of the diagonals.

5. *DEFG* is a rectangle, $DF = 5x + 15$, and $GE = 8x - 18$.

6. *QRST* is a square, $QS = 7n - 12$, and $RT = 3n + 8$.

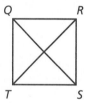

On Your Own

Use geometry software to draw each special parallelogram. Find the lengths of the diagonals and the measures of the angles formed by the intersections of the diagonals. What do you notice about each special parallelogram?

7. rectangle

8. rhombus

9. square

The photo shows the front door of a house. In rectangle *ABCD*, $AB = 36$ inches, and $BC = 80$ inches. Find each measure.

10. *DC*

11. *AD*

12. *AC*

13. *BD*

List each type of quadrilateral—*parallelogram, rectangle, rhombus,* and *square*—for which the property always applies.

14. The diagonals are perpendicular.

15. Opposite angles are congruent.

16. The diagonals are perpendicular and congruent.

17. All angles are right angles.

In Problems 18 and 19, show that the diagonals of a rhombus are perpendicular.

18. Prove that the diagonals of a rhombus are perpendicular.
   Given: *QRST* is a rhombus.
   Prove: $\overline{QS} \perp \overline{RT}$

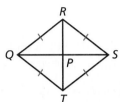

19. Graph *QRST* in the coordinate plane with vertices: $Q(-4.5, 2.2)$, $R(0.5, 2.2)$, $S(2.7, -2.3)$, $T(-2.3, -2.3)$.
   How can you use the diagonals to show the figure is not a rhombus?

20. **(MP) Construct Arguments** You have shown that a square is a rectangle and a rhombus. If you have proven the Diagonals of a Rectangle Theorem and the Diagonals of a Rhombus theorem, do you need to prove the Diagonals of a Square Theorem? Explain.

Each parallelogram is a rhombus. Find the side length.

21. *BC*

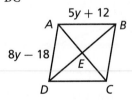

22. *ST*

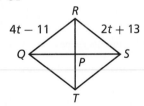

Each parallelogram is a rhombus. Find the angle measure.

23. $m\angle ABC = (10n + 5)°$

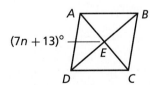

24. $m\angle RQT = (6z - 4)°$

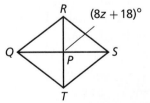

25. Draw a rectangle to represent a field hockey goal. Label the rectangle *ABCD* to show that the distance between the goal posts, $\overline{BC}$, is 2 feet less than twice the distance from the top goal post to the ground. If the perimeter of *ABCD* is 38 feet, what is the length of $\overline{BC}$?

26. **Construct Arguments** Trace the rectangle and fold as shown. Explain how the reflections show that the diagonals of a rectangle are congruent.

Step 1
Trace.

Step 2
Fold over vertical line.

Step 3
Fold over horizontal line.

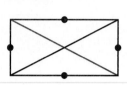

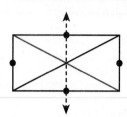

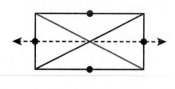

27. Open Ended Write a problem that requires solving for a variable to find a length in a special parallelogram. Solve your problem.

28. (Open Middle™) What is the fewest number of geometric markings needed to demonstrate that a quadrilateral is a rectangle? Give an example.

Spiral Review • Assessment Readiness

29. Which set of information guarantees that quadrilateral *ABCD* is a parallelogram?

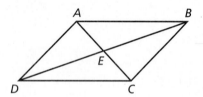

- (A) $\overline{AD} \cong \overline{AB}$, $\overline{BC} \cong \overline{DC}$
- (B) $\overline{DE} \cong \overline{BE}$, $\overline{AE} \cong \overline{CE}$
- (C) $\overline{AE} \cong \overline{BE}$
- (D) $\angle ADE \cong \angle DCB$

30. *JKLM* is a parallelogram with side lengths $JK = 17x + 5$, $KL = 3y - 7$, $LM = 20x - 1$, and $MJ = y + 11$. Find the length of $\overline{MJ}$.

- (A) 2
- (B) 9
- (C) 20
- (D) 39

31. Which theorem of congruence can you use to show that the triangles are congruent?

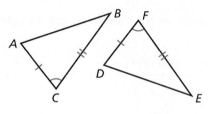

- (A) ASA
- (B) AAS
- (C) SAS
- (D) SSS

32. In $\triangle ABC$, $AB = 21$, $AC = 25$, and m$\angle A = 75°$. In $\triangle XYZ$, $XY = 21$ and $XZ = 25$. If $BC < YZ$, which of the following can be the measure of $\angle X$? Select all that apply.

- (A) 15°
- (B) 74°
- (C) 75°
- (D) 76°
- (E) 90°
- (F) 105°

I'm in a Learning Mindset!

How am I devoting my energy to learning about the properties of rectangles, rhombuses, and squares?

Conditions for Rectangles, Rhombuses, and Squares

(I Can) prove and use conditions for rectangles, rhombuses, and squares.

Spark Your Learning

As the accordion mirror extends, the shapes of the quadrilaterals formed on the sides of the extension change.

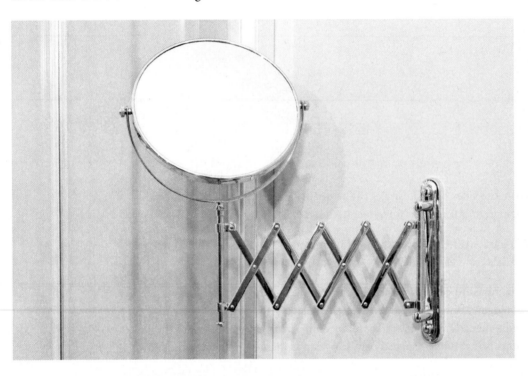

Complete Part A as a whole class. Then complete Parts B–D in small groups.

A. What is a mathematical question you can ask about the shapes formed by the folding side-pieces of the mirror?

B. How do the side lengths, angles, and diagonals of *ABCD* change as the mirror extends?

C. To answer your question, what strategy and tool would you use along with all the information you have? What answer do you get?

D. If you know the length of the full extension, what do you know about the length when the mirror is fulled retracted?

> **Turn and Talk** What must be true about the diagonals of *ABCD* as the shape changes? Explain.

Build Understanding

Determine Conditions for Special Parallelograms

You can use the definitions of special parallelograms to determine whether a quadrilateral is a rectangle, rhombus, or square. However, there are other conditions that guarantee that a quadrilateral is a rectangle, rhombus, or square.

  A. Use a compass to construct a circle and label the center. Use a straightedge to draw any two diameters. Then draw a quadrilateral by using a straightedge to connect the endpoints of the diameters. Is the quadrilateral a parallelogram? How do you know?

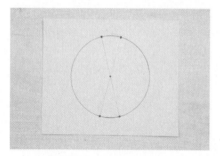 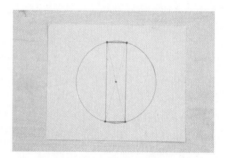

B. Measure the sides and the angles of the quadrilateral. What type of special parallelogram is formed? How do you know?

C. Repeat Part A using different pairs of diameters. Do you form the same type of parallelogram each time?

D. Use a compass to construct another circle and label the center. Use a straightedge to draw one diameter. Then construct the perpendicular bisector of the diameter. Draw a quadrilateral by connecting the endpoints of the segments. What type of special parallelogram is formed? How do you know?

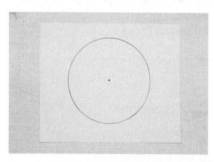 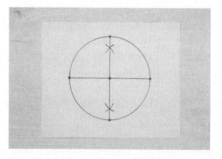

E. Is it possible to draw a rhombus that is not a square so that its vertices lie on a circle and its diagonals intersect at the center of the circle? Explain why or why not.

Turn and Talk Describe how information about the diagonals of a parallelogram can be used to classify the parallelogram as a rectangle, rhombus, or square.

Step It Out

Prove Conditions for Rectangles

The theorems below can be used to determine whether a parallelogram is a rectangle.

Theorems: Conditions for Rectangles	
If one angle of a parallelogram is a right angle, then the parallelogram is a rectangle.	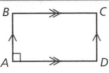
If the diagonals of a parallelogram are congruent, then the parallelogram is a rectangle.	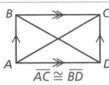

2 ▶ Prove that if the diagonals of a parallelogram are congruent, then parallelogram is a rectangle.

Given: $ABCD$ is a parallelogram and $\overline{AC} \cong \overline{BD}$.

Prove: $ABCD$ is a rectangle.

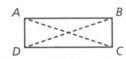

Because the opposite sides of a parallelogram are congruent, $\overline{AB} \cong \overline{CD}$.

It is given that $\overline{AC} \cong \overline{BD}$ and $\overline{AD} \cong \overline{AD}$ by the Reflexive Property of Congruence.

So, $\triangle ABD \cong \triangle DCA$.

> **A.** Which theorem can you use to show that the triangles are congruent?

$\angle BAD \cong \angle CDA$ by CPCTC. These angles are supplementary, so $m\angle BAD + m\angle CDA = 180°$.

> **B.** How do you know that these angles are supplementary?

By substitution, $m\angle BAD + m\angle BAD = 180°$.

A similar argument shows that the other angles of $ABCD$ are right angles, so $ABCD$ is a rectangle.

> **C.** What is $m\angle BAD$?

> **D.** Why does this tell you that $ABCD$ is a rectangle?

 Turn and Talk Suppose the given information did not state that $ABCD$ is a parallelogram. Can it be proven that $ABCD$ is a rectangle?

Prove Conditions for Rhombuses

The theorems below can be used to determine whether a parallelogram is a rhombus.

Theorems: Conditions for Rhombuses	
If one pair of consecutive sides of a parallelogram are congruent, then the parallelogram is a rhombus.	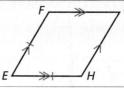
If the diagonals of a parallelogram are perpendicular, then the parallelogram is a rhombus.	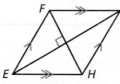
If one diagonal of a parallelogram bisects a pair of opposite angles, then the parallelogram is a rhombus.	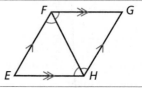

3 Shown below are the randomly ordered steps for proving that *If one pair of consecutive sides of a parallelogram are congruent, then the parallelogram is a rhombus.*

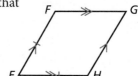

Given: *EFGH* is a parallelogram and $\overline{EH} \cong \overline{FE}$.

Prove: *EFGH* is a rhombus.

A. Write the statements in the correct order.

$\overline{EH} \cong \overline{FG}, \overline{FE} \cong \overline{GH}$

$\overline{EH} \cong \overline{GH} \cong \overline{FG} \cong \overline{FE}$

EFGH is a rhombus.

EFGH is a parallelogram and $\overline{EH} \cong \overline{FE}$.

B. Write the reasons in the correct order.

Transitive Property of Congruence

Given

Opposite sides of a parallelogram are congruent.

A quadrilateral is a rhombus if and only if it has four congruent sides.

 Turn and Talk Describe how you would prove that if the diagonals of a parallelogram are perpendicular, then the parallelogram is a rhombus.

Apply Conditions for Special Parallelograms

4 The flag of Brazil has a yellow quadrilateral.

Use the given information to determine whether the conclusion about the flag of Brazil is valid.

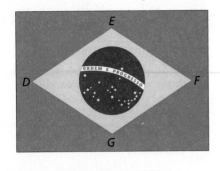

Given: $\overline{GE}$ and $\overline{DF}$ bisect each other, and $\overline{GE}$ bisects $\angle DGF$ and $\angle DEF$.

Conclusion: DEFG is a rhombus.

Step 1: Determine if DEFG is a parallelogram.

> **A.** Why do you need to determine if the quadrilateral is a parallelogram?

Because $\overline{GE}$ and $\overline{DF}$ bisect each other, DEFG is a parallelogram by the Diagonals of a Parallelogram Theorem.

Step 2: Determine if DEFG is a rhombus.

Because $\overline{GE}$ bisects $\angle DGF$ and $\angle DEF$, DEFG is a rhombus.

> **B.** Why can this conclusion be made?

Identify Special Parallelograms in the Coordinate Plane

5 Determine whether parallelogram PQRS is a rectangle, rhombus, or square. List all names that apply.

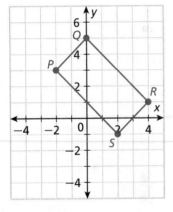

Step 1: Determine if PQRS is a rectangle.

$$PR = \sqrt{(-2-4)^2 + (3-1)^2} = \sqrt{36+4} = \sqrt{40}$$
$$QS = \sqrt{(0-2)^2 + (5-(-1))^2} = \sqrt{4+36} = \sqrt{40}$$

A. Explain why PQRS is a rectangle.

Step 2: Determine if PQRS is a rhombus.

$$\text{Slope of } \overline{PR} = \frac{y_2 - y_1}{x_2 - x_1} = \frac{1-3}{4-(-2)} = -\frac{1}{3}$$

$$\text{Slope of } \overline{QS} = \frac{y_2 - y_1}{x_2 - x_1} = \frac{5-(-1)}{0-2} = -3$$

B. Explain why PQRS is a not a rhombus.

C. Explain how you know that PQRS is a not a square.

Turn and Talk Determine the coordinates of a parallelogram that is a rhombus but not a rectangle. Explain how you know.

Check Understanding

Copy and complete each theorem.

1. If the diagonals of a parallelogram are perpendicular, then the parallelogram is a ___?___.

2. If one angle of a parallelogram is a right angle, then the parallelogram is a ___?___.

3. If one diagonal of a parallelogram bisects a pair of opposite angles, then the parallelogram is a ___?___.

Each quadrilateral is a parallelogram. Determine whether or not you have enough information to conclude that each parallelogram is a rectangle. Explain your reasoning.

4.

5.

6. Parallelogram *WXYZ* has vertices at $W(-1, 2)$, $X(2, -1)$, $Y(-1, -4)$, $Z(-4, -1)$. Determine whether *WXYZ* is a rectangle, rhombus, or square. List all names that apply.

On Your Own

Each quadrilateral is a parallelogram. Determine whether or not you have enough information to conclude that each parallelogram is a rhombus. Explain your reasoning.

7.

8.

9. Prove that if one diagonal of a parallelogram bisects a pair of opposite angles, then the parallelogram is a rhombus.

   Given: *ABCD* is a parallelogram.
   $\overline{AC}$ bisects ∠*DAB* and ∠*DCB*.
   $\overline{BD}$ bisects ∠*ADC* and ∠*ABC*.

   Prove: *ABCD* is a rhombus.

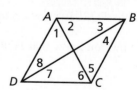

10. Prove that if one angle of a parallelogram is a right angle, then the parallelogram is a rectangle.

    Given: *ABCD* is a parallelogram. ∠*D* is a right angle.
    Prove: *ABCD* is a rectangle.

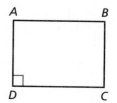

11. 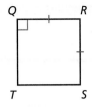 **(MP) Critique Reasoning** Lindsey believes she is given enough information to prove that parallelogram *QRST* is a square. Greg disagrees. Who is correct? Explain your reasoning.

12. Darren has a piece of fabric shaped like *WXYZ*. He makes the following conclusion about the fabric. Determine if the conclusion is valid. If not, tell what additional information is needed to make the conclusion valid.

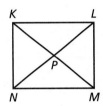

Given: $\overline{XZ}$ bisects $\angle WXY$ and $\angle WZY$.

Conclusion: *WXYZ* is a rhombus.

13. A surveyor is mapping a property and determines that the property is a parallelogram. Determine if the conclusion the surveyor makes is valid. If not, tell what additional information is needed to make the conclusion valid.

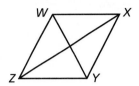

Given: *KLMN* is a parallelogram. $\overline{KP} \cong \overline{LP}$

Conclusion: *KLMN* is a rectangle.

14. A soccer player practices by kicking a ball at a parallelogram drawn on the side of a building. The sides are drawn so that $\overline{PQ} \cong \overline{RS}$ and $\overline{QR} \cong \overline{PS}$. A target is placed at point *Z*, so that *PZ, QZ, RZ,* and *SZ* are all equal lengths. Why must the parallelogram be a rectangle?

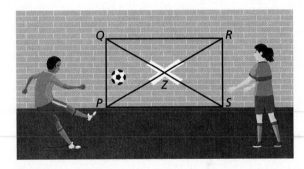

Determine whether the parallelogram is a rectangle, rhombus, or square. List all names that apply.

15.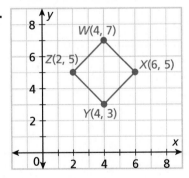

16.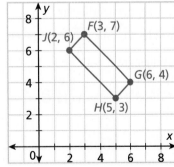

17. **(MP) Construct Arguments** Use the rotational symmetry of a square to justify the relationships between the diagonals of the square.

18. **(MP) Attend to Precision** Leon needs to cut a square out of a circular piece of paper. He wants the square to be as large as possible. Sketch how he can make sure that he cuts the largest possible square.

Find the value of x that makes each parallelogram the given type.

19. rhombus

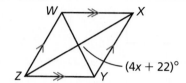

$(4x + 22)°$

20. square

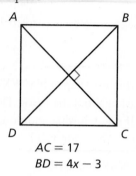

$AC = 17$
$BD = 4x - 3$

21. rhombus

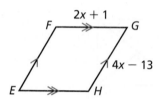

$2x + 1$

$4x - 13$

22. rectangle

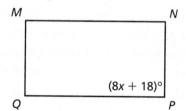

$(8x + 18)°$

23. (Open Middle™) Using the digits 1 to 9, at most one time each, fill in the boxes to create coordinates of the vertices of a square.

Spiral Review • Assessment Readiness

24. Which statement guarantees that $ABCD$ is a parallelogram?

Ⓐ Opposite sides $\overline{AB}$ and $\overline{CD}$ are congruent.

Ⓑ Diagonals $\overline{AC}$ and $\overline{BD}$ bisect each other.

Ⓒ $\overline{AB}$ and $\overline{BC}$ are perpendicular.

Ⓓ Opposite sides $\overline{BC}$ and $\overline{AD}$ are parallel.

25. $EFGH$ is a parallelogram with $EF = 4x + 11$, $FG = 3y + 15$, $HG = 7x - 1$, and $EH = 5y - 1$. Find the length of $\overline{HG}$.

Ⓐ 4

Ⓒ 27

Ⓑ 8

Ⓓ 39

26. The point $(4, 8)$ is the midpoint of which set of ordered pairs?

Ⓐ $(5, 9), (3, 10)$ Ⓒ $(3, 5), (5, 11)$

Ⓑ $(-4, -8), (8, 4)$ Ⓓ $(2, 6), (6, 2)$

27. Find the length of $\overline{SU}$.

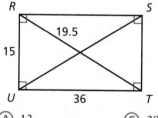

15

19.5

36

Ⓐ 13

Ⓒ 39

Ⓑ 21

Ⓓ 51

 I'm in a Learning Mindset!

How did I evaluate opposing views about conditions for rectangles, rhombuses, and squares?

Properties and Conditions for Trapezoids and Kites

(I Can) prove and apply theorems about trapezoids and kites.

Spark Your Learning

Anita is flying a kite at the beach.

Complete Part A as a whole class. Then complete Parts B–D in small groups.

   A. What is a geometric question you can ask about this situation?

   B. What information would you need to know to answer your question?

   C. To answer your question, what strategy and tool would you use along with all the information you have? What answer do you get?

   D. Use a different method to answer the question. Explain your reasoning.

> **Turn and Talk** Is it possible that the kite shown is a parallelogram? Explain why or why not.

Build Understanding

Understand Definitions of Kites and Trapezoids

In this lesson, you will learn about two special quadrilaterals, **kites** and **trapezoids**. Inclusive definitions for kite and trapezoid allow parallelograms to share the properties of kites and trapezoids. Exclusive definitions for kite and trapezoid do not allow parallelograms to share the properties of kites and trapezoids.

Definitions for Kite
Inclusive definition: A kite is a quadrilateral whose four sides can be grouped into two pairs of consecutive congruent sides.
Exclusive definition: A kite is a quadrilateral with two pairs of consecutive congruent sides, but opposite sides are not congruent.

Definitions for Trapezoid
Inclusive definition: A trapezoid is a quadrilateral with at least one pair of parallel sides.
Exclusive definition: A trapezoid is a quadrilateral with exactly one pair of parallel sides.

In this book, kite and trapezoid are defined using the inclusive definitions. That means a rhombus can be classified as a kite and as a trapezoid.

1 Consider the quadrilaterals shown.

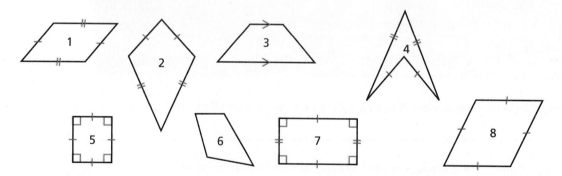

A. Which shape(s) are kites using the inclusive definition?

B. Which shape(s) are kites using the exclusive definition?

C. Which shape(s) are trapezoids using the inclusive definition?

D. Which shape(s) are trapezoids using the exclusive definition?

 Turn and Talk Another definition for kite is as follows: A kite is a quadrilateral with exactly two pairs of congruent consecutive sides. Is this an inclusive definition or exclusive definition? Explain.

Step It Out

Theorems About Kites

Consider the following theorems.

Theorems About Kites	
Diagonals of a Kite Theorem If a quadrilateral is a kite, then its diagonals are perpendicular. If *ABCD* is a kite, then $\overline{AC} \perp \overline{BD}$.	
Opposite Angles of a Kite Theorem If a quadrilateral is a kite, then at least one pair of opposite angles that are congruent. If *ABCD* is a kite, then $\angle B \cong \angle D$.	

2 ▶ Shown below are the randomly ordered steps for proving that *If a quadrilateral is a kite, then at least one pair of opposite angles are congruent.*

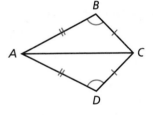

Given: $\overline{BC} \cong \overline{DC}$ and $\overline{AB} \cong \overline{AD}$.
Prove: $\angle B \cong \angle D$

A. Write the statements in the correct order.

$\triangle ABC \cong \triangle ADC$
$\overline{AC} \cong \overline{AC}$
$\overline{BC} \cong \overline{DC}$ and $\overline{AB} \cong \overline{AD}$.
$\angle B \cong \angle D$

B. Write the reasons in the correct order.

Corresponding parts of congruent figures are congruent.
Given
SSS Triangle Congruence Theorem
Reflexive Property of Congruence

C. Explain how to change the proof to show that $\overline{AC} \perp \overline{BD}$. What general result does your proof verify?

 Turn and Talk Using the inclusive definition for kite, what type of quadrilateral is a kite with both pairs of opposite angles congruent?

Theorems About Trapezoids

The **bases of a trapezoid** are the sides of the trapezoid that are parallel. The **base angles of a trapezoid** are a pair of consecutive angles whose common side is a base of the trapezoid. The **legs of a trapezoid** are the sides that are not the bases. An **isosceles trapezoid** is a trapezoid in which the legs are congruent but not parallel.

Theorems About Trapezoids	
Base Angles of a Trapezoid Theorem If a trapezoid has one pair of congruent base angles, then the trapezoid is isosceles. If $ABCD$ is a trapezoid and $\angle C \cong \angle D$, then $ABCD$ is an isosceles trapezoid.	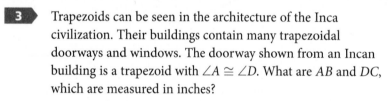
Isosceles Trapezoid Theorem If a quadrilateral is an isosceles trapezoid, then each pair of base angles are congruent. If $ABCD$ is an isosceles trapezoid, then $\angle A \cong \angle B$ and $\angle C \cong \angle D$.	
Diagonals of an Isosceles Trapezoid Theorem A trapezoid is isosceles if and only if its diagonals are congruent. $ABCD$ is an isosceles trapezoid if and only if $\overline{AC} \cong \overline{BD}$.	$\overline{AC} \cong \overline{BD}$

3 Trapezoids can be seen in the architecture of the Inca civilization. Their buildings contain many trapezoidal doorways and windows. The doorway shown from an Incan building is a trapezoid with $\angle A \cong \angle D$. What are AB and DC, which are measured in inches?

Find the value of x.

$18x + 11 = 24x - 7$
$\qquad 11 = 6x - 7$
$\qquad 18 = 6x$
$\qquad 3 = x$

A. Explain why $18x + 11 = 24x - 7$.

Find AB and DC.

Substitute $x = 3$ into the expression for one of the legs of the trapezoid.

$18x + 11 = 18(3) + 11 = 54 + 11 = 65$

B. Why was the value of x substituted in only one of the expressions?

The lengths of the legs of the trapezoid are 65 inches.

 Turn and Talk Explain how you can find all the angle measures of an isosceles trapezoid if you know the measure of one angle.

The Trapezoid Midsegment Theorem

The **midsegment of a trapezoid** is a segment whose endpoints are the midpoints of the legs of the trapezoid. The Trapezoid Midsegment Theorem below is similar to the Triangle Midsegment Theorem.

Trapezoid Midsegment Theorem	
The midsegment of a trapezoid is parallel to each base, and its length is one-half of the sum of the lengths of the bases. $\overline{XY} \parallel \overline{BC}$, $\overline{XY} \parallel \overline{AD}$, $XY = \frac{1}{2}(AD + BC)$	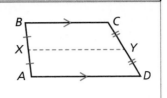

4 ▸ Find *DE*.

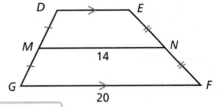

$$MN = \frac{1}{2}(DE + GF)$$

$$14 = \frac{1}{2}(DE + 20)$$

$$28 = DE + 20$$

$$8 = DE$$

> Why can the Trapezoid Midsegment Theorem be applied?

Transformations and Symmetry in Trapezoids and Kites

5 ▸ Consider the types of symmetry for the isosceles trapezoid and the kite shown.

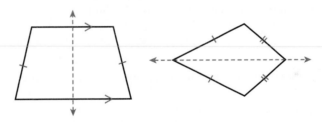

Rotational symmetry?	none	none
Line symmetry?	yes, across 1 vertical line	yes, across 1 horizontal line

A. Why do neither of the shapes have rotational symmetry?

B. Why do both shapes have line symmetry?

 Turn and Talk Suppose the trapezoid is not isosceles. How does this fact change the symmetry of the trapezoid?

Check Understanding

1. Explain why the words *inclusive* and *exclusive* are appropriate terms to describe the different definitions of kite and trapezoid.

In kite *KLMN*, m∠*KLM* = 140°. Find each measure.

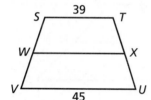

2. m∠*KNM*

3. m∠*KJN*

Do you have enough information to find the measure? If so, find the measure. If not, explain why.

4. *WX*

5. *AC*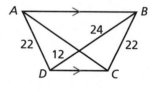

6. Is it possible to draw a kite that has no line symmetry? Explain why or why not.

On Your Own

7. **(MP) Reason** Using the inclusive definition for a trapezoid, are all parallelograms trapezoids? Are all trapezoids parallelograms? Explain.

8. **Art** In origami, a kite base is used as the starting point for many paper-folded creations. The steps for making a kite base out of a square piece of origami paper are shown. Explain how the paper folding justifies the fact that the diagonals of a kite are perpendicular.

Fold along one diagonal of the square and unfold.

Fold the left side to meet the crease in the center.

Fold the right side to meet the crease in the center.

9. **(MP) Critique Reasoning** Lexi believes that there is not enough information to determine the measure of ∠*Y*. Ally believes the measure of ∠*Y* is 117°. Who is correct? Explain your reasoning.

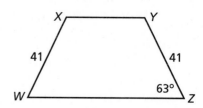

358

Find the value of *x* in the isosceles trapezoid. Then find the given measure.

10. *JL*

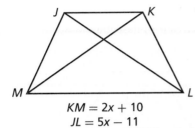

$KM = 2x + 10$
$JL = 5x - 11$

11. m∠*K*

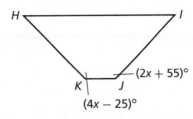

$(2x + 55)°$
$(4x - 25)°$

12. **STEM** An engineer is designing solar panels for a rover that will explore Mars. The solar panel unfolds to an isosceles trapezoid. The length of one leg is $0.1x - 0.5$ meters, and the length of the other leg is $0.3x - 2.1$ meters. What is the length of each of the legs of the solar panel?

Find the given measure.

13. *BC*

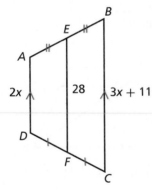

$2x$ 28 $3x + 11$

14. *RS*

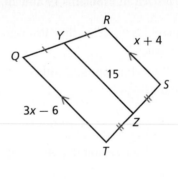

$x + 4$
15
$3x - 6$

Does the figure have rotational symmetry or line symmetry? If so, describe the symmetry.

15. kite *JKLM*

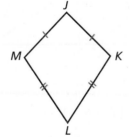

16. trapezoid *ABCD*

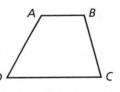

17. trapezoid *WXYZ*

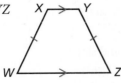

18. kite *QRST*

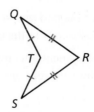

In Problems 19 and 20, prove each theorem for trapezoids using the diagram with an auxiliary segment and the plan for the proof.

19. Prove that if a quadrilateral is an isosceles trapezoid, then each pair of base angles are congruent.

Given: $\overline{BC} \parallel \overline{AD}$, $\overline{AB} \parallel \overline{EC}$, $\overline{AB} \cong \overline{CD}$

Prove: $\angle A \cong \angle D$, $\angle B \cong \angle BCD$

Plan for Proof: Show that $\triangle ECD$ is an isosceles triangle and $ABCE$ is a parallelogram. Use these facts to reason that $\angle A \cong \angle D$. The use the Congruent Supplements Theorem to show that $\angle B \cong \angle BCD$.

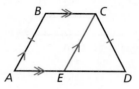

20. Prove that if a trapezoid has one pair of congruent base angles, then the trapezoid is isosceles.

Given: $\overline{GH} \parallel \overline{FJ}$, $\overline{GF} \parallel \overline{HK}$, $\angle F \cong \angle J$

Prove: $\overline{GF} \cong \overline{HJ}$

Plan for Proof: Show that $\triangle KHJ$ is an isoscleles triangle. Then reason that $\overline{GF} \cong \overline{HJ}$.

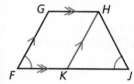

In Problems 21 and 22, prove each part of the third trapezoid theorem: *A trapezoid is isosceles if and only if its diagonals are congruent.* **Use the first two trapezoid theorems, which were proven in Problems 19 and 20.**

21. Prove that if a trapezoid is isosceles, then its diagonals are congruent, which is the first part of the theorem.

Given: $ABCD$ is an isosceles trapezoid with $\overline{BC} \parallel \overline{AD}$ and $\overline{AB} \cong \overline{CD}$.

Prove: $\overline{AC} \cong \overline{DB}$

Plan for Proof: Find a way to show that $\triangle ABD \cong \triangle DCA$. Then reason that $\overline{AC} \cong \overline{DB}$.

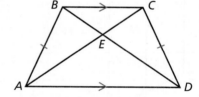

22. Prove that if the diagonals of a trapezoid are congruent, then it is an isosceles trapezoid, which is the second part of the theorem.

Given: $\overline{BC} \parallel \overline{AD}$ and $\overline{AC} \cong \overline{DB}$.

Prove: $ABCD$ is an isosceles trapezoid.

Plan for Proof: Show that $BCFE$ is a parallelogram. Then show that $\triangle DBE \cong \triangle ACF$. Use information about the congruent triangles to show that $\triangle ABC \cong \triangle DCB$. Then reason that the base angles of the trapezoid are congruent.

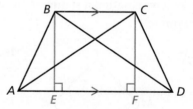

23. Quadrilateral $ABCD$ has vertices $A(-3, 4)$, $B(5, 2)$, $C(6, -4)$, and $D(-6, -1)$.

A. Show that $ABCD$ is a trapezoid.

B. Find the coordinates of the midsegment of $ABCD$ and use them to determine the length and slope of the midsegment.

C. Use the Trapezoid Midsegment Theorem to find the length and slope of the midsegment. Compare your answer to the answer for Part B.

Show that the statement about the figure in the coordinate plane is true.

24. *ABCD* is a trapezoid.

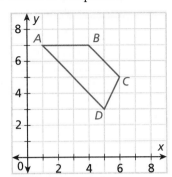

25. *ABCD* is a kite.

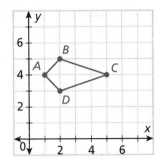

In Problems 26 and 27, use the diamond shown, which is in the shape of a kite.

26. Find the value of *x* when $y = 40°$ and $z = 92°$.

27. Write a general formula for finding the value of *x* for any values of *y* and *z*.

28. (MP) **Construct Arguments** Follow the steps below to prove the Trapezoid Midsegment Theorem.

Given: Trapezoid *FGHJ* with midsegment $\overline{MN}$

Prove: $\overline{MN} \parallel \overline{FJ}$, $\overline{MN} \parallel \overline{GH}$, $MN = \frac{1}{2}(FJ + GH)$

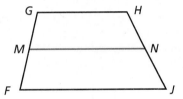

A. What does the given information tell you about the diagram?

B. $\overline{GN}$ is drawn to create △*GHN*. Then the triangle is rotated 180° about point *N* to create △*KJN* as shown below. Explain how you know that $\overline{GN} \cong \overline{KN}$.

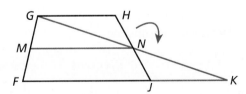

C. Use the fact that *N* is the midpoint of $\overline{GK}$ to explain why $\overline{MN} \parallel \overline{FK}$. (Hint: Consider how $\overline{MN}$ relates to △*GFK*.)

D. If you know that $\overline{MN} \parallel \overline{FK}$, then explain why $\overline{MN} \parallel \overline{GH}$.

E. How are $\overline{MN}$ and $\overline{FK}$ related? Use this relationship to show that $MN = \frac{1}{2}(FJ + GH)$.

29. Quadrilateral *PQRS* has vertices $P(-1, 3)$, $Q(2, 4)$, $R(5, 3)$, and $S(2, -6)$.

A. Find the side lengths of *PQRS*.

B. What do you notice about the side lengths?

C. Can you conclude that the quadrilateral is a kite? Explain your reasoning.

In Problems 30–36, determine whether the statement is *always,* *sometimes,* **or** *never* **true. Explain your reasoning.**

30. The bases of a trapezoid are parallel.

31. The legs of a trapezoid are congruent.

32. The midsegment of a trapezoid is parallel to the bases of the trapezoid.

33. The midsegment of a trapezoid is half the length of one of the bases.

34. The opposite sides of a kite are congruent.

35. The adjacent sides of a kite are perpendicular.

36. A trapezoid is a kite.

37. In kite *ABCD*, △*ABD* and △*CBD* can be rotated and translated, mapping $\overline{AD}$ onto $\overline{CD}$ and joining the remaining pair of vertices, as shown in the figure. Why does this process produce an isosceles trapezoid?

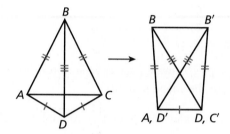

38. (Open Middle™) What is the fewest number of geometric markings needed to demonstrate that a quadrilateral is a trapezoid? Explain your reasoning.

Spiral Review • Assessment Readiness

39. Find the value of *x* that makes *WXYZ* a rhombus.

Ⓐ 11

Ⓑ 22.5

Ⓒ 90

Ⓓ 180

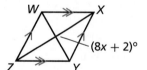

40. *WXYZ* is a rectangle with intersection of diagonals at point *V*. Find the length of $\overline{WY}$ if *ZV* = 26.

Ⓐ 13

Ⓑ 26

Ⓒ 39

Ⓓ 52

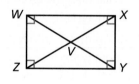

41. For each triangle, identify the dilation as an enlargement or reduction.

	Enlargement	Reduction
A. $(2,4), (0,2), (2,2) \rightarrow (3,6), (0,3), (3,3)$	?	?
B. $(6,2), (-2,4), (-1,-1) \rightarrow (12,4), (-4,8), (-2,-2)$	?	?
C. $(-2,2), (4,4), (2,-2) \rightarrow (-1,1), (2,2), (1,-1)$	?	?

I'm in a Learning Mindset!

What did I learn from the mistakes I made with the properties and conditions of trapezoids and kites?

Parallelograms

A parallelogram is a quadrilateral with opposite sides parallel.

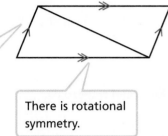

Each diagonal divides the parallelogram into 2 congruent triangles.

There is rotational symmetry.

- Opposite sides are congruent.
- Opposite angles are congruent.
- The diagonals bisect each other.

Rectangles

A rectangle is a parallelogram with right angles.

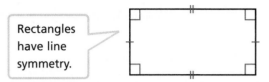

Rectangles have line symmetry.

- Rectangles have the same properties as parallelograms.
- The diagonals are congruent.

Rhombi

A rhombus is a parallelogram with all sides congruent.

- Rhombi have the same properties as parallelograms.
- The diagonals are perpendicular.

Squares

A square is both a rectangle and a rhombus.

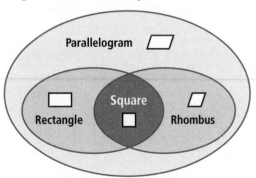

- Squares have the same properties as parallelograms, rectangles, and rhombi.

Kites

A kite is a quadrilateral with pairs of consecutive congruent sides.

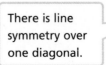

There is line symmetry over one diagonal.

- The diagonals are perpendicular.
- Kites have one pair of opposite angles that are congruent.

Isosceles Trapezoids

A quadrilateral with one pair of parallel sides is a trapezoid. An isosceles trapezoid has congruent legs.

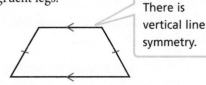

There is vertical line symmetry.

- The diagonals are congruent.
- Each pair of base angles are congruent.

Vocabulary

Choose the correct term from the box to complete each sentence.

1. A ___?___ is a ___?___ with four congruent sides.

2. A ___?___ is a quadrilateral whose four sides can be grouped into two pairs of consecutive congruent sides.

3. A ___?___ is a parallelogram with four right angles.

4. A ___?___ is a parallelogram with four congruent sides and four right angles.

Concepts and Skills

Consider parallelograms, rectangles, rhombi, squares, kites, and trapezoids. Identify which quadrilaterals always have the given property.

5. rotational symmetry

6. line symmetry

7. both rotational and line symmetry

8. Opposite sides are congruent.

9. Diagonals are congruent.

10. Diagonals are perpendicular.

Complete a proof given that opposite sides in a parallelogram are parallel.

11. Prove that opposite sides are congruent.

12. Prove that opposite angles are congruent.

Find the measure.

13. AC

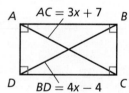

$AC = 3x + 7$
$BD = 4x - 4$

14. HG

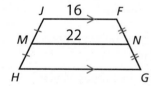

15. NP

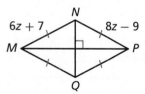

$6z + 7$ $8z - 9$

16. $m\angle C$

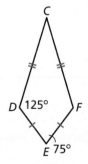

17. Parallelogram $WXYZ$ has vertices at $W(1, 3)$, $X(2, 5)$, $Y(6, 3)$, and $Z(5, 1)$. Determine whether $WXYZ$ is a rectangle, rhombus, or square. List all names that apply.

18. (MP) **Use Tools** A rectangular garden has a length of $(4x + 5)$ inches and a width of $(3x - 1)$ inches. Find the length and width of the garden if the perimeter is 36 feet. State what strategy and tool you will use to answer the question, explain your choice, and then find the answer.

Module Performance Task: *Spies and Analysts*™

MYSTERY
OF THE SEA

How big is the Bermuda Triangle?

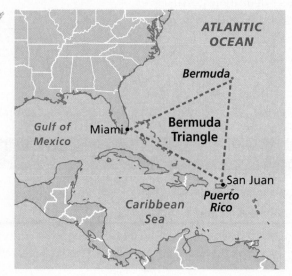

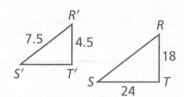

Are You Ready?

Complete these problems to review concepts and skills you will need for this module.

Scale Drawings

Triangle $R'S'T'$ is a scale of drawing of $\triangle RST$. Answer each question using the figures.

1. What is the length of $\overline{S'T'}$?

2. What is the length of $\overline{RS}$?

3. What is the scale factor from $\triangle RST$ to $\triangle R'S'T'$?

4. Assume $\triangle RST$ and $\triangle R'S'T'$ are right triangles. What is the area of each triangle?

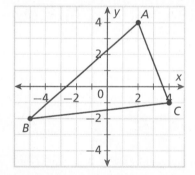

The Pythagorean Theorem and Its Converse

Determine if each triangle is a right triangle using the given side lengths. Explain.

5. $DE = 13.5$, $EF = 18$, $DF = 22.5$

6. $JL = 7$, $KL = 23$, $JK = 24$

7. $AB = 6$, $AC = 8$, $BC = 12$

8. $LM = 9$, $MN = 41$, $LN = 40$

Dilate Figures in the Coordinate Plane

Find the coordinates of $\triangle A'B'C'$ using the given center of dilation and scale factor.

9. Center of dilation: $(0, 0)$
Scale factor: 2.5

10. Center of dilation: $(2, 4)$
Scale factor: 40

Connecting Past and Present Learning

Previously, you learned:

- to use proportions to perform dilations,
- to develop criteria to prove figures are congruent, and
- to use transformations to prove figures are congruent.

In this module, you will learn:

- to use transformations to prove figures are similar,
- to develop criteria to prove figures are similar, and
- to identify and apply special relationships in similar right triangles.

Use Transformations to Prove Figures Are Similar

(I Can) use similarity transformations to prove figures are similar.

Spark Your Learning

The boundaries and lines on basketball courts are drawn to regulatory specifications to ensure the distances are the same.

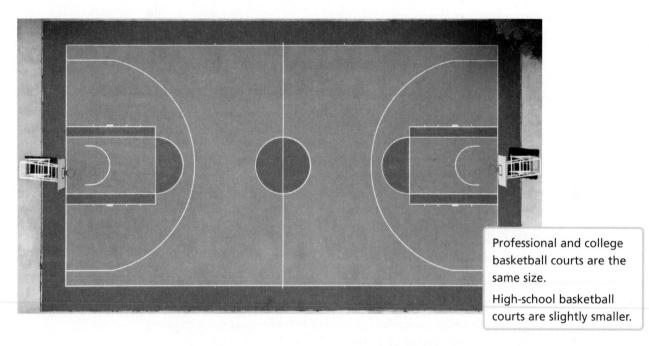

Professional and college basketball courts are the same size.

High-school basketball courts are slightly smaller.

Complete Part A as a whole class. Then complete Parts B–D in small groups.

A. What is a mathematical question you can ask about this basketball court?

B. Is it possible to use the pictured regulation court to determine the boundaries and lines on an actual court? What additional information do you need?

C. To answer your question, what strategy and tool would you use along with all the information you have? What answer do you get?

D. Is a transformation used to create the scale drawing? If so describe the transformation.

Turn and Talk Consider two congruent polygons. One of the polygons is enlarged by a ratio of 4. What are the relationships between corresponding angles and corresponding sides?

Build Understanding

Investigate Dilations

You learned a dilation is a transformation that changes the size of a figure but does not change the shape. The scale factor defines the ratio of the dilation. A scale factor greater than 1 enlarges the figure, and a scale factor between 0 and 1 reduces the figure.

1 Use a geometric drawing tool to construct $\triangle ABC$. Place point D in the interior of the triangle. Then use the dilation command to dilate $\triangle ABC$ by a scale factor of 2 with center of dilation D.

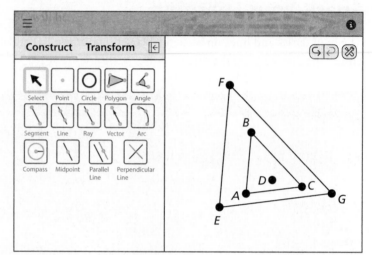

A. Measure the sides of the triangles. How can you use these measures to confirm that $\triangle EFG$ is a dilation of $\triangle ABC$ by a scale factor of 2? Do the sides of $\triangle ABC$ and $\triangle EFG$ have the same relationship as you drag one of the vertices of $\triangle ABC$? Explain.

B. Measure the angles of $\triangle ABC$ and $\triangle EFG$. What do you notice about the measure of each angle?

C. Construct a line parallel to $\overline{BC}$ through a point on $\overline{FG}$. How is this line related to $\overline{FG}$? Does this relationship change as you move one of the vertices of $\triangle ABC$? Does the same relationship exist between other corresponding sides of the image and the preimage?

 Turn and Talk Based on your results, what can you conclude about the slopes of the image and preimage of any segment that undergoes a dilation? Does the conclusion apply if the figure undergoes other types of transformations? Explain.

Find a Sequence of Similarity Transformations

A **similarity transformation** is a transformation in which the image has the same shape as the preimage. If a figure can be mapped to another figure using a sequence of similarity transformations, then the figures are **similar figures**. Two similar figures have the same shape but not necessarily the same size. You can write "$\triangle ABC$ is similar to $\triangle EFG$" as $\triangle ABC \sim \triangle EFG$. Similarity transformations are dilations and rigid motions.

Properties of Similar Figures

Corresponding angles of similar figures are congruent.

Corresponding sides of similar figures are proportional. The ratio of the lengths of two corresponding sides is the scale factor.

368

2 In the figure below, determine whether quadrilateral *ABCD* is similar to *LMNP*.

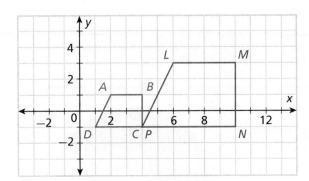

A. Is there a sequence of similarity transformations that maps *LMNP* onto *ABCD*? If so, would the dilation have a scale factor greater than 1 or between 0 and 1? Explain.

B. Write a ratio between two corresponding sides of *LMNP* and *ABCD* to determine a scale factor *k* of a possible dilation.

C. A transformation of *LMNP* is shown below as *L'M'N'P'*.

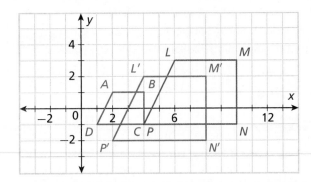

Explain how the coordinates of *LMNP* and *L'M'N'P'* show that a translation maps *LMNP* onto *L'M'N'P'*.

D. The graph shows *ABCD*, which is the image of *L'M'N'P'* after the dilation. What is true about all pairs of corresponding sides? Use examples from the graph to support your answer.

E. A sequence of transformations that maps *LMNP* onto *ABCD* is a translation $(x, y) \rightarrow (x - 2, y - 1)$ followed by a dilation $(x, y) \rightarrow \left(\frac{1}{2}x, \frac{1}{2}y\right)$. How do you know *LMNP* and *ABCD* are similar figures? Are there any angles in *ABCD* that must be congruent to ∠*M* in figure *LMNP*? Explain.

F. Is there only one sequence of similarity transformations that maps *LMNP* to *ABCD*? Explain.

 Turn and Talk In the graph above, suppose another quadrilateral *RMNP* has vertex *R*(4, 4). Would *RMNP* be similar to *ABCD*? Explain.

Prove All Circles Are Similar

You can use what you know about similarity to prove theorems about circles.

Circle Similarity Theorem
All circles are similar.

3 Prove the Circle Similarity Theorem.

Given: circle C with center C and radius r,

circle D with center D and radius s

Prove: Circle C is similar to circle D.

Suppose a company manufactures vinyl records. To prove similarity, show there is a sequence of similarity transformations that maps circle C, the label, to circle D, the vinyl.

A. How is the proof generalized by using variables to represents the radii?

B. To place the label on the record, the manufacturer translates circle C so its center coincides with the center of circle D. The image of circle C is circle C'. Is this transformation a similarity transformation? Explain.

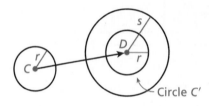

C. Transform circle C' with a dilation centered at point D and a scale factor of $\frac{s}{r}$. The image of circle C' after the dilation has a radius of $\frac{s}{r} \cdot r = s$. How are the images of circle C' after the dilation and circle D related?

D. Why can you conclude the circles are similar?

E. Show that the scale factor also transforms the diameters and circumferences in the same way as the radii.

$$\text{Diameter}_D \stackrel{?}{=} \frac{s}{r} \cdot \text{Diameter}_C$$

$$\text{Circumference}_D \stackrel{?}{=} \frac{s}{r} \cdot \text{Circumference}_C$$

 Turn and Talk Are all geometric shapes of the same type similar? Explain.

Step It Out

Apply Properties of Similar Figures

Recall that in similar figures, corresponding angles are congruent and pairs of corresponding sides are proportional. You can use these facts to find unknown angle measures or lengths of corresponding sides.

A pantograph is a tool that allows the user to make a copy of a figure by tracing. The copy can be smaller or larger and will be similar to the original.

 4 An artist used a pantograph to make figure *ABCDE* that is similar to *PQRST*.

Find the values of *x* and *y*.

Find the value of *x*.

$$\frac{AB}{PQ} = \frac{CD}{RS}$$

A. What are the pairs of corresponding sides?

$$\frac{4x}{35} = \frac{3x + 6}{30}$$

$$4x(30) = 35(3x + 6)$$

$$120x = 105x + 210$$

$$15x = 210$$

$$x = 14$$

B. Is it possible to use any other pairs of corresponding sides to write and solve a proportion to solve for *x*? Explain why or why not.

Find the value of *y*.

$$\angle B \cong \angle Q$$

C. How do you know that $\angle B \cong \angle Q$?

$$m\angle B = m\angle Q$$

$$120 = 2y$$

$$y = 60$$

D. What information must you know to determine the scale factor of the dilation that is part of the sequence of similarity transformations that maps *PQRST* onto *ABCDE*? Do you have enough information to determine the scale factor? If so, what is it?

 Turn and Talk If two polygons are similar, do the perimeters of the polygons have the same ratio as the corresponding pairs of sides? Why or why not?

Check Understanding

For Problems 1–3, use the graph where △PQR is a dilation of △LMN.

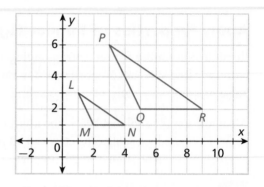

1. Which side of the image is parallel to $\overline{NL}$? Explain.

2. Which angle in △PQR is congruent to ∠L? Explain.

3. Is △LMN similar to △PQR? Explain why or why not.

4. Circle P has a radius of 3.6 mm. Circle Q has a radius of 10.8 mm. Is circle Q similar to circle P? If so, what is the scale factor?

5. Figure ABCD is similar to figure PQRS. What is the length of $\overline{CD}$?

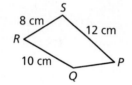
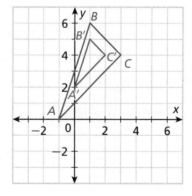

On Your Own

For Problems 6 and 7, determine whether the transformation is a dilation. If so, what is the scale factor? Explain your reasoning.

6.

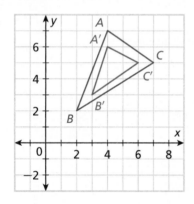

7.

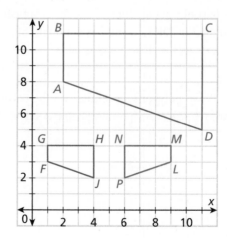

In the diagram, ABCD ∼ FGHJ.

8. Explain why ABCD ∼ FGHJ.

9. Is ∠J ≅ ∠D? Explain.

10. Is $\dfrac{AB}{BC}$ equal to $\dfrac{FG}{GH}$? Explain.

11. Is ABCD ∼ LMNP? Explain why or why not.

Determine whether each pair of figures is similar using similarity transformations. Explain your reasoning.

12. *JKLM* to *WXYZ*

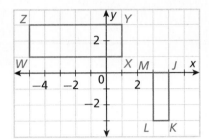

13. △*DEF* to △*LMN*

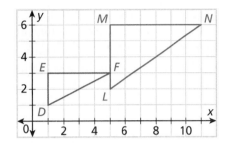

14. *ABCD* to *PQRS*

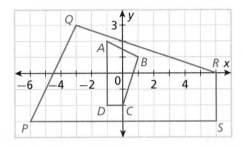

15. *MNPQR* to *ABCDE*

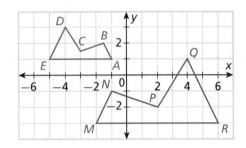

Social Studies For Problems 16–18, the photo shows the circular terraces at the Moray Ruins in Peru. It is widely believed that the ruins were used as an agricultural laboratory by the Incas. The circular terraces have the same center.

16. Are the circles in the terraces similar? Explain your reasoning.

17. Describe the similarity transformation that would take the largest terrace circle onto the smallest. Give an estimate of the scale factor.

18. How many times greater is the circumference of the largest terrace circle than the circumference of the smallest circle?

19. (MP) **Reason** Are congruent circles also similar circles? Explain your reasoning.

In the diagram, *JKLM* ~ *EFGH*.

20. Find the scale factor of *JKLM* to *EFGH*.

21. Find the values of *x*, *y*, and *z*.

22. Find the perimeter of each polygon.

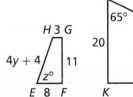

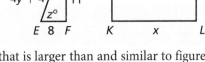

23. **Open Ended** Sketch a figure labeled *PQRS* that is larger than and similar to figure *JKLM*. What is the scale factor of *PQRS* to *JKLM*?

24. A. An Olympic-sized pool containing 10 lanes is shown. A shorter-sized pool contains only 8 lanes and is 25 m long by 18.3 m wide. Are the two pools similar in shape? Explain.

B. Financial Literacy It costs about $10.70 per square meter per year to maintain the Olympic-sized pool. Estimate the total cost per year to maintain a pool that is 75% of the area of the Olympic-sized pool.

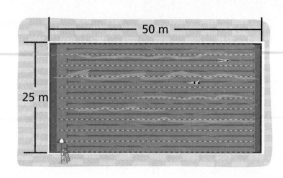

25. **(MP)** **Critique Reasoning** Michael and Sara are completing the following problem. Michael determines the answer is 3. Sara determines the answer is 2. Which student, if either, is correct? Justify your reasoning.

"A triangle on the coordinate plane is dilated from △LMN to △L'M'N'. $\overline{LM}$ lies along the line $y = 2x + 3$, $\overline{MN}$ lies along the line $y = -\frac{1}{3}x + 6$, and $\overline{NL}$ lies along the line $y = \frac{1}{4}x - 4$. The center of dilation is the origin. What is the slope of the line on which $\overline{M'N'}$ lies?"   ✓ ✗

26. A figure is transformed by $(x, y) \rightarrow (x + 2, y - 3)$ followed by $(x, y) \rightarrow (x, 3y)$. Does this sequence of transformations produce a pair of similar figures? Explain your reasoning.

Spiral Review • Assessment Readiness

27. In rectangle $ABCD$, $AC = (x + 15)$ ft and $BD = (3x - 10)$ ft. What is the length of $\overline{BD}$?

Ⓐ 2.5 ft   Ⓒ 12.5 ft

Ⓑ 6.25 ft   Ⓓ 27.5 ft

28. Kite $PQRS$ is symmetric across $\overline{PR}$. The diagonals intersect at point T. Which pairs of angles are congruent? Select all that apply.

Ⓐ $\angle PTS \cong \angle PTQ$ Ⓒ $\angle PSR \cong \angle PQR$

Ⓑ $\angle SPQ \cong \angle SRQ$ Ⓓ $\angle PTS \cong \angle RTQ$

29. A quadrilateral is described by the following: two consecutive sides are congruent, two sides are parallel, and an interior angle is 90°. What could be the shape? Select all that apply.

Ⓐ square   Ⓓ rhombus

Ⓑ rectangle   Ⓔ parallelogram

Ⓒ trapezoid   Ⓕ triangle

30. Two triangles have three corresponding congruent angles. Are the triangles similar?

Ⓐ always   Ⓒ sometimes

Ⓑ never   Ⓓ It cannot be determined.

 I'm in a Learning Mindset!

How can I improve my approach to solving transformation problems?

Develop AA Triangle Similarity

(I Can) prove AA, SSS, and SAS Similarity Theorems.

Spark Your Learning

An architect is designing a tree house that will have supports reaching to the top of a tree. Both the architect and the tree cast a shadow.

Complete Part A as a whole class. Then complete Parts B–D in small groups.

   A. What is a mathematical question you can ask about this situation?

   B. How can the shadows of the person and the tree be used to help determine the height of the tree?

   C. To answer your question, what strategy and tool would you use along with all the information you have? What answer do you get?

   D. What must be true about the angles of the triangles for you to show that the triangles are similar?

 Turn and Talk Compare and contrast the two shapes you used to model the scenario. What conclusion can you draw about the relationship between the shapes?

Build Understanding

Prove the AA Triangle Similarity Theorem

You have learned previously that two figures are similar when there is a sequence of similarity transformations that maps one figure to the other. You can also show that two triangles are similar by using theorems, such as the Angle-Angle Triangle Similarity Theorem.

> **Angle-Angle (AA) Triangle Similarity Theorem**
>
> If two angles of one triangle are congruent to two angles of another triangle, then the two triangles are similar.

1 Prove the AA Triangle Similarity Theorem.

Given: $\angle J \cong \angle P$ and $\angle K \cong \angle Q$.

Prove: $\triangle JKL \sim \triangle PQR$

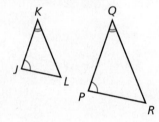

To prove that the triangles are similar, find a sequence of similarity transformations that maps $\triangle JKL$ to $\triangle PQR$.

A. Consider a dilation that maps $\triangle JKL$ to $\triangle J'K'L'$. What is the scale factor of the dilation so that $\triangle J'K'L'$ will be congruent to $\triangle PQR$? Why should $\triangle J'K'L'$ be congruent to $\triangle PQR$?

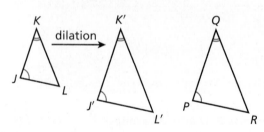

B. Why is $\triangle JKL$ similar to $\triangle J'K'L'$?

C. To complete the proof, you must show $\triangle J'K'L' \cong \triangle PQR$. Because $\triangle JKL \sim \triangle J'K'L'$, $J'K' = JK \cdot$ scale factor. What is the result when you substitute the scale factor from Part A, and simplify?

D. Because $\triangle JKL \sim \triangle J'K'L'$, $\angle J \cong \angle J'$ and $\angle K \cong \angle K'$. Explain why $\angle J' \cong \angle P$ and $\angle K' \cong \angle Q$.

E. Explain why you can conclude that $\triangle J'K'L' \cong \triangle PQR$.

F. Use the results from the steps above to describe how a sequence of similarity transformations maps $\triangle JKL$ to $\triangle PQR$.

 Turn and Talk Compare and contrast the AA Triangle Similarity Theorem and the ASA Triangle Congruence Theorem.

Step It Out

Apply the AA Triangle Similarity Theorem

You can use the AA Triangle Similarity Theorem to prove triangles are similar and find missing dimensions.

2 During time-lapse photography, a motorized camera slider stabilizer can be used. The camera moves along the slider while it records. Two positions of a camera slider are shown. What is *PQ*?

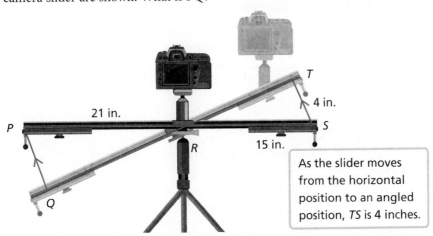

As the slider moves from the horizontal position to an angled position, *TS* is 4 inches.

Determine if △*PQR* and △*STR* are similar.

A. How can you use knowledge of parallel lines to prove ∠*P* and ∠*S* are congruent and ∠*Q* and ∠*T* are congruent?

B. Are there any other congruent angles in the triangles? If so, how do you know?

C. How can you prove the two triangles are similar?

Find *PQ*.

D. Name the corresponding pairs of sides between the two triangles.

E. Why can you use a proportion to find *PQ*?

$$\frac{RP}{PQ} = \frac{RS}{ST}$$

$$\frac{21}{PQ} = \frac{15}{4}$$

$$84 = 15 \cdot PQ$$

$$PQ = 5.6$$

Answer the question.

As the slider moves from the horizontal position to an angled position, *PQ* is 5.6 inches.

 Turn and Talk Is there more than one way to set up a proportion to find *PQ*? If so, give another proportion that can be used to find *PQ*.

Apply the SSS and SAS Triangle Similarity Theorems

In addition to the AA Triangle Similarity Theorem, there are two other theorems that can be used to prove triangle similarity.

> ### Side-Side-Side (SSS) Triangle Similarity Theorem
>
> If the three sides of one triangle are proportional to the corresponding sides of another triangle, then the triangles are similar.

> ### Side-Angle-Side (SAS) Triangle Similarity Theorem
>
> If two sides of one triangle are proportional to the corresponding sides of another triangle and their included angles are congruent, then the triangles are similar.

3 Find the value of x.

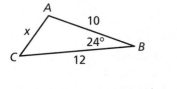 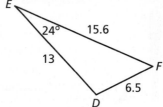

Determine whether the triangles are similar.

Start by investigating corresponding sides to determine if they are proportional.

$$\frac{ED}{AB} = \frac{13}{10} = 1.3 \qquad \frac{EF}{BC} = \frac{15.6}{12} = 1.3$$

> **A.** How do you know which corresponding sides are proportional?

Check for congruent corresponding angles.

$$\angle B \cong \angle E$$

> **B.** How do you know that the angles are congruent?

C. Why can you conclude that the triangles are similar? Write a similarity statement for the two triangles.

Find the value of *x*.

D. Which solution correctly determines the length of x? Explain.

$$\frac{ED}{AB} = \frac{FD}{x}$$

$$\frac{13}{10} = \frac{6.5}{x}$$

$$13x = 65$$

$$x = 5$$

$$\frac{ED}{CB} = \frac{FD}{x}$$

$$\frac{13}{12} = \frac{6.5}{x}$$

$$13x = 78$$

$$x = 6$$

 Turn and Talk Why isn't Angle-Side-Angle listed as a way to show two triangles are similar?

Use Indirect Measurement

You can use triangle similarity to find unknown measures in the real world when taking a direct measure may not be possible.

©F. Bilger Photodesign/F1online digitale Bildagentur GmbH/Alamy

4 ▶ A swimmer wants to find the distance across a lake to create a training plan. She wants to use indirect measurement to determine the distance across the lake.

The swimmer stands at point *U* and identifies a tree directly across the lake from her, and labels it point *T*. She then turns 90°, walks 300 feet, and marks point *V*.

She continues walking 200 feet in a straight line from *V* and marks point *W*. She then turns another 90° and walks until points *T* and *V* align with her location and marks the point as *Y*. She measures to find she had walked 290 feet from *W* to *Y*.

A. Which diagram correctly represents the situation?

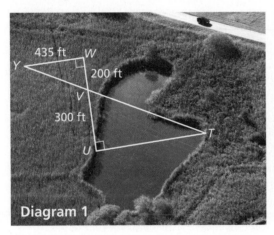

Diagram 1

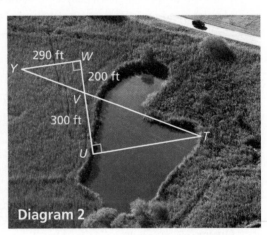

Diagram 2

B. Use each statement and give reasons to prove $\triangle TUV \sim \triangle YWV$.

$\angle UVT \cong \angle WVY$

$\angle TUV \cong \angle YWV$

$\triangle TUV \sim \triangle YWV$

C. To solve the problem, find *TU*. Which is the correct solution?

$$\frac{TU}{300} = \frac{200}{290}$$

$290 \cdot TU = 60{,}000$

$TU \approx 207$

The distance across the lake is about 207 feet.

$$\frac{TU}{290} = \frac{300}{200}$$

$200 \cdot TU = 87{,}000$

$TU = 435$

The distance across the lake is 435 feet.

D. Does your answer make sense in the context of the problem? Explain.

 Turn and Talk In the example, what is another proportion you can write to solve the problem?

Check Understanding

1. If $\triangle ABC \sim \triangle LMN$ and $\triangle LMN \sim \triangle XYZ$, is $\triangle ABC \sim \triangle XYZ$? Use the AA Triangle Similarity Theorem to support your answer.

2. Two triangular sculptures are similar. The leg of the first sculpture is 4.5 feet, and the base is 7.2 feet. The leg of the second sculpture is 6 feet. What is the length of the base for the second sculpture?

3. Are the triangles at the right similar? If so, what is x? If not, explain.

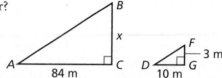

4. Explain how you can create a pair of similar triangles to measure an unknown distance across a canyon. Discuss landmarks, alignment of points, and measurements in your answer.

On Your Own

5. Are the two triangular flags similar? Explain.

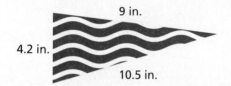

6. Prove the SAS Triangle Similarity Theorem using similarity transformations.

Given: $\dfrac{DE}{AB} = \dfrac{DF}{AC}$ and $\angle A \cong \angle D$.

Prove: $\triangle ABC \sim \triangle DEF$

Determine whether each set of triangles is similar. Justify your reasoning.

7. $\triangle ABC$ and $\triangle DEC$

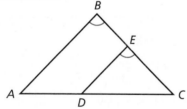

8. $\triangle XYZ$ and $\triangle PQR$

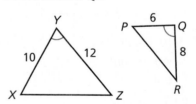

9. $\triangle LMN$ and $\triangle JKN$

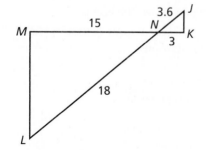

10. $\triangle ABC$ and $\triangle CDB$

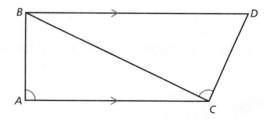

Determine whether each pair of triangles is similar. When possible, find the value of *x*.

11.

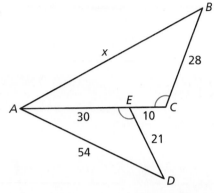

12.

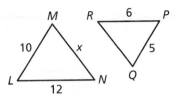

13.

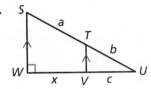

14.

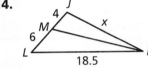

15. Find the value of *x* that makes $\triangle PQR$ similar to $\triangle TUV$.

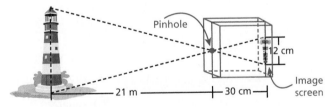

16. STEM In a pinhole camera, light from an object goes through a pinhole to produce an inverted image on its screen. A lighthouse is 21 m from the pinhole of a large pinhole camera. The 12 cm tall image is projected on the screen 30 cm from the pinhole.

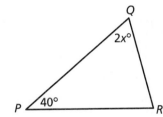

A. How tall is the lighthouse?

B. Suppose the same pinhole camera is moved closer to the lighthouse. If the lighthouse projects a 15 cm tall image, how much closer is the pinhole camera moved?

C. Suppose a different pinhole camera is placed 29.4 m from the lighthouse. If the image is 10 cm tall, how far is the camera screen from the pinhole?

17. Prove the SSS Triangle Similarity Theorem using similarity transformations.

Given: $\dfrac{DE}{AB} = \dfrac{DF}{AC} = \dfrac{FE}{BC}$

Prove: $\triangle ABC \sim \triangle DEF$

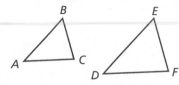

18. (MP) **Attend to Precision** An anthropologist studying an ancient society reaches a river that needs to be crossed. She locates a tree directly across the river at Point A, marks her location as Point B, then turns and walks to Point C. She continues walking to Point D, turns perpendicular to the river, and walks until Points A and C are directly in line with her final location, Point E. What is the width of the river?

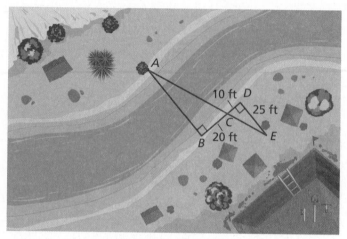

(MP) **Use Repeated Reasoning** Determine whether each of the following provides enough information to prove $\triangle ABC \sim \triangle DEC$. Justify your answer.

19. $\overline{AB} \parallel \overline{DE}$

20. $\angle B \cong \angle DEC$

21. $\text{m}\angle DEC = 90°$

22. $\dfrac{EC}{EC + EB} = \dfrac{DC}{DC + AD}$

Spiral Review • Assessment Readiness

23. A right triangle with a hypotenuse of 7 cm is dilated so that the hypotenuse is 4 cm. If k is the scale factor, then

Ⓐ $k < -1$ Ⓒ $k > 1$

Ⓑ $-1 < k < 0$ Ⓓ $0 < k < 1$

24. If a quadrilateral is a _____, then its diagonals are perpendicular. Select all that apply.

Ⓐ kite Ⓒ rhombus

Ⓑ rectangle Ⓓ trapezoid

25. If $\overline{AB}$ is the midsegment of $\triangle QRP$, what is AB?

Ⓐ $11\dfrac{1}{3}$

Ⓑ 17

Ⓒ 35

Ⓓ 68

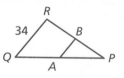

26. Which shape is not necessarily a parallelogram?

Ⓐ rhombus Ⓒ square

Ⓑ trapezoid Ⓓ rectangle

 I'm in a Learning Mindset!

When studying similarity in triangles, how do I react when my learning environment changes?

Develop and Prove Triangle Proportionality

(I Can) identify and use the connection between parallel lines and proportional segments in triangles.

Spark Your Learning

An A-frame house is styled with a very steep-angled roof that makes the front of the house resemble the letter A.

Complete Part A as a whole class. Then complete Parts B–D in small groups.

A. What is a mathematical question you can ask about the design of this house? What information do you need to answer the question?

B. How many triangles can you identify when looking at the front of the house?

C. To answer your question, what strategy and tool would you use along with all the information you have? What answer do you get?

D. How are the corresponding sides of the triangles related? How do you know?

 Turn and Talk Suppose you are only given the side lengths of the triangles formed. How could you use this information to answer the question?

Build Understanding

The Triangle Proportionality Theorem

The Triangle Proportionality Theorem describes how a line parallel to one of the sides of the triangle divides the two sides that it intersects.

Triangle Proportionality Theorem
If a line parallel to one side of a triangle intersects the other two sides, then it divides those sides proportionally.   If $\overleftrightarrow{DE} \parallel \overline{BC}$, then $\frac{AD}{DB} = \frac{AE}{EC}$. 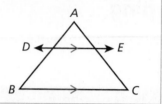

1 Prove the Triangle Proportionality Theorem.

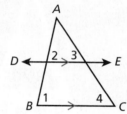

Given: $\overleftrightarrow{DE} \parallel \overline{BC}$

Prove: $\dfrac{AD}{DB} = \dfrac{AE}{EC}$

First, show that △ADE ~ △ABC.

A. Explain why $\angle 1 \cong \angle 2$ and $\angle 3 \cong \angle 4$.

B. Is there enough information to conclude that $\triangle ADE \sim \triangle ABC$? Explain.

Next, use the similar triangles to show that $\frac{AD}{DB} = \frac{AE}{EC}$.

$\dfrac{AB}{AD} = \dfrac{AC}{AE}$	Corresponding sides are proportional.
$\dfrac{AD + DB}{AD} = \dfrac{AE + EC}{AE}$	Segment Addition Postulate
$\dfrac{AD}{AD} + \dfrac{DB}{AD} = \dfrac{AE}{AE} + \dfrac{EC}{AE}$	Distributive Property of Division
$1 + \dfrac{DB}{AD} = 1 + \dfrac{EC}{AE}$	$\dfrac{a}{a} = 1$
$\dfrac{DB}{AD} = \dfrac{EC}{AE}$	Subtract 1 from each side.
$\dfrac{AD}{DB} = \dfrac{AE}{EC}$	Take the reciprocal of each side.

C. Suppose the proportion $\frac{AD}{AB} = \frac{AE}{AC}$ is used instead of $\frac{AB}{AD} = \frac{AC}{AE}$. Do you get the same result? Explain.

D. How could you state the Triangle Proportionality Theorem in terms of a dilation? Explain how your new version of the theorem is equivalent to the one given above.

 Turn and Talk Compare the Midsegment Theorem presented earlier to the Triangle Proportionality Theorem. How are they alike?

Step It Out

Apply the Triangle Proportionality Theorem

2 A light sensor is installed above the front door of a building at point *G*. If the light sensor is moved to point *J*, how far from the front door will the light from the sensor reach?

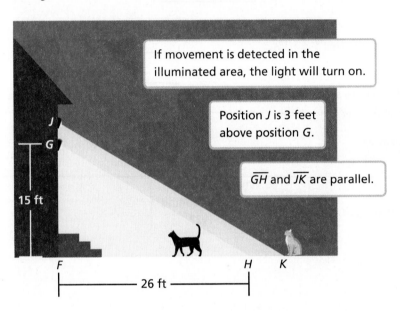

If movement is detected in the illuminated area, the light will turn on.

Position *J* is 3 feet above position *G*.

$\overline{GH}$ and $\overline{JK}$ are parallel.

15 ft

26 ft

Find *KH*.

$$\frac{JG}{GF} = \frac{KH}{HF}$$

A. How do you know this proportion is true?

$$\frac{3}{15} = \frac{KH}{26}$$

$$78 = 15 \cdot KH$$

$$KH = 5.2$$

Find *KF*.

B. What length in feet does *KF* represent?

$$KF = KH + HF$$

$$KF = 5.2 + 26$$

$$KF = 31.2$$

The light from the sensor will reach 31.2 feet after it is moved up to point *J*.

Turn and Talk The sensor is moved to position *M* in order to reach a horizontal distance of 33 feet from the building. Where is position *M* located on the wall in relation to position *G*?

The Converse of the Triangle Proportionality Theorem

Converse of the Triangle Proportionality Theorem

If a line divides two sides of a triangle proportionally, then it is parallel to the third side.

If $\frac{AD}{DB} = \frac{AE}{EC}$, then $\overleftrightarrow{DE} \parallel \overline{BC}$.

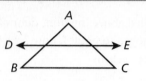

3 In the figure at the right, verify that $\overline{YZ} \parallel \overline{VX}$.

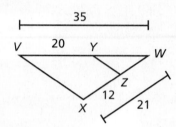

A. In order to use the Converse of the Triangle Proportionality Theorem to show that $\overline{YZ} \parallel \overline{VX}$, what must be true about the sides of the triangle?

Find WY, YV, WZ, and ZX.

$WY = 35 - 20 = 15$ $\qquad YV = 20$

$WZ = 21 - 12 = 9$ $\qquad ZX = 12$

> **B.** Why do you need to subtract to find WY and WZ?

Check for proportionality.

$$\frac{WY}{YV} \overset{?}{=} \frac{WZ}{ZX}$$

$$\frac{15}{20} \overset{?}{=} \frac{9}{12}$$

$$0.75 = 0.75 \checkmark$$

C. Is $\overline{YZ} \parallel \overline{VX}$? Explain.

Partition Segments

You can apply the Triangle Proportionality Theorem to **partition**, or divide, a line segment into shorter segments with a given ratio.

4 Find the coordinates of point P that divides $\overline{AB}$ into a ratio of 1 to 3 from $A(-6, -5)$ to $B(10, 7)$.

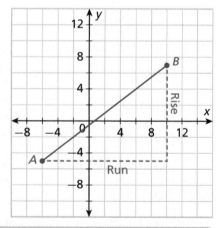

Write a ratio to describe the distance of point P along the segment from A to B.

Point P is $\frac{1}{3+1} = \frac{1}{4}$ of the distance from A to B.

Find the rise and the run between points A and B.

Run (horizontal distance): $10 - (-6) = 16$

Rise (vertical distance): $7 - (-5) = 12$

Find $\frac{1}{4}$ of the rise and run to determine the distance point P is from A.

$\frac{1}{4}$ of run $= \left(\frac{1}{4}\right)16 = 4$ $\qquad \frac{1}{4}$ of rise $= \left(\frac{1}{4}\right)12 = 3$

Point P is 4 units horizontally from Point A and 3 units vertically from Point A.

$P(x, y) = (-6 + 4, -5 + 3) = (-2, -2)$

The coordinates of point P are $(-2, -2)$.

> **A.** What does $\frac{1}{4}$ of the rise represent? $\frac{1}{4}$ of the run represent?

> **B.** Why is $\frac{1}{4}$ of the rise and $\frac{1}{4}$ of the run added to the coordinates of point A instead of the coordinates of point B?

5 ▶ You can use a construction to partition a segment into several equal parts. Then, you can locate a point that partitions the segment in a given ratio.

For $\overline{AB}$, construct point P that partitions the segment into a ratio of 2 to 3 from point A to point B.

A. Use a ruler to draw $\overrightarrow{AC}$. The exact length or angle is not important, but the construction may be easier if the measure of the angle is about 45° to 60°.

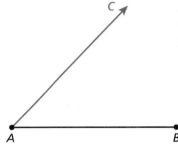

B. Placing your compass point on A, draw a small arc through $\overrightarrow{AC}$ and label that point D. The precise distance from A is not important, but for any construction, you will be drawing the number of arcs equal to the total number $a + b$ of portions in the ratio of a to b. Since the construction will divide $\overrightarrow{AB}$ in the ratio of 2 to 3, how many total arcs should you draw?

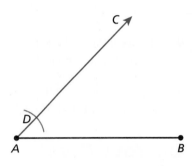

C. Using the same compass setting, place the compass point at D and draw a second arc and label the intersection E. Repeat the process 3 more times and label the points of intersection F, G, and H. Why is it necessary to draw an equal number of arcs as the total number of portions in the ratio?

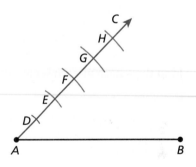

D. Use a straightedge to draw a segment from H to B. Construct an angle congruent to $\angle AHB$ with G as the vertex. Repeat the process for F, E, and D to create 5 segments.

E. The construction partitions $\overline{AB}$ into 5 equal parts. Why is point P located as shown?

F. Why is $\overline{EP}$ parallel to $\overline{HB}$?

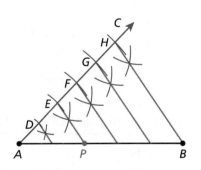

 Turn and Talk For the construction in Task 5, explain why this construction works using the Triangle Proportionality Theorem.

Check Understanding

1. Explain the criteria needed to use the Triangle Proportionality Theorem to find missing segment lengths when a line intersects two sides of a triangle.

2. What is the length of $\overline{AB}$?

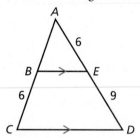

3. Are segments $\overline{BE}$ and $\overline{CD}$ parallel? Explain.

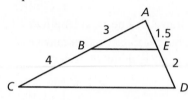

4. If a segment on a graph is divided into a ratio of 1 to 1 by point P, what can you conclude about point P?

5. If you divide $\overline{AB}$ in the ratio of 2:3 from A to B, is this the same as finding $\frac{2}{5}$ the distance from A to B? Explain.

On Your Own

6. $\overline{LM} \parallel \overline{QR}$. Construct a paragraph proof to show $\frac{PL}{LQ} = \frac{PM}{MR}$.

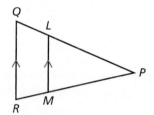

Find the length of each segment.

7. $\overline{AE}$

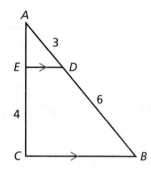

8. $\overline{VY}$

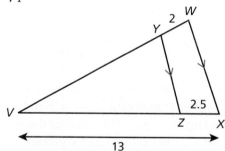

9. Write a two-column proof of the converse of the Triangle Proportionality Theorem.

   Given: $\dfrac{AD}{DB} = \dfrac{AE}{EC}$

   Prove: $\overline{DE} \parallel \overline{BC}$

   (Hint: Start by taking the reciprocal of each side, then adding 1 to each side. Remember to include the steps involving triangle similarity at the end.)

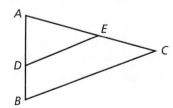

Find the coordinates of point P that divide $\overline{AB}$ into the given ratio from A to B.

10. $A(-7, -4)$, $B(8, 6)$; 3 to 2

11. $A(-10, 13)$, $B(5, -2)$; 3 to 12

12. (MP) **Use Structure** Two city streets are parallel. The measurements between the streets and a landmark are shown in the figure. Find the distance between 1st Street and 2nd Street along Pike Avenue and the distance between 2nd Street and the landmark along Pike Avenue.

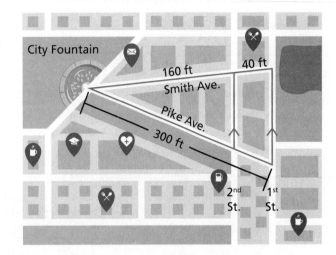

For each figure, determine if the segments are parallel. Explain.

13. $\overline{DE}$ and $\overline{BC}$

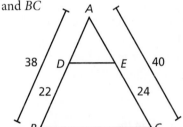

14. $\overline{LN}$ and $\overline{PQ}$

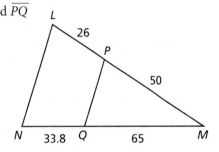

Copy segment $\overline{AB}$. Then show the construction of point P that divides the segment from A to B in the given ratio.

A •————————————————————————• B

15. 3 to 2

16. 1 to 2

17. (MP) **Use Repeated Reasoning** The exit for Hudsonville is 24 miles past the exit for Harper City. A new exit will be added for Westhaven that divides the highway from Harper City to Hudsonville in a 3 to 2 ratio. One new road sign will divide the section from Harper City to Westhaven in a 1 to 1 ratio, and a second road sign will divide the section from Westhaven to Hudsonville in a 1 to 1 ratio. Find the distances between all three exits and the locations of both new signs.

Harper City - Hudsonville

18. A corollary to the Triangle Proportionality Theorem states that if three or more parallel lines intersect two transversals, then the lines divide the transversals proportionally.
Prove the corollary.

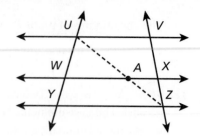

Given: $\overleftrightarrow{UV} \parallel \overleftrightarrow{WX}$, $\overleftrightarrow{WX} \parallel \overleftrightarrow{YZ}$

Prove: $\dfrac{UW}{WY} = \dfrac{UA}{AZ}, \dfrac{UA}{AZ} = \dfrac{VX}{XZ}, \dfrac{UW}{WY} = \dfrac{VX}{XZ}$

A. Complete the paragraph proof of the corollary.

B. What would be true about the ratios if the middle parallel line is the same distance from the other two parallel lines?

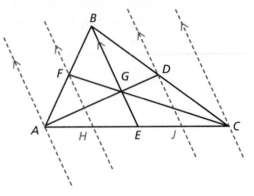

The diagram shows lines $\overline{UV}$, $\overline{WX}$, and $\overline{YZ}$ where $\overline{UV} \parallel \overline{WX}$ and $\overline{WX} \parallel \overline{YZ}$, as well as transversals $\overline{UY}$ and $\overline{VZ}$. I can draw a third transversal $\overline{UZ}$ because two points determine a line, and I can mark its intersection with $\overline{WX}$ as point A. In $\triangle UZY$, $\frac{UW}{WY} = \frac{UA}{AZ}$, and in $\triangle$ ___?___, $\frac{UA}{AZ} = \frac{VX}{XZ}$, by the Triangle ___?___ Theorem. Then, $\frac{UW}{WY} = \frac{VX}{XZ}$ by the Property of Equality, so the parallel lines divide transversals $\overline{UY}$ and $\overline{VZ}$ proportionally.

C. Use the corollary to show that the point where the medians of a triangle meet is $\frac{2}{3}$ of the way from each vertex to the midpoint of its opposite side.
(*Hint*: For a given median connecting a vertex and one midpoint, draw auxiliary parallel lines through the other two vertices and the other two midpoints. Notice how the parallel lines partition the other two medians.)

19. (Open Middle™) Using the digits 1 to 9, at most one time each, fill in the boxes to make segment lengths in the diagram. (Note: the diagram may not be drawn to scale.)

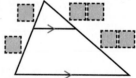

Spiral Review • Assessment Readiness

20. Two triangles with two pairs of congruent angles are similar.

Ⓐ always
Ⓒ sometimes
Ⓑ never
Ⓓ It cannot be determined.

21. A right triangle has legs that are 3 meters long and 4 meters long respectively. What is the length of the hypotenuse?

Ⓐ 4.25 m
Ⓒ 7 m
Ⓑ 5 m
Ⓓ 12 m

22. Which characteristic(s) are always true for two similar figures? Select all that apply.

Ⓐ congruent corresponding angles
Ⓑ congruent corresponding sides
Ⓒ noncongruent corresponding angles
Ⓓ proportional corresponding sides
Ⓔ equal areas

 I'm in a Learning Mindset!

Can my attitude in class when challenged to learn new concepts be changed? Why or why not?

Apply Similarity in Right Triangles

(I Can) identify similar right triangles, apply the Geometric Means Theorems, and recognize Pythagorean triples.

Spark Your Learning

When a tennis player hits the ball using an overhead smash serve, the goal is for the player to hit the ball close to a straight line that passes as close to the net as possible without hitting it.

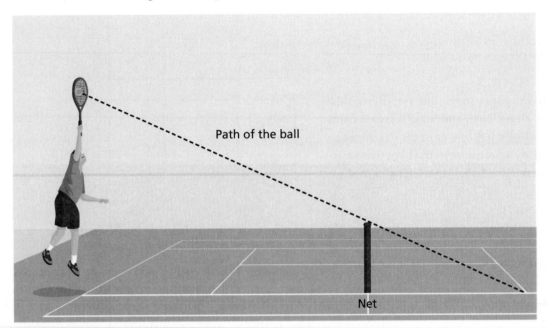

Path of the ball

Net

Complete Part A as a whole class. Then complete Parts B–D in small groups.

A. What is a mathematical question you can ask about the location of the player?

B. Is it possible to find a relationship between any of the triangles shown in the figure using the additional information? Explain.

C. To answer your question, what strategy and tool would you use along with all the information you have? What answer do you get?

D. What does your answer mean in the context of the situation?

 Turn and Talk Suppose the ball is served or hit from a height off the ground equal to the distance from the net to where the ball hits the ground. The total horizontal distance traveled by the ball stays the same. Determine the height of the ball when it is hit in this situation.

Build Understanding

Compare Corresponding Parts of Similar Figures

Right triangles have special features you can use to prove two triangles are similar.

1 ▶ **Use a ruler to draw a diagonal line on a rectangular piece of paper to form two congruent triangles.**

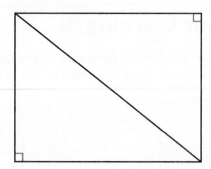

Fold the paper so the line you drew folds back along itself, and make a crease from the bottom left corner to the drawn line, creating an altitude to the hypotenuse of one triangle. Label your triangles as shown.

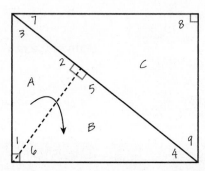

Cut out the three right triangles *A*, *B*, and *C*.

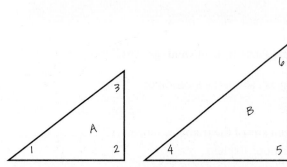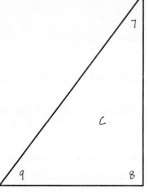

Place triangle *A* on triangle *B*. Move the triangles to match corresponding angles.

A. What do you observe about the angles of triangles *A* and *B*?

B. Are triangles *A* and *B* similar? Why or why not?

Move triangle *A* to triangle *C*. Move the triangles to match corresponding angles.

C. What do you observe about the angles of triangles *A* and *C*?

D. What relationship can you identify between triangles *B* and *C*. How do you know?

E. In general, what types of figures are created by drawing an altitude to the hypotenuse of a right triangle?

Step It Out

Identify Properties of Similar Right Triangles

The following theorem describes the figures formed when drawing the altitude to the hypotenuse of a right triangle.

> **Right Triangle Similarity Theorem**
>
> The altitude to the hypotenuse of a right triangle forms two triangles that are similar to each other and to the original triangle.

Segment lengths in the three triangles have a special proportional relationship. In a proportion of the form $\frac{a}{x} = \frac{x}{b}$, two numbers are the same. The x represents the *geometric mean* of a and b. The **geometric mean** of two numbers is the positive square root of their product. The following theorems involve the geometric mean and right triangles.

Geometric Means Theorems		
The length of the altitude to the hypotenuse of a right triangle is the geometric mean of the lengths of the segments of the hypotenuse.	$\frac{x}{h} = \frac{h}{y}$ or $h = \sqrt{xy}$	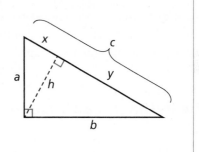
The length of the leg of a right triangle is the geometric mean of the lengths of the hypotenuse and the segment of the hypotenuse adjacent to that leg.	$\frac{x}{a} = \frac{a}{c}$ or $a = \sqrt{xc}$ $\frac{y}{b} = \frac{b}{c}$ or $b = \sqrt{yc}$	

 Prove the first Geometric Means Theorem.

Given: Right triangle ABC with altitude $\overline{BD}$

Prove: $\dfrac{CD}{BD} = \dfrac{BD}{AD}$

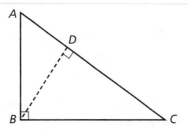

Statements	Reasons
1. Right triangle ABC with altitude $\overline{BD}$	**1.** Given
2. $\triangle ABD \sim \triangle BCD$	**2.** The altitude to the hypotenuse of a right triangle forms two triangles that are similar to each other and to the original triangle.
3. $\dfrac{CD}{BD} = \dfrac{BD}{AD}$	**3.** _____?_____

A. What property is used for the reason in Step 3 of the proof?

B. Is $BD = \sqrt{CD \cdot AD}$ equivalent to $\dfrac{CD}{BD} = \dfrac{BD}{AD}$? Explain why or why not.

Apply a Geometric Means Theorem

 3 To find the height of a rock-climbing tower, a climber uses a square of cardboard at eye level to line up the top and bottom of the tower. What is the height of the tower?

Write a proportion to find the missing portion of the height.

$$\frac{5}{9.5} = \frac{9.5}{y}$$

> **A.** Justify the proportion.

$$5y = 90.25$$

$$y = 18.05 \text{ ft}$$

Find the total height.

$$\text{height} = 18.05 + 5 = 23.05 \text{ ft}$$

> **B.** Why do you add 5 to y to find the total height?

> **Turn and Talk** A different person with an eye level at 6 ft is finding the height of the tower. Can this person stand at the same distance from the tower and estimate its height with this method? Explain.

Prove the Pythagorean Theorem

Recall the Pythagorean Theorem and its converse stated below.

Pythagorean Theorem: In a right triangle, the sum of the squares of the lengths of the legs equals the square of the length of the hypotenuse.

Converse of the Pythagorean Theorem: If the square of the length of the longest side of a triangle equals the sum of the squares of the lengths of the other two sides, then the triangle is a right triangle.

There are many proofs of the Pythagorean Theorem. One such proof uses a theorem presented in this lesson.

4 **Given:** $\triangle ABC$ is a right triangle.

Prove: $a^2 + b^2 = c^2$

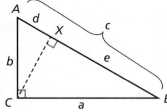

Relate the sides of the triangles.

A. $\overline{CX}$ is the altitude to the hypotenuse of $\triangle ABC$ that divides c into segments d and e. What theorem justifies the following equations?

$$\frac{e}{a} = \frac{a}{c} \text{ and } \frac{d}{b} = \frac{b}{c}$$

Derive the formula.

$\frac{e}{a} = \frac{a}{c}$ and $\frac{d}{b} = \frac{b}{c}$ Original proportions

$a^2 = ec \quad b^2 = cd$ Multiply.

$a^2 + b^2 = ec + cd$ Addition Property of Equality

$a^2 + b^2 = c(e + d)$ Distributive Property

$a^2 + b^2 = c(c)$ Substitute c for $e + d$.

$a^2 + b^2 = c^2$ Multiply.

> **B.** How do you know that $c = e + d$?

Use Pythagorean Triples

A **Pythagorean triple** is a set of three nonzero whole numbers a, b, and c that satisfy the equation $a^2 + b^2 = c^2$. Examples of Pythagorean triples are shown in the table.

Pythagorean triple	Used in $a^2 + b^2 = c^2$
3, 4, 5	$3^2 + 4^2 = 5^2$
5, 12, 13	$5^2 + 12^2 = 13^2$
8, 15, 17	$8^2 + 15^2 = 17^2$

5   Determine if the set of three values is a Pythagorean triple.

Set 1	Set 2
7, 24, 25	11, 14, 21
$7^2 + 24^2 \overset{?}{=} 25^2$	$11^2 + 14^2 \overset{?}{=} 21^2$
$49 + 576 \overset{?}{=} 625$	$121 + 196 \overset{?}{=} 441$
$625 = 625$	$317 \neq 441$

Both sides of the equation are equivalent, so 7, 24, 25 is a Pythagorean triple. | The sides of the equation are not equivalent, so 11, 14, 21 is not a Pythagorean triple.

A. How is the Converse of the Pythagorean Theorem used to determine whether a set of three numbers is a Pythagorean triple?

B. Make a sketch of a right triangle that has side lengths 7, 24, and 25. How do the numbers of a Pythagorean triple relate to the side lengths of a right triangle?

C. Explain why 5, 6, $\sqrt{61}$ is not a Pythagorean triple.

 Turn and Talk Suppose you multiply each of the numbers of a Pythagorean triple by the same number. Do the resulting numbers also form a Pythagorean triple? If so, give an example.

Check Understanding

1. Braden uses a ruler and protractor to draw a right triangle. He divides that triangle using the altitude to the hypotenuse. How many similar triangles does his drawing contain? Explain.

In Problems 2 and 3, use the diagram of the right triangle.

2. In a right triangle, how is the length of the altitude to the hypotenuse related to the lengths of the two segments it creates?

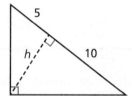

3. What is the value of h?

4. Explain how the Geometric Means Theorems are related to the Pythagorean Theorem.

5. Do the values 9, 40, and 41 describe the side lengths and hypotenuse of a right triangle? Explain why or why not.

On Your Own

Write a similarity statement comparing the triangles in each figure.

6.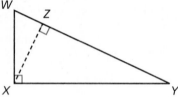

7.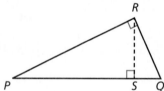

8.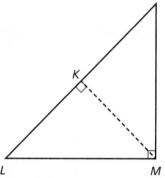

9. **Open Ended** Draw a right triangle with an altitude drawn to the hypotenuse and label the vertices of all the triangles formed. Redraw the triangle as three separate triangles, and write a similarity statement that relates the triangles. Why might redrawing the triangles be helpful when writing similarity statements for the triangles?

10. Prove the Right Triangle Similarity Theorem.
    Given: Right triangle ABC with altitude $\overline{BD}$

    A. Prove that $\triangle BDC \sim \triangle ABC$.
    B. Prove that $\triangle ADB \sim \triangle ABC$.
    C. Prove that $\triangle BDC \sim \triangle ADB$.

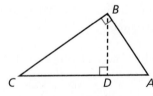

11. Prove the second Geometric Means Theorem.
    Given: Right triangle ABC with altitude $\overline{BD}$
    Prove: $\dfrac{AD}{AB} = \dfrac{AB}{AC}$ and $\dfrac{DC}{BC} = \dfrac{BC}{AC}$

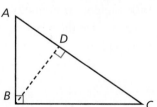

For Problems 12–15, find *x*, *y*, and *z*. Write your answer in simplest radical form.

12.

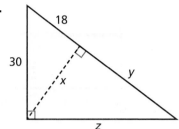

13.

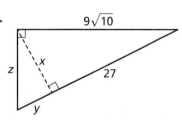

14.

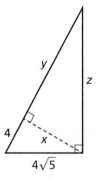

15.

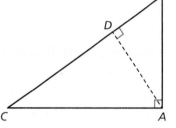

Find the length of $\overline{AD}$ using the given segment lengths.

16. $AC = 4$
    $AB = 3$

17. $AC = 80$
    $BC = 89$

18. $AB = 33$
    $BC = 65$

19. $BD = 3$
    $DC = 12$

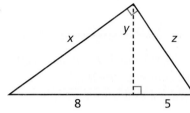

20. A 9 in. altitude divides the hypotenuse of a right triangle into two segments. One segment is 9 times as long as the other. What are the lengths for the two segments of the hypotenuse?

21. STEM One common style of bridge is a truss bridge, where a supporting framework adds strength to the bridge. Some truss members are under a compression load, and some truss members are under a tension load. What is the length of the shortest truss member under compression?

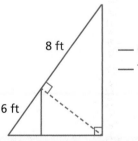

— Compression
— Tension

22. (MP) Repeated Reasoning An altitude to the hypotenuse of a right triangle divides it into two smaller right triangles. In the smallest triangle, the ratio of the hypotenuse to the longer leg is $\sqrt{2}$ to 1. In the original triangle, what is the ratio of the hypotenuse to the altitude?

Tell whether the numbers form a Pythagorean triple. Explain.

23. 4, 6, 10   **24.** 5, 12, 13   **25.** 8, 17, $\sqrt{353}$

26. 13, 24, 60   **27.** 24, 32, 40   **28.** 65, 72, 97

The lengths of the legs of a right triangle are a and b, and the length of the hypotenuse is c. Find the missing side length of the right triangle. Decide if the side lengths form a Pythagorean triple.

29. $a = 6, b = 8, c = ?$ **30.** $a = 10, b = ?, c = 26$ **31.** $a = ?, b = 32, c = 34$

32. (MP) **Attend to Precision** Kira has two plans for the frame of a small doghouse roof. She wants to choose the plan that requires the least amount of lumber.

     A. Which plan should she choose? Why?

     B. If lumber costs $2.50 per foot, what is her approximate total lumber cost for the frame?

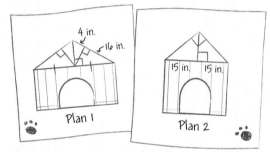

Spiral Review • Assessment Readiness

33. On a coordinate plane, A is at $(0, 0)$, B is at $(10, 4)$, and C is plotted so it divides the line segment from A to B in a 4 to 1 ratio. What are the coordinates of C?

     (A) $C(2.5, 1)$ (C) $C(8, 3.2)$

     (B) $C(2, 0.8)$ (D) $C(9, 3.6)$

34. In a right triangle with side lengths of 3 m, 4 m, and 5 m, what is the ratio of the length of the leg opposite the smallest interior angle to the length of the leg adjacent to the smallest interior angle?

     (A) $\frac{3}{4}$ (C) $\frac{3}{5}$

     (B) $\frac{4}{3}$ (D) $\frac{4}{5}$

35. In $\triangle ABC$, $m\angle A = 42°$, $m\angle B = 50°$, $AB = 4$ in., and $AC = 3$ in. In $\triangle XYZ$, $m\angle X = 42°$, $m\angle Y = 50°$, $XY = 14$ in., and $YZ = 9.5$ in. Match the part of each triangle with the correct measure.

Triangle part	Measure
A. $\overline{BC}$	**1.** 88°
B. $\overline{XZ}$	**2.** 10.5 in.
C. $\angle BCA$	**3.** 2.7 in.

 I'm in a Learning Mindset!

How am I responding to learning new material that builds on my previous understanding?

Similarity Transformations

A similarity transformation can use rigid transformations as well as dilations to map a pre-image onto a similar image.

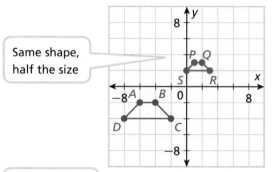

Same shape, half the size

Center: (0,0)
Scale Factor: $\frac{1}{2}$

Dilation: $(x, y) \rightarrow \left(\frac{1}{2}x, \frac{1}{2}y\right)$

Translation: $(x, y) \rightarrow (x + 4, y + 4)$

Similarity Theorems

Angle-Angle (AA) Similarity If two angles of one triangle are congruent to two angles of another triangle, then the two triangles are similar.

The third pair of angles are congruent by the Third Angle Theorem.

Side-Angle-Side (SAS) Similarity If two correspnding sides are proportional and the included angles are congruent, then the two triangles are similar.

Side-Side-Side (SSS) Similarity If all three pairs of corresponding sides are proportional, then the two triangles are similar.

Dilate to obtain congruent sides. Then apply SAS or SSS for congruence.

Triangle Proportionality

If a line parallel to one side of a triangle intersects the other two sides, then it divides those sides proportionally.

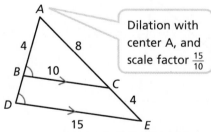

Dilation with center A, and scale factor $\frac{15}{10}$

$\overline{DE} \parallel \overline{BC}$, so corresponding angles are congruent. This means that $\angle D \cong \angle B$. $\angle A \cong \angle A$ by the Reflexive Property, so $\triangle ABC \sim \triangle ADE$.

$$\frac{DB}{BA} = \frac{EC}{CA} \rightarrow DB = \frac{EC}{CA}(BA) = \frac{4}{8}(4) = 2$$

The Pythagorean Theorem

Similarity can be used to prove the Pythagorean Theorem. Take a right triangle and draw in an altitude to the hypotenuse.

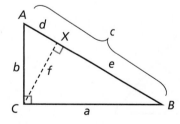

All 3 triangles are similar by AA similarity.

$$\triangle ABC \sim \triangle ACX \sim \triangle CBX$$

Set up equivalent ratios.

$$\frac{e}{a} = \frac{a}{c} \rightarrow a^2 = ec \text{ and } \frac{d}{b} = \frac{b}{c} \rightarrow b^2 = dc$$
$$\rightarrow a^2 + b^2 = ec + dc = (e + d)c = c^2$$

This proves that $a^2 + b^2 = c^2$.

Vocabulary

Choose the correct term from the box to complete each sentence.

1. A __?__ is a transformation that changes the size of a figure but leaves the shape unchanged.

2. When triangles have __?__ corresponding sides and congruent corresponding angles, they are said to be __?__

3. A __?__ produces an image that is similar to the preimage.

4. To __?__ a line segment is to divide it into equal segments.

Concepts and Skills

5. Compare and contrast the criteria used to prove two triangles are congruent with the criteria used to prove two triangles are similar.

Describe a sequence of transformations that proves each pair of figures are similar.

6.

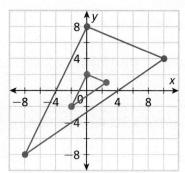

7.

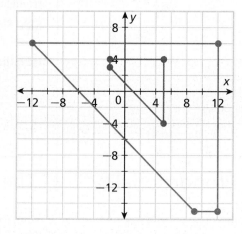

8. Find the value of x.

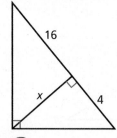

9. Is $\overline{LM}$ parallel to $\overline{PQ}$? Explain.

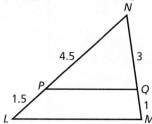

10. (MP) **Use Tools** A 30-foot pole casts a 12-foot shadow. Find the height of a nearby building that casts a shadow of 80 feet. State any assumptions you make. State what strategy and tool you will use to answer the question, explain your choice, and then find the answer.

11. $\triangle ABC \sim \triangle XYZ$, where $AB = 18$ cm, $BC = 30$ cm, and $CA = 42$ cm. The longest side of $\triangle XYZ$ is 25.2 cm. What is the perimeter of $\triangle XYZ$?

12. Line segment $\overline{AB}$ has endpoints $A(-6, 13)$ and $B(4, -2)$. Graph $\overline{AB}$ and plot point P that partitions the segment in the ratio 2:3 from A to B, and point Q that partitions the segment in the same ratio from B to A.

©Archimage/Alamy

Surveyor

A surveyor uses a variety of tools to make measurements and map out the physical features of a location that are used to assess the feasibility of construction and engineering projects involving land and property. Surveyors need to make precise measurements because their work ensures the safety of the general public.

STEM Task

Surveyors use a sight level with a sighting rod to measure vertical and horizontal distances. When you look through a sight level, the distance between the sight level and rod is proportional to the distance between the bottom and top sights by a ratio of 1:12.

Approximate your distance from the sight rod.

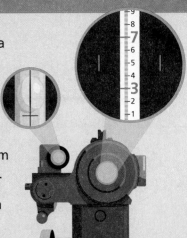

Learning Mindset

Perseverance Learns Effectively

Are your learning efforts effective? Make learning a priority. Use your social relationships to strengthen your involvement in a project rather than to distract from it. Be proactive in getting things done. We all experience failures, but we can recognize our failures or inefficiencies, reflect on them, and then use our experience to improve ourselves. Here are some questions you can ask yourself to monitor how effectively you are learning new material and progressing on a new task:

- How am I prioritizing my learning? What are my greatest strengths? What weaknesses might I need to address? How can I turn my weaknesses into strengths?

- Is a lack of organization affecting my learning outcomes? In what way? What steps can I take to become more organized?

- How do my social relationships affect my academic performance? How can I use these relationships to help me learn more effectively?

Reflect

Q When have you experienced an initial failure that led to growth and learning? How did you benefit from this experience in the long term? How can this experience help you approach new challenges?

Q As a surveyor, you would need to work with a team to make accurate measurements and precise calculations. What steps could you take to better organize your process? How would organization improve the outcome for your team?

13 Trigonometry with Right Triangles

Rising to the Challenge

How high does a firetruck's ladder reach?

Are You Ready?

Complete these problems to review prior concepts and skills you will need for this module.

Solve One-Step Equations

Solve each equation.

1. $6 + t = -17$

2. $7z = 84$

3. $b - 14 = 16$

4. $\dfrac{m}{8} = 11$

5. $-3x = 12$

6. $y + 14 = 2$

7. $\dfrac{a}{4} = -2$

8. $n - 3 = 1$

Angle Relationships in Triangles

Determine each value of x.

9.

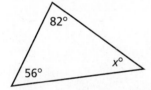

10.

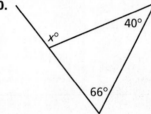

The Pythagorean Theorem and its Converse

11. A right triangle has a leg that is 11 feet long and hypotenuse that is 22 feet long. How long is the other leg of the triangle?

12. A triangle has sides with lengths 8 inches, 15 inches, and 17 inches. Is the triangle a right triangle? Explain how you know.

Connecting Past and Present Learning

Previously, you learned:

- to prove if figures are similar using proportionality,
- to use the Pythagorean Theorem to find missing side lengths of right triangles, and
- to use angle relationships in triangles to find the measure of missing angles.

In this module, you will learn:

- to use similarity to define trigonometric ratios of acute angles, and
- to use trigonometric ratios and the Pythagorean Theorem to solve right triangles in applied problems.

Tangent Ratio

(I Can) use the tangent ratio and its inverse to find side lengths and angle measures in right triangles.

Spark Your Learning

A group of students see the entrance as they walk toward the Taj Mahal.

The height of the Taj Mahal is 240 ft.

Complete Part A as a whole class. Then complete Parts B–D in small groups.

   A. What is a mathematical question you can ask about this situation? What information would you need to know to answer your question?

   B. What variable(s) are involved in this situation?

   C. To answer your question, what strategy and tool would you use along with all the information you have? What answer do you get?

   D. Does your estimate make sense in the context of the situation? How do you know?

> **Turn and Talk** What if the measure of the angle were a bit smaller? How would this affect the accuracy of your estimate?

Build Understanding

Investigate a Ratio in a Right Triangle

In the given right triangle $\triangle ABC$, the sides (or legs) are labeled in reference to $\angle C$. So side $\overline{AB}$ is the opposite leg of $\angle C$, and side $\overline{BC}$ is the adjacent leg to $\angle C$. The side that connects the opposite and adjacent legs is the hypotenuse.

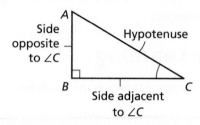

1 ▶ Analyze the relationships of opposite and adjacent side lengths of two right triangles that have the same acute angle.

A. Use tracing paper to create a copy of each triangle shown. What are the approximate side lengths, in inches, of $\overline{QR}$ and $\overline{YZ}$? Round to the nearest tenth of an inch.

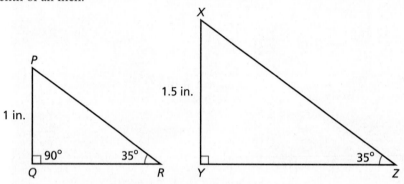

B. Complete the table below.

	Reference angle	Opposite side length (in.)	Adjacent side length (in.)	Ratio of $\frac{\text{opposite}}{\text{adjacent}}$
$\triangle PQR$	$m\angle R = 35°$	$PQ = 1.0$	$QR \approx ?$	$\frac{PQ}{QR} \approx ?$
$\triangle XYZ$	$m\angle Z = 35°$	$XY = 1.5$	$YZ \approx ?$	$\frac{XY}{YZ} \approx ?$

C. Compare the ratios of $\frac{\text{opposite}}{\text{adjacent}}$ of $\angle R$ and $\angle Z$. What do you notice?

D. Compare the triangles. What relationship exists between the triangles?

E. If you create a third right triangle with an angle of 35° and its opposite side is 3 in. long, how would your results be similar when comparing it to the triangles above? How would they be different?

F. Why do you think each ratio of the opposite side to the adjacent side between the two right triangles is the same?

 Turn and Talk Repeat the process for $\angle P$ and $\angle X$. What do you notice?

Understand Tangent Ratios

The ratio you calculated in Task 1 is called the tangent ratio. The **tangent** of an acute angle in a right triangle is the ratio of the length of the side opposite the angle to the length of the side adjacent to the angle. You can calculate the tangent, abbreviated tan, of any acute angle in a right triangle as shown.

Tangent Ratio

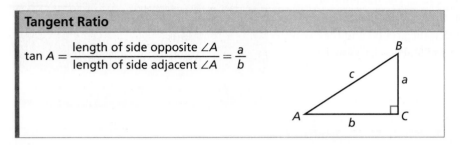

$$\tan A = \frac{\text{length of side opposite } \angle A}{\text{length of side adjacent } \angle A} = \frac{a}{b}$$

2 ▶ Use a geometric drawing tool to create the figures. Write each tangent ratio as a fraction and as a decimal rounded to the nearest hundredth. Then analyze your results.

A. Create the triangle shown. What is tan A?

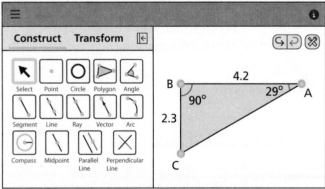

B. Drag point C down so BC is 3. Then measure ∠A. What is tan A?

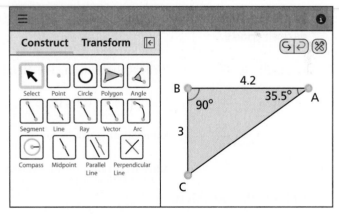

C. What happens to the tangent ratio as the measure of ∠A increases?

D. Because the triangles are right triangles, the other acute angle, ∠C, is complementary to ∠A. For each triangle, find the tangent of ∠C. What is the relationship between the tangent ratios of complementary angles?

 Turn and Talk A triangular support is being constructed for a new building. Will the tangent ratio most likely be used to find the opposite or adjacent side? Why do you think this is so?

Step It Out

Apply Tangent to Find a Length

3 Kathy is looking at the Washington Monument located in Washington, D.C. The monument is 555 feet tall. From where she is standing, the angle made between the ground and the top of the monument is 75°. How far away is she from the monument?

Draw a diagram of the situation.

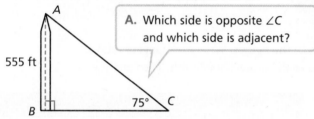

A. Which side is opposite ∠C and which side is adjacent?

Write the given information.

$\text{m}\angle C = 75°$

$AB = 555$ ft

$x = BC$

Write the tangent ratio.

$$\tan 75° = \frac{\text{length of side opposite } \angle C}{\text{length of side adjacent } \angle C} = \frac{555}{x}$$

B. What does the variable x represent?

Solve for the unknown distance. Be sure the calculator is in degree mode.

$\tan 75° = \dfrac{555}{x}$ Write the ratio using the identified values.

$x \cdot \tan 75° = \dfrac{555}{x} \cdot x$ Multiply both sides by x.

$x = \dfrac{555}{\tan 75°}$ Divide both sides by $\tan 75°$.

C. Why shouldn't we round the value of tangent?

≈ 149 Simplify. Round to the nearest foot.

Answer the question.

She is about 149 feet away from the monument.

 Turn and Talk How can you use what you know about the tangent of ∠C to find the tangent of ∠A? How can you verify this by using a calculator?

Apply Inverse Tangent to Find an Angle Measure

If you know the length of both legs of a right triangle, but an angle is unknown, you can use the **inverse tangent** to find the missing angle. The inverse tangent, written as $\tan^{-1}$ and read as "the inverse tangent of angle...", gives the acute angle that has a tangent equal to a given value.

Inverse Tangent

In a right triangle with acute angle A,

$\tan A = \dfrac{a}{b}$ and $\tan^{-1}\dfrac{a}{b} = \mathrm{m}\angle A$.

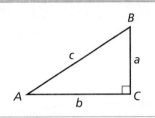

---

4 ▸ An angled wire supporting a wind turbine is anchored 10 ft away from the base of the turbine. For safety reasons, the wire must be attached 12 ft up the turbine. Find the measure of $\angle BAC$ between the turbine and the wire.

Draw and label a diagram.

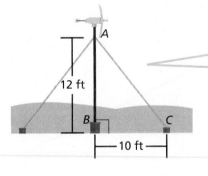

A. Explain the placement of each measurement in the diagram.

Write the given information.

Length of side opposite $\angle BAC$: 10 ft

Length of side adjacent to $\angle BAC$: 12 ft

B. Why is the opposite side the same as the horizontal side in this problem, while it was the vertical side in Task 3?

Write the tangent ratio.

$\tan BAC = \dfrac{10}{12} = \dfrac{5}{6}$

Solve using the inverse tangent.

$\mathrm{m}\angle BAC = \tan^{-1}\dfrac{5}{6}$ Write the inverse tangent equation.

$\approx 40°$ Use the inverse tangent function $\left(\tan^{-1}\right)$ to evaluate. Round to the nearest degree.

C. How was the inverse tangent equation written from the tangent ratio?

Answer the question.

The wire makes an angle of about $40°$ with the turbine.

 Turn and Talk Given that $\mathrm{m}\angle BAC \approx 40°$, find the measure of the base angle of the triangle without using trigonometry. Verify your answer using the inverse tangent.

Check Understanding

1. If two right triangles are similar, what is the relationship between the ratios of the length of the opposite side to the length of the adjacent side for any two corresponding acute angles?

2. Find the tangent of $\angle B$. What is the tangent of $\angle A$?

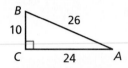

3. What is the length of $\overline{PR}$? Round to the nearest whole unit.

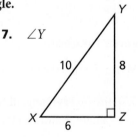

4. A ladder leaning against a wall reaches a vertical height of 14 ft. The base of the ladder is 3.5 ft from the wall. To the nearest degree, what is the angle that the ladder makes with the ground?

On Your Own

5. **(MP) Use Tools** Trace triangles *ABC* and *XYZ*. Using a centimeter ruler, measure the lengths of the sides opposite to and adjacent to both $\angle C$ and $\angle Z$.

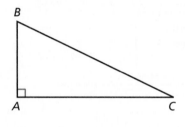

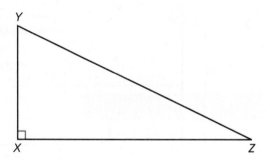

   A. Write the tangent ratio for $\angle C$ and $\angle Z$ as a fraction and as a decimal rounded to the nearest hundredth. Then compare the ratios.

   B. What can you conclude about m$\angle C$ and m$\angle Z$ without measuring?

   C. Use inverse tangent to verify your conclusions about m$\angle C$ and m$\angle Z$.

For each triangle, find the tangent of each given angle.

6. $\angle P$

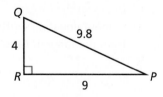

7. $\angle Y$

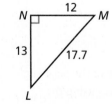

8. $\angle L$ and $\angle M$

9. $\angle B$ and $\angle C$

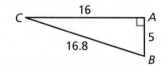

For each triangle, find the given side length. Round to the nearest tenth.

10. *AB*

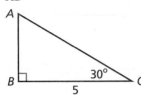

11. *PR*

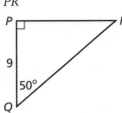

12. *MN*

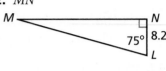

13. *ZY*

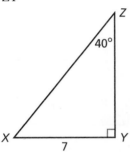

14. *AB*

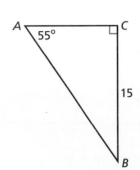

15. *YZ*

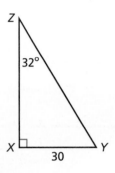

Use a calculator to find the measure of each given angle. Round the value to the nearest tenth of a degree.

16. m∠P

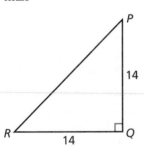

17. m∠Q

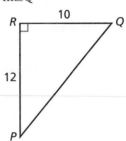

18. m∠Z

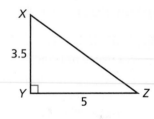

19. m∠L

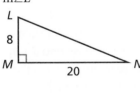

20. m∠B

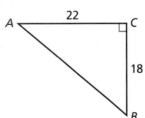

21. m∠T

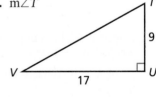

22. A kickball field is being set up by players in a nearby playground.

   A. What is the distance between home base where the kicker will kick the ball to the farthest base? Round to the nearest meter.

   B. After kicking the ball, a player ran from home plate to first base then to second base. The player was tagged out and walked straight back to home plate. What is the total distance the player traveled?

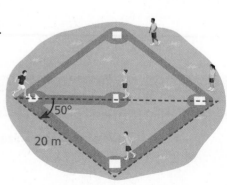

23. **(MP) Use Repeated Reasoning** Suppose △LMN and △OPQ are similar right triangles. For △LMN, the side opposite ∠M is 10 m, the side opposite ∠N is 24 m, and NM = 26 m.

   A. What is tan P and tan Q?

   B. What is a possible length of each side of △OPQ?

24. **(MP) Attend to Precision** The tangent ratios of the acute angles from three different right triangles are mixed together. Determine which angles belong to the same right triangle.

   tan∠3 = 1.25   tan∠4 = 0.6

   tan∠1 = 0.8   tan∠2 = 1.67

   tan∠5 = 0.25   tan∠6 = 4

25. Find the measure of ∠C. Round to the nearest tenth.

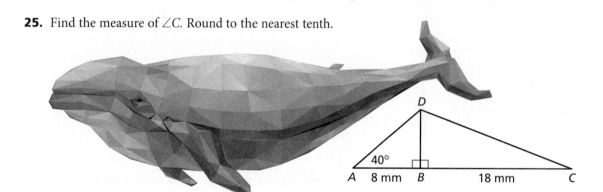

Spiral Review • Assessment Readiness

26. △ABC and △XYZ are similar, and △ABC is a scaled drawing of △XYZ. The length of $\overline{AB}$ is 7.2 cm, the length of $\overline{BC}$ is 6 cm, and the length of $\overline{XY}$ is 9.36 km. What is the length of $\overline{YZ}$?

   (A) 7.2 km   (C) 8.5 km

   (B) 7.8 km   (D) 12.2 km

27. Segment $\overline{AB}$ has endpoints $A(1, 3)$ and $B(5, 8)$. Point P divides $\overline{AB}$ into a 4 to 1 ratio from A to B. What are the coordinates of P?

   (A) $P(4, 6)$ (C) $P(4.2, 7)$

   (B) $P(2, 4)$ (D) $P(1.8, 4)$

28. In right triangle △XYZ, the side opposite ∠X is 6 m long, the side adjacent to ∠X is 8 m long, and the hypotenuse is 10 m long. What is the ratio of the length of the side opposite ∠X to the length of the hypotenuse?

   (A) 0.6   (C) 0.8

   (B) 0.75   (D) 1.33

29. The altitude to the hypotenuse of a right triangle divides the hypotenuse into a 3 in. segment and a 4 in. segment. What is the approximate length of the altitude?

   (A) 3.46 in.   (C) 5.5 in.

   (B) 5.28 in.   (D) 7 in.

 I'm in a Learning Mindset!

Does my lack of organization affect my learning outcomes? In what ways?

Sine and Cosine Ratios

(I Can) use sine and cosine ratios and their inverses to find side lengths and angle measures in right triangles.

Spark Your Learning

Steel cables are sometimes used to anchor a mast to a sailboat's deck.

Complete Part A as a whole class. Then complete Parts B–D in small groups.

A. What is a mathematical question you can ask about the cable?

B. What information do you need that can help you answer the question?

C. To answer your question, what strategy and tool would you use along with all the information you have? What answer do you get?

D. Does your answer make sense in the context of the situation? How do you know?

Turn and Talk Predict how your answer would change for each of the following changes in the situation:

• The cable is connected to the mast at a higher point but anchors to the deck at the same spot.
• The cable is connected to the mast at a lower point but anchors to the deck at the same spot.

©Plam Petrov/Shutterstock

Build Understanding

Investigate Ratios in a Right Triangle

Previously, you investigated the ratio between the sides opposite from and adjacent to a given acute angle in a right triangle. There are special ratios between the hypotenuse and the side adjacent to the referenced angle and between the hypotenuse and the side opposite from the referenced angle. The sides in the figure are labeled in relation to $\angle A$.

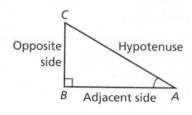

1 ▶ Use a geometric drawing tool to construct the figure by following these steps.

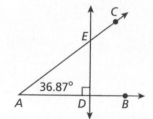

Step 1: Draw horizontal ray $\overrightarrow{AB}$.

Step 2: Draw $\overrightarrow{AC}$ so that $\angle A$ is acute.

Step 3: Draw line $\overleftrightarrow{ED}$ so that it is perpendicular to $\overrightarrow{AB}$.

A. Measure each side of $\triangle AED$. What are the lengths of both legs and the hypotenuse?

B. Calculate the ratio of each leg to the hypotenuse given by $\frac{ED}{AE}$ and $\frac{AD}{AE}$. Round to the nearest tenth.

C. If you slide $\overleftrightarrow{ED}$ horizontally along $\overrightarrow{AB}$, what values within $\triangle AED$ change and what values stay constant? How can you prove the different triangles that are created are similar to each other?

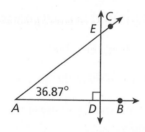

D. As you slide $\overleftrightarrow{ED}$ horizontally along $\overrightarrow{AB}$, what happens to the values of $\frac{ED}{AE}$ and $\frac{AD}{AE}$?

E. Explain your results from Part D using what you know about similar triangles. Do you think the same results would apply to any similar triangle? Why or why not?

 Turn and Talk For $\triangle AED$, predict how your answers would change if m$\angle A$ is increased.

Find the Sine and Cosine of an Angle

The ratios you calculated in Task 1 are called the sine and cosine ratios. The sine ratio is abbreviated as sin and read as "the sine of angle …". The cosine ratio is abbreviated as cos and read as "the cosine of angle …".

Trigonometric Ratios

A **trigonometric ratio** is a ratio of two sides of a right triangle. You have already studied the tangent ratio. The two additional trigonometric ratios, sine and cosine, involve the hypotenuse of a right triangle.

sine	$\sin A = \dfrac{\text{length of leg opposite } \angle A}{\text{length of hypotenuse}} = \dfrac{BC}{AB}$	$\sin A = \dfrac{a}{c}$	
cosine	$\cos A = \dfrac{\text{length of leg adjacent } \angle A}{\text{length of hypotenuse}} = \dfrac{AC}{AB}$	$\cos A = \dfrac{b}{c}$	

2 ▶ The figure represents a post $(\overline{IE})$ braced by four diagonal parallel supports.

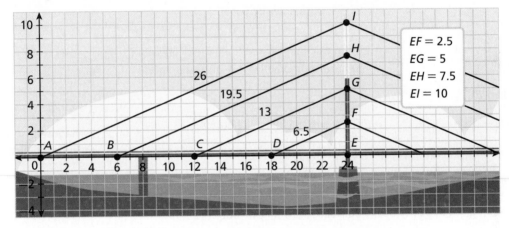

EF = 2.5
EG = 5
EH = 7.5
EI = 10

A. In $\triangle DEF$ and $\triangle CEG$, calculate the sine and cosine for $\angle D$, $\angle F$, $\angle C$, and $\angle G$. If necessary, round to the nearest thousandth.

B. What do you notice about the sines and cosines you found?

C. What relationship exists between the sine and cosine ratios of a pair of complementary angles in a right triangle—say $\angle D$ and $\angle F$ or $\angle C$ and $\angle G$? Is this relationship true for any pair of acute angles in a right triangle? Explain.

D. Verify your results from Parts A–C using different pairs of triangles such as $\triangle AEI$ and $\triangle BEH$.

 Turn and Talk In a right triangle, when one acute angle increases while the adjacent leg does not change, predict how the values change for each of the following:

- The length of the opposite leg as well as the measure of the complementary angle
- The sine and cosine of the angle as well as the sine and cosine of the complementary angle

Step It Out

Find Side Lengths and Perimeter Using Sine and Cosine

You can use the sine and cosine ratios to find unknown values in a right triangle.

3 ▶ Find the perimeter of $\triangle ABC$.

Start by finding the unknown side lengths in the triangle.

Given: m$\angle A$ and its adjacent side length.

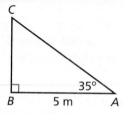

Find AC.

$$\cos A = \frac{AB}{AC}$$ Use the cosine ratio. **A.** Why do you use the cosine ratio?

$$\cos 35° = \frac{5}{AC}$$ Write the ratio using the given values.

$$AC \cdot \cos 35° = \frac{5}{AC} \cdot AC$$ Multiply both sides by AC.

$$AC = \frac{5}{\cos 35°}$$ Divide both sides by $\cos 35°$.

$$AC \approx 6.1$$ Use a calculator to evaluate the expression. Be sure your calculator is in degree mode.

Find BC.

$$AB^2 + BC^2 = AC^2$$ Use the Pythagorean Theorem. **B.** Why can we use the Pythagorean Theorem to find the missing leg?

$$5^2 + BC^2 = 6.1^2$$ Substitute.

$$25 + BC^2 = 37.21$$ Simplify.

$$BC^2 = 12.21$$ Subtract 25 from both sides.

$$BC \approx 3.5$$ Take the square root. Round to the nearest tenth.

Calculate the perimeter of $\triangle ABC$.

Perimeter of $\triangle ABC = AB + BC + AC$ Write the perimeter equation.

$$= 5 + 3.5 + 6.1$$ Substitute the known information.

$$= 14.6$$ Simplify.

Answer the question.

The perimeter of $\triangle ABC$ is approximately 14.6 m. **C.** Why is this an approximate value?

 Turn and Talk Can you solve for every side and angle in a right triangle when given any one angle and any one side length? Why or why not?

Find an Angle Measure Using Inverse Sine and Inverse Cosine

You can use the **inverse sine** and the **inverse cosine** to find an unknown angle when given the side lengths of a right triangle. Use a calculator to evaluate the inverse sine, written as $\sin^{-1}$, and inverse cosine, written as $\cos^{-1}$.

inverse sine	$\sin A = \dfrac{BC}{AB} = \dfrac{a}{c}$	$\sin^{-1}\left(\dfrac{a}{c}\right) = m\angle A$	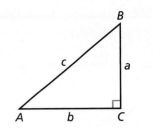
inverse cosine	$\cos A = \dfrac{AC}{AB} = \dfrac{b}{c}$	$\cos^{-1}\left(\dfrac{b}{c}\right) = m\angle A$	

4 ▶ A hot air balloon is tethered with cables that run from both sides of the basket to the ground. The tethers allow riders to experience a hot air balloon ride only up to a predetermined height. When the balloon is at the maximum height, what is $m\angle B$? Round to the nearest tenth of a degree.

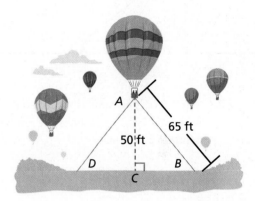

Write a trigonometric ratio for ∠B.

We are given the opposite side length and the hypotenuse. Use the sine ratio.

$\sin B = \dfrac{50}{65}$

> **A.** Why do you use the sine ratio in this situation?

Write the inverse sine ratio.

$\sin B = \dfrac{50}{65}$

$\sin^{-1}\left(\dfrac{50}{65}\right) = m\angle B$

> **B.** What does the "−1" represent?

Use a calculator to solve.

$m\angle B = \sin^{-1}\left(\dfrac{50}{65}\right)$

$= 50.3°$

Answer the question.

The tether makes a 50.3° angle with the ground.

> **C.** Does the answer make sense in this context?

 Turn and Talk Find one or both of the acute angles of a right triangle in a real-world problem given the length of the hypotenuse and one leg length.

Check Understanding

1. If two right triangles are similar, what is the relationship between the ratios of the lengths of the opposite side to the length of the hypotenuse for any two corresponding acute angles?

2. In $\triangle XYZ$, $\angle Y$ is a right angle. What is the relationship between $\angle X$ and $\angle Z$? What is the relationship between $\sin X$ and $\cos Z$?

3. Find the sine and cosine of $\angle A$.

4. What is the length of $\overline{QR}$? Round to the nearest hundredth.

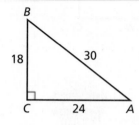

5. An 8-foot long ramp is placed so the end of the ramp is 5 feet from the base of a building. What angle does the ramp make with the ground? Round to the nearest tenth of a degree.

On Your Own

Determine whether each pair of right triangles is similar. Justify your reasoning.

6. $\dfrac{AC}{AB} = \dfrac{2}{3}$, $\dfrac{QR}{PR} = \dfrac{1.5}{2.5}$

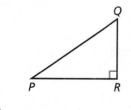

7. $\dfrac{AB}{AC} = \dfrac{5}{12}$, $\dfrac{QR}{PR} = \dfrac{6}{14.4}$

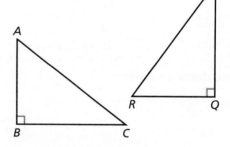

For Problems 8–13, the graph shows image $\triangle LMN$ which is a rotation and dilation of $\triangle GHI$. Write each pair of trigonometric ratios as a fraction and as a decimal.

8. $\sin G$, $\cos G$

9. $\sin I$, $\cos I$

10. $\sin L$, $\cos L$

11. $\sin N$, $\cos N$

12. In the figure, how can you prove that the triangles are similar?

13. What is the trigonometric relationship between the complementary angles within each triangle?

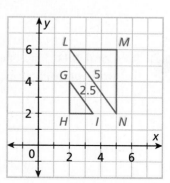

Find each side length. Round to the nearest tenth.

14. *LM*

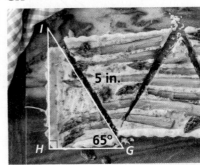

3 in.

40°

15. *RS*

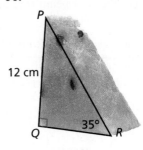

45°

4 in.

16. *GH*

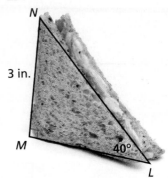

5 in.

65°

17. *PR*

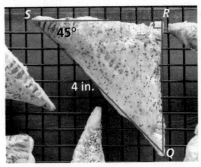

12 cm

35°

For each triangle, use a calculator to find the measure of the given angle. Round to the nearest tenth of a degree.

18. ∠K

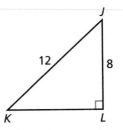

12

8

19. ∠B

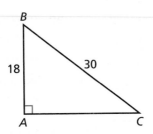

18

30

20. ∠P

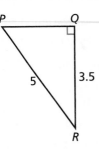

5

3.5

21. ∠X

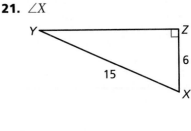

15

6

22. ∠M

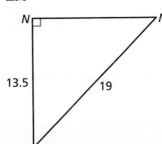

13.5

19

23. ∠V

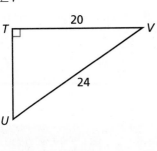

20

24

24. **(MP) Reason** Emerson wants to draw a right triangle with acute angles ∠1 and ∠2, where the sine of ∠1 is equal to the cosine of ∠2. How does this constrain the possible measures of the angles in the triangle?

25. (MP) **Attend to Precision** A farmer is building a set of new corrals. Corrals 1 and 2 share a side that is perpendicular to the barn. The barn serves as one side of each corral.

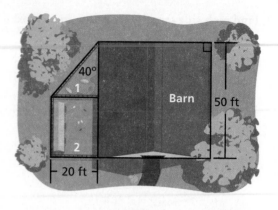

  A. To the nearest foot, about how many feet of fence material does the farmer need to build both corrals?

  B. What is the approximate total area of both corrals?

26. **STEM** In Tel Aviv, Israel, it took about a year to build a tower using construction toys. Andrea uses a laser measuring device to find the distance to the top of the tower at an angle of about 35°. If she moves forward so the angle is 45°, the length of the laser beam is reduced by 30 ft.

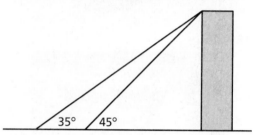

  A. What is the length of each laser beam? Round to the nearest foot.

  B. To the nearest foot, what is the height of the tower?

27. (Open Middle™) Using the digits 1 to 9, at most one time each, fill in the boxes to create two true statements.

$$\cos \frac{\boxed{}\, \pi}{\boxed{}} = \frac{\sqrt{\boxed{}}}{\boxed{}}$$

Spiral Review • Assessment Readiness

28. Which expression(s) represent the length of $\overline{AD}$? Select all that apply.

  Ⓐ $AB - DB$

  Ⓑ $\dfrac{AE \cdot AB}{AC}$

  Ⓒ $AE \cdot DB$

  Ⓓ $\dfrac{AE \cdot DB}{EC}$

29. What is the geometric mean of 5 and 45?

  Ⓐ 15   Ⓒ 40

  Ⓑ 25   Ⓓ 50

30. If the tangent of $\angle A$ is $\frac{10}{24}$, and the side adjacent to $\angle A$ is 36 cm, what is the length of the side opposite $\angle A$?

  Ⓐ 5 cm   Ⓒ 15 cm

  Ⓑ 12 cm   Ⓓ 18 cm

31. A skateboard ramp reaches a height of 2 feet and has a horizontal length of 4 feet. What is the angle the ramp makes with the ground?

  Ⓐ 63.4°   Ⓒ 30°

  Ⓑ 26.6°   Ⓓ 60°

 I'm in a Learning Mindset!

How am I prioritizing my learning? What do I do each day to prepare to learn tomorrow?

Special Right Triangles

(I Can) use trigonometric ratios and the Pythagorean Theorem to find the side lengths and angle measures of special right triangles.

Spark Your Learning

Triangles can be used to develop unique features in architectural design.

The window is an isosceles right triangle.

Complete Part A as a whole class. Then complete Parts B–D in small groups.

A. What is a mathematical question you can ask about this situation?

B. What previous knowledge do you have that could help you answer the question?

C. To answer your question, what strategy and tool would you use along with all the information you have? What answer do you get?

D. Does your answer make sense in the context of the situation? What trigonometric methods can you use to check your answer?

Turn and Talk Suppose the window doubled in height but the angles of the triangle are to be kept the same. How would the ratio of the new base to the new height compare to the ratio of the original base to the original height?

Build Understanding

Investigate 45°-45°-90° Triangles

1 ▸ Discover relationships that always apply to an isosceles right triangle.

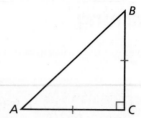

A. Construct an isosceles right triangle *ABC* as shown. Before you begin, what are the measurements of ∠*A* and ∠*B*? How do you know without measuring? Explain.

B. Label one leg length as *x*. What is the length of the other leg?

C. How can you determine the length of the hypotenuse in terms of *x*? What is the length? Show your work.

D. What is the relationship between the side length and the hypotenuse length in an isosceles right triangle? Is this relationship the same in a 45°-45°-90° triangle?

E. Given any one side of an isosceles right triangle, can you solve for the other two sides? Why or why not?

Investigate 30°-60°-90° Triangles

2 ▸ Discover relationships that always apply in a right triangle formed as half of an equilateral triangle.

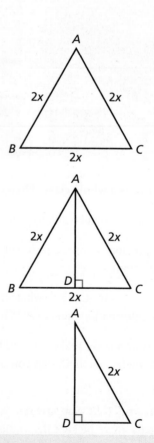

A. Construct an equilateral triangle *ABC* with side lengths of 2*x* as shown at the right. What are the measures of angles *A*, *B*, and *C*?

B. Draw an altitude $\overline{AD}$ from point *A* to $\overline{BC}$ and label the point of intersection *D*. How does this divide the triangle? Explain.

C. Examine one of the triangles created by the altitude as shown at the right. What are the three interior angles?

D. What is the length of base $\overline{DC}$? How can you find the length of $\overline{AD}$? Show your work.

E. From Part C, what is a three-term ratio (*f* : *g* : *h*, for example) for triangles given by the angle measures you found? Explain.

 Turn and Talk If the side length of an equilateral triangle is 4, what is the length of each leg and the hypotenuse of one of the 30°-60°-90° triangles created by an altitude to the base?

Step It Out

Find Trigonometric Ratios of Special Right Triangles

The 45°-45°-90° and 30°-60°-90° triangles are known as **special right triangles**.

45°-45°-90° Triangle Theorem

In a right isosceles triangle, the ratio of the angles is $45°:45°:90°$, and the ratio of the side lengths is $x:x:x\sqrt{2}$, where $x\sqrt{2}$ is always the hypotenuse.

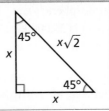

30°-60°-90° Triangle Theorem

In a right triangle where the ratio of the angles is $30°:60°:90°$, the ratio of the side lengths is $x:x\sqrt{3}:2x$, where $2x$ is always the hypotenuse.

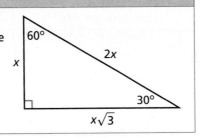

---

3 ▶ Consider the triangles above. Find the trigonometric ratios for 30°, 45°, and 60° when $x = 1$.

Sketch a 45°-45°-90° triangle with a leg length of 1. Then find the trigonometric ratios for either of the 45° angles.

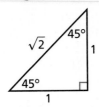

$$\sin 45° = \frac{\text{opp}}{\text{hyp}} = \frac{1}{\sqrt{2}} = \frac{\sqrt{2}}{2}$$

$$\cos 45° = \frac{\text{adj}}{\text{hyp}} = \frac{1}{\sqrt{2}} = \frac{\sqrt{2}}{2}$$

$$\tan 45° = \frac{\text{opp}}{\text{adj}} = \frac{1}{1} = 1$$

A. What is the extra step you need to take to find the sine and cosine ratios?

B. How could you use the sine and cosine of the 30° angle to find the sine and cosine of the 60° angle?

Sketch a 30°-60°-90° triangle in which the shortest leg is 1. Then find the trigonometric ratios for the 30° and 60° angles.

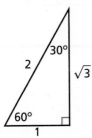

$$\sin 30° = \frac{\text{opp}}{\text{hyp}} = \frac{1}{2}$$

$$\cos 30° = \frac{\text{adj}}{\text{hyp}} = \frac{\sqrt{3}}{2}$$

$$\tan 30° = \frac{\text{opp}}{\text{adj}} = \frac{1}{\sqrt{3}} = \frac{\sqrt{3}}{3}$$

$$\sin 60° = \frac{\text{opp}}{\text{hyp}} = \frac{\sqrt{3}}{2}$$

$$\cos 60° = \frac{\text{adj}}{\text{hyp}} = \frac{1}{2}$$

$$\tan 60° = \frac{\text{opp}}{\text{adj}} = \frac{\sqrt{3}}{1} = \sqrt{3}$$

 Turn and Talk In both triangles, what would change if the side length x were not 1?

Model Real-World Measurements

From Task 3, you can use trigonometric relationships of special right triangles to find unknown side lengths.

4 Saturn's hexagon is a persisting cloud pattern around the north pole of Saturn. The cloud pattern is roughly a regular hexagon with a vortex at the center of the hexagon with rotating atmospheric gases. The shortest distance across the hexagon is 25,000 km. What is the length of one of the sides of the hexagon?

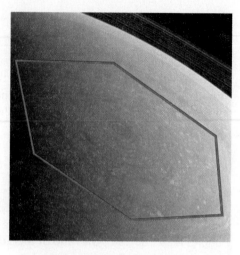

Sketch a regular hexagon. Then divide the hexagon into six equilateral triangles.

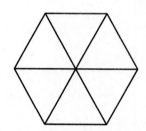

A. Why can you divide the hexagon into six equilateral triangles?

Use a 30°-60°-90° triangle to find the length of half of one of the sides of the hexagon.

B. Why can you use a 30°-60°-90° triangle to find half the length of one side of the hexagon?

The ratio of the shorter leg to the longer leg of the triangle is $x : x\sqrt{3}$.

Write and solve an equation.

Since the length of the longer leg is 12,500 kilometers, set 12,500 equal to $x\sqrt{3}$. Then solve for x. Round the measure to three significant digits since there are three significant digits in 12,500.

$$12{,}500 = x\sqrt{3}$$

$$\frac{12{,}500}{\sqrt{3}} = x$$

$$7220 \approx x$$

C. Why does the triangle show that the longer leg measures 12,500 kilometers?

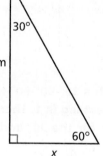

Answer the question.

The length of one of the sides of the hexagon is twice the length of the side of the triangle, so $2x \approx 2(7220) = 14{,}400$.

The length of one side of Saturn's hexagon is approximately 14,400 kilometers.

 Turn and Talk Without solving, describe how you could find the area of the top view of the cloud cover using trigonometry.

©JPL–Caltech/SSI/NASA Jet Propulsion Laboratory

Check Understanding

1. What is the relationship between side lengths in a 45°-45°-90° triangle? What does the ratio mean?

2. What is the relationship between side lengths in a 30°-60°-90° triangle? What does the ratio mean?

For Problems 3–5, use the diagram at the right.

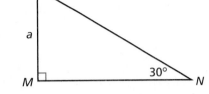

3. What is LN in terms of a?

4. How is sin N related to cos L? Explain.

5. What is MN in terms of a?

6. What is the length of $\overline{AC}$ in the rhombus shown?

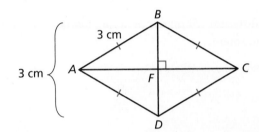

On Your Own

Determine whether each ratio of side lengths belongs to a 45°-45°-90° triangle, a 30°-60°-90° triangle, or neither.

7. $2:2\sqrt{3}:4$

8. $5:5:5\sqrt{2}$

9. $\sqrt{2}:\sqrt{6}:2\sqrt{2}$

10. $\sqrt{3}:3:2\sqrt{3}$

11. $2:3:2\sqrt{2}$

12. $4\sqrt{2}:4\sqrt{2}:8$

Determine whether each triangle is possible. Show your work.

13.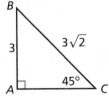

14.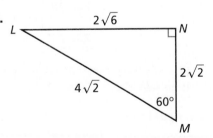

15.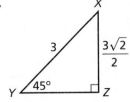

16.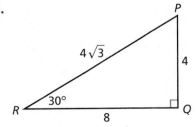

Find the unknown side lengths in each triangle. Give an exact answer.

17.

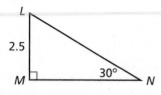

18.

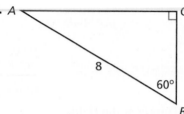

19.

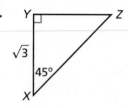

20.

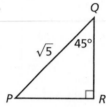

The illustration shows a site where three different triangular areas are being studied by archeologists. Find each measurement.

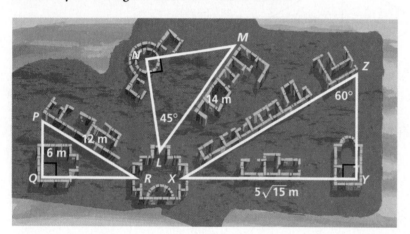

21. QR

22. $m\angle P$

23. MN

24. NL

25. YZ

26. XZ

27. Open Ended An acute angle has a sine ratio of $\frac{1}{2}$. Draw a right triangle that meets this criterion given that no side length is either 1 or 2.

Find the value of x in each right triangle.

28.

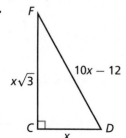

29.

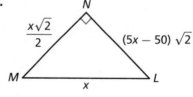

30. Is it true that if you know one side length of an isosceles right triangle, then you know all the side lengths? Explain.

For Problems 31–35, use the figure below to find the indicated values.

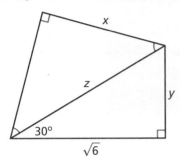

31. y **32.** z **33.** x

34. the perimeter of the composite figure (excludes z)

35. the area of the composite figure

36. (MP) **Construct Arguments** Using your knowledge of right isosceles triangles, prove the length of a diagonal of a square is always the side length multiplied by $\sqrt{2}$.

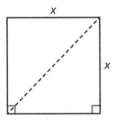

Find the range of acute angle measures x that satisfy each expression.

37. $\dfrac{\sqrt{2}}{2} < \cos x < 0$ **38.** $\dfrac{\sqrt{2}}{2} < \sin x < 1$ **39.** $\dfrac{\sqrt{3}}{2} < \sin x < 1$

40. $0 < \tan x < 1$ **41.** $\dfrac{\sqrt{3}}{2} < \cos x < \dfrac{1}{2}$ **42.** $1 < \tan x < \sqrt{3}$

43. (MP) **Critique Reasoning** Aiden is asked to sketch a right triangle with a 60° acute angle and a hypotenuse length of $24\sqrt{2}$. Identify, explain, and correct his error.

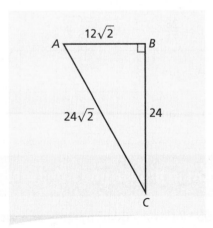

44. A rhombus on the Thai door is shown below. The length of $\overline{BD}$ is 4 inches.

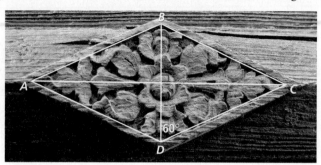

   A. Find the perimeter of the rhombus.

   B. Find the length of $\overline{AC}$.

45. Triangle XYZ is a 30°-60°-90° triangle with a right angle at point X. The longer leg $\overline{XY}$ has vertices $X(2, 2)$ and $Y(7, 2)$. Where is point Z in Quadrant I?

Spiral Review • Assessment Readiness

46. For the 20-foot wheelchair ramp shown, what is the approximate height h of the ramp? The diagram is not drawn to scale.

   (A) $h = 1.7$ ft

   (B) $h = 1.2$ ft

   (C) $h = 3.2$ ft

   (D) $h = 3.4$ ft

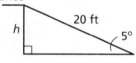

Entrance

20 ft

h

5°

47. For right triangle ABC, $\sin A = \frac{12}{13}$. Hypotenuse $\overline{AC}$ is 26 in. long. What is the area of $\triangle ABC$?

   (A) 30 in²

   (B) 60 in²

   (C) 90 in²

   (D) 120 in²

48. In right triangle ABC, m$\angle B = 90°$ and $\tan A = \frac{21}{28}$. Determine whether each statement is true or false.

Statement	True	False
A. $\tan C = \frac{28}{21}$	?	?
B. $\tan C = \frac{28}{35}$	?	?
C. m$\angle A = \tan^{-1}\frac{28}{21}$	?	?
D. m$\angle C = \tan^{-1}\frac{28}{21}$	?	?

I'm in a Learning Mindset!

Do I know my own strengths and weaknesses in learning? What is one example of each?

Keep Going to ▶ Journal and Practice Workbook

Solve Problems Using Trigonometry

(I Can) use trigonometric ratios, the area formula for a triangle in terms of its side lengths, and the Pythagorean Theorem to solve right triangles in applied problems.

Spark Your Learning

An artist created a sculpture made with several triangles.

The highlighted triangle is an obtuse scalene triangle.

Complete Part A as a whole class. Then complete Parts B–C in small groups.

A. What is a mathematical question you can ask about the highlighted triangle?

B. What information do you usually have that can help you answer the question?

C. To answer your question, what strategy and tool would you use along with all the information you have? What answer do you get?

 Turn and Talk
- How would your solution change if the angle provided is not the included angle?
- Can you determine how it could be possible to use a trigonometric ratio if the given triangle is not a right triangle?

Build Understanding

Derive an Area Formula

You can find the area of a triangle without knowing its height using trigonometric ratios.

The diagram shows a triangular pool. Use trigonometry and the lengths shown to find a formula for the area of the triangle.

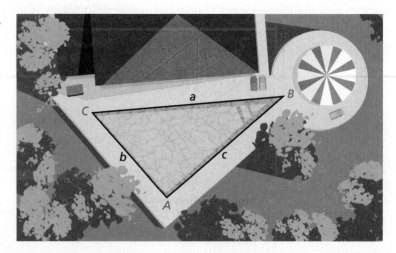

1 A. Redraw the triangle. Then draw an altitude h from vertex A to $\overline{BC}$. Make a conjecture as to why this altitude will help develop the formula.

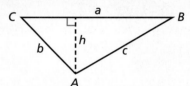

B. Write the equation for the sine of angle C. Then solve the equation for h.

C. Recall the general formula for the area of a triangle.

$$\text{area} = \frac{1}{2} \cdot \text{base} \cdot \text{height}$$

Which side of the triangle in the figure represents the base?

D. Write the formula in terms of the variables from the triangle in the figure.

E. Substitute the expression for h from Part B into the area formula.

F. What is the relationship between sides a and b and angle C? Would the formula still apply if you know sides a and c and angle B? Why or why not?

G. In the winter, a tarp is used to cover the pool. Find the area of the tarp if $a = 25$ feet, $b = 15$ feet, and $m\angle C = 47°$. Round your answer to the nearest hundredth.

Turn and Talk

- Does the area formula you found work if $\angle C$ is a right angle? Explain.
- Suppose you used a trigonometric ratio in terms of $\angle B$, h, and a different side length to find the area. How would this change your findings? What does this tell you about the choice of sides and included angle?

Step It Out

Solve a Right Triangle

To **solve a right triangle** means to find the length of each side of the triangle and the measure of each interior angle. You can use any of the methods you have learned to solve a right triangle, including trigonometric ratios, inverse trigonometric ratios, and the Pythagorean Theorem.

2 An eagle on top of a 65-foot cliff spots a fish in the water and dives toward it. The angle between the cliff and the eagle's path is 36°. Solve the right triangle that represents this situation. Round each value to the nearest tenth.

Determine the given information.

You are given an acute angle and an adjacent side length in a right triangle. Choose a trigonometric ratio that uses the given information.

A. What two trigonometric ratios use the side adjacent to the given angle?

Find _AB_.

$$\cos 36° = \frac{65}{AB}$$

$$AB \cos 36° = \frac{65}{AB} \cdot AB$$

$$AB = \frac{65}{\cos 36°}$$

$$AB \approx 80.3 \text{ ft}$$

B. Where did each value in this ratio come from?

Find _BC_.

$$\tan 36° = \frac{BC}{65}$$

$$65 \tan 36° = BC$$

$$BC \approx 47.2 \text{ ft}$$

C. Why do we start with our given information again and not use the value of _AB_?

Find the measure of _B_.

$$m\angle B = 90° - 36°$$

$$m\angle B = 54°$$

D. What allows us to use this equation to find the measure of angle _B_?

Answer the question.

Besides the given information, $AB \approx 80.3$ ft, $BC \approx 47.2$ ft, and $m\angle B = 54°$.

 Turn and Talk What is the minimum information you could use to solve the right triangle if you had not been given one of the acute angle measures?

Find an Angle of Elevation (or Depression)

You can use trigonometry to find angles of elevation and depression.

Angle of Elevation	
The **angle of elevation** is the angle formed by a horizontal line and a line of sight to a point above.	
Angle of Depression	
The **angle of depression** is the angle formed by a horizontal line and a line of sight to a point below.	

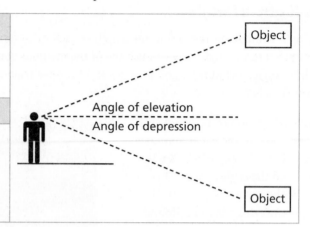

3   A boat on the surface of the water detects a whale 42 feet away at an angle of depression of 20°. What is the horizontal distance between the boat and the whale? What is the depth of the whale?

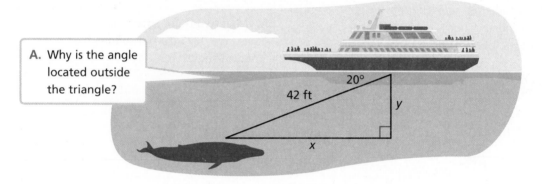

A. Why is the angle located outside the triangle?

The angle between the vertical and the line of sight is $90° - 20° = 70°$.

Use a trigonometric ratio of the 70° angle to find the horizontal distance.

$\sin 70° = \dfrac{x}{42}$

B. Why would you use the sine ratio?

$x = 42 \cdot \sin 70°$

$x \approx 39.5$ feet

The horizontal distance is 39.5 feet.

Use a different trigonometric ratio to find depth.

$\cos 70° = \dfrac{y}{42}$

C. Why can you use the cosine ratio? Can you also use the tangent ratio? Explain.

$y = 42 \cdot \cos 70°$

$y \approx 14.4$ feet

D. Is it possible to use another method to find y after x is determined? Explain.

The depth of the whale is 14.4 feet.

Turn and Talk From Task 3, what angle in the triangle can be considered an angle of elevation?

Solve a Right Triangle in the Coordinate Plane

When a right triangle is in the coordinate plane, you can use the distance formula in addition to trigonometric ratios to solve the triangle.

4 Triangle XYZ has vertices $X(-4, -3)$, $Y(5, -3)$, and $Z(-4, 2)$. Find the side lengths to the nearest tenth and the measure of each angle to the nearest degree.

Plot the coordinates on a graph.

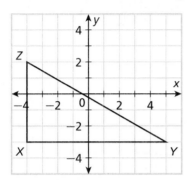

Find the side lengths.

$XY = 9$, $XZ = 5$

> **A.** Why is there no calculation needed to find these side lengths?

Use the distance formula to find the length of $\overline{YZ}$.

$$YZ = \sqrt{(-4-5)^2 + (2-(-3))^2}$$

$$YZ = \sqrt{(-9)^2 + (5)^2}$$

$$YZ = \sqrt{81+25} = \sqrt{106} \approx 10.3$$

Find the angle measures.

$m\angle X = 90°$

> **B.** How do you know this from the graph?

Use inverse tangent to find $m\angle Y$.

$$\tan Y = \frac{5}{9}$$

$$\tan^{-1}\left(\frac{5}{9}\right) = m\angle Y$$

$$m\angle Y \approx 29.1°$$

> **C.** Why do you use the inverse tangent to find $m\angle Y$ rather than the other inverse trigonometric functions?

$\angle Z$ and $\angle Y$ are complementary, so $m\angle Z \approx 90° - 29.1° = 60.9°$.

D. Is there only one correct method to solve this triangle? If not, outline a different series of steps you could use to solve this triangle.

 Turn and Talk What would change in the solution method if a right triangle has no horizontal or vertical sides?

Check Understanding

1. In an acute scalene triangle, you are given two adjacent side lengths and the included angle measure. How can you find the area of the triangle?

2. In $\triangle XYZ$, $\angle Y$ is a right angle, m$\angle X = 22°$, and YZ is 5 cm. Solve the triangle. Round to the nearest hundredth.

3. A tower casts a 24-meter long shadow. The sun is situated where an angle of depression is $67°$ from an imaginary horizontal line through the top of the tower. How tall is the tower?

4. Solve the triangle. Round to the nearest hundredth.

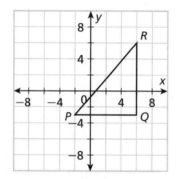

On Your Own

Find the area of each triangle. Round to the nearest tenth.

5. $\triangle PQR$, where $PR = 2.5$ in., $QR = 4$ in., and m$\angle R = 55°$

6. $\triangle XYZ$, where $XY = 7$ cm, $XZ = 4.2$ cm, and m$\angle X = 68°$

7.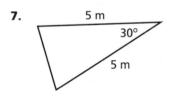

8.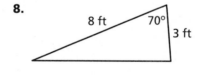

Solve each triangle. Round side lengths to the nearest tenth and angles to the nearest degree.

9. $\triangle ABC$, where $\overline{AB} \perp \overline{BC}$, $AC = 5.8$ in., and m$\angle C = 35°$

10. $\triangle LMN$, where m$\angle M = 90°$, m$\angle L = 24°$, and $LM = 11$ cm

11. A 12-foot ladder leans against a tree with an angle of elevation of $75°$. Round values to the nearest tenth.

    A. How far up the tree does the ladder go?

    B. What is the distance between the tree and the base of the ladder?

12. The main sail of the sailboat shown at the right has the shape of a right triangle. The boom is 20 feet in length. What is the measure of the angle of elevation of the sail when it is pulled 45 feet up the mast?

13. For Parts A–D, solve each triangle. Round side lengths to the nearest tenth and angles to the nearest degree.

    A. $\triangle JKL$: vertices $J(-3, -2)$, $K(6, -2)$, and $L(-3, 7)$

    B. $\triangle PQR$: vertices $P(-5, 9)$, $Q(5, 4)$, and $R(-1, 1)$

    C.
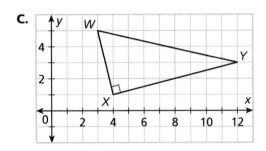

    D.
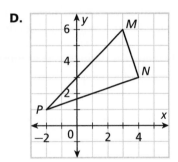

14. Open Ended Create a real-world problem involving angle of elevation or depression. Draw and label a diagram, then solve the problem.

15. History The dimensions of the Great Pyramid of Giza have changed with time. The original height was 146.5 m, and the base distance to the vertical was 115 m. The Egyptians believed that the pyramid would be most pleasing to the eye if the angle of elevation between one of the congruent sides and the ground were $\frac{1}{7}$ of the number of degrees of a full circle. Was the pyramid constructed correctly? Explain.

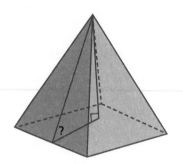

16. (MP) Critique Reasoning Paige and Bryan try to solve the following problem. Which student solved the problem incorrectly? Explain.

"A squirrel in a tree looks down toward a dog at a 52° angle of depression from the horizontal. The dog is 6 ft from the base of the tree. How high up the tree is the squirrel?"

Bryan's Work

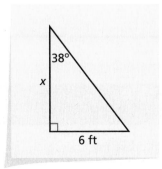

$$\tan 38° = \frac{6}{x}$$

$$x \tan 38° = 6$$

$$x = \frac{6}{\tan 38°}$$

$$x \approx 7.7 \text{ ft}$$

Paige's Work

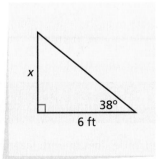

$$\tan 38° = \frac{x}{6}$$

$$x = 6 \tan 38°$$

$$x \approx 4.7 \text{ ft}$$

17. From the top of a lighthouse, a watchman sites a ship at an angle of depression of 10°. In the same direction, the watchman sees a second ship and measures the angle of depression to the ship as 14.2°. What is the distance between the two ships?

The top of the lighthouse is 180 feet above sea level.

18. (MP) **Attend to Precision** A tourist 20 miles from the base of a mountain looks up at the peak of the mountain at an angle of elevation of 15°. When the tourist is 10 miles away from the base of the mountain, what is the angle of elevation from his point of view to the peak of the mountain?

19. A man whose eye level is 6 feet off the ground looks up at an angle of elevation of 55° at his friend climbing a rock wall. The man is standing 8 feet from the base of the wall. How high up the rock wall is his friend?

20. (Open Middle™) Using the digits 1 to 9, at most two times each, fill in the boxes to create two similar right triangles.

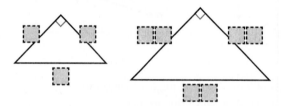

Spiral Review • Assessment Readiness

21. For what values is the statement true?
$$\sin(x + 20)° = \cos(y - 10)°$$
  Ⓐ $x = 70, y = 20$ Ⓒ $x = 45, y = 45$
  Ⓑ $x = 30, y = 60$ Ⓓ $x = 20, y = 60$

22. For which set of side lengths could the tangent ratio of an angle within a right triangle equal 1?
  Ⓐ $1:1\sqrt{3}:2$ Ⓒ $\sqrt{2}:\sqrt{2}:2\sqrt{2}$
  Ⓑ $3:3:3\sqrt{2}$ Ⓓ $\sqrt{2}:\dfrac{\sqrt{2}}{2}:2$

23. Match the trigonometric expression on the left with its approximate decimal value on the right.

Expression	Value
A. $\sin 38°$	**1.** 0.921
B. $\cos 38°$	**2.** 0.391
C. $\sin 67°$	**3.** 0.788
D. $\cos 67°$	**4.** 0.616

 I'm in a Learning Mindset!

How did an initial failure with learning trigonometric ratios improve my learning methods?

Trigonometric Ratios

Due to the proportionality of side lengths in similar figures, side ratios in right triangles are properties of the angles.

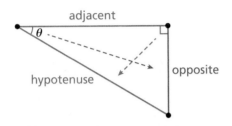

sine	$\sin(\theta) = \dfrac{\text{opposite}}{\text{hypotenuse}}$
cosine	$\cos(\theta) = \dfrac{\text{adjacent}}{\text{hypotenuse}}$
tangent	$\tan(\theta) = \dfrac{\text{opposite}}{\text{adjacent}}$

Missing Side Length

Ava and Nia are hiking up a mountain. The trail has a length of 20,643 feet and rises with a steady angle of elevation of 15 degrees.

At the summit, Ava and Nia wonder how tall the mountain is.

The height is opposite the angle of elevation.

Assume that the trail is a straight line.

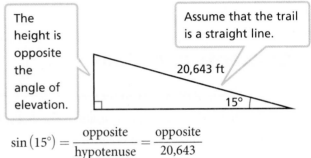

$$\sin(15°) = \frac{\text{opposite}}{\text{hypotenuse}} = \frac{\text{opposite}}{20{,}643}$$

$\rightarrow$ opposite $= 20{,}643 \sin(15°) \approx 5343$ ft

The height of the mountain is about 5343 feet.

Missing Angle Measure

Ava and Nia want to take the shortest distance back to town. They know that the town lies 5.3 miles north and 6.5 east of their current location.

This side is opposite the angle.

This side is adjacent to the angle.

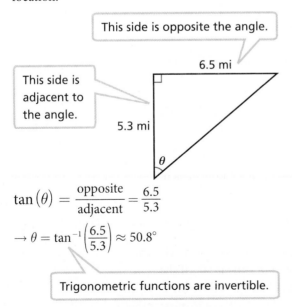

$$\tan(\theta) = \frac{\text{opposite}}{\text{adjacent}} = \frac{6.5}{5.3}$$

$$\rightarrow \theta = \tan^{-1}\left(\frac{6.5}{5.3}\right) \approx 50.8°$$

Trigonometric functions are invertible.

Ava and Nia should hike 50.8° east of north.

Special Right Triangles

There are two special right triangles that are helpful to remember.

45-45-90 triangle

This triangle can be considered as half of a square.

The x is the scale factor.

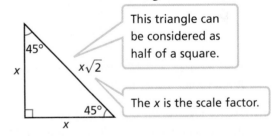

30-60-90 triangle

This triangle can be considered as half of an equilateral triangle.

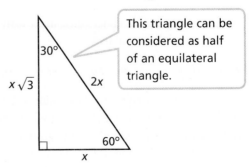

Vocabulary

Choose the correct term from the box to complete each sentence.

1. In a right triangle, the __?__ is the ratio of the length of the leg opposite an angle to the length of the leg adjacent to an angle.

2. In a right triangle, the __?__ is the ratio of the length of the leg adjacent to an angle to the length of the hypotenuse.

3. The __?__ is the angle between the horizontal and the line of sight when an observer is looking up at an object.

4. In a right triangle, the __?__ is the ratio of the length of the leg opposite an angle to the length of the hypotenuse.

Concepts and Skills

5. $\triangle DEF \sim \triangle ABC$ by a factor of k.

   A. Determine the sine, cosine, and tangent of $\angle A$ and $\angle B$.

   B. Determine $m\angle A$ and $m\angle B$.

   C. Explain the relationship between the sine and cosine of complementary angles and justify your reasoning.

   D. Determine $\sin(m\angle D)$ and justify your reasoning.

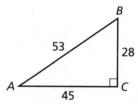

Solve each triangle.

6.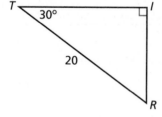

7.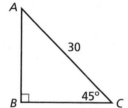

8. Find the area of $\triangle ABC$, with $a = 14$ inches, $b = 9$ inches, and $m\angle C = 42°$. Round your answer to the nearest tenth.

9. Haylee hikes to the top of a 120-foot vertical cliff. From the top of the cliff, the angle of depression to her campsite is 10°. How far away from the campsite is the base of the cliff? Round to the nearest foot.

10. A right triangle has an angle measure x with $\sin(x) = \frac{2}{3}$. Determine if each expression is also equal to $\frac{2}{3}$.

    A. $\cos(x)$ **B.** $\cos(90° - x)$ **C.** $\sin(90° - x)$ **D.** $\sin(45° - x)$

11. **(MP) Use Tools** Ashley is flying a kite and has let out 150 feet of string. The angle of elevation from where Ashley is holding the string to the kite is 50°. If she is holding the string 4 feet above the ground, how high is the kite above the ground? Round to the nearest foot. State what strategy and tool you will use to answer the question, explain your choice, and then find the answer.

Module Performance Task: *Spies and Analysts*™

Towering Over the Competition

How do you measure the height of the world's tallest cookie tower?

Are You Ready?

Complete these problems to review prior concepts and skills you will need for this module.

Find Equivalent Ratios

1. Carter walks 14 miles in 4 hours. How long will it take him to walk 24.5 miles?

2. A store sells 2 pounds of bananas for $1.58. How many pounds of bananas does the store sell for $3.95?

3. Jose earns $68 for working for 4 hours. How long will it take Jose to earn $153?

The Pythagorean Theorem and Its Converse

4. A right triangle has a leg that is 4 feet long and hypotenuse that is 6 feet long. How long is the other leg of the triangle?

5. A triangle has sides with lengths 10 inches, 24 inches, and 26 inches. Is the triangle a right triangle? Explain how you know.

6. A triangle has sides with lengths 8 inches, 10 inches, and 13 inches. Is the triangle a right triangle? Explain how you know.

Solve Quadratic Equations by Finding Square Roots

Solve each equation.

7. $x^2 = 64$

8. $\frac{1}{2}x^2 + 11 = 19$

9. $3x^2 - 17 = 55$

10. $2x^2 = 120$

11. $-5x^2 + 20 = 0$

Connecting Past and Present Learning

Previously, you learned:

• to use properties of similarity to define trigonometric ratios for acute angles, and

• to use trigonometric ratios and the Pythagorean Theorem to solve right triangles in applied problems.

In this module, you will learn:

• to prove the Law of Sines and Cosines, and

• to apply the Law of Sines and Cosines to find unknown measurements in right and non-right triangles.

Law of Sines

(I Can) use the Law of Sines to find side lengths and angle measures of non-right triangles and solve real-world problems.

Spark Your Learning

In a tower crane, the mast is the vertical part. The jib is the side of the horizontal section that lifts the weight. The other horizontal section is called the counter jib.

Both the jib and the counter jib are supported by suspension rods.

Complete Part A as a whole class. Then complete Parts B–D in small groups.

A. What is a mathematical question you can ask about the suspension rods? What information would you need to know to answer your question?

B. Is it possible to use right triangles to answer your question? Explain.

C. To answer your question, what strategy and tool would you use along with all the information you have? What answer do you get?

D. Does your answer make sense in the context of the situation? How do you know?

 Turn and Talk One way the tower crane can adjust its reach is to lengthen and shorten the jib as well as the height of the tower supporting it. How will these adjustments affect the angles of the triangles made by the mast, jib, counter jib, and the cables supporting them?

Build Understanding

Derive the Law of Sines

Previously, you used trigonometric ratios to find unknown measures in a right triangle. You can also use trigonometric ratios to find unknown measures in a triangle that is not a right triangle. The Law of Sines relates the sines of the angles of any triangle to the lengths of its sides.

Law of Sines

For $\triangle ABC$ with side lengths a, b, and c,
$$\frac{\sin A}{a} = \frac{\sin B}{b} = \frac{\sin C}{c}.$$

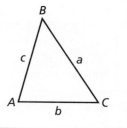

---

1 ▶ Use sine ratios to derive the Law of Sines.

A. In the triangle shown, h is the altitude from vertex A. Use the right triangles formed by the altitude to find each of the ratios.

$\sin C = \underline{\quad ? \quad}$

$\sin B = \underline{\quad ? \quad}$

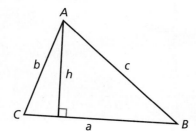

B. How can the two equations from Part A be used to write $\frac{\sin B}{b} = \frac{\sin C}{c}$?

C. In the triangle shown, t is the altitude from vertex C. Use the right triangles formed by the altitude to find each of the ratios.

$\sin A = \underline{\quad ? \quad}$

$\sin B = \underline{\quad ? \quad}$

Use your ratios to show that $\frac{\sin A}{a} = \frac{\sin B}{b}$.

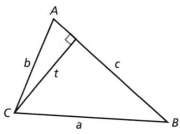

D. Use the equations from Parts B and C to explain the following result:

$$\frac{\sin A}{a} = \frac{\sin B}{b} = \frac{\sin C}{c}$$

 Turn and Talk Why would it be useful to rewrite the Law of Sines as $\frac{a}{\sin A} = \frac{b}{\sin B} = \frac{c}{\sin C}$? Explain how it is possible to rewrite the expression this way.

Determine when to Apply the Law of Sines

To find an unknown side length or angle measure in any triangle, you need to know the length of at least one side and two other measures in the triangle. There are five possible combinations of given information that are needed to solve a triangle.

- SSS: All three side lengths are known.
- SAS: Two side lengths and their included angle measure are known.
- SSA: Two side lengths and an angle measure opposite one of them are known.
- ASA: Two angle measures and an included side length are known.
- AAS: Two angle measures and a non-included side length are known.

The Law of Sines cannot be used to find unknown measures for all of the cases. The following task investigates when the Law of Sines can be applied.

 A. The triangle at the right shows only the lengths of the three sides, so it is an example of the SSS case. The Law of Sines is used to generate the equations below. Explain why it is not possible to apply the Law of Sines to find the value of $\sin A$, $\sin B$, or $\sin C$.

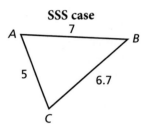

SSS case

$$\frac{\sin A}{6.7} = \frac{\sin B}{5} \qquad \frac{\sin B}{5} = \frac{\sin C}{7} \qquad \frac{\sin A}{6.7} = \frac{\sin C}{7}$$

B. For each triangle below, use the Law of Sines to write three equations that relate the side lengths to the sines of the angles. Can any of the equations be used to determine unknown angle measures or side lengths in the triangle? Explain.

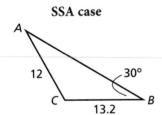

SSA case

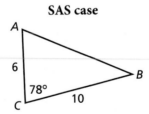

SAS case

C. For each triangle below, first find m∠B. Then use the Law of Sines to write three equations that relate the side lengths to the sines of the angles. Can any of the equations be used to determine unknown side lengths in the triangle? Explain.

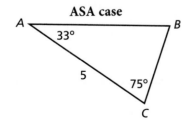

ASA case

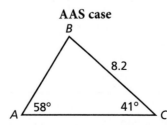

AAS case

D. Which of the five possible combinations of given information—SSS, SAS, SSA, ASA, AAS—can the Law of Sines be used to find unknown measures?

 Turn and Talk How can you figure out the side lengths of a triangle if you only know the measures of its angles? How do you know?

Explore the SSA Case

When given two side lengths and the angle measure of a non-included angle of a triangle (SSA case), the given measures may determine no triangle, one triangle, or two triangles. This is why the SSA case is called the ambiguous case.

Ambiguous Case

In each diagram, a, b, and m$\angle A$ are given. Side b and $\angle A$ are fixed, and then the possible positions of side a are considered.

$\angle A$ is acute.

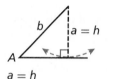

$a < h$
No triangle

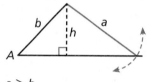

$a = h$
One triangle

$h < a < b$
Two triangles

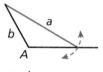

$a \geq b$
One triangle

$\angle A$ is right or obtuse.

$a \leq b$
No triangle

$a > b$
One triangle

---

3 **A.** Copy the table. Complete the table by using a calculator to find the sine of each angle measure in the table.

x	0°	30°	45°	90°	135°	150°	180°
sin(x)	?	?	?	?	?	?	?

B. Use the information in your table to make a conjecture about the sine values of supplementary angles.

C. For each of the sin(x) values in your table, evaluate the number using the inverse sine function on the calculator. Does the calculator always give the measure of the corresponding acute angle or obtuse angle? Explain.

D. For the SSA case, explain what has to be considered when using a calculator to find the measure of an unknown angle.

E. Do the considerations described in Part D apply to the ASA case or the AAS case? Explain why or why not.

Turn and Talk In $\triangle ABC$, suppose you are given AB, AC, and the measure of $\angle C$. For this triangle, there is only one possible measure for $\angle A$. What is true about $\angle C$? Explain your reasoning.

Step It Out

Apply the Law of Sines

The Law of Sines can be applied when given the following information about a triangle.

- SSA: Two side lengths and an angle measure opposite one of them are known.
- ASA: Two angle measures and an included side length are known.
- AAS: Two angle measures and a non-included side length are known.

4 Two scuba divers at points Y and Z are 15 meters apart when they start to ascend at the same rate to the surface at the angles shown. How far does each scuba diver travel when their paths cross?

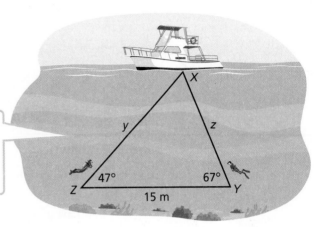

A. How do you know that you are able to use the Law of Sines to find the missing measures?

First, find the unknown angle measure.

$m\angle X + m\angle Y + m\angle Z = 180°$ Triangle Sum Theorem

$m\angle X + 67° + 47° = 180°$ Substitute the known angle measures.

$m\angle X = 66°$ Solve for the measure of $\angle X$.

Use the Law of Sines to find the distance traveled by each scuba diver.

B. Explain why $\frac{\sin X}{x}$ is used in both equations.

Find the value of y.

$$\frac{\sin Y}{y} = \frac{\sin X}{x}$$ **Law of Sines**

$$\frac{\sin 67°}{y} = \frac{\sin 66°}{15}$$ **Substitute.**

$$y = \frac{15 \sin 67°}{\sin 66°}$$ **Solve for the unknown.**

$$y \approx 15.114 \approx 15.1$$ **Evaluate.**

Find the value of z.

$$\frac{\sin Z}{z} = \frac{\sin X}{x}$$

$$\frac{\sin 47°}{z} = \frac{\sin 66°}{15}$$

$$z = \frac{15 \sin 47°}{\sin 66°}$$

$$z \approx 12.008 \approx 12.0$$

When the paths of the two scuba divers meet, the scuba diver who was at point Z traveled about 15.1 meters. The scuba diver who was at point Y traveled about 12 meters.

Turn and Talk In the triangle in Task 4, can you find the missing angle measure using the Law of Sines instead of using the Triangle Sum Theorem? Explain.

Apply the Law of Sines to the SSA Case

 5 In $\triangle ABC$, $AB = 9$ in., $BC = 6.8$ in., and $m\angle BAC = 42°$. What is AC?

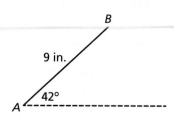

Determine how many triangles are possible.

Find the height.

$\sin 42° = \frac{h}{9}$, so $h = 9 \cdot \sin 42° \approx 6.022 \approx 6$ in.

There are two possible triangles because $h < a < c$.

> **A.** What are the values of h, a, and c?

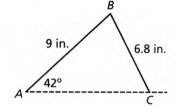 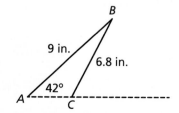

Use the Law of Sines to find the possible measures of $\angle C$.

$\dfrac{\sin 42°}{6.8} = \dfrac{\sin C}{9}$ **Law of Sines**

$\sin C = \dfrac{9 \sin 42°}{6.8}$ **Solve for sin C.**

> **B.** How are the two angles between 0° and 180° that have this sine value related?

Let $\angle C_1$ be the acute angle with the given sine, and let $\angle C_2$ be the obtuse angle. Use the inverse sine function on a calculator to find $m\angle C_1$. Then find the measure of $\angle C_2$.

$$m\angle C_1 = \sin^{-1}\left(\frac{9 \sin 42°}{6.8}\right) \approx 62.327° \approx 62.3°$$

$$m\angle C_2 \approx 180° - 62.327° \approx 117.673 \approx 117.7°$$

Find the measure of $\angle B$ and AC for each triangle.

> **C.** Why is it necessary to find $m\angle B$ in each triangle?

When $\angle C$ is acute

$m\angle B \approx 180° - 42° - 62.327°$

$\approx 75.673° \approx 75.7°$

$\dfrac{\sin 42°}{6.8} \approx \dfrac{\sin 75.673°}{AC}$

$AC \approx \dfrac{6.8 \sin 75.673°}{\sin 42°}$

$AC \approx 9.846 \approx 9.8$ in.

When $\angle C$ is obtuse

$m\angle B \approx 180° - 42° - 117.673°$

$\approx 20.327° \approx 20.3°$

$\dfrac{\sin 42°}{6.8} \approx \dfrac{\sin 20.327°}{AC}$

$AC \approx \dfrac{6.8 \sin 20.327°}{\sin 42°}$

$AC \approx 3.530 \approx 3.5$ in.

 Turn and Talk Suppose you are given AB, BC, and $m\angle BAC < 90°$ for $\triangle ABC$. How can you find the length BC that will produce only one triangle?

Check Understanding

1. Use the Law of Sines to write an equation that relates the ratios of each side length to the sine of the angle opposite the side length in △ABC.

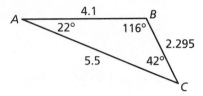

2. In △XYZ, you are given the measure of ∠X, XY and XZ. Can you use the Law of Sines to find YZ? Explain.

3. In △DEF, m∠D = 38°, DE = 3.1, and EF = 2.5. How many triangles are possible with the given measurements?

Find all the unknown side lengths and angle measures for each. Round your answers to the nearest tenth if necessary.

4.

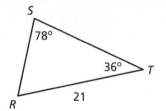

5.

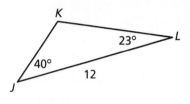

Find two angle measures that have the given sine value. Round each angle measure to the nearest tenth of a degree.

6. 0.9191

7. 0.0854

On Your Own

Match the altitude in △ABC with an equivalent expression.

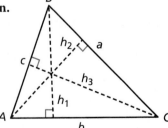

8. h_1

    A. $a \sin B$

9. h_2

    B. $c \sin A$

10. h_3

    C. $b \sin C$

11. (MP) **Reason** Triangle ABC is an obtuse triangle, and h is an altitude of the triangle.

    A. Write a ratio for the sine of ∠A.

    B. Write a ratio for the sine of ∠BCD. Use this ratio to find the sine of ∠C. Explain your reasoning.

    C. Draw altitude j from vertex C and find the sine of ∠B and the sine of ∠A using this altitude.

    D. Use the sine ratios to derive the Law of Sines for an obtuse triangle.

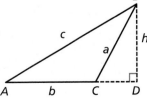

Determine whether the distance across each pond can be found using the Law of Sines and the given information. Explain your reasoning.

12.

13.

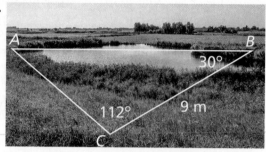

14.

15.

The measure of ∠D and side lengths d and f in △DEF are given. Also, the altitude h from vertex E is given. Determine how many triangles are possible for each set of given measures. Explain your reasoning.

16. $m\angle D = 110°$, $d = 5$, $f = 7$, $h = 6.6$

17. $m\angle D = 55°$, $d = 8$, $f = 6$, $h = 4.9$

18. $m\angle D = 30°$, $d = 7$, $f \approx 7.2$, $h = 7$

19. $m\angle D = 120°$, $d = 11$, $f = 10$, $h = 8.7$

Find the unknown measurements using the Law of Sines. Round your answers to the nearest tenth if necessary.

20.

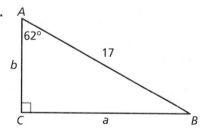

21.

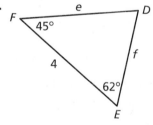

22.

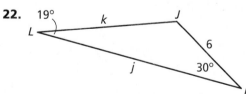

23.

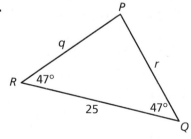

24. **(MP) Critique Reasoning** Two radio towers that are 65 miles apart track a satellite in orbit. The signal from Tower A forms a 76° angle between the ground and the satellite, and the signal from Tower B forms an 80.5° angle. Rylan says that Tower B is 4.5 miles closer to the satellite than Tower A. Is he correct? Explain.

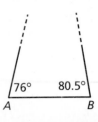

25. For a movie theater screen that is 50 feet wide, a high fidelity audio and visual company suggests that the center of the last row of seats forms the the angles shown with the left side *L* of the screen and the right side *R* of the screen.

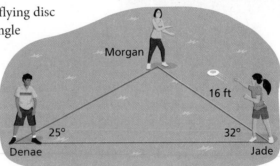

   A. Use the Law of Sines to find the distance from the center of the last row of seats to both the left side of the screen and to the right side of the screen to the nearest tenth of a foot.

   B. Is it possible to find the distances without using the Law of Sines? Explain.

26. Jade, Morgan, and Denae are tossing a flying disc in a park. Their locations form the triangle shown. Jade is 16 feet from Morgan.

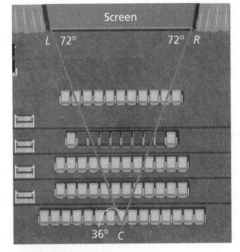

   A. How far apart are Morgan and Denae? Round to the nearest tenth of a foot.

   B. How far apart are Denae and Jade? Round to the nearest tenth of a foot.

Find the height *h* of each triangle to the nearest tenth.

27.

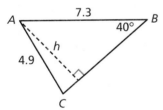

28.

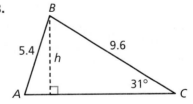

Find two angle measures that have the given sine value. Round your answer to the nearest tenth of a degree.

29. 0.6639   **30.** 0.2504   **31.** 0.9803

Use the given information to find the unknown angle measures and side lengths of △*ABC*, if possible. If more than one triangle is possible, find both sets of measures.

32. m∠*A* = 20°, *a* = 18, *b* = 14   **33.** m∠*A* = 64°, *a* = 13, *b* = 15

34. m∠*A* = 36°, *a* = 12, *b* = 18   **35.** m∠*A* = 106°, *a* = 11, *b* = 20

36. m∠*A* = 82°, *a* = 25, *b* = 20   **37.** m∠*A* = 45°, *a* = 27, *b* = 34

38. Open Ended Write the lengths of two sides and an angle measure that can form two different triangles. Find all dimensions of each triangle.

Find the area of each triangle. Round your answer to the nearest tenth of a square unit.

39.

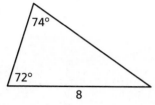

74°
72°
8

40.

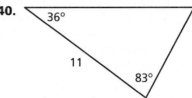

36°
11
83°

41. (Open Middle™) Using the digits 1 to 9 at most one time each, fill in the boxes three times. For the first set of numbers, fill in the boxes so that exactly two triangles exist. For the second set of numbers, fill in the boxes so that exactly one triangle exists. For the last set, fill in the boxes so no triangle exists.

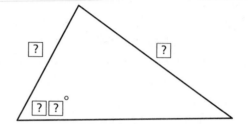

Spiral Review • Assessment Readiness

42. Find m∠C.

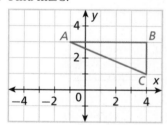

(A) 21.8°

(B) 42.9°

(C) 68.2°

(D) 90°

43. Find x.

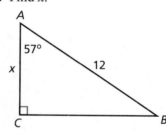

57°
x
12
C
B

(A) 0.05

(B) 6.5

(C) 10.1

(D) 18.5

44. Determine whether the side lengths of a triangle belong to a 45°-45°-90° triangle, a 30°-60°-90° triangle, or neither.

Side lengths	45°-45°-90° triangle	30°-60°-90° triangle	Neither
A. 3, 3√2, 3	?	?	?
B. 5, 5√3, 10√3	?	?	?
C. 2, 4, 2√3	?	?	?

 I'm in a Learning Mindset!

Did procrastination or lack of organization affect my learning outcomes? In what way?

Law of Cosines

(I Can) use the Law of Cosines to find side lengths and angle measures of non-right triangles and solve real-world problems.

Spark Your Learning

In a triathlon with a sprint format, competitors have to swim a course that is 750 meters long. An example of such a course is shown.

Complete Part A as a whole class. Then complete Parts B–D in small groups.

   A. What is a mathematical question you can ask about this situation? What information would you need to know to answer your question?

   B. Is it possible to use right triangle trigonometric ratios to answer your question?

   C. To answer your question, what strategy and tool would you use along with all the information you have? What answer do you get?

   D. Does your answer make sense in the context of the situation? How do you know?

   Turn and Talk How can you use the Law of Sines with the given information to find the unknown angle measures of the triangular course?

Build Understanding

Derive the Law of Cosines

You have learned how to find unknown angle measures and side lengths in a triangle using the Law of Sines. However, the Law of Sines cannot be used to solve triangles with the following combinations of given information:

- SSS: All three side lengths are known.
- SAS: Two side lengths and their included angle measure are known.

For these cases, you must apply a different law, the Law of Cosines.

> **Law of Cosines**
>
> For $\triangle ABC$, the Law of Cosines states that
>
> $a^2 = b^2 + c^2 - 2bc \cos A$
> $b^2 = a^2 + c^2 - 2ac \cos B$
> $c^2 = a^2 + b^2 - 2ab \cos C$

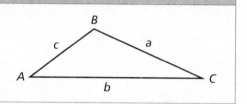

1 Use $\triangle ABC$ to derive the Law of Cosines.

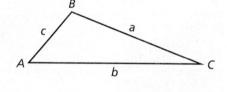

A. In the Law of Cosines, the equations contain the cosines of angles. Is it possible to write ratios for cosines of angles in $\triangle ABC$? Explain why altitude $\overline{BD}$ is drawn in the second triangle.

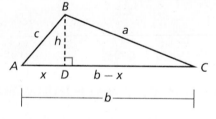

B. Use the Pythagorean Theorem to write a relationship for the side lengths of $\triangle ABD$ and for the side lengths of $\triangle CBD$.

C. Notice that both equations contain the variables x and h. Since these variables are not in the Law of Cosines, x and h need to be replaced. What does $x^2 + h^2$ equal? Replace $x^2 + h^2$ by this term in the equation for a^2.

D. Compare your revised equation for a^2 with the equation for a^2 given in the Law of Cosines. What should x be equivalent to? Explain how to use the ratio for the cosine of $\angle A$ to eliminate x from the equation for a^2.

> **Turn and Talk** Explain why the Pythagorean Theorem can be considered a special case of the Law of Cosines.

Investigate Cosine Values of Obtuse Angles

You have learned that supplementary angles have the same sine value. In $\triangle ABC$, the sine of $\angle ACB$ is equal to the sine of $\angle ACD$ because they form a linear pair.

The following task investigates how the cosines of supplementary angles are related.

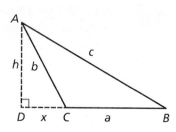

2 ▶ **A.** Copy the table. Complete the table by using a calculator to find the cosine of each angle measure in the table.

x	0°	30°	45°	90°	135°	150°	180°
cos(x)	?	?	?	?	?	?	?

B. Use the information in your table to make a conjecture about the cosine values of supplementary angles.

C. For each of the cos(x) values in your table, evaluate the number using the inverse cosine function on the calculator. Does the calculator always give the measure of the corresponding acute angle or obtuse angle?

Derive a Formula for the Area of a Triangle

You can use two side lengths of a triangle and their included angle to find the area of any triangle.

Area of a Triangle

The area of any triangle is one half the product of the lengths of two sides times the sine of their included angle.

For △ABC, there are three ways to calculate the area:

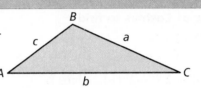

$$\text{Area} = \frac{1}{2}bc\sin A \qquad \text{Area} = \frac{1}{2}ac\sin B \qquad \text{Area} = \frac{1}{2}ab\sin C$$

3 ▶ Use △ABC to derive a triangle area formula. In △ABC, h is the height of the triangle.

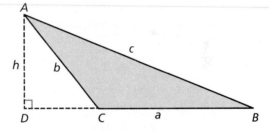

A. Use the formula for the area of a triangle, Area $= \frac{1}{2}bh$, to write the area of △ABC with base a. To generate an area formula that uses only two side lengths and the included angle, how does the formula need to change?

B. Write an equation for the value of h using ∠ACD. Use what you know about the value of the sines of supplementary angles to rewrite the expression for h using ∠C. Explain your reasoning.

C. Use your equation from Part B to eliminate the variable h from the original equation for the area found in Part A. Explain how you found the equation.

D. Explain how to use the diagram to show that $\frac{1}{2}ab\sin C = \frac{1}{2}bc\sin A$.

 Turn and Talk How can you use the equation you found for the area of a triangle in Part C to find the area of a right triangle, with ∠C being a right angle?

Step It Out

Solve a Triangle Using the Law of Cosines

When using the Law of Cosines to solve a triangle, start by finding the measure of the angle opposite the longest side. Recall that the largest angle in a triangle is opposite the longest side.

- If the largest angle in a triangle is acute, then the other two angles are acute.
- If the largest angle in a triangle is obtuse, then the other two angles are acute.

After using the Law of Cosines to find the measure of one angle, the Law of Sines can be used to find the measure of another angle. There are two angles between $0°$ and $180°$ that have the same sine value—an acute angle and its obtuse supplement. In this case, you will use the acute angle measure.

 4 In $\triangle XYZ$, $x = 4.6$, $y = 6.8$, and $z = 2.5$.
What are the angle measures of the triangle?

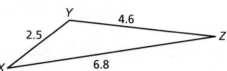

Use the Law of Cosines to find the measure of $\angle Y$.

$$y^2 = x^2 + z^2 - 2xz \cos Y$$

$$6.8^2 = 4.6^2 + 2.5^2 - 2(4.6)(2.5) \cos Y$$

$$46.24 = 21.16 + 6.25 - 23 \cos Y$$

$$18.83 = -23 \cos Y$$

$$\frac{18.83}{-23} = \cos Y$$

$$m\angle Y = \cos^{-1}\left(\frac{18.83}{-23}\right) \approx 144.954° \approx 145.0°$$

> **A.** Why is the measure of $\angle Y$ found first?

Use the Law of Sines to find the measure of $\angle X$.

$$\frac{\sin X}{x} = \frac{\sin Y}{y}$$

$$\frac{\sin X}{4.6} \approx \frac{\sin 144.954°}{6.8}$$

$$\sin X \approx \frac{4.6 \sin 144.954°}{6.8}$$

$$m\angle X \approx \sin^{-1}\left(\frac{4.6 \sin 144.954°}{6.8}\right) \approx 22.858° \approx 22.9°$$

> **B.** In a multi-step calculation, rounding one step's result, called an *intermediate result*, and using it in the next step can lead to round-off error. One way to avoid this type of error is to carry extra digits from one step to the next, as was done here. Check this by recalculating $m\angle X$ using 145.0° instead. What do you notice?

> **C.** How do you know that $m\angle X$ is about 22.9°, not 157.1°?

Use the Triangle Sum Theorem to find the measure of $\angle Z$.

$$m\angle X + m\angle Y + m\angle Z = 180°$$

$$22.858° + 144.954° + m\angle Z \approx 180°$$

$$m\angle Z \approx 12.188° \approx 12.2°$$

In $\triangle XYZ$, $m\angle X \approx 22.9°$, $m\angle Y \approx 145.0°$, and $m\angle Z \approx 12.2°$.

 Turn and Talk How can you check your answers without using the Triangle Sum Theorem?

Use the Law of Cosines to Solve a Real-World Problem

5 Tracking devices are used to monitor the elephants in a herd. An ecologist observes an elephant that has fallen behind the herd. Use the ecologist's distance from the herd and from the lone elephant to determine how far the elephant is from the herd.

Apply the Law of Cosines to find the distance between the elephant and the herd.

What do the variables *a*, *b*, and *c* represent?

$$a^2 = b^2 + c^2 - 2bc \cos A$$
$$a^2 = 57^2 + 11^2 - 2(57)(11) \cos 59°$$
$$a^2 = 3249 + 121 - 1254 \cos 59°$$
$$a^2 = 3370 - 1254 \cos 59°$$
$$a = \sqrt{3370 - 1254 \cos 59°} \approx 52.193 \approx 52.2$$

The elephant is about 52.2 meters from the herd.

 Turn and Talk Explain how each of the following will affect the estimate of the elephant's distance from the herd:

- The distance between the ecologist and the herd is underestimated
- The measure of the angle made by the herd, ecologist, and elephant is smaller

Find the Area of a Triangle

6 A triangular plot of land has the dimensions shown. Find the area of the plot to the nearest square foot.

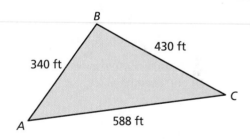

Find the measure of an angle.
$$b^2 = a^2 + c^2 - 2ac \cos B$$
$$588^2 = 430^2 + 340^2 - 2(430)(340) \cos B$$
$$45{,}244 = -292{,}400 \cos B$$
$$\frac{45{,}244}{-292{,}400} = \cos B$$
$$m\angle B = \cos^{-1}\left(\frac{45{,}244}{-292{,}400}\right) \approx 98.901° \approx 98.9°$$

Why is the measure of an angle needed to find the area?

Find the area of the triangle.
$$\text{Area} = \frac{1}{2}ac \sin B$$
$$\approx \frac{1}{2}(430)(340) \sin 98.901° \approx 72{,}219.669 \approx 72{,}220$$

The area of the plot is about 72,200 square feet.

 Turn and Talk Suppose $\overline{BD}$ is an altitude of the triangle in Task 6. How can you represent the lengths *AD* and *CD*? How can you find the length *BD*? How can you use this to find the area of the triangle in another way?

Check Understanding

1. Draw and label the diagram you would use to derive the form
$b^2 = a^2 + c^2 - 2ac \cos B$ from the Law of Cosines.

2. Suppose $m\angle K + m\angle J = 180°$. How is the sine of $\angle K$ related to the sine of $\angle J$?
How is the cosine of $\angle K$ related to the cosine of $\angle J$?

Solve each triangle. Round intermediate results to three decimal places and final answers to one decimal place.

3.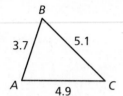

4.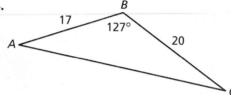

5. John owns a triangular piece of property. The lengths of two sides are 200 feet and 250 feet, and the included angle measures 85°.

   A. What is the length of the third side to the nearest foot?

   B. What is the area of the property to the nearest square foot?

On Your Own

6. (MP) **Reason** Solve the equation $c^2 = a^2 + b^2 - 2ab \cos C$ from the Law of Cosines for C. When would this form of the equation be useful?

7. (MP) **Reason** Suppose $\angle A$ in $\triangle ABC$ is an obtuse angle. What must be true about the value of x in the equation $\cos^{-1} x = A$?

8. (MP) **Reason** Explain how you can derive a formula for the area of an equilateral triangle with side length s using the formula Area $= \frac{1}{2} bc \sin A$.

Solve each triangle. Round intermediate results to three decimal places and final answers to one decimal place.

9.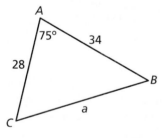

10.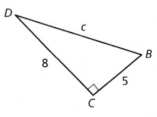

11.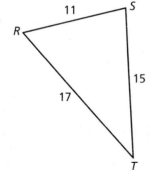

12.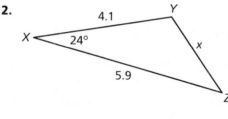

13. 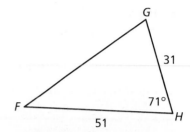 **(MP) Critique Reasoning** Melissa believes △*FGH* can be solved using only the Law of Sines. Sara believes △*FGH* can be solved using only the Law of Cosines. Who is correct? Explain your reasoning.

14. Open Ended Draw a triangle. Use a ruler to measure the lengths of two sides, and use a protractor to measure the included angle. Use the Law of Cosines to solve the triangle.

15. The distances from home plate to the pitcher's mound and from home plate to first base on a baseball field are shown. Alex is the pitcher, and he stands at point *B* on the pitcher's mound.

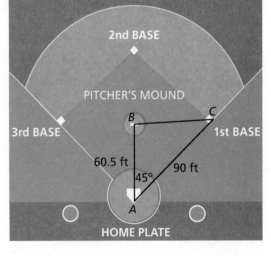

A. How far does Alex have to throw the ball from the pitcher's mound to reach first base?

B. Alex is facing home plate. Through what angle does he have to turn to face first base?

16. STEM In physics, vectors are used to represent forces. When two forces are applied to an object, the resultant force is the third side of a triangle. Suppose a motorboat that moves in still water at a velocity $\vec{b}$ with a magnitude of 8 feet per second is trying to travel directly across a river but is pushed by a current with a velocity $\vec{c}$ with a magnitude of 2 feet per second in a direction that makes a 70° angle with the direct path. What is the magnitude of the resultant velocity $\vec{r}$?

Use the given measures in △*ABC* to solve each triangle. Round intermediate results to three decimal places and final answers to one decimal place.

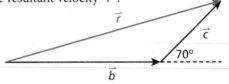

17. $a = 14$, $b = 9$, $c = 19$

18. $m\angle B = 62°$, $a = 5.3$, $c = 7.6$

19. $m\angle C = 132°$, $a = 11$, $b = 8$

20. $a = 6.8$, $b = 7.2$, $c = 12.1$

21. $m\angle A = 90°$, $b = 7$, $c = 24$

22. $a = 30$, $b = 18$, $c = 24$

23. **(MP) Critique Reasoning** Grant wants to find the area of the triangle. Martin says that he cannot find the area because he does not know the height of the triangle. Grant disagrees. Who is correct? Explain your reasoning.

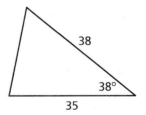

Find the area of each triangle. Round your answer to the nearest tenth of a square unit.

24.

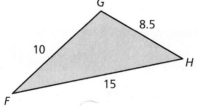

25.

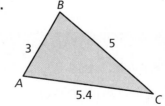

26. History The Historic Triangle in Virginia is a triangle formed by the historic communities of Jamestown, Williamsburg, and Yorktown as shown in the map. Use the distances between the communities to find the area of the Historic Triangle to the nearest tenth of a square mile.

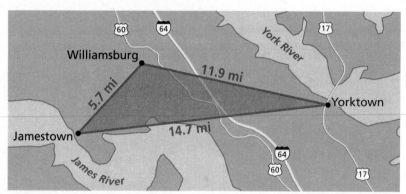

27. (**Open Middle™**) Using the digits 1 to 9, at most one time each, fill in the boxes to create a triangle with the greatest possible area.

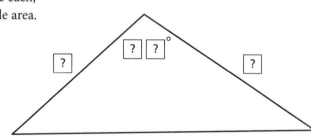

Spiral Review • Assessment Readiness

28. What is m∠B?

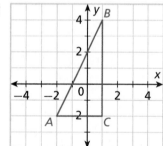

Ⓐ 26.6°

Ⓑ 30°

Ⓒ 63.4°

Ⓓ 90°

29. To the nearest tenth of an inch, what is the circumference of a circle that has a radius of 3.5 inches?

Ⓐ 5.5

Ⓑ 11.0

Ⓒ 22.0

Ⓓ 44.0

30. In $\triangle ABC$, m∠$A = 71°$, m∠$C = 68°$, and $b = 14$. What is the value c?

Ⓐ 9.9

Ⓒ 19.8

Ⓑ 13.7

Ⓓ 20.2

31. Which ratios of the side lengths of a triangle belong to a 30°-60°-90° triangle? Select all that apply.

Ⓐ $5 : 5\sqrt{3} : 10$

Ⓑ $3 : 6 : 3\sqrt{2}$

Ⓒ $4\sqrt{3} : 12 : 4$

Ⓓ $8 : 8 : 8\sqrt{3}$

Ⓔ $6 : 12 : 6\sqrt{3}$

 I'm in a Learning Mindset!

How am I prioritizing my learning? What are my greatest strengths?

Review

Law of Sines

Alicia is surveying a triangular park and takes measurements at two points, A and C.

She needs to find the remaining measurements to complete her report.

$m\angle B = 180° - 38° - 57° = 85°$

> Triangle Sum Theorem

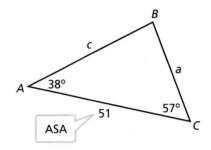

> ASA

	Law of Sines	
$\dfrac{\sin B}{b} = \dfrac{\sin A}{a}$	Law of Sines	$\dfrac{\sin B}{b} = \dfrac{\sin C}{c}$
$\dfrac{\sin(85°)}{51} = \dfrac{\sin(38°)}{a}$	Substitute.	$\dfrac{\sin(85°)}{51} = \dfrac{\sin(57°)}{c}$
$a = \dfrac{51\sin(38°)}{\sin(85°)}$	Solve for the unknown.	$c = \dfrac{51\sin(57°)}{\sin(85°)}$
$a \approx 31.5$	Evaluate.	$c \approx 42.9$

Law of Cosines

Alicia must include the triangular service shed that is in the park. She measures the outer dimensions and must determine the angle of each corner.

> SSS

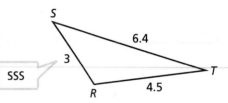

	Law of Cosines	
$r^2 = s^2 + t^2 - 2st\cos R$	Law of Cosines	$s^2 = r^2 + t^2 - 2rt\cos S$
$6.4^2 = 4.5^2 + 3^2 - 2(4.5)(3)\cos R$	Substitute.	$4.5^2 = 6.4^2 + 3^2 - 2(6.4)(3)\cos S$
$40.96 = 20.25 + 9 - 27\cos R$	Solve for the unknown.	$20.25 = 40.96 + 9 - 38.4\cos S$
$40.96 = 29.25 - 27\cos R$		$20.25 = 49.96 - 38.4\cos S$
$11.71 = -27\cos R$		$-29.71 = -38.4\cos S$
$\cos R = \dfrac{11.71}{-27}$		$\cos S = \dfrac{29.71}{38.4}$
$R = \cos^{-1}\left(\dfrac{11.71}{-27}\right) \approx 115.7°$	Evaluate.	$S = \cos^{-1}\left(\dfrac{29.71}{38.4}\right) \approx 39.3°$

> Triangle Sum Theorem

$m\angle T = 180° - 115.7° - 39.3° = 25°$

Vocabulary

Choose the correct term from the box to complete each sentence.

1. The Law of ___?___ can be used to find the unknown measures of triangle if you know the measure of two angles and a side length.

2. A ___?___ ratio is the ratio of two sides of a right triangle.

3. The Law of ___?___ can be used to find the unknown measures of triangle if you know the lengths of the three sides.

Concepts and Skills

For each case, identify if the Law of Sines, the Law of Cosines, or neither can be applied to solve the triangle.

4. SSS

5. SSA

6. SAS

7. AAA

8. AAS

9. ASA

Solve each triangle. Round each answer to the nearest tenth.

10.

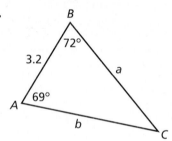

11.

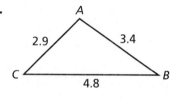

Find the area of each triangle. Round each answer to the nearest tenth.

12.

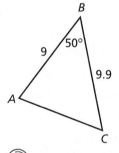

13.

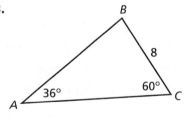

14. (MP) **Use Tools** Lamar is commissioned to build a fence around a municipal flower garden. The garden is triangle with two sides measuring 7 feet and 10 feet and the included angle measuring 55°. How much fencing does he need to enclose the flower garden? Round your answer to the nearest tenth of a foot. State what strategy and tool you will use to answer the question, explain your choice, and then find the answer. Round your answer to the nearest tenth of a foot.

15. Felicity walks around a nearly triangular lake and keeps track of each distance. What is the area of the lake? Round your answer to the nearest tenth of a square mile.

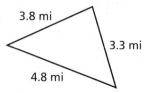

16. Explain why the SSA case of the Law of Sines is known as the ambiguous case.

Properties of Circles

Optical Lens Technician

An optical lens technician is a specialist in crafting lenses that must satisfy the exact specifications needed for a variety of imaging systems such as telescopes, microscopes, and cameras. They cut and shape materials with a high level of precision and care to craft lenses that will meet the needs of their clients.

STEM Task

The lens maker's equation is used to find the effective focal length, F, of a glass lens given the radii, R_1 and R_2.

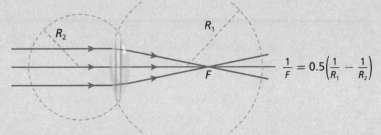

$$\frac{1}{F} = 0.5\left(\frac{1}{R_1} - \frac{1}{R_2}\right)$$

What is the effective focal length for a glass lens with $R_1 = 30$ cm and $R_2 = -20$ cm?

Learning Mindset
Resilience Identifies Obstacles

©Andrii Zhezhera/Dreamstime

Is something getting in the way of your learning or preventing you from achieving a specific goal? Sometimes we encounter obstacles and we need to find a way to overcome them. Having a plan to identify possible obstacles can help you prepare for these moments and minimize their impact on your learning outcome. Don't be afraid when you encounter an obstacle. Obstacles help bring about growth. Here are some questions you can ask yourself to help you identify obstacles that may impede your learning:

- What barriers are there to developing my understanding of the relationships between segments and angles in circles? Who can help me overcome these barriers?

- Are my obstacles externally based? Am I creating obstacles that are slowing me down? Which obstacles do I have control over?

- How does stress impact my ability to complete a project? What strategies can I use to reduce the impact of this obstacle?

- What strategies have I used that have been successful or unsuccessful? In what ways can they be improved?

Reflect

Q When have you had to overcome an obstacle when working on a task? How did you identify the obstacle? How did you grow from this experience?

Q As an optical lens technician, what obstacles might you face as you craft lenses for different clients? How can you learn from facing these obstacles?

15 Angles and Segments in Circles

©Mark Nazh/Shutterstock

Virtual Reality

To develop a virtual reality (VR) system, you need to have a geometric understanding of how the eye dynamically receives and composes images.

A horopter is the set of points that are imaged on the corresponding points of the retinas. Objects that lie on the horopter are seen as a single image. In this diagram, the large circle represents the horopter and the two smaller circles represent eyes with congruent radii.

A. What is the relationship between $\angle LAR$ and $\angle LBR$? Explain your reasoning.

B. Prove that $\triangle APL$ and $\triangle BPR$ are similar.

C. If $\overline{LD_L} \cong \overline{RD_R}$ and $\overline{LE_L} \cong \overline{RE_R}$, do you have enough information to show that $\overline{D_LE_L} \cong \overline{D_RE_R}$? Explain your reasoning.

D. What can you conclude about the images on the retinas at $\overparen{D_LE_L}$ and $\overparen{D_RE_R}$? Explain your reasoning.

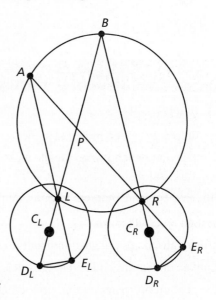

Are You Ready?

Complete these problems to review prior concepts and skills you will need for this module.

Multiply and Divide Rational Numbers

Simplify each expression.

1. $\frac{5}{4}(-56)$

2. $32 \div \frac{2}{3}$

3. 8.3×0.4

4. $\frac{9.6}{-1.2}$

5. $\frac{5}{8}(1.2)$

6. $6.4 \div \frac{4}{3}$

Types of Angle Pairs

Find the measure of each angle.

7. $\angle GED$

8. $\angle CEF$

9. $\angle GEC$

10. $\angle FEA$

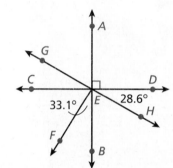

Distance and Midpoint Formulas

Find the distance and the midpoint of the segment between each set of points.

11. $(-4, -1)$ and $(3, -2)$

12. $(7, -3)$ and $(1, 7)$

13. $(5, 2)$ and $(-2, 4)$

14. $(-6, 3)$ and $(-3, -5)$

Connecting Past and Present Learning

Previously, you learned:

• to locate the circumcenter and incenter of triangles with constructions,

• to find unknown side lengths and angle measures in triangles and quadrilaterals, and

• to use the Pythagorean Theorem to find side lengths of right triangles.

In this module, you will learn:

• to identify relationships between segments and angles in circles,

• to find unknown lengths and angle measures in circles, and

• to write equations of circles on the coordinate plane.

Central Angles and Inscribed Angles

(I Can) determine the measures of central angles, inscribed angles, and arcs of a circle.

Spark Your Learning

An outdoor amphitheater has semicircular rows of seating around a semicircular stage. The tickets for the next performance have been sold out.

There are 30 rows in the amphitheater.

Complete Part A as a whole class. Then complete Parts B–C in small groups.

A. What is a mathematical question you can ask about this situation? What information would you need to know to answer your question?

B. To answer your question, what strategy and tool would you use along with all the information you have? What answer do you get?

C. Does your answer make sense in the context of the situation? How do you know?

Turn and Talk How much space would each attendee have if only $\frac{3}{4}$ of all tickets are sold? Explain.

©Lisa S. Engelbrecht/Alamy

Build Understanding

Investigate Central Angles and Inscribed Angles

A **circle** is the set of all points in a plane that are equidistant from a given point, called the center of the circle. A **chord** is a segment whose endpoints lie on a circle. A **diameter** is a chord that contains the center of the circle.

A **central angle** of a circle is an angle whose vertex is the center of the circle. An **inscribed angle** is an angle whose vertex is on a circle and whose sides contain chords of the circle.

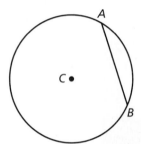
$\overline{AB}$ is a chord.

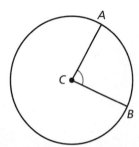
$\angle ACB$ is a central angle.

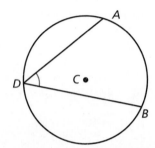
$\angle ADB$ is an inscribed angle.

1 ▶ Use a geometric drawing tool to draw a circle. Draw an acute inscribed angle on the circle. Then draw the corresponding central angle, which intersects the sides of the inscribed angle on the circle as shown.

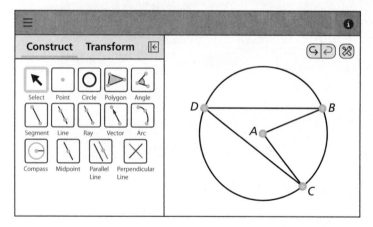

A. Measure the inscribed angle and the central angle. Drag the vertex of the inscribed angle around the circle. What do you notice about the angle measure as the vertex of the inscribed angle moves?

B. Observe the angle measures as you drag one of the points on the circle where the sides of the angles intersect. Make a conjecture about the relationship between the measures of an inscribed angle and its associated central angle.

 Turn and Talk Suppose $\overline{BC}$ is a diameter of a circle. An inscribed angle is drawn so that it intersects the diameter on the circle at points B and C. Make a conjecture about what type of angle the inscribed angle is. Explain your reasoning.

Understand Arcs and Arc Measures

An **arc** is an unbroken part of a circle consisting of two points on the circle, called the endpoints, and all the points on the circle between them.

Arc	Measure	Figure
A **minor arc** is an arc of a circle whose points are on or in the interior of a central angle.	The measure of a minor arc is equal to the measure of the central angle. $m\overset{\frown}{AB} = m\angle ACB$	
A **major arc** is an arc of a circle whose points are on or in the exterior of a central angle.	The measure of a major arc is equal to 360° minus the measure of the central angle. $m\overset{\frown}{ADB} = 360° - m\angle ACB$	
A **semicircle** is an arc of a circle whose points lie on a diameter.	The measure of a semicircle is 180°. $m\overset{\frown}{ADB} = 180°$	

Minor arcs are named by their two endpoints. Major arcs and semicircles are named by their two endpoints, and a point on the arc.

2 The minute hand of a circular clock sweeps out an arc as it moves from 9:10 to 9:25.

A. What fraction of a complete rotation did the minute hand travel?

B. A complete rotation of the minute hand corresponds to 360°. What is the degree measure that the minute hand traveled? What angle does this measure represent?

C. What is the measure of the arc formed on the clock as the minute hand moves from 9:10 to 9:25? Why?

Adjacent arcs are arcs of the same circle that have a common endpoint. You can add the measures of two adjacent arcs.

Arc Addition Postulate

The measure of an arc formed by two adjacent arcs is the sum of the measures of the two arcs.

$m\widehat{AB} = m\widehat{AD} + m\widehat{DB}$

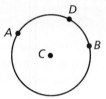

---

3   **A.** Two circles with different radii have their centers at A. Explain why $m\widehat{EB} = 40°$.

B. What arc measure is being calculated below?
$m\widehat{DC} + m\widehat{CF} = 40° + 79° = 119°$

C. What is $m\widehat{CDF}$? How do you know?

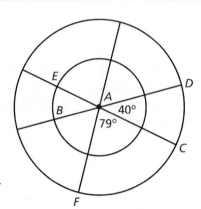

Construct a Regular Hexagon

Recall that a hexagon is a polygon with six sides, and that a regular hexagon is both equilateral and equiangular.

4   With a compass, construct a circle and place point A on the circle. Using the same compass setting, draw an arc from point A that intersects the circle. Label the point of intersection B. Continue this method back to point A, creating points C, D, E, and F. Use a straightedge to draw hexagon $ABCDEF$.

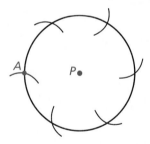 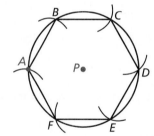 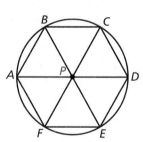

A. Explain why $AB = AP$. How do you know that the sides of the hexagon are congruent?

B. Use a straightedge to draw $\overline{AD}$, $\overline{BE}$, and $\overline{CF}$. Why do these line segments contain center P?

C. Each side of the hexagon along with the two sides connecting it to the center of the circle forms an equiangular triangle. Why?

D. Can you conclude that the hexagon is equiangular? Explain.

E. Why can you conclude that hexagon $ABCDEF$ is a regular polygon?

 Turn and Talk How can you use the regular hexagon construction to construct an equilateral triangle inscribed in a circle?

Step It Out

Prove the Inscribed Angle Theorem

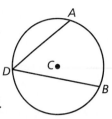

Two chords with a common endpoint form an inscribed angle. The other endpoints and all the points on the circle between them form an **intercepted arc**. $\angle ADB$ is the inscribed angle, and $\overset{\frown}{AB}$ is the intercepted arc.

Inscribed Angle Theorem
The measure of an inscribed angle is equal to half the measure of its intercepted arc. $m\angle ADB = \frac{1}{2}m\overset{\frown}{AB}$ 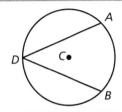

Inscribed Angle of a Diameter Theorem
The endpoints of a diameter lie on the endpoints of an inscribed angle if and only if the inscribed angle is a right angle. $\overline{AB}$ is a diameter of the circle if and only if $\angle ADB$ is a right angle. 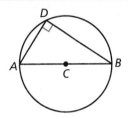

To prove the Inscribed Angle Theorem, the following three cases must be proven:

5 **Case 1:** The center of the circle is on a side of the inscribed angle.

Case 2: The center of the circle is inside the inscribed angle.

Case 3: The center of the circle is outside the inscribed angle.

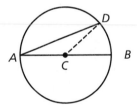

The proof for Case 1 is shown below.

Given: $\angle DAB$ is inscribed in circle C. $\overline{AB}$ contains C.

Prove: $m\angle DAB = \frac{1}{2}m\overset{\frown}{DB}$

Statements	Reasons
1. Draw $\overline{DC}$. $\overline{AC} \cong \overline{DC}$	**1.** $\overline{AC}$ and $\overline{DC}$ are radii for circle C.
2. $\triangle ADC$ is isosceles.	**2.** Definition of isosceles triangle
3. $\angle DAB \cong \angle ADC$	**3.** ___?___ **A.** Why are these angles congruent?
4. $m\angle DAB = m\angle ADC$	**4.** Congruent angles have equal measures.
5. $m\angle DAB + m\angle ADC = m\angle DCB$	**5.** The measure of an exterior angle equals the sum of the measures of its remote interior angles.
6. $2m\angle DAB = m\angle DCB$	**6.** $m\angle DAB = m\angle ADC$
7. $m\angle DAB = \frac{1}{2}m\angle DCB$ **B.** Which angle is the exterior angle?	**7.** Division Property of Equality
8. $m\angle DAB = \frac{1}{2}m\overset{\frown}{DB}$	**8.** Substitution **C.** Why can you substitute $m\angle DCB$ with $m\overset{\frown}{DB}$?

Use Inscribed Angles Theorems

6 Jana creates a circular rainbow art piece by wrapping strings with various colors around pins that are tacked to a board. She needs to know various angle measurements in order to design a fluid pattern.

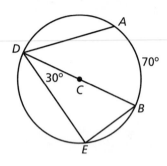

A. Find the measure of $\widehat{BE}$.

$$m\angle BDE = \frac{1}{2}m\widehat{BE}$$

$$30° = \frac{1}{2}m\widehat{BE}$$

$$60° = m\widehat{BE}$$

> **A.** What theorem or postulate can you use to determine $m\widehat{BE}$? What is $m\widehat{BE}$?

B. Find the measure of $\angle ADE$.

$$m\angle ADE = m\angle BDE + m\angle ADB$$

$$m\angle ADE = 30° + 35°$$

$$m\angle ADE = 65°$$

> **B.** Explain how you can determine $m\angle ADE$. What theorem or postulate did you use? What is $m\angle ADE$?

C. What type of triangle is $\triangle DBE$? What theorem or postulate did you use to determine this?

 Turn and Talk In each of the designs below, all of the inscribed angles are congruent. Find the measure of an inscribed angle for each design.

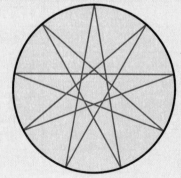

Check Understanding

Identify the chord(s), inscribed angle(s) and central angle(s) in each circle with center C.

1.

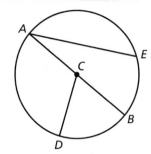

2.

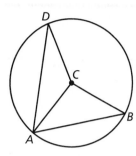

Name a major arc, a minor arc, and a semicircle in each circle with center C.

3.

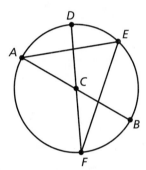

4.

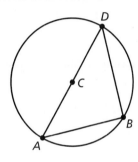

The center of the circle is A, and m∠EAC = 31°. Find each measure.

5. m$\widehat{CE}$

6. m∠BAC

7. m$\widehat{BC}$

8. m∠BDC

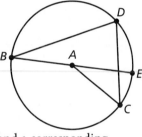

On Your Own

9. **Open Ended** Construct a circle with a central angle and a corresponding inscribed angle. Find the measures of the central angle and the inscribed angle.

10. The minute hand of a circular clock sweeps out an arc as it moves from 2:35 P.M. to 2:55 P.M. What is the measure of the arc?

$\overline{RV}$ and $\overline{QT}$ are diameters of circle P. Tell whether each arc is a *minor arc*, a *major arc*, or a *semicircle* of circle P. Then determine the measure of the arc.

11. $\widehat{QR}$

12. $\widehat{RS}$

13. $\widehat{QST}$

14. $\widehat{QTV}$

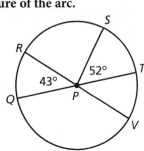

15. (MP) **Reason** In circle K, $m\overset{\frown}{AB} = 58°$, $m\overset{\frown}{BC} = 94°$, and $m\overset{\frown}{CD} = 80°$. Explain why 232° cannot be a possible value for $m\overset{\frown}{DA}$.

16. A. Construct a circle. Then construct an equilateral triangle inside the circle so that its vertices are on the circle.

    B. Explain two different ways to determine the measures of the arcs between the vertices.

17. (MP) **Construct Arguments** Use the regular pentagon $JKLMN$ inscribed in circle G.

    A. What are the measures of $\overset{\frown}{JK}$, $\overset{\frown}{KL}$, $\overset{\frown}{LM}$, $\overset{\frown}{MN}$, and $\overset{\frown}{NJ}$?

    B. Describe the rotational symmetry of pentagon $JKLMN$.

    C. How can you use the measures of arcs created by an inscribed regular polygon to determine the rotations that will map the polygon onto itself?

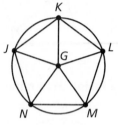

18. Complete the proof for the second case of the Inscribed Angle Theorem to show that $m\angle DBA = \frac{1}{2}m\overset{\frown}{DA}$.

    Given: $\angle DBA$ is inscribed in circle C, with diameter $\overline{BX}$.

    Prove: $m\angle DBA = \frac{1}{2}m\overset{\frown}{DA}$.

    Proof: Let $m\angle ABX = x°$ and $m\angle DBX = y°$.

Draw $\overline{AC}$ and $\overline{DC}$.

$\triangle ABC$ and $\triangle DBC$ are ___?___ triangles because radii of a circle are congruent, so $AC = BC = DC$. Then $m\angle BAC = x°$, and $m\angle BDC = $ ___?___ by the Isosceles Triangle Theorem.

$m\angle ACX = 2x°$ and $m\angle DCX = $ ___?___ by the Exterior Angle Theorem.

So, $m\angle DCA = (2x + 2y)°$ by the Angle Addition Postulate.

$m\overset{\frown}{AX} = 2x°$ and $m\overset{\frown}{DX} = $ ___?___ since the measure of a minor arc equals the measure of its central angle.

$m\overset{\frown}{DA} = $ ___?___ by the Arc Addition Postulate.

$m\angle DBA = $ ___?___ by the Angle Addition Postulate.

Since $m\overset{\frown}{DA} = (2x + 2y)° = 2(x + y)°$ and $m\angle DBA = (x + y)°$, then $m\angle DBA = \frac{1}{2}$ ___?___ .

19. Write a plan for how to prove the third case of the Inscribed Angle Theorem.

    Given: $\angle DBA$ is inscribed in circle C, where C is outside $\angle DBA$.

    Prove: $m\angle DBA = \frac{1}{2}m\overset{\frown}{DA}$.

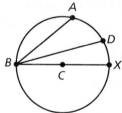

20. A circular garden is divided into three sections with different-colored flowers. The measure of ∠BCD is 21°. The measures of $\overset{\frown}{BC}$ and $\overset{\frown}{DC}$ are equal. What is the measure of each arc?

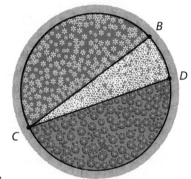

In Problems 21 and 22, use the diagram of the circle.

21. How does the measure of ∠ABD compare to the measure of ∠ACD? Explain your reasoning.

22. Points B and D are the endpoints of a diameter of the circle. How are the measures of $\overset{\frown}{AB}$ and $\overset{\frown}{AD}$ related? Explain.

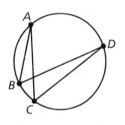

23. A right triangle is inscribed in a circle. How does the hypotenuse relate to the circle? What do you know about the arc formed by the endpoints of the hypotenuse?

24. A carpenter's square is a tool that is used to draw right angles. Suppose you are building a baby toy that has a circle the baby will spin. You need to drill a hole in the center of the circle to attach it to the rest of the toy. Explain how you can use a carpenter's square to find the center of the circle.

Carpenter's square

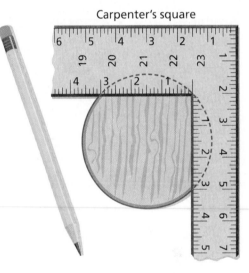

The center of the circle is C, and m∠EAD = 21°. Find each measure.

25. m$\overset{\frown}{ED}$

26. m∠DBE

27. m$\overset{\frown}{EB}$

28. m∠BFE

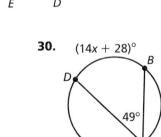

Find the value of x.

29.

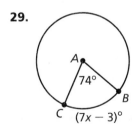

74°

(7x − 3)°

30.

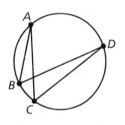

(14x + 28)°

49°

31.

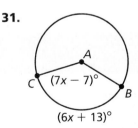

(7x − 7)°

(6x + 13)°

32.

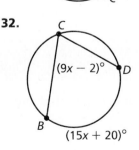

(9x − 2)°

(15x + 20)°

33. An inscribed angle with a diameter as a side has a measure of $x°$. If the ratio of $\overset{\frown}{mCD}$ to $\overset{\frown}{mDB}$ is 1:3, what is $\overset{\frown}{mDB}$? What is the value of x?

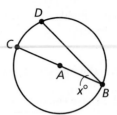

For Problems 34–36, use the two circles which have a common center, point A.

34. List three expressions that are equivalent to m∠DAB.

35. Describe how you could change the location of point F on the circle without changing the value of m∠CFE.

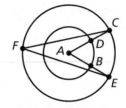

36. Find m∠CFE if $\overset{\frown}{m\ CFE} = 302°$.

37. (MP) **Construct Arguments** Inscribe acute, right, and obtuse triangles in a circle. Make a statement about the location of the center of the circle in relation to the triangle. What term have you learned previously that describes this point?

Spiral Review • Assessment Readiness

38. Find the missing length of the triangle.

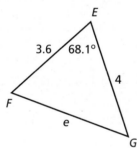

- (A) 4.3
- (C) 18.2
- (B) 5.4
- (D) 29.0

39. What is the measure of ∠A?

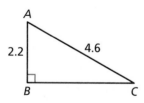

- (A) 0.49°
- (C) 28.6°
- (B) 25.6°
- (D) 61.4°

40. ABCD is a parallelogram. Which of the following pairs of angle measures could be the measures of ∠A and ∠B? Select all that apply.

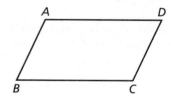

- (A) 32°, 148°
- (D) 60°, 110°
- (B) 63°, 117°
- (E) 90°, 90°
- (C) 45°, 45°
- (F) 100°, 100°

41. Find the value of y.

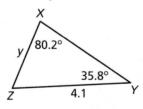

- (A) 2.4
- (C) 4.0
- (B) 3.7
- (D) 19.5

 I'm in a Learning Mindset!

What barriers are there to understanding central angles and inscribed angles?

Angles in Inscribed Quadrilaterals

(I Can) use the properties of angles of quadrilaterals inscribed in a circle to prove theorems and solve problems.

Spark Your Learning

The window is in the shape of a circle. A quadrilateral is inside the window.

The four corners of the quadrilateral touch the circle.

Complete Part A as a whole class. Then complete Parts B–C in small groups.

A. What is a geometric question you can ask about the garden in this photo? What information would you need to know to answer this question?

B. To answer your question, what strategy and tool would you use along with all the information you have? What answer do you get?

C. Does your answer make sense in the context of the situation? How do you know?

> **Turn and Talk** How can you use symmetry of a square to construct this design? Explain your process.

Build Understanding

Investigate Inscribed Quadrilaterals

You have already learned some properties of quadrilaterals. Inscribing them in circles reveals some special ones.

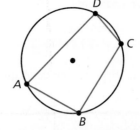

 A. Can all quadrilaterals be inscribed in a circle? Make a conjecture about the kinds of quadrilaterals that can be inscribed in a circle.

B. What relationships do you know about the measures of the angles in a quadrilateral?

C. Draw a circle and select 4 points on it. Label the points *A*, *B*, *C*, and *D*. Draw quadrilateral *ABCD*.

D. Measure the angles of the quadrilateral that you inscribed, then find the sums of the measures its adjacent and opposite pairs of angles.

$m\angle A + m\angle B =$ ___?___ $m\angle B + m\angle C =$ ___?___

$m\angle A + m\angle C =$ ___?___ $m\angle B + m\angle D =$ ___?___

$m\angle A + m\angle D =$ ___?___ $m\angle C + m\angle D =$ ___?___

E. Compare your results with others' in your class. What patterns do you notice about these sums of adjacent and opposite angle pairs?

F. Use what you know about inscribed angles in circles to justify your conjecture. Do you think this pattern is true for all quadrilaterals inscribed in a circle?

G. Does it matter if the center of the circle is inside or outside the inscribed quadrilateral for the relationship between the angles to hold? Explain.

 Turn and Talk Suppose you have a quadrilateral inscribed in a circle with opposite angles that are congruent. What do you know about those angles?

Prove the Inscribed Quadrilateral Theorem

The results of your investigation in the previous task can be summarized in the Inscribed Quadrilateral Theorem.

Inscribed Quadrilateral Theorem

If a quadrilateral is inscribed in a circle, then its opposite angles are supplementary.

If *A*, *B*, *C*, and *D* lie on circle *P*, then $m\angle A + m\angle C = 180°$ and $m\angle B + m\angle D = 180°$.

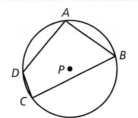

The converse of the Inscribed Quadrilateral Theorem is also true.

Converse of the Inscribed Quadrilateral Theorem

If the opposite angles of a quadrilateral are supplementary, then the quadrilateral can be inscribed in a circle.

If m∠A + m∠C = 180° and m∠B + m∠D = 180°, then A, B, C, and D lie on circle P.

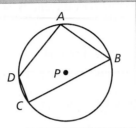

2 Prove the Inscribed Quadrilateral Theorem.

Given: Quadrilateral ABCD is inscribed in circle P.

Prove: ∠A and ∠C are supplementary.
∠B and ∠D are supplementary.

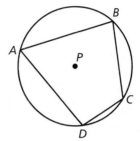

A. What is the sum of the measures of two arcs that together form a complete circle? What is the sum of the measures of the inscribed angles that form these two arcs?

Statements	Reasons
1. Quadrilateral ABCD is inscribed in circle P.	1. Given
2. m$\widehat{BCD}$ + m$\widehat{BAD}$ = 360°	2. Arc Addition Postulate and definition of a circle
3. m$\widehat{BCD}$ = 2m∠A m$\widehat{BAD}$ = 2m∠C	3. Inscribed Angle Theorem
4. 2m∠A + 2m∠C = 360°	4. Substitution Property of Equality
5. 2(m∠A + m∠C) = 360°	5. Distributive Property
6. m∠A + m∠C = 180°	6. Division Property of Equality
7. ∠A and ∠C are supplementary.	7. Definition of supplementary angles

B. The proof shows that ∠A and ∠C are supplementary. Use similar reasoning to show that ∠B and ∠D are supplementary.

C. Explain how the Inscribed Quadrilateral Theorem can be used to verify the Quadrilateral Sum Theorem presented previously for quadrilaterals that are inscribed in circles. This theorem states that the sum of the measures of the interior angles of a quadrilateral is 360°.

 Turn and Talk Is it possible for a parallelogram to be inscribed in a circle? Explain your reasoning.

Prove the Congruent Corresponding Chords Theorem

Two circles are **congruent circles** if they have the same radius. Two arcs are **congruent arcs** if they have the same measure and they are arcs of the same circle or of congruent circles.

Just as corresponding parts of congruent triangles are congruent, you can show that corresponding parts of congruent circles are also congruent.

Congruent Corresponding Chords Theorem

Two minor arcs in the same circle or in congruent circles are congruent if and only if their corresponding chords are congruent.

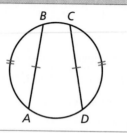

3 **A.** The Congruent Corresponding Chords Theorem is a biconditional statement. Rewrite the theorem as a conditional statement and its converse.

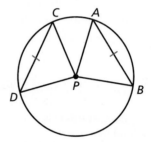

B. Which conditional statement from Part A is proven in the following proof?

Given: $\overline{AB} \cong \overline{CD}$, P is the center of the circle
Prove: $\overparen{AB} \cong \overparen{CD}$

Statements	Reasons
1. $\overline{AB} \cong \overline{CD}$	**1.** Given
2. Draw $\overline{AP}, \overline{BP}, \overline{CP}, \overline{DP}$	**2.** Through any two points exists one line.
3. $\overline{AP} \cong \overline{BP} \cong \overline{CP} \cong \overline{DP}$	**3.** Radii in the same circle are congruent.
4. $\triangle APB \cong \triangle CPD$	**4.** SSS Triangle Congruence Theorem
5. $\angle APB \cong \angle CPD$	**5.** Corresponding parts of congruent figures are congruent.
6. $m\angle APB = m\angle CPD$	**6.** Definition of congruent angles
7. $m\overparen{AB} = m\angle APB$ $m\overparen{CD} = m\angle CPD$	**7.** Definition of minor arc
8. $m\overparen{AB} = m\overparen{CD}$	**8.** Substitution Property of Equality
9. $\overparen{AB} \cong \overparen{CD}$	**9.** Definition of congruent arcs

C. Why can you state that the Congruent Corresponding Chords Theorem is true in congruent circles as well as in the same circle?

 Turn and Talk What statement can you make about the central angles formed by corresponding congruent chords in a circle?

478

Step It Out

Apply the Inscribed Quadrilateral Theorem

You can use the Inscribed Quadrilateral Theorem to find missing angle measures.

4 ▶ Find the measure of each angle in quadrilateral $WXYZ$.

Find the value of a.

$$m\angle X + m\angle Z = 180°$$
$$(5a + 7)° + (7a + 17)° = 180°$$
$$12a + 24 = 180$$
$$12a = 156$$
$$a = 13$$

> **A.** Why is this a true statement?

Substitute the value of a into the expression for each angle measure.

$$m\angle W = (8a - 1)° = (8(13) - 1)° = 103°$$
$$m\angle X = (5a + 7)° = (5(13) + 7)° = 72°$$
$$m\angle Z = (7a + 17)° = (7(13) + 17)° = 108°$$
$$m\angle Y = \underline{\quad ? \quad}$$

> **B.** How can you determine $m\angle Y$ even though you are not given an expression for this measure? What is $m\angle Y$?

Construct an Inscribed Square

5 ▶ Randall is making a tile design. He wants to inscribe a square in a circle as part of his pattern. How can he construct an inscribed square?

To construct a square, start by using a compass to draw a circle and label the center. Use a straightedge to draw a diameter of the circle. Then construct the perpendicular bisector of the diameter. Connect the endpoints of the two diameters to form the square.

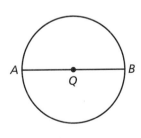
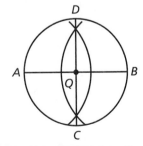
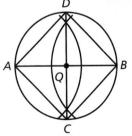

A. For $ADBC$ to be a parallelogram, its diagonals must bisect each other. Explain why $\overline{AB}$ bisects $\overline{CD}$.

B. For parallelogram $ADBC$ to be a square, its diagonals must be congruent and perpendicular. How do you know that $ADBC$ is a square?

 Turn and Talk How do you know that $ADBC$ is a rhombus?

Check Understanding

1. In quadrilateral $ABCD$, m$\angle A = 78°$, and m$\angle B = 116°$. What do the measures of $\angle C$ and $\angle D$ need to be in order for $ABCD$ to be able to be inscribed in a circle?

2. Circles A and B are congruent. List two pairs of congruent arcs.

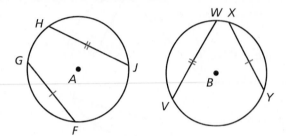

Find the value of x.

3.

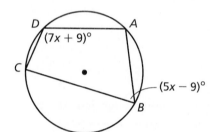

4.

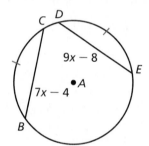

On Your Own

Find the interior angle measures of each inscribed quadrilateral.

5.

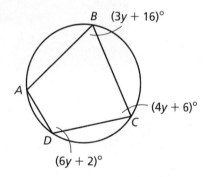

6.

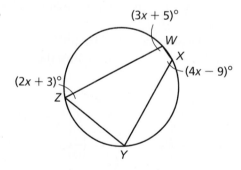

7.

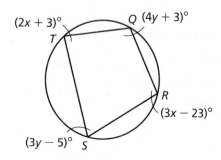

8.

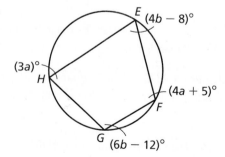

9. **(MP)** **Critique Reasoning** Marvin says it is not possible to inscribe a kite in a circle because each pair of opposite angles must be supplementary. Denise disagrees with Marvin. Explain why Denise is correct.

10. **(MP)** **Reason** What must be true about a rhombus that is inscribed in a circle? Explain your reasoning.

11. Donnie is programming a robot to walk in a quadrilateral-shaped path inscribed within a circular ring. He has the robot start at P toward Q, turn left $75°$ at Q, and then turn left $100°$ at R. How many degrees must the robot turn left at S to make it back to the starting point P?

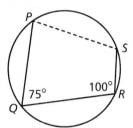

12. $GHJK$ is a quadrilateral inscribed in a circle. Angles H and K are opposite angles that are congruent. Is $\overline{GJ}$ a diameter of the circle? Explain your reasoning.

13. A company has a logo that contains a square inscribed in a circle. On the sign on the company's building, the circle has a diameter of 12 feet. What is the side length of the square?

14. One part of the Congruent Corresponding Chords Theorem was proven in Task 3. Use the statements below to prove the second part of the Congruent Corresponding Chords Theorem.

Given: $\overarc{AB} \cong \overarc{CD}$, P is the center of the circle.

Prove: $\overline{AB} \cong \overline{CD}$

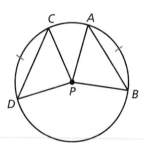

Find the measure of each chord or arc.

15. $\overline{DE}$

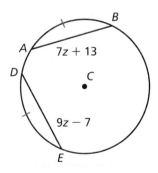

16. $\overarc{AB}$

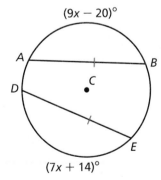

In Problems 17 and 18, tell whether the quadrilateral can be inscribed in a circle. If so, describe a method for doing so using a compass and a straightedge. If not, explain why not.

17. a parallelogram that is not a rectangle

18. a kite with two right angles

19. Chibenashi is making a dream catcher with his little brother. He shows him how to attach two pieces of string that are the same length to the ring. If the two pieces of string share one endpoint and the arc formed by the endpoints of one chord has the measure shown, what is the measure of the angle formed by the pieces of string?

140°

20. Use a compass to draw a circle. Then mark a point on the circle. Inscribe a square in the circle so that one of its vertices is the point marked on the circle. Explain your method.

21. (Open Middle™) What is the greatest possible area for a quadrilateral inscribed inside a circle with a circumference of 16π units?

Spiral Review • Assessment Readiness

22. Find the value of a.

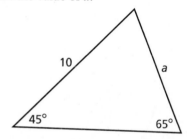

10

a

45°

65°

(A) 7.80   (C) 12.82

(B) 14.22   (D) 10.33

23. Find the value of c.

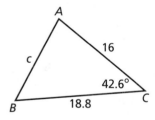

A

16

c

42.6°

B   18.8   C

(A) 12.9   (C) 16.6

(B) 14.2   (D) 20.2

24. Use the circle graph to find the measure of $\overset{\frown}{DEF}$ to the nearest degree.

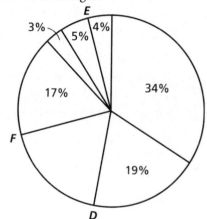

E

3%   5%   4%

17%   34%

F

19%

D

(A) 270°   (C) 295°

(B) 310°   (D) 328°

I'm in a Learning Mindset!

What strategies did I use to overcome barriers when solving problems with angles in inscribed quadrilaterals?

Tangents and Circumscribed Angles

(I Can) prove theorems about tangents to a circle and use them to solve mathematical and real-world problems.

Spark Your Learning

A communications satellite is in orbit around Earth.

Complete Part A as a whole class. Then complete Parts B–D in small groups.

  A. What is a mathematical question you can ask about this situation? What information would you need to know to answer your question?

  B. What quantities are you given in this situation? What unit of measurement is used for each quantity?

  C. To answer your question, what strategy and tool would you use along with all the information you have? What answer do you get?

  D. Does your answer make sense in the context of the situation? How do you know?

 Turn and Talk How would your answer change if the distance from the surface of Earth to the satellite increased by 10,000 miles?

Build Understanding

Investigate the Tangent-Radius Theorem

A **tangent of a circle** is a line that is in the same plane as the circle and intersects the circle in exactly one point. The point where the tangent and the circle intersect is called the **point of tangency**. In circle C, point P is the point of tangency.

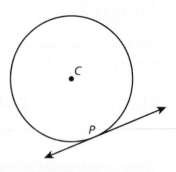

The **exterior of a circle** is the set of all points outside a circle. The **interior of a circle** is the set of all points inside a circle. All points on a line tangent to a circle other than the point of tangency are in the exterior of the circle.

1 Use a geometric drawing tool to draw a circle and a point on the circle. Then draw a line tangent to the circle at the point. Place an additional point on the tangent line.

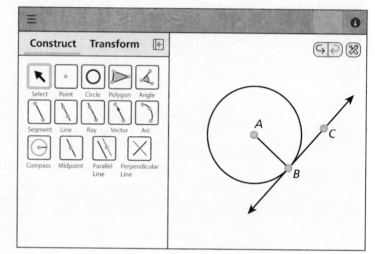

   A. What is the measure of $\angle ABC$?

   B. Change the location of point B on the circle to move the tangent line. What happens to the measure of $\angle ABC$ when you change the location of the point of tangency?

   C. Make a conjecture about the relationship between a tangent line and the radius at the point of tangency.

Prove the Tangent-Radius Theorem

The Tangent-Radius Theorem and its converse are both true.

2 An indirect proof is used to prove the Tangent-Radius Theorem. Recall that in an indirect proof, you begin by assuming that the conclusion is false. Then you show that this assumption leads to a contradiction.

   Given: Line m is tangent to circle C at point P.
   Prove: $\overline{CP} \perp m$

   A. What assumption should be made to start an indirect proof?

   B. What conclusion follows from this assumption?

   Proof:
   If $\overline{CP}$ is not perpendicular to line m, then there must be a point Q on line m such that $\overline{CQ} \perp m$.

   If $\overline{CQ}$ is perpendicular to m, then $\overline{CP}$ is the hypotenuse for $\triangle CPQ$. So, $CQ < CP$.

Since line *m* is a tangent line, it intersects circle *C* at the point of tangency *P*, and all other points of line *m* are in the exterior of the circle. This means point *Q* is in the exterior of the circle.

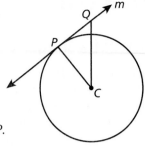

You can conclude that *CP* < *CQ* because $\overline{CP}$ is a radius of circle *C*.

CP < *CQ* contradicts *CQ* < *CP*. Thus, $\overline{CP} \perp m$.

C. Explain how exterior point *Q* leads to a contradiction of *CQ* < *CP*.

D. What does this contradiction mean?

 Turn and Talk How does an indirect proof demonstrate that an assertion must be true?

Prove the Circumscribed Angle Theorem

A **circumscribed angle** is an angle formed by two rays from a common endpoint that are tangent to a circle.

Circumscribed Angle Theorem
A circumscribed angle of a circle and its associated central angle are supplementary.

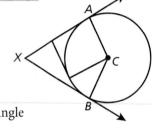

3 Prove the Circumscribed Angle Theorem.

Given: ∠*AXB* is a circumscribed angle of circle *C*.

Prove: ∠*AXB* and ∠*ACB* are supplementary.

A. How are the Circumscribed Angle Theorem and the Inscribed Angle Theorem alike? How are the theorems different?

Statements	Reasons
1. $\overline{XA}$ and $\overline{XB}$ are tangents to circle *C* at points *A* and *B*.	1. Definition of circumscribed angle
2. ∠*CAX* and ∠*CBX* are right angles.	2. Tangent-Radius Theorem
3. m∠*AXB* + m∠*CAX* + m∠*ACB* + m∠*CBX* = 360°	3. Sum of measures of interior angles of a quadrilateral is 360°.
4. m∠*AXB* + 90° + m∠*ACB* + 90° = 360°	4. Substitution Property of Equality
5. m∠*AXB* + m∠*ACB* = 180°	5. Subtraction Property of Equality
6. ∠*AXB* and ∠*ACB* are supplementary.	6. Definition of supplementary angles

B. Is it possible for *ACBX* to be a parallelogram? If so, what type?

 Turn and Talk Suppose that points *A* and *B* are endpoints of a diameter. Do the lines tangent to the circle at *A* and *B* form a circumscribed angle? How do you know?

Step It Out

Construct a Tangent to a Circle

4▶ Use a compass and a straightedge to construct tangents to a circle.

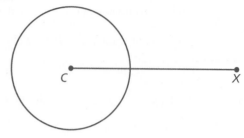

Step 1 Use a compass to draw a circle and label its center *C*. Mark a point *X* exterior to the circle, and use a straightedge to draw $\overline{CX}$.

Step 2 Bisect $\overline{CX}$ to find its midpoint. Label the midpoint *M*. Then use a compass to construct a circle centered at the point *M* that contains point *C*.

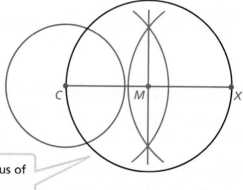

> **A.** What is a radius of circle *M*?

Step 3 From point *X*, use a straightedge to draw the tangents.

> **B.** What are the points of tangency? How are the points of tangency determined?

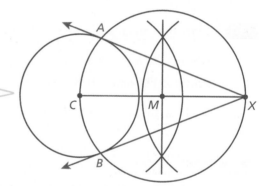

C. Consider the inscribed angle in circle *M* with vertex *A*. What type of angle is ∠*CAX*? How do you know?

D. How do you know that $\overrightarrow{XA}$ and $\overrightarrow{XB}$ are tangents to circle *C*?

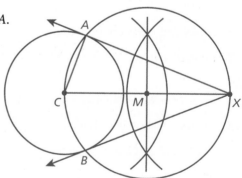

 Turn and Talk Does point *M* have to be in the exterior of circle *C* for $\overrightarrow{XA}$ and $\overrightarrow{XB}$ to be tangent lines? Explain your reasoning.

Prove the Two-Tangent Theorem

You can use the Tangent-Radius Theorem to prove the Two-Tangent Theorem.

> **Two-Tangent Theorem**
>
> If two segments from the same exterior point are tangent to a circle, then the segments are congruent.
>
> If $\overline{XA}$ and $\overline{XB}$ are tangents, then $\overline{XA} \cong \overline{XB}$.

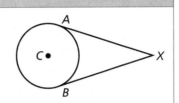

5 ▸ Prove the Two-Tangent Theorem.

Given: $\overline{XA}$ and $\overline{XB}$ are tangent to circle C.

Prove: $\overline{XA} \cong \overline{XB}$

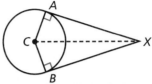

Statements	Reasons
1. $\overline{XA}$ and $\overline{XB}$ are tangent to circle C.	1. Given
2. $\overline{XA} \perp \overline{CA}$; $\overline{XB} \perp \overline{CB}$	2. ___?___
3. $\angle A$ and $\angle B$ are right angles.	3. Definition of perpendicular lines
4. $\triangle XAC$ and $\triangle XBC$ are right triangles.	4. Definition of a right triangle
5. $\overline{CA} \cong \overline{CB}$	5. ___?___
6. $\overline{CX} \cong \overline{CX}$	6. Reflexive Property of Congruence
7. $\triangle XAC \cong \triangle XBC$	7. ___?___
8. $\overline{XA} \cong \overline{XB}$	8. Corresponding parts of congruent figures are congruent.

A. What theorem justifies $\overline{XA} \perp \overline{CA}$ and $\overline{XB} \perp \overline{CB}$?

B. Why is $\overline{CA} \cong \overline{CB}$?

C. What theorem justifies $\triangle XAC \cong \triangle XBC$?

Apply the Two-Tangent Theorem

6 ▸ A bicycle is hung from the ceiling of an apartment using two wheel clips. One clip is attached to the ceiling, and the other is attached to the wall. The ceiling is tangent to the wheel at point J. The wall is tangent to the wheel at point L. The ceiling and the wall meet at point K. What are KJ and KL?

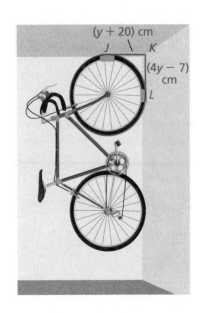

Find the value of y.

$KJ = KL$

$y + 20 = 4y - 7$

$27 = 3y$

$9 = y$

A. How do you know that $KJ = KL$?

Substitute 9 for y in the expression y + 20.

$KJ = y + 20$

$= 9 + 20$

$= 29$ cm

B. How can you use this information to find KL? What is KL?

Check Understanding

1. In the figure, $\overline{BC}$ is tangent to circle A at point B. What is m$\angle ACB$? Explain your reasoning.

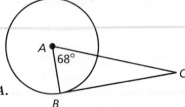

In each circle, A and B are points of tangency. Find the measure of $\angle BCA$.

2.

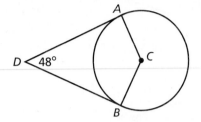

3.

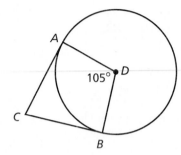

$\overline{AC}$ and $\overline{BC}$ are tangent to circle D. Find the value of x.

4.

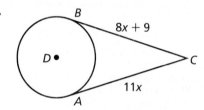

5.

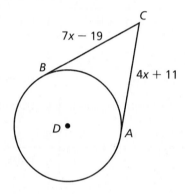

On Your Own

6. **(MP) Use Tools** Use a compass and a straightedge to create a diagram that demonstrates the Tangent-Radius Theorem.

7. **(MP) Reason** Prove the Converse of the Tangent-Radius Theorem.

   Given: Line t is in the plane of circle C, A is a point of circle C, and $\overline{CA} \perp t$.

   Prove: t is tangent to circle C at point A.

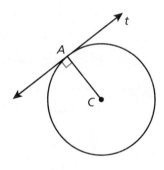

In circle F, G and J are points of tangency. Determine whether each statement in Problems 8–12 is *always* or *sometimes* true. Explain your reasoning.

8. $\angle GFJ$ and $\angle GHJ$ are supplementary.

9. $\angle HJF$ and $\angle GHJ$ are supplementary.

10. $\angle GHJ \cong \angle GFJ$

11. $\angle HGF \cong \angle HJF$

12. $\angle FGH \cong \angle GHJ$

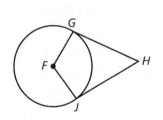

13. (MP) **Use Tools** A park in a town has a statue and a circular fountain. The town has built two sidewalks from the statue to the fountain that pass by the edges of the fountain. Use a compass and a straightedge to create a model of this situation.

14. Samantha is designing a logo with a circle and a circumscribed angle. The measure of the central angle is twice the measure of the circumscribed angle. What is the measure of each angle?

In each circle, *A* and *B* are points of tangency. Find the measures of the inscribed angle and the circumscribed angle.

15.

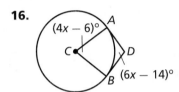

16.

17. Health and Fitness Rachel is standing at the center of a circle on a basketball court, and she has the ball. Derek and Ayush are standing on the circle. A line connecting Derek and Lia is tangent to the circle, and a line connecting Ayush and Lia is tangent to the circle. The ball can be passed along the blue path or the red path. Does one path cover more distance than the other? Explain your reasoning.

18. Given a circle with a diameter $\overline{CD}$, is it possible to construct tangents to points *C* and *D* from an external point *P*? If so, make a construction. If not, explain why it is not possible.

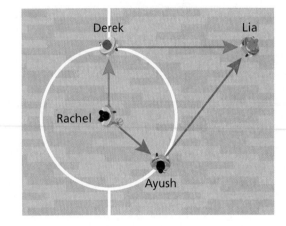

The segments in each figure are tangent to the circle at the points shown. Find each length.

19.

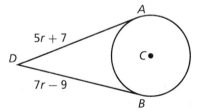

20.

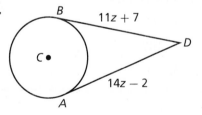

21.

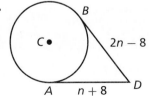

22.

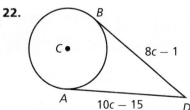

23. In circle A, m$\angle DCE = 48°$. Find m$\overset{\frown}{DBE}$.

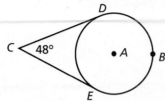

24. 🅼🅿 **Critique Reasoning** Given $CD = 41$, Rebecca says that $AC = 40$. Linda says that there is not enough information given to find AC. Who is correct? Explain your reasoning.

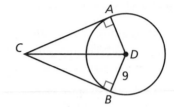

25. In the life preserver hanging from a rope, $\overline{BC}$ is tangent to circle A at B, $\overline{DC}$ is tangent to circle A at D, and m$\angle C = 58°$. Use the figure to find m$\angle EAH$ and m$\angle BAE$.

26. Suppose two tangents are drawn from a point Q to intersect a circle with center C at points P and R. Suppose a point T is on the major arc $\overset{\frown}{PSR}$. How are the measures of the circumscribed $\angle PQR$ and the inscribed $\angle PTR$ related? What if T is on the minor arc $\overset{\frown}{PR}$ instead?

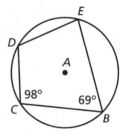

Spiral Review • Assessment Readiness

27. Find the value of a.

Ⓐ 3.8
Ⓑ 14.7
Ⓒ 40.6
Ⓓ 1648

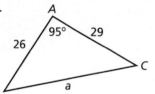

28. Find m$\angle D$.

Ⓐ 69°
Ⓑ 82°
Ⓒ 98°
Ⓓ 111°

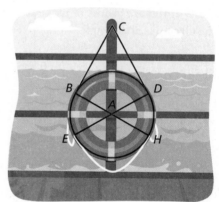

29. Match each item with its measurement.

Circle part	Measurement
A. $\angle CDB$	**1.** 50°
B. $\overset{\frown}{CDB}$	**2.** 100°
C. $\overset{\frown}{BC}$	**3.** 260°

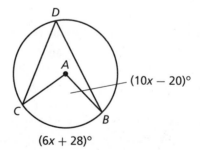

 I'm in a Learning Mindset!

What barriers are there to finding tangents and circumscribed angles?

Circles on the Coordinate Plane

(I Can) derive and write the equation of a circle with radius *r* and center (*h, k*).

Spark Your Learning

A traffic circle is an intersection where traffic moves in one direction around a central circular island.

Complete Part A as a whole class. Then complete Parts B–D in small groups.

A. What is a mathematical question you can ask about this situation?
   What information would you need to know to answer your question?

B. What variable(s) are involved in this situation? What unit of measurement
   would you use for each variable?

C. To answer your question, what strategy and tool would you use along with
   all the information you have? What answer do you get?

D. Does your answer make sense in the context of the situation? How do
   you know?

Turn and Talk A second traffic circle is constructed at a different location.
The diameter of this traffic circle is 250 feet. Compare an equation that would
describe this traffic circle to the equation that describes the original circle.

Build Understanding

Derive the Equation of a Circle

In the previous lessons, you have worked with circles. In this lesson, you will investigate circles on the coordinate plane and learn how to write an equation of a circle. Recall that a circle is the set of all points on the coordinate plane that are a fixed distance from the center (h, k).

1 ▶ Consider the circle on the coordinate plane that has its center at $C(h, k)$ and a radius r. Let P be any point on the circle with coordinates (x, y).

Draw a horizontal line through C and a vertical line through P and label their intersection A, as shown.

> **A.** If P can be any point on the circle, what does that mean about the maximum and minimum distances between C and A?

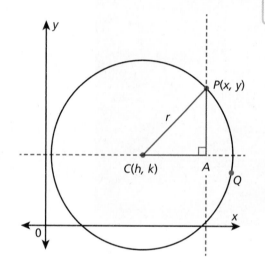

B. What are the coordinates of point A? Explain how you found them.

Right triangle $\triangle PCA$ has a hypotenuse of length r.

Its leg $\overline{CA}$ has length $|x - h|$.

Its leg $\overline{PA}$ has length $|y - k|$.

> **C.** Why are absolute values needed to express the lengths of $\overline{CA}$ and $\overline{PA}$?

Now apply the Pythagorean Theorem to write a relationship between the side lengths of $\triangle PCA$ and its hypotenuse.

$$(x - h)^2 + (y - k)^2 = r^2$$

> **D.** Why are absolute values now no longer needed for the lengths of $\overline{CA}$ and $\overline{PA}$?

This is the equation for a circle with center $C(h, k)$ and radius r.

Take the square root of both sides of this equation.

$$r = \sqrt{(x - h)^2 + (y - k)^2}$$

> **E.** Are these relationships true for values of x that are less than h, and for values of y that are less than k? Explain your reasoning.

This distance formula expresses the distance r between the center of the circle $C(h, k)$ and a point on its circumference $P(x, y)$.

Q is another point on the circle. Through it, draw a vertical line. Where that intersects the horizontal line through C, label the point of intersection B.

F. Compare and contrast this new $\triangle QCB$ with $\triangle PCA$. What will always be true about any triangle constructed in this way, provided that the point chosen on the circle does not lie directly right, left, above, or below the circle's center?

> **Turn and Talk** Suppose a circle has its center C at the origin. What is the equation of the circle in this case?

Step It Out

Write an Equation of a Circle

You can write the equation of any circle on a coordinate plane if you know its radius and the coordinates of its center.

Equation of a Circle
The equation of a circle with center (h, k) and radius r is $(x - h)^2 + (y - k)^2 = r^2$.

2 ▸ Fairy rings are growths that naturally take the shape of a circle. They begin when a fungal spore lands in a spot and begins to grow underground evenly in all directions, creating a circular organism. Mushroom caps then develop at the edges of the organism.

The center of a fairy ring is located in a field 7 feet east and 5 feet north from a stone trail marker. The ring has a radius of 3 feet.

Write an equation that represents the fairy ring on a coordinate plane with respect to the stone trail marker.

Identify the center of the circle and the radius.

The center of the circle is (7, 5), and the radius is 3 feet, as shown in the graph.

> **A.** Explain how the center of the circle was determined.

> **B.** What does the origin of the graph represent?

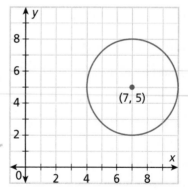

Write an equation for the circle.

Substitute the values for the center of the circle and radius into $(x - h)^2 + (y - k)^2 = r^2$.

$$(x - 7)^2 + (y - 5)^2 = 3^2 = 9$$

C. Another fairy ring is the same size but is located 4 feet west and 5 feet south of the stone trail marker. What is an equation that represents this fairy ring?

 Turn and Talk What does the transformation $(x, y) \rightarrow (x - h, y - k)$ represent in this context?

Find the Center and Radius of a Circle

The equation of a circle can also take the form $x^2 + ax + y^2 + by = c$. You can rewrite such an equation so that is in the form $(x - h)^2 + (y - k)^2 = r^2$ by completing the square. Then you can identify the center and radius of the circle.

3 Find the center and radius of the circle with equation $x^2 - 4x + y^2 + 12y = -24$. Then graph the circle.

Rewrite the equation in the form $(x - h)^2 + (y - k)^2 = r^2$ by completing the square twice.

$$x^2 - 4x + y^2 + 12y = -24 \qquad \text{Original equation}$$

$$x^2 - 4x + (\ )^2 + y^2 + 12y + (\ )^2 = -24 + (\ )^2 + (\ )^2 \qquad \text{Add spaces.}$$

$$x^2 - 4x + \left(\frac{-4}{2}\right)^2 + y^2 + 12y + \left(\frac{12}{2}\right)^2 = -24 + \left(\frac{-4}{2}\right)^2 + \left(\frac{12}{2}\right)^2$$

A. What expressions were added to both sides of the equation? Why?

$$x^2 - 4x + 4 + y^2 + 12y + 36 = -24 + 4 + 36 \qquad \text{Simplify.}$$

$$(x - 2)^2 + (y + 6)^2 = 16 \qquad \text{Factor.}$$

Identify h, k, and r.

$$(x - 2)^2 + (y + 6)^2 = 16$$

B. What is the benefit of rewriting the second squared term in this equation?

$$(x - 2)^2 + [y - (-6)]^2 = 16$$

C. How can you check that $(x - 2)^2 + (y + 6)^2 = 16$ is equivalent to $x^2 - 4x + y^2 + 12y = -24$?

So, $h = 2$, $k = -6$, and $r = 4$.

The center of the circle is $(2, -6)$, and the radius is 4.

Graph the circle.

Locate the center of the circle on the coordinate plane. Place the point of your compass at the center, open the compass to the radius, and then draw the circle.

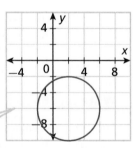

D. It is much easier to visualize this graph after completing the squares of the original equation to rewrite it as the equation of a circle. But, either equation can give you some information. For the equation in the form $x^2 + ax + y^2 + by = c$, how do the coefficients a and b and the constant c relate to the coordinates (h, k) of the center of the circle?

 Turn and Talk Change the sign of the constant on the right side of the original equation so that it becomes $x^2 - 4x + y^2 + 12y = 24$. Predict how this will affect the graph. Then graph it, and discuss your predictions and your results.

Write a Coordinate Proof

You can use a coordinate proof to show whether or not a given point lies on a given circle on the coordinate plane.

4 Does $\left(\sqrt{5}, 2\right)$ lie on a circle that is centered at the origin and contains the point $(0, -3)$?

Graph the circle.

Plot points at the origin and $(0, -3)$ to help you draw the circle.

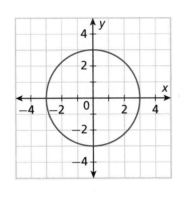

> **A.** Estimate the location of $\left(\sqrt{5}, 2\right)$ on the graph. Can you tell that it lies on the circle by inspection?

Determine the radius.

The radius of the circle is 3.

> **B.** How do you know that the radius is 3?

Write an equation for the circle.

Use the radius and the coordinates of the center to write the equation of the circle.

$$(x - h)^2 + (y - k)^2 = r^2$$

> **C.** How do you determine the values for h and k?

$$(x - 0)^2 + (y - 0)^2 = 3^2$$

$$x^2 + y^2 = 9$$

Substitute the given point in the equation.

Use the equation of the circle to check if the point $\left(\sqrt{5}, 2\right)$ lies on the circle.

$$x^2 + y^2 = 9$$

$$\left(\sqrt{5}\right)^2 + (2)^2 \stackrel{?}{=} 9$$

$$5 + 4 \stackrel{?}{=} 9$$

$$9 \stackrel{?}{=} 9$$

> **D.** Does $\left(\sqrt{5}, 2\right)$ lie on the circle? Explain.

 Turn and Talk Find another point that lies on the circle. Explain how you know that the point lies on the circle.

Check Understanding

1. What are the coordinates of the center of the circle represented by the equation $x^2 + y^2 = 25$?

Write the equation of the circle with the given center and radius.

2. center: $(-2, 7)$; radius: 2

3. center: $(-1, -4)$; radius: 8

Find the center and radius of the circle with the given equation.

4. $x^2 - 14x + y^2 - 2y + 41 = 0$

5. $x^2 - 8x + y^2 + 10y = 59$

6. Prove or disprove that the point $(7, \sqrt{29})$ lies on the circle that is centered at the origin and passes through the point $(0, -6)$.

7. Prove or disprove that the point $(\sqrt{21}, 2)$ lies on the circle that is centered at the origin and passes through the point $(5, 0)$.

On Your Own

8. **(MP) Reason** Describe how to use the Pythagorean Theorem to write the equation for a circle that is centered at $(2, -3)$ and passes through $(5, 1)$. What is the equation of the circle?

Write the equation of the circle with the given center and radius.

9. center: $(5, -1)$; radius: 1

10. center: $(6, 4)$; radius: 4

11. center: $(-2, -7)$; radius: $\sqrt{11}$

12. center: $(-3, 5)$; radius: $\sqrt{29}$

13. center: $(0, -4)$; radius: 9

14. center: $(7, 0)$; radius: $\sqrt{15}$

15. Chloe overlaid a coordinate plane on a photograph of a crop circle. The location of the center of the crop circle is at $(11, -4)$, and the radius of the circle is 3 units. Write an equation for a circle that represents the crop circle.

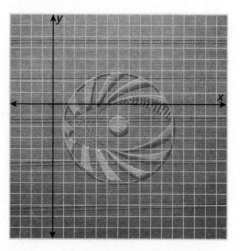

©Last Refuge/robertharding/Alamy

Determine whether each statement is true or false. If false, explain why.

16. The circle $(x - 4)^2 + (y + 1)^2 = 17$ has a radius of 17.

17. The center of the circle $(x + 5)^2 + (y - 2)^2 = 25$ lies in the second quadrant.

18. The equation of a circle centered at $(-3, 7)$ with a diameter of 8 is $(x + 3)^2 + (y - 7)^2 = 64$.

19. The circle $(x + 1)^2 + (y - 8)^2 = 25$ passes through the point $(-1, 3)$.

20. **Open Ended** Write an equation for your own circle. Identify the center and radius of your circle.

Write the equation of each circle.

21.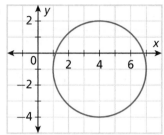

22.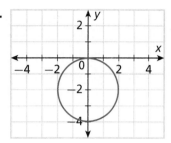

23.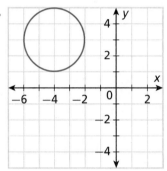

24.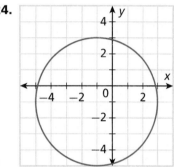

Find the center and radius of the circle with the given equation.

25. $x^2 + 6x + y^2 - 18y + 86 = 0$

26. $x^2 - 14x + y^2 - 2y = -25$

27. $x^2 + 8x + y^2 + 10y + 8 = 0$

28. $x^2 - 2x + y^2 + 2y - 20 = 0$

29. $x^2 + y^2 + 10y = -18$

30. $x^2 - 12x + y^2 = 5$

31. **STEM** An engineer is designing a Ferris wheel that has a diameter of 100 feet.

   A. If the center of the Ferris wheel is at the origin of a coordinate plane, what is the equation of the Ferris wheel?

   B. Is it possible for one of the cars of the Ferris wheel to be attached to the wheel at the point $(14, 48)$? Explain your reasoning.

Prove or disprove that the given point lies on the circle centered at the origin with a radius of 4.

32. $(-4, 0)$ 33. $(-2, -3)$ 34. $\left(\sqrt{15}, 1\right)$ 35. $\left(-3, -\sqrt{7}\right)$

36. (MP) **Critique Reasoning** Eve says that the point $\left(\sqrt{3}, \sqrt{7}\right)$ lies on a circle that is centered at the origin and passes through the point $(-4, 0)$. Brandy says that the point does not lie on the circle. Who is correct? Explain your reasoning.

37. Prove or disprove that the point $\left(-3\sqrt{3}, 3\right)$ lies on the circle that is centered at the origin and passes through the point $(0, -6)$.

38. (Open Middle™) Using the digits 1 to 9, at most one time each, fill in the boxes to create the equation of a circle and a point on the circle.

$$\left(x - \boxed{}\right)^2 + \left(y - \boxed{}\right)^2 = \boxed{}^2 \text{ with a point on the circle } \left(\boxed{}, \boxed{}\right)$$

Spiral Review • Assessment Readiness

39. Find m∠B.

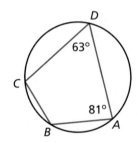

Ⓐ 63° Ⓒ 99°

Ⓑ 81° Ⓓ 117°

40. Find *XZ*.

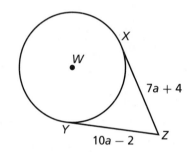

Ⓐ 2 Ⓒ 18

Ⓑ 14 Ⓓ 20

41. Classify each arc of circle C as a major arc, a minor arc, or a semicircle.

Circle part	Major arc	Minor arc	Semicircle
A. $\overset{\frown}{ADB}$	?	?	?
B. $\overset{\frown}{AE}$	?	?	?
C. $\overset{\frown}{ABE}$	?	?	?
D. $\overset{\frown}{AD}$	?	?	?

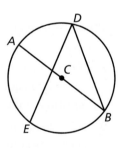

 I'm in a Learning Mindset!

What strategy did you use to overcome barriers to understanding a circle on a coordinate plane?

Central Angles and Inscribed Angles

Two inscribed angles, $\angle CDB$ and $\angle CEB$, of Circle A are shown with the associated arc, $\overset{\frown}{BC}$.

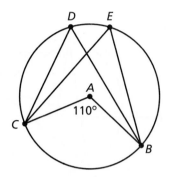

The central angle $\angle CAB$ has the same angle measure as its associated arc.

Each inscribed angle is equal to half the measure of the central angle.

$$m\angle CDB = m\angle CEB$$

$$= \frac{m\angle CAB}{2}$$

$$= \frac{110°}{2}$$

$$= 55°$$

Inscribed Quadrilaterals

A quadrilateral, $WXYZ$, is inscribed in Circle O.

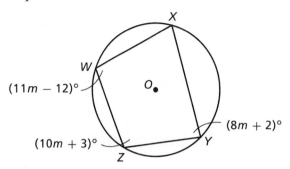

$\angle W$ and $\angle Y$ are supplementary by the Inscribed Quadrilateral Theorem.

$$m\angle W + m\angle Y = 180°$$

$$11m - 12 + 8m + 2 = 180$$

$$19m - 10 = 180$$

$$19m = 190$$

$$m = 10$$

$$m\angle W = \left(11(10) - 12\right)^\circ = \left(110 - 12\right)^\circ = 98°$$

$$m\angle Y = \left(8(10) + 2\right)^\circ = \left(80 + 2\right)^\circ = 82°$$

$$m\angle Z = \left(10(10) + 3\right)^\circ = \left(100 + 3\right)^\circ = 103°$$

$$m\angle X = 180° - 103° = 77°$$

Tangents

Circle O has a radius of 3. Tangent segments are drawn from A to Circle O.

The two tangent segments are congruent.

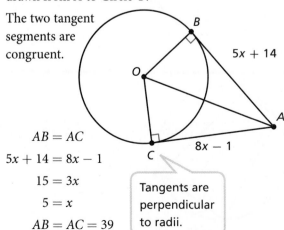

$$AB = AC$$

$$5x + 14 = 8x - 1$$

$$15 = 3x$$

$$5 = x$$

$$AB = AC = 39$$

Tangents are perpendicular to radii.

Equation of a Circle

Given a point on the circle $B\,(x, y)$, the horizontal distance to the center is $\left(x - (-1)\right) = x + 1$ while the vertical distance is $(y - 2)$.

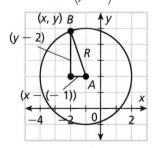

By the Pythagorean Theorem, the points on the circle must satisfy the equation

$$(x + 1)^2 + (y - 2)^2 = R^2 = 3^2 = 9.$$

Vocabulary

Choose the correct term from the box to complete each sentence.

1. A(n) ___?___ of a circle is a line that lies in the same plane as the circle and intersects the circle at exactly one point.

2. The set of points in a plane that are a fixed distance from a given point is a(n) ___?___.

3. An angle whose vertex is the center of a circle and whose sides contain ___?___ of the circle is a(n) ___?___.

4. An angle whose vertex is on a circle and whose sides contain ___?___ of the circle is a(n) ___?___.

Concepts and Skills

Given that m∠ABC = 38°, determine each angle measure and justify your reasoning.

5. m∠ACB
6. m∠CAB
7. m∠CDB

Given that Circle E has a radius of 5 and that $\overline{GF}$ and $\overline{GH}$ are tangent to Circle E, determine each measure and justify your reasoning.

8. m∠EFG
9. FG
10. EG

11. m∠FEG
12. m∠HEF
13. m∠FGH

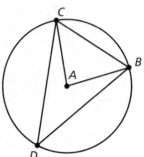

17x + 3

21x − 5

Find the center and radius each circle.

14. $(x + 3)^2 + (y - 4)^2 = 36.$

15. $x^2 + y^2 - 10y + 23 = 0$

16. In Circle S, an angle is inscribed along a diameter. Given that m∠PQR = (2x − 2) and m∠QRP = (3x + 12), determine the measures of all three angles in △PQR.

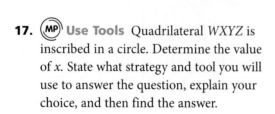

17. **(MP) Use Tools** Quadrilateral WXYZ is inscribed in a circle. Determine the value of x. State what strategy and tool you will use to answer the question, explain your choice, and then find the answer.

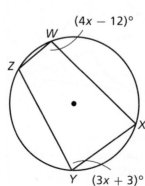

(4x − 12)°

(3x + 3)°

16 Relationships in Circles

Module Performance Task: Focus on STEM

Planetary Exploration

A space probe, *S*, approaches an unknown planet and takes measurements at different points.

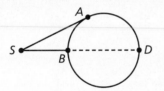

$\overline{SA}$ is tangent to the sphere at *A*.
$\overline{BD}$ is a diameter of the sphere.
Time for a radar signal to travel:

- from *S* to *A* and back to *S*: 0.0494 second
- from *S* to *B* and back to *S*: 0.0317 second

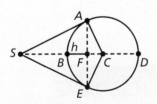

$\overline{SE}$ is tangent to the sphere at *E*.
$m\angle ASE = 52°$

A. Radar signals travel at the speed of light, approximately 186,000 miles per second. Use this information to determine the shortest distance to the surface, *SB*, and the distance to the horizon, *SA*. Round your answers to the nearest mile.

B. Approximate the radius of the planet to the nearest mile. Justify your reasoning.

C. The surface area of a sphere is given by the formula $A_{sphere} = 4\pi r^2$. Use this formula to approximate the surface area of the planet to the nearest square mile.

D. The portion of the planet that is viewable from *S* is a spherical cap with height *h*. The surface area of a spherical cap is given by the formula $A_{cap} = 2\pi rh$. What percentage of the planet's surface area is visible from the space probe? Justify your reasoning.

Are You Ready?

Complete these problems to review prior concepts and skills you will need for this module.

Solve Multi-Step Equations

Solve each equation.

1. $5x - 6 = 64$

2. $7 = 7(1 - 5n)$

3. $-5p = -2(8 + 6p)$

4. $-12(-3a - 3) = 8(5a + 12)$

5. $7(w + 3) = 5 - 4(5 - 2w)$

6. $2(3 - c) + 6c = 8 - 3(2c - 5)$

Solve Quadratic Equations by Finding Square Roots

Solve each equation by finding square roots.

7. $x^2 = 49$

8. $3x^2 = 48$

9. $25x^2 - 5 = 95$

10. $9x^2 + 7 = 23$

11. $40 - x^2 = 3x^2$

12. $8x^2 - 7 = 35$

Solve Quadratic Equations Using the Quadratic Formula

Solve each equation using the Quadratic Formula.

13. $x^2 - 5x + 6 = 0$

14. $2x^2 + 5x - 3 = -5$

15. $2x^2 - 14 = -3x$

16. $-3x^2 + 4 = 3x - 2x^2$

17. $3x^2 - x = x^2 + 1$

18. $-x^2 - 3 = 4 - 2x^2$

19. $x^2 - 4 = 2x$

20. $3x^2 - 4 = 2x - 1$

Connecting Past and Present Learning

Previously, you learned:

- to solve multi-step linear and quadratic equations,
- to prove theorems about lines and angles, and
- to prove relationships among inscribed angles, radii, and chords.

In this module, you will learn:

- to prove relationships formed by segments in circles and
- to use angle and segment relationships in circles to solve real-world problems.

Segment Relationships in Circles

(I Can) use segment relationships in circles to solve mathematical and real-world problems.

Spark Your Learning

A photographer is cropping a photograph into a circle. The photographer uses two chords to compose the image inside the circle.

Complete Part A as a whole class. Then complete Parts B–D in small groups.

A. What is a mathematical question you can ask about this situation? What information would you need to know to answer your question?

B. What are the shapes involved in this situation? What theorem in geometry could help you identify the relationship between these shapes?

C. To answer your question, what strategy and tool would you use along with all the information you have? What answer do you get?

D. Does your answer make sense in the context of the situation? How do you know?

Turn and Talk Would changing the intersection point of the chords affect the result of their relationship? Explain.

Build Understanding

Prove the Chord-Chord Product Theorem

Recall that a chord is a segment whose endpoints lie on a circle. The following theorem describes a relationship among the four segments formed when two chords intersect in a circle.

Chord-Chord Product Theorem

If two chords intersect inside a circle, then the products of the lengths of the segments of the chords are equal.

$$AE \cdot EB = CE \cdot ED$$

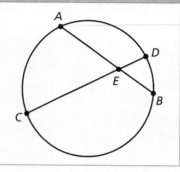

1 Prove the Chord-Chord Product Theorem.

Given: Chords $\overline{AB}$ and $\overline{CD}$ intersect in the interior of the circle. $\overline{AC}$ and $\overline{DB}$ are drawn to create triangles.

Prove: $AP \cdot BP = DP \cdot CP$

First, show that $\triangle APC \sim \triangle DPB$.

A. Why is $\angle APC \cong \angle DPB$?

B. Name at least one other pair of corresponding congruent angles shown in the triangles. Explain your reasoning.

C. Explain why $\triangle APC \sim \triangle DPB$.

Now, use the similar triangles to show that $AP \cdot BP = DP \cdot CP$.

D. Give a reason for each step in the calculation.

$$\frac{AP}{DP} = \frac{CP}{BP}$$
$$DP \cdot BP \cdot \frac{AP}{DP} = DP \cdot BP \cdot \frac{CP}{BP}$$
$$AP \cdot BP = DP \cdot CP$$

E. Suppose $\overline{AD}$ and $\overline{CB}$ are drawn instead of $\overline{AC}$ and $\overline{DB}$ to create triangles $\triangle DAP$ and $\triangle BCP$. Do you get the same result? Explain your reasoning.

 Turn and Talk Consider the triangles APD and CPA formed by connecting A to D and C to A. Can the Theorem be proven using these triangles?

Investigate Segment Relationships in Circles

A **tangent segment** is a segment of a tangent with one endpoint on the circle, such as $\overline{AB}$.

A **secant** of a circle is a line that intersects a circle at exactly two points, such as $\overleftrightarrow{DB}$. A **secant segment**, such as $\overline{DB}$, is a segment of a secant line with at least one endpoint on the circle. A secant segment that lies in the exterior of a circle with one point on the circle is called an **external secant segment**.

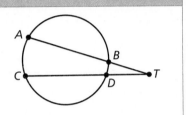

There is a special relationship in the lengths of secant segments drawn from the same point outside a circle.

Secant-Secant Product Theorem

If two secants intersect in the exterior of a circle, then the product of the lengths of one secant segment and its external segment is equal to the product of the lengths of the other secant segment and its external segment.

$$AT \cdot BT = CT \cdot DT$$

---

2 ▶ Investigate the Secant-Secant Product Theorem using a geometric drawing tool.

Draw a circle with two secants that intersect in the exterior of the circle as shown.

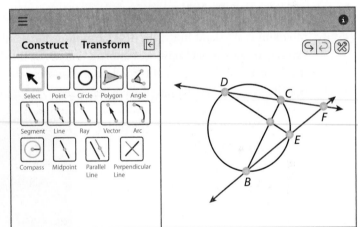

A. Use the Secant-Secant Product Theorem to write an equation that relates the lengths of the secant segments. Does this relationship remain true as points are moved around the circle?

B. Measure $\angle CDE$ and $\angle EBC$. What happens to the angle measures as you move point D closer to point C along the circle?

C. Explain why $\triangle FDE$ and $\triangle FBC$ are similar triangles. How does this relationship explain the result of the Secant-Secant Product Theorem?

 Turn and Talk Move point D along the circle until it coincides with point C, and name the new point D. Name a pair of similar triangles. Write an equation that relates DF, BF, and EF. Make a conjecture about the relationship between a tangent and a secant drawn from the same point outside the circle.

Step It Out

Use the Secant-Tangent Product Theorem

There is a special relationship in the lengths of a secant segment and a tangent that intersect outside a circle.

Secant-Tangent Product Theorem
If a secant and a tangent intersect in the exterior of a circle, then the product of the lengths of the secant segment and its external segment is equal to the square of the length of the tangent segment. $$AT \cdot BT = CT^2$$ 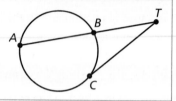

3 What is the value of x?

$$15 \cdot 8 = x^2$$
$$120 = x^2$$
$$\sqrt{120} = x$$
$$11 \approx x$$

Explain why this equation is true.

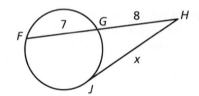

Apply Segment Relationships

4 Molokini is an island in the Pacific Ocean. It is the remains of the mouth of an extinct volcano. A geologist uses information about the distance BD to estimate the diameter of the mouth of the volcano. Assuming the mouth of the volcano is a circle, what is the length of diameter $\overline{AC}$?

A. What information is needed to determine AC?

B. What theorem is used to find AX?

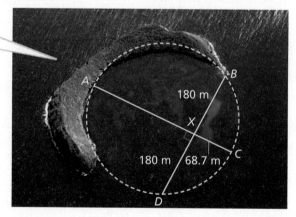

Find the length of $\overline{AX}$.

$$AX \cdot XC = DX \cdot XB$$
$$AX \cdot 68.7 = 180 \cdot 180$$
$$AX \cdot 68.7 = 32{,}400$$
$$AX \approx 471.6 \text{ m}$$

Find the length of $\overline{AC}$.

The diameter is about 540.3 meters.

C. How was the diameter determined?

Turn and Talk What segments can be drawn in the diagram to create two similar triangles? Write a similarity statement for the two triangles. Then justify the statement.

Check Understanding

1. Name two segments that can be drawn to create similar triangles in the diagram. What is a similarity statement that justifies the equation $XZ \cdot YZ = UZ \cdot VZ$?

2. Two secants intersect in the exterior of a circle and form four segments. What is the relationship between these four segments?

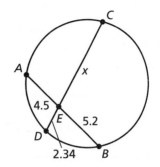

In Problems 3 and 4, find the value of x.

3.

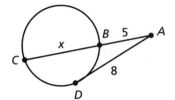

4.

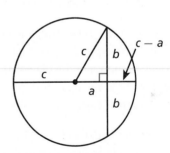

5. Chords $\overline{AB}$ and $\overline{CD}$ intersect inside a circle at point T. The chord $AB = 14$ centimeters, $AT = 5$ centimeters, and $\overline{CT} = 6$ centimeters. What is the length CD?

On Your Own

6. Two chords intersect inside a circle and form four segments. What is the relationship between these four segments?

7. (MP) **Construct an Argument** The circle in the diagram has radius c. Use the diagram and the Chord-Chord Product Theorem to prove the Pythagorean Theorem.

Use a geometric drawing tool to construct a circle and two chords $\overline{MN}$ and $\overline{PQ}$ that intersect inside the circle at C.

8. What do you know about the relationship between the lengths CM, CN, CP, and CQ?

9. Drag the points around the circle to change the lengths CM, CN, CP, and CQ. Does the relationship between the lengths CM, CN, CP, and CQ change?

10. Is there a place in the circle where you could place point C so that the lengths CM, CN, CP, and CQ are all equal?

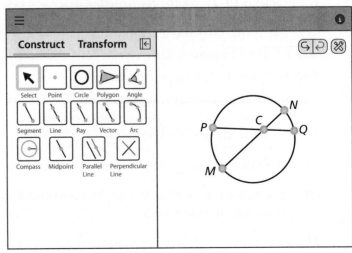

11. Prove the Secant-Secant Product Theorem.

Given: $\overline{AC}$ and $\overline{EC}$ are secant segments.

Prove: $AC \cdot BC = EC \cdot DC$

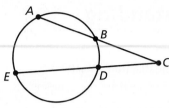

12. Can you apply the Secant-Secant Product Theorem to two secant segments that intersect on the circle? Explain.

13. Two secant segments intersect outside the circle. Their internal secant segments are congruent. Can you conclude that the secant segments are congruent? Explain.

14. Prove the Secant-Tangent Product Theorem.

Given: $\overline{CB}$ is the external segment to secant segment $\overline{DB}$. Secant $\overline{DB}$ and tangent $\overline{AB}$ intersect in the exterior of the circle. $\overline{DA}$ and $\overline{AC}$ are drawn to create triangles.

Prove: $AB^2 = BC \cdot DB$

15. A secant and a tangent intersect in the exterior of a circle and form two secant segments and a tangent segment. What is the relationship between these three segments?

16. What theorem is the basis for each of the product theorems in this lesson showing how segments in circles are related? Explain why.

17. Two secant segments intersect outside the circle where each of their corresponding external secant segments is equal, as shown in the diagram. What must be true about the relationship between the two secants? Justify your response.

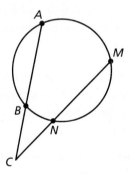

18. Can a tangent segment and a secant segment formed by a secant and a tangent intersecting in the exterior of a circle ever be equal? Explain.

For Problems 19–21, use the construction described below.

(**MP**) **Use Tools** Construct a perpendicular bisector of a chord.

Step 1: Use a compass to draw a circle. Mark the center.

Step 2: Use a straightedge to draw a chord.

Step 3: To construct the perpendicular bisector of the chord, draw two arcs with equal diameter, one with each endpoint as a center. Then connect the intersections of the arcs.

19. Does a diameter of the circle lie on the perpendicular bisector? Explain.

20. Draw a different chord in the circle and construct its perpendicular bisector. Do you have the same result?

21. Make a conjecture about the perpendicular bisector of a chord.

22. Find the diameter of a circular plate from an archeological dig. The length of the chord $\overline{LM}$ is 14 inches. $\overline{AB}$ is the perpendicular bisector of $\overline{LM}$.

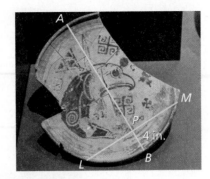

For Problems 23–26, find the length of the indicated segments.

23. *AB* and *CD*

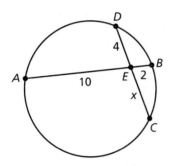

24. *TC*, *TB*, and *TD*

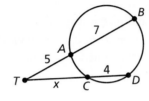

25. *CD*, *TD*, and *TB*

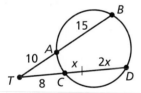

26. *AB*, *AQ*, and *CQ*

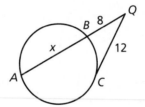

27. A secant and a tangent intersect in the exterior of a circle. The tangent segment is equal to the internal segment that is part of the secant. The external secant segment is 6 inches. What are the lengths of the tangent segment and secant segment to the nearest tenth of an inch?

28. A communication satellite's orbit is 6400 miles above the Earth. Its geographic range is the furthest distance it can reach on Earth at this orbit. This distance, shown by $\overline{SP}$, is a tangent segment. Find the geographic range of the satellite.

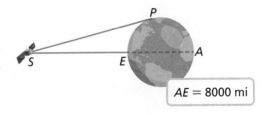

29. STEM A graphic arts designer is creating a logo for a company. The diagram shown is an outline of the logo that shows how much space the designer has for the company's slogan and name. According to the diagram, how many pixels are available for the company's name and for the company's slogan?

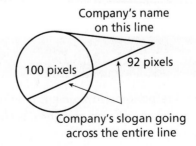

30. Lisa and Martha are in a park. The diagram shows how far each of them has to walk in order to reach a picnic table where they will eat lunch. How far is Lisa from the picnic table?

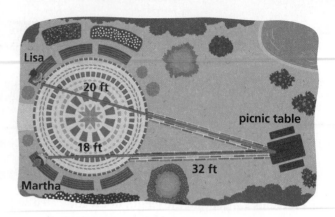

31. A student claims that all of the theorems in this lesson can be written as "When two lines intersect each other and intersect the same circle, the product of the distances between each intersection point of a line with the circle and the point where the lines intersect will be the same for both lines." Do you agree? Explain your reasoning.

Spiral Review • Assessment Readiness

32. Which angle measure is correct for the inscribed quadrilateral?

Ⓐ m∠B = 130°

Ⓑ m∠C = 100°

Ⓒ m∠A = 50°

Ⓓ m∠D = 40°

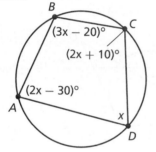

33. A Geostationary Operational Environmental Satellite is above Earth 26,199.5 miles from the center of the Earth. Earth's radius is approximately 3960 miles. What is the approximate distance from the satellite to Earth's horizon (which can be represented by a tangent segment)?

Ⓐ 25,898 mi   Ⓒ 702,095,400 mi

Ⓑ 26,497 mi   Ⓓ 909,565,281 mi

34. Which statement is true for the equation of the circle $x^2 + y^2 - 8x + 18y + 61 = 0$?

Ⓐ center $(-4, 9)$

Ⓑ center $(9, -4)$

Ⓒ radius 6 units

Ⓓ radius 12 units

35. In the diagram, $m\widehat{AC} = 34°$. What is the measure of angle ABC?

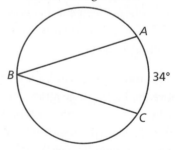

Ⓐ 34°   Ⓒ 17°

Ⓑ 76°   Ⓓ 6°

 I'm in a Learning Mindset!

How am I responding to segment relationships in circles instead of segment relationships of common polygons, such as rectangles?

Angle Relationships in Circles

(I Can) use angle relationships in circles to solve mathematical and real-world problems.

Spark Your Learning

John is observing the moon with a telescope. The two tangents drawn from Earth to the moon show the part of the surface of the moon John can see through the telescope.

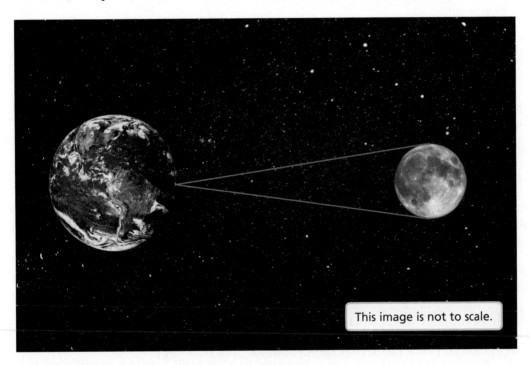

This image is not to scale.

Complete Part A as a whole class. Then complete Parts B–D in small groups.

A. What is a mathematical question you can ask about this situation? What information would you need to know to answer your question?

B. What shape can represent the situation? How can you use parts of the shape to solve the problem?

C. To answer your question, what strategy and tool would you use along with all the information you have? What answer do you get?

D. Does your answer make sense in the context of the situation? How do you know?

 Turn and Talk What happens to the measure of the arc of the moon that can be seen from Earth with the same points of tangency when the moon is closer to Earth, such as at lunar perigee when they are 221,559 miles apart?

(bg) ©guteksk7/Shutterstock; (l) ©Stocktrek Images, Inc./Brand X Pictures/Getty Images; (r) ©Tristan3D/Shutterstock

Build Understanding

Prove the Intersecting Chords Angle Measure Theorem

The following theorem describes a relationship among the measures of angles and arcs formed when two lines intersect inside a circle.

> **Intersecting Chords Angle Measure Theorem**
>
> If two secants or chords intersect in the interior of a circle, then the measure of each angle formed is half the sum of the measures of its intercepted arcs.
>
> Chords $\overline{AB}$ and $\overline{CD}$ intersect at E.
>
> $$m\angle AEC = \frac{1}{2}\left(m\widehat{AC} + m\widehat{DB}\right)$$

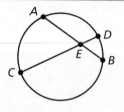

1 Prove the Intersecting Chords Angle Measure Theorem.

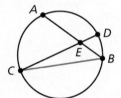

Given: Chords $\overline{AB}$ and $\overline{CD}$ intersect at E.

Prove: $m\angle AEC = \frac{1}{2}\left(m\widehat{AC} + m\widehat{DB}\right)$

A. How is the measure of $\angle AEC$ related to the measures of the angles in $\triangle CEB$? Write an equation for this relationship. What theorem justifies this equation?

B. Use the Inscribed Angle Theorem to express the measures of $\angle ABC$ and $\angle ACB$ in terms of the measures of $\widehat{AC}$ and $\widehat{DB}$.

C. How can the equations from Parts A and B help you write $m\angle AEC = \frac{1}{2}\left(m\widehat{AC} + m\widehat{DB}\right)$.

D. Describe a special case of intersecting chords in which $m\angle AEC = m\widehat{DB}$.

 Turn and Talk Could the theorem be proved using $\overline{AD}$ instead of $\overline{CB}$? Explain.

Explore the Tangent-Secant Interior Angle Measure Theorem

The following theorem describes the relationship between the measures of angles and the measures of arcs formed when two lines intersect on a circle.

> **Tangent-Secant Interior Angle Measure Theorem**
>
> If a tangent and a secant (or a chord) intersect on a circle at the point of tangency, then the measure of the angle formed is half the measure of the intercepted arc.
>
> Tangent $\overline{BC}$ and secant $\overline{BA}$ intersect at B.
>
> $$m\angle ABC = \frac{1}{2}m\widehat{AB}$$

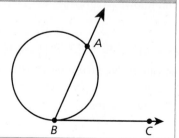

2 ▶ Consider what happens to the segments and angles as *C* approaches *B* in the circles.

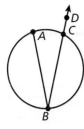

Circle 1

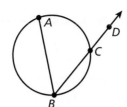

Circle 2

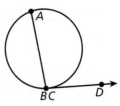

Circle 3

A. Describe the location of point *C* in relation to point *B* as you move from the first to the third circle.

B. What do you know about the measure of the intercepted arc of an inscribed angle?

C. How does the measure of the intercepted arc of an inscribed angle relate to the Tangent-Secant Interior Angle Measure Theorem?

Prove the Tangent-Secant Interior Angle Measure Theorem

There are three cases of the Tangent-Secant Interior Angle Measure Theorem.

Case 1	Case 2	Case 3
secant is diameter of circle	center is interior to angle	center is exterior to angle

3 ▶ Prove Case 1 of the Tangent-Secant Interior Angle Measure Theorem.

Given: Secant $\overrightarrow{BC}$ tangent to circle *K* at point *B* and diameter $\overline{AB}$.

Prove: $m\angle ABC = \frac{1}{2}m\widehat{APB}$

First, find the measure of ∠ABC.

A. What is $\overline{BK}$ for the circle? Explain.

B. Why is $\overline{BC} \perp \overline{BK}$? What is $m\angle KBC$? What is $m\angle ABC$? Explain.

Now, find the measure of $\widehat{APB}$.

C. Why is $m\widehat{APB} = 180°$?

Finally, show you have enough information to prove Case 1.

D. How does $m\angle ABC$ compare to $m\widehat{APB}$?

 Turn and Talk If you use the Angle Addition Postulate to prove the two other cases, what postulate will you have to use for the arcs?

Step It Out

Prove the Tangent-Secant Exterior Angle Measure Theorem

The following theorem relates the measures of angles and arcs formed when two lines intersect outside of a circle.

Tangent-Secant Exterior Angle Measure Theorem

If a tangent and a secant, two tangents, or two secants intersect in the exterior of a circle, then the measure of the angle formed is half the difference of the measures of its intercepted arcs.

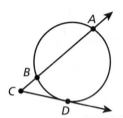 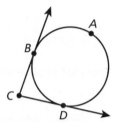 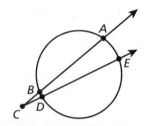

$$m\angle ACD = \frac{1}{2}\left(m\widehat{AD} - m\widehat{BD}\right) \qquad m\angle BCD = \frac{1}{2}\left(m\widehat{BAD} - m\widehat{BD}\right) \qquad m\angle ACE = \frac{1}{2}\left(m\widehat{AE} - m\widehat{BD}\right)$$

 The statements in the left column of the proof of the Tangent-Secant Exterior Angle Measure Theorem for two secants are scrambled below.

Given: Secants $\overrightarrow{AC}$ and $\overrightarrow{AE}$

Prove: $m\angle CAE = \frac{1}{2}\left(m\widehat{CE} - m\widehat{BD}\right)$

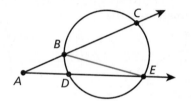

Put the proof statements in the correct sequence.

Statements	Reasons
1. Secants $\overrightarrow{AC}$ and $\overrightarrow{AE}$	1. Given.
$m\angle CAE = \frac{1}{2}m\widehat{CE} - \frac{1}{2}m\widehat{BD}$	2. Exterior Angle Theorem
$m\angle CAE = m\angle CBE - m\angle BEA$	3. Subtraction Property of Equality
$m\angle CAE + m\angle BEA = m\angle CBE$	4. Inscribed Angle Theorem
$m\angle BEA = \frac{1}{2}m\widehat{BD}$ and $m\angle CBE = \frac{1}{2}m\widehat{CE}$	5. Substitution Property of Equality
$m\angle CAE = \frac{1}{2}\left(m\widehat{CE} - m\widehat{BD}\right)$	6. Distributive Property

---

 Turn and Talk Can the same reasoning that was used to prove the Tangent-Secant Exterior Angle Measure Theorem for two secants be used to prove the case with the secant and the tangent? Explain why or why not.

Apply Angle Relationships in Circles

5 Find $x°$, the measure of $\angle DTC$.

$x° = \frac{1}{2}\left(m\overset{\frown}{AB} + m\overset{\frown}{DC}\right)$ **A.** Why was this equation chosen?

$x° = \frac{1}{2}(48° + 86°)$ Substitute the measures from the diagram.

$x° = \frac{1}{2}(134°)$ Add.

B. What measurements do you substitute into the equation? Explain.

$x° = 67°$ Multiply.

C. Which theorem is used for the problem, and what is the measure of $\angle DTC$?

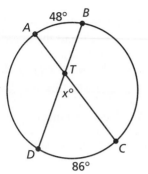

6 **Archaeology** Stonehenge is a circular arrangement of massive stones near Salisbury, England. The diagram represents a viewer at V that observes the monument from a point where two of the stones A and B are aligned with stones at the endpoints of a diameter of the circular shape. If $m\overset{\frown}{AB} = 48°$, then what is $m\angle AVB$?

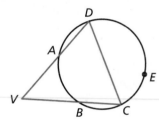

$m\angle AVB = \frac{1}{2}\left(m\overset{\frown}{DC} - m\overset{\frown}{AB}\right)$ **A.** Why was this equation chosen?

$= \frac{1}{2}(180° - 48°)$ Substitute the given measures.

B. Why 180°?

$= \frac{1}{2}(132°)$ Subtract.

$= 66°$ Multiply.

C. Which theorem is used for the problem, and what is the measure of $\angle AVB$?

Turn and Talk If $\overset{\frown}{AB}$ was formed with two tangent lines instead of two secant lines, does $m\angle AVB$ change? Explain why or why not.

Check Understanding

1. Explain the relationship between angles formed by lines intersecting inside a circle and the intercepted arcs.

2. What is the relationship between an angle whose vertex is on the circle and its intercepted arc? Explain.

3. How are tangent-secant interior angles different from inscribed angles?

4. Use a theorem and the diagram shown to find the measures of $\overset{\frown}{EB}$ and $\angle ABC$.

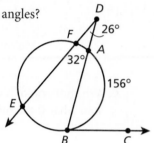

On Your Own

5. Is the equation in the Intersecting Chords Angle Measure Theorem an equation for finding an average? Explain.

In Problems 6 and 7, use the diagram and given information. Given: Chords $\overline{AB}$ and $\overline{CD}$ intersect at the center of the circle, point E .

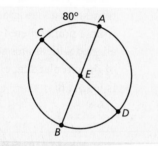

6. **(MP)** **Construct Arguments** Show that $m\angle AEC = \frac{1}{2}\left(m\overset{\frown}{CA} + m\overset{\frown}{BD}\right)$ using the diagram and a two-column proof.

7. How does your proof for Problem 6 use different geometric relationships and theorems than the proof in Task 1?

8. Prove the Tangent-Secant Interior Angle Measure Theorem, where the center of the circle is exterior to $\angle ABC$

   Given: $\overline{BC}$ is tangent to circle Z at point B.
   $\overline{AB}$ is a secant and intersects $\overline{BC}$ at B.

   Prove: $m\angle ABC = \frac{1}{2}m\overset{\frown}{AB}$

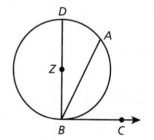

9. Which theorem would you apply to find the measure of an angle formed by two secants that intersect on a circle like in the diagram? Explain.

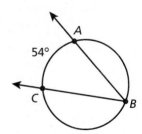

10. $\overrightarrow{XA}$ and $\overrightarrow{XB}$ are tangent to a circle with center C. Use a theorem and what you know about central angles to show the relationship between $\angle AXB$ and $\angle ACB$ in the diagram.

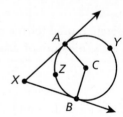

11. Prove the Tangent-Secant Exterior Angle Measure Theorem for a secant and tangent, and then compare the proof for two tangents.

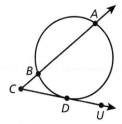

A. Write a proof for a secant and tangent that intersect in the exterior of the circle.

Given: Tangent $\overleftrightarrow{CD}$ and secant $\overrightarrow{CA}$ intersect at C in the exterior of the circle.

Prove: $m\angle ACD = \frac{1}{2}\left(m\widehat{AD} - m\widehat{BD}\right)$

B. Suppose two tangents intersect outside the circle. Describe how you can modify the proof in part A to prove that $m\angle BCD = \frac{1}{2}\left(m\widehat{BAD} - m\widehat{BD}\right)$

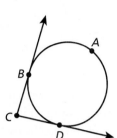

Find the indicated measure.

12. $m\widehat{AEB}$

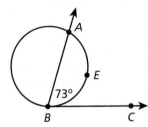

13. $m\angle ACD$

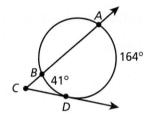

14. $m\angle AEC$

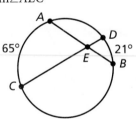

15. $m\angle ACE$

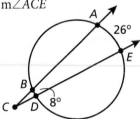

16. Sean designed the necklace shown. It is a circular stone held by a triangular wire. The measure of the angle at vertex C where the triangle attaches to a chain is 72°. The base of the wire crosses the stone across its center. What is the measure of $\widehat{BD}$?

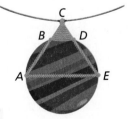

17. The outline of a symmetrical logo is shown in the diagram. It is an X, W, and O layered on top of each other. $\overrightarrow{BA}$ and $\overrightarrow{DE}$ are tangent to the circle. The difference between $m\widehat{BD}$ and $m\widehat{FG}$ is 84°. What is $m\widehat{FG}$ and $m\angle ABG$?

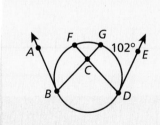

18. STEM The superior oblique and inferior rectus are two muscles that help control eye movement. They intersect behind the eye to create ∠*ACB*. If m$\widehat{AEB}$ = 200° what is m∠*ACB*?

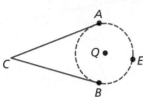

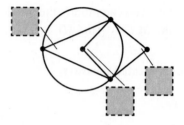

Superior oblique
Medical rectus
Superior rectus
Lateral rectus
Inferior rectus   Inferior oblique

19. **(Open Middle™)** Using the digits 0 to 9, at most one time each, fill in the boxes so that the central angle, the inscribed angle, and the angle formed by two tangent segments have the correct relationship. The diagram is not shown to scale.

Spiral Review • Assessment Readiness

20. During an orbit of Saturn, the Cassini satellite was 1,680 miles from Saturn. The radius of Saturn is approximately 33,780 miles where Cassini was directly above Saturn. What is the approximate distance from the satellite to Saturn's horizon (which can be represented by a tangent segment)?

(A) 10,785 mi   (C) 33,911 mi

(B) 33,738 mi   (D) 48,974 mi

21. Which statement is true for the equation of the circle $x^2 + y^2 + 12x + 4y + 24 = 0$?

(A) radius 16

(B) radius 8

(C) center $(2, 6)$

(D) center $(-6, -2)$

22. Given the circle, the secant, and the tangent shown in the diagram, what is the length of the tangent segment to the nearest tenth?

(A) 6.7

(B) 8.4

(C) 11.2

(D) 20.1

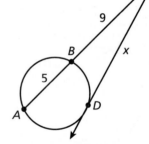

23. A decorative circular plate has a circumference of 33.9 inches. What is the plate's radius to the nearest tenth of an inch?

(A) 3.3 inches   (C) 10.8 inches

(B) 5.4 inches   (D) 17 inches

I'm in a Learning Mindset!

How am I responding to angle relationships in circles instead of segment relationships in circles?

Segment Relationships in Circles

Jasmine plants a circular garden. She places steppingstones along $\overline{AC}$ and $\overline{BD}$.

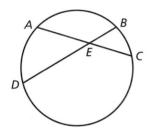

Given $AE = 11$ feet, $EC = 9$ feet, and $EB = 7$ feet, you can use the Chord-Chord Product Theorem to find DE.

$$AE \cdot EC = DE \cdot EB$$
$$11 \cdot 9 = DE \cdot 7$$
$$99 = DE \cdot 7$$
$$14.14 \approx DE$$

DE is approximately 14 feet.

Jasmine's cousin also plants a circular garden.

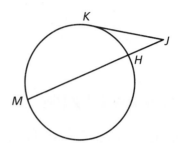

He builds a tool shed at point J. Given $HM = 18$ feet and $JH = 4$ feet, you can use the Secant-Tangent Product Theorem to find the distance from point K to the tool shed.

$$JH \cdot JM = JK^2$$
$$4 \cdot (4 + 18) = JK^2$$
$$4 \cdot 22 = JK^2$$
$$88 = JK^2$$
$$9.38 \approx JK$$

The tool shed is approximately 9.4 feet from point K.

Angle Relationships in Circles

Jasmine is planning to place a statue at E. Given $m\widehat{AD} = 15°$ and $m\widehat{BC} = 9.8°$, you can use the Intersecting Chords Angle Measure Theorem to find $m\angle AED$.

$$m\angle AED = \frac{1}{2}\left(m\widehat{AD} + m\widehat{BC}\right)$$
$$m\angle AED = \frac{1}{2}\left(15° + 9.8°\right)$$
$$m\angle AED = \frac{1}{2}\left(24.8°\right)$$
$$m\angle AED = 12.4°$$

Jasmine's cousin places a spotlight on the corner of his tool shed. Given $m\widehat{MK} = 135°$ and $m\angle KJM = 24°$, you can use the Tangent-Secant Exterior Angle Measure Theorem to find the amount of the garden's edge illuminated by the spotlight.

$$m\angle KJM = \frac{1}{2}\left(m\widehat{MK} - m\widehat{HK}\right)$$
$$24° = \frac{1}{2}\left(135° - m\widehat{HK}\right)$$
$$48° = 135° - m\widehat{HK}$$
$$m\widehat{HK} = 87°$$

Approximately 87° of the garden's edge is illuminated by the spotlight.

Vocabulary

Choose the correct term from the box to complete each sentence.

1. A(n) ___?___ is a line that intersects a circle at two points. A segment of this line that is outside of the circle with only one endpoint on the circle is a(n) ___?___.

2. A(n) ___?___ is a segment whose endpoints lie on a circle.

3. A(n) ___?___ is a line that is in the same plane as a circle and intersects the circle in exactly one point. A segment of this line that has one endpoint on the circle is a(n) ___?___.

Concepts and Skills

4. **A.** What theorem can be used to find *x*?

   B. What is *BD*?

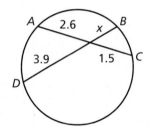

5. Myra and Leonard are sitting on the edge of a circular pool and batting a beach ball back and forth. A sudden gust of wind blows the ball across the pool, and it comes to rest at point *B*. Myra and Leonard swim across the pool, hop over the side, and walk to reach the ball.

   A. Who has farther to travel? How much farther?

   B. Who has farther to swim? How much farther?

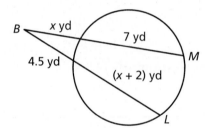

6. (**MP**) **Use Tools** Divers are exploring the areas surrounding a shipwreck. The points *X*, *Y*, and *Z* mark spots at the circular bottom of the lake where the divers locate artifacts. What is the horizontal distance from the artifact located at point *Z* and basecamp, *W*? Round to the nearest meter. State what strategy and tool you will use to answer the question, explain your choice, and then find the answer.

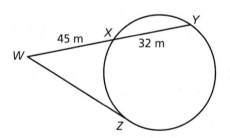

A fountain with a circumference of 300 feet has several points of interest.

7. Given m∠*DMA* = 84° and m$\widehat{DA}$ = 72°, find m$\widehat{EC}$.

8. Given m$\widehat{ET}$ = 85° and m$\widehat{AT}$ = 155°, find m∠*S*.

9. The wall of the fountain along $\widehat{TC}$ needs to be repaired. Given m∠*STC* = 69°, what length of the fountain wall needs to be repaired? Explain your reasoning.

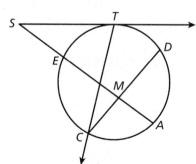

Circumference and Area of a Circle

Module Performance Task: Focus on STEM

The Coriolis Effect

Earth rotates as an airplane flies from Buffalo, New York, to Quito, Ecuador. The radius of Earth is 3959 miles and the speed of the plane is 525 miles per hour.

Buffalo, New York
latitude: 43° N
longitude: 78° W

Quito, Ecuador
latitude: 0°
longitude: 78° W

A. What is the distance between Buffalo and Quito? How long does it take the plane to fly this distance?

B. While the plane is in flight, Earth continues to rotate. How far around the circumference of Earth will Quito have moved while the plane is in flight? Has the rotation of Earth also moved the plane? Explain your reasoning.

C. How can the pilot change the flight path so that the plane arrives at Quito? Draw a sketch of your proposed flight path. Explain your reasoning.

D. How would this situation change if the plane were flying north from a location in the Southern Hemisphere to Quito? Draw a sketch of your proposed flight path. Compare and contrast this flight path with the flight path from Buffalo.

Are You Ready?

Complete these problems to review prior concepts and skills you will need for this module.

Write Equations for Proportional Relationships

Write an equation for each proportional relationship.

1.

x	5	10	15	20
y	−3	−6	−9	−12

2. One inch is equal to 2.54 centimeters. Write an equation that can be used to convert n inches to c centimeters.

Circumferences of Circles

Use Figures 1 and 2 for Problems 3, 4, 7, and 8. Round to the nearest hundredth.

3. What is the circumference of Figure 1?

4. What is the circumference of Figure 2?

5. What is the circumference of a circle with diameter 4 feet?

6. What is the circumference of a circle with radius 2.5 meters?

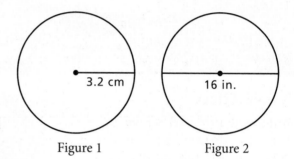

Figure 1   Figure 2

Areas of Circles

7. What is the area of Figure 1?

8. What is the area of Figure 2?

9. What is the area of a circle with diameter 6 feet?

10. What is the area of a circle with radius 1.8 meters?

Connecting Past and Present Learning

Previously, you learned:

- to use proportional relationships to determine side lengths of similar figures,
- to derive the relationship between the circumference and the radius of a circle, and
- to use similarity criteria to solve applied problems.

In this module, you will learn:

- to derive the fact that the length of an arc in a circle intercepted by an angle is proportional to the radius of the circle,
- to define the radian measure of an angle as the constant of proportionality given by the ratio of the length of the subtended arc and the length of the radius, and
- to give an informal argument to develop the formula for the area of a sector.

Measure Circumference and Area of a Circle

(I Can) justify and use the circumference and area of a circle formulas to solve real-world problems.

Spark Your Learning

Maintenance hole covers allow workers to access underground systems such as water lines and maintenance tunnels.

Complete Part A as a whole class. Then complete Parts B–D in small groups.

A. What is a mathematical question you can ask about the cover? What information would you need to know about the cover to precisely answer your question?

B. What estimates can you make using information in the photo?

C. To answer your question, what strategy and tool would you use along with all the information you have? What answer do you get?

D. How can you determine if your estimates are reasonable?

Turn and Talk Suppose the diameter doubled in length.
- How would you adjust your estimate?
- How would your new estimate relate to your original estimate?

Build Understanding

Justify the Formula for the Circumference of a Circle

The **circumference** of a circle is the distance around the circle. The ratio of the circumference of any circle to its diameter is a constant that is defined as pi (π), which is the irrational number 3.14159. . . . Throughout this book, you should use a calculator when performing calculations with π.

Circumference of a Circle

The circumference C of a circle is $C = \pi d$ or $C = 2\pi r$, where d is the diameter of the circle and r is the radius of the circle.

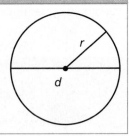

---

1 ▶ **A.** The diagrams show regular n-gons inscribed in circles with radius 1. Consider the perimeter of each n-gon. As n increases, what value should the perimeters approach? Explain your reasoning.

  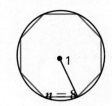

B. Consider the circle with an inscribed regular hexagon. The hexagon can be divided into six congruent triangles. Each triangle has a vertex angle measuring $\frac{360°}{6} = 60°$ and legs with length 1. Then each triangle can be divided into two right triangles. Use trigonometric ratios to write an expression for the value of x. Then use the value of x to write the perimeter of the hexagon.

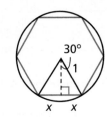

C. Consider an inscribed regular polygon with n sides. The triangle shown is from a regular n-gon inscribed in a circle with radius 1. What is an expression for the value of x? Use this expression to write a formula for the perimeter of the n-gon.

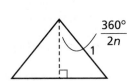

D. Use the formula in Part C to find the perimeters of regular n-gons inscribed in circles with radius 1 for large values of n. What value do the perimeters approach as n gets very large? How does this justify the formula $C = 2\pi r$?

 Turn and Talk Suppose you know the diameter and circumference of two different-sized circles. Would you expect the ratio of the circumference to the diameter of the circles to be the same or to be different? Explain your reasoning.

Justify the Formula for the Area of a Circle

Area of a Circle

The area A of a circle is $A = \pi r^2$, where r is the radius of the circle.

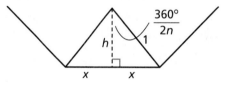

In mathematics, a **limit** is a value that the output of a function approaches as the input increases or decreases without bound or approaches a given value. From the diagram in the previous task, it appears that the perimeters of the inscribed n-gons approach the limit of the circumference of the circle as n increases.

2 **A.** In Task 1, the formula for circumference is justified using the perimeters of regular n-gons inscribed in circles with radius 1 for large values of n. Explain how this method can be used to justify the formula for the area of a circle.

B. A regular n-gon is inscribed in a circle with radius 1. The n-gon is divided into n congruent triangles, one of which is shown. What is the area of the triangle in terms of h and x? Use this expression to write the area of the n-gon.

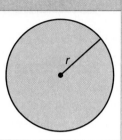

C. Use trigonometric ratios to write expressions for h and x in terms of n. Then use the expressions to write the area of the n-gon in terms of n.

D. Suppose a regular n-gon is inscribed in a circle with radius 1. Use a spreadsheet to find the area of the n-gon as n increases to very large numbers. What value does the area approach for larger values of n?

B2	fx = A2*SIN(RADIANS(360/(2*A2)))*COS(RADIANS(360/(2*A2)))		
	A	**B**	**C**	**D**
1	n	Area of n-gon		
2	50	3.1333308		
3	100			
4	150			
5	200			

E. Explain how the result from Part D justifies the formula for the area of a circle.

 Turn and Talk Is it possible for n to be a large enough value such that the area of the n-gon is equal to the area of the circle? Why or why not?

Justify π

As you have learned, π (pi) represents the ratio of the circumference of any circle to its diameter.

3 ▶ Consider a circle with radius r that has an inscribed regular hexagon and a circumscribed regular hexagon.

A. Suppose P_1 is the perimeter of the smaller hexagon, P_2 is the perimeter of the larger hexagon, and C is the circumference of the circle. This relationship can be represented as shown.

$$P_1 < C < P_2$$

Explain how to rewrite the inequality in terms of π.

$$\underline{\quad ? \quad} < \pi < \underline{\quad ? \quad}$$

B. What would be true about the inequalities in Part A if regular polygons with larger numbers of sides were used?

C. Consider a circle with radius 1 that has an inscribed regular n-gon and a circumscribed regular n-gon. The n-gons are divided into n congruent triangles, and one triangle from each n-gon is shown below. Explain how the formulas for the perimeters of the n-gons were derived.

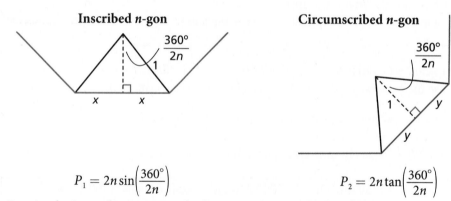

Inscribed n-gon

Circumscribed n-gon

$$P_1 = 2n \sin\left(\frac{360°}{2n}\right) \qquad\qquad P_2 = 2n \tan\left(\frac{360°}{2n}\right)$$

D. Rewrite the inequality in terms of π from Part A using the formulas from Part C and a radius of 1. Then use a spreadsheet to calculate a lower bound for π, an upper bound for π, and the average of the two bounds for different n-gons. What do you observe?

B2	✕ ✓	fx	= AVERAGE(B2:C2)	
	A	**B**	**C**	**D**
1	n	Lower Bound	Upper Bound	Average
2	50	3.1395260	3.1457334	3.1426297
3	100			
4	150			
5	200			

Turn and Talk Explain why an alternate definition of π is the area of a circle with radius 1.

Step It Out

Apply the Circumference Formula

4 A new traffic circle will have an outer circumference of $\frac{1}{4}$ mile. What should the radius of the traffic circle be to the nearest foot? Use the fact that there are 5280 feet in 1 mile.

Determine the circumference in feet.

$\frac{1}{4}\,\text{mi} \cdot \frac{5280 \text{ ft}}{1 \text{ mi}} = 1320 \text{ ft}$ ⟵ **A.** Why would you choose to convert the circumference from miles to feet?

Use the circumference formula.

$C = 2\pi r$ ⟵ **B.** Why is this version of the formula used?

$1320 = 2\pi r$

$r = \frac{1320}{2\pi} \approx 210 \text{ ft}$

Apply the Area Formula

5 The plan for a splash pad shows a concrete area with circular nonslip surfaces. The diameter d for each circle is given. The nonslip surfaces cost \$11 per square foot. What is an estimate for the cost for the nonslip surfaces?

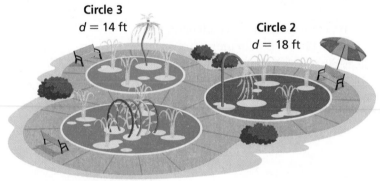

Circle 3
$d = 14$ ft

Circle 2
$d = 18$ ft

Circle 1
$d = 20$ ft

Find the area of each circle.

Area of Circle 1 $= \pi r^2$ Area of Circle 2 $= \pi r^2$ Area of Circle 3 $= \pi r^2$

$= \pi \cdot 10^2$ $= \pi \cdot 9^2$ $= \pi \cdot 7^2$

$= 100\pi$ $= 81\pi$ $= 49\pi$

Find the total area.

$100\pi + 81\pi + 49\pi = 230\pi \approx 723 \text{ ft}^2$

A. Why are the answers left in terms of π?

Estimate the cost.

$723 \times 11 = \$7953$ ⟵ **B.** What are the units in the cost equation?

 Turn and Talk Suppose the cost of the circular surfaces should be close to but not exceed \$7500. How can the design change to meet the budget?

Check Understanding

1. A regular 20-gon is inscribed in a circle with radius 2 units. A regular 30-gon is inscribed in another circle with radius 3. Which inscribed polygon has a perimeter closer to the circumference of the circle in which it is inscribed? Explain.

2. How do you justify and use the formula for the area of a circle?

3. Is it possible to draw a circle whose ratio of circumference to diameter is not π? Explain why or why not.

A pair of sunglasses has circular lenses that each have a diameter of 1.8 inches.

4. Determine the length of wire that frames each lens. Round to the nearest tenth.

5. A polarized film is embedded in each lens to filter sunlight. How many square inches of polarized film is needed for both lenses? Round to the nearest tenth of a square inch.

On Your Own

6. **(MP) Reason** A regular n-gon is inscribed in a circle with radius r. Is there any value of n that will produce an n-gon with a perimeter of $2\pi r$? Explain why or why not.

7. **(MP) Critique Reasoning** Disha states that the circumference and the area of the larger circle are both double the circumference and the area of the smaller circle. Is she correct? Explain why or why not.

8. A pizza with radius r is divided into congruent triangles. The triangular pieces are rearranged to form a parallelogram.

    A. How are the base and the height of the parallelogram related to the circle?

    B. How can the parallelogram be used to justify the formula for the area of a circle?

    C. Suppose the circle is divided into 16 congruent triangles. Will the new parallelogram formed by these pieces be a better estimate for the area of the circle? Explain.

9. **(MP) Reason** Refer back to Task 3. If you only inscribed a regular n-gon in the circle, is that enough to find an approximate value of π? Explain.

Find the circumference of each circle with the given radius r or diameter d. Round answers to the nearest hundredth.

10. A circle with $r = 4$ in.

11. A circle with $d = 7.5$ m

12. A circle with $r = 16.2$ mm

13. A circle with $d = 15$ cm

14. A circular horse pen is used to provide rehabilitation exercise for a horse recovering from an injury.

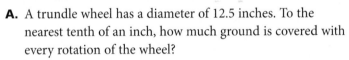

The horse trots at 15 feet per second 20 feet from the center of the pen.

20 ft

A. To the nearest foot, what is the total distance the horse travels during one lap around the pen?

B. How many seconds does it take to complete 5 laps around the pen?

C. Suppose the horse trots around the pen 18 feet from the center at the same speed. How much less time would it take the horse to complete 5 laps?

15. STEM A trundle wheel is used by a surveyor to measure distances by rolling it on the ground and counting the number of revolutions.

A. A trundle wheel has a diameter of 12.5 inches. To the nearest tenth of an inch, how much ground is covered with every rotation of the wheel?

B. The trundle wheel measures a distance of 78.6 feet. How many rotations did the wheel make while measuring this distance?

C. Suppose a trundle wheel is designed so one revolution measures 1 meter. What is the radius of the wheel in centimeters? Round to the nearest centimeter.

Find the area of each circle with radius r or diameter d. Round answers to the nearest tenth.

16. $r = 7$ mm

17. $d = 22$ yd

18. $d = 37$ cm

19. $r = 5.3$ ft

Find the circumference of the circle with the given area A. Round answers to the nearest hundredth.

20. $A = 121\pi$ in^2

21. $A = 49\pi$ cm^2

22. $A = 400\pi$ mm^2

23. $A = 16\pi$ ft^2

In Problems 24 and 25, use the figure which shows two circles with the same center.

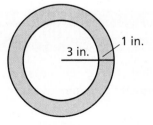

1 in.

3 in.

24. What percent of the circle's area is within the shaded region?

25. Suppose the radius of the white circle changes so the shaded area represents half of the total area. What is the new radius of the white circle?

26. (MP) **Reason** A pizzeria charges $10.50 for a medium cheese pizza and $12.50 for a large cheese pizza. The medium pizza has a diameter of 12 inches, while the large pizza has a diameter of 14 inches. Which pizza is a better buy? Explain.

27. A weather advisory states that the orange circular region with an average diameter of 72 miles is sustaining tropical storm force winds. The diameter of the circular region is increasing at a rate of 5 miles per hour. At this rate, how long will it take for the circular region to cover 6650 square miles?

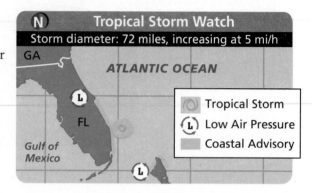

28. **STEM** An engineer designs a circular gasket with a manufacturing tolerance of ± 1.5 mm, which means that any dimension of a gasket produced in the factory must be within the range of 1.5 mm bigger than or smaller than the drawing specifications to pass quality control. If the outer diameter of the gasket is labeled as 50 mm on the engineering drawing, what is the acceptable range of the circumference of the part?

Spiral Review • Assessment Readiness

29. Which of the following are true statements? Select all that apply.

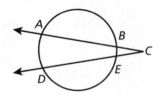

Ⓐ $BC = \dfrac{DE \cdot EC}{AC}$ Ⓓ $EC = \dfrac{AC \cdot BC}{DC}$

Ⓑ $m\angle C = m\widehat{AD}$ Ⓔ $m\angle C = AD \cdot DE$

Ⓒ $m\angle C \le 180°$ Ⓕ $m\widehat{AD} = 2 \cdot m\widehat{BE}$

30. Diameters of a circle are drawn to divide the circle into congruent parts as shown. What is the value of x?

Ⓐ 22.5°

Ⓑ 30°

Ⓒ 45°

Ⓓ 60°

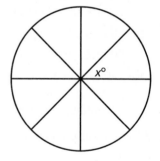

31. Match the equation of a circle on the left to its description on the right.

Equation

A. $(x - 2)^2 + (y + 1)^2 = 9$
B. $(x - 1)^2 + (y + 2)^2 = 3$
C. $(x + 1)^2 + (y - 2)^2 = 1$
D. $(x + 2)^2 + (y - 1)^2 = 9$

Description

1. center at $(1, -2)$, radius of $\sqrt{3}$ units
2. center at $(-2, 1)$, radius of 3 units
3. center at $(-1, 2)$, radius of 1 unit
4. center at $(2, -1)$, radius of 3 units

⬡ **I'm in a Learning Mindset!**

What strategy did I use to overcome difficulties with applying previous knowledge in new ways to justify the circumference and area formulas?

Measure Arc Length and Use Radians

(I Can) use similarity of circles to find arc length.

Spark Your Learning

Portions of circles called arcs are often used in architectural design to add visual interest.

Complete Part A as a whole class. Then complete Parts B–D in small groups.

A. What is a mathematical question you can ask about the border of this entrance? What information would you need to know to answer your question?

B. How can you determine which arc to analyze? Are both the same size?

C. To answer your question, what strategy and tool would you use along with all the information you have? What answer do you get?

D. Does the answer make sense in the context of the situation? How do you know?

Turn and Talk Consider the following changes to the intercepted arc.

- How would your answer change if the intercepted arc were 180°, or exactly half the circle? How would the size of the arc relate to the circumference?
- How would your answer change if the intercepted arc were 270°? How would the size of the arc relate to the circumference?

©HelloRF Zcool/Shutterstock

Build Understanding

Derive the Formula for Arc Length

An **arc** is an unbroken part of a circle consisting of two points, called endpoints, and all the points on the circle between them. The distance along an arc, measured in linear units such as centimeters, is called the **arc length**. You can apply the fact that there are 360° in a circle to find the length of an arc given the radius of the circle.

1 The table shows information about two circles.

Circle	$C = 2\pi r$	$m\widehat{AB}$	Fraction of circle	Length of $\widehat{AB}$
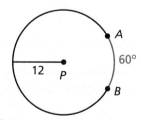	$C = 2 \cdot \pi \cdot 10$ $= 20\pi$	90°	$\frac{1}{4}$	$\frac{1}{4}(20\pi) = 5\pi$
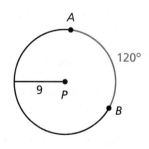	$C = 2 \cdot \pi \cdot 7$ $= 14\pi$	180°	$\frac{1}{2}$	$\frac{1}{2}(14\pi) = 7\pi$

A. How can you find the fraction of the circle that each arc represents?

B. Describe how the arc length in the last column is calculated.

C. What units are used to measure arc length? Explain.

D. Create a similar table for the circles shown.

E. Suppose $m\widehat{AB} = x°$. What fraction of the circumference is contained within the arc?

F. Using the same reasoning, what formula can you write to determine the arc length s for any arc measuring $x°$ with radius r?

 Turn and Talk Explain in your own words how the arc length relates to the diameter in terms of the arc measure and 360°.

Derive an Expression for Radian Measure

Angles are commonly measured using degrees, and there are 360° in a circle. Another measure that can be used for angles is *radian measure*, which is defined using the relationship between the length of an arc intercepted by a central angle in a circle and the radius of the circle.

Radian measure can be investigated using **concentric circles**, which are coplanar circles that have the same center. The radar screen shown uses concentric circles to mark distances from a specific point.

2 ▶ Consider the concentric circles shown. The central angle of 60° cuts off arcs that each measure 60°.

A. The table shows the ratio of the arc length to the radius for the circles with radii 2 and 3. Find the arc length and the ratio of the arc length to the radius for the arcs in the circles with radii 4 and 5.

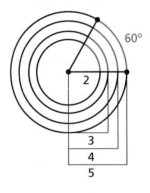

Radius r	Arc length	$\dfrac{\text{arc length}}{\text{radius}}$
2	$\dfrac{60°}{360°} \cdot 2\pi(2) = \dfrac{2}{3}\pi$	$\dfrac{\frac{2}{3}\pi}{2} = \dfrac{\pi}{3}$
3	$\dfrac{60°}{360°} \cdot 2\pi(3) = \pi$	$\dfrac{\pi}{3}$

B. What do you notice about the ratio of the arc length to the radius of a circle for an arc defined by a central angle of 60°?

C. Suppose the concentric circles have a central angle of 90° instead of 60°. What should be true about the ratios of the corresponding arc lengths and radii? Explain.

D. As you have learned, all circles are similar. Use what you know about the ratios of corresponding parts of similar figures to explain the relationship between the arc lengths and the radii in the concentric circles.

E. The expression $s = \dfrac{x°}{360°} \cdot 2\pi r$ gives the arc length s for an arc intercepted by a central angle of $x°$ in a circle with radius r. When $x°$ is fixed, the expression $\dfrac{x°}{360°} \cdot 2\pi$ is the constant of proportionality, and this constant is defined as the **radian measure** of the fixed angle. How is the radian measure of an angle related to the ratio of an arc's length to the radius of the circle? Explain.

Turn and Talk Write an ordered pair of the form (radius, arc length) for each circle in Part A, using a decimal to the nearest tenth for each arc length. Should the points lie on a line? If so, what should be the slope of the line?

Step It Out

Apply the Formula for Arc Length

Arc Length

The arc length s of an arc with measure $x°$ and radius r is given by the formula $s = \frac{x°}{360°} \cdot 2\pi r$.

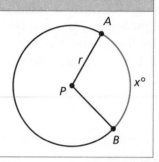

3 ▶ The Palace of Westminster in London, England, has a tower with a circular clock face set in an iron frame. The tip of the minute hand sweeps across the iron frame as the time changes. How far does the tip of the minute hand travel as the clock progresses from 10:05 to 10:25? Round your answer to the nearest tenth.

The circular frame of the clock face has a diameter of 23 feet.

Find the radius.

The radius is half of the diameter.

$r = \frac{23}{2} = 11.5$ ft

10:05

10:25

Find the arc measure.

The minute hand sweeps an arc over 20 minutes, which is $\frac{1}{3}$ of a complete rotation. So, the measure of the arc is $\frac{1}{3} \cdot 360° = 120°$.

A. Why is 20 minutes $\frac{1}{3}$ of a complete rotation of the minute hand?

Find the arc length.

$s = \frac{x°}{360°} \cdot 2\pi r$

$= \frac{120°}{360°} \cdot 2\pi(11.5)$

$= \frac{23}{3}\pi$

≈ 24.1 ft

B. What is another way to find the arc length given that the arc is $\frac{1}{3}$ of a complete rotation of the minute hand?

The minute hand of the clock travels about 24.1 feet as the clock progresses from 10:05 to 10:25.

 Turn and Talk Would the results change if you were asked to find the distance as the clock progressed from 1:32 to 1:52? Why or why not?

Convert Between Radian Measure and Degree Measure

As you learned in Task 2, the radian measure of an angle that measures $x°$ is $\frac{x°}{360°} \cdot 2\pi$. Because there are $360°$ in a circle, there are 2π radians in a circle. That means $360° = 2\pi$ radians and $180° = \pi$ radians. This proportional relationship can be used to convert between radians and degrees.

Convert Degrees to Radians	Convert Radians to Degrees
Multiply the degree measure by $\frac{\pi \text{ radians}}{180°}$ and simplify the fraction.	Multiply the radian measure by $\frac{180°}{\pi \text{ radians}}$ and simplify the fraction.

Radian measures are usually given in terms of π. When giving an angle measure in radians, the unit "radians" is often not included. For example, $\frac{\pi}{2}$ radians can be written as $\frac{\pi}{2}$.

Working with radian measures will be useful in future coursework in math and physics that involves trigonometry functions and circular and angular motion.

4 Convert $270°$ to radian measure.

$$270° = 270°\left(\frac{\pi \text{ radians}}{180°}\right)$$

$$= \frac{270° \cdot \pi \text{ radians}}{180°}$$

$$= \frac{3\pi}{2} \text{ radians}$$

> Why are there no degree measures in the final answer?

 Turn and Talk Give answers in radian measure.
- What is the sum of the measures of the angles in a triangle?
- What is the sum of the measures of the angles in a quadrilateral?

5 Convert $\frac{\pi}{6}$ to degree measure.

$$\frac{\pi}{6} = \left(\frac{\pi}{6} \text{ radians}\right)\left(\frac{180°}{\pi \text{ radians}}\right)$$

$$= \frac{180°}{6}$$

$$= 30°$$

> How do you know that the degree measure of $\frac{\pi}{6}$ will be less than $180°$?

 Turn and Talk Use the fact that $180° = \pi$ radians to set up and solve a proportion to find the degree measure of $\frac{\pi}{6}$ radians.

Check Understanding

1. Describe the difference between the measure of an arc and the length of an arc.

Answer each question about the formula for the arc length s of an arc $s = \frac{x°}{360°} \cdot 2\pi r$.

2. What part of the circle does the expression $2\pi r$ represent?

3. What does $x°$ represent?

4. What does $\frac{x°}{360°}$ represent?

5. For a fixed angle that measures $x°$, what does $\frac{x°}{360°} \cdot 2\pi$ represent?

Find the length of $\overset{\frown}{AB}$ using the given measure of $\overset{\frown}{AB}$ in a circle with a radius of 5 meters. Round to the nearest hundredth.

6. $m\overset{\frown}{AB} = 135°$

7. $m\overset{\frown}{AB} = 80°$

Complete each statement with the equivalent angle measure.

8. $120° = $ _____?_____ radians

9. _____?_____ $= \frac{\pi}{5}$ radians

On Your Own

Tell whether each statement is *always*, *sometimes*, or *never* true. Explain.

10. Two arcs with the same measure have the same arc length.

11. The length of the arc of a circle is greater than the circumference of the circle.

12. In a circle, two arcs with the same length have the same measure.

Find each length of $\overset{\frown}{AB}$. Round to the nearest hundredth.

13.
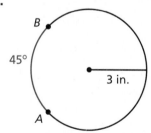

14.
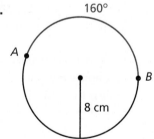

15.
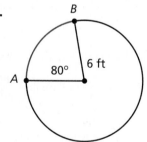

16. **MUSIC** Metronomes provide a tempo for musicians by producing clicks at a set interval. Each swing of the inverted pendulum produces a click. With each swing, the pendulum sweeps through an angle of 70°. What distance does the tip of the pendulum travel on each swing? Round to the nearest centimeter.

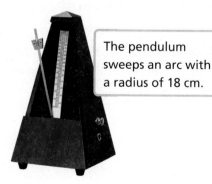

The pendulum sweeps an arc with a radius of 18 cm.

In Problems 17 and 18, two concentric circles on a pocket watch are shown. Find the unknown measure. Round to the nearest hundredth.

17. length of $\overset{\frown}{AB} = 3.87$ cm,
length of $\overset{\frown}{CD} = 6.9$ cm,
$PA = 1.85$ cm,
$PD = \underline{\quad?\quad}$

18. length of $\overset{\frown}{AB} = \underline{\quad?\quad}$,
length of $\overset{\frown}{CD} = 8.38$ cm,
$PA = 1.7$ cm,
$PD = 3$ cm

19. Snow skis have curved edges. The curve is determined by the sidecut radius, which is the radius of a very large circle. The ski shown has an effective edge of 150.1 cm, and the measure of $\overset{\frown}{AB}$ is 6.14°. What is its sidecut radius in meters?

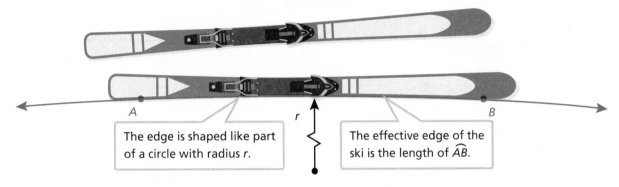

The edge is shaped like part of a circle with radius r.

The effective edge of the ski is the length of $\overset{\frown}{AB}$.

20. Belt drives transmit power between drive shafts in equipment. In the belt drive shown, the smaller pulley is being driven by a power source and is delivering power to the larger pulley through the belt. The difference in size is used to change the speed at which the larger pulley turns. For each full turn of the smaller pulley, through what angle does the larger pulley turn? Round to the nearest tenth.

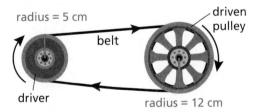

radius = 5 cm
belt
driver
driven pulley
radius = 12 cm

Convert each angle from degree measure to radian measure.

21. $15°$ **22.** $55°$ **23.** $110°$ **24.** $200°$

25. STEM The angular velocity ω of an object gives the radians traveled per unit of time. This can be applied to objects traveling a circular path. To find the linear velocity when given the angular velocity, use the formula $v = r\omega$, where v is the linear velocity, r is the radius, and ω is the angular velocity. If a racecar on a circular track with a radius of 500 ft travels an arc of 30° per second, what is the linear velocity of the car in feet per second?

26. **(MP)** **Reason** In circle Q, the length of $\widehat{CD}$ is equal to its radius.

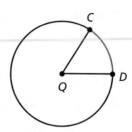

   A. How many times does $\widehat{CD}$ fit around the circle? Leave your answer in terms of π.

   B. Is it possible that the terms *radians* and *radius* are related to each other? Use your observations to explain your answer.

Convert each angle from radian measure to degrees.

27. $\dfrac{3\pi}{2}$ **28.** $\dfrac{\pi}{6}$ **29.** $\dfrac{7\pi}{8}$ **30.** $\dfrac{7\pi}{9}$

31. **(MP)** **Use Repeated Reasoning** Complete the table to find the angle measure in radians for the benchmark angles.

Benchmark Angles									
Degree measure	0°	30°	45°	60°	90°	120°	135°	150°	180°
Radian measure	?	?	?	?	?	?	?	?	?

32. **(Open Middle™)** Using the digits 1 to 9, at most one time each, fill in the boxes so that the radius and angle measure result in the arc length measure.

$r = \boxed{}$ cm $\theta = \boxed{}\boxed{}^{\circ}$ $\widehat{AB} = \boxed{}\pi$ cm

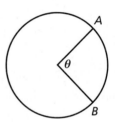

Spiral Review • Assessment Readiness

33. Find the value of x.

   (A) 8
   (B) 11
   (C) 12
   (D) 16

35. What is the measure of $\angle ABC$?

   (A) 20°
   (B) 40°
   (C) 80°
   (D) 160°

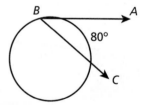

34. A circle has a circumference of 25 feet. What is the approximate area of the circle?

   (A) 13.2 ft²   (C) 36.2 ft²
   (B) 25.6 ft²   (D) 49.7 ft²

36. A circle has a radius of 6 inches. What is the area of the circle?

   (A) 9π in²   (C) 27π in²
   (B) 20π in²   (D) 36π in²

 I'm in a Learning Mindset!

What barriers are there to understanding how radian measure and degree measure relate to each other?

Measure Sector Area

(I Can) use sector area to solve real-world problems.

Spark Your Learning

The neighborhood is divided by concentric circular streets and streets along radii.

Complete Part A as a whole class. Then complete Parts B–D in small groups.

A. What is a mathematical question you can ask about the neighborhood? What information would you need to know to answer your question?

B. How does the shape of one portion of the neighborhood compare to the shape of a circle with the same radius?

C. To answer your question, what strategy and tool would you use along with all the information you have? What answer do you get?

D. Does the answer make sense in the context of the situation? How do you know?

Turn and Talk How would the area of one portion of the neighborhood relate to the area of the complete circle if the central angle were 180°, or exactly half the circle?

Build Understanding

Derive the Formula for Sector Area

A **sector** of a circle is a portion of the circle bounded by two radii and their intercepted arc. A sector is named using the ends of each radius and the center of the circle. You have learned how to find the area of a circle. You can use proportional reasoning to find the area of a sector of a circle.

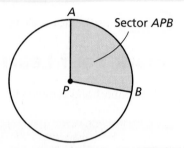
Sector APB

1 Find the area of each sector.

A. Find the area of the circle at the right. Leave your answer in terms of π. Suppose a sector represents $\frac{1}{5}$ of the area of the circle. What is the area of the sector?

B. The table shows the areas of two sectors of a circle with radius 10 cm. How is the fraction of the circle represented by the sector calculated? How is the fraction used to find the area of the sector?

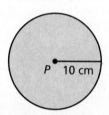

Circle	Central angle	Fraction of circle	Area of whole circle	Area of sector APB
 90° P 10 cm B A	90°	$\frac{90°}{360°} = \frac{1}{4}$	100π cm²	$\frac{1}{4}(100\pi) = 25\pi$ cm²
A P B 20 cm	180°	$\frac{180°}{360°} = \frac{1}{2}$	100π cm²	$\frac{1}{2}(100\pi) = 50\pi$ cm²

C. Create a similar table for the circles shown.

D. Suppose m∠APB = x°. What fraction of the circle's area is represented by the sector?

E. The area A is the area of a sector of a circle with central angle x° and radius r. Write a proportion that relates A, x°, the total area of the circle, and the number of degrees in a circle. Then solve the proportion for A.

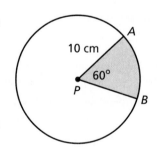

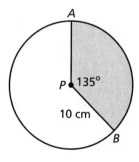

 Turn and Talk Compare the formulas for finding arc length and sector area. How are they the same? How are they different?

Step It Out

Use the Formula for Sector Area

The proportional reasoning used to find the area of a sector in the previous task can be generalized by the following formula.

> ### Area of a Sector
> The area A of a sector with a central angle of $x°$ of a circle with radius r is given by $A = \frac{x°}{360°} \cdot \pi r^2$.
>
>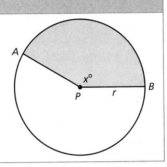

2 The bristles of a fan brush are a sector of a circle. Find the area of the bristles.

$$A = \frac{x°}{360°} \cdot \pi r^2$$

$$= \frac{120°}{360°} \cdot \pi(3)^2$$

$$\approx 9.42 \text{ cm}^2$$

> Why is it helpful to use an estimate for π in real-world problems?

3 One part of a pizza is topped with only green peppers, and the other part is topped with only mushrooms. The part topped with mushrooms has an area of 40π in². What is the radius of the pizza?

Identify the given information.
$A = 40\pi$ in², $x° = 225°$

> A. What do A and $x°$ represent?

Use the formula for area of a sector.

$$A = \frac{x°}{360°} \cdot \pi r^2 \qquad \text{Write the formula.}$$

$$40\pi = \frac{225°}{360°} \cdot \pi r^2 \qquad \text{Substitute the given values.}$$

$$\frac{360°}{225°} \cdot 40\pi = \frac{225°}{360°} \cdot \pi r^2 \cdot \frac{360°}{225°} \qquad \text{Multiply to clear the fraction.}$$

$$64\pi = \pi r^2 \qquad \text{Simplify.}$$

$$64 = r^2 \qquad \text{Divide both sides by } \pi.$$

$$8 = r$$

> B. How can you check the answer?

> **Turn and Talk** Why can your answer contain either π or an approximated decimal? Explain a situation where you would use each method. What does it mean if a problem asks for either an exact or approximate answer?

Check Understanding

1. Describe the process you can use to find the area of a sector of a circle when you know the area of the circle and the central angle of the sector.

2. If the angle measure of a sector is 210°, what fraction of the circle is the sector?

In Problems 3 and 4, find the area of each shaded sector. Give your answer in terms of π.

3.

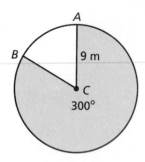

4.

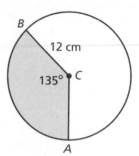

5. A circular stained-glass window is divided into 10 congruent wedge-shaped panes that meet at the center of the circle. The radius of the window is 2 ft. What is the area of one pane? Round the answer to the nearest hundredth.

On Your Own

6. **(MP) Reason** Suppose you are given the angle measure of a sector and the radius of the circle, but you have forgotten the formula for finding the area of a sector. Explain how you can use proportional reasoning to find the area of the sector.

7. **Open Ended** Two congruent circles each have a sector. The area of one sector is twice the area of the other sector. Draw and label two different scenarios that meet the criteria, including the central angle of each sector and the radius of the circles.

8. **(MP) Critique Reasoning** Parisa says that when you double the radius of a sector while keeping the central angle constant, you double the area of the sector. Do you agree or disagree? Explain.

Find the exact area of each sector.

9.

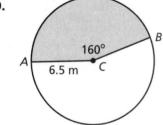

10.

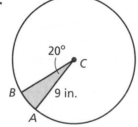

11.

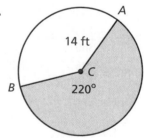

Find the approximate area of each sector with the given measure $x°$ in a circle with diameter d or radius r. Round the answer to the nearest hundredth.

12. $x° = 25°$, $d = 13$ mm

13. $x° = 73°$, $r = 8.2$ ft

14. $x° = 205°$, $r = 4$ in.

15. $x° = 315°$, $d = 27$ m

16. Sundar makes the logo shown for a florist. It consists of a rectangle with two sectors on top of the rectangle and 3 sectors below.

A. Estimate the area of the logo to the nearest hundredth.

B. One ounce of ink in Sundar's printer can cover 625 square inches. About how many times can the logo be printed at the given size to use 1 ounce of ink?

2 in.

1 in.

AK Florist

17. A semicircular window is mounted over a rectangular entryway. The diameter of the window is 48 inches. To the nearest square inch, what is the area of the window?

Find each area occupied by the sprouts between the concentric circles. Round the answer to the nearest hundredth.

18.

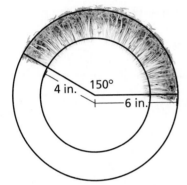

4 in.   150°

6 in.

19.

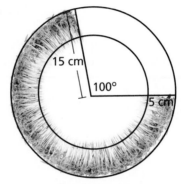

15 cm   100°

5 cm

20. (MP) **Model with Mathematics** Sectors from two different circles are outlined on a construction site. The radius of sector A is 10 feet, and the radius of sector B is 12 feet. The area of sector B is twice as much as the area of sector A. The central angle of sector A is 14° less than the central angle of sector B.

A. Using the area of a sector formula, write an equation that could be used to solve for the central angle of one sector. (Hint: Use the given information to write the equation in terms of just one variable.)

B. What are the measures of the central angles of sector A and of sector B?

C. What are the areas of sector A and of sector B? Round to the nearest tenth.

21. A farmer uses an irrigation system that covers an equal distance from the center of a crop. This irrigation method produces circular regions of crops. An irrigation system has a radius of 1300 feet and covers a sector of 20° every 45 seconds. What is the rate of coverage of the system in square feet per second? Round to the nearest tenth.

22. The spokes on the rim of a bicycle wheel are equally spaced. Each spoke is connected from the center of the wheel to the rim of the wheel. There are 24 spokes connected to the rim.

A. What is the angle formed between each spoke?

B. If each spoke is 14 inches long, what is the area of the sector formed between any two consecutive spokes? Round to the nearest hundredth.

C. Suppose the area of the sector formed by two consecutive spokes is 6π square inches. What is the length of each spoke?

23. Financial Literacy A college student creates a table to track monthly budgeting. If the student creates a pie chart with a radius of 6 cm to represent the monthly budget, what is the area of each sector? Round to the nearest tenth.

Category	% of Budget
Rent	25%
Bills	10%
Food	15%
Savings	20%
Other	30%

Estimate the radius *r* of each sector with the given measure *x*° in a circle with the given area. Round the answer to the nearest whole unit.

24. $x° = 50°$, area $= 85.5 \text{ m}^2$

25. $x° = 85°$, area $= 107 \text{ ft}^2$

26. $x° = 210°$, area $= 148 \text{ cm}^2$

27. $x° = 315°$, area $= 1718 \text{ in}^2$

28. The area of the shaded sector is 51.3 square feet. What is an estimate for the radius of the circle? Round the answer to the nearest foot.

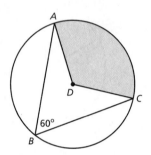

29. The base of a single-serving pizza box is shown. What are the radius, angle measurement, and base area of the largest pizza slice that can fit in the box?

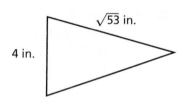

Spiral Review • Assessment Readiness

30. What is the value of *x*?

Ⓐ 64
Ⓑ 32
Ⓒ 128
Ⓓ 74

212°

x°

31. What is the degree measure of 2π radians?

Ⓐ 180°   Ⓒ 360°

Ⓑ 270°   Ⓓ 540°

32. Which expressions describe the area of a circle with radius *r* or diameter *d*? Select all that apply.

Ⓐ $r(\pi r)$

Ⓑ $\dfrac{360°}{360°} \cdot \pi r^2$

Ⓒ πd^2

Ⓓ $2\pi r$

Ⓔ $\pi\left(\dfrac{d}{2}\right)^2$

Ⓕ $x \cdot \pi r^2$

33. If a cube is sliced parallel to a face, what is the shape of the surface of the slice?

Ⓐ rectangle   Ⓒ circle

Ⓑ square   Ⓓ triangle

 I'm in a Learning Mindset!

How did procrastination impact my ability to perform my best today?

Review

Circumference and Area

Jenna draws five circles to model a dream catcher she saw at a local craft fair.

- The large circle has a radius of 5 inches.
- The medium circle has a diameter of 4.5 inches.
- The small circles each have a radius of 1 inch.

Jenna calculates the circumference of the large circle to determine how much ribbon she would need to cover it.

To find the circumference of the large circle, use the formula for the circumference of a circle with $r = 5$.

$C = 2\pi r = 2\pi(5) \approx 31.4$ in.

Jenna wonders whether the area covered by the medium circle will be large enough to cover a mark on the wall.

To find the area of the medium circle, use the formula for the area of a circle with $r = 2.25$.

$A = \pi r^2 = \pi(2.25)^2 \approx 15.9$ in^2

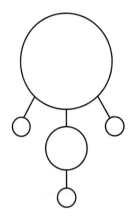

Arc Length

Jenna decides to paint the dream catcher on her wall. She divides the large and medium circles symmetrically into sectors to paint them.

The two red sectors in the large circle are congruent. The red and yellow sectors in the medium circle are congruent.

She wants to line the arc formed by the red sector in the medium circle with patterned duct tape.

To find the length of the arc formed by the red sector in the medium circle, use the formula for arc length with $x° = 140°$ and $r = 2.25$.

$s = \dfrac{x°}{360°} \cdot 2\pi r = \left(\dfrac{140°}{360°}\right) \cdot 2\pi(2.25) \approx 5.5$ in.

Area of a Sector

Jenna estimates she only has about one-fourth of a bottle of blue paint left and that an entire bottle can cover up to 16 square feet.

To find the area of the blue sector in the large circle, use the formula for the area of a sector with $x° = 166°$ and $r = 5$.

$A = \dfrac{x°}{360°} \cdot \pi r^2 = \dfrac{166°}{360°} \cdot \pi(5)^2 \approx 36.2$ in^2

Find the area of the blue sector in the medium circle.

$A = \dfrac{80°}{360°} \cdot \pi(2.25)^2 \approx 3.5$ in^2

Find the area of the small blue circle.

$A = \pi(1)^2 \approx 3.1$ in^2

The area Jenna wants to cover with blue paint is the sum.

$36.2 + 3.5 + 3.1 = 42.8$ in^2

Because $\dfrac{1}{4} \cdot 16$ ft$^2 \cdot \dfrac{144 \text{ in}^2}{1 \text{ ft}^2} = 576$ in^2 is greater than 43 in^2, she won't need more blue paint.

Vocabulary

Choose the correct term from the box to complete each sentence.

1. ___?___ is the constant of proportionality that relates the radius to arc length for a fixed value m.

2. A(n) ___?___ is an unbroken part of a circle consisting of two endpoints and all the points on the circle between them.

3. A portion of a circle bounded by two radii and their intercepted arc is a(n) ___?___.

4. Circles that share a center are called ___?___ circles.

Concepts and Skills

5. Find the area of a circle with a circumference of 18 inches. Round to the nearest tenth.

6. Find the circumference of a circle with an area of 25π m².

7. Andrew sells seats made from tree stumps. He only uses stumps with a diameter between 1.5 feet and 2 feet. Andrew weatherproofs the top of the seats by sealing them with lacquer. A can of lacquer will cover 200 square feet. How many seats can Andrew weatherproof if he has only one can of lacquer left?

Convert each angle from degrees to radian measure or from radian measure to degrees.

8. 80°

9. $\dfrac{5\pi}{6}$

Approximate each shaded sector area and corresponding arc length. Round to the nearest hundredth.

10.

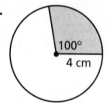

100°
4 cm

11.

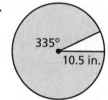

335°
10.5 in.

12. A security camera is attached to the corner of a store building. The camera is guaranteed to see with a radius of 100 feet. It rotates around an arc measuring 245°. What distance around the perimeter of the building does the security camera cover? Round to the nearest foot.

13. (MP) **Use Tools** Josiah is designing a mural for a contest. The mural consists of a circle with radius 3 feet, in which he sketches a central angle of 65°. Josiah intends to paint the sector purple but paints only one-fourth of the sector before he runs out of purple paint. What is the unpainted area of the sector? Round to the nearest tenth of a square foot. State what strategy and tool you will use to answer the question, explain your choice, and then find the answer.

14. A window is in the shape of a circle and divided into 12 equal-sized sectors. Five of the sectors are tinted blue. The diameter of the window is 50 inches. What is the area of the window that is tinted blue? Round to the nearest square inch.

Surface Area and Volume

Naval Architect

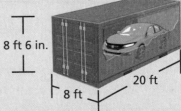 **STEM** POWERING INGENUITY

Naval architects design, build, and maintain ships of many different sizes, including sailboats, cruise ships, oil tankers, submarines, cargo ships, and aircraft carriers. They lead teams through prototyping blueprints; constructing the hull, propulsion system, and navigation system; and testing and revising strategies to ensure that each ship is safe, stable, and efficient.

©Aun Photographer/Shutterstock

STEM Task

Large cargo ships frequently stack standardized cargo containers or TEUs (twenty-foot equivalent units), allowing smaller and irregularly shaped cargo to be transported more efficiently.

8 ft 6 in.

8 ft

20 ft

What is the total volume available for cargo on a ship that can hold 21,413 TEUs?

Learning Mindset

Strategic Help-Seeking Identifies Need for Help

©fotohunter/Shutterstock

How do you know when you need help? Learning is both an individual and collaborative experience. When learning a new concept, it is important to develop your own initial understanding. Then, discussing the concept with your classmates can help you assess and grow your understanding. Collaboration allows you to build a deeper understanding of concepts by approaching them from different viewpoints. Here are some questions you can ask yourself when thinking about whether you need help:

- Is something preventing me from achieving my learning goal? How have I approached the problem? How have others approached the problem?

- How can I benefit from receiving and giving help in learning about surface area and volume? What impact can this have on my learning goals?

- What skills do I have that help in collaborating with others? Which collaboration skills do I still need to improve?

Reflect

Q Think of a time when you needed help but did not realize it until after you completed your task. What signs could have helped you identify that you needed help earlier?

Q Imagine you are a naval architect designing a new container ship. Will you be able to complete the task entirely by yourself? How would you know when you need to ask for help from others? How could it be beneficial to seek help with some parts of the task?

Module Performance Task: *Spies and Analysts*™

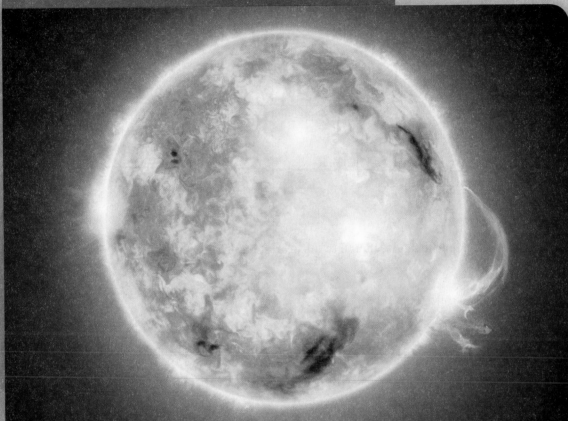

On the
SPOT

How can you describe the
area of a sunspot?

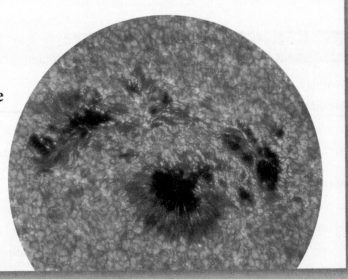

Are You Ready?

Complete these problems to review prior concepts and skills you will need for this module.

Nets and Surface Area

Find the surface area of the three-dimensional figure represented by the given net. Round to the nearest hundredth.

1.

8 in.

2 in.

1.73 in.

2 in.

2 in.

2.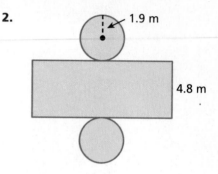

1.9 m

4.8 m

Areas of Composite Figures

Find the area of each composite figure. Round to the nearest hundredth.

3.

3 cm

4 cm

5 cm

11 cm

4.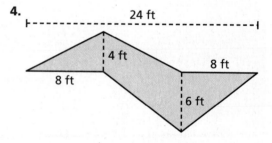

24 ft

4 ft

8 ft

8 ft

8 ft

6 ft

Cross Sections of Solids

Name the shape of each two-dimensional cross section.

5. A cylinder is sliced parallel to its base.

6. A square pyramid is sliced perpendicular to its base.

Connecting Past and Present Learning

Previously, you learned:

- to create nets to model the surface areas of three-dimensional figures,
- to solve problems involving areas of figures composed of polygons, and
- to describe cross-sections that result from slicing three-dimensional solids.

In this module, you will learn:

- to model real-world objects using geometric shapes and their properties,
- to use formulas to find the surface areas of three-dimensional figures, and
- to apply concepts of density based on area and volume in modeling situations.

Three-Dimensional Figures

(I Can) identify the characteristics of three-dimensional figures and represent them using drawings.

Spark Your Learning

A photographer takes a long-exposure photo of a carnival ride.

Complete Part A as a whole class. Then complete Parts B and C in small groups.

A. What is a mathematical question you can ask about this situation? What information would you need to know to answer your question?

B. To answer your question, what strategy and tool would you use along with all the information you have? What answer do you get?

C. What shape do the outermost lights appear to form? How do you know?

   Turn and Talk What kinds of solid shapes can be generated this way? Are there shapes that cannot be generated?

©Tami Freed/Alamy

Build Understanding

Identify Solids of Rotation

Right solids have an axis or lateral edges that are perpendicular to their base(s).
Oblique solids have an axis or lateral edges that are not perpendicular to their base(s).

A **prism** has two parallel congruent polygonal bases connected by lateral faces. Prisms are named by the shapes of their bases. A **cylinder** has two parallel congruent circular bases connected by a curved lateral surface. Its axis connects the centers of the bases.

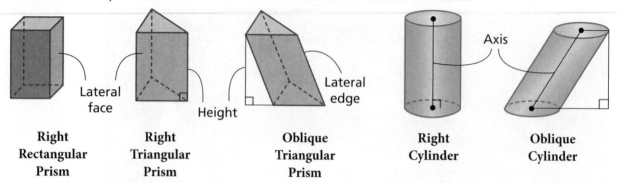

| Right Rectangular Prism | Right Triangular Prism | Oblique Triangular Prism | Right Cylinder | Oblique Cylinder |

A **pyramid** has a polygonal base with triangular faces that meet at a vertex. A **cone** has a circular base and a curved surface that connects the edge of the circular base to its vertex. A **sphere** is the locus of points that are a fixed distance from its center.

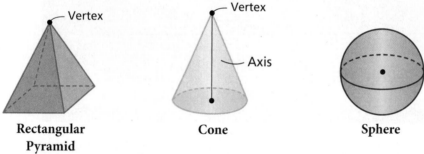

| Rectangular Pyramid | Cone | Sphere |

1 **A.** Suppose a right triangle is rotated about a line that contains one of its legs. This line is called the axis of rotation. You can model the rotation by taping a right triangular piece of paper to a pencil and spinning the pencil. What solid is formed by the rotation?

B. Suppose a rectangle is rotated about a line that contains one of its sides. What solid is formed by the rotation?

C. When a polygon is rotated about a line containing one of its sides, what shape is swept out in space by a point on another side of the polygon?

D. A solid that is formed by rotating a shape about an axis is a **solid of rotation**. Which of the eight solids above are solids of rotation?

Turn and Talk What happens if the rotated shape crosses the axis of rotation? Does it matter whether the axis of rotation is a line of symmetry for the shape?

Cross Sections of Solids

A **cross section** is the intersection of a three-dimensional figure and a plane.

The cross sections of three-dimensional figures can be simple figures, such as triangles, rectangles, or circles.

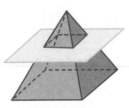

2 > A. In each figure shown, a plane parallel to the base intersects the solid. Describe the cross section of each figure. Compare the cross sections of the figures. What can you conclude?

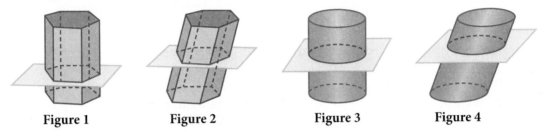

Figure 1   **Figure 2**   **Figure 3**   **Figure 4**

B. In each figure shown, a plane parallel to the base intersects the solid. Describe the cross section of each figure. What type of transformation maps the shape of the base to the cross section in each figure?

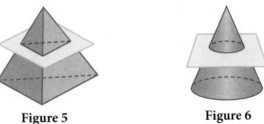

Figure 5   **Figure 6**

C. Suppose a rectangle is drawn on the coordinate plane. Describe how to use transformations of the rectangle to generate a rectangular pyramid.

D. Consider the different intersections of a plane and a cylinder as shown. What is true about the cross sections formed when a plane intersects a cylinder along its lateral surface? What is true about the cross sections formed when a plane intersects a cylinder through its two bases?

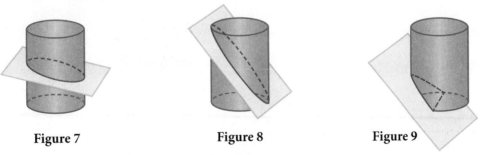

Figure 7   **Figure 8**   **Figure 9**

E. What is true about all cross sections of a sphere?

 Turn and Talk Determine whether it is possible to create a cross section that is a triangle in a prism, cylinder, pyramid, cone, and sphere. Explain your reasoning.

Step It Out

Apply Cross Sections

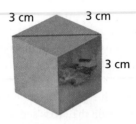

3cm   3cm

3cm

3 One form of the mineral pyrite naturally forms shiny metallic cubes. A cube of pyrite is cut in half along the diagonal of one of its faces and perpendicular to that face. What is the area of the newly exposed cross section?

The cross section is a rectangle. ⟵ **A.** Why is the cross section a rectangle but not a square?

Use the Pythagorean Theorem to find the length of the rectangle.

$a^2 + b^2 = c^2$

$3^2 + 3^2 = c^2$

$18 = c^2$

$3\sqrt{2} = c$

B. Why is the width of the rectangle 3 cm?

Use the length of the rectangle and its width, 3 cm, to find the area of the rectangle.

$A = \ell w = \left(3\sqrt{2}\right)(3) = 9\sqrt{2} \approx 12.7 \text{ cm}^2$

 Turn and Talk Describe a different way to cut the pyrite cube in half so that the area of the cross section formed is less than the area of the cross section found in the task.

Model a Real-World Solid

4 A carpenter needs to replace several turned balusters to repair a staircase. The carpenter uses a contour gauge to draw the profile of each existing baluster and delivers the profile drawings shown to the shop to get the balusters turned on a lathe. Match the profile drawings with the balusters.

A.    **B.**    **C.**

1.    **2.**    **3.**

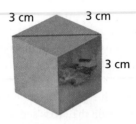

(t) ©Marcel Clemens/Shutterstock; (b) ©Josch/Shutterstock

Check Understanding

1. What solid will be created by rotating the shape about the given axis of rotation?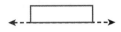

In Problems 2–4, use the figure of the rectangular pyramid. The plane is perpendicular to the base of the pyramid.

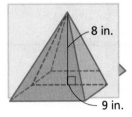

2. Describe the cross section shown.

3. Find the area of the cross section.

4. Suppose a plane intersects the pyramid parallel to its base. What shape is formed by the cross section?

5. Raheem used a drafting application on a computer to generate the solid shown. He created the solid by rotating a two-dimensional shape around a horizontal axis of rotation. Draw the shape that was rotated.

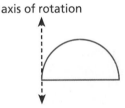

On Your Own

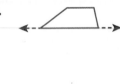

6. **(MP) Critique Reasoning** Kyle believes that rotating the given shape about the axis of rotation will produce a sphere. Juan believes the shape that will be formed is round in certain aspects, but not a sphere. Who is correct? Explain your reasoning.

Sketch the figure created by rotating each given shape about the axis.

7.

8.

9.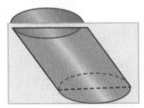

Describe each cross section.

10.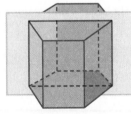

11.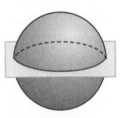

12.

13. A plane intersects a prism and forms a cross section that is congruent to its base. What is true about the plane?

14. A plane intersects a prism perpendicular to the base and forms a cross section that is congruent to its base. What is true about the prism?

15. **Open Ended** Sketch the intersection of a solid and a plane with a cross section that is a triangle.

An art teacher uses a piece of yarn to slice through a block of clay. Find the area of the rectangular cross section created by each slice.

16.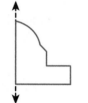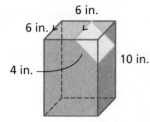

6 in.
6 in.
4 in.
10 in.

17.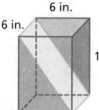

6 in.
6 in.
10 in.

Match each shape with its solid of rotation.

18.

19.

20.

A.

B.

C.

Spiral Review • Assessment Readiness

21. Find the circumference of a circle that has a radius of 4.

Ⓐ 2π Ⓒ 8π

Ⓑ 4π Ⓓ 16π

22. What is the area of a rectangle with a height of 3 inches and a length of 4π inches?

Ⓐ π in²   Ⓒ 7π in²

Ⓑ 6π in²   Ⓓ 12π in²

23. What is $\frac{2\pi}{3}$ in degrees?

Ⓐ 30°   Ⓒ 120°

Ⓑ 60°   Ⓓ 240°

24. A circular game piece 1.5 inches in diameter is divided into sectors. Each sector has a central angle of 60°. What is the area of one sector of the game piece?

Ⓐ 0.29 in²   Ⓒ 2.36 in²

Ⓑ 1.18 in²   Ⓓ 7.07 in²

 I'm in a Learning Mindset!

Was collaboration an effective tool for describing cross sections of three-dimensional figures? Explain.

Surface Areas of Prisms and Cylinders

(I Can) find the surface area of a prism or cylinder.

Spark Your Learning

Caleb is folding gift boxes and wrapping gifts.

Complete Part A as a whole class. Then complete Parts B–D in small groups.

A. What is a mathematical question you can ask about this situation? What information would you need to know to answer your question?

B. What variable(s) are involved in this situation? What unit of measurement would you use for each variable?

C. To answer your question, what strategy and tool would you use along with all the information you have? What answer do you get?

D. Does your answer make sense in the context of the situation? How do you know?

Turn and Talk Make a copy of the image of the unfolded box. Shade the sections that are not included in the surface area of the built box. How does the surface area of the built box compare to the area of the unfolded box?

Build Understanding

Develop a Surface Area Formula for a Right Prism

Surface area is the total area of all faces and curved surfaces of a three-dimensional figure. The **lateral area** of a prism is the sum of the areas of the lateral faces.

A **net** is a diagram of a three-dimensional figure arranged in such a way that the diagram can be folded to form the three-dimensional figure.

1 Consider the net of the right rectangular prism.

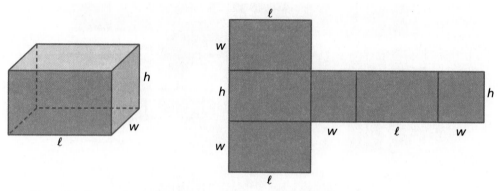

A. Describe the surface area of the prism represented by the net.

B. Use your description of the surface area of the prism to write a formula for the surface area of a right rectangular prism.

Consider the net of the oblique rectangular prism shown.

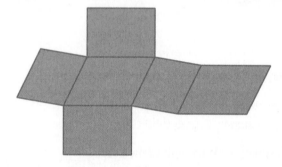

C. Draw a sketch of the oblique prism that you would get if you folded the net.

D. Describe how the surface area of the prism represented by the net is the same as the right rectangular prism. How is it different?

E. Is it possible to write a general formula for the surface area of an oblique prism using the dimensions of the net? Explain your reasoning.

Turn and Talk
- For the prism in Parts A and B, if $w\ell$ represents the area of the bases, what is the lateral area of the prism that does not include base areas?
- Describe how to find the surface area of a prism with a base that is a regular polygon but not a square.

Develop a Surface Area Formula for a Right Cylinder

You can also use a net of a right cylinder to develop a formula for the surface area of a right cylinder.

2 Consider the net of a right cylinder.

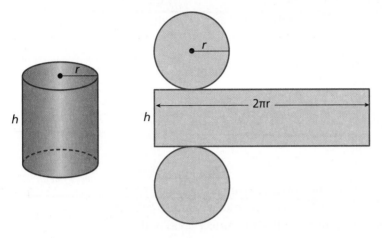

A. What shapes make up the surface of the cylinder?

B. Describe the surface area of the cylinder represented by the net.

C. Why is the length of the rectangle represented by the expression $2\pi r$? Explain your reasoning.

D. Use your description of the surface area of the cylinder to write a formula for the surface area of a right cylinder.

Consider an oblique cylinder.

E. Would the lateral area of the oblique cylinder be represented by a rectangle?

F. Can you write a general formula for the surface area of an oblique cylinder? Explain your reasoning.

 Turn and Talk Suppose you squeeze a right cylinder so that the shape of each base is an ellipse or oval shape, not a circle. What would you need to know in order to calculate the surface area?

Step It Out

Find the Surface Area of a Composite Figure

Surface Area of a Right Prism

The surface area of a right prism is the sum of the lateral area L and the area of the two bases $2B$.

$S = L + 2B$

Surface Area of a Right Cylinder

The surface area of a right cylinder is the sum of the lateral area L and the area of the two bases $2B$.

$S = L + 2B$

Recall that a **composite figure** is a three-dimensional figure made up of prisms, cones, pyramids, cylinders, and other simple three-dimensional figures. You can find the surface area of a composite figure by finding the surface areas of the individual figures that make up the composite figure.

3 ▸ Find the surface area of the small house.

> **A.** What are the three-dimensional figures that make up the house?

First, find the surface area of the rectangular prism.

$S = 2\ell w + 2\ell h + 2wh$

$S = 2(16)(12) + 2(16)(6) + 2(12)(6)$

$S = 384 + 192 + 144$

$S = 720 \text{ ft}^2$

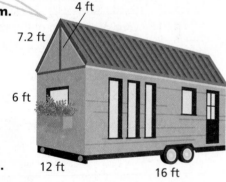

4 ft

7.2 ft

6 ft

12 ft

16 ft

Then, find the surface area of the triangular prism.

$S = 2\left(\frac{1}{2}(4)(12)\right) + 2(7.2)(16) + (16)(12)$

$S = 48 + 230.4 + 192$

$S = 470.4 \text{ ft}^2$

> **B.** What does each term in this equation represent in the triangular prism?

Find the surface area of the composite figure.

The surface area is the sum of the areas of all surfaces on the exterior of the figure.

$S = 720 + 470.4 - 2(16)(12)$

$S = 806.4 \text{ ft}^2$

> **C.** Why is 2(16)(12) subtracted from this equation?

 Turn and Talk Another model of this small house has a rectangular prism that is 6.5 feet high. How would the equation for the surface area change?

Apply a Surface Area Formula

Surface area can be used to answer many real-world questions. One use of surface area is in population density problems. **Population density** is the number of organisms of a particular type per square unit of area.

4 ▶ A treasure chest in an aquarium is covered with algae. If the algae covered the entire treasure chest, the population would be about 30,000,000 cells. What would be the population density of the algae?

3 cm

5 cm

6 cm

First, find the surface area of the rectangular prism.

$S = 2\ell w + 2\ell h + 2wh$

$S = 2(6)(5) + 2(6)(3) + 2(5)(3)$

$S = 60 + 36 + 30$

$S = 126$

The surface area of the treasure chest is 126 square centimeters.

Answer the question.

To find the population density of the algae on the entire treasure chest, divide the total population of algae by the surface area of the treasure chest.

> **A.** Why do you divide the total population by the surface area?

$$\text{Population Density} = \frac{30,000,000}{126}$$

$$\approx 238,000$$

> **B.** What do the units mean in this situation?

If 30,000,000 cells of algae covered the entire chest, the population density would be about 238,000 algae cells per square centimeter.

C. How many algae would you expect to be on the top of an algae-covered treasure chest? Explain your reasoning.

D. What would the population density of the algae be if 30,000,000 algae cells covered all except the bottom of the treasure chest?

 Turn and Talk Suppose the treasure chest had dimensions of 12 cm, 10 cm, and 6 cm, with the same population of algae. How would the population density of this chest compare to the population density of the original treasure chest? Explain.

Check Understanding

Find the surface area. Round your answer to the nearest tenth, if necessary.

1.

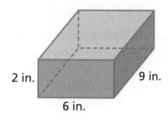

2 in. 9 in.
6 in.

2.

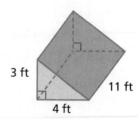

3 ft 11 ft
4 ft

3.

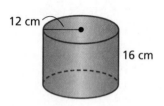

12 cm
16 cm

4.

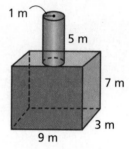

1 m
5 m
7 m
3 m
9 m

5. Raul is wrapping a gift that is a box shaped like a rectangular prism. The box is 14 inches long, 8 inches wide, and 3 inches tall. How much wrapping paper does he need to cover the box?

On Your Own

6. Dante has a vase that is shaped as shown.

   A. (MP) **Critique Reasoning** He says that the surface area of the vase is about 50.3 square inches. Is he correct? Explain your reasoning.

   B. If he wants to redecorate the lateral part of the vase only, what is the lateral area of the vase? Round to the nearest square inch

7 in.
2 in.

Find the surface area. Round your answer to the nearest tenth, if necessary.

7.

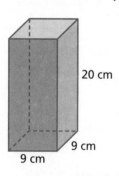

20 cm
9 cm
9 cm

8.

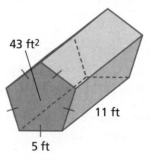

43 ft²
11 ft
5 ft

9.

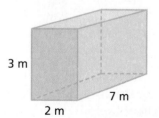

3 m
7 m
2 m

10.

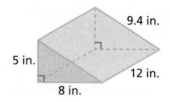

9.4 in.
5 in.
12 in.
8 in.

Find the surface area of each figure. Leave your answer in terms of π.

11.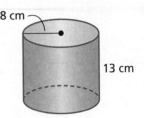
8 cm
13 cm

12.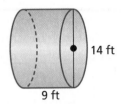
14 ft
9 ft

13.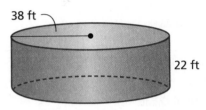
38 ft
22 ft

14.
9 in.
4 in.
3 in.
8 in.
3 in.

15. **STEM** A scientist is conducting an experiment with bacteria. The growth medium is shaped like a rectangular prism as shown.

   A. What is the entire surface area of the block?

   B. What is the population density of the bacteria on the block after 24 hours?

   C. What change in the surface area would decrease the population density?

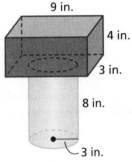

After 24 hours, 63,000 bacteria have colonized on the block.

3 in.

3 in.

4 in.

16. Compression socks are used on horses to increase circulation, to support the tendons and ligaments, and to provide stress relief from standing. Ryan's horse's lower front legs are 9 inches around and 11 inches long.

   A. What three-dimensional figure could model a horse's leg?

   B. Identify what the given information represents in the figure you chose.

   C. Determine the amount of fabric needed to make a pair of socks for the horse's front legs.

17. (MP) **Reason** Erica draws and labels the rectangle and wants to know what the surface area would be if it is rotated about the line. Does she have enough information to calculate the surface area? Explain your reasoning. If she has enough information, what is the surface area?

8 ft
12 ft

18. After performing market research, a box manufacturing company determined that their consumers most often purchase boxes that have a surface area of at least 234 square inches but at most 278 square inches. The given net represents a pattern for the company's boxes. What is the range of possible widths of the boxes that the company should produce in order to make only boxes of the most popular sizes?

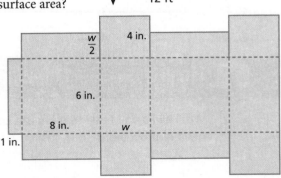

$\frac{w}{2}$
4 in.
6 in.
8 in.
w
1 in.

19. Find the height of a right cylinder with a radius of 24 centimeters and a surface area of 1632π square centimeters.

20. Find the surface area of a hexagonal prism with regular hexagons as the bases. The area of the base is 210 square inches. Each side of the base is 9 inches, and the height of the prism is 6 inches.

21. **Geology** Volcanic activity near basalt rock formations sometimes results in naturally occurring columns. The columns shown are slowly eroding because of exposure to rain and other elements. Suppose the bases of the columns that are labeled can be modeled by regular hexagons. The area of the base of the taller labeled one is approximately 1.5 square feet. Each side of its base is 9 inches.

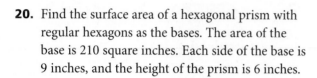

A. Draw a net that represents the taller hexagonal column. Then shade the area of the net that appears to be exposed to the elements.

B. From Part A, what is the surface area that is exposed to the elements?

22. Find the width of a right rectangular prism with a length of 16 inches, a height of 4 inches, and a surface area of 368 square inches.

23. (Open Middle™) What is the greatest possible volume for a cylinder with a surface area of 24π square units? (The formula for the volume of a cylinder is $V = \pi r^2 h$.)

Spiral Review • Assessment Readiness

24. Find the area of the sector.

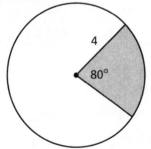

Ⓐ 6.28

Ⓑ 11.17

Ⓒ 12.57

Ⓓ 50.27

25. Which of the following could be a vertical or horizontal cross section of a cylinder? Select all that apply.

Ⓐ rectangle   Ⓓ circle

Ⓑ triangle   Ⓔ cone

Ⓒ trapezoid   Ⓕ pyramid

26. Match the angle measure on the left with its equivalent radian measure on the right.

A. 135°   1. $\dfrac{2\pi}{3}$

B. 120°   2. $\dfrac{\pi}{3}$

C. 45°   3. $\dfrac{\pi}{4}$

D. 60°   4. $\dfrac{3\pi}{4}$

 I'm in a Learning Mindset!

What skills do I have that benefit collaboration? Which collaboration skills still need improvement?

Surface Areas of Pyramids and Cones

(I Can) use formulas for the surface area of pyramids and cones to solve real-world problems.

Spark Your Learning

Geno is shingling the roof of an octagonal gazebo.

Complete Part A as a whole class. Then complete Parts B–D in small groups.

A. What is a mathematical question you can ask about this situation? What information would you need to know to answer your question?

B. What variable(s) are involved in this situation? What unit of measurement would you use for each variable?

C. To answer your question, what strategy and tool would you use along with all the information you have? What answer do you get?

D. Does your answer make sense in the context of the situation? How do you know?

> **Turn and Talk** How would your method to find the area change if the gazebo had 6 sides instead of 8 sides?

©CEW/Shutterstock

Build Understanding

Develop a Surface Area Formula for a Regular Pyramid

A **regular pyramid** is a pyramid whose base is a regular polygon and whose lateral faces are congruent isosceles triangles. The **slant height** ℓ of a regular pyramid is the height of each lateral face. Three examples of regular pyramids are shown.

Square Pyramid

4 congruent lateral faces

Triangular Pyramid

3 congruent lateral faces

Hexagonal Pyramid

6 congruent lateral faces

1 ▶ A. How is the slant height different from the height of a pyramid?

Consider the regular square pyramid as shown.

B. Describe the base and the lateral faces of the pyramid. What are the dimensions of the base and a lateral face?

C. Use the description of the base and lateral faces of the square pyramid to draw a net of the pyramid.

D. Suppose the side length s of the pyramid is 7 centimeters and the slant height ℓ is 5 centimeters. Use your net to calculate the surface area of the pyramid. Then write a general formula for the surface area of a square pyramid.

Consider a regular hexagonal pyramid as shown.

E. Can you generalize the formula you wrote for the surface area of a square pyramid to find the surface area of a hexagonal pyramid? If so, write the formula. If not, what additional information do you need?

F. Describe a general formula for the surface area of any regular pyramid. Do you think this formula would apply to the surface area of a cone?

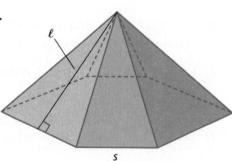

 Turn and Talk What shapes make up the net of a cone?

Develop a Surface Area Formula for a Right Cone

A **right cone** is a cone whose axis is perpendicular to its base. The slant height ℓ is the length from the base to the vertex along the lateral edge.

2 ▶ Consider the glass-blown right cone displayed.

A. Describe the base of the cone. What does r represent in the figure? What attributes of the base can you determine using r?

B. The lateral area of the cone is a sector of a circle as shown. What is the radius of the sector?

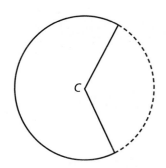

C. From Part B, what is the arc length of the sector? How do you know?

D. Mackenzie and Cole both draw nets to represent the glass-blown cone. Which is the correct net you would use to find the surface area of the cone?

Mackenzie's Drawing   **Cole's Drawing**

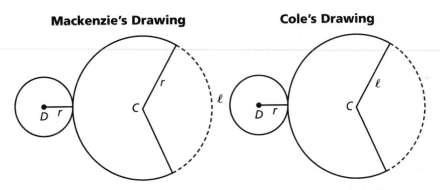

E. Suppose the radius of the cone is 2 inches and the slant height is 6 inches. Use the correct net from Part D to find the surface area of the cone.

F. Can you write a general formula for the surface area of a right cone? If so, write the formula. If not, what additional information do you need?

G. How are the surface area formulas of a cone and a pyramid similar? How are they different?

⬡ **Turn and Talk** How are cones and pyramids related?

Step It Out

Find the Surface Area of a Composite Figure

Surface Area of a Regular Pyramid

The lateral area of a regular pyramid with perimeter P and slant height ℓ is $L = \frac{1}{2} P\ell$.

The surface area of a regular pyramid with lateral area L and base area B is $S = L + B$, or $S = \frac{1}{2} P\ell + B$.

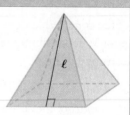

Surface Area of a Right Cone

The lateral area of a right cone with a radius r and slant height ℓ is $L = \pi r \ell$.

The surface area of a right cone with a lateral area L and base area B is $S = L + B$, or $S = \pi r \ell + \pi r^2$.

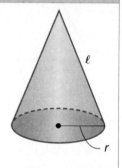

You learned previously how to find the surface area of composite figures made up of prisms and cylinders. Now you can find the surface area of composite figures with pyramids and cones as well.

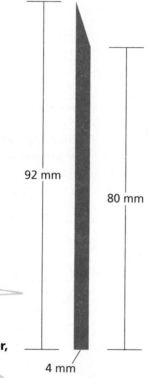

92 mm

80 mm

4 mm

3 A crayon can be modeled by rotating the two-dimensional shape shown about an axis. Find the surface area of the crayon.

> **A.** What simple shapes make up this shape? What figures are formed when this is rotated about an axis?

Find the lateral area of the cone, the lateral area of the cylinder, and the area of the base of the cylinder.

The height of the cone is $92 - 80 = 12$.

The slant height of the cone is $\ell = \sqrt{4^2 + 12^2} = 4\sqrt{10}$.

The lateral area of the cone is $\pi r \ell = \pi(4)(4\sqrt{10}) \approx 50.6\pi$.

> **B.** Why do you not need to find the area of the base of the cone?

The lateral area of the cylinder is $2\pi rh = 2\pi(4)(80) = 640\pi$.

The area of the base of the cylinder is $\pi r^2 = \pi(4^2) = 16\pi$.

Answer the question.

> **C.** Why is approximating the value of π done only at the last step?

The surface area of the crayon is $50.6\pi + 640\pi + 16\pi = 706.6\pi$, or about 2220 square millimeters.

Apply a Surface Area Formula

Recall that the population density is the number of organisms of a particular type per square unit of area. Surface density is similar in that it is the number of objects per square unit of area. You can find the surface density by dividing the number of objects by the area of the solid.

4 Evan is decorating a crystal square pyramid paperweight. He has a bottle of 250 gold flakes to cover the paperweight. He covers the pyramid with glue and rolls it into the flakes, making sure that all flakes in the bottle stick to the surface of the pyramid. What is the surface density—the number of gold flakes per square centimeter?

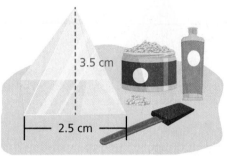

3.5 cm

2.5 cm

Find the surface area of the pyramid.

$S = \frac{1}{2} P\ell + B$

$S = \frac{1}{2}(10)(3.5) + 2.5^2$

> **A.** What do each of the variables in the formula mean in terms of the crystal pyramid?

$S = 17.5 + 6.25 = 23.75$

The surface area is 23.75 square centimeters.

Calculate the density.

$D = \frac{250}{23.75} \approx 11$

> **B.** What are the units of the density?

Answer the question.

Evan uses about 11 flakes per square centimeter to cover the paperweight.

C. How would the calculation of the density be different if there were no flakes added to the bottom of the paperweight? What would the density be in this situation?

D. How many flakes would be on one of the triangular faces of the pyramid? Explain how you found your answer.

E. When Evan is rolling the paperweight in the flakes, suppose he knocks some of the flakes on the floor and loses them. How would the density of the flakes that end up on the paperweight compare to the calculated population density? Explain.

Turn and Talk

- How would the density change if the bottle of flakes contained 100 flakes instead?
- If you know the surface density is 20 flakes per square centimeter, and you use the bottle of 250 flakes to cover the surface of the square pyramid, estimate the area of the base of the pyramid if the slant height is 2 centimeters. Show your work.

Check Understanding

Find the surface area of each figure. All pyramids have a regular base. Round to the nearest tenth, if necessary.

1.

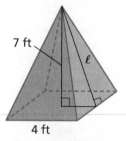

7 ft ℓ

4 ft

2.

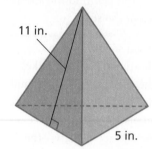

11 in.

5 in.

3.

16 cm

12 cm

4.

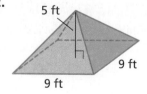

9 in.

20 in.

5 in.

5. Jake wants to decorate a ceramic right cone. The base radius of the cone is 4 inches, and the slant height is 6 inches tall. There are 2000 golden metallic flakes inside a jar. If he uses the entire jar to cover the cone, what is the surface density of the flakes on the cone?

On Your Own

6. The Luxor Hotel in Las Vegas, Nevada is a square pyramid with a height of 350 ft.

A. What is the slant height of one of its faces? Round to the nearest foot.

B. What is the lateral area of the pyramid?

C. (MP) **Model with Mathematics** A model of the hotel uses a scale of 1 in^2 = 1000 ft^2. To the nearest square inch, what is the surface area of the model?

646 ft

Find the surface area of each regular pyramid. Round to the nearest tenth, if necessary.

7.

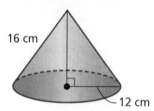

12 ft

7 ft

7 ft

8.

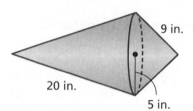

22 cm

14 cm

14 cm

9.

12 in.

11 in.

11 in.

10.

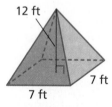

11 in.

8 in.   110 in^2

11.

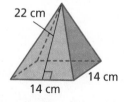

5 m

2 m

12.

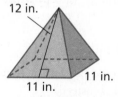

5 ft

9 ft

9 ft

Find the surface area of each right cone. Leave your answer in terms of π.

13.

16 ft

14 ft

14.

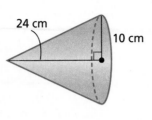

24 cm

10 cm

15.

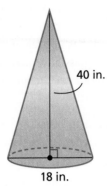

40 in.

18 in.

Find the surface area of each figure. If necessary, round to the nearest tenth.

16.

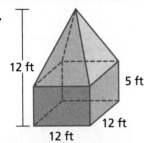

12 ft

5 ft

12 ft

12 ft

17.

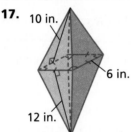

10 in.

6 in.

12 in.

18.

8 cm

5 cm

4 cm

19. (MP) **Reason** A regular pyramid has a surface area of 212 square feet. What would the surface area of the figure be if you multiplied each dimension of the pyramid by 2? Explain your reasoning.

20. Suppose a mooring buoy shown in the diagram is attached to an anchor and is pulled underwater by a chain malfunction. While underwater, the buoy collected about 1 million algae cells on its surface. What is the approximate population density of the algae on the buoy?

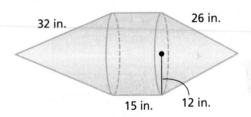

32 in.   26 in.

15 in.   12 in.

21. A square pyramid has a surface area of 272 square feet, and one of the side lengths of the square base is 8 feet. What is the slant height of the pyramid?

22. A cone has a surface area of 1650 square centimeters, and the radius of the base is 15 centimeters. What is the slant height of the cone? Round to the nearest tenth.

23. (MP) **Reason** An ice tray makes ice "cubes" that are square pyramids with height of 1.5 centimeters and with each side of the base 2.5 centimeters.

   A. Find the surface area of the ice cube to the nearest tenth of a centimeter.

   B. Suppose an ice cube tray makes ice cubes in the shape of a right cone which has the same surface area as the pyramid. The diameter of the base is 3 cm. Find the height of the cone to the nearest tenth of a centimeter.

24. Suppose the greenhouse shown has two seven-sided pyramids with corresponding faces connected by trapezoids. Each of the seven trapezoids has an area of 88 ft². Find the amount of glass, in square feet, needed for the exterior surface area of the greenhouse.

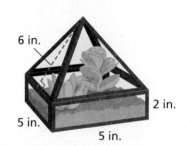

25. A chocolatier makes chocolates in the shape of cubes with an edge length of 1 inch.

A. The chocolatier is considering packaging in the shape of a pyramid with a square base. The pyramid would hold 30 chocolates in four square layers: 16 in the bottom layer, 9 in the second layer, 4 in the third layer, and 1 at the top. What would be the pyramid's minimum surface area? Explain.

B. If a rectangular prism is used to hold 30 chocolates, what would be the minimum surface area? Explain.

26. Emily is designing a terrarium for a contest at her school as shown. The terrarium has a base that is a rectangular prism and a top that is a square pyramid. What is the surface area of the terrarium?

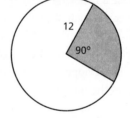

Spiral Review • Assessment Readiness

27. Find the surface area, in square feet, of the cylinder.

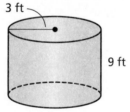

- (A) 18π
- (B) 54π
- (C) 63π
- (D) 72π

28. Which of the following could be a vertical or horizontal cross section of a cone? Select all that apply.

- (A) rectangle
- (B) triangle
- (C) square
- (D) circle
- (E) trapezoid
- (F) parallelogram

29. Find the area of the sector.

- (A) 113.1
- (B) 226.2
- (C) 339.3
- (D) 452.4

30. Find the diameter of a circle with an area of 615.44 cm².

- (A) 14 cm
- (B) 28 cm
- (C) 196 cm
- (D) 392 cm

 I'm in a Learning Mindset!

How did I benefit by giving help with finding the surface area of a composite figure? What impact did it have on my learning outcome?

Surface Areas of Spheres

(I Can) use the formula for the surface area of a sphere to calculate the surface areas of composite figures.

Spark Your Learning

The baseballs used in Major League Baseball games must be covered in two strips of white leather, tightly stitched together.

The baseball has a radius of 1.45 in.

Complete Part A as a whole class. Then complete Parts B–D in small groups.

A. What is a mathematical question you can ask about this situation? What information would you need to know to answer your question?

B. Suppose you could take the leather covering off of the baseball and lay the pieces flat. Make a sketch of what the pieces would look like.

C. To answer your question, what strategy and tool would you use along with all the information you have? What answer do you get?

D. Does your answer make sense in the context of the situation? How do you know?

> **Turn and Talk** In Major League Baseball, the rules state that the circumference of a baseball must be 9 inches or greater but not exceed 9.25 inches. What are the minimum and maximum surface areas that a baseball can have?

Build Understanding

Investigate the Formula for the Surface Area of a Sphere

Surface Area of a Sphere

The surface area of a sphere with a radius r is given by $S = 4\pi r^2$.

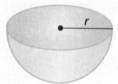

A **hemisphere** is half of a sphere. The surface area of a hemisphere is half the surface area of the related sphere plus the area of its circular base.

1 A cylinder and a sphere have the same radius r. The sphere fits inside the cylinder so that the sphere intersects each base of the cylinder in exactly one point.

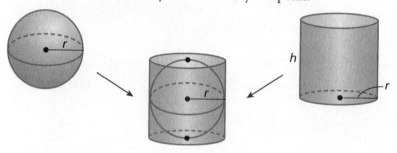

A. Write the lateral area of the cylinder in terms of the radius r and height h of the cylinder.

B. What is the height of the cylinder in terms of the radius r?

C. Write the lateral area of the cylinder in terms of r only. How is the lateral area of the cylinder related to the surface area of the sphere?

D. A hemisphere with radius r fits inside a cylinder with radius r and height r. One base of the cylinder is the circular surface of the hemisphere, and the hemisphere intersects the other base in one point. Is the surface area of the hemisphere half the surface area of the cylinder? Explain.

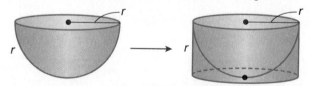

 Turn and Talk Suppose you wanted to construct a solid that approximates the shape of a sphere by stacking cross sections on top of each other. Describe the cross sections that you could use.

Step It Out

Use the Surface Area of a Sphere

2 ▶ Gold beads like the ones shown are used to make earrings. Each gold bead is a stainless steel sphere with a 24-carat gold coating. The density of gold in the coating is 0.009 milligrams of gold per square millimeter. About how much gold is in the coating of one gold bead?

The radius of each bead is 6 mm.

Surface area of sphere $= 4\pi r^2 = 4\pi(6)^2 \approx 452$ mm^2

Total amount of gold ≈ 0.009 mg/mm$^2 \cdot 452$ mm$^2 \approx 4.068$ mg

How do the units of 0.009 and 452 produce the units of the total amount of gold?

One gold bead is covered with about 4.1 milligrams of gold.

Find the Surface Area of a Composite Figure

Recall that you can find the surface area of composite figures by using appropriate formulas to find the areas of the different surfaces of the figure.

3 ▶ Find the surface area of the silo to the nearest square foot.

Determine the different surfaces of the silo.
The surface area of the silo is composed of the lateral area of a cylinder and the surface area of the spherical part of a hemisphere.

$$\boxed{\begin{array}{c} \text{Surface area} \\ \text{of silo} \end{array}} = \boxed{\begin{array}{c} \text{Lateral area} \\ \text{of cylinder} \end{array}} + \boxed{\begin{array}{c} \text{Surface area of} \\ \text{spherical part of} \\ \text{hemisphere} \end{array}}$$

20 ft

60 ft

Find the lateral area of the cylindrical part of the silo.

$L = 2\pi rh$
$= 2\pi(10)(60)$
$= 1200\pi$ ft^2

A. Why is 10 substituted for r instead of 20?

Find the surface area of the spherical part of the silo. Then answer the question.

$S = \frac{1}{2}(4\pi r^2)$
$= \frac{1}{2}[4\pi(10^2)]$
$= 200\pi$ ft^2

B. Why is this expression multiplied by $\frac{1}{2}$?

C. Why is approximating the value of π done in the last step?

The surface area of the silo $= 1200\pi + 200\pi \approx 4398$ square feet.

 Turn and Talk Some silos have conical caps instead of hemispherical caps. If you keep the height the same, which design would minimize the amount of material needed to build the cap? Explain.

Check Understanding

1. Explain how two-dimensional shapes can be used to represent the surface area of a sphere that has a radius of 8 centimeters.

Find the surface area of each sphere. Leave answers in terms of π.

2.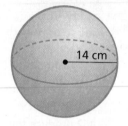
   14 cm

3.
   22 m

4. A polystyrene sphere representing the moon has a radius of 18 inches. The sphere is coated with extra fine glitter. If 1 ounce of glitter covers 900 square inches, how many ounces of glitter are needed to cover the sphere? Round your answer to the nearest tenth of an ounce.

Find the surface area of each composite figure. Round answers to the nearest tenth.

5.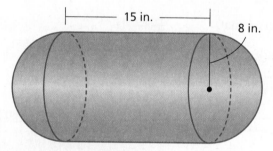
   15 in.
   8 in.

6.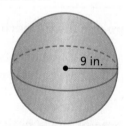
   2 ft
   2 ft
   9 ft
   4 ft

On Your Own

Find the surface area of each figure. Leave answers in terms of π.

7.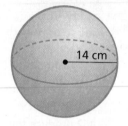
   8 ft

8.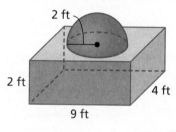
   9 in.

9.
   24 yd

10.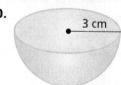
    3 cm

11. The figure shows how a long piece of rope was wrapped around the cylinder to completely cover its lateral surface. Then the rope is taken from the cylinder and wrapped around the sphere. Will the rope completely cover the surface of the sphere? Why or why not?

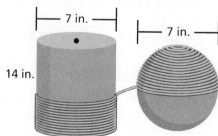
7 in.
7 in.
14 in.

576

12. **Open Ended** Draw a sphere and label the radius of the sphere. Find the surface area of your sphere.

13. (MP) **Critique Reasoning** Glen and Nancy both attempt to calculate the surface area of the closed hemisphere shown. The results are shown below. Who is correct? Explain your reasoning.

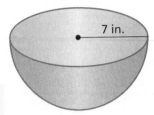
7 in.

Nancy's Calculations
$$S = \frac{1}{2}\left(4\pi r^2\right) + \pi r^2$$
$$= \frac{1}{2}\left[4\pi (7^2)\right] + \pi (7)^2$$
$$= 147\pi \text{ in}^2$$

Glen's Calculations
$$S = \frac{1}{2}\left(4\pi r^2\right)$$
$$= \frac{1}{2}\left[4\pi (7^2)\right]$$
$$= 98\pi \text{ in}^2$$

14. If two pieces of ice have the same volume, the one with the greater surface area will melt faster. One piece of ice shown is a sphere, and the other piece is a cube. Given that the pieces of ice have approximately the same volume, which will melt faster? Explain.

A side length is 24.2 mm.

The radius is 15 mm.

15. **STEM** In the figure shown, an engineer sketches a two-dimensional image to be used to create a three-dimensional model of a toy. The image will be rotated about an axis to create the model. Find the surface area of the model. Round to the nearest tenth.

16. (MP) **Reason** What happens to the surface area of a sphere if you triple its radius? Explain your reasoning.

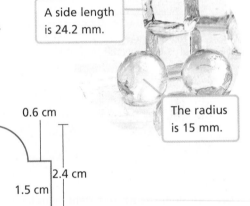
0.6 cm
2.4 cm
1.5 cm
1.5 cm

17. **Art** The fountain shown is called a floating sphere fountain because a person can easily spin a granite sphere weighing thousands of pounds. This is due to the force provided by the water in the socket that the sphere rests in.

   A. In one such fountain, 5% of the surface of the sphere is in contact with the water in the socket. How many square inches of the sphere is in contact with the water?

   B. The water in the socket applies a force of 15 pounds per square inch to the sphere. How much force is applied to the sphere?

The diameter of the sphere is 48 in.

Find the surface area of each composite figure. Round answers to the nearest tenth.

18.
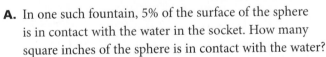
5 cm
12 cm
2 cm

19.
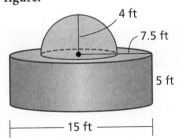
4 ft
7.5 ft
5 ft
15 ft

20. Find the radius of the globe shown. If you want to purchase a globe with a radius 50% larger, what is the approximate surface area of the new globe?

21. A dog has a ball that is 2.7 in. wide. A scientist estimates that the population of bacteria on the surface of the ball is about 41,000 cells. What is the approximate population density of bacteria on the ball?

22. Earth's rotation about its polar axis causes it to bulge at the equator. Its radius at the equator is about 6378 km, while its radius at the poles is about 6357 km. What is Earth's approximate surface area? Explain your reasoning.

23. (Open Middle™) Sphere A has a volume of 36π units^3. Sphere B has a surface area of 36π units^2. Which sphere is bigger? $\left(\text{Volume of a sphere: } V = \frac{4}{3}\pi r^3\right)$

The globe has a surface area of about 452.4 in².

Spiral Review • Assessment Readiness

24. What is the surface area of the cone?

Ⓐ 85π in^2

Ⓑ 90π in^2

Ⓒ 220π in^2

Ⓓ 230π in^2

12 in.

10 in.

25. ___?___ have an axis or lateral edges that are perpendicular to its base(s). Select all that apply.

Ⓐ Spheres

Ⓑ Oblique solids

Ⓒ Right solids

Ⓓ Cones

26. Consider the net of a right cylinder. Can you use the given shape to show the surface of the cylinder?

Shape	Yes	No
A. rectangle	?	?
B. circle	?	?
C. triangle	?	?
D. trapezoid	?	?

©D. Hurst/Alamy

I'm in a Learning Mindset!

How did I benefit by giving help with finding surface area of a composite figure? What impact did it have on my learning outcome?

Cross Sections

A cross section is the intersection of a three-dimensional figure and a plane.

A cross section that is made parallel to the base of a prism or pyramid is similar to the base.

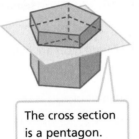

The cross section is a pentagon.

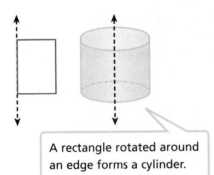

A rectangle rotated around an edge forms a cylinder.

A two-dimensional shape and an axis of rotation can determine a three-dimensional figure.

Surface Area of Prisms and Cylinders

The surface area of right prisms and right cylinders is $S = L + 2B$, where L is the lateral area and B is the area of a base.

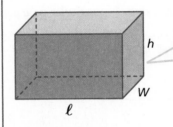

You can also find the area of each of the six faces of a prism and add them together.

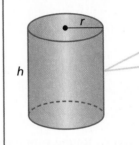

The lateral area of a cylinder is $L = 2\pi rh$. The area of the base of a cylinder is $B = \pi r^2$.

Surface Area of Pyramids and Cones

The surface area of regular pyramids and right cones is $S = L + B$, where L is the lateral area and B is the area of the base.

For a regular pyramid, the lateral area is half the product of the perimeter of the base and the slant height, or $L = \frac{1}{2}P\ell$.

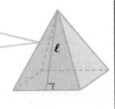

For a cone, the lateral area is the product of π, the radius, and the slant height, or $L = \pi r\ell$.

Surface Area of Spheres

The surface area of a sphere is $S = 4\pi r^2$.

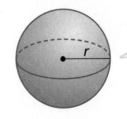

The curved part of a hemisphere has half the surface area of a sphere.

One base of the cylinder is not exposed. Omit this area.

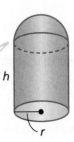

Vocabulary

Choose the correct term from the box to complete each sentence.

1. The ___?___ of a prism is the sum of the areas of the lateral faces.

2. Half a sphere is a(n) ___?___.

3. A(n) ___?___ is a solid that has an axis or sides that are not perpendicular to its base.

4. A solid whose base is a regular polygon and whose five lateral faces are congruent isosceles triangles is a(n) ___?___.

5. The number of organisms of a particular type per square unit of area is the ___?___.

Vocabulary
hemisphere
lateral area
oblique solid
population density
regular pyramid

Concepts and Skills

6. Describe the cross section.

7. What solid will be created by rotating the shape about the given axis of rotation?

Find the surface area of each figure. Round your answers to the nearest tenth, if necessary.

8.

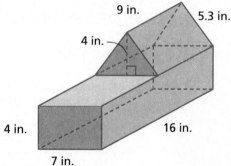

9in.   5.3 in.
4 in.
4 in.   16 in.
7 in.

9.

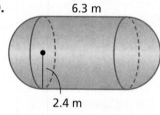

6.3 m
2.4 m

10. Travis uses a 3D printer to create a regular square pyramid with a base length of 6 centimeters and a slant height of 6 centimeters. Rhonda uses the printer to create a cone with a radius of 4 centimeters and a slant height of 5 centimeters. Whose figure has a smaller surface area? Explain.

11. (MP) **Use Tools** Nadia is making a scale model of a disco ball. She has a plastic-foam sphere with a radius of 5.2 inches. She has a package that contains 1400 sequins. She covers the sphere with glue and rolls it in the sequins, making sure that all the sequins stick to the sphere. Find the density of sequins on the sphere. State what strategy and tool you will use to answer the question, explain your choice, and then find the answer.

PAY Per CHEW

How many gumballs fit in the gumball machine?

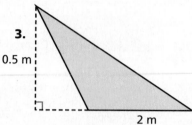

Are You Ready?

Complete these problems to review prior concepts and skills you will need for this module.

Areas of Triangles

Calculate the area of each triangle.

1.

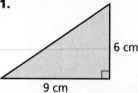

6 cm
9 cm

2.

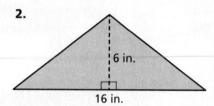

6 in.
16 in.

3.

0.5 m
2 m

Volumes of Right Rectangular Prisms

Calculate the volume of each right rectangular prism.

4.

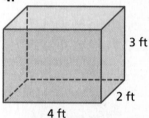

3 ft
2 ft
4 ft

5.

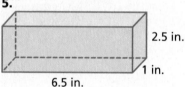

2.5 in.
1 in.
6.5 in.

6.

15 cm
7 cm
9 cm

Areas of Circles

Calculate the area of each circle. Leave answers in terms of π.

7.

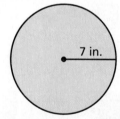

7 in.

8.

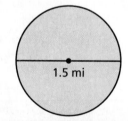

1.5 mi

9.

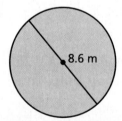

8.6 m

Connecting Past and Present Learning

Previously, you learned:

- to construct arguments for the circumference and area of a circle,
- to identify the shapes of two-dimensional cross sections of three-dimensional objects, and
- to apply surface area to solve design problems.

In this module, you will learn:

- to give an informal argument for the formulas for the volume of prisms and cylinders,
- to give an informal argument using Cavalieri's principle for the formulas for the volume of solid figures, and
- to use volume formulas for cylinders, pyramids, cones, and spheres to solve problems.

Volumes of Prisms and Cylinders

(I Can) develop and use formulas for the volume of a prism and a cylinder.

Spark Your Learning

Circular containers can be stacked to save storage space. The stacked containers are in the shape of a cylinder.

A typical stack includes 4 containers.

Complete Part A as a whole class. Then complete Parts B–D in small groups.

   A. What is a mathematical question you can ask about this situation? What information would you need to know to answer your question?

   B. What variables are involved in this situation? What unit of measurement would you use for each variable?

   C. To answer your question, what strategy and tool would you use along with all the information you have? What answer do you get?

   D. Does your answer make sense in the context of the situation? How do you know?

> **Turn and Talk** How does finding the volume of one layer of a cylinder help you find the volume of the entire cylinder?

Build Understanding

Develop a Basic Volume Formula

The **volume** of a three-dimensional figure is the number of nonoverlapping cubic units contained within the figure.

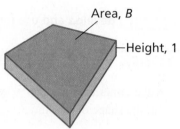
Area, *B*
Height, 1

1. Consider the right prism shown, with a base area of *B* square units and a height of 1 unit.

  A. Each side of a unit cube is 1 unit. How many unit cubes could you place in the prism? What is the volume of this prism?

  Suppose you stack another identical prism on top of this prism.

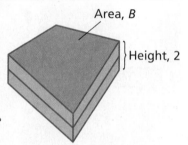
Area, *B*
Height, 2

  B. What is the volume of the stacked prism? Explain your reasoning.

  C. Suppose you continue adding prisms on top of each other until you have *h* prisms stacked. What is the volume of the full prism?

  D. Can you use the same method to find the volume of a three-dimensional figure if the base is a circle with an area of *B* square units and a height of 1 unit? What is the volume of a right cylinder made by stacking four of these cylinders?

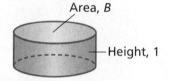
Area, *B*
Height, 1

  E. What is a general rule you can use to find the volume of a right prism or a right cylinder? Write an equation for this rule.

Justify the Procedure for Finding Volumes of Oblique Prisms and Cylinders

You can use the same formula you found for the volume of a prism and a cylinder to find the volume of an oblique prism and an oblique cylinder.

2. Consider a stack of ten nickels.

  A. The diameter of a nickel is 21.21 millimeters, and the height is 1.95 millimeters. What is the volume of a nickel? What is the volume of this stack of nickels? Write your answer to the nearest cubic millimeter.

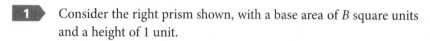

  B. How are these stacks of nickels similar to the previous stack of nickels? How are they different?

  C. What is the volume of each stack of nickels? Explain your reasoning.

  D. Use what you found to make a general statement about any stack of 10 nickels.

  E. The volume of the right cylinder shown is 80π cubic inches. Can you determine the volume of the oblique cylinder? Explain.

 Turn and Talk How does the volume of the stack of nickels change if you add three more nickels?

Investigate the Volume of a Solid Formed by Rotation

In Tasks 1 and 2, you investigated the formulas for the volumes of prisms and cylinders with vertical edges and those with slanted edges. Cavalieri's Principle guarantees that those oblique solids have the same volumes as their corresponding right solids.

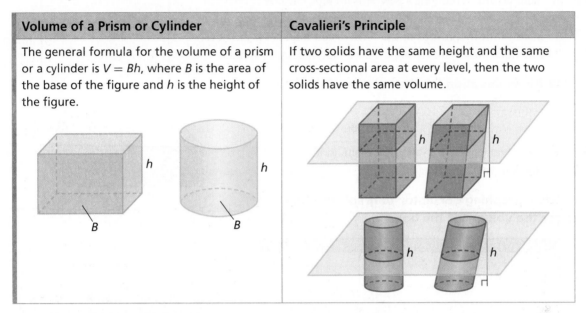

Volume of a Prism or Cylinder	Cavalieri's Principle
The general formula for the volume of a prism or a cylinder is $V = Bh$, where B is the area of the base of the figure and h is the height of the figure.	If two solids have the same height and the same cross-sectional area at every level, then the two solids have the same volume.

Recall that you have explored revolving two-dimensional shapes about an axis or a line to form three-dimensional figures. You have also found the surface area of these three-dimensional figures.

 Suppose you form a cylinder by rotating a rectangle with length h and width r about a vertical axis.

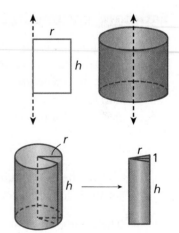

A. What are the dimensions of the cylinder shown?

B. Approximate the volume of the cylinder by cutting the cylinder into a series of triangular prisms. Let the short base edge of each triangular prism be 1 unit and the height of the triangular base be equal to the radius of the base of the cylinder. How many of these triangular prisms can the cylinder be divided into? Explain your reasoning.

C. What is the volume of each triangular prism?

D. Show how you can use the volume of the triangular prism and the number of triangular prisms formed to estimate the volume of the cylinder.

E. Compare the volume estimate you found in part D to the volume of a cylinder found by using the formula $V = Bh$. What do you notice?

 Turn and Talk Suppose you approximated the volume of the cylinder in Task 3 by dividing the cylinder into triangular prisms with a base of 2 units. How would this affect the resulting volume formula?

Step It Out

Maximize the Volume of a Rectangular Prism

4 A manufacturer is building a box with no top. The box is constructed from a piece of cardboard that is 10 inches long and 15 inches wide by cutting out the corners and folding up the sides. The manufacturer wants to build a box with maximum volume.

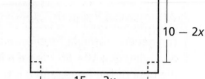

Write an equation for the volume of the box.

$V = x(10 - 2x)(15 - 2x)$

A. How was this equation developed?

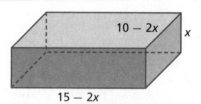

B. What values of x are valid in this situation? Explain your reasoning.

Use a graphing calculator to graph the function for the volume of the box.

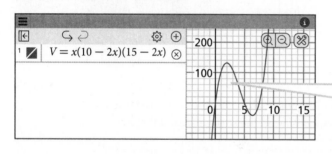

C. Explain why a box with approximate dimensions of height 2 inches, width 6 inches, and length 11 inches will give the maximum volume. What is that volume?

Estimate Volume in a Real-World Scenario

5 A craftsperson wants to make a wooden drinking vessel for wild animals that holds approximately 3 gallons of water (1 gallon ≈ 231 cubic inches) by cutting a portion of a log and hollowing it out. One inch of wood will be retained on the bottom and lateral part (side) of the vessel. What should be the height of the vessel?

The drinking vessel will be a cylinder, so use the formula $V = \pi r^2 h$.

To find the height, substitute the values of the radius and volume in the formula for the volume and solve for h. The radius of the drinking vessel is 7 inches.

The volume of the drinking vessel is 3 gallons, or about 693 cubic inches.

A. Why is the radius 7 inches?

$$V = \pi r^2 h$$
$$693 = \pi(7^2)h$$

B. Why is 693 cubic inches used for the volume instead of 3 gallons?

$$693 = 49\pi h$$
$$\frac{693}{49\pi} = h$$
$$h \approx 4.5$$

C. Explain why the height of the vessel is 1 inch more than the height of the water.

So, the drinking vessel will be about 5.5 inches high.

 Turn and Talk What would be the height of the drinking vessel if the amount of wood retained on the bottom and side were 0.5 inch?

©Oleg Dudko/Dreamstime

Check Understanding

1. Explain how you can find the volume of a prism or cylinder.

Find the volume of each figure. Round your answer to the nearest hundredth.

2.

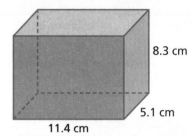

8.3 cm

5.1 cm

11.4 cm

3.

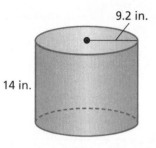

9.2 in.

14 in.

4. The diameter of a dime is 17.91 millimeters, and the height is 1.35 millimeters. What is the volume of a dime? What is the volume of an oblique cylinder formed by stacking 50 dimes? Round your answers to the nearest hundredth.

5. A rectangle with a height of 6 inches and a width of 6 inches is rotated around an axis along one side. Find the volume of the solid that is created by this rotation. Round your answer to the nearest hundredth.

6. Find the maximum volume of a box with side lengths of x, $24 - 2x$, and $16 - 2x$. What are the approximate dimensions that produce the maximum volume and what is that volume? Round all answers to the nearest hundredth.

7. Mike has a shoe box that is 14.75 inches long, 10 inches wide, and 5.5 inches tall. What is the volume of his shoe box?

On Your Own

8. (MP) **Critique Reasoning** Francisco believes that the volume of an oblique cylinder with a height of 3 inches and a radius of 1 inch is the same as the volume of a right cylinder with a height of 3 inches and a radius of 1 inch. Is Francisco correct? Explain your reasoning.

9. A rectangle is rotated about a line containing one of its long sides. The rectangle has a length of 5 inches and a width of 2 inches. Find the volume of the solid that is created by this rotation. What type of solid is created?

2 in.

5 in.

10. (MP) **Reason** Deanna is studying two cylindrical blocks. The radius of the base of one block is 6 inches. The diameter of the base of the other block is 10 inches. Each block has a height of 12 inches. Without calculating, identify which block has the greater volume. Explain your reasoning.

11. Ramon has a cylindrical can of chili with the dimensions shown. How much chili can fit in the can? Round your answer to the nearest hundredth.

3.25 in.

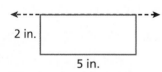

4.25 in.

Find the volume of each prism or cylinder. Round your answer to the nearest hundredth.

12.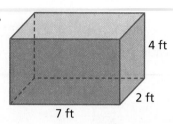
4 ft
2 ft
7 ft

13.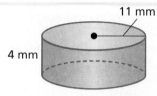
11 mm
4 mm

14.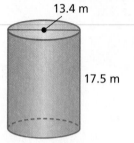
13.4 m
17.5 m

15.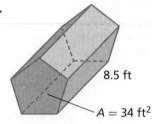
8.5 ft
$A = 34$ ft^2

16.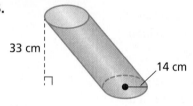
33 cm
14 cm

17.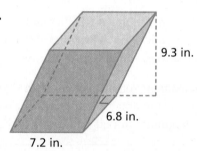
9.3 in.
6.8 in.
7.2 in.

18.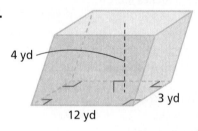
4 yd
3 yd
12 yd

19.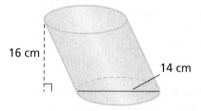
16 cm
14 cm

Find the maximum volume of each box and the dimensions that produce the maximum volume. Round all answers to the nearest hundredth.

20.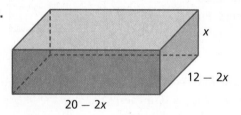
x
$12 - 2x$
$20 - 2x$

21.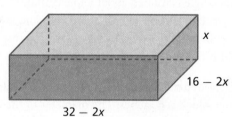
x
$16 - 2x$
$32 - 2x$

22. An aquarium is 40 centimeters long, 20 centimeters wide, and 25 centimeters high. When filled with water, the mass of the water in the aquarium is 20 kilograms. What is the volume of the aquarium? What is the density of the water in the aquarium in grams per cubic centimeter?

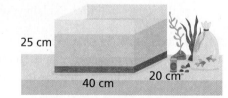
25 cm
40 cm
20 cm

Find the volume of each composite figure. Round your answer to the
nearest hundredth.

23.

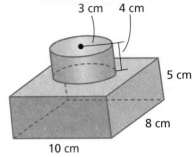

3 cm   4 cm

5 cm

8 cm

10 cm

24.

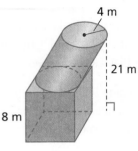

4 m

21 m

8 m

25.

2.5 in.

4.5 in.

3 in.

26.

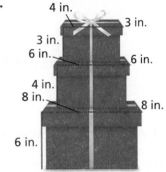

4 in.   3 in.

3 in.
6 in.   6 in.

4 in.
8 in.   8 in.

6 in.

27. Dwight is digging a hole for a post for a mailbox. The post is 4 inches wide and 4 inches
long. The post must be buried between 12 inches and 18 inches deep in the ground.
What is the minimum and maximum volume of the hole that Dwight must dig?

Find the missing dimension of each figure. Round your answer to the nearest tenth.

28. $V = 706.86 \text{ ft}^3$

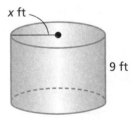

x ft

9 ft

29. $V = 436.05 \text{ in}^3$

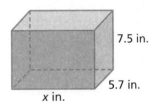

7.5 in.

5.7 in.

x in.

30. Cylinder A and cylinder B are similar solids. What is the volume of cylinder B?

4 m

7 m

Cylinder A

6 m

Cylinder B

31. STEM An engineer designs an oil filter. The filter is a cylinder with a base diameter of
3.5 inches. The filter must fit in a space that is 5 inches long by 5 inches wide by 5 inches
tall. What is the greatest volume the filter can have and still fit in the space?

32. A homeowner orders 3 cubic yards of mulch that will be stored in a box. The box is a rectangular prism with a base 1.5 yards wide and 1.5 yards long. What minimum height must the box have to hold all of the mulch?

33. A can manufacturer wants to make a cylindrical can that holds 355 cm³ (which is 355 mL, or about 12 fl oz) of liquid. Use a graphing calculator or a spreadsheet to find the base radius that minimizes the can's surface area.

34. (Open Middle™) Using the digits 1 to 9 at most two times each, fill in the boxes for the length of the radius and height such that it creates a true statement where the volume of a cone plus the volume of a sphere equals the volume of a cylinder.

$$r = \boxed{}$$
$$h = \boxed{}$$

cone + sphere = cylinder: $$\frac{\boxed{}}{\boxed{}}\pi + \frac{\boxed{}}{\boxed{}}\pi = \frac{\boxed{}}{\boxed{}}\pi$$

Spiral Review • Assessment Readiness

35. Which of the following expressions could be used to find the surface area of the cylinder? Select all that apply.

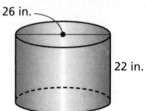
26 in.
22 in.

(A) $\pi r^2 h$

(B) $L + 2\pi r^2$

(C) $L + 2B$

(D) $2\pi r^2$

(E) Bh

(F) $2L + B$

36. Find the length of $\overline{BC}$.

(A) 2.64

(B) 3.26

(C) 3.4

(D) 4.2

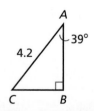
A
39°
4.2
C   B

37. Find the surface area of the cone.

(A) 85π m²

(B) 105π m²

(C) 261π m²

(D) 281π m²

5 m
16 m

38. Find the surface area of the sphere.

(A) 11π mm²

(B) 121π mm²

(C) 242π mm²

(D) 484π mm²

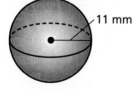
11 mm

I'm in a Learning Mindset!

What skills do I have that benefit collaboration? Which collaboration skills still need improvement?

Keep Going to▶ Journal and Practice Workbook

Volumes of Pyramids and Cones

(I Can) show the relationship between the volume formulas for pyramids and cones.

Spark Your Learning

Brooke is researching the pyramids of ancient Egypt. The Great Pyramid of Giza is the largest one.

The height of the pyramid is 147 meters.

Complete Part A as a whole class. Then complete Parts B–D in small groups.

A. What is a mathematical question you can ask about this situation? What information would you need to know to answer your question?

B. A pyramid is related to what other three-dimensional figure? About what fraction of the space inside that figure does a pyramid take up—more than half as much space, half as much space, or less than half as much space? Give an approximate fraction and explain your reasoning.

C. What variable(s) are involved in this situation about the Giza Pyramid? What unit of measurement would you use for each variable?

D. To answer your question, what strategy and tool would you use along with all the information you have? What answer do you get?

Turn and Talk What would it mean to find the volume of one of the pyramids at Giza? What would you need to know to find this volume?

Build Understanding

Develop a Formula for the Volume of a Pyramid

The following postulate is helpful when developing a formula for the volume of a pyramid.

Postulate
Pyramids that have equal base areas and equal heights have equal volumes.

1 Consider a triangular pyramid with vertex G directly over vertex D of the base HCD. This triangular pyramid can be thought of as part of triangular prism with $\triangle EFG \cong \triangle HCD$. Let the area of the base of the pyramid be B and let $GD = h$.

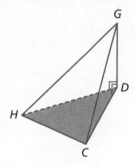 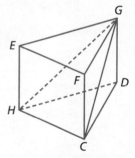

A. What is the volume of the triangular prism in terms of B and h?

B. Draw $\overline{EC}$. Consider the three pyramids: $G\text{-}EHC$, $G\text{-}CFE$, and $G\text{-}HCD$. Explain why the sum of the volumes of these pyramids is equal to the volume of the prism.

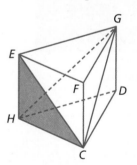 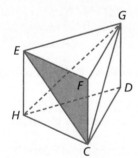 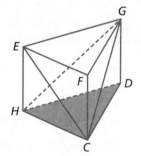

C. $\overline{EC}$ is the diagonal of a rectangle, so $\triangle EHC \cong \triangle CFE$. Explain why pyramids $G\text{-}EHC$ and $G\text{-}CFE$ have the same volume. Explain why pyramids $G\text{-}HCD$ and $C\text{-}EFG$ have the same volume.

D. $G\text{-}CFE$ and $C\text{-}EFG$ are two names for the same pyramid, so you have shown that the three pyramids that form the triangular prism have the same volume. Compare the volume of pyramid $G\text{-}HCD$ to the volume of the triangular prism. Write the volume of pyramid $G\text{-}HCD$ in terms of B and h.

 Turn and Talk If the bases of a pyramid and a prism are congruent, is it always true, sometimes true, or never true that the volume of the pyramid is $\frac{1}{3}$ the volume of the prism?

Develop a Formula for the Volume of a Cone

Volume of a Pyramid

The volume V of a pyramid with base area B and height h is given by $V = \frac{1}{3}Bh$.

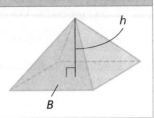

You can approximate the volume of a cone by finding the volume of inscribed pyramids.

Base of inscribed pyramid has 3 sides

Base of inscribed pyramid has 4 sides

Base of inscribed pyramid has 5 sides

2 **A.** Consider pyramids with regular polygon bases: equilateral triangles, squares, regular pentagons, and so on. As the number of sides increases, what shape does the base begin to resemble?

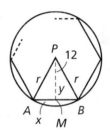

B. The base of the pyramid is inscribed in the base of the cone and is a regular n-gon. Let P be the center of the cone's base, let r be the radius of the cone's base, and let h be the height of the cone.

Construct $\overline{PM}$ from P to the midpoint M of $\overline{AB}$. How do you know that the non-central angles of triangle PAB, angles 1 and 2, are congruent? What do you know about $\angle AMP$ and $\angle BMP$?

C. There are n triangles congruent to $\triangle APB$ in the n-gon, so $m\angle APB = \frac{360°}{n}$ and $m\angle 1 = \frac{180°}{n}$. Using the fact that $\sin(\angle 1) = \frac{x}{r}$ and $\cos(\angle 1) = \frac{y}{r}$, you know that $x = r\sin\left(\frac{180°}{n}\right)$ and $y = r\cos\left(\frac{180°}{n}\right)$. Using these equations for x and y, and the formula for the area of a triangle, write an equation for the area of the n-gon.

D. The expression for the area of the base of the pyramid includes the expression $n\sin\left(\frac{180°}{n}\right) \cdot \cos\left(\frac{180°}{n}\right)$. Use a spreadsheet to discover what happens to this expression as n gets larger.

- Use column A for the n-values. Enter 3 in cell A1 and "= A1 + 1" in cell A2, then fill down column A.

- Enter this formula in cell B1, then fill down column B:
  = A1 * SIN(RADIANS(180/A1)) * COS(RADIANS(180/A1))

What happens to the expression as n gets very large?

E. Use your answer from Part D. What happens to the expression for the volume of the inscribed pyramid as n increases?

Step It Out

Model a Real-World Structure to Estimate Volume

Volume of a Cone

The volume of a cone with base radius r and base area $B = \pi r^2$ and height h is given by $V = \frac{1}{3}Bh$ or $V = \frac{1}{3}\pi r^2 h$.

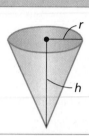

3 An ice cream shop has a large decorative cone next to its front door. What is the volume of the cone?

Use the formula $V = \frac{1}{3}\pi r^2 h$ for the volume of the cone and substitute the values of the height and the radius.

$$V = \frac{1}{3}\pi r^2 h$$

$$V = \frac{1}{3}\pi (1.5^2)(4.5)$$

> **A.** Why is 1.5 substituted for r?

$$V = 3.375\pi$$

$$V \approx 10.6$$

The volume of the cone is about 10.6 cubic feet.

A second cone with the same dimensions is added upside down on a cylinder with a diameter of 3 feet and a height of 2 feet. Find the volume of the composite figure.

Find the volume of the cylinder.

$$V = \pi r^2 h$$

$$V = \pi (1.5^2)(2)$$

> **B.** How can you find the volume of the composite figure?

$$V = 4.5\pi$$

$$V \approx 14.1$$

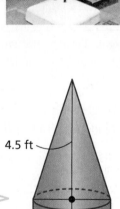

Add the volume of the cylinder and the cone to find the volume of the composite figure.

The volume of the composite figure is about $10.6 + 14.1 = 24.7$ cubic feet.

Turn and Talk Given a cylinder and a cone with the same height and radius, is the volume of the cylinder always, sometimes, or never greater than the volume of the cone?

Apply a Volume Formula to Find Density of a Real-World Object

A crystal is cut into a shape formed by two square pyramids joined at the base.

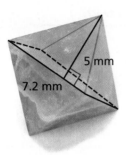

5 mm

7.2 mm

The mass of the crystal is 3 grams. Find the density of the crystal in grams per cubic millimeter.

A. How do the units inform the process of finding the density?

Find the volume of one of the pyramids.

$V = \frac{1}{3}Bh$

$V = \frac{1}{3}(7.2^2)(5)$ **B.** Why is 7.2^2 substituted for B?

$V = 86.4$

The volume of a pyramid is 86.4 cubic millimeters.

Find the volume of the crystal.

The volume of the crystal is $2(86.4) = 172.8$ cubic millimeters.

C. Why is the volume of the crystal two times the volume of the pyramid?

Find the density.

$\text{density} = \frac{\text{mass}}{\text{volume}}$

$d = \frac{3}{172.8} \approx 0.0174$

The density is about 0.0174 gram per cubic millimeter.

D. What is the density of the crystal if the mass of the crystal is 5 grams?

 Turn and Talk Suppose a different crystal has the same edge length and mass, but double the height. How would that affect the density?

©Reika/Shutterstock

Check Understanding

1. How does the volume of a pyramid compare to the volume of a prism with the same base and height as the pyramid?

Find the volume of each pyramid. Round your answer to the nearest tenth.

2.

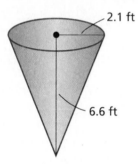
5 cm
12 cm   12 cm

3.

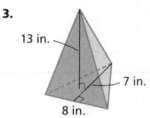
13 in.
7 in.
8 in.

Find the volume of each cone. Round your answer to the nearest tenth.

4.

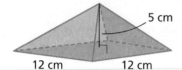
2.1 ft
6.6 ft

5.

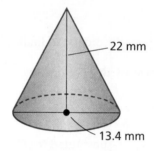
22 mm
13.4 mm

6. Julian is making candles. Each has the same volume. The dimensions of the candles are shown. If he has 200 cubic centimeters of wax, how many candles can he make?

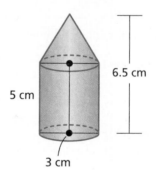
6.5 cm
5 cm
3 cm

On Your Own

7. (MP) **Critique Reasoning** Malcolm states that it takes 3 cones to fill a cylinder with the same base. Angus states that it takes $\frac{1}{3}$ of a cylinder to fill a cone with the same base. Who is correct? Explain your reasoning.

8. (MP) **Reason** Dana knows the volume of a pyramid. How can she find the volume of a prism with the same base and the same height as the pyramid?

9. (MP) **Reason** How is finding the volume of a composite figure with a pyramid removed different from finding the surface area of a composite figure with a pyramid removed?

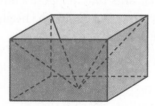

10. Find the volume of a hexagonal pyramid with a base area of 147 square meters and a height of 4 meters.

Find the volume of each pyramid. Round your answer to the nearest tenth.

11.

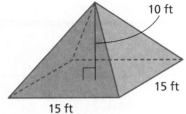

10 ft

15 ft

15 ft

12.

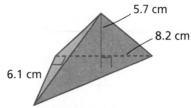

5.7 cm

8.2 cm

6.1 cm

13.

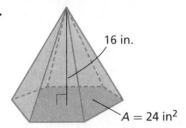

16 in.

$A = 24$ in^2

14.

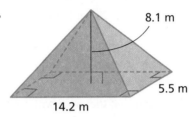

8.1 m

5.5 m

14.2 m

Find the volume of each cone. Round your answer to the nearest tenth.

15.

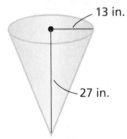

13 in.

27 in.

16.

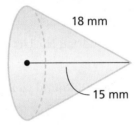

18 mm

15 mm

17.

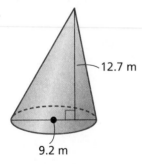

12.7 m

9.2 m

18.

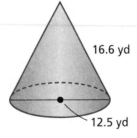

16.6 yd

12.5 yd

Find the volume of each composite figure. Round your answer to the nearest tenth.

19.

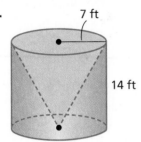

7 ft

14 ft

20.

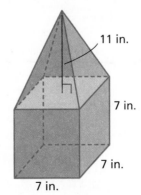

11 in.

7 in.

7 in.

7 in.

21. STEM A water tower is built on top of a building. The dimensions of the water tower are shown.

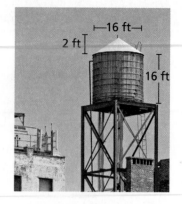

A. What is the volume of the water tower?

B. Assume the entire volume of the water tower is filled with water. The weight of the water in the tower is about 209,193 pounds. What is the density of the water in the water tower?

22. A garage is constructed as a rectangular prism with a roof that is a pyramid. The rectangular prism is 42 feet long, 20 feet wide, and 9 feet tall. The pyramid is 3 feet tall. What is the volume of the garage?

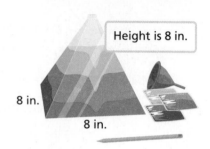

23. Hope is creating sand art. She is using a pyramid-shaped mold. The base of the mold is shaped like a square and has a side length of 8 inches. The height of the mold is 8 inches.

A. What is the volume of sand that the mold will hold? Round your answer to the nearest tenth of a cubic inch.

B. When the mold is full, the sand weighs 9.43 pounds. What is the density of the sand in the mold? Round your answer to three decimal places.

Height is 8 in.

8 in.

8 in.

24. Open Ended Draw a square pyramid and label its dimensions. Find the volume of your pyramid.

Find the missing dimension of each figure. Round your answer to the nearest tenth.

25. $V = 66.7$ ft^3

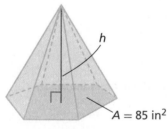

8 ft

x

x

26. $V = 79.7$ cm^3

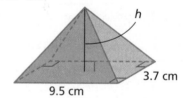

h

3.7 cm

9.5 cm

27. $V = 481.7$ in^3

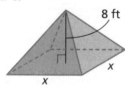

h

$A = 85$ in^2

28. $V = 15,500$ mm^3

h

38 mm

29. $V = 14.3$ ft^3

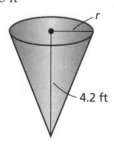

r

4.2 ft

30. $V = 3468$ cm^3

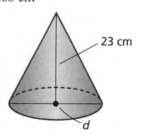

23 cm

d

31. Dan has a plastic cup that is shaped as shown.

   A. How much plastic is needed to make his cup?

   B. The cup cost Dan $4. What is the cost per cubic inch of plastic?

   C. Dan buys another cup with the same radius but a height of 6 inches. Using your result in Part B, what should Dan pay for this cup?

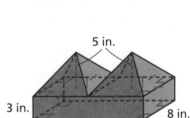

32. (MP) **Reason** A prism has a square base with sides of 4 inches and a height of 8 inches. Without calculating the volumes, find the height of a pyramid with the same base and the same volume as the prism. Explain your reasoning.

33. Consider the volume of a cone. How does the volume of the cone change if the height of the cone is doubled? How does the volume of the cone change if the radius of the cone is doubled?

34. A composite figure is formed by a rectangular prism with two square pyramids on top of it. What is its volume? Round your answer to the nearest tenth of a cubic inch.

35. Randall needs 50 pounds of sand. He is scooping it with a cone-shaped tool whose dimensions are shown. The density of the sand is 0.055 pound per cubic inch. How many times does Randall need to fill his tool to get the amount of sand he needs?

Find the volume of each composite figure. Round your answer to the nearest tenth.

36.

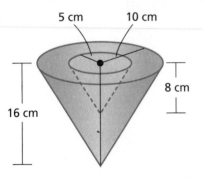

37.

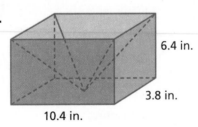

38. The frustum of a right cone is the portion of the cone between the base and a cross section of the cone parallel to the base. A manufacturing company produces paper cups in the shape of a frustum. The radius R of the cup's rim is 1.5 times the radius r of the cup's base. The volume V of the cup is 236 cm³ (about 8 fl oz).

   A. Use the volume formula to solve for h in terms of r^2. Then express the slant height ℓ in terms of r.

   B. Rewrite the formula for the outer surface area S in terms of r.

   C. Use a graphing calculator or spreadsheet to find the base radius r that minimizes the surface area of the cup.

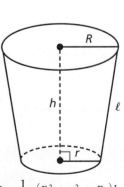

39. A square pyramid has a volume of 132 cubic inches. If the height of the pyramid is 11 inches, what is the length of a side of the base?

$$V = \frac{1}{3}\pi(R^2 + r^2 + Rr)h$$

$$S = \pi(R + r)\ell + \pi r^2$$

$$\ell = \sqrt{(R - r)^2 + h^2}$$

40. Social Studies Some pastoral nomads of central Asia live in portable structures adapted to a mobile life on the windy Great Steppe. A *ger*, the Mongolian word for "home," consists of a cylindrical frame under a conical crown. This one is 4 meters in diameter. Its cylindrical frame is 40 cm taller than its crown. If this *ger* has a total volume of 8π cubic meters, how tall is its crown?

41. (**Open Middle™**) Using the digits 1 to 9, at most one time each, fill in the boxes for a square pyramid's height and base edge length so that the volume has the greatest possible value.

Base edge = ☐

Height = ☐

Volume = ☐ ☐ ☐

Spiral Review • Assessment Readiness

42. Find the area of the circle.

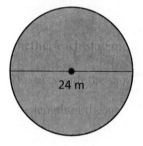

24 m

 Ⓐ 24π m²   Ⓒ 144π m²

 Ⓑ 48π m²   Ⓓ 576π m²

43. Find the volume of the cylinder.

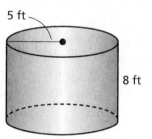

5 ft

8 ft

 Ⓐ 40 ft³   Ⓒ 200 ft³

 Ⓑ 125.6 ft³   Ⓓ 628 ft³

44. Match the quantity with what it measures.

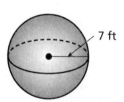

7 ft

Quantity	Measurement
A. 14π ft	**1.** area of maximum cross-section
B. $\dfrac{1372\pi}{3}$ ft³	**2.** volume
C. 49π ft²	**3.** circumference of maximum cross-section
D. 196π ft²	**4.** surface area

I'm in a Learning Mindset!

Was collaboration an effective tool for finding volumes of cylinders and pyramids? Explain.

Volumes of Spheres

(I Can) use the formula for the volume of a sphere to calculate the volumes of composite figures.

Spark Your Learning

Cherry tomatoes are often sold in pint baskets.

Basket dimensions: 3.25 in. by 3.25 in. by 2.875 in.

Complete Part A as a whole class. Then complete Parts B–D in small groups.

A. What is a mathematical question you can ask about this situation? What information would you need to know to answer your question?

B. What variable(s) are involved in this situation? What unit of measurement would you use for each variable?

C. To answer your question, what strategy and tool would you use along with all the information you have? What answer do you get?

D. Does your answer make sense in the context of the situation? How do you know?

 Turn and Talk Suppose the cherry tomatoes of another variety have, on average, the same volume as the ones above, but are shaped more like eggs than spheres. How could you decide whether more or fewer would fit in the same size basket?

©David Kay/Shutterstock

Build Understanding

Develop a Formula for the Volume of a Sphere

1 ▶ To develop a formula for the volume of a sphere, compare one of its hemispheres to a cylinder with the same height and radius from which a cone has been removed.

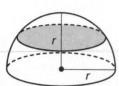
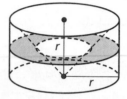

A. Use the Pythagorean Theorem to find the area of a cross section of the hemisphere.

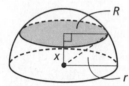

B. A cross section of the cylinder with the cross section of the cone removed is a ring. How can you find the area of the ring? What is the area of the ring?

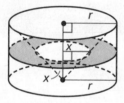

C. What do you notice about the area of the cross section of the hemisphere and the area of the cross section of the cylinder with the cone removed?

D. Find the volume of the cylinder with the cone removed. Explain the steps you use and your reasoning.

E. How can you use Cavalieri's Principle to find the volume of the hemisphere? Use this result to write a formula for the volume of a sphere with radius r.

F. Find the volume of the sphere using your formula from Part E. Leave your answer in terms of π.

9 in.

Turn and Talk How can you determine the increase in volume if the radius of a sphere doubles?

Step It Out

Use a Volume Formula to Solve a Real-World Problem

Volume of a Sphere
The volume of a sphere with radius *r* is given by $V = \frac{4}{3}\pi r^3$. 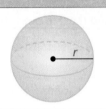

2 ▶ BTU (British Thermal Units) is a common unit in the United States for measuring the amount of heat energy or heat capacity used.

The spherical propane storage tank shown is full of propane. What is the heating capacity of the propane in BTUs? Use the fact that 1 cubic foot of propane contains 2516 BTUs.

The radius of the tank is 30 feet.

A. What steps do you need to take to answer this question?

Find the volume of propane.

$$V = \frac{4}{3}\pi r^3$$

$$V = \frac{4}{3}\pi (30)^3$$

$$V = 36{,}000\pi$$

B. What information in the problem statement tells you that you need to find the volume?

$$V \approx 113{,}097$$

The volume of the propane is about 113,097 cubic feet.

Find the number of BTUs.

$$113{,}097 \cdot 2516 = 284{,}552{,}052$$

C. What are the units of the conversion factor?

The heating capacity of the propane is about 284,552,052 BTUs.

D. What is the heating capacity of a full spherical propane storage tank with a radius of 2 feet?

> **Turn and Talk** How would the process to find the heating capacity change if you were given the diameter instead of the radius of the propane storage tank?

©Jochen Tack/Alamy

Estimate Volume in a Real-World Situation

You can use the volume formula to estimate the volume of a real-world object.

3 Consider the tree shown.

A. What three-dimensional shapes can be used to model the tree trunk and the tree canopy?

The diameter of the canopy is 25 feet. Estimate the volume of the canopy.

You can use the formula for the volume of a sphere to estimate the volume.

$$V = \frac{4}{3}\pi r^3$$

Substitute the value of the radius of the canopy and simplify.

$$V = \frac{4}{3}\pi(12.5)^3$$

> B. Why is 12.5 substituted for r instead of 25?

$$V = \frac{4}{3}\pi(1953.125)$$

$$V \approx 8181.2$$

The volume of the canopy of the tree is about 8181 cubic feet.

Suppose a landscaping company trims the tree so that the canopy is still spherical but has a new volume of 5000 cubic feet. What is the diameter of the canopy after trimming?

$$V = \frac{4}{3}\pi r^3$$

> C. Why is this formula used when it doesn't involve the diameter of the tree?

$$5000 = \frac{4}{3}\pi r^3$$

$$1193.66 \approx r^3$$

> D. How is the equation with r^3 solved for r?

$$10.6 \approx r$$

The radius of the canopy is about 10.6 feet after trimming, so the diameter is about 21.2 feet.

When the diameter of the canopy grows to 24 feet, it will be trimmed again. How many cubic feet of the canopy must be trimmed so the canopy's diameter is cut back to 21.2 feet?

$$V = \frac{4}{3}\pi r^3$$

$$V = \frac{4}{3}\pi(12)^3$$

$$V = \frac{4}{3}\pi(1728)$$

> E. What does this value represent?

$$V \approx 7238.2$$

> F. How is this value determined?

About 2238 cubic feet of the canopy must be trimmed for the diameter to be 21.2 feet.

Find the Volume of a Composite Figure

You can use the formula for the volume of a sphere to help find the volume of composite figures that contain hemispheres.

4 ▶ Find the volume of the composite figure.

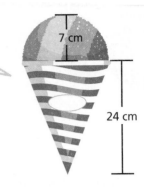

7 cm

24 cm

> A. What figures make up the composite figure?

Find the volume of the cone.

$V = \frac{1}{3}\pi r^2 h$

$V = \frac{1}{3}\pi (7)^2 (24)$

> B. How do you know that the radius of the base of the cone is 7 cm?

$V = 392\pi$

$V \approx 1231.5$

The volume of the cone is approximately 1,231.5 cubic centimeters.

Find the volume of the hemisphere.

$V = \frac{2}{3}\pi r^3$

$V = \frac{2}{3}\pi (7)^3$

> C. Why is the formula for the volume of a hemisphere $V = \frac{2}{3}\pi r^3$?

$V \approx 718.4$

The volume of the hemisphere is approximately 718.4 cubic centimeters.

Find the volume of the composite figure.

Add the volumes of the cone and the hemisphere.

$V = 1231.5 + 718.4 = 1949.9$

The volume of the composite figure is approximately 1950 cubic centimeters.

The composite figure below shows a hemisphere on top of a cube.

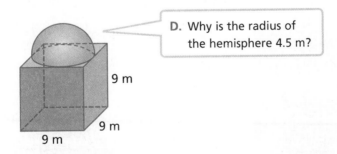

9 m

9 m

9 m

> D. Why is the radius of the hemisphere 4.5 m?

 Turn and Talk How would you find the volume of a composite figure?

Check Understanding

Find the volume of each sphere. Round your answer to the nearest tenth.

1.

5 cm

2.

12 ft

3. Su is making a model of Earth out of papier mâché. The diameter of her model is 13 inches. What is the volume of her model? Round your answer to the nearest tenth of a cubic inch.

4. A chickpea is approximately spherical. Chickpeas have a diameter of about 9 millimeters. Estimate the volume of a chickpea. Round your answer to the nearest tenth of a cubic millimeter.

Find the volume of each composite figure. Round your answer to the nearest tenth.

5.
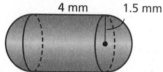
4 mm   1.5 mm

6.
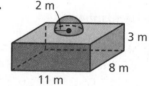
2 m
3 m
8 m
11 m

On Your Own

7. (MP) **Critique Reasoning** Dawn states that if you double the radius of a sphere, you double the volume of the sphere. Is she correct? Explain your reasoning.

8. A trout lays eggs that are approximately spherical. The eggs have a diameter of about 3.5 millimeters. Estimate the volume of one egg. Round your answer to the nearest tenth of a cubic millimeter.

Find the volume of each sphere. Leave the answer in terms of π.

9.
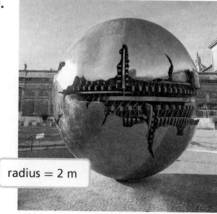
radius = 2 m

10.
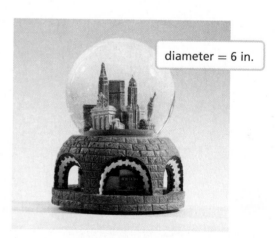
diameter = 6 in.

Find the volume of each hemisphere. Leave the answer in terms of π.

11.

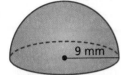

9 mm

12.

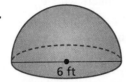

6 ft

13. A homeowner installs a propane tank with the dimensions shown. The tank is then filled with propane. What is the heating capacity of the propane in BTUs? Round your answer to the nearest whole number. (1 cubic foot of propane contains 2516 BTUs.)

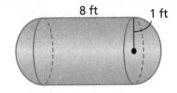

8 ft   1 ft

14. A landscaper is trimming shrubs. Each shrub is nearly spherical, with a diameter of 4 feet. Estimate the volume of a shrub. Round your answer to the nearest tenth of cubic foot.

15. A sphere has a volume of 697 cubic meters. What is the radius of the sphere? Round your answer to the nearest tenth of a meter.

16. A sphere has a volume of 2482 cubic inches. What is the diameter of the sphere? Round your answer to the nearest tenth of an inch.

The diameter of each shrub is about 4 feet.

17. A basketball has a circumference of 29.5 inches. What is the volume of the basketball? Round your answer to the nearest cubic inch.

Find the volume of each composite figure. Round your answer to the nearest tenth.

18.

8 in.
8 in.
8 in.

19.

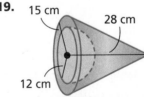

15 cm   28 cm
12 cm

20. Jenna has a scoop that is shaped like a hemisphere. She is filling the scoop with water and is dumping the water in a bucket that is a cylinder with the dimensions shown. How many scoops of water will it take to fill the bucket?

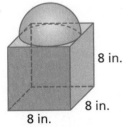

6 in.

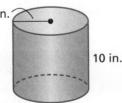

6 in.
10 in.

21. A cube has a side length of 14 centimeters. What is the volume of the largest sphere that can fit inside of the cube? Leave your answer in terms of π.

22. A bead is formed by drilling a cylindrical hole with a 2-millimeter diameter through a sphere with a 6-millimeter diameter. Estimate the volume of the bead to the nearest cubic millimeter.

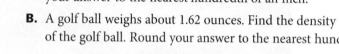

23. A cube-shaped box has sides 24 centimeters long. A sphere with a diameter of 24 centimeters is placed inside the box. How much empty space is in the box? Round your answer to the nearest cubic centimeter.

24. A golf ball is nearly spherical. The volume of a golf ball is about 2.48 cubic inches.

   A. Estimate the diameter of a golf ball. Round your answer to the nearest hundredth of an inch.

   B. A golf ball weighs about 1.62 ounces. Find the density of the golf ball. Round your answer to the nearest hundredth.

Spiral Review • Assessment Readiness

25. Find the volume of the pyramid.

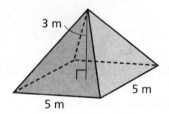

3 m

5 m

5 m

Ⓐ 13 m³   Ⓒ 55 m³

Ⓑ 25 m³   Ⓓ 75 m³

26. Find the volume of the cylinder

Ⓐ 37π in³   Ⓒ 110π in³

Ⓑ 55π in³   Ⓓ 275π in³

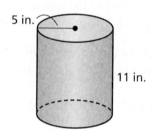

5 in.

11 in.

27. Classify each triangle given the following characteristics.

Characteristics	Isosceles	Equilateral	Scalene
Each vertex angle measures 60°.	?	?	?
Has side lengths of 3–3–5.	?	?	?
Has side lengths of 3–5–7.	?	?	?

 I'm in a Learning Mindset!

How did I benefit by giving help with finding the volume of a sphere? What impact did it have on my learning outcome?

©FenrisWolf/Shutterstock

Volume of Prisms and Cylinders

The volume of a prism and a cylinder is $V = Bh$, where B is the area of the base and h is the height.

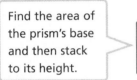
Find the area of the prism's base and then stack to its height.

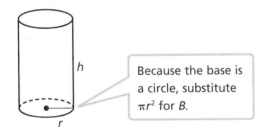

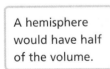
Because the base is a circle, substitute πr^2 for B.

Volume of Pyramids and Cones

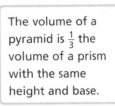
The volume of a pyramid is $\frac{1}{3}$ the volume of a prism with the same height and base.

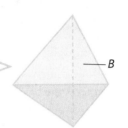

The volume of a pyramid and a cone is $V = \frac{1}{3}Bh$ with base area B and height h.

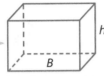

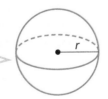
The volume of a cone is $\frac{1}{3}$ the volume of a cylinder with the same height and radius.

Volume of Spheres

The volume of a sphere with radius r is given by $V = \frac{4}{3}\pi r^3$.

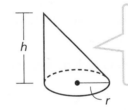
A hemisphere would have half of the volume.

The radius of a hamster ball is 7 inches. The amount of space a hamster would have to run around in is $V = \frac{4}{3}\pi(7)^3 \approx 1437$ cubic inches.

Volume of Composite Figures

Decompose a complex figure into simpler parts. The volume of the complex figure is the sum of the volumes of the parts. Consider a hamster cage with a climbing tube.

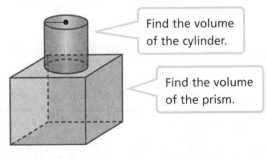
Find the volume of the cylinder.

Find the volume of the prism.

$V_{\text{total}} = V_{\text{cylinder}} + V_{\text{prism}}$

Vocabulary

Choose the correct term from the box to complete each sentence.

1. A three-dimensional figure with a polygonal base and triangular sides that meet at a point is a ___?___.

2. A three-dimensional figure with two circular bases and one curved side is a ___?___.

3. A three-dimensional figure with two congruent polygonal bases and rectangular sides is a ___?___.

4. A three-dimensional figure with a circular base and a curved lateral surface that connects the base to the vertex is a ___?___.

Concepts and Skills

5. Melanie has stacked multiple decks of cards on a slant with a height of 5 inches. The length of each card is 3.5 inches. Jorge has also created a straight stack of cards with a height of 5 inches and the length of each card is 4.5 inches. All cards have the same width. Without making calculations, whose stack of cards has a greater volume? Explain your reasoning.

Find the missing dimension of each figure. Round your answer to the nearest whole number.

6. $V = 7,100$ in³

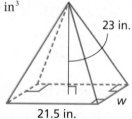

23 in.

21.5 in.

w

7. $V = 450$ cm³

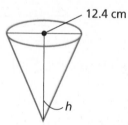

12.4 cm

h

8. (MP) **Use Tools** A cylindrical tank of emergency water has a radius of 12.6 meters and a height of 10 meters. The mass of the water is 4,972,630 kilograms. What is the density of the water? Round to the nearest whole number. State what strategy and tool you will use to answer the question, explain your choice, and then find the answer.

Find the volume of each composite figure. Round your answer to the nearest whole number.

9.

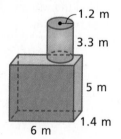

1.2 m

3.3 m

5 m

1.4 m

6 m

10.

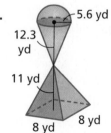

5.6 yd

12.3 yd

11 yd

8 yd

8 yd

11. A melon ball with a circumference of 7.85 centimeters is placed in a cylindrical bowl with a diameter of 12 centimeters and a height of 7 centimeters. How much space is left in the bowl? Round your answer to the nearest tenth.

Probability

Genetic Counselor

Genetic counselors help people understand the facts of their genetic makeup. They analyze genetic information to identify risks for passing on certain medical conditions. They discuss the risks, benefits, and limitations of genetic testing options for individuals and families, and write detailed reports of test results.

©Rafal Rodzoch/Caia Image/Alamy

STEM Task

Colorblindness is the decreased ability to see differences in color. The most common cause is genes on the X chromosome. A person will not be colorblind if they have at least one gene for unaffected sight.

B = Unaffected Sight
b = Colorblindness

		Carrier Mother	
		X^B	X^b
Not Colorblind Father	X^B	$X^B X^B$	$X^B X^b$
	Y	$X^B Y$	$X^b Y$

What is the chance that a child of these two parents will be colorblind?

Learning Mindset

Perseverance Collects and Tries Multiple Strategies

How do you know what strategy will work best to solve a given problem? You can brainstorm different strategies or ask others about strategies they use. It is important to have strategies that will help you work faster when you need to or that will help you identify ways to get started when you are stuck. For example, you may choose to use flash cards to help you learn new material. If you are having difficulty managing your time, you may use a planner to help you find the time to study. Here are some questions you can ask yourself when thinking about using different strategies:

- Is the strategy I chose working out? How can I identify different strategies to use?

- How can I find organizational tools that will help me learn?

- Will I be able to reach my goal fully and on time?

- How can I organize a set of strategies to use for solving problems and learning new material?

Reflect

Q Think of a time when you needed to persevere. What strategies did you use to help you persevere? How did you find or choose those strategies?

Q Imagine that you are a genetic counselor. What if your presentation style doesn't work for a client? How can you work with the client to develop a successful strategy? Why is it important to have different communication strategies?

Probability of Multiple Events

Module Performance Task: *Spies and Analysts*™

Personalized **Plates, Probably**

What is the likelihood of seeing a license plate with your initials?

Are You Ready?

Complete these problems to review prior concepts and skills you will need for this module.

Write Decimals and Fractions as Percents

Express each rational number as a percent.

1. 1.2

2. 0.065

3. $\frac{7}{10}$

4. $\frac{24}{5}$

5. $\frac{5}{8}$

6. $\frac{133}{400}$

Probability of Simple Events

Calculate each theoretical probability.

7. What is the probability of rolling a number greater than 4 on a number cube?

8. What is the probability of drawing a silver marble from a bag that contains 4 blue marbles, 7 silver marbles, and 5 green marbles?

9. A high school debate team has 5 seniors, 4 juniors, 4 sophomores, and 3 freshmen. What is the probability of randomly selecting a junior from the debate team?

Probability of Compound Events Involving *Or*

Calculate each probability.

10. The letters of the word MATHEMATICS are written on slips of paper and placed in a bowl. What is the probability of drawing an M or a vowel?

11. Andrew has several pairs of socks in a drawer: 6 are black, 4 are gray, 3 are blue, and 8 are white. He chooses a pair of socks without looking. What is the probability Andrew chooses a black pair or a gray pair of socks?

Connecting Past and Present Learning

Previously, you learned:

- to apply concepts of density based on area and volume in modeling situations,
- to describe events as subsets of a sample space using characteristics of the outcomes, and
- to summarize categorical data in two-way frequency tables.

In this module, you will learn:

- to describe events as subsets of a sample space, including unions and complements of other events,
- to calculate the probabilities of mutually exclusive events, and
- to use two-way tables as a sample space to approximate conditional probabilities.

Probability and Set Theory

(I Can) use sets and their relationships to understand and calculate probabilities.

Spark Your Learning

Dogs can be categorized into seven groups—terrier, toy, working, sporting, nonsporting, hound, and herding. Each group will have different types of coats.

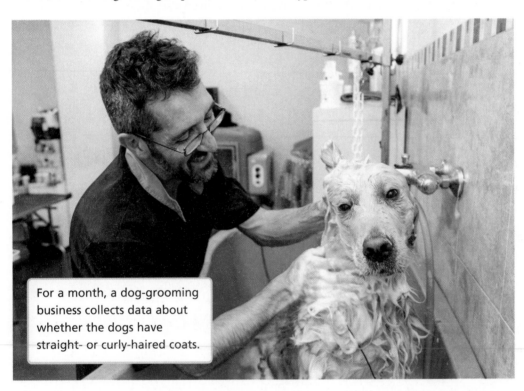

For a month, a dog-grooming business collects data about whether the dogs have straight- or curly-haired coats.

Complete Part A as a whole class. Then complete Parts B–D in small groups.

A. What is a mathematical question you can ask about this situation? What information would you need to know to answer your question?

B. What variable(s) are involved in this situation?

C. To answer your question, what strategy and tool would you use along with all the information you have? What answer do you get?

D. Does your answer make sense in the context of the situation? How do you know?

Turn and Talk During the month, what ratio of groomings for large dogs were for large dogs with straight hair?

Build Understanding

Work with Sets

A **set** is a collection of distinct objects. Each object in a set is called an **element** of the set. A set is often denoted by writing the elements in braces. A set with no elements is called the **empty set**, denoted by $\varnothing$ or $\{\}$. The set of all elements in a particular context is called the **universal set**.

To denote the number of elements in a set, use the letter n. For example, given a set A, $n(A)$ denotes the number of elements in set A.

For example, consider the natural numbers less than 10.

Set	Set Notation	Number of Elements
the universal set	$U = \{1, 2, 3, 4, 5, 6, 7, 8, 9\}$	$n(U) = 9$
the set of even numbers	$A = \{2, 4, 6, 8\}$	$n(A) = 4$
the set of multiples of 3	$B = \{3, 6, 9\}$	$n(B) = 3$
the set of multiples of 12	$C = \{\}$	$n(C) = 0$

Term	Definition	Symbol	Venn Diagram
subset	A **subset** is a set that is contained entirely within another set. Set A is a subset of set B if every element of A is contained in B.	$A \subset B$	
intersection	The **intersection** of sets A and B is the set of all elements that are in both set A and set B.	$A \cap B$	
union	The **union** of sets A and B is the set of all elements that are in set A or set B, including elements that are in both sets.	$A \cup B$	
complement	The **complement** of set A is the set of all elements in the universal set U that are not in set A.	A^c	

1 ▶ Consider the parrots on the branch.

A. What is the universal set shown in the photo? How many elements are in the universal set?

B. Describe a subset of the universal set.

C. Let event *A* be the set of all parrots with blue and yellow body color. Let event *B* be the set of all parrots with green color on the top of their head, called the crown. Copy and complete the Venn diagram.

D. How many elements are in each set?

E. How many elements are in a union of *A* and *B*? Intersection of *A* and *B*? Complement of *A*?

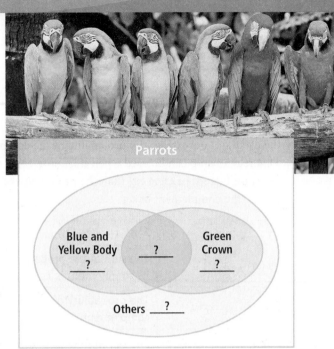

Parrots

Blue and Yellow Body ___?___   ___?___   Green Crown ___?___

Others ___?___

Calculate Theoretical Probabilities

A **probability experiment** is an activity involving chance. Each repetition of the experiment is called a **trial**, and each possible result of the experiment is called an **outcome**. A set of outcomes is known as an **event**, and the set of all possible outcomes is called a **sample space**.

Impossible   Unlikely   As likely as not   Likely   Certain

0        $\frac{1}{2}$ 1

Probability measures how likely an event is to occur. The probability of an event occurring is a number between 0 and 1.

If all of the outcomes of a probability experiment are equally likely to occur, the **theoretical probability** of an event *A* in the sample space *S* is

$$P(A) = \frac{\text{number of outcomes in the event}}{\text{number of outcomes in the sample space}} = \frac{n(A)}{n(S)}.$$

2 ▶ Kurt and Isaac are performing probability experiments. Kurt flips a coin. Isaac randomly chooses a marble from a bag of 4 red marbles and 6 blue marbles.

A. Identify the trial, an event, a possible outcome of the event, and the sample space for each of the probability experiments.

B. Within each probability experiment, are all of the possible outcomes in the sample space equally likely? Explain your reasoning.

C. What is the theoretical probability of Kurt flipping heads on the coin? What is the theoretical probability of Isaac choosing a blue marble?

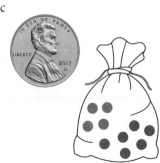

Turn and Talk Suppose Isaac's bag has 5 red marbles and 5 blue marbles. Are all the outcomes in the sample space equally likely? Explain.

Step It Out

Use the Complement of an Event

You may have noticed that the probability of an event occurring and the probability of the event not occurring (the probability of the complement of the event) have a sum of 1. This relationship can be used when it is more convenient to calculate the probability of the **complement of an event** than the probability of the event. Use a superscript c to denote the complement of set.

Probabilities of an Event and Its Complement	
$P(A) + P(A^c) = 1$	The sum of the probability of an event and the probability of its complement is 1.
$P(A) = 1 - P(A^c)$	The probability of an event is 1 minus the probability of its complement.
$P(A^c) = 1 - P(A)$	The probability of the complement of an event is 1 minus the probability of the event.

Use the complement to calculate the probabilities.

3 Lamar rolls a six-sided number cube once. What is the probability that he rolls a number greater than 1?

Let A^c be that he rolls a 1.

> **A.** Why is rolling a 1 the complement of rolling a number greater than 1?

$$P(A) = 1 - P(A^c)$$
$$P(A) = 1 - \frac{1}{6} = \frac{5}{6}$$

> **B.** Why is it easier to use the complement to find the probability of this event?

The probability of rolling a number greater than 1 is $\frac{5}{6}$.

Erica spins the spinner shown once. The spinner is divided into 12 equal sections. Find the probability that the pointer lands on red.

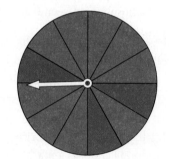

Let A^c be the event that the pointer lands on blue.

> **C.** Why is it easier to use the complement to find the probability of this event?

$$P(A) = 1 - P(A^c)$$
$$P(A) = 1 - \frac{3}{12} = \frac{9}{12} = \frac{3}{4}$$

> **D.** What is the complement of A^c?

The probability of spinning red is $\frac{3}{4}$.

 Turn and Talk Use the complement of the event to find the probability of rolling a number less than 5 on a six-sided number cube.

Calculate Probability in a Real-World Scenario

 4 Veronica attends a conference where there is a possibility that she can win a prize as described. What is the probability that Veronica does not win a prize?

There are 120 people attending the conference.

Eight people will be randomly selected to win a prize.

To find the probability that Veronica does not win a prize, find the probability of the complement of the event that she wins a prize.

A. Why is it easier to use the complement to find the probability of this event?

Let _A_ be the event that Veronica wins a prize.

$$P(A) = \frac{\text{attendees that win a prize}}{\text{total number of attendees}} = \frac{8}{120}$$

$$= \frac{1}{15}$$

B. What is the sample space?

Find the probability that Veronica does not win a prize.

$$P(A^c) = 1 - P(A)$$

$$= 1 - \frac{1}{15}$$

$$= \frac{14}{15}$$

C. What does A^c represent?

Answer the question.

The probability that Veronica does not win a prize is $\frac{14}{15}$.

 Turn and Talk

- The next day, Veronica attends a conference that has 30 fewer attendees. Ten people are selected at random to win a prize. Find the probability that she wins a prize. Then find the probability that she does not win a prize.
- Does Veronica have a better chance to win a prize on the first or the second day?

Check Understanding

1. Let *A* be the set of natural number multiples of 3 that are less than 25. Let *B* be the set of even natural numbers less than 25. Find *A* ∩ *B*, the intersection of the sets.

2. Cameron has a bag with 8 green marbles and 7 yellow marbles. If Cameron chooses a marble at random, what is the probability that he chooses a yellow marble?

3. Lindsey is writing a report about one of the 50 states. She chooses a state at random. What is the probability that the state she chooses isn't Ohio, Oregon, or Oklahoma?

4. Nancy's school is selecting 4 students from each class at random to attend a presentation. There are 28 students in Nancy's class. What is the probability that Nancy will be selected to attend the presentation? What is the probability that she will not be selected?

On Your Own

5. A store marks certain items with special colored tags. Suppose you choose an item at random. Find the probability of each event.

   A. the item has a white tag

   B. the item has a red or black tag

6. (MP) **Critique Reasoning** Zack says that the probability of rolling a number less than 4 on a six-sided number cube is $\frac{4}{6}$. Valeria says that the probability is $\frac{3}{6}$. Who is correct? Explain.

There are 8 red tags, 3 blue tags, 5 white tags and 4 black tags.

Let *A* be the set of factors of 10, *B* be the set of even natural numbers less than or equal to 10, *C* be the set of odd natural numbers less than or equal to 10, and *D* be the set of factors of 9. The universal set is the set of natural numbers less than or equal to 10.

7. Write sets *A*–*D* using set notation.

8. Is *D* ⊂ *C*? Explain.

9. What is *A* ∩ *B*?

10. What is *A* ∩ *C*?

11. What is *A* ∪ *B*?

12. What is *A* ∪ *C*?

13. What is *B* ∩ *C*?

14. What is *A* ∪ *D*?

15. What is C^c?

16. What is D^c?

A set of 12 cards is numbered 1 to 12. A card is chosen at random. Event *A* is choosing a card greater than 4. Event *B* is choosing an even number. Calculate each probability.

17. $P(A)$

18. $P(B)$

19. $P(A \cap B)$

20. $P(A \cup B)$

21. $P(A^c)$

22. $P(B^c)$

23. Kiera has a bag with 20 chips in it. There are 3 red chips and 4 yellow chips. The rest of the chips are blue. If she chooses a chip at random from the bag, use the complement of the event to find each probability.

  A. She chooses a blue chip.

  B. She chooses a blue or red chip.

  C. She does not choose a red chip.

The spinner is divided into 8 equal sections. Suppose you spin the spinner once. Find the probability of the pointer landing on each number described.

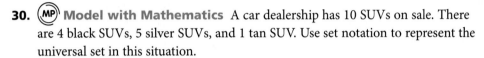

24. odd

25. less than 3

26. greater than or equal to 4

27. not less than 8

28. greater than 10

29. less than 9

30. (MP) **Model with Mathematics** A car dealership has 10 SUVs on sale. There are 4 black SUVs, 5 silver SUVs, and 1 tan SUV. Use set notation to represent the universal set in this situation.

31. Anita randomly chooses a marble from a bag. The bag contains 6 red marbles, 4 blue marbles, and 5 green marbles.

  A. What are the possible outcomes of the event "not choosing a blue marble"?

  B. What is the probability of not choosing a blue marble?

Social Studies In a recent survey, parents and teens were asked about their cellphone use. Some of the results are shown in the table.

Cellphone Habits		
Parents (%)	Teens (%)	Said that they...
36	54	spend too much time on their cellphone.
26	44	check their phone as soon as they wake up.
14	30	feel their teen/parent is distracted when having in-person conversations.
15	8	lose focus at work/school because they are checking their cellphone.

32. Describe the sample space in the study.

33. What is an event in the study?

34. According to this study, what is the probability that a parent surveyed does not lose focus at work/school because they are checking their cellphone?

35. According to this study, what is the probability that a teen surveyed does not feel their parent is distracted when having in-person conversations?

36. According to this study, what is the probability that a teen surveyed spends too much time on their cellphone?

37. According to this study, what is the probability that a parent surveyed spends too much time on their cellphone?

38. (MP) **Reason** Greg buys a ticket for a raffle. On the ticket, it states that the probability of winning a prize is $\frac{1}{25}$. He wants to know what the probability is that he will not win a prize. Explain how he can determine this probability.

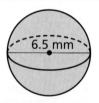

Observe the jar of marbles at the right.

39. The jar has the 10 marbles shown. What is the probability that a randomly selected marble is not yellow? Use the complement to find the probability.

40. Suppose one marble of each color is removed from the jar. What is the probability that a randomly selected marble is red?

41. Jerome is going to randomly select one of his friends to go to an amusement park with him. The list shows the names of his friends. What is the probability that he chooses a name that does not start with a J, A, or D?

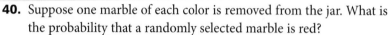

Ana   Calvin   Deandre

Donna   Jorge   Jake

Kim   Bruce   Phu

Jasmine

Spiral Review • Assessment Readiness

42. Find the volume of the cone.

Ⓐ 42π cm^3

Ⓑ 294π cm^3

Ⓒ 882π cm^3

Ⓓ 1176π cm^3

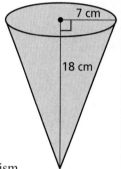

7 cm

18 cm

43. Find the volume of the prism.

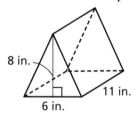

8 in.

6 in.

11 in.

Ⓐ 25 in^3 Ⓒ 264 in^3

Ⓑ 132 in^3 Ⓓ 528 in^3

44. Use the two-way table to find the number of people in the east side of a street who swim.

	East	West	Total
Swims	28	24	52
Does not swim	17	19	36
Total	45	43	88

Ⓐ 17   Ⓒ 28

Ⓑ 24   Ⓓ 45

45. A ball bearing has a diameter of 6.5 mm. What is its volume? Round to the nearest whole.

Ⓐ 144 mm^3

Ⓑ 575 mm^3

Ⓒ 863 mm^3

Ⓓ 1150 mm^3

6.5 mm

 I'm in a Learning Mindset!

Did I manage my time effectively while I was calculating probabilities? What steps did I take to manage my time?

Disjoint and Overlapping Events

(**I Can**) calculate probabilities for both disjoint and overlapping events.

Spark Your Learning

Fruits can be classified in many ways, such as the type of seeds they contain, the type of core they have, or what type of climate they grow in. You can also categorize fruits by the color of their surfaces.

Complete Part A as a whole class. Then complete Parts B–D in small groups.

- **A.** What is a mathematical question you can ask about this situation? What information would you need to know to answer your question?

- **B.** What variable(s) are involved in this situation?

- **C.** To answer your question, what strategy and tool would you use along with all the information you have? What answer do you get?

- **D.** Does your answer make sense in the context of the situation? How do you know?

 Turn and Talk What are two groups of fruit characteristics that have items in common?

Build Understanding

Recognize Disjoint Events

Two events are **disjoint**, or **mutually exclusive**, if they cannot occur in the same trial at the same time.

If you flip a coin, it cannot have a result of both heads and tails in the same trial. If you roll a number cube, you cannot roll a number that is both even and odd. These events are disjoint.

The Venn diagram shows two events A and B that are disjoint. Observe that the circles do not intersect.

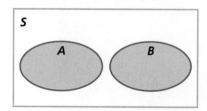

1 Haylee randomly chooses a marble from the jar of marbles.

A. What is the probability that she chose an orange marble?

B. What is the probability that she chose a purple marble?

C. What is the probability that she chose a marble that is orange and purple? Explain your reasoning.

It is not possible to choose an orange and purple marble on the same trial, so these events are disjoint.

D. What is the probability that Haylee will randomly choose a marble that is orange or purple? Explain how you found your answer.

E. What relationship do you notice about the probability of choosing an orange marble, the probability of choosing a purple marble, and the probability of choosing an orange marble or a purple marble?

F. Use the relationship you found in Part E to write an equation to determine the probability of randomly choosing an orange marble or a green marble from the jar of marbles.

 Turn and Talk

- For Part D, sketch a Venn diagram that would be helpful in finding the probability.
- What is the probability that Haylee chooses a green marble or a purple marble? How can you calculate this probability in two different ways?

Recognize Overlapping Events

Two or more events are **overlapping events** if they share one or more outcomes in common.

If you roll a six-sided number cube, you can roll a number that is both even and a multiple of 3. If you randomly choose a car from a lot, you can choose a car that is blue and is a sedan. These are overlapping events.

The Venn diagram shows two events A and B that are overlapping. Notice that the circles intersect.

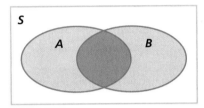

> **2** Dylan spins the spinner once.

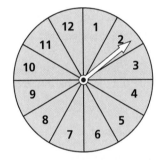

A. What is the probability that the result is an odd number?

B. What is the probability that the result is a factor of 6?

It is possible that the result is both an odd number and a factor of 6, so these events are not disjoint. They are overlapping events.

C. Sketch a Venn diagram that represents the overlapping events. What is the probability that the result is an odd number or a factor of 6?

D. Compare the probability that the result is an odd number or a factor of 6 to the sum of the individual event probabilities. What do you notice?

E. Use your response in Part D to find the probability that the number is even or a multiple of 5. Write an equation that shows how you determined this probability.

Turn and Talk
- What does *and* represent when describing the probability of multiple events?
- What does *or* represent when describing the probability of multiple events?

Step It Out

Find the Probability of Disjoint Events

The probability of disjoint events can be determined by adding the probabilities of the individual events.

> **Disjoint Events**
>
> If A and B are disjoint events, then $P(A \text{ or } B) = P(A) + P(B)$.

The probability of overlapping events can be determined by adding the probabilities of the individual events and subtracting the probability of both events occurring.

> **The Addition Rule**
>
> $P(A \text{ or } B) = P(A) + P(B) - P(A \text{ and } B)$.

3   Jana has slips of paper with the numbers 1–25 written on them. She randomly chooses one slip of paper. What is the probability that she chose a number that is a multiple of 6 or greater than 15?

Let A be the event that the number is a multiple of 6. Let B be the event that the number is greater than 15.

A. Are A and B disjoint events? Explain your reasoning.

Make a table to organize the different probabilities.

Probability	Value
$P(A)$	$\dfrac{4}{25}$
$P(B)$	$\dfrac{10}{25} = \dfrac{2}{5}$
$P(A \text{ and } B)$	$\dfrac{2}{25}$

B. Explain why you can use the Addition Rule even if A and B were disjoint.

Use the Addition Rule to find the probability.

$$P(A \text{ or } B) = P(A) + P(B) - P(A \text{ and } B)$$
$$= \frac{4}{25} + \frac{10}{25} - \frac{2}{25} = \frac{12}{25}$$

C. Explain why you subtract the probability of A and B in terms of the number of outcomes.

Answer the question.

The probability that she chose a number that is a multiple of 6 or greater than 15 is $\frac{12}{25}$.

 Turn and Talk How can you use probability to determine whether or not two events are disjoint? Explain.

Find a Probability from a Two-Way Table of Data

You can use a two-way table to determine the probabilities of events.

4 ▶ Alyssa took a survey of some students in her school. She asked them what their favorite season is. The results of the survey are shown in the table.

<table>
<tr><td rowspan="2"></td><td rowspan="2"></td><td colspan="5">Year in High School</td></tr>
<tr><td>Freshman</td><td>Sophomore</td><td>Junior</td><td>Senior</td><td>Total</td></tr>
<tr><td rowspan="5">Favorite Season</td><td>Spring</td><td>14</td><td>22</td><td>19</td><td>21</td><td>76</td></tr>
<tr><td>Summer</td><td>56</td><td>55</td><td>46</td><td>63</td><td>220</td></tr>
<tr><td>Fall</td><td>12</td><td>3</td><td>24</td><td>7</td><td>46</td></tr>
<tr><td>Winter</td><td>8</td><td>11</td><td>0</td><td>10</td><td>29</td></tr>
<tr><td>Total</td><td>90</td><td>91</td><td>89</td><td>101</td><td>371</td></tr>
</table>

What is the probability that a randomly selected student is a junior or their favorite season is winter?

Find each of three probabilities—the student is a junior, their favorite season is winter, and they are both a junior and their favorite season is winter.

Let A be the event that a student is a junior.
Let B be the event that a student said winter.

$P(A) = \frac{89}{371}$; $P(B) = \frac{29}{371}$; $P(A \text{ and } B) = \frac{0}{371} = 0$

> **A.** How did you use the table to find the values in the numerator and dominator of these probabilities?

Use the Addition Rule to find $P(A \text{ or } B)$.

$P(A \text{ or } B) = P(A) + P(B) - P(A \text{ and } B)$

> **B.** Do you have to use the Addition Rule to find this probability? Explain.

$= \frac{89}{371} + \frac{29}{371} - 0 = \frac{118}{371}$

The probability that the student is a junior or their favorite season is winter is $\frac{118}{371}$.

What is the probability that a randomly selected student is a sophomore or their favorite season is summer?

$P(\text{sophomore}) = \frac{91}{371}$; $P(\text{summer}) = \frac{220}{371}$; $P(\text{sophomore and summer}) = \frac{55}{371}$

$P(A \text{ or } B) = P(A) + P(B) - P(A \text{ and } B)$

> **C.** Do you have to use the Addition Rule to find this probability? Explain.

$= \frac{91}{371} + \frac{220}{371} - \frac{55}{371} = \frac{256}{371}$

The probability that the student is a sophomore or their favorite season is summer is $\frac{256}{371}$.

 Turn and Talk What does a 0 in a cell of the two-way table indicate to you?

Check Understanding

Determine if the events are disjoint or overlapping.

1. You roll a six-sided number cube once and the result is less than 4 and a factor of 4.

2. You roll a six-sided number cube once and the result is odd or greater than 5.

Find the probability of each event.

3. Juanita has a bag that contains 5 red marbles, 9 yellow marbles, and 6 green marbles. She randomly chooses a yellow marble or a green marble.

4. Jun spins a spinner with equal sized sections labeled 1–10. The result is a number that is a multiple of 3 or a factor of 6.

Use the two-way table to find each probability.

		Enjoys Cooking		
		Yes	No	Total
Tries New Foods	Yes	4	18	22
	No	13	23	36
	Total	17	41	58

5. $P($enjoys cooking or tries new foods$)$

6. $P($does not enjoy cooking or does not try new foods$)$

On Your Own

7. **(MP) Critique Reasoning** Mario is rolling a six-sided number cube. He states that rolling an even number and rolling less than 2 are disjoint events. Is he correct? Explain your reasoning.

A bag contains slips of paper with the numbers 1–20 on them. A slip of paper is selected at random. Find each probability.

8. $P($less than 7 or even$)$

9. $P($multiple of 4 or less than 10$)$

10. $P($even or factor of 15$)$

11. $P($greater than 14 or $\leq 2)$

12. A bag contains 26 tiles, each with a different letter of the alphabet written on it. Consider the letters a, e, i, o, or u as vowels. You choose a tile without looking. What is the probability of each event?

    A. a vowel or a letter in the word MATH

    B. a consonant or a letter not in the word MATH

13. **Open Ended** Write two events that are disjoint. Write two events that are overlapping. Find the probability of your events.

The table shows the results of a survey asking residents of three towns if they had attended college. You randomly choose one person from the survey. Find the probability of each event.

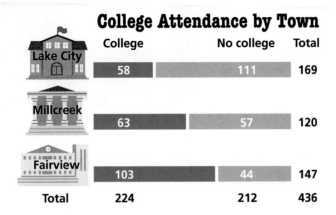

College Attendance by Town

	College	No college	Total
Lake City	58	111	169
Millcreek	63	57	120
Fairview	103	44	147
Total	224	212	436

14. The person is a resident of Lake City.

15. The person attended college.

16. The person is a resident of Millcreek and attended college.

17. The person is a resident of Fairview or attended college.

18. The person is a resident of Lake City or did not attend college.

19. The person attended college or is not a resident of Millcreek.

STEM The table shows partial climate data in Honolulu, Hawaii throughout the year. If a meteorologist chooses a month at random to analyze the climate, find the probability that she chooses a month with the given data.

Average Climate Data—Honolulu, Hawaii												
	Jan	Feb	Mar	Apr	May	Jun	Jul	Aug	Sep	Oct	Nov	Dec
High (°F)	80	80	81	83	85	87	88	89	89	87	84	81
Low (°F)	66	66	68	69	71	73	74	75	74	73	71	68
Sunshine (h)	227	202	250	255	276	280	293	290	279	257	221	211
Precipitation (in.)	2.3	2.0	2.0	0.6	0.6	0.3	0.5	0.6	0.7	1.9	2.4	3.2

20. The high temperature is above 80 °F and below 87 °F.

21. The low temperature is below 70 °F or the precipitation is above 2.0 inches.

22. The number of hours of sunshine is 280 h or the precipitation is below 0.5 in.

23. The high temperature is 80 °F or the number of hours of sunshine is above 225 h.

24. Jessica surveys middle school and high school students and asks if they play video games. Construct a two-way table showing her results. For a randomly selected student, find the probability of each event.

A. a middle school student or does not play video games

B. a high school student or plays video games

C. any student who plays video games or does not play video games

> 54 out of 60 middle school students and 48 out of 55 high school students play video games.

25. (MP) **Reason** Explain why it makes sense to subtract the probability of events *A* and *B* from the sum of the probabilities of *A* and *B* for overlapping events when using the Addition Rule.

26. Last year, Michael painted 17 portraits, drew 11 sketches, and made 7 sculptures. This year, he painted 21 portraits and made 14 sculptures. Construct a two-way table showing his artwork types. Michael chooses a piece of artwork at random. Find the probability of each event.

A. chooses a sketch or the piece of artwork was made this year

B. chooses a portrait or the piece of artwork was made last year

Spiral Review • Assessment Readiness

27. Find $\frac{2}{3} \times \frac{9}{16}$.

Ⓐ $\frac{3}{8}$ Ⓒ $\frac{11}{19}$

Ⓑ $\frac{11}{48}$ Ⓓ $\frac{59}{48}$

28. Find the volume of the sphere.

Ⓐ 4608π in^3

Ⓑ 9216π in^3

Ⓒ $18{,}432\pi$ in^3

Ⓓ $55{,}296\pi$ in^3

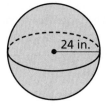

24 in.

29. A standard deck of 52 cards has 13 cards $(2, 3, 4, 5, 6, 7, 8, 9, 10,$ jack, queen, king, ace$)$ in each of 4 suits (hearts, clubs, diamonds, spades). Suppose you select a card at random. Match the event on the left with its probability on the right.

Event

A. select a 2, 3, or 4

B. select an ace

C. do not select a card from 2 through 8

D. do not select a diamond

Probability

1. $\frac{3}{13}$ **3.** $\frac{1}{13}$

2. $\frac{6}{13}$ **4.** $\frac{3}{4}$

⊹⊹ **I'm in a Learning Mindset!**

How effective is making a table to find the probability of overlapping events?

Events

Students are picking natural numbers less than or equal to 20. Set D contains multiples of 6. Set E contains multiples of 3.

$D = \{6, 12, 18\}$ — Subset

$E = \{3, 6, 9, 12, 15, 18\}$ $D \subset E$

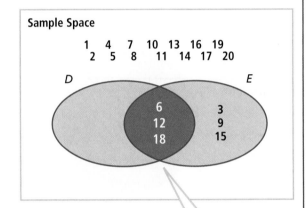

Sample Space

1 4 7 10 13 16 19
 2 5 8 11 14 17 20

D E

6
12
18

3
9
15

Union
"or"
$D \cup E =$
$\{3, 6, 9, 12, 15, 18\}$

Intersection
"and"
$D \cap E = \{6, 12, 18\}$

Theoretical Probability

The theoretical probability of an event D in the sample space S is

$$P(D) = \frac{\text{number of outcomes in the event}}{\text{number of outcomes in the sample space}}.$$

$P(D) = \dfrac{3}{20}$ — probability of picking a multiple of 6

$P(E) = \dfrac{6}{20}$ — probability of picking a multiple of 3

An event and its complement contain all elements of a sample space, with no overlapping elements.

Complement
$D^C = \{1, 2, 3, 4, 5, 7, 8, 9, 10, 11, 13, 14, 15,$
$\quad 16, 17, 19, 20\}$
$E^C = \{1, 2, 4, 5, 7, 8, 10, 11, 13, 14, 16, 17,$
$\quad 19, 20\}$

The sum of the probability of picking a number from set D and the probability of its complement is 1.

$P(D) + P(D^c) = 1$

$\dfrac{3}{20} + \dfrac{17}{20} = 1$

Mutually Exclusive Events

Students can also pick from the set of odd numbers, F. Students cannot pick a multiple of 6 and an odd number in a single pick. Thus, the events D and F are mutually exclusive events.

$P(D \cup F) = P(D) + P(F)$

$= \dfrac{3}{20} + \dfrac{10}{20}$

$= \dfrac{13}{20}$

Take the sum of the probabilities of each event.

Overlapping Events

$P(D \cup E) = P(D) + P(E) - P(D \cap E)$

$= \dfrac{3}{20} + \dfrac{6}{20} - \dfrac{3}{20}$

$= \dfrac{6}{20} = \dfrac{3}{10}$

6, 12 and 18 would be counted twice because they are in both sets.

The probability of overlapping events can be found by adding the probabilities of picking a number from set D and set E individually and subtracting the probability of both events occurring.

Vocabulary

Choose the correct term from the box to complete each sentence.

1. Two events are __?__ if they cannot both occur in the same trial of an experiment.

2. A __?__ is a set that is contained entirely within another set.

3. The set of all possible __?__ is called a __?__.

4. The __?__ of sets F and G is the set of all __?__ that are in set F or set G.

5. Two or more events are __?__ if they have one or more outcomes in common.

Concepts and Skills

6. **(MP) Use Tools** Denny and his friends are using a spinner. State what strategy and tool you will use to answer the questions, explain your choice, and then find the answers.

   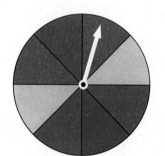

   A. What is the probability that the spinner lands on green?

   B. What is the probability that the spinner lands on yellow?

   C. What is the probability that the spinner lands on red or blue?

7. Elaine is choosing a shirt for school. She has 3 red shirts, 8 blue shirts, 4 green shirts, and 6 white shirts.

   A. What is the probability that a shirt is not blue? Explain your reasoning.

   B. What is the probability that a shirt is red or white? Explain your reasoning.

   C. What is the probability that a shirt is red and white? Explain your reasoning.

8. The table shows the food in the school refrigerator and freezer. Keith cannot decide what he wants to eat, so he randomly chooses an item.

		Food		
		Vegetable	Fruit	Meat	Total
Location	**Refrigerated**	7	8	2	17
	Frozen	11	3	5	19
	Total	18	11	7	36

   A. Determine the probability that the item is a piece of fruit.

   B. Determine the probability that the item is refrigerated.

   C. Determine the probability that the item is a piece of fruit and refrigerated.

   D. Explain how to use these probabilities to determine the probability that the item is a piece of fruit or refrigerated.

Conditional Probability and Independence of Events

Module Performance Task: *Spies and Analysts*™

Birthday BASH!

What are the chances that two people in this group have the same birthday?

NOVEMBER				
Mon.	Tues.	Wed.	Thur.	Fri.
31	1	2	3	4
6	7	8 John and Bobby's Birthday!	9	10
13	14	15	16	17
20	21	22	23	24

Are You Ready?

Complete these problems to review prior concepts and skills you will need for this module.

Multiply and Divide Rational Numbers

Simplify each expression.

1. 5.03×14.1

2. $125.248 \div 30.4$

3. $\dfrac{2}{3} \div \dfrac{7}{9}$

4. $\dfrac{5}{12} \times \dfrac{4}{15}$

Probability of Simple Events

Calculate each theoretical probability.

5. A spinner has five congruent sections numbered 1 through 5. What is the probability of spinning a 2?

6. A bowl contains 15 strawberries, 32 red raspberries, 27 black raspberries, and 24 blackberries. What is the probability of randomly selecting a red raspberry?

Probability of Compound Events Involving *And*

Calculate each probability.

7. Laiken can choose one sandwich (ham and cheese, egg salad, peanut butter and jelly) and one side (apple, carrots, pretzels) for her lunch. If she chooses each item at random, what is the probability she chooses the egg salad sandwich and the apple?

8. On a field trip, students can choose one free item from each of three tables. At the first table, students can choose a pen or a keychain. At the second table, they can choose a notepad, a bottle of water, or a coupon. At the third table, they can choose a T-shirt or a hat. If Trevor chooses an item from each table at random, what is the probability he chooses a pen, a notepad, and a hat?

Connecting Past and Present Learning

Previously, you learned:

- to describe events as subsets of a sample space,
- to calculate probabilities of disjoint and overlapping events, and
- to represent data on two quantitative variables and describe the association between the variables.

In this module, you will learn:

- to find and interpret conditional probabilities,
- to understand and determine independence between two events, and
- to recognize and explain the concepts of conditional probability and independence in everyday language and everyday situations.

Conditional Probability

(I Can) calculate conditional probability and use it to solve real-world problems.

Spark Your Learning

Miguel and Bryn play a video game. In the game, each player collects and hatches dragon eggs.

Dragons can be red, green, or blue.

Some dragons have wings. Some dragons do not.

Complete Part A as a whole class. Then complete Parts B–D in small groups.

A. What is a mathematical question you can ask about this situation? What information would you need to know to answer your question?

B. What variables are involved in this situation?

C. To answer your question, what strategy and tool would you use along with all the information you have? What answer do you get?

D. Does your answer make sense in the context of the situation? How do you know?

 Turn and Talk Predict how your answer would change for each of the following changes in the situation:

- The game designer adds 10 more eggs that contain red dragons.
- The game designer adds 20 more eggs that contain blue dragons with no wings.
- The game designer adds 2 eggs that contain blue, winged dragons.

Build Understanding

Find Conditional Probabilities from a Two-Way Frequency Table

For two events A and B, the probability that event B occurs given that event A has already occurred is the **conditional probability** of B given A and is written $P(B \mid A)$.

1 Suppose 30 people choose a playing card at random from a standard deck and then return the card to the deck before the next person chooses. The two-way frequency table shows how many times each outcome occurred.

	Face card	Other card	Total
Red card	6	3	9
Black card	10	11	21
Total	16	14	30

A. Describe $P(\text{face} \mid \text{red})$ in words.

B. Which parts of the table would you use to find $P(\text{red})$ and $P(\text{face} \mid \text{red})$? What is $P(\text{face} \mid \text{red})$?

C. Which parts of the table would you use to find $P(\text{red} \mid \text{face})$? What is $P(\text{red} \mid \text{face})$?

D. What is a difference between finding $P(\text{face} \mid \text{red})$ and finding $P(\text{red} \mid \text{face})$?

2 In an experiment, one group of participants uses a new toothpaste and another group uses their old toothpaste. After a year, both groups are examined to see if they have any new cavities. The two-way frequency table shows the results.

	No new cavities	At least 1 new cavity	Total
New toothpaste	46	9	55
Old toothpaste	16	29	45
Total	62	38	100

A. What do the values 16, 45, and 100 represent in this situation?

B. Let A be the event that a person uses the new toothpaste. Let B be the event that a person has no new cavities. Which values from the table would you use to find $P(B \mid A)$?

C. What is $P(B \mid A)$?

D. Did you need to use any values from the second row to find $P(B \mid A)$? Explain why or why not.

 Turn and Talk What does $P(A \mid B)$ represent in the toothpaste experiment? Is $P(A \mid B)$ equivalent to $P(B \mid A)$? Explain your reasoning.

Derive the Conditional Probability Formula

3 Recall the experiment in Task 1 where 30 people chose a card from a standard deck. Let event A be choosing a red card. Let event B be choosing a face card.

You can use set notation to describe each cell of the two-way frequency table. The first cell is the intersection of event A and event B. The value 6 in that cell tells you that 6 people chose a card that is both a red card and a face card.

	Face card	Other card	Total
Red card	$A \cap B$	?	A
Black card	?	?	A^C
Total	?	?	?

A. Copy and complete the table using set notation to describe the remaining cells.

B. Do any of the cells represent a union? Explain your thinking.

C. What is the value of $A \cap B^C$? What does the value of $A \cap B^C$ represent in this situation? What is $P(A \cap B^C)$?

D. What does $P(B^C \mid A)$ represent in this situation? How does this compare to $P(A \cap B^C)$?

Relative frequency is the frequency of one outcome divided by the frequency of all outcomes. To get the relative frequency table for the toothpaste experiment in Task 2, divide each value in the table by the total number of participants in the experiment.

E. Copy and complete the relative frequency table for the experiment in Task 2.

	No new cavities	At least 1 new cavity	Total
New toothpaste	$\frac{46}{100} = 0.46$	?	?
Old toothpaste	?	?	?
Total	?	?	?

F. Recall that event A is that a participant used the new toothpaste and event B is that a participant has no new cavities. What is $P(A)$? $P(A \cap B)$?

G. Which values from the table would you use to find $P(B \mid A)$?

H. What is $P(B \mid A)$? Use set notation to show how you found your answer.

 Turn and Talk What is the difference between frequency and relative frequency? What does each represent?

Step It Out

Use the Conditional Probability Formula

The previous task explores the relationship between the probability of an event given that a second event has already occurred, the probability of the intersection of the two events, and the probability of the event that has already happened. The equation that describes this relationship is the conditional probability formula.

Conditional Probability Formula

For events A and B, the conditional probability of B given A is the probability of the intersection of A and B divided by the probability of A.

$$P(B \mid A) = \frac{P(A \cap B)}{P(A)}$$

---

4 Dr. Lin studies a group of patients with insomnia. She has some of the patients do exercise like yoga before they go to bed. The other patients do not exercise before bed. In the morning, patients record how well they had slept.

Exercise vs. Insomnia Study

	Slept well 😴	Slept poorly 😞	Total
Exercise	10	18	28
No exercise	7	15	22
Total	17	33	50

Let A be the event that a patient did not exercise before bed and B be the event that a patient slept well. Match each probability with its value.

Probability	Value
A. $P(A)$	**1.** $\dfrac{7}{50}$
B. $P(B)$	**2.** $\dfrac{7}{22}$
C. $P(A \cap B)$	**3.** $\dfrac{7}{17}$
D. $P(B \mid A)$	**4.** $\dfrac{17}{50}$
E. $P(A \mid B)$	**5.** $\dfrac{11}{25}$

 Turn and Talk What do $P(A \cap B)$, $P(B \mid A)$, and $P(A \mid B)$ represent in the study?

Use the Conditional Probability Formula to Solve a Real-World Problem

Quality control is the process of checking a sample of a factory's output for defects. A high percentage of defects shows that there is a problem with a machine or process in the factory.

 Julia buys a pair of ListenUp! earbuds, but they are defective. What is the probability that Julia's earbuds were made on a Friday?

Only 2.8% of ListenUp! earbuds made are defective.

	ListenUp! Earbuds Manufacturing Defects in Q3					
	M	**T**	**W**	**Th**	**F**	**Total**
Earbuds manufactured	6000	6000	6000	6000	6000	30,000
Defective earbuds (average based on daily samples)	90	72	80	99	510	851
Percent defective earbuds (average for the quarter)	0.3%	0.2%	0.3%	0.3%	1.7%	2.8%

Describe each event.

Let A be the event that a pair of earbuds is defective. Let B be the event that a pair of earbuds is made on a Friday.

Identify the given probabilities.

$P(A) = 0.028$

$P(A \cap B) = 0.017$

A. What does $P(A \cap B)$ represent in this situation?

Solve.

$P(B \mid A) = \dfrac{P(A \cap B)}{P(A)}$?

B. What is the justification for this step?

$ = \dfrac{0.017}{0.028}$ Substitute.

$ \approx 0.607$ Divide.

Answer the question.

The probability that Julia's earbuds were made on a Friday is about 61%.

Turn and Talk Suppose Julia's earbuds were not defective.

- Do you have enough information to find the probability that her earbuds were made on a Friday?
- If yes, what is the probability? If not, what additional information do you need?

Check Understanding

Use the table for Problems 1–3. A computer assigns a randomly selected letter of the alphabet to 100 people. The table shows the results. Assume the letter Y is a vowel.

	First letter of name	Not first letter	Total
Vowel	5	21	26
Consonant	9	65	74
Total	14	86	100

1. What is $P(\text{first letter} \mid \text{consonant})$? Round to the nearest whole percent.

2. Let A be the event that a person receives the first letter of their name. Let B be the event that a person receives a vowel. What is $P(B \mid A^C)$? Round to the nearest whole percent.

3. Create a relative frequency table for the two-way frequency table.

4. Ivan tosses an icosahedron, numbered from 1 to 20. Let event A be tossing a number less than or equal to 7. Let event B be tossing an odd number. Find $P(A)$, $P(A \cap B)$, and $P(B \mid A)$ to the nearest whole percent.

5. Darren and Paula are dishwashers at a restaurant. On a randomly selected night, there is a 0.64% probability that Darren breaks a plate, and a 0.4% probability that Darren and Paula each break a plate. What is the probability that on a randomly selected night, Paula will break a plate given that Darren has also broken a plate?

On Your Own

On each turn in a game, a player spins a spinner and tosses a 6-sided number cube. The spinner has same-sized sectors colored red, blue, red, green, red, white, and red. Use the table below that shows the relative frequencies for one game.

	Multiple of 3	Not a multiple of 3	Total
Red	0.13	0.47	?
Not red	?	0.23	0.40
Total	0.30	?	1.00

6. What is the missing value in each row? What does the value represent?

7. Let A be the event that a player spins a red sector, and let B be the event that a player does not toss a multiple of 3. What is $P(A)$ to the nearest whole percent?

8. What does $P(A \cap B)$ represent? What is $P(A \cap B)$ to the nearest whole percent?

9. What does $P(B \mid A)$ represent? What is $P(B \mid A)$ to the nearest percent?

10. (MP) **Use Structure** Is it possible to use the table to find how many turns are taken in the game? Explain.

You have 26 hand-carved wooden letters—one for each letter in the alphabet. You choose a letter at random. Let event *A* represent choosing a letter in the range V–Z. Let event *B* represent choosing a consonant (assume Y is a vowel). Let event *C* represent choosing a letter in the range N–W. Write each probability as a fraction.

11. $P(A \mid B)$

12. $P(B \mid C)$

13. $P(C \mid A)$

14. $P(A \mid C)$

15. $P(B \mid A)$

16. $P(C \mid B)$

17. A survey asks 1000 people to choose their favorite movie from a list of comedy and drama movies. Overall, 420 of the people in the survey choose a comedy. For Parts A–D, find each probability to the nearest percent.

200 people choose a drama and are less than 21 years old.

170 people choose a comedy and are at least 21 years old.

A. chooses a drama given that the person is at least 21 years old

B. chooses a comedy given that the person is under 21 years old

C. is under 21 years old given that the person chooses a comedy

D. is at least 21 years old given that the person chooses a drama

18. In a carnival game, Carl randomly pulls two ducks from a box of yellow and green ducks. To win, he must pull a yellow duck first, then a green duck. To the nearest whole percent, what is Carl's probability of winning if he pulls a yellow duck on his first draw?

19. (MP) **Attend to Precision** A company has a website that sells only jeans and T-shirts. During a recent month, 61% of customers buy jeans and T-shirts, while 83% of customers buy jeans. What is the probability that a customer who buys jeans also buys a T-shirt? Round to the nearest percent.

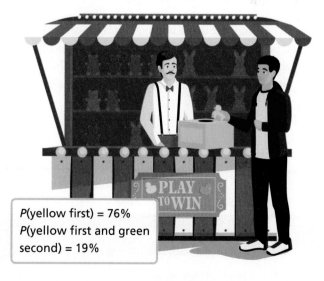

P(yellow first) = 76%
P(yellow first and green second) = 19%

20. (MP) **Critique Arguments** Mark surveys 100 cell phone owners about whether their phone is new (less than 1 year old) or old, and whether they had problems with their phone.

	No problems	Problems (one or more)	Total
New phone	46	9	55
Old phone	16	29	45
Total	62	38	100

Mark calculates $P(\text{problems} \mid \text{new cell phone}) = \frac{9}{38}$, or about 24%.

A. What is Mark's error?

B. What is the correct probability to the nearest whole percent?

21. (Open Middle™) Using the digits 1 to 9, at most one time each, fill in the boxes to make a true statement.

There is a bag of ▢ marbles with ▢ blue marbles and ▢ white marbles. The probability of picking a white marble first and picking a blue marble second (without replacement) is ▢▢%. Round to the nearest whole percent.

Spiral Review • Assessment Readiness

22. A number from 1 to 50 is chosen at random. What is the probability that the number is not divisible by 4?

Ⓐ $\frac{4}{25}$ Ⓒ $\frac{14}{25}$

Ⓑ $\frac{6}{25}$ Ⓓ $\frac{19}{25}$

23. If you randomly choose a factor of 30, what is the probability of choosing an odd number or a multiple of 3?

Ⓐ $\frac{1}{4}$ Ⓒ $\frac{3}{4}$

Ⓑ $\frac{1}{2}$ Ⓓ $\frac{7}{8}$

24. Let event A be that a puppy weighs more than 6 pounds, event B be that the puppy weighs no more than 8 pounds, and event C be that the puppy weighs 5 pounds or less. For each pair of events, identify whether the events are disjoint or overlapping.

Events	Disjoint	Overlapping
A. A and B	?	?
B. B and C	?	?
C. C and A	?	?

 I'm in a Learning Mindset!

How effective was using the conditional probability formula in finding probabilities?

Independent Events

(**I Can**) determine whether two events are independent and find their probabilities.

Spark Your Learning

Tasha surveyed 245 students at her school.

Eighty-seven students own a dog.

Thirty-eight students get 60 minutes or more of aerobic activity each day.

Complete Part A as a whole class. Then complete Parts B–D in small groups.

A. What is a mathematical question you can ask about this situation? What information would you need to know to answer your question?

B. What probabilities are involved in this situation? How can you use these probabilities to answer your question?

C. To answer your question, what strategy and tool would you use along with all the information you have? What answer do you get?

D. Does your answer make sense in the context of the situation? How do you know?

Turn and Talk Predict how the answer to your question would change if the following numbers changed as described:

- The number of students who own dogs and get 60 or more minutes of aerobic activity each day is 15.
- The number of students who own dogs is 125.
- The number of students who get 60 or more minutes of exercise is 54.

Build Understanding

Understand Independence of Events

Two events are called **independent events** when the occurrence
of one event does not influence the occurrence of the other.

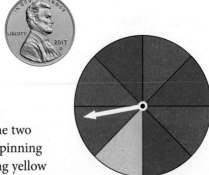

1 ▶ Consider the two simple events of flipping a coin
and spinning a spinner where the result is heads and
spinning yellow. Any outcome from flipping the coin
does not influence the outcome of spinning the spinner,
so the events are independent.

A. Suppose that you want to use probability to show that the two
events are independent. How should the probability of spinning
yellow compare to the conditional probability of spinning yellow
given that the result of the coin flip is heads? Explain your reasoning.

B. How should the probability of flipping heads compare to the conditional
probability of flipping heads given that yellow is spun? Explain your reasoning.

C. How can you calculate the conditional probabilities? Do the results agree
with your expectations?

 Turn and Talk If A and B are independent events, what must be true about the
conditional probabilities $P(A \mid B)$ and $P(B \mid A)$?

Derive the Formula for the Probability of the Intersection of Independent Events

Events A and B are independent if and only if $P(A \mid B) = P(A)$ and $P(B \mid A) = P(B)$.

2 ▶ From Task 1, suppose you spin the spinner twice. Let R be the event that
you spin red first and Y be the event that you spin yellow second.

A. Why are events R and Y independent?

B. What are $P(R)$, $P(Y)$, and $P(R \cap Y)$?

C. Find the product of $P(R)$ and $P(Y)$. How does it compare to $P(R \cap Y)$?

D. Recall from the definition of conditional probability that for any events
A and B, $P(A \mid B) = \frac{P(A \cap B)}{P(B)}$. Suppose events A and B are independent so that
$P(A \mid B) = P(A)$. Use the definition of conditional probability to show that
$P(A \cap B) = P(A) \cdot P(B)$.

 Turn and Talk Suppose that for two events A and B, $P(A \cap B) = P(A) \cdot P(B)$.
How can you show that events A and B are independent?

Step It Out

Find the Probability of Independent Events

Your findings from Task 2 give the following result.

Probability of Independent Events
Events A and B are independent if and only if $P(A \cap B) = P(A) \cdot P(B)$.

3 ▶ A bag contains 12 marbles as shown. You select a marble, return it, and then select another marble. What is the probability that you select a red marble first and a blue marble second?

Let R be the event of selecting a red marble first and B be the event of selecting a blue marble second.

So, $P(R) = \frac{1}{3}$, and $P(B) = \frac{1}{2}$. ◁——— **A. How do you find $P(R)$ and $P(B)$?**

The events are independent, so multiply their probabilities to find $P(R \cap B)$.

$P(R \cap B) = P(R) \cdot P(B) = \frac{1}{3} \cdot \frac{1}{2} = \frac{1}{6}$ ◁——— **B. Why are the two events independent?**

Show that Two Real-World Events are Independent

To show that two events A and B are independent, you can either show that $P(A \mid B) = P(A)$ or show that $P(A \cap B) = P(A) \cdot P(B)$.

4 ▶ A local theater wants to determine if the event that a youth ticket is sold is independent of the event that the ticket sold is for a musical.

Let Y be the event that a youth ticket is sold and M be the event that the ticket sold is for a musical.

From the table, $P(Y) = \frac{84}{280} = 30\%$, and $P(Y \mid M) = \frac{36}{120} = 30\%$. Since $P(Y) = P(Y \mid M)$, the events are independent.

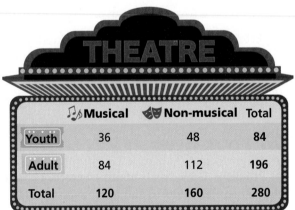

	♫ Musical	🎭 Non-musical	Total
Youth	36	48	84
Adult	84	112	196
Total	120	160	280

A. How do you use data in the table to find $P(Y)$ and $P(Y \mid M)$?

Likewise, you can find $P(M)$ and $P(Y \cap M)$ to show that $P(Y \cap M) = P(Y) \cdot P(M)$. ◁——— **B. How do you show that $P(Y \cap M) = P(Y) \cdot P(M)$ using the data in the table?**

Check Understanding

1. Give an example of two simple independent events. Use conditional probability to explain why the events are independent.

2. For two standard 6-sided number cubes, you roll the green number cube and the red number cube. Let A be the event that you roll an even number on the green number cube and B be the event that you roll a 4 or 5 on the red number cube. Show that events A and B are independent by finding $P(A)$, $P(B)$, $P(A \mid B)$, and $P(B \mid A)$.

3. A box has 20 tiles with shapes etched on them. Three tiles have triangles, 12 tiles have squares, and the rest have circles. You randomly select a tile, put it back in the box, and then randomly select again. Let T be the probability that you select a tile with a triangle first and C be the probability that you select a tile with a circle second. What is $P(T \cap C)$?

4. A bookstore owner surveyed customers on whether they regularly read science fiction and mystery books. The two-way frequency table shows the survey results.

	Reads mystery books	Does not read mystery books	Total
Reads science fiction books	45	54	99
Does not read science fiction books	35	42	77
Total	80	96	176

Let M be the event that the customer reads mystery books. Let S be the event that the customer reads science fiction books. Determine if M and S are independent in two ways. Show the following:

A. $P(M \mid S) = P(M)$ **B.** $P(M \cap S) = P(M) \cdot P(S)$

On Your Own

For Problems 5–9, a bag contains 10 green, 12 yellow, and 8 red marbles. You randomly select a marble, return it, and then randomly select another marble. Let G be the event that you select a green marble first, Y be the event that you select a yellow marble second, and R be the event that you select a red marble second.

5. Explain why G and Y are independent events.

6. Explain why R and G are independent events.

7. Find $P(G \cap Y)$. What does $P(G \cap Y)$ represent?

8. Find $P(G \cap R)$. What does $P(G \cap R)$ represent?

9. Explain why Y and R are not independent events.

10. **(MP) Use Structure** Events M and N are independent. Show that $P(M \cap N \mid N) = P(M)$.

11. **STEM** Gregor Mendel was an early pioneer in using probability in genetics. He discovered that various traits in pea plants, such as flower color, were inherited independently. As shown, each parent has purple flowers and can donate either B or b to the new plant. A pea plant can have purple flowers (BB or Bb) or white flowers (bb) depending on what it inherits from the parents. If the events of inheriting either B or b from each parent are independent and equally likely, what is the probability that the new pea plant inherits b from each parent and has white flowers?

For Problems 12–14, determine if the events are independent.

12. A restaurant manager wants to know if the event that a customer orders dessert at dinner is independent of the event that the customer is dining on the weekend.

	Weekend diners	Weekday diners	Total
Dessert	81	36	117
No dessert	459	204	663
Total	540	240	780

13. Town officials are considering a property tax increase to finance a new park. They want to know if the event that a person has children is independent of the event that person supports the tax.

	Supports tax	Does not support tax	Total
Has children	100	40	140
Does not have children	20	60	80
Total	120	100	220

14. The school cafeteria takes orders for a field trip. Students have a choice to order a salad or a sandwich and water or juice. Determine if the event that a student orders a sandwich is independent of the event that the student orders water.

	Water	Juice	Total
Salad	27	12	39
Sandwich	54	24	78
Total	81	36	117

15.  **(MP) Reason** You randomly select a sock from the laundry basket shown. Let D be the event that the sock has dots, R be the event that the sock has some red in its pattern, and S be the event that the sock has stripes.

A. Are events D and R independent events? Explain.

B. Are events D and S independent events? Explain.

> **Dotted socks:**
> 2 red and 2 blue
> **Striped socks:**
> 4 red and 4 blue

16. Explain why $P(B \mid A) = P(B)$ is true if $P(A \mid B) = P(A)$ is true.

17. (Open Middle™) Using the digits 1 to 9, at most one time each, fill in the boxes to make a true statement.

Rolling a sum of ⬚ on two ⬚-sided dice is the same probability

as rolling a sum of ⬚ on two ⬚-sided dice.

Spiral Review • Assessment Readiness

18. Suppose you select a number at random from 1 to 20. Let A be the event of selecting a multiple of 3. Let B be the event of selecting a number greater than 12. What is $P(A \cap B)$?

Ⓐ $\frac{1}{20}$　　　Ⓒ $\frac{3}{20}$

Ⓑ $\frac{1}{10}$　　　Ⓓ $\frac{1}{5}$

19. You roll two 4-sided dice, each numbered from 1 to 4. What is the probability that the two numbers rolled are the same or that the sum of the two numbers is odd?

Ⓐ $\frac{1}{4}$　　　Ⓒ $\frac{5}{8}$

Ⓑ $\frac{1}{2}$　　　Ⓓ $\frac{3}{4}$

20. You randomly select a card from a standard 52-card deck of playing cards. Let event A be selecting a king, queen, or jack, event B be selecting a red card, and event C be selecting a club. Match the probability on the left with its value on the right.

A. $P(A \mid C)$　　　**1.** 0

B. $P(B \mid A)$　　　**2.** $\frac{3}{13}$

C. $P(B \mid C)$　　　**3.** $\frac{1}{4}$

D. $P(C \mid A)$　　　**4.** $\frac{1}{2}$

 I'm in a Learning Mindset!

Which strategy works best to determine whether two events are independent when I am given information in a two-way frequency table?

Dependent Events

(I Can) determine whether two events are dependent and find their probabilities.

Spark Your Learning

Evanston, Illinois, is a suburb north of Chicago. Many residents of Evanston drive to and from Chicago every weekday for work.

> On average, the drive from Evanston to Chicago takes about 30 minutes.

> Drive times today are longer than average.

Complete Part A as a whole class. Then complete Parts B–D in small groups.

A. What is a mathematical question you could ask about this situation? What information would you need to know to answer your question?

B. What events could you define in this situation?

C. To answer your question, what strategy and tool would you use along with all the information you have? What answer do you get?

D. Does your answer make sense in the context of this situation? How do you know?

Turn and Talk What does it mean if two events are not independent? What other situations can you think of where two events might not be independent?

Build Understanding

Derive a Formula for the Probability of the Occurrence of Two Dependent Events

Sometimes the probability of an event depends on the occurrence of another event. For example, suppose you have 3 red marbles and 2 blue marbles as shown in the diagram. You choose a marble at random. When you select another marble at random, the probability of selecting blue can be either $\frac{2}{4}$ or $\frac{1}{4}$. Events are **dependent events** if the occurrence of one event affects the probability of the other.

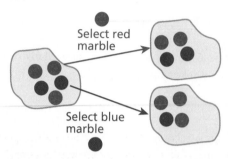

Select red marble

Select blue marble

You have learned two ways to test whether events A and B are independent:

1. If $P(A \mid B) = P(A)$, then A and B are independent.

2. If $P(A \cap B) = P(A) \cdot P(B)$, then A and B are independent.

If either of these tests fails, then the two events are dependent.

1 ▶ The two-way frequency table shows the numbers of people in two age categories who went to different restaurants at a mall. Let Y be the event that a person is 20 years old or younger. Let A be the event that the person ate at the casual dining restaurant.

	Casual dining	Family style	Total
20 years old or younger	25	15	40
Over 20 years old	30	30	60
Total	55	45	100

A. Find $P(Y)$, $P(A)$, and $P(Y \cap A)$ as fractions. Are events Y and A independent or dependent events?

B. What are the conditional probabilities $P(Y \mid A)$ and $P(A \mid Y)$?

C. Copy and complete the multiplication table using the probabilities you computed.

×	P(Y)	P(A)
P(Y | A)	?	?
P(A | Y)	?	?

D. Do any of the products equal $P(Y \cap A)$? What does this suggest about computing the probability of dependent events?

Turn and Talk How are the products $P(Y) \cdot P(A \mid Y)$ and $P(Y) \cdot P(A)$ alike and how are they different?

Step It Out

Find the Probability of Two Dependent Events

When events are dependent, you can use the Multiplication Rule to find the probability of the events occurring.

> **Multiplication Rule**
>
> $P(A \cap B) = P(A) \cdot P(B \mid A)$ where $P(B \mid A)$ is the conditional probability of event B given that event A has occurred.

2 A board game includes tiles with circles and squares. On each turn, players place all the tiles in a bag, select a tile, then select a tile again without replacing the first tile.

Find the probability that the player selects a circle and then a square.

Let C be the event that the first tile is a circle. Let S be the event that the second tile is a square. There are 3 circles and 3 squares.

After the first tile is removed, the probability of event S depends on whether event C occurred, so S and C are dependent.

$$P(C) = \frac{3}{6} = \frac{1}{2}$$

$$P(S \mid C) = \frac{3}{5}$$

> **A.** Why is $P(S \mid C)$ equal to $\frac{3}{5}$ and not $\frac{3}{6}$ or $\frac{2}{5}$?

Apply the Multiplication Rule.

$$P(C \cap S) = P(C) \cdot P(S \mid C) = \frac{1}{2} \cdot \frac{3}{5} = \frac{3}{10}$$

Find the probability that the player selects a circle followed by another circle.

Let $C1$ be the event that the first tile is a circle.

Let $C2$ be the event that the second tile is a circle.

> **B.** Why are $C1$ and $C2$ dependent events?

$$P(C1) = \frac{3}{6} = \frac{1}{2}$$

$$P(C2 \mid C1) = \frac{2}{5}$$

> **C.** Why are $P(C2 \mid C1)$ and $P(S \mid C)$ not equal?

Apply the Multiplication Rule.

$$P(C1 \cap C2) = P(C1) \cdot P(C2 \mid C1) = \frac{1}{2} \cdot \frac{2}{5} = \frac{1}{5}$$

 Turn and Talk How would the probabilities be different if the player put the first tile back in the bag before drawing the second tile?

Find the Probability of Three or More Dependent Events

The Multiplication Rule can be extended to three or more dependent events. For dependent events A, B, and C, $P(A \cap B \cap C) = P(A) \cdot P(B \mid A) \cdot P(C \mid A \cap B)$.

3 Suppose you keep your passwords for secure websites on an encrypted list. The list contains five passwords, and you have forgotten which one to use for your bank website. You try the passwords one at a time, without repeating any.

What is the probability that the third password you try is correct?

GeoBank
Account Login
Username: myaccount224
Password: **********
☐ Remember me on this computer

Sign in

ⓧ The password is not valid.
I cannot access my account
OK

Let $W1$ be the event that the first password you try is incorrect: $P(W1) = \frac{4}{5}$.	Let $W2$ be the event that the second password you try is incorrect: $P(W2 \mid W1) = \frac{3}{4}$.	Let R be the event that the third password you try is correct: $P(R \mid W1 \cap W2) = \frac{1}{3}$

A. Why are $W1$, $W2$, and R dependent events?

Apply the Multiplication Rule. Then answer the question.

$$P(W1 \cap W2 \cap R) = P(W1) \cdot P(W2 \mid W1) \cdot P(R \mid W1 \cap W2)$$
$$= \frac{4}{5} \cdot \frac{3}{4} \cdot \frac{1}{3} = \frac{1}{5}$$

The probability that the third password you try is correct is $\frac{1}{5}$.

What is the probability that any one of the first three passwords is correct?

Find the probability of the complement: *none of the first three passwords are correct.*

Let $W1$, $W2$, and $W3$ be the events that the first, second, and third passwords are incorrect. From above, $P(W1) = \frac{4}{5}$, and $P(W2 \mid W1) = \frac{3}{4}$. On the third try, three passwords remain, so $P(W3 \mid W1 \cap W2) = \frac{2}{3}$.

B. Why is *none of the first three passwords are correct* the complement of *one of the first three passwords is correct*?

Apply the Multiplication Rule. Then answer the question.

$$P(W1 \cap W2 \cap W3) = P(W1) \cdot P(W2 \mid W1) \cdot P(W3 \mid W1 \cap W2)$$
$$= \frac{4}{5} \cdot \frac{3}{4} \cdot \frac{2}{3} = \frac{2}{5}$$

This is the probability that none of the first three passwords are correct. To find the probability that one of the first three passwords is correct, subtract from 1. So, $1 - \frac{2}{5} = \frac{3}{5}$.

The probability that one of the first three passwords is correct is $\frac{3}{5}$.

Check Understanding

1. The two-way frequency table shows the numbers of 9th and 10th graders who are on the track team and the robotics team.

	9th graders	10th graders	Total
On track team	50	20	70
On robotics team	10	20	30
Total	60	40	100

Let N be the event that a person is in 9th grade. Let R be the event that the person is on the robotics team. Find $P(N)$, $P(R)$, and $P(N \cap R)$. Are events N and R independent or dependent events?

There are 5 orange bumper cars and 3 green bumper cars that are being tested for safety for a ride at an amusement park. Two bumper cars are tested at random, one at a time, without retesting the same car.

2. Find the probability that both cars are orange.

3. Find the probability that the first car is green and the second is orange.

There are 6 chemical elements represented by Li, Na, Mg, Rb, Cs, and Fr that are written on separate pieces of paper. You randomly choose 3 elements, one at a time, without replacement.

4. Find the probability that the third element is Na.

5. Find the probability that the first element is Fr, the second element is Rb, and the third element is Li.

On Your Own

6. A survey at a high school asked students and teachers whether they read books for entertainment. The two-way frequency table shows the results of the survey. Let S be the event that a person is a student. Let N be the event that the person does not read for entertainment.

	Teacher	Student	Total
Reads books for entertainment	28	57	85
Does not read books for entertainment	2	113	115
Total	30	170	200

   A. Find $P(S)$, $P(N)$, and $P(S \cap N)$ as fractions. What does each probability represent? Are events S and N independent or dependent events?

   B. What are the conditional probabilities $P(S \mid N)$ and $P(N \mid S)$?

   C. Which probabilities can you multiply to find $P(S \cap N)$?

7. **Geography** The two-way frequency table shows the number of states by area and population density.

	Population density less than 200 people per square mile	Population density greater than or equal to 200 people per square mile	Total
Land area less than 50,000 square miles	10	12	22
Land area greater than or equal to 50,000 square miles	25	3	28
Total	35	15	50

A. Let D be the event that a state has a population density greater than or equal to 200 people per square mile. Let A be the event that a state has an area less than 50,000 square miles. Are events D and A independent or dependent? Explain how you know.

B. Find $P(D \mid A)$ and $P(A \mid D)$. How can you use these probabilities to find $P(A \cap D)$?

8. A box of cereal bars contains 4 blueberry bars and 4 apple bars. Jason reaches into the box and takes a cereal bar. Then Amanda reaches into the box and takes a bar. What is the probability that both Jason and Amanda take a blueberry bar? Let $B1$ be the event that Jason takes a blueberry bar and $B2$ be the event that Amanda takes a blueberry bar.

9. There are 8 singers, 4 instrumentalists, and 3 stage hands in a traveling musical group. They randomly select one member to be interviewed by a local TV station and a different member to be interviewed by a local newspaper. Find each probability.

A. the member interviewed by the TV station is a singer and the member interviewed by the newspaper is an instrumentalist

B. both members are stage hands

10. Andrew is a volunteer dog walker at an animal shelter. He has been asked to walk Rex, Lulu, Spot, and Skipper today, one at a time, in any order he chooses.

A. If he randomly chooses the order, what is the probability that Skipper will be second?

B. Is the probability that any specific dog will be walked in any specific order position the same as the probability you found in Part A? Justify your answer.

Andrew walks four dogs today in any order he chooses.

11. (MP) **Reason** If $P(A) = P(B \cap A)$, what can you conclude? Give an example of events where $P(A) = P(B \cap A)$.

12. **Open Ended** In your own words, describe the difference between independent and dependent events. Give an example of two events that are independent and two events that are dependent.

13. (MP) **Critique Reasoning** Robert solved the problem shown at the right. His work is shown below. Is his answer correct? Explain your answer.

> There are 4 girls (Ana, Charise, Greta, and Jane) and 3 boys (Ethan, Pablo, and Tom) in the Spanish club. If they randomly select a student to be president and a different student to be secretary, what is the probability that a girl will be the president and Greta will be the secretary?

> Let A be the event that a girl is president. Let B be the event that Greta is secretary. There are 4 girls out of 7 total members, so $P(A) = \frac{4}{7}$. If a girl is selected as president, there are 6 members left, and Greta is one of them, so $P(B|A) = \frac{1}{6}$. $P(A \cap B) = P(A) \cdot P(B|A) = \frac{4}{7} \cdot \frac{1}{6} = \frac{2}{21}$.

14. You randomly select three tiles, one at a time without replacement, from a bag containing the tiles shown.

A. Let B be the event that the first tile is B, G be the event that the second tile is G, and A be the event that the third tile is A. What is $P(B \cap G \cap A)$?

B. Let V be the event that the first tile is a vowel, $C1$ be the event that the second tile is a consonant, and $C2$ be the event that the third tile is a consonant. What is $P(V \cap C1 \cap C2)$?

C. What do $P(B \cap G \cap A)$ and $P(V \cap C1 \cap C2)$ represent in the given context?

15. Ann, Ben, Chandra, Diondre, Emma, Franklin, and Gina will be giving presentations in English class today. The teacher randomly selects the order in which the students will give their presentations.

A. Show how to find the probability that Emma will be one of the first three students by computing the probability of the complement and subtracting from 1.

B. Show how to find the probability that Emma will be one of the first three students by adding the probabilities that (1) Emma will be first, (2) Emma will be second, and (3) Emma will be third.

C. Which method do you prefer? Why?

16. A basketball coach randomly assigns players to Team A or Team B for a practice game. She writes "A" on 10 slips of paper and "B" on 10 slips of paper and then places the slips in a bag. The players take turns removing one slip of paper to be assigned to a team. What is the probability that the first three players will be assigned to the same team?

17. A bag contains 3 red marbles, 3 green marbles, and 2 blue marbles. You remove 3 marbles, one at a time, without replacement. What is the probability that the first marble is blue, the second marble is green, and the third marble is not red?

18. (MP) **Construct Arguments** Given that $P(A \cap B \cap C) = P\big((A \cap B) \cap C\big)$, use the Multiplication Rule for two dependent events to prove the Multiplication Rule for three dependent events.

19. (Open Middle™) Using the digits 1 to 9, at most one time each, fill in the boxes to find the conditions with the greatest probability.

There is a bag of ▢ marbles with ▢ blue marbles and ▢ white marbles.

The probability of getting 1 white marble and 1 blue marble without replacement

(rounding to the nearest percent) is ▢▢ %.

Spiral Review • Assessment Readiness

20. If $P(A) = \frac{1}{2}$ and $P(B) = \frac{1}{6}$, which probability shows that A and B are independent?

Ⓐ $P(B \mid A) = \frac{2}{3}$

Ⓑ $P(A \mid B) = \frac{1}{6}$

Ⓒ $P(A \cap B) = \frac{1}{12}$

Ⓓ $P(A \cap B) = \frac{1}{3}$

21. You randomly pull a card from a deck of playing cards. Which events are mutually exclusive? Select all that apply.

Ⓐ pulling a 7 and pulling a heart

Ⓑ pulling a 5 and pulling a face card

Ⓒ pulling a red card and pulling a number card

Ⓓ pulling a club and pulling a number card divisible by 5

Ⓔ pulling a heart and pulling a spade

Ⓕ pulling a black card and pulling a face card.

22. You roll a 10-sided number cube with the numbers 2 through 11. Let A be the event that the number is even. Let B be the event that the number is prime. Let C be the event that the number is divisible by 4. Match the probability on the left with its value on the right.

Probability	Value
A. $P(A \mid B)$	**1.** $\frac{2}{5}$
B. $P(B \mid C)$	**2.** 1
C. $P(C \mid A)$	**3.** 0
D. $P(A \mid C)$	**4.** $\frac{1}{5}$

 I'm in a Learning Mindset!

What different strategies can I use to find the probability of dependent events?

Review

Conditional Probability

At Lakeview High, juniors and seniors must join one of three academies.

	Juniors	Seniors	Total
Engineering	103	142	245
Medical	173	228	401
Arts	91	137	228
Total	367	507	874

To find the probability that a student is in the medical academy given that the student is a senior, $P(\text{medical} \mid \text{senior})$, divide the number of seniors who are in the medical academy by the total number of seniors: $\frac{228}{507} \approx 45.0\%$. To find $P(\text{junior} \mid \text{arts})$, divide the number of juniors in the arts academy by the total number of students in the arts academy: $\frac{91}{228} \approx 39.9\%$.

Independent Events

Events A and B are independent if and only if

$$P(A \cap B) = P(A) \cdot P(B).$$

> the probability that a student is a junior and in the engineering academy

$$P(J \cap E) \overset{?}{=} P(J) \cdot P(E)$$

$$\frac{103}{874} \overset{?}{=} \frac{367}{874} \cdot \frac{245}{874}$$

$$0.118 = 0.118$$

Being a junior and being in the engineering academy are independent.

At a university near Lakeview High, three-fifths of all students live on campus. Living on campus, C, and a student's major are independent events.

From Lakeview's senior class, 78 students have been accepted into the university's engineering program.

> the probability that a student in the senior class will major in engineering and live on campus

$$P(E \cap C) = P(E) \cdot P(C)$$

$$= \frac{78}{507} \cdot \frac{3}{5} \approx 9.2\%$$

Dependent Events

The university has a large summer internship program for high school students considering careers in the medical field. The university only accepts 12% of the students who apply. The funding sources for the program require that exactly 25% of the accepted students are high school juniors.

> the probability that a student who applies is accepted and is a junior

$$P(A \cap J) = P(A) \cdot P(J \mid A)$$

$$= (0.12) \cdot (0.25)$$

$$= 0.03, \text{ or } 3\%$$

Vocabulary

Choose the correct term from the box to complete each sentence.

1. Two events for which the occurrence of one event does not influence the occurrence of the other are __?__.

2. For two events A and B, the probability that event B occurs given that event A has already occurred is the __?__ of B given A and is written $P(B \mid A)$.

3. __?__ is the frequency of one outcome divided by the frequency of all outcomes.

4. Events are __?__ if the occurrence of one event affects the probability of the other.

Concepts and Skills

You create a game that uses the spinner shown. Find each probability.

5. $P(\text{blue} \mid \text{even})$

6. $P(\text{red} \mid \geq 7)$

7. $P(< 6 \mid \text{yellow})$

8. $P(\text{blue} \mid \text{odd})$

9. $P(\text{odd} \mid \text{green})$

10. $P(\text{green} \mid \text{even})$

11. Students attending a summer camp get to choose between climbing a rock wall or practicing archery. Determine whether the event that a student chooses archery is independent of the event that the student is 10–12 years old. Show your work.

	Rock wall	Archery	Total
7–9 years	45	32	77
10–12 years	38	27	65
Total	83	59	142

12. A student polled her class. Let M be the event that a student has more than two siblings and C be the event that the student takes a drafting class.

    A. What would it mean for M and C to be dependent or independent in this context?

    B. Determine $P(M \cap C)$.

    C. Are M and C independent? Explain your reasoning.

	Drafting class	No drafting class	Total
≤ 2 siblings	109	53	162
> 2 siblings	16	31	47
Total	125	84	209

13. **(MP) Use Tools** There are 12 yellow, 21 blue, and 17 red marbles in a bag. You take three marbles out of the bag, one at a time, without replacement. What is the probability that the first marble is yellow and the next two marbles are red? State what strategy and tool you will use to answer the question, explain your choice, and then find the answer.

UNIT 1

MODULE 1, LESSON 1.1
On Your Own

5. A. undefined; B. undefined; C. defined; D. defined; E. undefined; F. defined

7. Possible answer: Point A, Point B, Point C, Point D

11. $AB = 35$

13. $x = 8$

15. No, $AB \neq BC$

17. $(-3, -2)$

19. Yes, they are both 6 units long.

21. Yes, they are both 4 units long.

23. $(-2, -5)$

25. $(-11, 6)$

27. $(-5.5, 11.5)$

29. $C(5, -12)$ and $D(-4, -12)$

31. Quadrant III

33. Possible answer: He did not use the Midpoint Formula correctly. The correct answer should be $(-3, 3)$.

35. $(1, 2), (1, 10), (-3, 6), (5, 6)$; Possible answer: I found the points by adding and subtracting 4 units from either the y-axis or the x-axis. The midpoint is 2 units from each side, therefore the other endpoint is 2 units away from that point.

Spiral Review • Assessment Readiness

39. A

41. B

MODULE 1, LESSON 1.2
On Your Own

5. $\angle ABC$, $\angle B$, or $\angle 4$

7. $\angle LMN$, $\angle M$, or $\angle 6$

9.

11.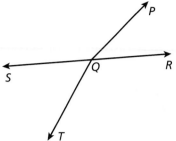

Other angles: $\angle PQS$ and $\angle RQT$

13. Possible answer:

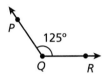

15.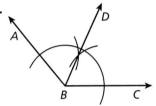

17. $20°$

19. $50°$

21. $90°$

23. $m\angle ABD = 42°$ and $m\angle DBC = 35°$

25. $27°$

27. $134°$ and $46°$

29. $20°$; $80°$

31.

Obtuse angle: $121°$; Acute angle: $59°$

Spiral Review • Assessment Readiness

33. A

MODULE 1, LESSON 1.3
On Your Own

5. Possible answer: a circle; because it contains a curve rather than only straight lines

7. No, because both bases must be perpendicular to the height. Jason could divide the yard into a triangle and trapezoid and use the Area Addition Postulate.

9. no

11. yes; 4 in.

13. Possible answers: *PQRST; QPTSR; STPQR*

15. Possible answers: *DEFGHI; GHIDEF; HGFEDI*

17. about 112 ft²

19.A. Mr. Edwards's class has a greater population density. The population density of Ms. Chang's class is approximately 0.06 students per square foot. The population density of Mr. Edwards's class is approximately 0.11 students per square foot.

   B. 18 square feet of classroom space per student

   C. $\dfrac{x}{270} = \dfrac{23}{208}$

      $208x = 6210$

        $x \approx 30$

   Approximately 15 students need to be added to Ms. Chang's class to make the population density of the two classrooms equal.

Spiral Review • Assessment Readiness

23. C

25. D

MODULE 1, LESSON 1.4

On Your Own

5. yes; The parallelograms share a base, and the sides opposite the base lie on the same line, so the parallelograms have the same height and therefore the same area.

7. The farther you move one segment along the line that contains it, the more "stretched" the figure becomes. The perimeter will continue to increase while the area remains the same.

9. about 17.1 units

11. $P \approx 26.1$ units; $A = 33.75$ units²

13. $P = 20.8$ units; $A = 15.5$ units²

15. 14 units²

17. 3 units²

19. A. no; he needs 70 more feet; **B.** 1700 ft²; **C.** $B(8, 3)$, $C(8, -2)$; $P \approx 254$ feet

21. $P \approx 15.8$ units

23. Area C is the closest.

Spiral Review • Assessment Readiness

27. A

MODULE 2, LESSON 2.1

On Your Own

5. If the three points are noncollinear, then the statement is true and only one plane can pass through them. Counterexample: If the points are collinear, then an infinite number of planes can pass through them.

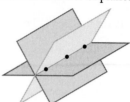

7. If $x = 2$, then $4x + 7 = 15$.

9. If two angles are supplementary angles, then the sum of their measures is 180 degrees.

11. If the dog performs the trick, then it gets a treat. Converse: If the dog gets a treat, then it performed a trick. Inverse: If the dog does not perform a trick, then it did not get a treat. Contrapositive: If the dog does not get a treat, then it did not perform a trick.

13. A triangle is a scalene triangle if and only if it has three sides with different lengths.

15. Two lines are perpendicular if and only if they intersect at a 90° angle.

17. Possible answer: $-5 - (-8) = 3$

19. Answers will vary.

21. Statement: If the job wasn't done by us, then it wasn't done right; Converse: If the job wasn't done right, then it wasn't done by us. Inverse: If the job was done by us, then it was done right. Contrapositive: If the job was done right, then it was done by us.

Spiral Review • Assessment Readiness

23. A

25. A. 3; **B.** 5; **C.** 1; **D.** 2; **E.** 4

MODULE 2, LESSON 2.2

On Your Own

5. The conclusion is based on observing three numbers.

7. The conclusion is based on observing the scores of 7 soccer games.

9. The conclusion is based on observing the pattern in 3 different images.

11. deductive reasoning; The definition of a right angle is used to draw the conclusion.

13. inductive reasoning; The conclusion is based on observing Cindy's six rolls of a number cube.

15. inductive reasoning; The conclusion is based on observing Tammy's 3 bowling scores.

17. Line m and line n intersect at one point.

19. 17 is an odd number.

21. 54 is divisible by 2.

23. If $x - 7 = 22$, then $x = 29$.

25. If $3a + 4 = 10$, then $a = 2$.

27. If $x = 7$, then $2x - 13 = 1$.

29. If $n = 12$, then $n - 20 = -8$.

31. cannot

33. may

35. may

37. always

39.

Statements	Reasons
1. $n + 14 = 19$	**1.** Given
2. $n + 14 - 14 = 19 - 14$	**2.** Subtraction Property of Equality
3. $n = 5$	**3.** Simplify.

41.

Statements	Reasons
1. $2r - 11 = 1$	**1.** Given
2. $2r - 11 + 11 = 1 + 11$	**2.** Addition Property of Equality
3. $2r = 12$	**3.** Simplify.
4. $\dfrac{2r}{2} = \dfrac{12}{2}$	**4.** Division Property of Equality
5. $r = 6$	**5.** Simplify.

43. Given: $\overrightarrow{EG}$ is the angle bisector of $\angle DEF$.

Prove: $m\angle DEF = 2 \cdot m\angle DEG$

Statements	Reasons
1. $\overrightarrow{EG}$ is the angle bisector of $\angle DEF$.	**1.** Given
2. $m\angle DEG = m\angle GEF$	**2.** Definition of angle bisector
3. $m\angle DEF = m\angle DEG + m\angle GEF$	**3.** Angle Addition Postulate
4. $m\angle DEF = m\angle DEG + m\angle DEG$	**4.** Substitution Property
5. $m\angle DEF = 2 \cdot m\angle DEG$	**5.** Simplify.

45. false

47. true

49.A. $n - 1, n + 1$

B. $(n - 1) + n + (n + 1) = 3n$

C. The sum of the three numbers is 3 times n which is the middle number.

D. yes; n can be any integer.

51. Rectangle $JKLM$ is a square.

Rectangle $WXYZ$ is not a square.

Spiral Review • Assessment Readiness

53. B

55. A

MODULE 2, LESSON 2.3

On Your Own

7. A

9. A

11. B

13. 2

15. 27

17. yes

19. no

21. first group: $\overline{XY}, \overline{YZ}, \overline{XZ}$; second group: $\overline{YW}, \overline{WZ}$

23.

Statements	Reasons
1. Triangle DEF is an equilateral triangle. $\overline{FG} \cong \overline{DE}$	**1.** Given
2. $\overline{DE} \cong \overline{EF}$	**2.** Definition of an equilateral triangle
3. $\overline{EF} \cong \overline{FG}$	**3.** Transitive Property of Segment Congruence

25. first group: $\overline{AB}, \overline{CD}$; second group: $\overline{AC}, \overline{BD}, \overline{CE}, \overline{DF}$

27. $x = 5$

29. $x = 4$

31. $x = 15$

33. 91 ft

35. 12 miles

37. $a = 5$; $XY = 31$, $YZ = 31$, $XZ = 62$

Spiral Review • Assessment Readiness

39. C

41.A. Contrapositive

B. Converse

C. Inverse

© Houghton Mifflin Harcourt Publishing Company

MODULE 2, LESSON 2.4

On Your Own

5. C

7. C

9. B

11. m∠1 = 148°, m∠2 = 32°, m∠3 = 148°

13. m∠1 = 132°, m∠2 = 48°

15. m∠1 = 103°, m∠2 = 103°

17.

Statements	Reasons
1. ∠DEF ≅ ∠FEB	1. Given
2. m∠DEF = m∠FEB	2. Definition of congruent angles
3. ∠AEC ≅ ∠DEB	3. Vertical Angles Theorem
4. m∠AEC = m∠DEB	4. Definition of congruent angles
5. m∠DEB = m∠DEF + m∠FEB	5. Angle Addition Postulate
6. m∠AEC = m∠DEF + m∠FEB	6. Transitive Property
7. m∠AEC = m∠FEB + m∠FEB	7. Substitution
8. m∠AEC = 2m∠FEB	8. Combine like terms.

19.

Statements	Reasons
1. ∠1 ≅ ∠2	1. Given
2. ∠2 is a complement of ∠3.	2. Given
3. m∠2 + m∠3 = 90°	3. Definition of complementary angles
4. m∠1 = m∠2	4. Definition of congruent angles
5. m∠1 + m∠3 = 90°	5. Substitution
6. ∠1 is a complement of ∠3.	6. Definition of complementary angles

21. $x = 9$

23. $x = 21$

25. $x = 12$

27. $x = 3$

29. m∠2 ≅ m∠3 ≅ m∠6 ≅ m∠7
m∠1 ≅ m∠4 ≅ m∠5 ≅ m∠8

31. 3; ∠1 and ∠4, ∠2 and ∠5, ∠3 and ∠6

33. Statements: ∠AFE ≅ ∠BFD, m∠BFD = m∠BFC + m∠CFD; Reasons: ∠AFE and ∠BFD are opposite angles sharing a vertex at the intersection of two lines.; Definition of congruent angles; Transitive Property

35. 139°; The angle is the sum of half of each of the two given angles.

Spiral Review • Assessment Readiness

39. D

UNIT 2

MODULE 3, LESSON 3.1

On Your Own

5. *See below.*

7. ∠2, ∠4, ∠6, ∠8

9. Consecutive Exterior Angles Theorem

11. Consecutive Interior Angles Theorem

13. m∠1 = 80°, m∠2 = 100°

17. $x = 11$

19. $x = 13$

21. $x = 21$

23.A. ∠2

B. Corresponding Angles Postulate

C. m∠1 = 105°, m∠2 = 75°, m∠3 = 105°

25. m∠3 = m∠9 = 125°

5.

Corresponding angles	Consecutive interior angles	Consecutive exterior angles	Alternate interior angles	Alternate exterior angles
∠1 and ∠5 ∠2 and ∠6 ∠3 and ∠7 ∠4 and ∠8	∠3 and ∠6 ∠4 and ∠5	∠1 and ∠8 ∠2 and ∠7	∠3 and ∠5 ∠4 and ∠6	∠1 and ∠7 ∠2 and ∠8

27.

Statements	Reasons
1. Line *a* is parallel to line *b*. Line *x* is parallel to line *y*.	1. Given
2. $\angle 2 \cong \angle 6$	2. Corresponding Angles Postulate
3. $\angle 6$ is supplementary to $\angle 7$.	3. Linear Pairs Theorem
4. $\angle 7 \cong \angle 13$	4. Alternate Interior Angles Theorem
5. $\angle 6$ is supplementary to $\angle 13$.	5. Congruent Supplements Theorem
6. $\angle 2$ is supplementary to $\angle 13$.	6. Congruent Supplements Theorem

Spiral Review • Assessment Readiness

29. A

31. D

MODULE 3, LESSON 3.2

On Your Own

7. no

9. yes; the Converse of the Consecutive Interior Angles Theorem

11. $\angle 1 \cong \angle 3$; Converse of the Corresponding Angles Postulate

13. $x = 7$

15. $x = 9$

17.

Statements	Reasons
1. $\angle 4$ and $\angle 5$ are supplementary.	1. Given
2. $\angle 5$ and $\angle 8$ are supplementary.	2. Linear Pairs Theorem
3. $\angle 4 \cong \angle 8$	3. Congruent Supplements
4. $a \parallel b$	4. Converse of Corresponding Angles Postulate

19. Possible answer: The corresponding angles are all congruent.

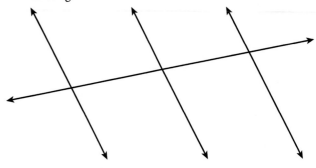

21.A. $b \parallel c$; The measure of the angle that is vertical to the 45° angle is also 45°. 45° and 135° angles are supplements, so the lines are parallel by the converse of Consecutive Exterior Angles Theorem.

B. Line *a* is not parallel with the other lines. Because 46° and 135° are not supplementary or congruent, the lines are not parallel by any of the converses of the parallel lines theorems.

Spiral Review • Assessment Readiness

23. A

MODULE 3, LESSON 3.3

On Your Own

5. No, you need to know if $PR = PQ$.

7.

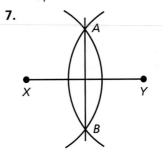

9. $a = 4$

11. $d = 7$

13.

Statements	Reasons
1. $AC = BC$ $AD = BD$	1. Given
2. C lies on the perpendicular bisector of $\overline{AB}$.	2. Converse of the Perpendicular Bisector Theorem
3. D lies on the perpendicular bisector of $\overline{AB}$.	3. Converse of the Perpendicular Bisector Theorem
4. $\overleftrightarrow{AB} \perp \overleftrightarrow{CD}$	4. Definition of Perpendicular Bisector

15. 15

17. 28

19.

Statements	Reasons
1. $a \perp t$ and $a \parallel b$	1. Given
2. $m\angle 1 = 90°$	2. Definition of Perpendicular Lines
3. $m\angle 1 = m\angle 2$	3. Corresponding Angles Postulate
4. $m\angle 2 = 90°$	4. Transitive Property of Equality
5. $b \perp t$	5. Definition of Perpendicular Lines

21. 3

23. 17

25. By the Converse of the Perpendicular Bisector Theorem, you know that oxygen atom is on the perpendicular bisector.

27. $w = 5$, $v = 7.2$; the linear pair formed are congruent angles, so the lines are perpendicular. $15w + 15 = 90$, so $w = 5$. $\frac{25v}{2} = 90$, so $v = 7.2$.

Spiral Review • Assessment Readiness

29. D

31. B

MODULE 4, LESSON 4.1

On Your Own

7. $m = \frac{3}{5}$

9. $m = -4$

11.

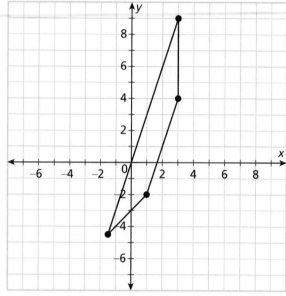

13. not parallel

15. not parallel

17. 1. C, 2. A, 3. B, 4. E, 5. D

19. $y = -\frac{1}{17}x + \frac{1}{68}$

21. $y = -\frac{1}{3}x + \frac{29}{6}$

23. $y = 2x - 22$

25. $y = x + 1.75$

27. Answers will vary.

29. Undefined; $x = 1.4$

31. $m = 0$; $y = 3$

33. $m = 0$; $y = \frac{3}{5}$

35.A. no; The two lines do not have the same slope.

B. $y = -\frac{1}{3}x + 3$

C. The two lines would be parallel.

37. light rail: $y = -0.25x + 107$; community walking path: $y = -0.25x + 160.9$

Spiral Review • Assessment Readiness

39. A

41. A. 2; B. 1; C. 3; D. 4

MODULE 4, LESSON 4.2

On Your Own

7. $y = x + 6$

9. $y = -\frac{2}{3}x + \frac{29}{3}$

11. $y = 0$

13. always

15. sometimes

17. never

19.A. $y = -\frac{2}{3}x + 6$

B. $y = -\frac{2}{3}x + \frac{5}{3}$

C. perpendicular; $\frac{3}{2}\left(-\frac{2}{3}\right) = -\frac{6}{6} = -1$

21. no; You need two sets of parallel lines, perpendicular to each other, to create a rectangle.

23. Possible answer: Given: The slopes of two lines are opposite reciprocals. Prove: The lines are perpendicular. If the two slopes are opposite reciprocals, I can name them $\frac{a}{b}$ and $-\frac{b}{a}$. I can draw two lines on the coordinate plane to represent these slopes. The distances a and b create right triangles with each line and represent the rise and run of each line. A rotation of $90°$ maps one triangle to the other. Therefore, the angle between the two lines is $90°$. The lines are perpendicular.

25. $x = 4$

Spiral Review • Assessment Readiness

29. B, E

31. C

MODULE 4, LESSON 4.3

On Your Own

7. Possible answer: If you subtract x_1 from x_2 and divide by 2, you will find the horizontal distance between x_1 and the midpoint, not the actual x-coordinate of the midpoint, which is the horizontal distance between the origin and the midpoint.

9. They are congruent. AB: $2\sqrt{5}$; CD: $2\sqrt{5}$

11. They are congruent. AB: $\sqrt{109}$; CD: $\sqrt{85}$

13. They are congruent. AB: $3\sqrt{2}$; CD: $3\sqrt{2}$

15. They are not congruent. AB: $\sqrt{85}$; CD: $\sqrt{74}$

17. length: $4\sqrt{2}$; midpoint: $(3, 2)$

19. No, it is not an equilateral triangle; The legs are not equal lengths.

21.A. Approximately 1307 feet per lap

B. 12 laps

23.A. 6.5 miles; 9:41 a.m.

B. about 4 miles

25.A. $\overline{PQ}$ and $\overline{PR}$ are congruent.

B. 3 whole supports

Spiral Review • Assessment Readiness

27. D

UNIT 3

MODULE 5, LESSON 5.1

On Your Own

7. always

9. $(x, y) \rightarrow (x - 2, y + 8)$

11.

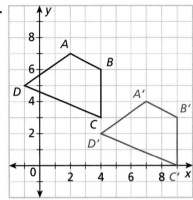

13. C

15. B

17. $\langle 5, -3 \rangle$

19. $A \rightarrow B$: $\langle 0, -10 \rangle$;
$A \rightarrow C$: $\langle 10, -5 \rangle$;
$A \rightarrow D$: $\langle 10, -15 \rangle$

21. Yes, he will use 120 black and 120 white tiles.

23. Possible answer: The x-coordinate translates in a positive direction, not a negative one. The correct vector should be $\langle 3, -3 \rangle$.

Spiral Review • Assessment Readiness

25. A

27. A. Right; **B.** Obtuse; **C.** Acute

MODULE 5, LESSON 5.2

On Your Own

7. Always; rotations are rigid motions, so the preimage and image will always be congruent.

9. Sometimes; $\angle GHF$ and $\angle HFG$ are angles in the same triangle. They could be congruent. But, whether they are congruent or not, is not determined by a rotation.

11. No; possible answer: Rocco located vertex L' correctly, but he translated the triangle instead of rotating it.

13.

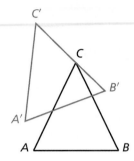

15.

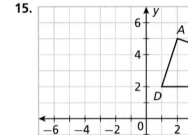

17.

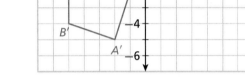

19. $A'(-5, -7)$, $B'(-9, -6)$ and $C'(-6, -3)$

21. $45°, 90°, 135°, 180°, 225°, 270°, 315°, 360°$

23. $210°$

25. 22.5 minutes

27. Possible answer: $R_{C(0, 0), 90°}(P) = P'; P'(-3, 2)$

Spiral Review • Assessment Readiness

29. D

31. A

MODULE 5, LESSON 5.3

On Your Own

7.

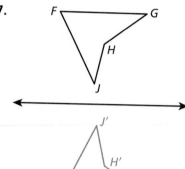

9. A–B.

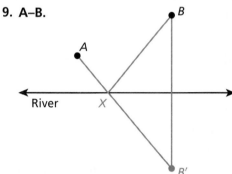

11. Possible answer:

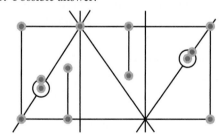

13.

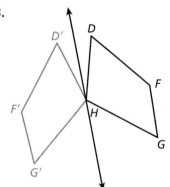

15. $A'(1, 1)$, $B'(-2, 3)$, $C'(2, -2)$

17. Possible answer: Reflect $\triangle ABC$ in the x-axis. Then reflect the image across the y-axis.

19.A. $y = \frac{1}{2}x + 3$

B. Because $\overline{AA}{}'$ is perpendicular to the line of reflection, the slope of $\overline{AA}{}'$ is the opposite reciprocal of the slope of the line of reflection; -2.

21. Possible answer: The student reflected the image across $y = 0$ instead of $y = -2$. The student should have translated the image up two units, reflected the image across $y = 0$, and then translated the image down two units. The correct image is $A'(-2, -10)$, $B'(5, -9)$, and $C'(5, -7)$.

Spiral Review • Assessment Readiness

23. A

25. D

MODULE 5, LESSON 5.4

On Your Own

7.

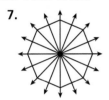

9.

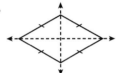

11. Yes; 90°, 180°, 270°, 360°

13. Yes; 72°, 144°, 216°, 288°, 360°

15. Possible answer: It must be formed so that all six of its "branches" are identical.

17.

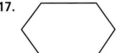

19. 7 sides

21. 12 sides

23. True

25. False

27.A.

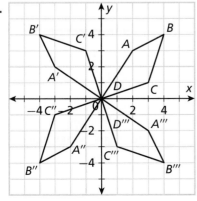

B. no

29. 1 line of symmetry through the body

31. Many of lines of symmetry and rotational symmetry

Spiral Review • Assessment Readiness

33. C

35. A. 3; B. 1; C. 4; D. 2

MODULE 6, LESSON 6.1

On Your Own

7.A. Maya can compare the coordinates for the corresponding vertices of the triangles.

B. The scales of the graphs are different, which makes it hard to determine what happened just by looking at the images.

C. A horizontal stretch

9. No. Bridget dilated by a scale factor of 2 instead of $\frac{1}{2}$.

11. Horizontal stretch with scale factor 7

13. Vertical compression with scale factor of one-half and translation to the right 2 units

15. Translation right 1 unit and down 2 units and then dilated by scale factor of two

17. Construct a triangle and write down the coordinates of the vertices. Use the function notation to construct the dilation. Multiply the x- and y-values of the vertices B and C by the scale factor $k = 0.5$. Vertex A is the center of dilation, so its coordinates remain the same. Construct the dilated triangle on the coordinate plane.

19.A. Moving the second finger toward the first should shrink the figure. Moving the second finger away from the first should enlarge the figure.

B. When the first finger (at the center of dilation) is on the figure: Any side of the figure that includes the center of dilation will be mapped to the line containing that side. Any side of the figure that does not include the center of dilation will be mapped to a line parallel to that side of the figure.

When the first finger (at the center of dilation) is not on the figure: Any side of the figure will be mapped to a line parallel to that side of the figure.

21. no; The lanes are different sizes, and translations preserve the size of the figure.

23.A. This is a translation, so the measures of the angles and the lengths of the sides of the image remain the same as the preimage. The vertices of the image are $A'(-5, 1)$, $B'(-7, -2)$, $C'(0, 1)$.

B. This is a horizontal stretch, so the measures of the angles and the lengths of the sides are different than in the preimage. The vertices of the image are $A'(-3, 1)$, $B'(-9, -2)$, $C'(12, 1)$.

C. This is a dilation, so the measures of the angles are the same as the preimage; however, the lengths of the sides are longer than the lengths of the sides of the preimage. The vertices of the image are $A'(-2, 2)$, $B'(-6, -4)$, $C'(8, 2)$.

D. Rigid transformations (translations, rotations, reflections) all preserve angle measure and distance. Some non-rigid transformations (dilations) preserve angle measure but do not preserve distance. Some non-rigid transformations (horizontal stretches or compressions and vertical stretches or compressions) do not preserve angle measure or distance.

Spiral Review • Assessment Readiness

25. D

27. reflection, no reflection, no reflection, reflection

MODULE 6, LESSON 6.2

On Your Own

5. Reflect across x-axis, translate left 4 units and down 2 units

7.

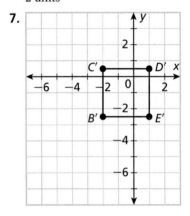

9. He is not correct because it changes whether the scale factor will be inside or outside the parentheses.

11. $(x, y) \rightarrow (-x + 5, y - 6)$

13. $A'(6, -18)$, $B'(-14, -2)$, $C'(-14, -18)$

15. Sample answer: $(x, y) \rightarrow (-x, y)$ then $(x, y) \rightarrow (x, -y)$; $(x, y) \rightarrow (-x, y)$ then $(x, y) \rightarrow (x, -y)$

17. Possible answer: Rotate the figure 90° counterclockwise each time.

19. $(x, y) \rightarrow (-y + 1, -x - 4)$

21. $(x, y) \rightarrow (-0.5y - 1.5, 0.5x + 2.5)$

23.A. isosceles; Two of the sides have the same length.

B. $A'\left(-\frac{5}{2}, \frac{1}{2}\right)$, $B'\left(-\frac{3}{2}, -3\right)$, $C'\left(-\frac{1}{2}, \frac{1}{2}\right)$

C. yes; $\triangle A'B'C'$ is an isosceles triangle.

D. Possible answer: translation down 1 unit, vertical compression by a factor of $\frac{2\sqrt{3}}{7}$. The image will be an equilateral triangle.

25. $(x, y) \rightarrow (2y - 20, -2x + 4)$

Spiral Review • Assessment Readiness

27. C

29. C

MODULE 7, LESSON 7.1

On Your Own

5. Yes; corresponding parts of congruent figures are congruent.

7.A. 120°

B. $A'B'$ and $C'B'$

9. no; The figures are not the same size and shape.

11. yes; Possible answer: translation then rotation

13. not congruent; Not all pairs of corresponding angles are congruent.

15. She could use a sequence of rigid motions to map one shape to the other.

17.A. The design is created from 16 congruent triangles. Each quarter of the design consists of 4 of the triangles joined to form a square.

B. Possible answer: There are many ways to transform the triangle with base $\overline{AB}$ to the position of the triangle with base $\overline{CD}$. One way is to translate it to the position of the triangle directly beneath it, then, rotate it 90° counterclockwise about C, then translate to the right.

C. $\overline{CD} \cong \overline{AB}$ because corresponding parts of congruent figures are congruent.

Spiral Review • Assessment Readiness

19. C

MODULE 7, LESSON 7.2

On Your Own

5. She is right; since the corresponding sides of congruent triangles are congruent, the sum of the total lengths of the sides (perimeter) will be the same for both triangles.

7. A. and B.

Translate *ABCD* so that *A* corresponds with *X*.	Definition of translation
Rotate *A′B′C′D′* counterclockwise about *A′* by m∠*B′A′W* so that $\overline{A'B''}$ corresponds with $\overline{XW}$.	Definition of rotation
Reflect *A′B″C″D″* over $\overline{XW}$ so that $\overline{B''C'''}$ corresponds with $\overline{WZ}$.	Definition of reflection
ABCD ≅ *XWZY*	Definition of congruence
$\overline{AD} \cong \overline{XY}$	CPCFC

9. The triangles *XYZ* and *PQR* are congruent because all corresponding sides are marked as congruent along with 2 of the pairs of corresponding angles. By the Third Angles Theorem, the third pair of corresponding angles are also congruent, so the triangles are congruent; $w = 27$

11. ∠*T* ≅ ∠*W*, but $\overline{TU}$ is not congruent to $\overline{WX}$ or $\overline{WV}$ (by counting). So, the triangles are not congruent.

13. The correct puzzle piece will be light blue in color, and will have two indentations on opposite sides and two protrusions on opposite sides. Pieces A and C fit this description. Piece C fits in the empty space.

15.

Statements	Reasons
1. △*STU* ≅ △*VTU*	1. Given
2. $\overline{ST} \cong \overline{SV}$	2. Given
3. $\overline{ST} \cong \overline{VT}$	3. CPCFC
4. $\overline{SV} \cong \overline{VT}$	4. Transitive Property of Congruence
5. △*STV* is equilateral.	5. Definition of equilateral triangle

17. A. First, rotate A 90° clockwise about the origin. Then, reflect the image over the line $x = 3$.

B. no; Translate C down 3 units and left 3 (so that the point that touches shape B moves to the origin). Then, rotate the image of C 180° about the origin.

Spiral Review • Assessment Readiness

19. D

MODULE 7, LESSON 7.3

On Your Own

3. Yes. The congruence statement determines the corresponding parts of the congruent figures.

5. Possible answer: Map △*ABC* to △*DEF* with a rotation of 180° around the origin, followed by a

translation; rotation: $(x, y) \rightarrow (-x, -y)$; translation: $(x, y) \rightarrow (x + 2, y + 6)$.

7. Possible answer: Map △*WXY* to △*CED* with a rotation of 180° around the origin, followed by a horizontal translation. rotation: $(x, y) \rightarrow (-x, -y)$; translation: $(x, y) \rightarrow (x - 2, y)$.

9. Possible answer: You can map *WXYZ* to *DEFG* with a reflection across the *x*-axis, followed by a horizontal translation. So, the two figures are congruent; reflection: $(x, y) \rightarrow (x, -y)$; translation: $(x, y) \rightarrow (x + 10, y)$.

11. There is no sequence of rigid transformations that will map one figure onto the other, so they are not congruent.

13. 45°, 90°, 135°, 180°, 225°, 270°, and 315° rotations about the center of the logo

15. Map *PQRSTU* to *ABCDEF* with a translation. The coordinate notation for the translation is $(x, y) \rightarrow (x + 6, y + 10)$.

17. Answers will vary.

Spiral Review • Assessment Readiness

19. D

MODULE 8, LESSON 8.1

On Your Own

7. A translation that maps *M* to *Y*, then a rotation about point *Y* using ∠*L′M′X* as the angle of rotation.

9. Yes; We can find the missing side using the Pythagorean theorem. The triangles are congruent by ASA Triangle Congruence Theorem.

11. No; We are not given two congruent angles and a congruent side.

13.1. $\overline{WX}$ bisects ∠*YWZ* and ∠*YXZ*.: Given

4. $\overline{XW} \cong \overline{XW}$: Reflexive Property of Congruence

5. △*YWX* ≅ △*ZWX*: ASA Triangle Congruence Theorem

15.

Statements	Reasons
1. $\overline{BD} \perp \overline{AC}$	1. Given
2. m∠*BDA* = m∠*BDC* = 90°	2. Definition of perpendicular lines
3. ∠*BDA* ≅ ∠*BDC*	3. Definition of congruent angles
4. *D* is the midpoint of $\overline{AC}$.	4. Given
5. $\overline{AD} \cong \overline{CD}$	5. Definition of midpoint
6. ∠*A* ≅ ∠*C*	6. Given
7. △*ADB* ≅ △*CDB*	7. ASA Triangle Congruence Theorem

17. $x = 10$

$y = 4$

19. No; one pair of corresponding angles are congruent, and one pair of corresponding sides are congruent $\left(\overline{LN} \cong \overline{LN}\right)$, but no other information is known.

21. Yes; here, two pairs of angles are congruent $\left(\angle MNL \cong \angle KNL \text{ [Given] and } \angle MLN \cong \angle KLN\right)$[Definition of angle bisector] and the included side $\left(\overline{LN} \cong \overline{LN}\right)$

Spiral Review • Assessment Readiness

23. B

25. A

MODULE 8, LESSON 8.2

On Your Own

5. Yes; Possible answer: The triangles have congruent 3 inch sides, a congruent included angle, and a congruent shared side. They are congruent by the SAS Triangle Congruence Theorem.

7. Yes; Possible answer: They have congruent 20 mm sides, a congruent included angle, and a congruent shared side. They are congruent by the SAS Triangle Congruence Theorem

9. Yes; The triangles have two pairs of congruent sides and pair of included congruent angles, so you can prove the triangles are congruent by the SAS Triangle Congruence Theorem.

11. Zach left a step out of his proof. He has only proved one pair of congruent sides and one pair of congruent angles. He could prove $\angle A$ and $\angle E$ are congruent by a transversal through parallel lines to complete the proof.

13.

Statements	Reasons
1. $\overline{PQ} \| \overline{RS}$	**1.** Given
2. $PQ = RS$	**2.** Given
3. $\angle PQS \cong \angle RSQ$	**3.** Alternate Interior Angles Theorem
4. $\overline{SQ} \cong \overline{SQ}$	**4.** Reflexive Property of Congruence
5. $\triangle PQS \cong \triangle RSQ$	**5.** SAS Triangle Congruence Theorem

15. $x = -8$

17. No; Possible answer: There is not enough information given to use SAS Congruence; She can't use ASA because we don't know if the 9 in. side is the included side. No theorem can prove congruence.

19. Not enough information to prove congruency; Possible answer: The student would need to know the

actual length of either the longest side or shortest side of Triangle 1.

21. It is possible to create two different triangles when given two sides and an angle that is not included between those two sides. Two triangles with the same SSA criteria would not necessarily be congruent.

23. Let D be the point where the angle bisector intersects $\overline{BC}$. We know that $\overline{AB} \cong \overline{AC}$ by the definition of congruent segments and the given information. Since D is on the bisector of $\angle A$, $\angle CAD \cong \angle BAD$. Also, $\overline{AD} \cong \overline{AD}$. Using this information, $\triangle ACD \cong \triangle ABD$ by SAS.

Spiral Review • Assessment Readiness

25. A

27. B

MODULE 8, LESSON 8.3

On Your Own

5. Yes, they are congruent.

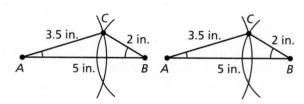

7. Congruent; SSS Triangle Congruence Theorem; Possible answer: The triangles have two sides marked as congruent and share a third side, which must be congruent.

9. Congruent; ASA Triangle Congruence; There is a congruent pair of angles, a pair of congruent included sides, and a congruent pair of vertical angles.

11. Not congruent. Possible answer: There are 4 side lengths shown. Two congruent triangles have a maximum of 3 different side lengths.

13. Translate $\triangle ABC$ along $\overrightarrow{AD}$ to map A to D. Rotate $\triangle ABC$ clockwise about D with an angle of rotation of $\angle CDF$ to map $\triangle ABC$ to $\triangle DEF$.

15. $x = 4$

17. $x = 4.5, y = 9$ or $x = 3, y = 6$

19. $x = 12, y = 3$ or $x = 18, y = 2$

21. No; Possible answer: Many triangles have the same angle measurements but different side lengths. For example, the triangles could have side lengths of 2-3-4 and 4-6-8 and have congruent corresponding angles.

23.

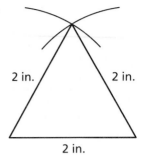

2 in.   2 in.

2 in.

Possible answer: I drew a 2-inch segment, then set my compass to 2 inches, put the compass on each endpoint, and drew an arc. I put a point where the arcs intersected and drew a triangle using the point as the third vertex.

25. Create two triangles with the center of the circle, the satellite, and the signal distance points as the vertices. The length of the sides from the center to the signal distance points is r. The shared side from the center to the satellite is $35{,}700 + r$. Both triangles have a corresponding included angle of $90° - 9° = 81°$, so the triangles are congruent by the SAS Triangle Congruence Theorem. Therefore all corresponding sides are congruent, and the signal is proven to travel the same distance in both directions.

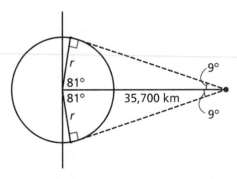

r
81°
81°   35,700 km
r
9°
9°

27. No; You cannot prove two triangles are congruent using only information about the angles.

Spiral Review • Assessment Readiness

29. C

31. A. 1 or 4, B. 4 or 1, C. 3, D. 2, E. 5

MODULE 8, LESSON 8.4

On Your Own

7. Yes, by AAS Congruence

9. Yes, by HL Congruence

11. cannot be determined

13. $x = 3$; HL Congruence

15.

Statements	Reasons
1. $\angle A \cong \angle C$	1. Given
2. $\overline{DB}$ bisects $\angle ABC$.	2. Given
3. $\angle ABD \cong \angle CBD$	3. Definition of Angle Bisector
4. $\overline{DB} \cong \overline{DB}$	4. Reflexive Property of Congruence
5. $\triangle ABD \cong \triangle CBD$	5. AAS Triangle Congruence Theorem

17.

Statements	Reasons
1. $\angle E$ and $\angle C$ are right angles.	1. Given
2. $\overline{AE} \cong \overline{BC}$	2. Given
3. $\triangle ABC$ and $\triangle BAE$ are right triangles.	3. Definition of right triangles
4. $\overline{AB} \cong \overline{AB}$	4. Reflexive Property of Congruence
5. $\triangle ABC \cong \triangle BAE$	5. HL Triangle Congruence Theorem

19. The king post is 10 ft tall, and the bottom chord is 25 ft long.

21. 36 m; The two triangles are congruent right triangles. By using the Pythagorean Theorem, I can find $YW = 8$. The sum of the sides is $10 + 10 + 8 + 8 = 36$ m.

Spiral Review • Assessment Readiness

23. D

25. C

UNIT 5

MODULE 9, LESSON 9.1

On Your Own

7. Yes; the exterior angle of the right angle in a right triangle is a right angle.

9.

Statements	Reasons
1. $\angle B \cong \angle C$	1. Given
2. Draw $\overline{AD}$ so that it bisects $\angle A$.	2. An angle has one angle bisector.
3. $\angle DAB \cong \angle DAC$	3. Definition of angle bisector
4. $\overline{AD} \cong \overline{AD}$	4. Reflexive Property of Congruence
5. $\triangle ADB \cong \triangle ADC$	5. AAS Triangle Congruence Theorem
6. $\overline{AB} \cong \overline{AC}$	6. Corresponding Parts of Congruent Triangles Are Congruent

11. 59°

13. $x = 34$

15. $x = 70$

17. $x = 118$

19. Answers will vary. Sample answer: The entrance to a tent is shaped like an isosceles triangle. One of the congruent angles has a measure of 57°. What are the measures of the other two angles?

21. 42°, 84°

23. no; The Exterior Angle Theorem only helps you find the sum of the measures.

25. $m\angle A = 53°$, $m\angle B = 28°$, $m\angle C = 99°$

27. $m\angle A = 52°$, $m\angle B = 68°$, $m\angle C = 60°$

29. $m\angle A = 28°$, $m\angle B = 28°$, $m\angle C = 124°$

31. 35

Spiral Review • Assessment Readiness

35. B

37. C

MODULE 9, LESSON 9.2

On Your Own

7. The circumcenter of an obtuse triangle is located outside of the triangle.

9.

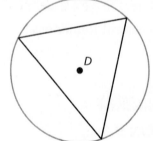

11.

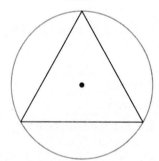

13. The measures of opposite angles of the quadrilateral are supplementary.

15. $(2, -3)$

17. $(1, 0)$

19. Possible answer: It is fairly easy to find an equation for a line perpendicular to a horizontal or vertical through a given point.

21. 4 or 0

23. 1 or 3

25. $x = 10$

27. $x = 5$

29. $BE = 24$, $DC = 25$

31. $\overline{DA}$ or $\overline{DB}$ or $\overline{DC}$

33. justified

35. $PA = 81$

37. $PA = 53$

Spiral Review • Assessment Readiness

39. D

41. C

MODULE 9, LESSON 9.3

On Your Own

9. No; possible explanation: For $AQ = CQ$, point Q needs to be on the angle bisector of $\angle ABC$. There is no information given about $\angle ABC$.

11. Yes; possible explanation: Because $\overline{AQ} \perp \overline{AB}$, $\overline{CQ} \perp \overline{CB}$, and $AQ = CQ$, the Converse to the Angle Bisector Theorem can be applied to conclude that $\overrightarrow{BQ}$ bisects $\angle ABC$.

15. Answers will vary.

17. 50°

19. 37

21. Eve is correct. The incenter of a triangle is always within the triangle.

23. 47°

25. true

Spiral Review • Assessment Readiness

27. D

29. D

MODULE 9, LESSON 9.4

On Your Own

7.

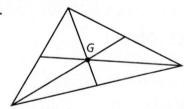

9. Possible answer: In each triangle, the side opposite vertex A is point Z. So, each triangle has $\overline{AZ}$ as a median. By the Centroid Theorem, the centroid is located $\frac{2}{3}$ down $\overline{AZ}$ from A.

11. no; The medians of a triangle are inside the triangle, so the intersection of the medians has to be inside the triangle.

13. inside

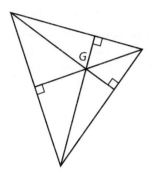

15. on

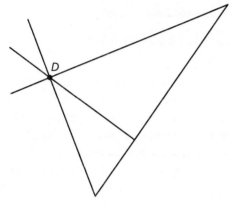

17. 10

19. 51

21. 36

23. Yes, the distance you are given is $\frac{2}{3}$ of the length of the median. You can find the length of the median by multiplying the given length by $\frac{3}{2}$.

25. $n = 9$

27. $a = 4$

29. $w = 10$

31. $(1, -0.5)$

33. $(4, 0)$

35. $(4, 4)$

37. $(2, -1)$

39. $(0, 0)$

41. $(8, 1)$

43. $(-1, 2)$

45. $(6, -2)$

47. $(6, 4)$

Spiral Review • Assessment Readiness

51. B

MODULE 9, LESSON 9.5

On Your Own

7.A.

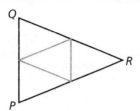

B. Isosceles triangle; Two of the midsegments will be congruent since their lengths are half the length of the congruent sides.

9. The lengths of the midsegments of an equilateral triangle are equal. So, the triangle is equilateral.

11. 28.5

13. 30

15. 30

17. 80 cm; Yes; the new side is parallel to the hypotenuse, so it is also a right triangle.

19. $(1, 7), (3, 4)$

21. $(-2, 1), (0, -2)$

23. Slope of $\overline{LM} = -\frac{3}{4}$ and slope of $\overline{AB} = -\frac{3}{4}$. So, $\overline{LM} \parallel \overline{AB}$; $LM = 5$ and $AB = 10$. So, $LM = \frac{1}{2}AB$.

25. $v = 5$

27. $n = 9$

Spiral Review • Assessment Readiness

29. A

31. A. 3, B. 1, C. 4, D. 2

MODULE 10 LESSON 10.1

On Your Own

11. AC decrease as point C moves counterclockwise towards point A.

13. $6 < x < 20$

15. $9 < x < 37$

17. $0 < AC < 16$

19. If $\overline{AB}$ is the longest side, then the length of any other side added to AB will be greater than the length of the third side.

21. $\overline{KL}, \overline{JL}, \overline{JK}; \angle J, \angle K, \angle L$

23. $\angle G, \angle F, \angle H; \overline{FH}, \overline{GH}, \overline{FG}$

25. $m\angle Z < m\angle X < m\angle Y$, so $XY < YZ < XZ$. Therefore, the safest route is to avoid sailing between the islands at X and Y.

27. $AB + BC > x$

   $AB + x > BC$

   $x > BC - AB$

$BC + x > AB$

$x > AB - BC$

Since $AB > BC$, $BC - AB < 0$, so the second inequality is not relevant. Combining the first and last inequalities gives $AB - BC < x < AB + BC$.

29.

Statements	Reasons
1. $\triangle ABC$	1. Given
2. Draw $\overline{BX}$ so that $m\angle XBC = m\angle XCB$.	2. By construction
3. $XB = XC$	3. Sides opposite angles of equal measure are equal in length.
4. $AX + XB = AX + XC$	4. Addition Property of Equality
5. $AC = AX + XC$	5. Segment Addition Postulate
6. $AC = AX + XB$	6. Substitution
7. $AX + XB > AB$	7. The sum of the lengths of any 2 sides of a triangle is greater than the length of the 3rd side.
8. $AC > AB$	8. Substitution

Spiral Review • Assessment Readiness

33. C

MODULE 10, LESSON 10.2

On Your Own

9. $ST > VW$

11. $VW > CZ$

13. $m\angle L > m\angle D$

15. $2 < x < 10$

17. $-18 < x < 34$

19. Pair 2; Both sides of the triangles created by their paths are congruent, but the included angle is greater for Pair 2, so the distance from camp is greater.

17.

Statements	Reasons
1. $ABCD$ is a parallelogram	1. Given
2. $\overline{AB} \parallel \overline{DC}$, $\overline{AD} \parallel \overline{BC}$	2. Definition of parallelogram
3. $\angle A$ is supplementary to $\angle B$, $\angle B$ is supplementary to $\angle C$, $\angle C$ is supplementary to $\angle D$, $\angle D$ is supplementary to $\angle A$	3. Consecutive Interior Angles Theorem.

21.A. $\frac{5}{3} < x < \frac{13}{2}$

B. 5

C. The length of the side represented by $4x + 3$ is 23, and the length of the side represented by $6x - 10$ is 20.

23. Assume that both $\angle 1$ and $\angle 2$ can be obtuse. If $\angle 1$ and $\angle 2$ are both obtuse, then $m\angle 1 > 90°$ and $m\angle 2 > 90°$, so $m\angle 1 + m\angle 2 > 180°$. But $\angle 1$ and $\angle 2$ are supplementary, so $m\angle 1 + m\angle 2 = 180°$. So, $\angle 1$ and $\angle 2$ cannot both be obtuse.

Spiral Review • Assessment Readiness

27. D

29. B, D, F

UNIT 6

MODULE 11, LESSON 11.1

On Your Own

9. Draw diagonal $\overline{GJ}$ to form two triangles. By the Triangle Sum Theorem, you know that $m\angle 1 + m\angle 2 + m\angle 3 = 180°$ and $m\angle 4 + m\angle 5 + m\angle 6 = 180°$. Add these two equations to find $m\angle 1 + m\angle 2 + m\angle 3 + m\angle 4 + m\angle 5 + m\angle 6 = 360°$. Use Commutative Property to rewrite the equation as $m\angle 1 + m\angle 2 + m\angle 4 + m\angle 3 + m\angle 5 + m\angle 6 = 360°$. For the Angle Addition Postulate, $m\angle J = m\angle 3 + m\angle 5$ and $m\angle G = m\angle 2 + m\angle 4$. Substitute to find $m\angle F + m\angle G + m\angle J + m\angle H = 360°$.

11. $70°$

13. 2.5

15. $76°$

17. *See below.*

19. $117°$

21. 43

23. $34°$

25. *See below.*

25.

Statements	Reasons
1. $ABCD$ and $AXYZ$ are parallelograms.	1. Given
2. $\angle C \cong \angle A$, $\angle A \cong \angle Y$	2. Opposite angles of parallelograms are congruent.
3. $\angle C \cong \angle Y$	3. Transitive Property of Congruence

27. *See below.*

Spiral Review • Assessment Readiness

29. A, B

MODULE 11, LESSON 11.2

On Your Own

9. *See below.*

11. No, you do not know any information about the angles opposite the given angle measures.

13. No. A pair of opposite sides is congruent, but the other pair of opposite sides is parallel.

15. yes

17. no

19. yes

21. Yes, because each pair of opposite sides has the same length.

23. No, because *MJ* is not equal to *KL*.

25. $a = 8, b = 5$

27. $m = 11, n = 6$

29. Answers will vary.

31.A. The triangles are congruent, because a rotation does not change the size or shape of the triangle. So, the opposite sides of the quadrilateral are congruent because they are corresponding parts of congruent triangles. Therefore, the quadrilateral is a parallelogram.

B. The parallelogram will map onto itself after a 180° rotation; therefore, the parallelogram has 180° rotational symmetry. There is not one single reflection that will map a parallelogram onto itself.

C. yes; All parallelograms will have 180° rotational symmetry, because if you rotate a parallelogram around its center 180°, it will always map onto itself.

33. Draw $\overline{AC}$. $\overline{ZW}$ is the midsegment of $\triangle ADC$, so $\overline{ZW} \parallel \overline{AC}$ and $ZW = \frac{1}{2}AC$. Also, $\overline{YX}$ is the midsegment of $\triangle BAC$, so $\overline{XY} \parallel \overline{AC}$ and $XY = \frac{1}{2}AC$. So, $\overline{XY} \parallel \overline{ZW}$ and $\overline{XY} \cong \overline{ZW}$, so $WXYZ$ is a parallelogram.

27.

Statements	Reasons
1. $\triangle ABC$ with medians $\overline{CD}$ and $\overline{BE}$ that intersect at G.	**1.** Given
2. E is the midpoint of $\overline{AC}$. D is the midpoint of $\overline{AB}$.	**2.** Definition of median
3. Draw a segment $\overline{AH}$ through G so that $AG = GH$. Then draw $\overline{CH}$ and $\overline{BH}$.	**3.** Two points determine a line.
4. G is the midpoint of $\overline{AH}$.	**4.** Definition of midpoint
5. $\overline{EG}$ is a midsegment of $\triangle ACH$ and $\overline{DG}$ is a midsegment of $\triangle ABH$.	**5.** Definition of midsegment
6. $\overline{EG} \parallel \overline{CH}$ and $\overline{DG} \parallel \overline{BH}$	**6.** Triangle Midsegment Theorem
7. Because $\overline{GC}$ lies on the same line as $\overline{DG}$ and $\overline{GB}$ lies on the same line as $\overline{EG}$, then $\overline{GB} \parallel \overline{CH}$ and $\overline{GC} \parallel \overline{BH}$.	**7.** Definition of collinear and Substitution Property
8. $CHBG$ is a parallelogram.	**8.** Definition of parallelogram
9. $CJ = JB$	**9.** Diagonals of a Parallelogram Theorem
10. J is the midpoint of $\overline{CB}$.	**10.** Definition of midpoint
11. $\overline{AJ}$ is the third median of $\triangle ABC$.	**11.** Definition of median
12. G is the point of intersection of the three medians.	**12.** Definition of concurrent

9.

Statements	Reasons
1. $\overline{AD} \cong \overline{BC}$, $\overline{AD} \parallel \overline{BC}$	**1.** Given
2. Draw $\overline{AC}$.	**2.** Through any two points, there is exactly one line.
3. $\overline{AC} \cong \overline{AC}$	**3.** Reflexive Property of Congruence
4. $\angle DAC \cong \angle BCA$	**4.** Alternate Interior Angles Theorem
5. $\triangle DAC \cong \triangle BCA$	**5.** SAS Triangle Congruence Theorem
6. $\overline{AB} \cong \overline{DC}$	**6.** Corresponding Parts of Congruent Triangles are Congruent.
7. $ABCD$ is a parallelogram.	**7.** If both pairs of opposite sides of a quadrilateral are congruent, then the quadrilateral is a parallelogram.

Selected Answers

Spiral Review • Assessment Readiness

35. A, C, E

37. A

MODULE 11, LESSON 11.3

On Your Own

7. Answers will vary. The lengths of the diagonals will be equal. The diagonals of a rectangle have the same length.

9. Answers will vary. The lengths of the diagonals will be equal and the angles formed by the diagonals will all measure 90°. The diagonals of a square have the same length and are perpendicular.

11. 80 inches

13. about 87.7 inches

15. parallelogram, rectangle, rhombus, square

17. rectangle, square

19.

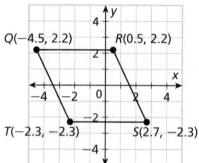

If the diagonals are perpendicular, their slopes will be opposite reciprocals.

slope of $\overline{RT} = \dfrac{2.2 - (-2.3)}{0.5 - (-2.3)} = \dfrac{4.5}{2.8} \approx 1.6$

slope of $\overline{QS} = \dfrac{-2.3 - 2.2}{2.7 - (-4.5)} = \dfrac{-4.5}{7.2} = -0.625$

These are not exactly opposite reciprocals. So, the diagonals are not perpendicular and the figure is not a rhombus.

21. 62

23. 115°

25. 12 ft

27. Answers will vary. Possible answer:

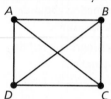

$ABCD$ is rectangle, $AC = 4x + 1$, and $BD = 5x - 6$. Find BD. $BD = 29$

Spiral Review • Assessment Readiness

29. B

31. C

MODULE 11, LESSON 11.4

On Your Own

7. Yes. A parallelogram with consecutive congruent sides is a rhombus.

9. *See below.*

11. Lindsey is correct. You are given that the parallelogram has one right angle, so $QRST$ is a rectangle. You are also given that consecutive sides are congruent, so $QRST$ is a rhombus. Because $QRST$ is a rectangle and a rhombus, it is a square.

13. The conclusion is valid. Because $KLMN$ is a parallelogram, the diagonals bisect each other. It was further given that the diagonals are congruent. Therefore, the parallelogram is a rectangle.

9.

Statements	Reasons
1. *ABCD* is a parallelogram. $\overline{AC}$ bisects ∠*DAB*, ∠*DCB*. $\overline{BD}$ bisects ∠*ADC*, ∠*ABC*.	**1.** Given
2. ∠1 ≅ ∠2, ∠3 ≅ ∠4, ∠5 ≅ ∠6, ∠7 ≅ ∠8	**2.** Definition of Angle Bisector
3. $\overline{AB} \cong \overline{DC}$, $\overline{AD} \cong \overline{BC}$	**3.** Opposite Sides of a Parallelogram are Congruent
4. $\overline{BD} \cong \overline{BD}$, $\overline{AC} \cong \overline{AC}$	**4.** Reflexive Property of Congruence
5. △*ABC* ≅ △*CDA*, △*ADB* ≅ △*CBD*	**5.** SSS Triangle Congruence Theorem
6. ∠1 ≅ ∠5, ∠2 ≅ ∠6, ∠3 ≅ ∠7, ∠4 ≅ ∠8	**6.** CPCTC
7. ∠1 ≅ ∠6, ∠2 ≅ ∠5, ∠3 ≅ ∠8, ∠4 ≅ ∠7	**7.** Transitive Property of Congruence
8. $\overline{AB} \cong \overline{AD}$, $\overline{DC} \cong \overline{BC}$, $\overline{AB} \cong \overline{BC}$, $\overline{DC} \cong \overline{AD}$	**8.** Converse of Isosceles Triangle Theorem
9. $\overline{AB} \cong \overline{DC} \cong \overline{AD} \cong \overline{BC}$	**9.** Transitive Property of Congruence
10. *ABCD* is a rhombus.	**10.** Definition of Rhombus

15. rectangle, rhombus, square

17. A rotation of 90° will map each diagonal onto the other, so it shows that the diagonals are congruent. Because this rotation maps one side of an angle formed by the diagonals onto the other side of the angle, it shows that the measure of the angle is 90°. So the diagonals are perpendicular.

19. 17

21. 7

Spiral Review • Assessment Readiness

25. C

27. C

MODULE 11, LESSON 11.5

On Your Own

7. yes; A parallelogram has two pairs of opposite parallel sides. The inclusive definition of a trapezoid only requires one pair of opposite parallel sides; no; A trapezoid with noncongruent bases is not a parallelogram.

9. Lexi is correct. Even though the figure appears to be an isosceles trapezoid, the bases are not labeled parallel, so you cannot assume they are parallel.

11. $x = 40$; m$\angle K = 135°$

13. 38

15. There is line symmetry across the vertical diagonal. There is no rotational symmetry.

17. There is line symmetry across the vertical line through the midpoints of the bases. There is no rotational symmetry.

19. Because $\overline{BC} \parallel \overline{AD}$ and $\overline{AB} \parallel \overline{EC}$, $ABCE$ is a parallelogram. So, $\overline{AB} \cong \overline{EC}$. Using the Transitive Property of Congruence, $\overline{CE} \cong \overline{CD}$, so $\triangle ECD$ is an isosceles triangle and $\angle D \cong \angle CED$. By Corresponding Angles Postulate, $\angle A \cong \angle CED$, therefore $\angle A \cong \angle D$ by the Transitive Property of Congruence. By Consecutive Interior Angles, $\angle A$ and $\angle B$ are supplementary and $\angle D$ and $\angle BCD$ are supplementary. $\angle B \cong \angle BCD$ are congruent by Congruent Supplements Theorem.

21. It is given that $\overline{AB} \cong \overline{CD}$. By the base angles of an isosceles triangle are congruent, $\angle BAD \cong \angle CDA$ and by the Reflexive Property of Congruence, $\overline{AD} \cong \overline{AD}$. By SAS Triangle Congruence Theorem, $\triangle ABD \cong \triangle DCA$. By CPCTC, $\overline{AC} \cong \overline{DB}$.

23.A. slope of $\overline{AB} = \frac{2-4}{5-(-3)} = -\frac{1}{4}$, slope of $\overline{CD} = \frac{-4-(-1)}{6-(-6)} = -\frac{1}{4}$. Since one pair of opposite sides of the quadrilateral are parallel, the quadrilateral is a trapezoid.

B. midpoint of $\overline{AD}$: $\left(\frac{-3+(-6)}{2}, \frac{4+(-1)}{2}\right) = \left(-\frac{9}{2}, \frac{3}{2}\right)$; midpoint of $\overline{BC}$: $\left(\frac{5+6}{2}, \frac{2+(-4)}{2}\right) = \left(\frac{11}{2}, -1\right)$. The midsegment has endpoints of $\left(-\frac{9}{2}, \frac{3}{2}\right)$ and $\left(\frac{11}{2}, -1\right)$. Using the Distance Formula, the length of the midsegment is $\frac{5\sqrt{17}}{2}$. The slope is $-\frac{1}{4}$.

C. Based on the Trapezoid Midsegment Theorem, the slope of the midsegment is equal to the slope of the bases, $-\frac{1}{4}$. The lengths of the bases are $AB = 2\sqrt{17}$ and $CD = 3\sqrt{17}$. Using the Trapezoid Midsegment Theorem, the length of the midsegment is the average of the lengths of the bases, $\frac{5\sqrt{17}}{2}$. This is the same as the result found in Part B.

25. $AB = AD$, $BC = CD$, so $ABCD$ is a kite.

27. $x = 180° - \frac{y+z}{2}$

29.A. $PQ = \sqrt{10}, QR = \sqrt{10}, RS = 3\sqrt{10}, PS = 3\sqrt{10}$

B. $PQ = QR$ and $RS = PS$

C. Yes. By definition, a kite has two pairs of congruent consecutive sides. In this case, $\overline{PQ}$ and $\overline{QR}$ are consecutive sides with the same length, and $\overline{RS}$ and $\overline{PS}$ are consecutive sides with the same length.

31. Sometimes. If the trapezoid is isosceles, the legs will be congruent.

33. Never. One of the bases would have to be 0 for this to be true.

35. Sometimes. If the kite is a square, adjacent sides are perpendicular.

37. $\overline{AB} \cong \overline{CB}$ and $\angle BAD \cong \angle BCD$. $\overline{AD} \parallel \overline{BB'}$ so $ABB'D$ is an isosceles trapezoid.

Spiral Review • Assessment Readiness

39. A

41. A. enlargement, B. enlargement, C. reduction

MODULE 12, LESSON 12.1

On Your Own

7. a dilation; Possible answer: The slopes of $\overline{AB}$ and $\overline{A'B'}$ are equal to 3. The slopes of $\overline{BC}$ and $\overline{B'C'}$ are equal to -1. The slopes of $\overline{CA}$ and $\overline{C'A'}$ are equal to 1. So, $\triangle A'B'C'$ is a dilation of $\triangle ABC$. The scale factor is $\frac{A'B'}{AB} = \frac{B'C'}{BC} = \frac{C'A'}{CA} = \frac{1}{2}$.

9. Yes. Possible answer: The sides of both angles have the same slopes, so the angles are congruent.

11. Yes. Possible answer: Since $FGHJ \cong LMNP$ and $ABCD \sim FGHJ$, corresponding sides have the same scale factor and corresponding angles are congruent. So $ABCD \sim LMNP$.

13. no; Possible answer: The ratios of corresponding side lengths are not equal, so the triangles are not similar. Therefore, $\triangle LMN$ cannot be obtained from a sequence of similarity transformations performed on $\triangle DEF$.

15. yes; Possible answer: The transformations are dilation, reflection, and translation.

17. Possible answer: The circumference of the largest circle is about 4 times as big as the circumference of the smallest circle. The transformation will have a scale factor of $\frac{32}{120} \approx \frac{1}{4}$.

19. Possible answer: Congruent circles, or any congruent figures, are similar with a scale factor of 1.

21. $x = 27.5$

$\frac{11}{x} = \frac{8}{20}$; $220 = 8x$; $x = \frac{220}{8} = 27.5$

$y = 2$

$\frac{4y+4}{30} = \frac{8}{20}$; $80y + 80 = 240$; $80y = 160$; $y = 2$

$z = 65$

25. Neither student is correct. The slope of $\overline{M'N'}$ is $-\frac{1}{3}$; Possible answer: After a dilation, corresponding sides are parallel, so $\overline{MN}$ and $\overline{M'N'}$ would have the same slope.

Spiral Review • Assessment Readiness

27. D

29. A, B, C, D, E

MODULE 12, LESSON 12.2

On Your Own

5. no; $\frac{4.2}{2} = \frac{10.5}{5} = 2.1$, $\frac{9}{4.8} \neq 2.1$

7. yes; The triangles share $\angle C$ and $\angle B \cong \angle E$. The triangles are similar by the AA Triangle Similarity Theorem.

9. yes; The triangles have two pairs of proportional sides and a pair of included congruent angles by the Vertical Angles Theorem. The triangles are similar by the SAS Triangle Similarity Theorem.

11. $\triangle ABC \sim \triangle ADE$; $x = 72$

13. $\triangle UTV \sim \triangle USW$; $x = \frac{ac}{b}$

15. $x = 42.5$

17. Possible answer: Dilate $\triangle ABC$ using the scale factor $k = \frac{DE}{AB}$. The image of $\triangle ABC$ is $\triangle A'B'C'$. The length of $\overline{A'B'}$ is the length of $\overline{AB}$ multiplied by the scale factor k. So $A'B' = k \cdot AB = \frac{DE}{AB} \cdot AB = DE$. By the same logic, $A'C' = k \cdot AC = \frac{DF}{AC} \cdot AC = DF$, and $C'B' = k \cdot CB = \frac{FE}{CB} \cdot CB = FE$. Therefore $\triangle A'B'C' \cong \triangle DEF$ by the SSS Triangle Congruence Theorem. Because a dilation maps $\triangle ABC$ to $\triangle A'B'C'$ and is followed by a sequence of rigid motions that maps $\triangle A'B'C'$ to $\triangle DEF$, this shows there is a sequence of similarity transformations that maps $\triangle ABC$ to $\triangle DEF$. So, $\triangle ABC \sim \triangle DEF$.

19. yes; AA Triangle Similarity Theorem

21. no; only 1 pair of congruent angles is known

Spiral Review • Assessment Readiness

23. D

25. B

MODULE 12, LESSON 12.3

On Your Own

7. $AE = 2$

9. *See below.*

9.

Statements	Reasons
1. $\frac{AD}{DB} = \frac{AE}{EC}$	1. Given
2. $\frac{DB}{AD} = \frac{EC}{AE}$	2. Take the reciprocal of each side. (Multiplication/Division Properties of Equality)
3. $1 + \frac{DB}{AD} = 1 + \frac{EC}{AE}$	3. Addition Property of Equality
4. $\frac{AD}{AD} + \frac{DB}{AD} = \frac{AE}{AE} + \frac{EC}{AE}$	4. $\frac{a}{a} = 1$
5. $\frac{AD + DB}{AD} = \frac{AE + EC}{AE}$	5. $\frac{a}{c} + \frac{b}{c} = \frac{a+b}{c}$
6. $\frac{AB}{AD} = \frac{AC}{AE}$	6. Segment Addition Postulate
7. $\angle A \cong \angle A$	7. Reflexive Property of Congruence
8. $\triangle ABC \sim \triangle ADE$	8. SAS Triangle Similarity Theorem
9. $\angle ADE \cong \angle ABC$	9. Corresponding angles in similar triangles are congruent.
10. $\overline{DE} \parallel \overline{BC}$	10. Converse of Corresponding Angles Postulate

11. $(-7, 10)$

13. no; $\frac{AD}{DB} \neq \frac{AE}{EC}$

15. 2. Two points; 3. Triangle Proportionality Theorem; 4. $\frac{UA}{AZ} = \frac{VX}{XZ}$; 5. Transitive

17.

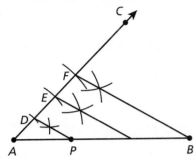

Spiral Review • Assessment Readiness

21. B

MODULE 12, LESSON 12.4

On Your Own

7. $\triangle QSR \sim \triangle RSP \sim \triangle QRP$

9. $\triangle ABC \sim \triangle ADB \sim \triangle BDC$

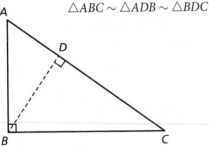

11. *See below.*

13. $x = 2\sqrt{26}$, $y = 2\sqrt{10}$, $z = \sqrt{65}$

15. $x = 9$, $y = 3$, $z = 2\sqrt{209}$

17. $AD = \frac{3120}{89} \approx 35.1$

19. $AD = 6$

21. $4\sqrt{3}$, or approximately 6.93 feet

23. No; $4^2 + 6^2 \neq 10^2$

25. No, $\sqrt{353}$ is not a whole number.

27. Yes; $24^2 + 32^2 = 40^2$

29. $c = 10$; Yes

31. $a = \sqrt{132} = 2\sqrt{33}$; No

Spiral Review • Assessment Readiness

33. C

35. A. 3; B. 2; C. 1

UNIT 7

MODULE 13, LESSON 13.1

On Your Own

5.A. Possible answers:

$\tan C \approx \frac{2\text{ cm}}{4.3\text{ cm}} \approx 0.47$; $\tan Z \approx \frac{3\text{ cm}}{6.4\text{ cm}} \approx 0.47$;

The tangent ratios are the same.

  B. They have the same measurement.

  C. $\tan^{-1} C \approx \tan^{-1}\frac{2}{4.3} \approx 25°$; $\tan^{-1} Z \approx \tan^{-1}\frac{3}{6.4} \approx 25°$

7. $\tan Y = \frac{6}{8} = 0.75$

9. $\tan B = \frac{16}{5} = 3.2$;

  $\tan C = \frac{5}{16} = 0.3125$

11. $PR = 10.7$

13. $ZY = 8.3$

15. $YZ = 56.6$

17. $m\angle Q = 50.2°$

19. $m\angle L = 68.2°$

21. $m\angle T = 62.1°$

23.A. $\tan P = \frac{10}{24} = 0.417$; $\tan Q = \frac{24}{10} = 2.4$

  B. Possible answer: $OP = 12$ m, $PQ = 13$ m; $OQ = 5$ m

25. $m\angle C \approx 20.5°$

Spiral Review • Assessment Readiness

27. C

29. A

11.

Statements	Reasons
1. *ABC* is a right triangle with altitude $\overline{BD}$.	**1.** Given
2. $\triangle ABC \sim \triangle ADB \sim \triangle BDC$	**2.** Right Triangle Similarity Theorem
3. $\frac{AD}{AB} = \frac{AB}{AC}$	**3.** Corresponding sides of similar triangles are proportional.
4. $\frac{DC}{BC} = \frac{BC}{AC}$	**4.** Corresponding sides of similar triangles are proportional.

MODULE 13, LESSON 13.2

On Your Own

7. Yes, given that $\frac{AB}{AC} = \frac{5}{12}$ and $\frac{QR}{PR} = \frac{6}{14.4}$, the triangles are similar because $\frac{AB}{QR} = \frac{AC}{PR}$.

9. $\sin I = \frac{2}{2.5} = 0.8$, $\cos I = \frac{1.5}{2.5} = 0.6$

11. $\sin N = \frac{3}{5} = 0.6$, $\cos N = \frac{4}{5} = 0.8$

13. For any pair of complementary angles, the sine ratio of one angle is equal to the cosine ratio of its complementary angle, and vice versa. For example, $\sin G = \cos I$ and $\sin L = \cos N$.

15. 2.8 in.

17. 20.9 in.

19. $m\angle B = 53.1°$

21. $m\angle X = 66.4°$

23. $m\angle V = 33.6°$

25.A. 97 ft

  B. about 760 ft^2

Spiral Review • Assessment Readiness

29. A

31. B

MODULE 13, LESSON 13.3

On Your Own

7. 30°-60°-90°

9. 30°-60°-90°

11. neither

13. Yes; $3:3:3\sqrt{2} = x:x:x\sqrt{2}$

15. Yes; $\frac{3\sqrt{2}}{2} : \frac{3\sqrt{2}}{2} : 6 = x:x:x\sqrt{2}$

17. $LN = 5$, $MN = 2.5\sqrt{3}$

19. $YZ = \sqrt{3}$, $XZ = \sqrt{6}$

21. $6\sqrt{3}$ m

23. $7\sqrt{2}$ m

25. $5\sqrt{5}$ m

27. Answers will vary.

29. $x = \frac{100}{9}$

31. $y = \sqrt{2}$

33. $x = 2$

35. $2 + \sqrt{3}$

37. $45° < x < 90°$

39. $60° < x < 90°$

41. $30° < x < 60°$

43. BC should be $12\sqrt{2} \cdot \sqrt{3} = 12\sqrt{6}$.

45. $\left(2, 2 + 5\frac{\sqrt{3}}{3}\right)$, or approximately $(2, 4.89)$

Spiral Review • Assessment Readiness

47. D

MODULE 13, LESSON 13.4

On Your Own

5. about 4.1 in^2

7. about 6.3 m^2

9. $AB \approx 3.3$ in., $BC \approx 4.8$ in., $m\angle A = 55°$

11.A. 11.6 ft

  B. 3.1 ft

13.A. $JK = 9$, $JL = 9$, $LK = 12.7$, $m\angle J = 90°$, $m\angle K = 45°$, $m\angle L = 45°$

  B. $QR = 6.7$, $PR = 8.9$, $PQ = 11.2$, $m\angle P = 37°$, $m\angle R = 90°$, $m\angle Q = 53°$

  C. $WX = 4.1$, $WY = 9.2$, $XY = 8.2$, $m\angle W = 63°$, $m\angle X = 90°$, $m\angle Y = 27°$

  D. $MN = 3.2$, $MP = 7.0$, $NP = 6.3$, $m\angle M = 63°$, $m\angle N = 90°$, $m\angle P = 27°$

15. Yes; since $\frac{1}{7}$ of $360° \approx 51.4°$, and the angle of elevation is $\tan^{-1}\frac{146.5}{115} \approx 51.87°$, the pyramid was build as the Egyptians had planned.

17. about 309 ft

19. about 17.4 ft

Spiral Review • Assessment Readiness

21. D

23.A. 4

  B. 3

  C. 1

  D. 2

MODULE 14, LESSON 14.1

On Your Own

9. C

11.A. $\sin A = \frac{h}{c}$
  $\sin \angle BCD = \frac{h}{a}$; $\sin C = \frac{h}{a}$;

  B. $\angle BCD$ and $\angle C$ are supplementary, so they have the same sine value.

  C. $\sin B = \frac{j}{a}$, $\sin A = \frac{j}{b}$

  D. Using the sine ratios from Parts A and B, $c \sin A = a \sin C$, or $\frac{\sin A}{a} = \frac{\sin C}{c}$. Using the ratios from Part C, $b \sin A = a \sin B$, or $\frac{\sin A}{a} = \frac{\sin B}{b}$. The Transitive Property of Equality can be used to write $\frac{\sin A}{a} = \frac{\sin B}{b} = \frac{\sin C}{c}$.

13. Yes; The given measures are an ASA case, and the Law of Sines can be applied to this case.

15. No; The given measures are an SAS case, and the Law of Sines cannot be applied to this case.

17. 1 because $\angle D$ is acute and $d \geq f$.

19. 1 because $\angle D$ is obtuse and $d > f$.

21. $m\angle D = 73°; e = 3.7, f = 3.0$

23. $m\angle P = 86°; q = 18.3, r = 18.3$

25.A. 80.9 feet for both distances

　B. Yes; Because the triangle is isosceles, the height bisects the 50 foot side forming two congruent right triangles. Trigonometric ratios can be used to find the distances in the right triangles.

27. 4.7

29. $41.6°, 138.4°$

31. $78.6°, 101.4°$

33. not possible

35. not possible

37. first case: $m\angle B = 62.9°$, $m\angle C = 72.1°$, $c = 36.3$
second case: $m\angle B = 117.1°$, $m\angle C = 17.9°$, $c = 11.8$

39. 17.7 square units

Spiral Review • Assessment Readiness

43. B

MODULE 14, LESSON 14.2

On Your Own

7. x is negative.

9. $a = 38$, $m\angle B = 45.3°$, $m\angle C = 59.7°$

11. $m\angle R = 60.4°$, $m\angle S = 80°$, $m\angle T = 39.6°$

13. Sara is correct. The given information is a case of side-angle-side, so the Law of Cosines is used to solve the triangle.

15.A. about 63.7 feet

　B. about 92.8°

17. $m\angle A = 44°$, $m\angle B = 26.5°$, $m\angle C = 109.5°$

19. $m\angle A = 28°$, $m\angle B = 20°$, $c = 17.4$

21. $m\angle B = 79.7°$, $m\angle C = 42.3°$, $a = 19.0$

23. Grant is correct. Because two sides and the included angle are given, the area formula $A = \frac{1}{2} ac \sin B$ can be used to find the area.

25. 7.4 square units

Spiral Review • Assessment Readiness

29. C

31. A, E

UNIT 8

MODULE 15, LESSON 15.1

On Your Own

9. Answers will vary.

11. minor arc; $43°$

13. semicircle; $180°$

15. Possible answer: major arc: $232°$, minor arc $128°$

17.A. $m\widehat{JK} = m\widehat{KL} = m\widehat{LM} = m\widehat{MN} = m\widehat{NJ} = 72°$

　B. rotational symmetry of $72°$

　C. Divide $360°$ by the number of arcs.

19. Possible answer: Construct $\triangle ABC$ and $\triangle BCD$. Show that these triangles are isosceles triangles. Use the fact that the base angles of an isosceles triangle are the same measure, and the fact that the measure of an exterior angle equals the sum of the remote interior angles to show that the measure of the central angle is twice the measure of the inscribed angle. Use the Angle Addition Postulate to subtract the smaller angles from the larger angles.

21. The measures of the angles are equal because the intercepted arc of both angles is the same.

23. The hypotenuse of the triangle is a diameter of the circle. The measure of the arc is $180°$, and the arc is a semicircle.

25. $42°$

27. $180°$

29. $x = 11$

31. $x = 20$

33. $135°, x = 22.5$

35. F can be anywhere on $\widehat{CFE}$. As long as the C and E are in the same location, the angle measure will remain the same.

Spiral Review • Assessment Readiness

39. D

41. A

MODULE 15, LESSON 15.2

On Your Own

5. $m\angle A = 102°$, $m\angle B = 70°$, $m\angle C = 78°$, $m\angle D = 110°$

7. $m\angle Q = 107°$, $m\angle R = 97°$, $m\angle S = 73°$, $m\angle T = 83°$

9. Since a kite must have a pair of congruent opposite angles, it is possible to inscribe a kite in a circle as long as the two congruent opposite angles are right angles.

11. $105°$

13. $6\sqrt{2}$ feet

15. 83

17. It is not possible to inscribe a parallelogram that is not a rectangle in a circle because the opposite angles must be congruent and supplementary, which means they are right angles.

19. $40°$

Spiral Review • Assessment Readiness

23. B

MODULE 15, LESSON 15.3

On Your Own

7. Let B be any point on t other than A.

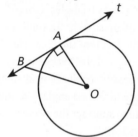

Then $\triangle OAB$ is a right triangle with hypotenuse $\overline{OB}$. Therefore, $\overline{OB} > \overline{OA}$ since the hypotenuse is the longest side of a right triangle. Since $\overline{OA}$ is a radius, point B must be in the exterior of circle O. So, A is the only point of line t that is on circle O. Since line t intersects circle O at exactly one point, line t is tangent to the circle at A.

9. sometimes $\angle GHJ$ is a right triangle;

11. always; by the Tangent-Radius Theorem

13. Possible model:

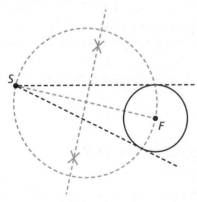

15. $m\angle A = 131°$; $m\angle ADB = 49°$

17. no; The paths are the same length. The two radii of the circle are the same length and the two tangent lines are the same length by the Two-Tangent Theorem.

19. Each length is 47 units.

21. Each length is 24 units.

23. $228°$

25. $m\angle EAH = 122°$, $m\angle BAE = 58°$

Spiral Review • Assessment Readiness

27. C

29. A: 1; B: 3; C: 2

MODULE 15, LESSON 15.4

On Your Own

9. $(x - 5)^2 + (y + 1)^2 = 1$

11. $(x + 2)^2 + (y + 7)^2 = 11$

13. $x^2 + (y + 4)^2 = 81$

15. $(x - 11)^2 + (y + 4)^2 = 9$

17. true

19. true

21. $(x - 4)^2 + (y + 1)^2 = 9$

23. $(x + 4)^2 + (y - 3)^2 = 4$

25. center: $(-3, 9)$; radius: 2

27. center: $(-4, -5)$; radius: $\sqrt{33}$

29. center: $(0, -5)$; radius: $\sqrt{7}$

31.A. $x^2 + y^2 = 2500$

    B. Yes; $14^2 + 48^2 = 196 + 2304 = 2500 = 50^2$

33. $(-2, -3)$ does not lie on the circle;
$(-2)^2 + (-3)^2 = 4 + 9 \neq 4^2$

35. $(-3, -\sqrt{7})$ lies on the circle;
$(-3)^2 + (-\sqrt{7})^2 = 9 + 7 = 4^2$

37. $(-3\sqrt{3}, 3)$ does lie on the circle.
$(-3\sqrt{3})^2 + 3^2 = 27 + 9 = 36 = 6^2$

Spiral Review • Assessment Readiness

39. D

41.

Circle part	Major arc	Minor arc	Semicircle
A. $\overset{\frown}{ADB}$	?	?	?
B. $\overset{\frown}{AE}$	?	?	?
C. $\overset{\frown}{ABE}$	?	?	?
D. $\overset{\frown}{AD}$	?	?	?

MODULE 16, LESSON 16.1

On Your Own

7. Since the diameter of a circle is perpendicular to a chord, then the diameter bisects the chord. So, the lengths of the segments on either side of the diameter are equal. That means one side of the equation by the Chord-Chord Product Theorem is b^2. The other chord (which is the diameter) is the product c^2 because the radius is c. Since a leg of the right triangle lies on one side of the center of the diameter, you can rewrite the radius as $c + a - a$. The chord intersects the diameter so that one side of the chord is $c + a$ and the other side is $c - a$. Now the diameter can be written as the product $(c + a)(c - a)$. By the Chord–Chord Product Rule

$$b^2 = (c + a)(c - a)$$
$$b^2 = c^2 - a^2$$
$$a^2 + b^2 = c^2$$

9. No. The Chord–Chord Product rule still holds, so the relationship would stay the same.

11.

Statements	Reasons
1. Draw segments $\overline{AD}$ and $\overline{EB}$.	1. Through any two points, there is exactly one line.
2. $\angle CAD \cong \angle CEB$	2. Tangent Chord Theorem
3. $\angle C \cong \angle C$	3. Reflexive Property
4. $\triangle CAD$ and $\triangle CEB$	4. AA Triangle Similarity Theorem
5. $\dfrac{AC}{EC} = \dfrac{DC}{BC}$	5. Definition of Similar Figures
6. $AC \cdot BC = EC \cdot DC$	6. Cross Products Property

13. Yes; There are two places on the circle (only one if the secant's internal segment is the diameter of the circle) where the internal secant segments are equal. In both cases the secant segments are equal also.

15. The product of the lengths of the secant segment and its exterior segment equals the square of the tangent segment.

17. *See below.*

19. yes; The perpendicular bisector passes through the center of the circle.

21. The perpendicular bisector of a chord is also a diameter of the circle.

23. $AB = 12$ and $CD = 9$

25. $CD = 23.25$, $TD = 31.25$, and $TB = 25$

27. The tangent segment is about 9.7 inches, and the secant segment is about 15.7 inches.

29. Approximately 132 pixels for the company's name and 192 pixels for the company's slogan.

31. Possible answer: yes; When the intersection in inside the circle, this is just a restatement of the theorem. When the intersection is outside the circle, then the distance from one intersection with the circle to the intersection of the lines is the whole secant segment and the other is the external secant segment. When one of the intersecting lines is tangent to the circle, you can think of the two points of intersection as being the same point, so the lengths are the same.

17. The secant segments must also be equal since $(AB + BC) \cdot BC = (MN + NC) \cdot NC$, and $BC = NC$. Then you can rewrite the product as follows:

$(AB + NC) \cdot NC = (MN + NC) \cdot NC$	Substitute NC for BC.
$AB \cdot NC + NC \cdot NC = MN \cdot NC + NC \cdot NC$	Distributive Property
$AB \cdot NC = MN \cdot NC$	Subtract $NC \cdot NC$ from both sides.
$AB = MN$	Divide both sides by NC.

© Houghton Mifflin Harcourt Publishing Company

Spiral Review • Assessment Readiness

33. A

35. C

MODULE 16, LESSON 16.2

On Your Own

5. Yes. You are finding the average of the lengths of the intercepted arcs because multiplying the sum of the arcs by one-half is the same as adding the two arcs and dividing by 2.

7. In the proof in Task 1, the Exterior Angle Theorem and inscribed angles were used. In this proof, central angles and verticals angles can be used instead since the chords intersect at the center of the circle.

9. Tangent-Secant Interior Angle Measure because the angle that is formed is an inscribed angle. The measure of an inscribed angle is half the arc it intercepts.

11.A.

Statements	Reasons
1. $\overrightarrow{CA}$ is a secant and $\overline{CD}$ is a tangent. Point C is in the exterior of the circle.	1. Given
2. Draw $\overline{DA}$.	2. Through any two points there is exactly one line.
3. $m\angle DCA + m\angle CAD = m\angle UDA$	3. Exterior Angle Theorem
4. $m\angle DCA = m\angle UDA - m\angle CAD$	4. Subtract $m\angle CAD$ from both sides.
5. $m\angle CAD = \frac{1}{2}m\widehat{BD}$	5. Inscribed Angle Theorem
6. $m\angle UDA = \frac{1}{2}m\widehat{AD}$	6. Tangent-Secant Interior Angle Measure Theorem
7. $m\angle DCA = \frac{1}{2}m\widehat{AD} - \frac{1}{2}m\widehat{BD}$	7. Substitution
8. $m\angle DCA = \frac{1}{2}\left(m\widehat{AD} - m\widehat{BD}\right)$	8. Distributive Property

B. The segment that is drawn connects to the points of tangency, but you still use the Exterior Angles Theorem and substitute the inscribed angles.

13. 61.5°

15. 9°

17. $m\widehat{FG} = 36°$ and $m\angle ABG = 69°$

Spiral Review • Assessment Readiness

21. D

23. B

MODULE 17, LESSON 17.1

On Your Own

7. No; The circumference of the larger circle (20π) is double the circumference of the smaller circle (10π). However, the area of the larger circle (100π) is four times as large as the area of the smaller circle (25π).

9. no; Possible answer: If you only use an inscribed regular n-gon, you can generate a sequence of approximations of the value of π, but you wouldn't know the accuracy of those approximations because you have nothing against which to compare them. The inscribed regular n-gon will provide just a lower bound on the value of π. When finding an approximate value of π, you should both inscribe a regular n-gon in the circle and circumscribe a regular n-gon about the circle to get both a lower bound and an upper bound on the value of π.

11. 23.56 m

13. 47.12 cm

15.A. 39.3 inches

B. 24 rotations

C. 16 cm

17. 380.1 yd²

19. 88.2 ft²

21. 43.98 cm

23. 25.13 ft

25. $\sqrt{8}$, or $2\sqrt{2} \approx 2.83$ in.

27. about 4 hours

Spiral Review • Assessment Readiness

29. C, D

31.A. 4

B. 1

C. 3

D. 2

MODULE 17, LESSON 17.2

On Your Own

11. Never; An arc is part of a circle, so its length will be less than the circumference.

13. 2.36 in.

15. 8.38 ft

17. 3.30 cm

19. 14 m

21. $\frac{\pi}{12}$ radians

23. $\frac{11\pi}{18}$ radians

25. 261.8 feet per second

27. 270°

29. 157.5°

31. *See below.*

Spiral Review • Assessment Readiness

33. C

35. B

MODULE 17, LESSON 17.3

On Your Own

7. Check students' work. Key elements are two sectors drawn on the same circle, where one has a central angle twice the other sector. Any radius is acceptable.

9. $\frac{169\pi}{9}$ m²

11. $\frac{1078\pi}{9}$ ft²

13. 42.83 ft²

15. 500.99 m²

17. 905 in²

19. 283.62 cm²

21. 6554.7 ft²/sec

23.

Category	Central angle	Area (cm²)
Rent	90°	28.3
Bills	36°	11.3
Food	54°	17
Savings	72°	22.6
Other	108°	33.9

25. about 12 ft

27. about 25 in.

29. $r = 7$ in.; 31.89°; 13.64 in²

Spiral Review • Assessment Readiness

31. C

33. B

UNIT 9

MODULE 18, LESSON 18.1

On Your Own

7.

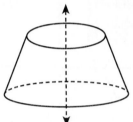

9.

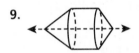

11. parallelogram

13. The plane is parallel to the base.

15. Answers will vary.

17. $12\sqrt{34}$ in²

19. A

Spiral Review • Assessment Readiness

21. C

23. C

MODULE 18, LESSON 18.2

On Your Own

7. 882 cm²

9. 82 m²

11. 336π cm²

13. 4560 ft²

15.A. 66 in²

B. approximately 955 bacteria per square inch

C. an increase in surface area

31.

	Benchmark Angles								
Degree measure	0°	30°	45°	60°	90°	120°	135°	150°	180°
Radian measure	0	$\frac{\pi}{6}$	$\frac{\pi}{4}$	$\frac{\pi}{3}$	$\frac{\pi}{2}$	$\frac{2\pi}{3}$	$\frac{3\pi}{4}$	$\frac{5\pi}{6}$	π

17. The figure after it is rotated is a cylinder, and because she knows the height and radius of the cylinder, she can calculate the surface area. The surface area is about 1508 square feet.

19. 10 centimeters

21.A.

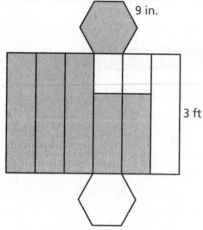

B. Possible answer: 11.25 square feet

Spiral Review • Assessment Readiness

25. A, D

MODULE 18, LESSON 18.3

On Your Own

7. 224 ft^2

9. 385 in^2

11. 16.7 m^2

13. $161\pi \text{ ft}^2$

15. $450\pi \text{ in}^2$

17. 264 in^2

19. 848 ft^2; If each dimension is multiplied by 2, when finding the surface area, each product would be $2 \times 2 = 4$ times as great as in the original figure, so the surface area would be 4 times as great.

21. 13 ft

23.A. 16 cm^2

   B. 1.2 cm

25.A. $25 + 25\sqrt{5} \approx 80.9 \text{ in}^2$

   B. 62 in^2

Spiral Review • Assessment Readiness

27. D

29. A

MODULE 18, LESSON 18.4

On Your Own

7. $64\pi \text{ ft}^2$

9. $432\pi \text{ yd}^2$

11. Yes, the lateral surface area of the cylinder is equal to the surface area of the sphere.

13. Nancy is correct. Because the hemisphere is a closed hemisphere, the area of the circular base is included in the surface area. Glen found the surface area of the curved surface, but Nancy found the sum of the curved surface plus the circular base of the closed hemisphere.

15. 30.8 cm^2

17.A. 362 in^2

   B. 5430 pounds

19. 639.3 ft^2

21. 1790 bacteria per square inch

Spiral Review • Assessment Readiness

25. C, D

MODULE 19, LESSON 19.1

On Your Own

9. 62.83 in^3; right cylinder

11. 35.26 in^3

13. 1520.53 mm^3

15. 289 ft^3

17. 455.33 in^3

19. 2463.01 cm^3

21. Maximum volume is about 788.28 in^3. Dimensions of box are 3.38 in. by 9.24 in. by 25.24 in.

23. 513.10 cm^3

25. 131.95 in^3

27. Minimum: 192 in^3, Maximum: 288 in^3

29. 10.2 inches

31. about 48.11 in^3

33. $r \approx 3.8 \text{ cm}$

Spiral Review • Assessment Readiness

35. B, C

37. B

MODULE 19, LESSON 19.2

On Your Own

7. They are both correct. The volume of a cone with the same base as a cylinder is $\frac{1}{3}$ of the volume of the cylinder. The volume of the cylinder is 3 times the volume of the cone.

9. When finding the volume of the composite figure, you subtract the volume of the pyramid from the volume of the prism. When finding the surface area, you add the lateral area to the surface area of the prism.

11. 750 ft^3

13. 128 in^3

15. 4778.4 in^3

17. 281.4 m^3

19. 1436.8 ft^3

21.A. About 3351 ft^3

  B. about 62.4 pounds per cubic foot

23.A. about 170.7 in^3

  B. about 0.055 pound per cubic inch

25. Base lengths: 5 ft

27. Height: 17 in.

29. Radius: 1.8 ft

31.A. 37.7 in^3

  B. about $0.11 per cubic inch

  C. about $3.11

33. If the height of the cone is doubled, the volume of the cone is doubled. If the radius of the cone is doubled, the volume of the cone is four times as great.

35. 7 times

37. 168.6 in^3

39. 6 inches

Spiral Review • Assessment Readiness

43. D

MODULE 19, LESSON 19.3

On Your Own

7. Dawn is incorrect. If you double the radius of a sphere, the volume is 8 times as large.

9. $\frac{32}{3}\pi$ m^3

11. 486π mm^3

13. 73,773 BTUs

15. 5.5 m

17. 434 in^3

19. 2978.2 cm^3

21. $\frac{1372}{3}\pi$ cm^3

23. 6586 cm^3

Spiral Review • Assessment Readiness

25. B

27. Each vertex angle measures 60°: Equilateral

  Has side lengths of 3–3–5: Isosceles

  Has side lengths 3–5–7: Scalene

UNIT 10

MODULE 20, LESSON 20.1

On Your Own

5.A. $\frac{1}{4}$

  B. $\frac{3}{5}$

7. $A = \{1, 2, 5, 10\}$, $B = \{2, 4, 6, 8, 10\}$, $C = \{1, 3, 5, 7, 9\}$, $D = \{1, 3, 9\}$

9. $A \cap B = \{2, 10\}$

11. $A \cup B = \{1, 2, 4, 5, 6, 8, 10\}$

13. $B \cap C = \{ \ \}$

15. $C^C = \{2, 4, 6, 8, 10\}$

17. $\frac{2}{3}$

19. $\frac{1}{3}$

21. $\frac{1}{3}$

23.A. $\frac{13}{20}$

  B. $\frac{4}{5}$

  C. $\frac{17}{20}$

25. $\frac{1}{4}$

27. $\frac{1}{8}$

29. 1

31.A. {red, green}

  B. $\frac{11}{15}$

33. Possible answer: A parent often checks their phone as soon as they wake up.

35. 70%

37. 36%

39. $\frac{4}{5}$

41. $\frac{2}{5}$

Spiral Review • Assessment Readiness

43. C

45. A

MODULE 20, LESSON 20.2

On Your Own

7. Mario is correct. It is not possible to roll an even number less than 2, so the events are disjoint.

9. $\frac{3}{5}$

11. $\frac{2}{5}$

13. Answers will vary.

15. $\frac{56}{109}$

17. $\frac{67}{109}$

19. $\frac{379}{436}$

21. $\frac{1}{2}$

23. $\frac{5}{6}$

25. When adding the probabilities of each event, the outcomes that are in both events are counted twice, so you need to subtract the probability of both events so they are only counted once.

Spiral Review • Assessment Readiness

27. A

29. A. 1, B. 3, C. 2, D. 4

MODULE 21, LESSON 21.1

On Your Own

7. 60%

9. the probability that a person who spins a positive number does not toss a multiple of 3; 78%

11. $\frac{1}{5}$

13. $\frac{2}{5}$

15. $\frac{4}{5}$

17.A. $\frac{380}{550} \approx 69\%$

B. $\frac{250}{450} \approx 56\%$

C. $\frac{250}{420} \approx 60\%$

D. $\frac{380}{580} \approx 66\%$

19. 73%

Spiral Review • Assessment Readiness

23. C

MODULE 21, LESSON 21.2

On Your Own

5. $P(G) = \frac{1}{3}$ and $P(G\,|\,Y) = \frac{1}{3}$, so $P(G) = P(G\,|\,Y)$, and the events are independent.

7. $\frac{2}{15}$; $P(G \cap Y)$ represents the probability of selecting a green marble first and a yellow marble second.

9. $P(Y) = \frac{2}{5}$ and $P(Y\,|\,R) = 0$, so $P(Y) \neq P(Y\,|\,R)$, and the events are not independent.

11. $\frac{1}{4}$

13. not independent

15.A. yes; $P(D) = \frac{4}{12} = \frac{1}{3}$, $P(R) = \frac{6}{12} = \frac{1}{2}$, $P(D \cap R) = \frac{2}{12}$ $= \frac{1}{6}$, so $P(D \cap R) = P(D) \cdot P(R)$. Since $P(D \cap R) = P(D) \cdot P(R)$, D and R are independent.

B. no; $P(D) = \frac{4}{12} = \frac{1}{3}$, $P(S) = \frac{8}{12} = \frac{2}{3}$, $P(D \cap S)$ $= \frac{0}{12} = 0$, so $P(D \cap S) \neq P(D) \cdot P(S)$.

Spiral Review • Assessment Readiness

19. D

MODULE 21, LESSON 21.3

On Your Own

7.A. dependent; $P(D) = \frac{3}{10}$, $P(A) = \frac{11}{25}$, $P(D \cap A) = \frac{6}{25}$; since $P(D) \cdot P(A) \neq P(D \cap A)$, the events are dependent.

B. $P(D\,|\,A) = \frac{6}{11}$, $P(A\,|\,D) = \frac{4}{5}$; multiply $P(A)$ and $P(D\,|\,A)$, or multiply $P(D)$ and $P(A\,|\,D)$ to find $P(D \cap A)$.

9.A. $\frac{16}{105}$

B. $\frac{1}{35}$

11. You can conclude that $P(B \mid A) = 1$, which means that event B always occurs if event A occurs. For example, you roll a number cube. Let event A be rolling a 4, and let event B be rolling an even number. If you roll a 4, you also roll an even number.

13. no; Event A should be the event that a girl other than Greta is president. Since the president and secretary are different, Greta can only be the secretary if she is not the president. If event A is the event that a girl other than Greta is president, and event B is the event that Greta is secretary, then $P(A) = \frac{3}{7}$, $P(B \mid A) = \frac{1}{6}$, and $P(A \cap B) = \frac{1}{14}$.

15.A. Let $N1$ be the event that Emma is not first, $N2$ be the event that Emma is not second, and $N3$ be the event that Emma is not third. $P(N1) = \frac{6}{7}$, $P(N2 \mid N1) = \frac{5}{6}$, $P(N3) \mid (N1 \cap N2) = \frac{4}{5}$, $P(N1 \cap N2 \cap N3) = \frac{6}{7} \cdot \frac{5}{6} \cdot \frac{4}{5} = \frac{4}{7}$. The probability that Emma will be one of the first three students is $1 - \frac{4}{7} = \frac{3}{7}$.

B. Let F be the event that Emma is first: $P(F) = \frac{1}{7}$. Let $N1$ be the event that Emma is not first and S be the event that Emma is second: $P(N1) = \frac{6}{7}$, $P(S \mid N1) = \frac{1}{6}$, $P(N1 \cap S) = \frac{1}{7}$. Let $N1$ be the event that Emma is not first, $N2$ be the event that Emma is not second, and T be the event that Emma is third: $P(N1) = \frac{6}{7}$, $P(N2 \mid N1) = \frac{5}{6}$, $P(T \mid N1 \cap N2) = \frac{1}{5}$, $P(N1 \cap N2 \cap T) = \frac{1}{7}$. The probability that Emma will be one of the first three is $\frac{1}{7} + \frac{1}{7} + \frac{1}{7} = \frac{3}{7}$.

17. $\frac{3}{56}$

Spiral Review • Assessment Readiness

21. B, E

A

English	Spanish	Examples
acute angle An angle that measures greater than 0° and less than 90°.	**ángulo agudo** Ángulo que mide más de 0° y menos de 90°.	
adjacent angles Two angles in the same plane with a common vertex and a common side, but no common interior points.	**ángulos adyacentes** Dos ángulos en el mismo plano que tienen un vértice y un lado común pero no comparten puntos internos.	∠1 and ∠2 are adjacent angles.
adjacent arcs Two arcs of the same circle that intersect at exactly one point, which is a shared endpoint.	**arcos adyacentes** Dos arcos del mismo círculo que se cruzan en un punto exacto, que es un extremo compartido.	RS and ST are adjacent arcs.
alternate exterior angles For two lines intersected by a transversal, a pair of angles that lie on opposite sides of the transversal and outside the intersected lines.	**ángulos alternos externos** Dadas dos líneas cortadas por una transversal, par de ángulos no adyacentes ubicados en los lados opuestos de la transversal y fuera de las otras dos líneas.	∠4 and ∠5 are alternate exterior angles.
alternate interior angles For two lines intersected by a transversal, a pair of nonadjacent angles that lie on opposite sides of the transversal and between the intersected lines.	**ángulos alternos internos** Dadas dos líneas cortadas por una transversal, par de ángulos no adyacentes ubicados en los lados opuestos de la transversal y entre las líneas cortadas.	∠3 and ∠6 are alternate interior angles.
altitude of a triangle A perpendicular segment from a vertex to the line containing the opposite side.	**altura de un triángulo** Segmento perpendicular que se extiende desde un vértice hasta la línea que forma el lado opuesto.	
angle bisector A ray that divides an angle into two congruent angles.	**bisectriz de un ángulo** Rayo que divide un ángulo en dos ángulos congruentes.	$\overrightarrow{JK}$ is an angle bisector of ∠LJM.

Glossary/Glosario

English	Spanish	Examples
angle of depression The angle formed by a horizontal line and a line of sight to a point below.	**ángulo de depresión** Ángulo formado por una línea horizontal y una línea de visión dirigida a un punto ubicado por debajo de la primera.	
angle of elevation The angle formed by a horizontal line and a line of sight to a point above.	**ángulo de elevación** Ángulo formado por una línea horizontal y una línea de visión dirigida a un punto ubicado por encima de la primera.	
angle of rotation The angle through which a figure is turned when a rotation is applied.	**ángulo de rotación** Ángulo a través del cual una figura gira cuando se aplica una rotación.	
angle of rotational symmetry The smallest angle through which a figure with rotational symmetry can be rotated to coincide with itself.	**ángulo de simetría de rotación** El ángulo más pequeño alrededor del cual se puede rotar una figura con simetría de rotación para que coincida consigo misma.	
arc An unbroken part of a circle consisting of two points on the circle, called the endpoints, and all the points on the circle between them.	**arco** Parte continua de una circunferencia formada por dos puntos de la circunferencia denominados extremos y todos los puntos de la circunferencia comprendidos entre éstos.	
arc length The distance along an arc measured in linear units.	**longitud de arco** Distancia a lo largo de un arco medida en unidades lineales.	
area The surface contained within the boundaries of a two-dimensional object such as a triangle, rectangle, or trapezoid.	**área** Superficie comprendida dentro de los límites de un objeto bidimensional, como un triángulo, un rectángulo o un trapecio.	

English	Spanish	Examples
auxiliary line A line drawn in a figure to aid in a proof.	**línea auxiliar** Línea dibujada en una figura como ayuda en una demostración.	
axiom *See* postulate.	**axioma** *Ver* postulado.	
axis of a cone The segment with endpoints at the vertex and the center of the base.	**eje de un cono** Segmento cuyos extremos se encuentran en el vértice y en el centro de la base.	
axis of a cylinder The segment with endpoints at the centers of the two bases.	**eje de un cilindro** Segmentos cuyos extremos se encuentran en los centros de las dos bases.	

B

English	Spanish	Examples
base angle of a trapezoid One of a pair of consecutive angles whose common side is a base of the trapezoid.	**ángulo base de un trapecio** Uno de los dos ángulos consecutivos cuyo lado en común es la base del trapecio.	
base angle of an isosceles triangle One of the two angles that have the base of the triangle as a side.	**ángulo base de un triángulo isósceles** Uno de los dos ángulos que tienen como lado la base del triángulo.	
base of a geometric figure A side of a polygon; a face of a three-dimensional figure, by which the figure is measured or classified.	**base de una figura geométrica** Lado de un polígono; cara de una figura tridimensional por la cual se mide o clasifica la figura.	
bases of a trapezoid Two sides of a trapezoid that are parallel.	**bases de un trapecio** Los dos lados de un trapecio que son paralelos.	
between Given three points A, B, and C, B is between A and C if and only if all three of the points lie on the same line and $AB + BC = AC$.	**entre** Dados tres puntos A, B y C, B está entre A y C si y sólo si los tres puntos se encuentran en la misma línea y $AB + BC = AC$.	

Glossary/Glosario

English	Spanish	Examples
biconditional statement A statement that can be written in the form "p if and only if q," where p is the hypothesis and q is the conclusion.	**enunciado bicondicional** Enunciado que puede expresarse en la forma "p si y sólo si q", donde p es la hipótesis y q es la conclusión.	A figure is a triangle if and only if it is a three-sided polygon.
bisect To divide a figure into two congruent parts.	**trazar una bisectriz** Dividir una figura en dos partes congruentes.	$\overrightarrow{JK}$ bisects ∠LJM.

C

English	Spanish	Examples
center of dilation The fixed point in the plane that does not change when the dilation is applied.	**centro de dilatación** Punto fijo en el plano que no cambia cuando se aplica la dilatación.	
center of rotation The point around which a figure is rotated.	**centro de rotación** Punto alrededor del cual rota una figura.	
central angle of a circle An angle with measure less than or equal to 180° whose vertex is the center of a circle.	**ángulo central de un círculo** Ángulo con medida inferior o igual a 180° cuyo vértice es el centro de un círculo.	
centroid of a triangle The point of concurrency of the three medians of a triangle. Also known as the *center of gravity*.	**centroide de un triángulo** Punto donde se encuentran las tres medianas de un triángulo. También conocido como *centro de gravedad*.	The centroid is *P*.
chord A segment whose endpoints lie on a circle.	**cuerda** Segmento cuyos extremos se encuentran en un círculo.	

English	Spanish	Examples
circle The set of points in a plane that are a fixed distance from a given point called the center of the circle.	**círculo** Conjunto de puntos en un plano que se encuentran a una distancia fija de un punto determinado denominado centro del círculo.	
circumcenter of a triangle The point of concurrency of the three perpendicular bisectors of a triangle.	**circuncentro de un triángulo** Punto donde se cortan las tres mediatrices de un triángulo.	The circumcenter is *P*.
circumcircle *See* circumscribed circle.	**circuncírculo** *Ver* círculo circunscrito.	
circumference The distance around a circle.	**circunferencia** Distancia alrededor del círculo.	
circumscribed angle An angle formed by two rays from a common endpoint that are tangent to a circle	**ángulo circunscrito** Ángulo formado por dos semirrectas tangentes a un círculo que parten desde un extremo común.	
circumscribed circle A circle that intersects all vertices of a polygon and intersects no other points of the polygon.	**círculo circunscrito** Círculo que interseca todos los vértices de un polígono y no interseca otros puntos del polígono.	
circumscribed polygon A polygon in which each side is tangent to a circle drawn in the interior of the polygon.	**polígono circunscrito** Todos los lados del polígono son tangentes al círculo.	
collinear Points that lie on the same line.	**colineal** Puntos que se encuentran sobre la misma línea.	*K*, *L*, and *M* are collinear points.
complement of an event All outcomes in the sample space that are not in an event E, denoted E^C.	**complemento de un suceso** Todos los resultados en el espacio muestral que no están en el suceso E y se expresan E^C.	In the experiment of rolling a number cube, the complement of rolling a 3 is rolling a 1, 2, 4, 5, or 6.

English	Spanish	Examples
complement of set *A* The set of all elements in the universal set *U* that are not in set *A*.	**complemento del conjunto A** Conjunto de todos los elementos del conjunto universal *U* que no están en el conjunto *A*.	
complementary angles Two angles whose measures have a sum of 90°.	**ángulos complementarios** Dos ángulos cuyas medidas suman 90°.	The complement of a 53° angle is a 37° angle.
component form The form of a vector that lists the vertical and horizontal change from the initial point to the terminal point.	**forma de componente** Forma de un vector que muestra el cambio horizontal y vertical desde el punto inicial hasta el punto terminal.	The component form of $\overrightarrow{CD}$ is $\langle 2, 3 \rangle$.
composite figure A plane figure made up of triangles, rectangles, trapezoids, circles, and other simple shapes, or a three-dimensional figure made up of prisms, cones, pyramids, cylinders, and other simple three-dimensional figures.	**figura compuesta** Figura plana compuesta por triángulos, rectángulos, trapecios, círculos y otras figuras simples, o figura tridimensional compuesta por prismas, conos, pirámides, cilindros y otras figuras tridimensionales simples.	
composition of transformations A transformation that directly maps a preimage to the final image after each image is used as a preimage in a sequence of two or more transformations.	**composición de transformaciones** Transformación que establece una correspondencia directa entre una imagen original y la imagen final tras usar cada imagen como imagen original en una sucesión de dos o más transformaciones.	
compression A nonrigid transformation that changes the shape of a figure in one direction by a factor greater than 0 and less than 1.	**compresión** Transformación no rígida que cambia la forma de una figura en una dirección por un factor mayor que 0 pero menor que 1.	vertical compression
concentric circles Coplanar circles that have the same center.	**círculos concéntricos** Círculos coplanares que tienen el mismo centro.	

English	Spanish	Examples
conclusion The part of a conditional statement following the word *then*.	**conclusión** Parte de un enunciado condicional que sigue a la palabra *entonces*.	If $x + 1 = 5$, then $\underline{x = 4}$. Conclusion
concurrent lines Three or more lines that intersect at one point.	**líneas concurrentes** Tres o más líneas que se cortan en un punto.	
conditional probability The probability of event B, given that event A has already occurred or is certain to occur, denoted $P(B \mid A)$; used to find probability of dependent events.	**probabilidad condicional** Probabilidad del suceso B, dado que el suceso A ya ha ocurrido o es seguro que ocurrirá, expresada como $P(B \mid A)$; se utiliza para calcular la probabilidad de sucesos dependientes.	
conditional statement A statement that can be written in the form "if p, then q," where p is the hypothesis and q is the conclusion.	**enunciado condicional** Enunciado que se puede expresar como "si p, entonces q", donde p es la hipótesis y q es la conclusión.	If $\underline{x + 1 = 5}$, then $\underline{x = 4}$. Hypothesis Conclusion
cone A three-dimensional figure with a circular base and a curved lateral surface that connects the base to a point called the vertex.	**cono** Figura tridimensional con una base circular y una superficie lateral curva que conecta la base con un punto denominado vértice.	
congruence transformation *See* rigid motion.	**transformación de congruencia** *Ver* movimiento rígido.	
congruent Having the same size and shape, denoted by $\cong$.	**congruente** Que tiene el mismo tamaño y la misma forma, expresado por $\cong$.	 $\overline{PQ} \cong \overline{SR}$
congruent arcs Two arcs that have the same measure and are arcs of the same circle or of congruent circles.	**arcos congruentes** Dos arcos que tienen la misma medida y que son arcos del mismo círculo o de círculos congruentes.	
congruent circles Two circles that have the same radius.	**círculos congruentes** Dos círculos que tienen el mismo radio.	
congruent Two figures whose corresponding sides and angles are congruent. One figure can be obtained from the other by a sequence of rigid motions.	**polígonos congruentes** Dos figuras cuyos lados y ángulos correspondientes son congruentes. Una figura se puede obtener de la otra mediante una sucesión de movimientos rígidos.	

English	Spanish	Examples
conjecture A statement that is believed to be true.	**conjetura** Enunciado que se supone verdadero.	A sequence begins with the terms 2, 4, 6, 8, 10. A reasonable conjecture is that the next term in the sequence is 12.
consecutive exterior angles For two lines intersected by a transversal, a pair of angles that lie on the same side of the transversal and outside the intersected lines.	**ángulos externos consecutivos** Dadas dos líneas cortadas por una transversal, el par de ángulos ubicados en el mismo lado de la transversal y del lado externo de las otras líneas cortadas.	$\angle 1$ and $\angle 4$ are consecutive exterior angles.
consecutive interior angles For two lines intersected by a transversal, a pair of angles that lie on the same side of the transversal and between the intersected lines.	**ángulos internos consecutivos** Dadas dos líneas cortadas por una transversal, el par de ángulos ubicados en el mismo lado de la transversal y entre las líneas cortadas.	$\angle 2$ and $\angle 3$ are consecutive interior angles.
contrapositive The statement formed by both exchanging and negating the hypothesis and conclusion of a conditional statement.	**contrarrecíproco** Enunciado que se forma al intercambiar y negar la hipótesis y la conclusión de un enunciado condicional.	Statement: If $n + 1 = 3$, then $n = 2$. Contrapositive: If $n \neq 2$, then $n + 1 \neq 3$.
converse The statement formed by exchanging the hypothesis and conclusion of a conditional statement.	**recíproco** Enunciado que se forma intercambiando la hipótesis y la conclusión de un enunciado condicional.	Statement: If $n + 1 = 3$, then $n = 2$. Converse: If $n = 2$, then $n + 1 = 3$.
coordinate proof A style of proof that uses coordinate geometry and algebra.	**prueba de coordenadas** Tipo de demostración que utiliza geometría de coordenadas y álgebra.	
coplanar Figures that lie in the same plane.	**coplanar** Figuras que se encuentran en el mismo plano.	
corollary A theorem whose proof follows directly from another theorem.	**corolario** Teorema cuya demostración proviene directamente de otro teorema.	
corresponding angles of lines intersected by a transversal For two lines intersected by a transversal, a pair of angles that lie on the same side of the transversal and on the same sides of the intersected lines.	**ángulos correspondientes de líneas cortadas por una transversal** Dadas dos líneas cortadas por una transversal, el par de ángulos ubicados en el mismo lado de la transversal y en los mismos lados de las otras dos líneas.	$\angle 1$ and $\angle 3$ are corresponding angles.

English	Spanish	Examples
corresponding angles of polygons Angles in the same position in two different polygons that have the same number of angles.	**ángulos correspondientes de los polígonos** Ángulos que tienen la misma posición en dos polígonos diferentes que tienen el mismo número de ángulos.	 $\angle A$ and $\angle D$ are corresponding angles.
corresponding sides of polygons Sides in the same position in two different polygons that have the same number of sides.	**lados correspondientes de los polígonos** Lados que tienen la misma posición en dos polígonos diferentes que tienen el mismo número de lados.	 $\overline{AB}$ and $\overline{DE}$ are corresponding sides.
cosine In a right triangle, the cosine of $\angle A$ is the ratio of the length of the leg adjacent to $\angle A$ to the length of the hypotenuse. It is the reciprocal of the secant function.	**coseno** En un triángulo rectángulo, el coseno del ángulo A es la razón entre la longitud del cateto adyacente al ángulo A y la longitud de la hipotenusa. Es la inversa de la función secante.	 $\cos A = \dfrac{\text{adjacent}}{\text{hypotenuse}} = \dfrac{1}{\sec A}$
counterexample An example that proves that a conjecture or statement is false.	**contraejemplo** Ejemplo que demuestra que una conjetura o enunciado es falso.	
CPCTC An abbreviation for "Corresponding Parts of Congruent Triangles are Congruent," which can be used as a justification in a proof after two triangles are proven congruent.	**PCTCC** Abreviatura que significa "Las partes correspondientes de los triángulos congruentes son congruentes", que se puede utilizar para justificar una demostración después de demostrar que dos triángulos son congruentes (CPCTC, por sus siglas en inglés).	
cross section The intersection of a three-dimensional figure and a plane.	**sección transversal** Intersección de una figura tridimensional y un plano.	
cylinder A three-dimensional figure with two parallel congruent circular bases and a curved lateral surface that connects the bases.	**cilindro** Figura tridimensional con dos bases circulares congruentes y paralelas y una superficie lateral curva que conecta las bases.	

D

English	Spanish	Examples
deductive reasoning The process of using logic to draw conclusions.	**razonamiento deductivo** Proceso en el que se utiliza la lógica para sacar conclusiones.	

© Houghton Mifflin Harcourt Publishing Company

English	Spanish	Examples
definition A statement that describes a mathematical object and can be written as a true biconditional statement.	**definición** Enunciado que describe un objeto matemático y se puede expresar como un enunciado bicondicional verdadero.	
density The amount of matter that an object has in a given unit of volume. The density of an object is calculated by dividing its mass by its volume.	**densidad** La cantidad de materia que tiene un objeto en una unidad de volumen determinada. La densidad de un objeto se calcula dividiendo su masa entre su volumen.	$\text{density} = \dfrac{\text{mass}}{\text{volume}}$
dependent events Events for which the occurrence or nonoccurrence of one event affects the probability of the other event.	**sucesos dependientes** Dos sucesos son dependientes si el hecho de que uno de ellos se cumpla o no afecta la probabilidad del otro.	From a bag containing 3 red marbles and 2 blue marbles, drawing a red marble, and then drawing a blue marble without replacing the first marble.
diagonal of a polygon A segment connecting two nonconsecutive vertices of a polygon.	**diagonal de un polígono** Segmento que conecta dos vértices no consecutivos de un polígono.	
diameter A segment that has endpoints on the circle and that passes through the center of the circle; also, the length of that segment.	**diámetro** Segmento que atraviesa el centro de un círculo y cuyos extremos están sobre la circunferencia; longitud de dicho segmento.	
dilation A transformation in which the lines connecting every point P with its preimage P' all intersect at a point C known as the center of dilation, and $\frac{CP'}{CP}$ is the same for every point P; a transformation that changes the size of a figure but not its shape.	**dilatación** Transformación en la cual las líneas que conectan cada punto P con su imagen original P' se cruzan en un punto C conocido como centro de dilatación, y $\frac{CP'}{CP}$ es igual para cada punto P; transformación que cambia el tamaño de una figura pero no su forma.	
disjoint Two events are disjoint, or mutually exclusive, if they cannot occur in the same trial at the same time.	**disjunto** Dos sucesos son disjuntos o mutuamente excluyentes si no pueden ocurrir en la misma prueba al mismo tiempo.	
distance between two points The absolute value of the difference of the coordinates of the points. The length of the shortest line segment that can connect two points.	**distancia entre dos puntos** Valor absoluto de la diferencia entre las coordenadas de los puntos. La longitud del segmento de recta más corto que puede conectar dos puntos.	 $AB = |a - b| = |b - a|$

English	Spanish	Examples
distance from a point to a line The length of the perpendicular segment from the point to the line.	**distancia desde un punto hasta una línea** Longitud del segmento perpendicular desde el punto hasta la línea.	 The distance from P to $\overleftrightarrow{AC}$ is 5 units.

E

English	Spanish	Examples
element of a set An item in a set.	**elemento de un conjunto** Componente de un conjunto.	4 is an element of the set of even numbers. $4 \in \left\{ \text{even numbers} \right\}$
empty set A set with no elements.	**conjunto vacío** Conjunto sin elementos.	The solution set of $\lvert x \rvert < 0$ is the empty set, $\{\}$, or $\varnothing$.
endpoint A point at an end of a segment or the starting point of a ray.	**extremo** Punto en el final de un segmento o punto de inicio de un rayo.	
event An outcome or set of outcomes in a probability experiment.	**suceso** Resultado o conjunto de resultados en un experimento de probabilidad.	In the experiement of rolling a number cube, the event "an odd number" consists of the outcomes 1, 3, 5.
exterior of a circle The set of all points outside a circle.	**exterior de un círculo** Conjunto de todos los puntos que se encuentran fuera de un círculo.	
exterior angle of a polygon An angle formed by one side of a polygon and the extension of an adjacent side.	**ángulo externo de un polígono** Ángulo formado por un lado de un polígono y la prolongación del lado adyacente.	 $\angle 4$ is an exterior angle.
external secant segment A segment of a secant that lies in the exterior of the circle with one endpoint on the circle.	**segmento secante externo** Segmento de una secante que se encuentra en el exterior del círculo y tiene un extremo sobre el círculo.	 $\overline{NM}$ is an external secant segment.

F

English	Spanish	Examples
flow proof A proof format that uses boxes and arrows to show the structure of a logical argument.	**demostración de flujo** Formato de demostración que utiliza recuadros y flechas para mostrar la estructura de un argumento lógico.	

G

English	Spanish	Examples
geometric mean For positive numbers a and b, the positive number x such that $\frac{a}{x} = \frac{x}{b}$. In a geometric sequence, a term that comes between two given nonconsecutive terms of the sequence.	**media geométrica** Dados los números positivos a y b, el número positivo x tal que $\frac{a}{x} = \frac{x}{b}$. En una sucesión geométrica, un término que está entre dos términos no consecutivos dados de la sucesión.	$\frac{a}{x} = \frac{x}{b}$ $x^2 = ab$ $x = \sqrt{ab}$
glide reflection A composition of a translation and a reflection across a line parallel to the translation vector.	**deslizamiento con inversión** Composición de una traslación y una reflexión sobre una línea paralela al vector de traslación.	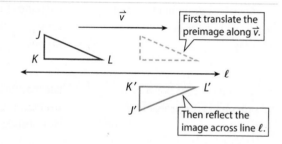 First translate the preimage along $\vec{v}$. Then reflect the image across line ℓ.

H

English	Spanish	Examples
hemisphere Half of a sphere.	**hemisferio** Mitad de una esfera.	
hypothesis The part of a conditional statement following the word *if*.	**hipótesis** La parte de un enunciado condicional que sigue a la palabra *si*.	If $\underline{x + 1 = 5}$, then $x = 4$. Hypothesis

I

English	Spanish	Examples
image A shape that results from a transformation of a figure known as the preimage.	**imagen** Forma resultante de la transformación de una figura conocida como imagen original.	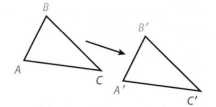

English	Spanish	Examples
incenter of a triangle The point of concurrency of the three angle bisectors of a triangle.	**incentro de un triángulo** Punto donde se encuentran las tres bisectrices de los ángulos de un triángulo.	P is the incenter.
incircle *See* inscribed circle.	**incírculo** *Ver* círculo inscrito.	
included angle The angle formed by two adjacent sides of a polygon.	**ángulo incluido** Ángulo formado por dos lados adyacentes de un polígono.	$\angle B$ is the included angle between $\overline{AB}$ and $\overline{BC}$.
included side The common side connecting two consecutive angles of a polygon.	**lado incluido** Lado común que conecta dos ángulos consecutivos de un polígono.	$\overline{PQ}$ is the included side between $\angle P$ and $\angle Q$.
independent events Events for which the occurrence or nonoccurrence of one event does not affect the probability of the other event.	**sucesos independientes** Dos sucesos son independientes si el hecho de que se produzca o no uno de ellos no afecta la probabilidad del otro suceso.	From a bag containing 3 red marbles and 2 blue marbles, drawing a red marble, replacing it, and then drawing a blue marble.
indirect proof A proof in which the statement to be proved is assumed to be false and a contradiction is shown.	**demostración indirecta** Prueba en la que se supone que el enunciado a demostrar es falso y se muestra una contradicción.	
inductive reasoning The process of reasoning that a rule or statement is true because specific cases are true.	**razonamiento inductivo** Proceso de razonamiento por el que se determina que una regla o enunciado son verdaderos porque ciertos casos específicos son verdaderos.	
initial point of a vector The starting point of a vector.	**punto inicial de un vector** Punto donde comienza un vector.	Initial point
inscribed angle An angle whose vertex is on a circle and whose sides contain chords of the circle.	**ángulo inscrito** Ángulo cuyo vértice se encuentra sobre un círculo y cuyos lados contienen cuerdas del círculo.	

English	Spanish	Examples
inscribed circle A circle drawn inside a polygon so that each side of the polygon is tangent to the circle.	**círculo inscrito** Círculo trazado dentro de un polígono de tal forma que cada lado del polígono es tangente al círculo.	
inscribed polygon A polygon drawn inside a circle so that every vertex of the polygon lies on the circle.	**polígono inscrito** Polígono trazado dentro de un círculo de tal forma que todos los vértices se encuentran sobre el círculo.	
intercepted arc An arc that consists of endpoints that lie on the sides of an inscribed angle and all the points of the circle between the endpoints.	**arco abarcado** Arco cuyos extremos se encuentran en los lados de un ángulo inscrito y consta de todos los puntos del círculo ubicados entre dichos extremos.	$\widehat{DF}$ is the intercepted arc.
interior angle An angle formed by two sides of a polygon with a common vertex.	**ángulo interno** Ángulo formado por dos lados de un polígono con un vértice común.	∠1 is an interior angle.
interior of a circle The set of all points inside a circle.	**interior de un círculo** Conjunto de todos los puntos que se encuentran dentro de un círculo.	Interior
intersection of two sets The set of all elements that are in both set A and set B.	**intersección de dos conjuntos** Conjunto de todos los elementos compartidos por los conjuntos A y B.	
inverse The statement formed by negating the hypothesis and conclusion of a conditional statement.	**inverso** Enunciado formado al negar la hipótesis y la conclusión de un enunciado condicional.	Statement: If $n + 1 = 3$, then $n = 2$. Inverse: If $n + 1 \neq 3$, then $n \neq 2$.
inverse cosine The trigonometric function used to find the measure of an angle whose cosine ratio is known.	**coseno inverso** La función trigonométrica utilizada para hallar la medida de un ángulo cuya razón coseno es conocida.	If $\cos A = x$, then $\cos^{-1} x = m\angle A$.
inverse sine The trigonometric function used to find the measure of an angle whose sine ratio is known.	**seno inverso** La función trigonométrica utilizada para hallar la medida de un ángulo cuya razón seno es conocida.	If $\sin A = x$, then $\sin^{-1} x = m\angle A$.

English	Spanish	Examples
inverse tangent The trigonometric function used to find the measure of an angle whose tangent ratio is known.	**tangente inversa** La función trigonométrica utilizada para hallar la medida de un ángulo cuya razón tangente es conocida.	If $\tan A = x$, then $\tan^{-1} x = \text{m}\angle A$.
isometry *See* rigid motion.	**isometría** *Ver* movimiento rígido.	Reflections, translations, and rotations are all examples of isometries.
isosceles trapezoid A trapezoid in which the legs are congruent but not parallel.	**trapecio isósceles** Trapecio cuyos lados no paralelos son congruentes.	
isosceles triangle A triangle with at least two congruent sides.	**triángulo isósceles** Triángulo que tiene al menos dos lados congruentes.	

K

kite A quadrilateral whose four sides can be grouped into two pairs of consecutive congruent sides.	**cometa o papalote** Cuadrilátero cuyos cuatro lados se pueden agrupar en dos pares de lados congruentes consecutivos.	Kite *ABCD*

L

lateral area The sum of the areas of the lateral faces of a prism or pyramid, or the area of the lateral surface of a cylinder or cone.	**área lateral** Suma de las áreas de las caras laterales de un prisma o pirámide, o área de la superficie lateral de un cilindro o cono.	12 cm, 6 cm, 8 cm. Lateral area $= 2(6)(12) + 2(8)(12)$ $= 336\ \text{cm}^2$
leg of an isosceles triangle One of the two congruent sides of an isosceles triangle.	**cateto de un triángulo isósceles** Uno de los dos lados congruentes del triángulo isósceles.	leg, leg
legs of a trapezoid The sides of a trapezoid that are not the bases.	**catetos de un trapecio** Los lados del trapecio que no son las bases.	Leg, Leg

English	Spanish	Examples
length The distance between the two endpoints of a segment.	**longitud** Distancia entre los dos extremos de un segmento.	A ●————————● B a b $AB = |a - b| = |b - a|$
limit A value that the output of a function approaches as the input increases or decreases without bound or as the input approaches a given value.	**límite** Valor al que se aproxima el valor de salida de una función a medida que el valor de entrada aumenta o disminuye sin límite o se aproxima a un valor determinado.	
line An undefined term in geometry, a line is a straight path that has no thickness and extends forever in one dimension.	**línea** Término indefinido en geometría; una línea es un trazo recto que no tiene grosor y se extiende infinitamente en una dimensión.	←————————→ ℓ
line of reflection A line over which a figure is reflected. The line of reflection is the perpendicular bisector of each segment joining each point and its image.	**línea de reflexión** Línea sobre la cual se refleja una figura. La línea de reflexión es la mediatriz de todos los segmentos que unen cada punto y su imagen.	m is the line of reflection.
line of symmetry A line that divides a plane figure into two congruent reflected halves.	**eje de simetría** Línea que divide una figura plana en dos mitades reflejas congruentes.	
line segment *See* segment of a line.	**segmento** *Ver* segmento de recta.	
line symmetry A property of a figure that means it can be reflected across a line so that the image coincides with the preimage.	**simetría axial** Propiedad de una figura que implica que puede reflejarse sobre una línea de forma tal que la imagen coincida con la imagen original.	
linear pair A pair of adjacent angles whose noncommon sides are opposite rays.	**par lineal** Par de ángulos adyacentes cuyos lados no comunes son rayos opuestos.	$\angle 3$ and $\angle 4$ form a linear pair.

M

major arc An arc of a circle whose points are on or in the exterior of a central angle.	**arco mayor** Arco de un círculo cuyos puntos están sobre un ángulo central o en su exterior.	$\overset{\frown}{ADC}$ is a major arc of the circle.

English	Spanish	Examples
mapping An operation that matches each point in a plane with another point in the plane, and which is often used to describe an operation used to match a figure (the preimage) to another figure (the image).	**correspondencia** Operación que establece una correlación entre cada elemento de un conjunto con otro elemento, su imagen, en el mismo conjunto.	
median of a triangle A segment whose endpoints are a vertex of the triangle and the midpoint of the opposite side.	**mediana de un triángulo** Segmento cuyos extremos son un vértice del triángulo y el punto medio del lado opuesto.	
midpoint The point that divides a segment into two congruent segments.	**punto medio** Punto que divide un segmento en dos segmentos congruentes.	 B is the midpoint of $\overline{AC}$.
midsegment of a trapezoid The segment whose endpoints are the midpoints of the legs of the trapezoid.	**segmento medio de un trapecio** Segmento cuyos extremos son los puntos medios de los catetos del trapecio.	
midsegment of a triangle A segment that joins the midpoints of two sides of the triangle.	**segmento medio de un triángulo** Segmento que une los puntos medios de dos lados del triángulo.	
minor arc An arc of a circle whose points are on or in the interior of a central angle.	**arco menor** Arco de un círculo cuyos puntos están sobre un ángulo central o en su interior.	 $\overarc{AC}$ is a minor arc of the circle.
mutually exclusive events Two events are mutually exclusive if they cannot both occur in the same trial of an experiment.	**sucesos mutuamente excluyentes** Dos sucesos son mutuamente excluyentes si ambos no pueden ocurrir en la misma prueba de un experimento.	In the experiment of rolling a number cube, rolling a 3 and rolling an even number are mutually exclusive events.

N

English	Spanish	Examples
net A diagram of the faces of a three-dimensional figure arranged in such a way that the diagram can be folded to form the three-dimensional figure.	**plantilla** Diagrama de las caras de una figura tridimensional que se puede plegar para formar la figura tridimensional.	

English	Spanish	Examples
n-gon An n-sided polygon.	**n-ágono** Polígono de n lados.	
nonpolygon A two-dimensional geometric object that does not meet the definition of a polygon.	**no polígono** Objeto geométrico bidimensional que no cumple con la definición de un polígono.	

O

English	Spanish	Examples
oblique solid A three-dimensional figure that has an axis or lateral edge that is not perpendicular to its base(s).	**sólido oblicuo** Figura tridimensional que tiene un eje o arista lateral que no es perpendicular a su(s) base(s).	
obtuse angle An angle that measures greater than 90° and less than 180°.	**ángulo obtuso** Ángulo que mide más de 90° y menos de 180°.	
opposite rays Two rays that have a common endpoint and form a line.	**rayos opuestos** Dos rayos que tienen un extremo común y forman una línea.	F E G $\overrightarrow{EF}$ and $\overrightarrow{EG}$ are opposite rays.
orthocenter of a triangle The point of concurrency of the three altitudes of a triangle.	**ortocentro de un triángulo** Punto de intersección de las tres alturas de un triángulo.	P is the orthocenter. P
outcome A possible result of a probability experiment.	**resultado** Resultado posible de un experimento de probabilidad.	In the experiment of rolling a number cube, the possible outcomes are 1, 2, 3, 4, 5, and 6.
overlapping events Events that have one or more outcomes in common. Also called inclusive events.	**sucesos superpuestos** Sucesos que tienen uno o más resultados en común. También se denominan sucesos inclusivos.	Rolling an even number and rolling a prime number on a number cube are overlapping events because they both contain the outcome rolling a 2.

P

English	Spanish	Examples
parallel lines Lines in the same plane that do not intersect.	**líneas paralelas** Líneas rectas en el mismo plano que no se cruzan.	r s r ∥ s

English	Spanish	Examples
parallel planes Planes that do not intersect.	**planos paralelos** Planos que no se cruzan.	Plane *AEF* and plane *CGH* are parallel planes.
parallelogram A quadrilateral with two pairs of parallel sides.	**paralelogramo** Cuadrilátero con dos pares de lados paralelos.	
partition a segment To divide a line segment into shorter segments with a given ratio.	**dividir un segmento** Fraccionar un segmento de recta en segmentos más cortos de acuerdo con una razón determinada.	
perpendicular Intersecting to form 90° angles, denoted by $\perp$.	**perpendicular** Que se cruza para formar ángulos de 90°, expresado por $\perp$.	$m \perp n$
perpendicular bisector A line perpendicular to a segment or to a side of a triangle at the segment's midpoint.	**mediatriz** Línea perpendicular a un segmento o a un lado de un triángulo, trazada en el punto medio del segmento.	ℓ is the perpendicular bisector of $\overline{AB}$.
perpendicular lines Lines that intersect to form 90° angles.	**líneas perpendiculares** Líneas que se cruzan para formar ángulos de 90°.	$m \perp n$
pi The ratio of the circumference of a circle to its diameter, denoted by the Greek letter π (pi). The value of π is irrational, often approximated by 3.14 or $\frac{22}{7}$.	**pi** Razón entre la circunferencia de un círculo y su diámetro, expresado por la letra griega π (pi). El valor de π es irracional y por lo general se aproxima a 3.14 ó $\frac{22}{7}$.	If a circle has a diameter of 5 inches and a circumference of C inches, then $\frac{C}{5} = \pi$, or $C = 5\pi$ inches, or about 15.7 inches.
plane An undefined term in geometry, it is a flat surface that has no thickness and extends forever in two dimensions.	**plano** Término indefinido en geometría; un plano es una superficie plana que no tiene grosor y se extiende infinitamente en dos dimensiones.	plane *R* or plane *ABC*

Glossary/Glosario

English	Spanish	Examples
point An undefined term in geometry, it names a location and has no size. A point has no dimension.	**punto** Término indefinido de la geometría que denomina una ubicación y no tiene tamaño. Un punto no tiene dimensión.	P • point P
point of concurrency A point where three or more lines coincide.	**punto de concurrencia** Punto donde se cruzan tres o más líneas.	
point of tangency The point of intersection of a circle or sphere with a tangent line or plane.	**punto de tangencia** Punto de intersección de un círculo o esfera con una línea o plano tangente.	 Tangent C Point of tangency
polygon A closed plane figure formed by three or more segments such that each segment intersects exactly two other segments only at their endpoints and no two segments with a common endpoint are collinear.	**polígono** Figura plana cerrada formada por tres o más segmentos tal que cada segmento se cruza únicamente con otros dos segmentos sólo en sus extremos y ningún segmento con un extremo común a otro es colineal con éste.	
polyhedron A closed three-dimensional figure formed by four or more polygons that intersect only at their edges.	**poliedro** Figura tridimensional cerrada formada por cuatro o más polígonos que se cruzan sólo en sus aristas.	
population density The number of organisms of a particular type per square unit of area.	**densidad de población** Número de organismos de un tipo particular por unidad cuadrada de área.	
postulate A statement that is accepted as true without proof. Also called an *axiom*.	**postulado** Enunciado que se acepta como verdadero sin demostración. También denominado *axioma*.	
preimage The original figure in a transformation.	**imagen original** Figura original en una transformación.	
prism A polyhedron formed by two parallel congruent polygonal bases connected by lateral faces that are parallelograms.	**prisma** Poliedro formado por dos bases poligonales congruentes y paralelas conectadas por caras laterales que son paralelogramos.	

English	Spanish	Examples
probability experiment An activity that has a defined set of possible outcomes and which can be repeated.	**experimento de probabilidad** Actividad que tiene un conjunto definido de resultados posibles que pueden repetirse.	
proof An argument that uses logic to show that a conclusion is true.	**demostración** Argumento que se vale de la lógica para probar que una conclusión es verdadera.	
proof by contradiction *See* indirect proof.	**demostración por contradicción** *Ver* demostración indirecta.	
pyramid A polyhedron formed by a polygonal base and triangular lateral faces that meet at a common vertex.	**pirámide** Poliedro formado por una base poligonal y caras laterales triangulares que se encuentran en un vértice común.	
Pythagorean triple A set of three nonzero whole numbers a, b, and c such that $a^2 + b^2 = c^2$.	**Tripleta de Pitágoras** Conjunto de tres números enteros distintos de cero a, b y c tal que $a^2 + b^2 = c^2$.	$\{3, 4, 5\}$ $\quad 3^2 + 4^2 = 5^2$

Q

quadrilateral A four-sided polygon.	**cuadrilátero** Polígono de cuatro lados.	

R

radial symmetry *See* rotational symmetry.	**simetría radial** *Ver* simetría de rotación.	
radian A unit of angle measure based on arc length. In a circle of radius r, if a central angle has a measure of 1 radian, then the length of the intercepted arc is r units. 2π radians $= 360°$ 1 radian $\approx 57°$	**radián** Unidad de medida de un ángulo basada en la longitud del arco. En un círculo de radio r, si un ángulo central mide 1 radián, entonces la longitud del arco abarcado es r unidades. 2π radians $= 360°$ 1 radian $\approx 57°$	r r O $\theta = 1$ radian
ray A part of a line that starts at an endpoint and extends forever in one direction.	**rayo** Parte de una línea que comienza en un extremo y se extiende infinitamente en una dirección.	D
rectangle A parallelogram with four right angles.	**rectángulo** Paralelogramo con cuatro ángulos rectos.	

© Houghton Mifflin Harcourt Publishing Company

English	Spanish	Examples
reflection A transformation across a line, called the line of reflection, such that the line of reflection is the perpendicular bisector of each segment joining each point and its image.	**reflexión** Transformación sobre una línea, denominada la línea de reflexión. La línea de reflexión es la mediatriz de cada segmento que une un punto con su imagen.	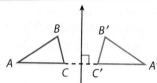
reflection symmetry *See* line symmetry.	**simetría de reflexión** *Ver* simetría axial.	
reflex angle An angle with measure greater than 180° and less than 360°.	**ángulo reflejo** Ángulo cuya medida es mayor que 180° y menor que 360°.	
regular polygon A polygon that is both equilateral and equiangular.	**polígono regular** Polígono equilátero de ángulos iguales.	
regular pyramid A pyramid whose base is a regular polygon and whose lateral faces are congruent isosceles triangles.	**pirámide regular** Pirámide cuya base es un polígono regular y cuyas caras laterales son triángulos isósceles congruentes.	
relative frequency The ratio of the frequency of one outcome to the frequency of all outcomes.	**frecuencia relativa** Razón entre la frecuencia de un resultado y la frecuencia de todos los resultados.	
remote interior angle An interior angle of a polygon that is not adjacent to the exterior angle.	**ángulo interno remoto** Ángulo interno de un polígono que no es adyacente al ángulo externo.	The remote interior angles of ∠4 are ∠1 and ∠2.
rhombus A parallelogram with four congruent sides.	**rombo** Paralelogramo con cuatro lados congruentes.	
right angle An angle that measures 90°.	**ángulo recto** Ángulo que mide 90°.	
right cone A cone whose axis is perpendicular to its base.	**cono recto** Cono cuyo eje es perpendicular a su base.	Axis

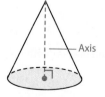

English	Spanish	Examples
right solid A three-dimensional figure that has an axis or lateral edge that is perpendicular to its base(s).	**sólido recto** Figura tridimensional que tiene un eje o arista lateral que es perpendicular a su(s) base(s).	
rigid motion A transformation that does not change the size or shape of a figure.	**movimiento rígido** Transformación que no cambia el tamaño ni la forma de una figura.	Reflections, translations, and rotations are all examples of rigid motions.
rigid transformation *See* rigid motion.	**transformación rígida** *Ver* movimiento rígido.	
rotation A transformation about a point *P*, also known as the center of rotation, such that each point and its image are the same distance from *P*. All of the angles with vertex *P* formed by a point and its image are congruent.	**rotación** Transformación sobre un punto *P*, también conocido como el centro de rotación, tal que cada punto y su imagen estén a la misma distancia de *P*. Todos los ángulos con vértice *P* formados por un punto y su imagen son congruentes.	
rotational symmetry A property of a figure that can be rotated about a point by an angle less than 360° so that the image coincides with the preimage.	**simetría de rotación** Propiedad de una figura que puede rotarse alrededor de un punto en un ángulo menor de 360° de forma tal que la imagen coincide con la imagen original.	Order of rotational symmetry: 4

S

sample space The set of all possible outcomes of a probability experiment.	**espacio muestral** Conjunto de todos los resultados posibles de un experimento de probabilidad.	In the experiment of rolling a number cube, the sample space is {1, 2, 3, 4, 5, 6}.
scale factor The multiplier used on each dimension to change one figure into a similar figure.	**factor de escala** El multiplicador utilizado en cada dimensión para transformar una figura en una figura semejante.	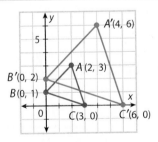 Scale factor: 2
secant of a circle A line that intersects a circle at two points.	**secante de un círculo** Línea que corta un círculo en dos puntos.	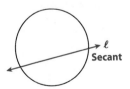

English	Spanish	Examples
secant segment A segment of a secant with at least one endpoint on the circle.	**segmento secante** Segmento de una secante que tiene al menos un extremo sobre el círculo.	$\overline{NM}$ is an external secant segment. $\overline{JK}$ is an internal secant segment.
sector of a circle A region inside a circle bounded by two radii of the circle and their intercepted arc.	**sector de un círculo** Región dentro de un círculo delimitado por dos radios del círculo y por su arco abarcado.	
segment bisector A line, ray, or segment that divides a segment into two congruent segments.	**bisectriz de un segmento** Línea, rayo o segmento que divide un segmento en dos segmentos congruentes.	
segment of a circle A region inside a circle bounded by a chord and an arc.	**segmento de un círculo** Región dentro de un círculo delimitada por una cuerda y un arco.	
segment of a line A part of a line consisting of two endpoints and all points between them.	**segmento de una línea** Parte de una línea que consiste en dos extremos y todos los puntos entre éstos.	
semicircle An arc of a circle whose endpoints lie on a diameter.	**semicírculo** Arco de un círculo cuyos extremos se encuentran sobre un diámetro.	
set A collection of items called elements.	**conjunto** Grupo de componentes denominados elementos.	$\{1, 2, 3\}$
similar Two figures are similar if they have the same shape but not necessarily the same size.	**semejantes** Dos figuras con la misma forma pero no necesariamente del mismo tamaño.	
similar figures If a figure can be mapped to another figure using a sequence of similarity transformations, the figures are similar.	**figuras semejantes** Si se puede establecer una correspondencia entre una figura y otra usando una sucesión de transformaciones de semejanza, las figuras son semejantes.	

English	Spanish	Examples
similarity transformation A transformation that produces similar figures.	**transformación de semejanza** Una transformación que resulta en figuras semejantes.	Dilations are similarity transformations.
sine In a right triangle, the ratio of the length of the leg opposite $\angle A$ to the length of the hypotenuse.	**seno** En un triángulo rectángulo, razón entre la longitud del cateto opuesto a $\angle A$ y la longitud de la hipotenusa.	$$\sin A = \frac{\text{opposite}}{\text{hypotenuse}}$$
skew lines Lines that are not coplanar.	**líneas oblicuas** Líneas que no son coplanares.	$\overleftrightarrow{AE}$ and $\overleftrightarrow{CD}$ are skew lines.
slant height The height of each lateral face of a right pyramid or the lateral surface of a right cone.	**altura inclinada** Altura de cada cara lateral de una pirámide recta o superficie lateral de un cono recto.	The slant height is ℓ.
slide *See* translation.	**deslizamiento** *Ver* traslación.	
slope A measure of the steepness of a line. If (x_1, y_1) and (x_2, y_2) are any two points on the line, the slope of the line, denoted m, is represented by the equation $m = \frac{y_2 - y_1}{x_2 - x_1}$.	**pendiente** Medida de la inclinación de una línea. Dados dos puntos (x_1, y_1) y (x_2, y_2) en una línea, la pendiente de la línea, denominada m, se representa con la ecuación $m = \frac{y_2 - y_1}{x_2 - x_1}$.	
solid A three-dimensional figure.	**cuerpo geométrico** Figura tridimensional.	
solid of rotation A solid that is formed by rotating a two-dimensional shape about an axis.	**sólido de rotación** Cuerpo geométrico que se forma al rotar una figura bidimensional sobre un eje.	

Glossary/Glosario

English	Spanish	Examples
solving a triangle Using given measures to find unknown angle measures or side lengths of a triangle.	**resolución de un triángulo** Utilizar medidas dadas para hallar las medidas desconocidas de los ángulos o las longitudes de los lados de un triángulo.	
special right triangle A $45°-45°-90°$ triangle or a $30°-60°-90°$ triangle.	**triángulo rectángulo especial** Triángulo de $45°-45°-90°$ o triángulo de $30°-60°-90°$.	
sphere The set of points in space that are a fixed distance from a given point called the center of the sphere.	**esfera** Conjunto de puntos en el espacio que se encuentran a una distancia fija de un punto determinado denominado centro de la esfera.	
square A parallelogram with four congruent sides and four right angles.	**cuadrado** Paralelogramo con cuatro lados congruentes y cuatro ángulos rectos.	
straight angle A 180° angle.	**ángulo llano** Ángulo que mide 180°.	
stretch A nonrigid transformation that changes the shape of a figure in one direction by a factor greater than 1.	**estiramiento** Transformación no rígida que cambia la forma de una figura en una dirección por un factor mayor que 1.	horizontal stretch
subset A set that is contained entirely within another set. Set B is a subset of set A if every element of B is contained in A, denoted $B \subset A$.	**subconjunto** Conjunto que se encuentra dentro de otro conjunto. El conjunto B es un subconjunto del conjunto A si todos los elementos de B son elementos de A; se expresa $B \subset A$.	The set of integers is a subset of the set of rational numbers.
supplementary angles Two angles whose measures have a sum of 180°.	**ángulos suplementarios** Dos ángulos cuyas medidas suman 180°.	$\angle 3$ and $\angle 4$ are supplementary angles.

English	Spanish	Examples
surface area The total area of all faces and curved surfaces of a three-dimensional figure.	**área total** Área total de todas las caras y superficies curvas de una figura tridimensional.	Surface area $= 2(8)(12) + 2(8)(6) + 2(12)(6) = 432$ cm^2
symmetry A property of a figure that can be mapped to itself using a rigid motion such as a reflection or rotation.	**simetría** Propiedad de una figura que puede establecer una correspondencia consigo misma mediante un movimiento rígido, como la reflexión o la rotación.	

T

English	Spanish	Examples
tangent of an angle In a right triangle, the ratio of the length of the leg opposite $\angle A$ to the length of the leg adjacent to $\angle A$.	**tangente de un ángulo** En un triángulo rectángulo, razón entre la longitud del cateto opuesto a $\angle A$ y la longitud del cateto adyacente a $\angle A$.	$\tan A = \dfrac{\text{opposite}}{\text{adjacent}}$
tangent segment A segment of a tangent with one endpoint on the circle.	**segmento tangente** Segmento de una tangente con un extremo en el círculo.	$\overline{BC}$ is a tangent segment.
tangent of a circle A line that is in the same plane as a circle and intersects the circle at exactly one point.	**tangente de un círculo** Línea que se encuentra en el mismo plano que un círculo y lo cruza únicamente en un punto.	
terminal point of a vector The endpoint of a vector.	**punto terminal de un vector** Extremo de un vector.	
theorem A statement that has been proven.	**teorema** Enunciado que ha sido demostrado.	

Glossary/Glosario

English	Spanish	Examples
theoretical probability The ratio of the number of equally-likely outcomes in an event to the total number of possible outcomes.	**probabilidad teórica** Razón entre el número de resultados igualmente probables de un suceso y el número total de resultados posibles.	In the experiment of rolling a number cube, the theoretical probability of rolling an odd number is $\frac{3}{6} = \frac{1}{2}$.
transformation A function that changes the position, size, or shape of a figure or graph.	**transformación** Función que cambia la posición, tamaño o forma de una figura o gráfica.	Preimage / Image $\triangle ABC \rightarrow \triangle A'B'C'$
translation A transformation that shifts or slides every point of a figure or graph the same distance in the same direction.	**traslación** Transformación en la que todos los puntos de una figura o gráfica se mueven la misma distancia en la misma dirección.	
transversal A line that intersects two or more coplanar lines at two different points.	**transversal** Línea que corta dos o más líneas coplanares en dos puntos diferentes.	Transversal
trapezoid A quadrilateral with at least one pair of parallel sides.	**trapecio** Cuadrilátero con al menos un par de lados paralelos.	
trial In probability, a single repetition or observation of an experiment.	**prueba** En probabilidad, una sola repetición u observación de un experimento.	In the experiment of rolling a number cube, each roll is one trial.
trigonometric ratio A ratio of two sides of a right triangle.	**razón trigonométrica** Razón entre dos lados de un triángulo rectángulo.	$\sin A = \frac{a}{c}$; $\cos A = \frac{b}{c}$; $\tan A = \frac{a}{b}$

U

undefined term A basic figure that is not defined in terms of other figures. The undefined terms in geometry are *point*, *line*, and *plane*.	**término indefinido** Figura básica que no está definida en función de otras figuras. Los términos indefinidos en geometría son el punto, la línea y el plano.	

© Houghton Mifflin Harcourt Publishing Company

English	Spanish	Examples
union of two sets The set of all elements that are in either set, denoted by ∪.	**unión de dos conjuntos** Conjunto de todos los elementos que se encuentran en ambos conjuntos, expresado por ∪.	$A = \{1, 2, 3, 4\}$ $B = \{1, 3, 5, 7, 9\}$ $A \cup B = \{1, 2, 3, 4, 5, 7, 9\}$
universal set The set of all elements in a particular context.	**conjunto universal** Conjunto de todos los elementos de un contexto determinado.	

V

English	Spanish	Examples
vector A quantity that has both magnitude and direction.	**vector** Cantidad que tiene magnitud y dirección.	
vertex of an angle The common endpoint of the sides of an angle.	**vértice de un ángulo** Extremo común de los lados del ángulo.	 *A* is the vertex of ∠*CAB*.
vertex of a cone The point opposite the base of a cone.	**vértice de un cono** Punto opuesto a la base del cono.	
vertex of a polygon The intersection of two sides of a polygon.	**vértice de un polígono** La intersección de dos lados del polígono.	 *A, B, C, D,* and *E* are vertices of the polygon.
vertex of a pyramid The point opposite the base of a pyramid.	**vértice de una pirámide** Punto opuesto a la base de la pirámide.	
vertex of a three-dimensional figure The point that is the intersection of three or more faces of a figure.	**vértice de una figura tridimensional** Punto que representa la intersección de tres o más caras de la figura.	

English	Spanish	Examples
vertex of a triangle The intersection of two sides of a triangle.	**vértice de un triángulo** Intersección de dos lados del triángulo.	 *A, B,* and *C* are vertices of △*ABC*.
vertical angles The nonadjacent angles formed by two intersecting lines.	**ángulos opuestos por el vértice** Ángulos no adyacentes formados por dos rectas que se cruzan.	 ∠1 and ∠3 are vertical angles. ∠2 and ∠4 are vertical angles.
volume The number of nonoverlapping unit cubes of a given size that will exactly fill the interior of a three-dimensional figure.	**volumen** Cantidad de cubos unitarios no superpuestos de un determinado tamaño que llenan exactamente el interior de una figura tridimensional.	 4 ft 3 ft 12 ft Volume $= (3)(4)(12) = 144$ ft³

density, volume formula in finding, of a real-world object, 595

dependent events, 649–656, 657
probability of three or more, 652
probability of two, 650, 651

depression, angle of, 432

descriptions, making sketches from, 42

diagonals
of an isosceles trapezoid, 356
of a kite, 355

Diagonals of a Kite Theorem, 355

Diagonals of an Isosceles Trapezoid Theorem, 356

Diagonals of a Parallelogram Theorem, 324
converse of, 331

Diagonals of a Rectangle Theorem, 338

Diagonals of a Rhombus Theorem, 339

Diagonals of a Square Theorem, 339

diameter, 466

dilations, 174, 189, 368
center of, 175
in the coordinate plane, 172, 176, 366
investigating, 368
properties of, 176

disjoint events, 624
probability of, 626

distance formula, 31, 104, 124, 131, 256, 464
applying to a real-world problem, 127
in finding segment length and proving congruence, 126
proving, 124

division of rational numbers, 634

Division Property of Equality, 49, 51

drawings, scale, 172

E

elements of a set, 616

elevation, angle of, 432

empty sets, 616

endpoints, 6, 14

equality
Addition Property of, 49, 51, 54
Division Property of, 49, 51
Multiplication Property of, 49
Subtraction Property of, 49

equation(s)
of a circle, 499
justifying steps for solving, 40
multi-step, 76, 502
solving one-step, 404

writing, for proportional relationships, 522

equilateral triangles
angle of rotational symmetry in, 164
image of, 164
lines of symmetry in, 164
sides in, 164

events, 617, 631
complement of, 618
compound
involving *and,* 634
involving *or,* 614
dependent, 649–656, 657
formula for the probability of the occurrence of two, 650
probability of, 651
probability of three or more, 652
disjoint, 624
probability of, 626
independent, 643–648, 657
deriving formula for the probability of the intersection of, 644
probabilities of, 645
real-world events as, 645
mutually exclusive, 624, 631
overlapping, 625, 631
probability of, 626
probability of compound, involving *or,* 614
probability of simple, 614, 634
simple
probability of, 614, 634

experiments, probability, 617

exterior angles, 78, 258

Exterior Angle Theorem, 258

exterior of a circle, 484

external secant segments, 505

F

figures
composite, 560
areas of, 550
surface area of, 560, 568, 575
volume of, 605, 609
reflecting, in the coordinate plane, 136
rotating, in the coordinate plane, 136
three-dimensional, 551–556
translating, in the coordinate plane, 136

financial literacy, 374, 544

flow proofs, 80

formula
for arc length, 532, 534
for the area of a circle, 525
for the area of a triangle, 453
for the circumference of a circle, 524

for conditional probability, 638, 639
deriving area, 430
deriving conditional probability, 637
distance, 31, 104, 124, 126, 127, 131, 256, 464
midpoint, 9, 104, 125, 256, 464
for probability of the intersection of independent events, 644
for probability of the occurrence of two dependent events, 650
for sector area, 540, 541
for surface area, 561, 569
of a composite figure, 560, 568
of a cone, 567
of a cylinder, 559
of a prism, 558
of a pyramid, 566
of a sphere, 574
for volume, 584
of a cone, 593, 594
of a cylinder, 585
of a prism, 585
of a pyramid, 592
in solving a real-world problem, 603
of a sphere, 602

fractions
writing, as percents, 614
writing decimals as, 614

frequency, relative, 637

functions, writing a composition of, 184

G

Geometric Means Theorem, 394

geometric optics, 171

geometric relationships, proving, 205

geometry
The development of geometry skills and concepts is found throughout the book.
angles in, 13–17
arc in, 5
coordinate plane in, 29–36
defined, 5
endpoints in, 6
line segments in, 6, 7–9
lines in, 5, 6
midpoints in, 8, 9
planes in, 6
points in, 5, 6, 9
polygons in, 21–25
postulates of, 7, 42
rays in, 6
terms in, 6, 10
theorems in, 50
tools in, 7

Glossary, GL1–GL31

gravity, finding center of, 284

Index

© Houghton Mifflin Harcourt Publishing Company

Index

© Houghton Mifflin Harcourt Publishing Company

Tables of Measures, Symbols, and Formulas

LENGTH

1 meter (m) = 1000 millimeters (mm)

1 meter = 100 centimeters (cm)

1 meter ≈ 39.37 inches

1 kilometer (km) = 1000 meters

1 kilometer ≈ 0.62 mile

1 inch = 2.54 centimeters

1 foot (ft) = 12 inches (in.)

1 yard (yd) = 3 feet

1 mile (mi) = 1760 yards

1 mile = 5280 feet

1 mile ≈ 1.609 kilometers

CAPACITY

1 liter (L) = 1000 milliliters (mL)

1 liter = 1000 cubic centimeters

1 liter ≈ 0.264 gallon

1 kiloliter (kL) = 1000 liters

1 cup (c) = 8 fluid ounces (fl oz)

1 pint (pt) = 2 cups

1 quart (qt) = 2 pints

1 gallon (gal) = 4 quarts

1 gallon ≈ 3.785 liters

MASS/WEIGHT

1 gram (g) = 1000 milligrams (mg)

1 kilogram (kg) = 1000 grams

1 kilogram ≈ 2.2 pounds

1 pound (lb) = 16 ounces (oz)

1 pound ≈ 0.454 kilogram

1 ton = 2000 pounds

TIME

1 minute (min) = 60 seconds (s)

1 hour (h) = 60 minutes

1 day = 24 hours

1 week = 7 days

1 year (yr) = about 52 weeks

1 year = 12 months (mo)

1 year = 365 days

1 decade = 10 years

Tables of Measures, Symbols, and Formulas

SYMBOLS

$=$	is equal to	x^2	x squared
$\neq$	is not equal to	x^3	x cubed
$\approx$	is approximately equal to	$\lvert x \rvert$	absolute value of x
$>$	is greater than	$\frac{1}{x}$	reciprocal of x $(x \neq 0)$
$<$	is less than	$\sqrt{x}$	square root of x
$\geq$	is greater than or equal to	$\sqrt[3]{x}$	cube root of x
$\leq$	is less than or equal to	x_n	x sub n $(n = 0, 1, 2, \ldots)$

FORMULAS

Perimeter and Circumference

Polygon	$P = $ sum of the lengths of sides
Rectangle	$P = 2\ell + 2w$
Square	$P = 4s$
Circle	$C = \pi d$ or $C = 2\pi r$

Area

Rectangle	$A = \ell w$
Parallelogram	$A = bh$
Triangle	$A = \frac{1}{2}bh$
Trapezoid	$A = \frac{1}{2}h(b_1 + b_2)$
Square	$A = s^2$
Circle	$A = \pi r^2$

Volume

Right Prism	$V = \ell wh$ or $V = Bh$
Cube	$V = s^3$
Pyramid	$V = \frac{1}{3}Bh$
Cylinder	$V = \pi r^2 h$
Cone	$V = \frac{1}{3}\pi r^2 h$
Sphere	$V = \frac{4}{3}\pi r^3$

Surface Area

Right Prism	$S = Ph + 2B$
Cube	$S = 6s^2$
Square Pyramid	$S = \frac{1}{2}P\ell + B$

Pythagorean Theorem

$$a^2 + b^2 = c^2$$